THE GERMAN PEOPLE

VOL. XIV.

HISTORY OF THE GERMAN PEOPLE at the
Close of the Middle Ages. By JOHANNES JANSSEN.

Vols. I. and II. Translated by M. A. MITCHELL and
A. M. CHRISTIE.

Vols. III.—XVI. Translated by A. M. CHRISTIE.

HISTORY OF THE GERMAN PEOPLE AT THE CLOSE OF THE MIDDLE AGES

By Johannes Janssen

VOL. XIV.

SCHOOLS AND UNIVERSITIES, SCIENCE, LEARNING AND CULTURE DOWN TO THE BEGINNING OF THE THIRTY YEARS' WAR

TRANSLATED BY A. M. CHRISTIE

LONDON

KEGAN PAUL, TRENCH, TRUBNER & CO. Ltd.

BROADWAY HOUSE, CARTER LANE, E.C.

B. HERDER BOOK CO.

15-17 SOUTH BROADWAY, ST. LOUIS, MO.

1909

TRANSLATOR'S NOTE.

These Volumes (*XIII.* and *XIV.*) are translated from *Vol. VII.* of the German [*Fifteenth and Sixteenth Editions, improved and added to by Ludwig Pastor*].

CONTENTS

OF

THE FOURTEENTH VOLUME

HISTORY

OF

THE GERMAN PEOPLE

AT THE CLOSE OF THE MIDDLE AGES

———◦◦———

CHAPTER VI

THE HEALING ART

SIDE by side with botanical literature there runs all
through the sixteenth and seventeenth centuries another
kind of writing which is concerned with medicinal
superstition, especially the so-called signature of plants.
It was believed, namely, that from certain external
features, from the similarity of some of their parts
with human organs, the effects of these plants on certain
parts of human bodies or on certain diseases could be
ascertained. This doctrine was carried to absurdity
by Paracelsus and his followers.[1] The disciples of this

---

[1] So Haeser, ii³. 98 ; cf. Meyer, iv. 431 f. Concerning Paracelsus
see present work, vol. xii. p. 278 ff. ; Hirsch, *Gesch. der Medizin*, p. 50 ff. ;
R. Netzhammer, *Theoph. Paracelsus*, Einsiedeln, 1901 ; F. Strunz,
Th. Paracelsus, sein Leben und seine Persönlichkeit, Leipzig, 1903. Concerning Paracelsus and the Paracelsists, see also Baas, p. 203 ff. It is
undeniable that Paracelsus, in spite of all eccentricities, deserves credit
in manifold ways for the introduction of powerful materia medica ;
still ' the aim of his scientific endeavours was a mistaken one ; not less
mistaken also was the way by which he sought to reach his end (Haeser,

'Reformer of Einsiedeln' were extremely numerous, especially in Germany. From Basle, where Adam von Bodenstein worked in the spirit of the 'Master,' the new teaching spread with extraordinary rapidity over South and West Germany, and thence on into the northern districts.[1]

'The Paracelsists may be divided into two classes : 1. People without any general or medical education,

ii. 105 ; cf. Roth, *Vesalius*, p. 56 ; ' and equally certain it is that with Paracelsus, and still more with his followers, what was really true was so enveloped and choked with nonsense and superstition that it is very difficult to get at the kernel of sense. Cf. Finckenstein in the *Deutsche Klinik*, 1868, No. 11 ; Petersen, *Therapie*, pp. 26–27. Baas criticises Paracelsus as follows (p. 203 f.) : ' That Theophrastus did homage to the philosophical and natural (or as the case may be occult) science of his day, as well as to its current humanistic tendency, is evidenced outwardly by his change of name (the adoption of the name Paracelsus), and inwardly and in a more important manner by his emphatic opposition to the system of Arabism (and of Galenism), and by the fact that he was an enlightened adherent of the empiricism and physiotherapy of Hippocrates. For him experience was science (*scientia est experientia*), in which respect he was the precursor of Bacon. But nothing more clearly proves his physiotherapeutic tendency and his insight (based on clear observation as well as deep thinking) into the known, and yet unknown, workings of nature and the ' power ' of the doctor than his surgical confession : ' Every surgeon must know that it is not he who heals the wounds, but the balsam in the body which does the work of healing, and that wherein you, O surgeon ! are of use is to give help and protection to nature in the injured part.' See also Stange, *Einführung in die Gesch. der Chemie*, Münster, 1902, p. 35 ff. ; *Paracelsus und das Zeitalter der medizinischen Chemie*. ' Paracelsus is one of those fiery heads,' says Stange (p. 37), ' which are always found on the borderland of two epochs, full of a new spirit like seers, looking out with prophetic gaze into the future, and yet having many of their hearts' tendrils rooted in the past. . . . Brimful of contradictions, Paracelsus is at one moment a strict investigator, at another a downright visionary. Here he demands in his disciples a natural science training, there he insists that his teaching can be understood by the unlearned also ; he is actually proud to think that he is on very strained terms with the scholasticism of his day. His writings now attract by their novelty and originality of thought, now repel by the incredible coarseness of tone in very many passages.'

[1] Fränkel, p. 18.

who adopted the practical teaching of their leader, and proclaimed it, some of them with the zeal of genuine enthusiasts, some as cunning impostors ; 2. Men of education, mostly doctors, who believed in the Paracelsist theories as well as in their practical results. These brought the teaching into connexion with the mystical and theosophical doctrines prevalent in the sixteenth and seventeenth centuries, and endeavoured to harmonise them (the teachings of the Arcana) with the progress of chemistry.' [1] Among zealous Paracelsists of the last class, besides Adam von Bodenstein († 1577 at Basle of the plague) and Melanchthon's son-in-law Caspar Peucer, who suffered twelve years' hard imprisonment on account of his crypto-Calvinist views, we must above all mention the Calvinist Oswald Croll, who died in 1609 as house-physician to Prince Christian of Anhalt-Bernburg.[2] His work ' Basilica Chymica,' published in 1609, contains directions for the preparation of new and effectual medicines, and also a passionate defence of Paracelsus and his teaching. ' No mortal man,' says Croll, ' in the whole domain of philosophy and medicine has fathomed such deep and hidden secrets as,

---

[1] Haeser, ii[3]. 106 ; cf. Rosenbaum in Ersch-Gruber's *Enzyklopädie* (third section), xi. 284. Hirsch (*Gesch. der Medizin*, p. 64 f.) divides the followers of Paracelsus into four categories : (1) swindlers ; (2) half-ruined theologians ; (3) scientifically trained doctors ; (4) spagyric doctors. Hirsch, moreover, is not quite accurate when (*l.c.*) he counts M. Bapst of Rochlitz among the Paracelsists. See below, p. 18 ff.

[2] Concerning Bodenstein and Peucer see Schmieder, p. 278 f. ; *Allgem. deutsche Biographie*, iii. 7 ff., and iv. 604, as also vol. viii. of the present work, p. 173 ff. For the wonderful assertions which Bodenstein reproduces concerning Paracelsus, see Mook, *Paracelsus*, Würzburg, 1876, p. 11 f. The little that is known about Croll's life has been put together by Fränkel (p. 88 f.). The credit which Croll deserves for the introduction of effectual *medica materia* is insisted on by Hirsch, *Gesch. der Medizin*, pp. 65–66.

by undoubted grace of heaven, this Theophrastus has done ; he is the true monarch of the healing art and the first doctor of the microcosm, the first and only man who has written about the inner astral man and its functions created by God, and also about the great and incurable diseases of natural and of metaphysical origin, things that the doctors of the earlier ages never even dreamt of, still less our adherents of the pagan philosophy.   In the science of chemistry Paracelsus was a distinguished scholar, but he was not its originator ; on the contrary he borrowed much in secret from his precursors. As, however, he was a chosen instrument of God for restoring and extending the true philosophical science of healing, and whereas he endeavoured to bring all the sciences back to their centre, the devil, this perpetual enemy of the human race and the wicked attendant of all budding truth forthwith sent out his halberdiers against him [Theophrastus], and goaded and seduced the doctors into the opinion that the cures performed by him were devil's works. And whereas it is the great failing of the Germans that they only prize highly what is foreign, and disparage what belongs to their own country, they rejected their countryman Paracelsus, while foreign nations were admiring and wondering at his knowledge ; as, for instance, Severinus among the Danes, Bovius among the Italians, Muffet among the English, and among the French my honoured friend Joseph Quercetanus (house-physician to Henry IV), who were all his adherents.'[1]

That Croll also should have defended the theological views of Paracelsus is not a matter of surprise, seeing that he himself believed in a pantheistic philosophy.

[1] Fränkel, p. 93.

'In therapeutics his highest ideal was the healing of diseases through spiritual means by the power of faith, the might of prayer, and the direct magnetic influence of the doctor.' 'Every agency,' he taught, ' aspires after its like. If a medicament is to exercise curative power it must of necessity (seeing that disease is something spiritual) be itself spiritual, be drawn out of its natural gross conditions, purified and spiritualised. For in nature there is nothing, however noble, which does not contain in itself a poison, and *vice versa* : *ubi virus, ibi virtus* [where poison is, there is virtue]. But all cleansing and purifying occur through fire. Through Vulcan the creature of God is perfected. The art of distillery separates the good from the bad, the visible from the invisible, the earthly, the impure, the rind and the shell, the body of medicine from its soul, from its superearthly mystery and quintessence. It is not the plant, it is not the metal which is the medicament, but the word of God which dwells in them. The first life of the plant and the metal must be destroyed in order that out of the foulness and corruption the new life may come forth and grow. The old nature must die in order that the new may be born. Chemistry is the true and living anatomy of nature ; fire is the genuine anatomical knife, which pierces through bone and marrow, separates body, soul and spirit, and sets free the three fundamental principles of all things, which correspond with body, soul, and spirit, viz. salt, brimstone, and mercury. From the breaking-up of the unity of these three basic principles into microcosm, from the exaltation and segregation of any one of them, disease arises. The doctor restores the unity of the three substances, the normal mixture of the original

fluid, by introducing into the microcosm the same
substance which has segregated, or a similar one, from
the macrocosm. Hence the doctor must be a chemist
also, and medicine and chemistry cannot be separated
from each other.[1]

In the same year (1609) there appeared also Croll's
pamphlet, ' Von den Signaturen.' In nature, he here explains, nothing is formed for nothing, or for mere sport :
the smallest things have their signification. This
applies especially to plants, which God has designed,
like the symbols of a mute language, to indicate their
hidden inward forces, viz. the symbols of form and
colour by which they speak to us in magic wise. Now
just as man is the object and centre of nature, so all
similarity and signatures of the other terrestrial creatures
relate ultimately to him and his requirements. From
the similarity of a plant, or a part of one, to a particular
organ of the human body, the healing power of this
plant, or this part of it, for the organ in question may
be deduced. Thus the walnut, the paeony, the poppy,
have the signature of head and brain, the *Rhizoma
galangae* that of the stomach, and so they serve as
means of healing for these respective organs. But
besides the human organs, all the symptoms of different
diseases have also their symbols and counterparts in
the natural bodies. The saxifrage root bears the
mark of the disease called stone ; all resinous growths
which are subject to the bursting of their rinds are
good for curing wounds and scars.[2]

The ideas of Paracelsus had been most widely accepted by Protestant doctors, and in like manner they

[1] Fränkel, pp. 97–98.
[2] *Ibid.* pp. 99–100 ; cf. Sprengel, *Arzneikunde*, iii. 530.

found most favour with the Protestant theologians. The well-known Valentine Weigel (since 1567 preacher in Zschopau near Chemnitz, where he died in 1588) was also a great admirer of the medical reformer of Einsiedeln.[1] The Zschopau preacher knew well what he had to expect from the persecuting spirit of Protestant orthodoxy. ' It is not well-pleasing to God,' he said to himself, ' that one should cast pearls before swine or throw one's treasures to the dogs ; for reward they would have rent and devoured me ; I should barely have escaped with my life ; my knowledge would have been of no use to anyone among the crowd ; none would have given up the false teaching they believed in. I should have suffered injury, and they would not have been helped.' For these reasons he carefully kept his writings secret. His mystical gnostic books were not published till after his death, when they gained him numerous followers. Very serious from the medical point of view must have been Weigel's teaching that numbers of diseases could not be cured on earth, and that their healing salves grew in heaven.

Principles similar to Weigel's were put forward by the theosophist Aegidius Gutmann from Suabia, who claimed to possess ' the universal means by which human nature could be ennobled, all illness warded off and healed, and besides all this, gold produced. It was only a matter of faith, he asserted, to be able to fly through the air, to transform metals, and to practise all the secret arts.'

The ideas of Paracelsus and Weigel received further development through the pantheist Jacob Böhme, a shoemaker at Görlitz. He is the first man who com-

---

[1] See Herzog, *Real-Enzyklopädie*, xvi². 477 ff. ; cf. Zöckler, p. 593.

posed great philosophical writings in the German
language. Not so prudent as Weigel, this fantastic
visionary, in 1612, came into conflict with Lutheran
orthodoxy shortly after the completion of his first
pamphlet, 'Die Morgenröte im Aufgange' ('The
Dawn of Day '). The Görlitz superior pastor, Gregory
Richter, compelled him to deliver up the manuscript
of this work. In order to escape banishment Böhme
was obliged to promise (1613) not to write anything
further. When, after the year 1619 he returned to
the work of authorship, and in 1624 published his
' Weg zu Christo,' a new storm broke out upon him from
orthodox Lutheran quarters. Richter now called on
the Görlitz Council ' to punish this agitator and criminal
heretic, so that God might not have cause to visit the
town of Görlitz with the same judgment that He sent
on Korah, Dathan, and Abiram.' An early death
(November 17, 1624) saved Weigel from further persecution. His writings and teaching, however, found
numerous adherents, especially in Silesia. Much as
Weigel deviated from Luther, especially as to the
doctrine of justification, he was nevertheless a true
disciple of his as regards abuse of Catholic doctrines
and of the popes.[1]

Virulent invectives against the Pope and the Church
were also contained in the work ' Bekenntnis der

---

[1] Menzel, vi. 29 ff. ; Kard. Rauscher in Wetzer and Welte's *Kirchenlexikon*, ii². 954 f. ; Grünhagen, ii. 336 ; Sprengel, ii. 526 ; Zöckler,
pp. 593, 755, where also the literature on Böhme is summarised. Concerning the new work of John Claassen, *J. Böhme*, Stuttgart, 1885, 3 vols.,
see *Histor.-polit. Blätter*, xcvii. 472 ff. It is worthy of mention that all
the doctors with whom Böhme was on friendly terms were lovers of
alchemy and occult wisdom. Harless, *J. Böhme und die Alchymisten*,
Berlin, 1870, p. 43.

löblichen Brüderschaft des hochgeehrten Rosenkreuzes'
('Profession of the learned Order of Rosicrucians).
About the same time there had appeared anonymously
the 'Entdeckung der Brüderschaft des hochloblichen
Orden des R.C.,' and on the top of this, in 1616, came out
the book 'Chymische Hochzeit Christiani Rosenkreutz'
('Chemical Wedding Feast of Christian Rose-Cross'),
which was announced as a book aiming at the reformation of the world. The author was said to be Christian
Rosenkreuz (born in 1388), who had become versed in
occult knowledge in Palestine and Egypt, and on his
return home had enlisted seven men to form a brotherhood of the 'Rose-Cross.' The members of this union
had 'gone on journeys for the objects of the society,
but once a year they had met together. Each member
had to procure himself a successor, and for a hundred
years the society was to remain a secret one. Thus
the brothers had worked on, until the grave of the
founder was discovered in the house of the brotherhood,
and his written records were also found. The object
of the union was the diminution of human misery by
leading the race to true philosophy and religion, by
showing men how to attain to the highest wisdom, and
how by pure lives and morals they could keep free
from pain and sickness.'[1]

The author of these writings was probably the
Protestant theologian John Valentine Andreä, whose
intention was to turn into ridicule the credulity of
the world and the search after occult mysteries.[2] Most

[1] Kopp, *Alchemie*, ii. 1 ff.
[2] Kopp also (*Alchemie*, ii. 3) does not consider the authorship of Andreä
positively certain. See also Henke in the *Allgem. deutsche Biographie*,
i. 444, and Hefele in Wetzer and Welte's *Kirchenlexikon*, i². 824 ; see also
ix. 399 f.

people of the time, however, believed firmly in the existence of the ' Rosenkreuz brotherhood.' It was in vain that Andreä himself declared the writings to be fictitious. Numbers of people came forward wanting to be admitted into the secret society, and there were also no lack of persons who gave themselves out as members of the union, and wanted to heal all manner of complaints with their universal panacea. A perfect deluge of Rosenkreuz writings now flooded the land, and had a very deleterious effect on the sciences, and especially on that of medicine.[1]

The most just judgment on these new fanatics was pronounced by the Franconian pastor, Andrew Forner. These ' so-called Rosenkreuz brethren,' he said, ' do nothing but dabble in occult arts, such as gold-making, discovering secrets, finding treasures, healing diseases. They are downright impostors.' [2]

While prominent men among the Jesuits combated alchemy, the Marian congregations under their lead did fierce battle with the superstitions of the day, the medical superstition not excepted ; [3] but the tendency of the age was too strong for them, the heads even of

[1] Cf. Sprengel, iii. 519, 523 f. ; Petersen, *Therapie*, p. 28.

[2] *Panoplia*, p, 71.

[3] The students who belonged to the *Marienbund* (Marian congregation) considered it one of the duties of their society, especially in holiday time, to keep watch in their parental homes and among their youthful friends, ' that forbidden literature, such as heretical, immoral, superstitious books should not be read or kept in possession.' They were above all pledged to keep a vigilant eye on *Wound Salves* or other superstitious booklets and songs, also on prayers in which fables of Christ or His apostles were related with a view to driving away illnesses, &c. ' Ansprache an die kleine Kongregation zu Ingolstadt am 8. Juli, 1590,' published in the *Katholische Bewegung*, 19 Jahrg., pp. 149–152. Among the Jesuits who opposed alchemy were Benedict Pereirius, a Spaniard († 1610), Balthasar Hagelius, professor at Ingolstadt († 1616), and Gretser ; see Kopp, *Alchemie*, i. 251 ; Huber, p. 420.

the wisest were so confused that the efforts of the Jesuits could not have any great result. At any rate, however, the stand they made against alchemistical and medicinal superstition shows what value is to be attached to the charge brought forward by the enemies of their Order that it had itself edited the *Rosenkreuz* writings, or at least used them in an altered form to deceive the Protestants or lull them to sleep.

Most of the Rosenkreuzers were also zealous Paracelsists ; as, for instance, Henning Scheunemann, practising doctor at Bamberg and later at Aschersleben, ' a man without any learning or knowledge of languages,' and the Protestant preacher John Gramann, who sold white vitriol with a conserve of roses as a panacea. To their number belonged also Julius Sperber, house-physician of the Prince of Anhalt ; Henry Kunrath, physician at Hamburg and later at Dresden ; Michael Maier, house-medicus to the Emperor Rudolf II and the Landgrave Maurice of Hesse-Cassel, and many others. John Heunemann of Reussing also († 1614), house-physician of the Emperor Rudolf II, gave himself up in later years to Paracelsist and alchemistical pursuits, but fell into ill-favour with the Emperor because he could not discover the philosopher's stone. At the beginning of the seventeenth century Germany was deluged with fanatics and swindlers of every kind and description ; Rosicrucians, alchemists, gold-makers, astrologers, expounders of dreams, Weigelians, and Paracelsists carried on everywhere their sinister trades, and spread abroad the most absurd and preposterous theories in floods of pamphlets. Mountebanks, quacks, hernia-curers, stone-curers, cataract-couchers, perambulated the market-places and had their arts proclaimed

in public by means of their harlequin.[1] Even men
of European fame, such as Crato von Krafftheim
(1586), the house-physician of Maximilian II, had to
compete with the most miserable charlatans and
quacks, and lived in ' brilliant misery.'

Other able and esteemed doctors of that period,
who rank with Crato, are John Schenck of Grafenberg,
John Lange, Felix Platter, William Fabricius Hildanus († 1634) and Hippolytus Guarinoni.[2] The last of
these is of such immense importance in the domain
of public culture of health that a fuller account of his
work seems indispensable.

Born at Trent in 1571, he received his education
in the Prague Jesuit College and at Padua; later on
he acted as town physician at Hall in Tyrol, where
he was house-physician to the Archduchesses Maria
Christina and Eleonora von Steiermark (Styria) in
the *Damenstift* (convent for noble ladies) of the place,
and where he died in 1654 at the age of eighty-three.[3]
He published his principal work at Ingolstadt in 1610
under the significant title ' Die Grewel der Verwüstung
Menschlichen Geschlechts' ('The Abomination of Deso-
lation in Mankind ').

[1] See Sprengel, iii. 519, 527, 531 f., 533 f. ; Hirsch, *Lexikon*, ii. 628 ;
Deutsche Klinik, 1868, No. 14 ; Schmieder, p. 353 f. ; Haeser, iii³. 226 ;
Kopp, i. 220; Hefele in Wetzer and Welte's *Kirchenlexikon*, ix³. 399;
Peters, N.F. pp. 224, 227, and vol. vi. of the present work, p. 285 ff.

[2] Haeser, ii³. 142 ; H. H. Beer, ' Krato von Krafftheim ' in the *Beilage
zu Jahrg. 8 der Österreich. Zeitschr. für praktische Heilkunde*, Vienna, 1862 ;
Archiv für Geschichte der Medizin, i. 107 f. ; *Deutsche Klinik*, 1868, No. 17 ;
concerning Lange.   Maier, *Schenck*, p. 37 ff. ; *Sammlung bernischer Bio-
graphien*, i. Bern, 1887, 276–284, for Hildanus; see *Archiv für Gesch.
der Medizin*, vi. 1 ff., and Henschel's *Zeitschr. der Medizin*, iii. 225 ff. ;
Pichler, *Guarinoni*, 12 f. ; Nagl-Zeidler, p. 611 f.

[3] See our remarks, vol. xi. p. 389 ff., and vol. xiii. p. 545 ff.

In the introduction to this book Guarinoni puts the question : Whence does it arise that in several places in Germany there is such a lack of old people, ' and that all the rest who are young are either weak and inert, or pale and thin ? Some have crippled hands, some lame feet, some of them are gouty, some have diseased bladders and kidneys, and are afflicted with other serious complaints. And all this, notwithstanding that through the length and breadth of Germany, and especially in our beloved fatherland Tyrol, such excellent and admirable gifts of medicine and nostrums are provided.'

On account of ' the love and loyalty he bears towards the German nation, but especially to his fatherland,' Guarinoni intends to point out the causes of this melancholy absence of health, and he fulfils the task in an admirable manner. The work is written in the German language and is addressed to the whole country, but especially the ruling authorities, whose business it is to take measures against the miseries which he describes. Accordingly the proofs he adduces are not taken from book-learning. Of medical authorities, only Aristotle, Galen and Hippocrates are quoted ; Guarinoni is in antagonism to the new empiricists and followers of Paracelsus, and he gladly seizes the opportunity of showing ' what sort of *Geselle* without the *G* these men are.' [1] But the actual convincing element of the book does not lie in the theoretical developments, but in the pungent descriptions of all the miserable conditions which the experienced author observed in his coming and going as doctor in town and village, among rich and poor.

[1] A play on the words *Geselle* (fellow) and *Esel* (donkey).—(TRANSLATOR.).

Guarinoni's accounts of the uncleanliness in houses and streets, of the disorder and viciousness of daily life, make it easy to understand the complaints raised as to the bad condition of the health of the people.

First among the things injurious to health he mentions the small, cramped, low rooms, especially when they are dirty and dark into the bargain, as is so common in Germany, where there are no good builders, and the masons are allowed to work in their own ignorant fashion.[1] Besides this, these smallrooms are wanting in proper ventilation, and Guarinoni takes a great deal of trouble to explain the necessity for remedying this evil. ' If stagnant air is unwholesome and injurious even under the open sky,' he says, ' how much more must it be so in the confinement of a town, a house, above all a room which is often kept shut for several months, sometimes not ventilated for one or more years ? With what an amount of dirt, impurity, and poison such an atmosphere must be loaded, and all this filth remains boxed up in the dirty, stinking rooms ! What wonder is it, then, that so many people complain of being constantly out of health, weak, and sickly, although they do not commit any excesses ? What greater disorder can there be indeed than to be always inhaling poisonous air ? What numbers of people I might mention, one after another, whom I have ordered out of such abominable conditions, with the result that they have afterwards been healthier and stronger ! ' [2]

As in private houses, so 'in almost all German schools, the windows and doors were kept religiously

---

[1] Guarinoni, p. 490.   [2] *Ibid.* p. 489.

closed, and everything turned on saving firewood and losing health. And so the parents had no need to wonder if their dear children sometimes came back from school pale and ill ; many a time the horrible stench of the school was to blame.' [1]

At the colleges it was the business of the professors to keep the beadles up to the work of ventilation. ' But there were some beadles so abominably lazy that they scarcely liked to open the school doors when people had to go in, still less could they be got to turn out the rooms and clean them now and then during the year ; and so the dust often lay as thick as a finger on the benches, and filth and mess of all sorts were found underneath.' [2]

In the streets of the Tyrolese towns the state of things seems to have been much worse even than in the houses. Heaps of dung lay ' collected in mounds in front of the houses and on the public places, and under the rays of the sun they gave out clouds of putrid, poisonous vapours, which floated all over the town and produced noxious fevers, and often downright pestilences. The spring was an especially unhealthy season, for then these heaps of dung and refuse were carted into waggons and taken into the fields, and the stench stirred up in the streets during the process of removal made many people sick and faint, and they had enough to do to stop up their noses and mouths.' [3] ' Filth and cattle dung,' Guarinoni said, ' must therefore not be tolerated in the town. The villages and peasants' farms are the proper place for them.' [4]

The civil authorities must also take into considera-

---

[1] Guarinoni, p. 492. [2] *Ibid.* p. 492.
[3] *Ibid.* p. 517. [4] *Ibid.* p. 516.

tion ' the putrid carcases which may be seen, and still more smelt, not only on and by the common country highways, but also lying exposed in towns and streets, and even outside private houses.[1] Such offal must not be thrown at haphazard by the street side or into streams or ponds. Putrefying carcases of animals ' must be buried deep under the earth.' Cemeteries also must not be within the town walls, especially as in some places ' the graves are dug scarcely deep enough to take in the coffins, and leave room to cover them over lightly with mould.' [2]

In still stronger language Guarinoni attacks another abuse, which indeed he shrinks from dealing with in more than a few hints : the pollution of the streets arising from the want of closets in many houses. 'Shall I speak, or shall I be silent ? Shall I bear witness to the truth, or shall I dissemble to please the dirty folk ? But how can I hold my tongue when I myself am sometimes one of the injured ones ? Of what use is it for me and other respectable men and householders to be careful to keep our own houses clean, when dirt and filth are thrown back again outside our houses and in front of our windows, making such a horrible stench that we are like to faint with sickness and are obliged to stop up our noses ? Go to, go to, sharpen thyself, my pen, thou must verily write the truth. Oh, unheard-of monstrosity ! I cannot find words with which to describe aright this inhuman dirt and filthiness, let alone the endless misery, ill-health, and bodily suffering that result from it. O pestilence ! where else shouldest thou abide than there where so rich and free a sacrifice

[1] Guarinoni, p. 515.   [2] *Ibid.* p. 514.

is daily offered up unto thee, there where thou art honoured, enticed, summoned ? . . .' [1]

In like graphic manner Guarinoni describes the stupidity with which the fountains are polluted, food made poisonous, and daily life in thousands of small ways sacrificed to insensate prejudices. At every turn there shines forth the noble character of the author, who, in spite of occasional coarseness of language, means it all heartily well for the welfare of the German nation, whose merits above other nations he frequently emphasises. That he will be mocked and ridiculed on account of his book he knows full well. He is not restrained, however, by dread of his fellow-creatures from frank criticism of public conditions, and his fearless, manly character shows itself still more by the courage with which he pronounces the chief blame of these unhealthy conditions to lie in the general immorality of the nation and in the abomination of taverns and bathing-houses ; he applies the lash as fearlessly to intemperance and immorality as to uncleanliness in the streets and houses. Thus in the first book he treats of the work of God, showing that without divine protection all care for health is vain, insisting again and again that a necessary means to the preservation of physical strength and health is a regular life, and the observation of the Ten Commandments of God, especially as to purity and chastity. On the very first page the author attests that ' this most humble little book of healing' is dedicated to the Mother of the ' Heil und Heiland ' (Health and Health-bringer = the Saviour), since ' there never has been dis-

---

[1] Guarinoni, pp. 504–505. Guarinoni says expressly that the description of this unsanitary state of things applies chiefly to Tyrol.

covered any stronger or better preserver and defender
of the common health, salvation, and truth, after God
than the ' Virgin Majesty ' of the Mother of God.[1]

In strong contrast to this Catholic Tyrolese doctor
stood Michael Bapst of Rochlitz, Protestant preacher
at Mohorn in the Meissen district.   A layman in medical

---

[1] Fragments of a second volume of the *Grewel der Verwüstung menschlichen Geschlechts* are to be seen in manuscript at the Innsbruck university
library among *Guarinoni's MSS*. vol. iv. fol. 390 f.   Not till the last
years of his life does the author appear to have taken in hand the contemplated continuation of his principal work.   At the end of the second
book stands the date : 15 July 1652.   Book III. chap. xviii., as the introductory words state, was begun forty-four years after the completion
of the first volume.   While the first volume is concerned with the ' horrors
of devastation ' arising from irregular living in days of health, the second
treats of *Irrungen in Krankheiten* (mistakes in illnesses).   Of the second
volume there is still extant ' the second book : *Den Kranken und sein
Amt betreffend*, and (mutilated at the end) the third book : *Den Doktor
der Arznei und sein hohe Kunst und Wissenschaft und Amt und Würde
betreffend*.   In the second book, chaps. i.–v. deal with hospitals ;
chap. xiv. (fol. 440ᵇ f.) with the ' abomination of lying soothsayers, cheating planet-readers and astrologists, palmists, wound and disease-charmers,
exorcists and bringers of disease on men, cattle and crops, witches riding
on forks and goats, and such-like monstrosities.   Chap. xv. (fol. 453):
' Of the abominable horror of the worldly-political, Machiavellian, bestial
patients who deny God, the eternal life and the immortality of the soul.'
Chap. xix. (fol. 471.ᵇ f.): ' Of the abomination of the dissolute, insolent,
and highly dangerous, apish counsellors and doctors.'   In the third book we
may specially mention the chapters against the Paracelsists, and such-like.
Chap. xviii. (fol. 513ᵇ): ' Whether the young men coming from college as
doctors of medicine are to be trusted.'   Chap. xviii. (fol. 517): *Vom
unleidentlichen, sträflichen Greuel der hermetisch unmenschlichen, ungeheuern
metallisch purgirenden Mord- und Tod Giften ; item wessen man sich zu
deren andern (ausser benannten Plutonischen Gespenstern) Gutes oder Böses
zu versehen habe.*   Chap. xix. : *Vom unchristlichen Greuel der ertzenden
verruchten, treulosen Juden.* . . . Chap. xxi. (fol. 530ᵃ): *Vom Greuel der
liederlichen täglichen Eingeb- und Einnehmung der purgirenden Arzneien und
der täglichen elenden Dies und Jenes Doktoren oder Alls Pillenschlucker,
dadurch der Leib verwelkt, der Farb und Kraft ermatt und der Magen zur
Apotheker Büchs Werden.*

matters, this preacher-doctor wrote numbers of books intended for the people, which contained on the one hand receipts for the cure of illnesses both of men and animals, and on the other instructions for every possible technical and economic business and detail of human life ; he announces especially that information on alchemistic matters was to be obtained from him. He introduces the most fabulous matter into this book, so much so that he often grows anxious himself as to what the reader's judgment will be. Thus he says once : [1] ' Whereas in this book I have for the most part borrowed from other writers, and had not time or ability enough to test everything, whether it was true or untrue, it may well have happened that now and then there be some mistakes. If therefore the reader should discover any incorrectnesses, I ask him not to ascribe it to me, but to the writers from whom I have copied, and to be assured of my own industry and well-intentioned spirit.' [2]

Of anything like order or method there is no question in the books of extracts of this scribbling preacher. In his ' Neues und nützliches Ertznei-,Kunst- und Wunderbuch,' published at Mühlhausen in 1590, ' there follow in delightful confusion recipes for nose-bleeding and menorrhagies, taming of leopards, constipation, sting of scorpion, tooth-ache, dog-bite, spider sting, discerning pregnancy in a woman, how to give copper the appearance of silver, visible and invisible writing, fishing, horses' diseases, against fever at night,' and so forth.[3] An equally motley collection of the most different and eccentric fruits of his reading

[1] *Leib und Wund Artzneibuch*, part II. pp. 171ᵇ, 172ᵃ.
[2] Schubert-Sudhoff, pp. 94–95.   [3] *Ibid.* pp. 86–87.

is contained in Bapst's 'Giftjagendes Kunst- und
Hausbuch' (Leipzig, 1591 and 1592). Of personal experience there is scarcely a trace in this book. It ' begins
with the snake-bite (first the serpent in Paradise)
and the medicinal use of snakes, spider stings, bait on
the fishing rod, bites of lion and wolf, catching foxes,
driving out wolves, fishing frogs, bites of scorpion,
a great deal about worms, accustoming pigeons to the
dove-cot and teaching them to bring other doves with
them, preserving fruits, producing plant-varieties,
preserving meat, driving away flies, &c., diarrhœa in
chickens, to keep bees in the hive, to kill bats, to get
rid of hairs and warts, wound-plaisters, to destroy
moths, maggots and lice ; the catching of birds, fish
and crawfish, with which the cure of cancer is connected,
and so forth. Among the thousands of nostrums of
all sorts there are scattered here and there, to suit the
taste of the time, a few alchemistical and chemiatric
receipts.' [1]

Exactly similar in character is the first part of the
' Wunderbarliches Leib und Wund Artzneibuch,' published at Eisleben in 1596. In addition to epilepsy the
Protestant divine here deals with all manner of complaints, fistulas, gout, pestilences ; he also discusses in
detail the means for raising the sexual functions, and
the ways for discerning the pregnancy of women. He
further goes into the questions of human dung as a
means of healing, of cement for distilling ovens, of
drinkable gold, the time for bleeding, and sympathy
methods.[2]

---

[1] Schubert-Sudhoff, p. 88.
[2] *Ibid.* pp. 89–90. Concerning Bapst's *Pimelotheca* (Eisleben, 1599,
it is said here at p. 91 : ' This, too, is another collection of recipes)

Sometimes even Bapst himself 'finds the prescriptions of his authorities too crazy.' Thus, for
instance, he says, after quoting the Count of Hohen-
lohe's prescription for cramp and pains in the limbs,
'Five lice and eight sheep-lice to be eaten between
slices of bread,' 'Let him who fancies it try it ; I myself
would rather be excused.' [1]

The charlatan Thurneissen zum Thurn was an
out-and-out Paracelsist.[2] In his 'Quinta Essentia'
he laments with profound sorrow that God should have
taken the 'Master Paracelsus in the prime of life.'

> His writings scattered here and there
> Are daily read with greatest care ;
> Many a science-loving man
> Will be thankful that he can
> See them, for they teach the art
> How to heal and soothe each part
> Of the body, be it sick or well.
> And not of medicine doth it tell
> Alone, but also about alchemy
> And many another mystery,
> Of star, soul, element he's laid
> Before us : oh, had he but stayed
> On earth a little longer, what
> Might not the world from him have got !
> But honours plenty on his head
> Have fallen, and the great man's dead.
> When 1500 years had fled

into which are introduced all sorts of delicate things, some of which
one would not at all have expected to find in this author, especially
from the department of the *Aphrodisiaka*. " Soot from a comet as a cure
for scab " is a nice piece of therapeutic information which he has picked
up in a book.'

[1] ' Of the psychic effect of this nostrum, still in use among the people,
he has no idea.' Schubert-Sudhoff, pp. 92–93.

[2] For supplementing the statements concerning Thurneissen in
vol. xii. p. 297 ff. of the present work, I refer readers to the article of
J. J. Merlo in the *Kölnische Volkszeitung*, 1886, No. 238, third sheet. Some
notes from the Cologne town archives which authentically confirm this
quack's death at Cologne in either 1595 or 1596 are given there.

> And forty-one, he did decease
> Christianly, in perfect peace.
> The day he died, September four
> And twenty ; the great name he bore
> Aureolus Theophrastus.
> Many a noble art he's left us.

In the epilogue of his strange work Thurneissen again speaks of his master in verse :

> For what Theophrastus has distilled,
> That he has to such a fineness reduced,
> That he was alone (what I say
> Is truly true) in fact,
> Without any other substance (near or about him)
> It became pure, translucid, clear and altogether subtile
>   [= bodiless or spirit-like],
> He did extract (the fifth essence or the empyrean fire)
> By the power of which he wrought prophet's wonders ;
> And before him there was not his equal.
> Maybe of his kind he will be the last.[1]

Valentine Antagrassus Siloranus went still further ; he declared Paracelsus to be an infallible ambassador of God. The Frankfort doctor, Gerhard Dorn, rendered an equal tribute to his master in boundless abuse of all his gainsayers : ' He, as an expert, could prepare the philosopher's stone in fifteen months ; others took years to do it.' In a publication which appeared at Frankfort in 1583, Dorn deduced the whole system of alchemy from the Book of Moses. Andrew Ellinger, professor at Jena, furthered the spread of Paracelsian crazes by his ' Apothekerbuch ' (Zerbst, 1602), as also by his pamphlet ' Von rechter Extraktion der seelischen und spiritualischen Kräfte aus allerlei Kräutern ' (Wittenberg, 1609). Another of these charlatans who enjoyed as great repute as did Thurneissen was

---

[1] L. Thurneissen, *Quinta Essentia*, Leipzig, 1574, pp. 34, 203.

the ' occult miracle-doctor ' Bartholomew Carrichter, patronised even by princes and kings.

Maximilian II appointed him his house-physician ; however, the celebrated doctor Crato von Krafftheim declared that Carrichter was to blame for the death of the Emperor Ferdinand I. In Carrichter's herb books, which were published by Michael Toxites, the plants are classified according to the twelve signs of the zodiac, and their effects are variously described according to the constellation at the time of their being gathered.[1]

In the preface of one of these herbals the publisher says : ' Doctor Carrichter was a man of learning and experience, although some doctors, but unjustly, look on him with contempt, as is sufficiently evident from his other books. In spite of his having taken his fundamentals from Theophrastus Paracelsus, he afterwards deviated from them and put forward a different method in his writings ; nevertheless I praise all that he has bequeathed to us of good in medicine, and above all I praise him for having described everything so plainly and lucidly in his books.' [2]

How far the praise lavished on the ' Kräutel-doctor ' Carrichter is justifiable let some passages from his herb books decide.

' Magic,' he says here, ' is nothing else than a stoppage of blood-spirit [*Blutgeist*] in human beings, in the

---

[1] Besides Sprengel, iii. 501 f., cf. *Allgem. Biographie*, iv. 27 ; v. 351 ; vi. 53 f. ; Wunderlich, *Gesch. der Medizin*, Stuttgart, 1859, p. 95 ; and Isensee, *Gesch. der Medizin*, i. Berlin, 1840, p. 250. Concerning Carrichter see Meyer, iv. 432 f., and Hirsch, *Lexikon*, i. 671. See also Gillet, ii. 38.

[2] Cf. herewith Schmidt, *Toxites*, p. 98 f., who says : ' It is scarcely comprehensible that Toxites, who only pretended to rave about Paracelsus, should have been able to praise such a senseless system of healing.'

veins. To this belongs also *Topasius*, the marrow of
young foals of horses, and the blood and marrow from
the legs of young wild goats or of young sucking pup-
pies, which must be carried about one's person or dried
above it ; carry it in a silk handkerchief, or a piece
of clean linen which has not been washed. Also the
blood of moles, taken from them while alive and laid
on the person dry or fresh, is equally good. Also the
spleen of young foals taken from their tongues. Also
the milk of young mares, churned into butter in May,
and then made into balsam with hazel-nut medlars,
gathered in May, before sunrise, or made into an
unguent with the juice of small Durant or the flowers
of hazel-nut trees, applied as above prescribed. These
things, used in this way, drive off all ills that come
from magic.' [1]

About the herb ' true love ' Carrichter says : ' The
royal art of " signature " tells great things of this little
herb, and no less indeed than that these herbs are very
poisonous on account of their earth-damp, but that
they are marvellous herbs for outward application ;
as an aconite is to the feet, so is this to the hands.
It is " signed " as follows : If anyone is suffering from
the plague and it presses from the arms to the heart,
so that there is a red stripe from the arm to the heart,
and it has the shape of a star in the heart of this flower ;
if the juice is extracted from this herb [true love] and
spread out on the hand whence the red mark starts
(not more than two or three berries, a little bruised,
when green), and this is done once, twice, or thrice,
even if anyone is in the pangs of death, either man or
woman, it brings him or her back to life, and extracts

[1] Carrichter, *Kräuterbuch*, Strassburg, 1617, pp. 12–13.

all the poison. And so each herb has its own virtue.
Hence, if any person has the whole " Harmonia and
Sympathia" of any herbs, he should regard these as
the noblest of all herbs. There is nothing nobler than
these herbs, for every one of them has its three " Har-
monias," and, *vice versa*, its three " Antipathias," from
which it may be seen what these herbs can do for
poisonous wounds or atmosphere, which can easily be
corrected by the figural triplicity, as aforesaid ; but
first of all they must be slightly distilled with vinegar
and wine, and afterwards added to from the last degree
of Leo and the highest degree of Virgo.' [1]

Still stranger things are found in Carrichter's pamphlet, ' Von gründlicher Heylung der zauberischen
Schäden.' [2] ' All who read this little treatise,' the
author assures his readers, ' and who gather and collect
the herbs and other things appertaining thereto at the
right time, will be serviceable to God and man, and no
magic or witchcraft will be able to hurt them.' Two
salves, ' otherwise called balsams,' are especially recommended here ' in all cases of magic.'

The first of these, the balsam of filbert mould, is
made as follows : ' Item, take of the fat of a puppy,
after it has been well clarified, 8 lot ; of bear-grease,
well clarified, 16 lot ; capon fat, 24 lot, well clarified ;
filbert mould three handfuls ; mix all in a mortar with
a pestle of linden-wood, with berries and leaves, so
that it may be juicy ; put it into some vase, leave it
in the sun for nine weeks, till it becomes a light green
salve ; with this you may smear all wounds and hurts
caused by magic, and they will all disappear.

[1] Carrichter, *Kräuterbuch*, pp. 173–174.
[2] See present work, vol. xii. p. 290 ff.

'Now follows the second balsam of linden-wood mould.

'Item, capon fat, well clarified, to which add four handfuls of linden-wood mould, and do just as above described. The process is then complete.'[1]

'When anyone is crooked and deformed, so that his knees grow into his breasts, which also comes from witchcraft,' Carrichter recommends the following cure : 'If there is burning and heat, it must be cooled with fern roots and oak-ash lye ; shake it over the place, cold, and take the fine Durant water ; if this cannot be had take Widerthon water, in a morning before getting up ; it must be dug up and burnt, so that no one may see it ; put into this three or four drops of the blood of a young puppy ; do this several times over, and lay it on the burnt place till the scald disappears (the blood must be taken from the left ear of the puppy) ; if, however, the wound is open or begins to suppurate, take of Widerthon one part, of Durant three parts, powdered fine, till the man is healed. He will be thoroughly healed.'[2]

'People who are afraid of being victims of magic,' says Carrichter, 'or who live with bad people from whom they are afraid of being infected with bad thoughts, must take sprigs of the noble hypericon and the noble Durant, which have been dug up under the right celestial influence, and they must hang it in four corners of the house, rooms, and cellar, and lay it in their beds ; they must also wear it at their throats, and I do assure them that no magic will have power to hurt them ; they may

[1] Carrichter, *Von gründlicher Heylung der zauberischen Schäden*, pp. 6, 7.
[2] Carrichter, *ibid.* pp. 8, 9.

also use it like powder for eight days. Also if people give it to their cattle with salt, they themselves will be proof against all magic arts.' [1]

In another place Carrichter writes : ' If one man has stabbed or murdered another, let him go quickly and throw the blood that is running from him three times into a fire of dry oak-wood of the greatest heat, and change his shoes, putting the right shoe on the left foot, and the left shoe on the right foot ; he will then become blind and think he is riding in water up to his mouth, and he will come back to the murdered man be he who he may.' [2]

' I have been obliged to give these examples,' says the herb-doctor, ' in order that people may see that the remedies that have been used hitherto are without foundation and truth, and are only old wives' arts, and that they have gone on being altered more and more into syrups, pillules, juleps, electuaries and such-like, and that by this means the highly laudable art of medicine has fallen into contempt with the Avicennists and Galenists, who say that they have derived all their facts and principles from Hippocrates, who certainly, as the discoverer *locorum morborum et simptomatum*, also of the humours, has originated something, which he caused to be discussed with his disciples and so shaped into a book. But as regards the "Sympathia," herbs, shrubs and trees he was thoroughly ignorant, except in so far as he had learnt from old wives.' [3]

In view of such utterances it is easy to understand

---

[1] Carrichter, pp. 31, 32.
[2] Carrichter, *Practica aus den fürnemsten Secretis* (Strassburg, 1614), ii. 42.
[3] Carrichter, *Practica*, ii. 121.

how the botanist and Heidelberg Professor Tabernaemontanus wrote : ' The new pretended, self-made doctors, who call themselves Paracelsists, boast hugely of
their tinctures and of all the wonderful things they can
do with them. I myself, however, have never seen or
heard of any one of them who either has or could make
a proper tincture. I will not speak of the great marvels
which they pretend to work with them, but mixing
three parts of lies with one part of truth, they still
have some standing, and do such wonders in the way
of curing diseases, which are otherwise as they say
incurable, that many people complain of these quacks,
that they have been ruined and made into cripples by
them, and that many of their patients have lost their
lives in a dreadful way through their practices.' [1]

Still stronger language concerning the decline of
medicine and the practice of the Paracelsists was used
by the renowned physician Caspar Hofmann, at Frankfort-on-the-Oder. In a lecture on the invasion of
barbarism in all departments of learning (' Über die
hereinbrechende Barbarei auf allen Gebieten der Wissenschaft '), which was printed in 1578, he said respecting
the science of healing : ' Into this sacred science also,
which is so beneficial to the human race, cheating
swindlers are forcing an entrance. Driven by hunger,
lured by gain, people who have acquired no learning
whatever flock to this profession as a last anchor of
hope, when all other attempts have failed. Without
humanistic culture, without philosophical training of
the mind, they actually venture on the treatment of
the sick, while they are ignorant of the most ordinary
medical prescriptions, and have never had any ex-

---

[1] Tabernaemontanus, *New Kreuterbuch*, i. 17–18.

perience in the practical application of the science of medicine.   No disease is too serious for their audacious experiments.   Their art, so they declare even in cases of the utmost danger, will bring healing—healing which in reality they sacrifice to every sport of chance.   They take no account whatever of what is required by different diseases in view of their special nature and their different stages, or what the physical characteristics of different individuals demand.   These men use fixed remedies, the essence and nature of which are unknown to them, without inquiring into the particular constitution and strength of the patient, without any distinction between different temperaments, without regard to the seat of the disease, or to age, bodily condition, habits, and all the other considerations which experienced doctors look upon as guides to treatment.

' And nevertheless these shameless quacks set themselves up above all others, and, relying on the senseless credulity of the masses, they lie boldly about the secrets of their art, praise up, like criers in the market-place, their mighty deeds and wondrous cures— *i.e.* the cures of those who thanks to their vigorous constitutions have overcome the disease ; of the rest who fell victims to death owing to the audacious ignorance of their doctors no mention is made.   If, however, the cure does not prosper, and fear of worse complications drives the sick persons to seek advice from more experienced doctors, because they see that the result does not justify the glowing assurances that had been made to them, then words can scarcely describe the shamelessness with which these puffed-up wind-bags insult and revile the men who have grown grey in honourable practice of their profession.   As

a matter of fact they are afraid of being convicted of
ignorance and blunders.   Hence they carefully conceal
the secrets of their healing methods, and with wicked
cunning have recourse to equivocation, so as not to be
condemned.

' We cannot, however, help wondering how all these
charlatans, who spring up everywhere like mushrooms,
obtain such high repute with the great masses.   For
the latter all flock to them, and make a tremendous
fuss with them ; they are worshipped by the people,
and exalted to heaven by all those who let themselves
be bewitched by popular opinions, although they have
no claim at all to the title of scholars.   Their training
for practising the art of healing does not consist in the
study of philosophy, but in learning the art of deception.

' But the inexperienced crowd, always on the
look-out for something new, listen with wide-open ears
to these presumptuous promises, and indulge in the
keenest hopes of being healed.   They look at the few
successful cases, judge the whole matter by a single
fact, and do not consider how many lives have been
shortened to one that has been saved.   The repute
of the quacks, therefore, has its origin in the utter
want of judgment of the multitude.   Meanwhile the
" salvation " which they promise they do not as a rule
bring to the sick, until their complaints are hidden
under the damp earth.

' But from these deceivers let us now pass to the
smoke-blackened sons of Vulcan, who had no good luck
at the forge, and in their despair turned to the art
of healing.   From their melting furnace they promised
themselves to produce marvellous cures, and they
boasted of glorious achievements in the field of medicine.

' For these uneducated alchemists nature, as it
was formerly known, was too limited ; they therefore
conceived a dream of a new and a truer world.

' So they found for themselves a new way of healing,
all done through metals.

' Besides this they had still other means for making
themselves a name and for emptying purses. They
gained repute, for instance, by appealing to Paracelsus,
whose name is all-powerful with all the friends of
novelty, just as if before him alone Nature had risen
reverentially and unveiled herself. And yet this very
man, though he promised length of life to others,
hastened on his own death by his metallic methods.
Another way by which the quacks exalt themselves is to
look down with contempt on the works of the princes
of our art, while arrogating to themselves acquaintance
with the whole of nature, intimacy with all true learning, imputing ignorance to all the rest, and wickedly
undermining their repute by making the uneducated
classes believe that their pretended knowledge is mere
verbiage and word-tinkling. At the same time, however, they take good care to inform themselves of the
different mental tendencies of all those they pretend
to despise, to note accurately their various talents
and characters, and they flee religiously from those
who are likely to see through their own hollowness
and to cast suspicion on them, while to those who
admire and praise their charlatanry they cringe in
servile reverence. For the wealthy they prepare drinks
and concoctions made from precious stones, and gain
their favour through soothsaying, and claim to be
honoured and esteemed because they can see into the
future and disclose hidden secrets. Not least among

their means of self-advancement are the amulets which, as they pretend, will drive away all diseases if hung on the person at prescribed hours.' [1]

Closely connected with this kind of doctoring were the astrological illusions, which were disseminated in the widest circles by the universal custom of having calendars prepared by doctors of medicine, with weather forecasts and explanations of the constellations. Those calendars with their rules for house and home procured an entry for astrological nonsense as well as medicinal superstitions into the homes of burghers and peasants. In this way the most preposterously absurd things were spread abroad among the people.[2]

'Yes, indeed,' says Tabernaemontanus, 'if it all went on without injuring the sick, one could put up with it ; but through their gross ignorance many people's lives are ruined, and then the planets and the stars are called to account, and the wicked aspects are held guilty, as though the stars had given warning beforehand of what was to happen ; and so they charge the beautiful constellations with their own guilt and ignorance. It is high time for a Christian government to interfere and put a stop to the work of these ignorant fanatics and calendar-makers ; yea, verily, men who have graduated at universities ought to be ashamed of all these rubbishy tricks which any wretched bacchant is capable of performing, and not thus belittle their reputation.' [3] 'Our present-day astrologers and calendar-makers, who forsake their callings and set

[1] C. Hofmanus, *De barbarie imminente*, Francof. 1578, and as appendix to Dornavius, *Ulysses Scholasticus*, pp. 109–115.

[2] See Hellmann, *Meteorologische Volksbücher*, Berlin, 1891 ; Sprengel, ii. 409 f. ; Haeser, ii³. 218 ; Schindler, pp. 84, 210, 235.

[3] Tabernaemontanus, *New Kreuterbuch*, i. 225.

about to discover the nature and workings of the firmament of heaven, get involved in such a labyrinth of error that they no longer know one herb from another, and do not even recognise a nettle unless they are stung by touching it.   And yet they write out for their patients great and lengthy receipts, with twenty or more different things brought into them of which they themselves scarcely know two or three ; and so the true and genuine knowledge of the simple herbs and vegetable growths is becoming greatly corrupted and obscured.' [1]

While Paracelsus and his followers were busy with the explanation of the magic forces of medicinal substances, and while the astrologers were questioning the stars concerning the diseases of mankind, a saviour of the true science of medicine arose in Andrew Vesalius, physician in ordinary to Charles V, in 1544, and later on to Philip II, and who died in 1564 on the island of Zante after his return from a pilgrimage to Jerusalem. Born of a German family of Wesel, he is ' the actual founder of modern anatomy, the first who with his scientific knowledge broke through and abolished the almighty power of mere book-lore.'   His work, entitled ' Sieben Bücher vom Bau des menschlichen Korpers ' ('Seven Books on the Construction of the Human Body '), published at Basle in 1543, contains the foundations of modern anatomy ; they are still an object of admiration to the most eminent experts ; ' open the work where you will, and as often as you will, always and everywhere you will find instruction, stimulus, and enjoyment.' [2]

[1] Tabernaemontanus, Preface.
[2] Roth, *Vesalius*, pp. v and 130 ; see p. 140 f. ; and Haeser, ii³. 39 f. ; cf. Dr. Aug. Froriep, *Zur Gesch. der anatomischen Anstalt zu Tübingen*

On the title-page of this monumental work,[1] which
covers about 700 pages of large folio, is depicted the
anatomical theatre of Vesalius ; the master stands in
the middle, surrounded by numerous onlookers, occupied
with the dissection of a female corpse.   In the border
round the title there are two grinning apes and a
human face, which represent the opposite anatomical
systems of Galen and of Vesalius.   Above, in the
middle, are displayed the laurel-decked arms of the
author : three weasels.[2]

In the preface Vesalius complains in bitter language
of the decline of all branches of the science of healing.
Anatomy, he says, comes off worst of all.   The professors consider it beneath their dignity to handle a
knife and the prosectors are ignorant barbarians ;
hence the universal ignorance of the wonderful
mechanism of the human body.   And yet for the
doctor of medicine, the investigator of nature, the
thinking human being, anatomy was of essential importance.   The principal reason why anatomy was
proscribed and put down was, according to Vesalius,
the fact that everywhere people treated as infallible
the authority of a man who had never dissected a
human corpse, viz. Galen.   ' No doctor,' he writes,

(Brunswick, 1902), vi. Concerning Vesalius see also Baus, p. 230 ff.
Ro h (p. 151 f.) shows how all the different departments, which have
since detached themselves from anatomy, have their origin in the work
of Vesalius.   The above-named investigator shows also that, besides the
already mentioned great and important work intended for the professional people who attend the dissections, the abridgment of this work
(*Suorum de fabrica corporis humani librorum Epitome*, Basileae, 1543)
must not be neglected.   This last, compiled for beginners, gives more
than it promises.

[1] *De corporis humani fabrica libri septem*, Basileae, 1543.
[2] Roth, *Vesalius*, pp. 178–179.

'considers it possible that the slightest mistake has ever been or could ever be found in the anatomical works of Galen. As a matter of fact, however, Galen never in his life cut up a human corpse, because he "never had access to more than two dried-up corpses." Led astray by his monkeys, Galen frequently, but unjustly, attacks the Alexandrian doctors who were experienced in human anatomy. Moreover Galen very often did not rightly understand the anatomy of monkeys. It is a remarkable fact that in spite of the enormous difference between the structure of men and of monkeys Vesalius only recognised a distinction in the toes and the bend of the knee. And even these points doubtless would not have been learnt by him if the knowledge had depended on a post-mortem.' [1]

In the work itself Vesalius begins with the bones and cartilages, deals next with the ligaments and muscles, the blood-vessels and nerves, and ends with the three cavities of the body. Each organ is described in regard to number, position, shape, size, composition, connexion, use—in short, in every one of its aspects. Side by side with the description there is always a steady refutation and explanation of the Galenian anatomy. Galen is tested by the true standard, the human body. In like manner the knowledge of all the other medical classics is shown up and refuted by nature and by anatomy. The descriptions are illustrated by pictures which, ' while perfectly true to nature, are as far removed from over-careful individualisation as from superficiality, and are adapted alike to the demands of anatomy and to those of art.' [2]

---

[1] Haeser, ii[3]. 40–41 ; Roth, pp. 131, 143–144.

[2] *Ibid.* pp. 132, 143–144 ; Haeser, ii[3]. 40.

This master-work of Vesalius was published in a German translation by Albinus Thorinus, professor of medicine at Basle, in 1551, at Nuremberg.

In the Basle university this much misunderstood master of anatomy found warm adherents and disciples. By the combined efforts of a number of scholars the medical faculty at Basle had made notable strides since 1532 ; but their actual period of prosperity began towards the end of the first half of the sixteenth century, when two men, thenceforth to shine as radiant stars, started on their careers of activity : Felix Platter and Theodore Zwinger.   The second of these two remained for thirty years in the medical faculty and filled six times the post of dean.   The new statutes drawn up by him for the faculty, which were adopted by the academic senate in 1570, retained their authority almost down to the present time.   It was not only by his instructional work, but also by his organisation of free disputations for the students, and by his management of the finances of the faculty, that this excellent man made himself invaluable.[1]

The labours of Felix Platter, the earliest representative on German soil of the tendency followed by Vesalius, were of still greater importance.   In 1557, on his return to his native town after a residence of four and a half years at the university of Montpellier, Platter started his medical practice, as well as his instructional work at the college.   In both lines he achieved important results.   In 1562 he was already able to write in his diary, ' My practice grows more and more—brings me nearly all the nobles living at Basle ; also many strangers, some of whom soon leave, taking with them

[1] Miescher, *Medizinische Facultät in Basel*, p. 19 f.

my methods and advice ; some of them invite me to
their courts and castles.' Later on the help of the distinguished Basle doctor was requisitioned by numbers
of princes, as, for instance, the Margraves of Baden
and Brandenburg, the Dukes of Lorraine and Saxony,
Katherine, sister of King Henry IV of France, and
above all the Dukes of Württemberg.[1]

Platter was still more distinguished as an anatomist.
As a teacher of this subject he did work of immense
importance. In 1559, when a young man of twenty-
three, he gave a public anatomical demonstration.

' It happened on April 1,' he himself relates, ' that
a prisoner was to be executed for theft, and I asked
my brother-in-law, who was a member of the council,
to help me to secure his corpse. As, however, he
thought that the corpse would be wanted by the
university, or perhaps he thought I should not be
able to dissect it, I said no more to him but went
straight to the burgomaster, Franz Oberieth, to whom
I made my request, and begged for the corpse after the
execution. He was surprised that I should undertake
this alone, but promised to do his best and to bring the
matter before the council the next morning. The evil-
doer was to be executed on April 5 ; he was condemned
to death by the sword. As soon as the council broke
up my brother-in-law came to me and told me they
had consented to let me have the corpse, and that they
would convey it to the church of St. Elsbethen, after
the execution, where I was to dissect it ; but that I was
to inform the doctors and surgeons, so that they might

---

[1] Miescher, pp. 41–44. See also Albert, *Beiträge zur Gesch. der Chir-
urgie,* ii. Vienna, 1878, p. 193, and Hirsch, *Gesch. der medizinischen
Wissenschaften,* p. 42 ff.

attend if they wished, besides a great many people
who were also present.   This brought me great renown,
because for a great many years only one dissection
(post-mortem) had been held by one member of our
university, viz. by Dr. Vesalius at Basle.   I was engaged
on it for three days ; afterwards I boiled the bones that
had been well cleaned, and put them together and
made a skeleton out of them, which I still have in my
possession after fifty-three years, for I had a case made
for it in which it stood in my room.' [1]

Platter held another public anatomical demonstration in 1563 and two in 1571, while at the same time he
went on diligently dissecting in private.   In the preface to his work ' Über den Bau und die Verrichtungen
des menschlichen Körpers ' he speaks of having dissected fifty corpses.   ' With such ardour,' he says
here, ' did I carry on anatomical studies that neither
the horror nor the repulsiveness of the work, nor the
dangers to which it often exposed me, nor my other
extremely arduous occupations, were able to keep me
back from experiments of this sort.'   Besides the
above-mentioned work, Platter also published a ' Handbuch der Pathologie und Therapie,' and a volume of
' Beobachtungen über die Krankheiten des Menschen.'
In the preface of the handbook he says : ' I have made
it a rule always to search into the truth for myself, as
far as lies in my power, and never blindly to follow any
so-called authority ; that which on sure grounds and
reliable experience I have recognised as truth, I have
stated as such ; when anything has appeared to me
only probable, or else uncertain, or very doubtful, even

[1] Miescher, pp. 46–47.   Concerning Platter's art of making skeletons
as compared with that of Vesalius, see Roth, p. 471 f.

though others should hold it to be certain, I have
honestly given my own opinion. With regard to
things not yet known I have preferred to draw my
conclusions from results rather than from causes, and
not to make what is already obscure still more so by
unintelligible theories, as is often done because people
are ashamed of owning their ignorance.' The chief interest of these observations of Platter is their evidence
of the author's efforts to trace the causes of disease
by means of anatomical investigation. Special attention is given in these pages to mental disturbances.[1]

It was of vital importance to the improvement of
the medical faculty at Basle that Platter was able,
in 1589, to carry through the establishment of a third
professorship. Up till then there had been only two
professors of medicine—one for theory, the other for
practice ; but in 1589 a third chair was founded for
anatomy and botany, and at the same time an anatomical theatre and a botanical garden were started.
The new professorship was given to Caspar Bauhin,[2]
who now began a career of labour no less important
than that of his teacher Platter. Bauhin's public
anatomical dissections of human corpses were attended
not by the students only but by interested spec-
tators of all classes, even the highest. In the Deaconate
book of 1596 there is mention of an ' anatomical performance ' which was attended by princes, counts,
barons, nobles, doctors, and a great crowd of students.[3]
The study of anatomy suffered a drawback from

---

[1] Miescher, *Medizinische Facultät in Basel*, pp. 47, 49–50.

[2] See vol. xiii. p. 541 ff.

[3] Hess, *K. Bauhin*, p. 53. Here (p. 58 f.) there are fuller details
concerning Bauhin's anatomical writings.

the difficulties in the way of procuring human corpses ;
the professors were often obliged to content themselves
with the carcases of animals.   Felix Platter, who in all
undertakings aiming at the improvement of the faculty
and of the study of anatomy was invariably the great
motive power, exerted himself most energetically to
overcome this obstacle.   Under his deanship, in 1604,
it was arranged that visitation of the poor patients in
the hospital should be instituted as a return for the
grant of corpses.   Platter himself (1612) made a
beginning by undertaking the new duties.   Finally,
also, he took up the smaller business details and nego-
tiated with the council and the executioner concerning the price of the burials of the dead bodies.[1]   By
the introduction of regular anatomical teaching and
thanks to the distinguished tuitional work of Platter
and Bauhin, the Basle college outstripped all the
German universities.   When Platter came to Basle in
1557 he found only two students of medicine ; in 1575
the number had risen to fifteen, in 1580 to twenty-one,
in 1588 to twenty-nine, in 1606 to thirty-four, and in
1609 to fifty-one.   Still more gratifying was the increase in ' Doctor-promotions.'   In the period between
1532 and 1560 only nine men had taken the degree of
doctor ; in the next twenty-five years the number rose
to 114, and in the following twenty-four years, from
1586 to 1610, it rose to 454.[2]

Platter died in 1614, and Bauhin succeeded him
in the chair of practical medicine.   The brilliance of
the medical faculty in the ' Helvetian Alps ' now began

[1] Miescher, pp. 21–22.
[2] His, ' Zur Gesch. des anatomischen Unterrichtes in Basel ' in the
Gedenkschrift zur Eröffnung des Vesalianum, Leipzig, 1885, p. 6.

gradually to fade, as is shown by the decrease in the number of doctor's degrees taken. The pursuit of anatomy also came to a standstill. Here, as everywhere in Germany, the greatest difficulties were placed in the way of study. In the first place, the fact that only the corpses of people who had been executed were allowed to be used for scientific experimentalising was an immense hindrance to regular demonstrations ; added to which, before a corpse could be secured after an execution, endless correspondence and transactions had to be carried on with an unintelligent bureaucracy.[1] The common people, moreover, then, as before, had the greatest prejudice against opening corpses. The stubbornness with which this feeling was kept up is astounding. Even in the middle of the seventeenth century the anatomical zeal of the Jena professor, Werner Rolfink, stirred the peasants of the neighbourhood to such a frenzy of excitement, that they instituted strict watch over their corpses to prevent their being ' gerolfinkt ' (Rolfinked). At the college at Würzburg, the splendid institution of the Prince-bishop Julius Echter of Mespelbrunn, very shortly after its foundation, the dissection of human corpses had been initiated by the medical faculty ; but as late as 1661 report said concerning the professor Becher : ' At Würzburg the town has become hostile towards anatomy, because, with the sanction of the authorities, he subjected to anatomical dissection a woman who had been executed ; the townspeople did not desist till they had driven him out of the place.' [2]

---

[1] His, pp. 6–7 ; Puschmann, p. 331.
[2] Haeser, ii³. 280.   Kölliker, *Zur Gesch. der medizinischen Facultät an der Universität Würzburg*, Würzburg, 1871, pp. 8 and 11.   At Strassburg

These prejudices gradually diminished, especially
among the upper classes; but another serious difficulty
arose ' in the shape of unworthy scientific curiosity,
bound up with objectionable sensuality.' ' The dissections came to be looked on as edifying spectacles
to which crowds flocked for entertainment; the chief
point of excitement lay in the demonstrations on the
sexual organs, for which a higher entrance fee was
charged.   When the reigning Duke of Württemberg,
in 1604, was visited by three Saxon princes, in order to
provide them with an entertainment he took them to
Tübingen to see the dissection of a human corpse, an
operation which lasted for eight days.' [1]

In the department of practical medicine also Vesalius was in advance of all his contemporaries.[2]   In the
preface to his celebrated work he delineates the position
of both anatomy and medicine at that period.   ' The
ancient doctors of medicine,' he says, ' with Hippocrates at their head, cultivated the entire art of healing,
including dialectics, the knowledge and application of
materia medica, and surgery, with which they were as
familiar as with the other branches; Galen practised
surgery with his own hands.   Gradually, however,
under the influence of the Romans, the physicians gave
away their science, handed over the preparation of the
patients' food to the attendants, that of the medicines

it was not till 1690 that the corpses of hospital patients were granted for
anatomical purposes.   Wieger, *Gesch. der Medizin in Strassburg*, Strassburg, 1885, p. 82.   All the great anatomical discoveries of the sixteenth
and seventeenth centuries were made from animals only, says Hyrtl,
*Vergangenheit und Gegenwart des Museums für menschliche Anatomie
an der Wiener Universität*, Vienna, 1869, p. xiii.

[1] Puschmann, pp. 331–332.

[2] Roth (*Vesalius*, pp. 200–201) might indeed claim that he knew more
than most of the medical men of the eighteenth century.

to the apothecaries, the surgical work to the barbers, and kept to themselves nothing more than the prescription of drugs and diet in cases of internal diseases. They neglected the most important part of medical treatment which is most dependent on observation of nature, viz. surgery, and at the same time they treated the surgeons worse than servants. The physicians themselves have been the cause that they and our sacred art of healing have come to be despised, for of their own accord they let the best part of the work slip out of their hands. The students must at all costs be prevailed on to master the art of the surgery. This is all the more necessary because those among them who are most highly educated have as great a horror of surgery as of the plague, and the chief cause of this is that they do not wish to be held up to the common people by the other doctors as barbers, which would make them lose caste and profits. This detestable prejudice of the common people is in great measure to blame for the fact that the doctors nowadays do not themselves practise the whole of their art, but, to the injury of mankind, confine themselves to a small part of it.' Vesalius himself had to suffer from this ' disgusting prejudice,' as imperial physician he was only allowed to treat internal complaints ; to his great grief he was usually obliged to abstain from surgery. With unflinching courage and frankness he calls the surgeons of the time thoroughly uneducated men, barely even semi-doctors, medical syrup-writers and gold-makers.[1] Hard words these, but altogether justifiable. Quacks and charlatans, who performed the most difficult operations without any training, or any knowledge of

[1] Roth, pp. 197–199.

the construction of the human body, had become a regular plague in the land. It is pitiful to think of the numbers of human lives sacrificed in those days because doctors innumerable were given up to astrology and deduced the symptoms of disease from the influence of the stars.

True, there were not wanting opponents to all this quackery, but how could the common-sense doctors make any headway when even so intellectual and significant a man as Philip Melanchthon eulogised his friend Jacob Milich, professor of medicine at Wittenberg, chiefly for the reason that he was seeking to combine astrology with medicine in the minutest manner, and that he considered astrology quite as certain and unillusive as any other human science ? It was a pupil of Melanchthon and Milich, John Moibanus of Berlin, who, from the opposition of Saturn, prophesied his own speedy death, which prophecy chanced to come true. The defenders of such superstition were enormously greater in number than were those who saw through the error and baselessness of astrology. To what hostility the latter class were exposed is shown from the biography of the botanist Cordus. Thomas Erastus, also, had much to suffer at the court of Count von Henneberg because he held aloof from astrological charlatanry. Those doctors, on the other hand, who devoted themselves to casting nativities, to the preparation of alchemical miracle-tinctures, occult medicines and talismans, stood in the greatest repute with both high and low, and reaped rich harvests of gold.[1]

[1] Sprengel, iii. 412–413, 417–418. Concerning Cordus see vol. xiii. pp. 509–511. For Erast, see Bonnard, *Th. Eraste et la discipline ecclésiastique*, Lausanne, 1894. Respecting the miracle-tinctures see also our present work, vol. xii. p. 282 ff.

This decline of practical medicine was in great part
due to the absence of regular clinical instruction at
the German universities. Only here and there—for
instance, at Vienna, Heidelberg, Ingolstadt and Würzburg—were the students conducted to the hospitals
for study ; as a rule instruction in diseases lay outside
the university curriculum. The lectures were for the
most part only theoretical. Even the practical instruction in anatomy consisted chiefly in the demonstration of sections of corpses ; only in exceptional cases
did the students have the opportunity of taking part
in the dissections.[1]

Quite apart from these deficiencies, it is undoubtedly
true that the medical faculties, in every respect, were
no more than step-children to the universities of that
time. Generally there were only two professors appointed, and often not more than one. With regard to
salaries also the professors of medicine were beneath
those of theology and jurisprudence. The scarcity of
attendance in the medical faculties is astounding. At
Leipzig there were seldom more than from four to six
students of medicine. The Basle university in 1556
counted only two professors and two students of
medicine. All who were able to do so went abroad ;

---

[1] Haeser, ii[3]. 129 ; Puschmann, pp. 274, 277–278 ; J. Schneller, *Historische Entwickelung der medizinischen Facultät in Wien*, Vienna, 1856,
p. 5. In the medical faculty at Vienna from the year 1557, Professor
John Aichholtz had to undertake the dissection of corpses for purposes
of study for more than twenty years. Cf. *Nachträge zu Aschbachs
Gesch. der Wiener Universität*, i. 1, 4 ff. ' There is no proportion whatever
between this long period of time, and the number of cases of dissection,
not more than nine, which are quoted, and it may be inferred from these
figures how seldom teachers and students had the opportunity of gaining
closer acquaintance with the human body by observation and practice '
(p. 6).

the Montpellier and Padua universities especially were largely attended by medical students. It is true that grave abuses prevailed there also ; for instance, at Padua it was customary for the candidates for examination to bring with them assistants who whispered to them the answers to the questions asked. The arrangements were even more convenient at Helmstadt, where, according to the statement of the Augustinian Leyser, the answers were written side by side with the question and handed to the examinees. No wonder that prominent physicians, such as Sylvius and Vesalius, did not exert themselves to win honours such as these.[1]

In the German colleges surgery was quite an exceptional branch of study—as, for instance, at Vienna, it was almost entirely relegated to the barbers and shavers, and scarcely ever placed above the level of handwork.[2]

This was all the worse because the actual learned doctors who had been trained at the universities scarcely practised any surgery (under which maternity cases were then included), and, moreover, were themselves

---

[1] Puschmann, pp. 263, 265–266, 279–281, where proofs are given.

[2] Puschmann, p. 282. See also Baas, pp. 189 ff., 225 ff. The able Felix Würtz († 1574 or 1575 ; cf. Haeser, ii[3]. 165) stands quite alone. See concerning him also Hirsch, *Gesch. der Medizin*, p. 74 f. ; *ibid.* p. 73, the examination of surgeons and the appointment of town surgeons, and p. 77 f., concerning the interesting compendium of the oculist's art by George Bartisch, court oculist at Dresden († 1607), who, moreover, was so deeply plunged in superstition that he considered many eye-diseases brought on by ' sorcery, witches, magic and devil's work.' Concerning the treatise of Bartisch see also d'Elvert, p. 118, who remarks : ' Almost incredible are the author's tales of the shamelessness and ignorance of the " cataract couchers," who perambulated the market-places, and who in the public streets, without troubling themselves even to make a show of a diagnosis, for a slight fee (three, six, or at the most twelve groschen !) operated on the blind with instruments which Bartisch himself calls clumsy, and then left the patients to their fate.'

few in number. By far the greater part of the popu-
lace were at the mercy of the barber-surgeons whose
art was of a very questionable character. The
melancholy condition of the surgical art in Germany
is still more striking if compared with the high status
to which surgery attained in Italy and Spain in the
sixteenth century.

' The surgeons of our day,' says John Lange at
about the middle of the century, ' have scarcely ever
witnessed the process of disembowelling a calf or a pig.
And yet, although completely ignorant of anatomy,
they have no scruple in cauterising and cutting up
human bodies in the most barbarous manner.' [1]

That this complaint is not an exaggeration is shown
by the reports of other medical writers. The celebrated
Bernese town physician, Wilhelm Fabricius Hildanus,
was horrified at seeing how ' ignorant men without
any training, without any knowledge of the construction
of the human body, who had spent only a short time
in the shops of their masters, undertook the most
difficult surgical operations. Failures and mishaps did
not frighten off these people. " We must experiment-
alise and learn even if it costs the lives of a hundred
peasants ! " said one such practitioner.' ' The itinerant
surgeons proceeded even more insanely than the local
ones. Up and down the land they trudged, chiefly with
the object of crying up their art at the yearly fairs,
which they did with great profusion of market-criers'

---

[1] Haeser, ii[3]. 157. Concerning the magic-medicine art at Nuremberg
see Mummenhoff in the *Festschrift der* 65. *Versammlung deutscher Naturforscher und Arzte*, p. 81 ff. ' The bathers, barbers and surgeons did
not always keep strictly within the limits of their art, but not seldom
encroached on the province of the learned doctors ; in other words they
carried on quackery and charlatanism.'

tricks. Even the most thorough-going vagrants and vagabonds gained the confidence of suffering humanity. Charlatans doctored them, without scruple, for diseases wholly unknown to them with the most incisive methods.' Through the doings of such mountebanks, who were patronised by the highest classes, and even to a great extent by the rulers of the land, ' the blind Germans,' according to Hildanus, ' lost as much in money and in men as would have sufficed to fight the Turks with good success.' [1]

In bitter language the Heidelberg professor and house-physician James Theodore Tabernaemontanus inveighs against the proceedings of the surgeons in his ' Kräuterbuch,' which appeared in the years 1588 and 1591. ' It has come to this,' he says, ' with a number

---

[1] Müller, ' Hildanus' Leben und Wirken ' in the *Archiv für Gesch. der Medizin*, vi. 10–11. See also *Mitteilungen des Vereins für Gesch. von Steiermark*, xxxiii. 32 f., concerning the theatrical and laughable proceedings of the perambulating healers there. ' The practice of medicine,' says Baas (p. 184), ' was in many places, at any rate at the beginning of the sixteenth century, quite exempt from licence, so that academically trained doctors, among whom, for instance, Felix Platter must be included, and uneducated popular doctors were, so to say, perfectly legitimate competitors. This exemption from licence applied to German practitioners both at home and abroad. But in many places new or revived medical ordinances came into vogue, for instance at Würzburg and Nuremberg. In university towns especially, and in the free towns, the system of concession was introduced and the irregular practitioners were watched ; thus at Heidelberg it was decided (1588) that the latter must be " examined," restrained or even abolished. The possession of a university degree was a mark of a scientifically trained doctor ; the doctor's degree bestowed unconditional authority to practise ; a licentiate was only excluded from certain functions—for instance, the inspection of lepers ; but a bachelor was only allowed to practise under the supervision of a doctor. In reality, however, as may easily be imagined, this university prescript was not always respected. The number of fully fledged doctors was still small ; . . . these were only available for wealthy merchants, councillors, patricians and burghers, and inaccessible as a rule to the common people and the peasants.'

of asses' heads, that when they have been for a year in a barber's shop and have washed the peasants' heads, shaved them, cleaned their noses and ears, they set themselves up above all the physicians, and pose as skilful and experienced surgeons.'

Tabernaemontanus also speaks very indignantly in his description of the Tormentil root. ' Our barbers, shavers, and such-like pretended surgeons, ought to use this and the other herbs to make their wound salves and plaisters ; but they act like the great fools and donkeys they are, and are determined to stick to their yellow, green and red carriage grease. And although we have already offered to give these knife-grinders, jobbers and bathing attendants some instruction in the use of these and other wholesome herbs for the cure of wounds, in order that they may learn a short and quick method, and may be able to heal their patients without the aforesaid carriage-grease plaister and without a long process of smearing, corroding and burning, and also at great saving of expense, they are such proud, inex-perienced, ignorant donkeys' heads that they behave as if they had eaten their fill of all the arts and sciences, feel offended since they have not seen such things in the barbers' shops or the bathing-rooms, and so they go on in their stupid ignorance, smearing on for ever, as boots are smeared ; and, smear as long as they may, the poor, wounded, suffering men and women are not helped, and many people are so greatly injured that they remain cripples down to their graves. But all this is the fault of the ruling authorities, whose business it is to look into the matter, for they might well procure other people who understand what they are about, and who would send to the right-abouts all these mountebanks, beard-shavers, old wives, hangman's attendants, Jews, renegade priests, and such-like cheats and impostors.' [1]

In 1555 the apothecary Humelius wrote from Basle to Felix Platter, then studying at Montpellier, that ' very few orders for drugs were given; there was no respect for skilled physicians at Basle; more German than Latin prescriptions were written out; the *Medici* chiefly used senna, liquorice and other such rubbish for purging. D. Isaac made up common prescriptions for the patients himself; he would rather be a beggar at Basle than an apothecary. They do not understand anything else but giving purgatives, they use no proper sort of remedies as at Montpellier.' [2]

The abuse of colocynth (bitter apple) was especially flagrant. ' The vagrants and the Jews give this as a purgative (not without the greatest injury) to the people who trust in them,' we read in an herbal.[3] ' Colocynth,' writes the botanist Leonard Fuchs, ' is beyond measure injurious to the stomach. Therefore the magistrates ought well to punish the vagrants, Jews,

---

[1] Tabernaemontanus, i. 116, 451–452. At ii. 275, the author complains of the abuse of opium : ' Whereas these vagrants and mischievous Jews make constant use of this drug and habitually perform great wonders with it, since they can very quickly quiet and allay all pains with it, and thus gain great credit with the common people, as the Jews do most especially, I would have all people warned that they should be on their guard against such individuals who have no conscience whatever.'

[2] Boos, p. 242 f. The excessive use of purgatives was largely connected with the excessive eating and drinking that was customary. Cf. Carrichter, *Der Teutschen Speisskammer*, Strassburg, 1614, pp. 247–248.

[3] (J. de Cuba) *Kreuterbuch*, newly published by Adam Lonicerus, Frankfort, 1587, p. ccxii. Against colocynth, hawthorn roots, &c., Dr. Balthasar Conradinus of Schwatz in Tyrol says indignantly : ' Such things are only fit for horses and pigs.' But this did not hinder the learned man from using the excrement of birds, dried toads, and other such delicacies in certain cases. *Mitteilungen des Vereins für Gesch. von Steiermark*, xxxiii. 30.

and other quack doctors who purge the people to such
an extent with this violent medicine that many of them
give up the ghost. But there is nobody who at all
takes to heart all this injury and loss of life to so many
people. Yea, verily, numbers of preachers, who call
themselves evangelical, entirely forget their vocation,
which they ought to attend to, and fulfil truly and
diligently according to their own and to Christ's
teaching, and set up their fairs and dispose of more
medicine than would a couple of honest, genuine
physicians.' ' The latter, indeed, never act like this,
but the tramps and vagabonds who will not remain at
their books, of which indeed they have not many, mix
themselves up in all sorts of affairs, as, alas ! everybody
sees.' ' This I have desired, with good intentions, to
point out, in order that the ruling authorities may be
moved to look into the matter in a Christian manner,
and put a stop to such abuses.' [1]

The defective supervision of materia medica on the
part of the magistrates and the doings of the Jew
doctors are also complained of by Adam Lonicerus.[2]
' Nowadays,' he writes, ' it is a lamentable fact, and
a source of pitiful harm to numbers of people, that
everywhere anybody can so easily pose as a doctor,
and administer medicine. And to the Jews especially
this is allowed, the Jews who daily curse Christian
blood, and who are not admitted to any other useful
trade, but freely practise usury and sell fraudulent
medicine, sucking the blood of the Christians. The Jew
doctors here are clumsy, inexperienced blockheads and

---

[1] L. Fuchs, *New Kräuterbuch*, chap. 139.

[2] Roth, ' Die Botaniker Euch, Rösslin, Theodor Dorsten und Adam
Lonicerus ' in the *Zentralblatt für Bibliothekswesen*, 1901, pp. 271 ff., 338 ff.

clownish bacchanals, who have never studied anything
and have no understanding about illnesses, nor do they
even understand one word of the prescriptions which
they write, but copy these out like asses from German
" Praktica," and give them to the sick on the chance of
their answering the purpose : would that every pious
Christian would take this to heart and consider how
justice can be done in the matter, and how iniquitous it
is for a government to allow its subjects to be exposed
to such serious injury. For it is undeniable, and may
be proved daily, that these pretended Jew doctors
cheat and ruin the people by selling them the medicines on which they grow rich, for they say they require
no payment for their trouble and their advice, they only
ask to be paid for the medicine, which is no common
medicine and cannot be got at the apothecaries ; they
ask and take from the people three or four florins for
small doses, which they have procured at the chemist's
for three or four farthings. Such cheating as this they
are guilty of day after day, and these statements can be
proved true.' [1]

---

[1] (J. de Cuba) *Kreuterbuch*, newly published by Adam Lonicerus,
Frankfort (1587), Preface. See Stricker's article on the Jew doctors
in Germany in the *Zeitschr. für Kulturgesch.* iii. 222. The apothecaries
in Germany had to a great extent become grocery dealers, and they
met the medical requirements of the people very inefficiently. The
Reichstagsabschied of 1548 instituted better regulations for the business
of apothecaries, and in some places—at Nuremberg, for instance—these
rules were observed ; see Peters in the *Mitteilungen aus dem germanischen
Museum*, i. 36 f. Concerning the sale of false and rotten drugs in the
sixteenth century at Graz, see *Mitteilungen des Vereins für Gesch. von
Steiermark*, xxxiii. 38 f. The ' Apothecary Ordinances ' of Ferdinand I,
Maximilian II and Rudolf II contained stringent regulations : see Macher,
Das Apothekerwesen, Vienna, 1846, i. 23 f. For the history of the
apothecaries' trade at Nuremberg, see H. Peters in the *Festschrift der 65.
Versammlung deutscher Naturforscher und Ärzte*, p. 97 ff.

'Nowadays,' says Tabernaemontanus, 'there are a lot of conceited, impudent, puffed-up fellows, who pretend to concoct useful mixtures out of their own ignorant heads, and declare that not one of these is to be got from the apothecaries, as if they were cleverer and more learned than all *Doctores Medici* who have lived for a thousand years down to the present time, and it is time the government looked into these things and punished these presumptuous hypocrites : indeed, all the universities ought to set themselves against such fellows and write against them, so that this great abuse and falsification of medicine may be put an end to, for anybody of the smallest intelligence can easily understand how very harmful all this charlatanism must be, especially the lavish use of laxatives and purgatives.' [1]

In another place Tabernaemontanus complains that the physicians have no knowledge of the different medicines. 'Yes, indeed, there are many common vendors of roots who have more knowledge of herbs and their differences than many a doctor of medicine, who thinks, forsooth, when he has obtained his doctor's hat, and wears a long superintendent's cloak, and struts along the pavement and can write a prescription *ex quam phoribus*, of things that are wholly unknown to him, that he is an experienced, learned doctor, lacking nothing, knowing everything that he ought to know—while all the time, concerning the most essential thing appertaining to his art, viz. the genuine simples and their differences, he is wholly ignorant.' [2]

---

[1] Tabernaemontanus, Preface to the *New Kreuterbuch*, II Parts, Frankfort, 1588 and 1591.
[2] *Ibid.* i. 317

No wonder that the ' professors of the healing art '
are used as comic figures for the carnival plays. Hans
Sachs especially has given us many extremely coarse
pictures ridiculing the doings of quacks and miracle-
doctors. The best known of these is his farce ' Der
Bauer mit dem Säumagen.' A doctor is cutting out
a patient's stomach in order to cleanse it; in place of
the one that has suddenly been removed he gives him
a pig's stomach: hence the enormous voracity of the
peasants. The conclusion forms an emphatic warning
against cow and horse doctors, ' who have not studied
and taken their degrees in medicine and who consequently bring many people to their graves.' [1] The
extent to which a learned physician of that period
thought himself capable of healing disease, is shown by
a written communication addressed to the town council
by Samuel Mylius, who died in 1616 : ' Nevertheless,
that it may be known what I, God be praised, can do,
as my deeds attest, herewith I declare that I have cured
headache, vertigo, blindness, fistulas in the eye and the
nose, gout, ulcers, excessive nose-bleeding, indigestion,
loss of memory, insanity, idiotcy, apoplexy, crooked
mouths, insensibility, or lameness of limbs, epilepsy,
croup and ulcers on the tongue and in the throat,
scorbutic and other malignant sores, which suddenly
develop in the mouth and throat and from which
people may very quickly be suffocated, cramp, paralysis,
flushings which come and go, female ulcers of the
breast and uterus, and other malignant diseases, which
have been made worse by other doctors and barbers,
pleurisy, ulcers on the liver, consumption, coughs and

---

[1] H. Sachs (published by Keller), ix. 308–311 ; cf. Lier, *Studien zur
Gesch. des Nürnberger Fastnachtspiels*, pp. 61–62.

asthma, suppuration and hemorrhage, faintings, heart-beatings, ruptures ; besides all which I have succeeded in allaying hemorrhoids, and alleviating the pains of gout ; I have set right nerves, bones and joints which were out of order or injured, cured leprosy and other sorts of scabies of the body when the evil had not gone too far, as well as all sorts of fevers and plague, indigestion and vomiting, dysentery, dropsy, gravel ; I have cured kidneys and bladder by operations, lessened the pains of gout, saved weak and sickly children in their mother's wombs and preserved them alive, stopped flooding after child-birth, which can put an end to life so rapidly, made lame limbs sound, in most extreme danger revived the four elements of life, diminished and allayed the after pains of labour, healed foul and stinking sores and cleansed them, cured insomnia, overcome abnormal sleep in feverish illnesses, stopped unnatural perspirations, destroyed and driven out worms, deadened and relieved the abnormal pains and hindrances to childbirth by which mother and child may be killed, allayed great obstructions and swelling in the body and gripes in the bowels, opened them and stopped the pain, cured jaundice, croup, abnormal growths, great boils from which gout and other troubles arise, incontinence and retention of urine ; I have successfully treated cases of death and decay of the child's body in the mother's womb, which had gone on for four, five and even more years, and which had caused great danger and excessive suffering : with God's help I have removed the source of evil and restored the mother to permanent health.' [1]

If in this lamentable state of practical medicine the

[1] *Anzeiger für Kunde deutscher Vorzeit*, 1882, pp. 267–268.

position of sick people was melancholy enough even at ordinary times, it became thoroughly unbearable in periods of infectious diseases and great plagues. It was precisely in this last respect that the age of Church schisms was visited in the most frightful manner. The Apocalyptic riders, war, hunger and death, which Dürer depicted at the close of the fifteenth century as a prophecy of things to come, held now here, now there, their gruesome course.

An account of all the plagues and epidemics since the close of the Middle Ages would require a work to itself ; only a survey of the most important ones, with special regard to the features that are individually characteristic, can be given here.[1]   By the people as well as by the chroniclers, all epidemics at that period were called ' plague ' or ' pestilence.' On closer observation the different forms of pestilence were gradually distinguished. The most important of all chronic diseases of the Middle Ages—leprosy—begins indeed to diminish with the sixteenth century, but it was

---

[1] This was also Janssen's intention, as his memoranda show.   For the rest what Lammert (p. v) remarks, holds good here : ' The annals of a people's sufferings are closely interwoven with the history of its civilisation ; the data which we get from them are in intimate connexion with the varying manifestations of political and social life.   In the history of the diseases of a nation we have a most significant and interesting volume of the great universal history of the world, the importance and wide bearing of which deserve more attention and study.'   ** Cf. B. M. Lersch, *Gesch. der Volksseuchen*, Berlin, 1896, who collects together in chronological order the accounts of national plagues handed down from the earliest ages to the present day ; G. Bloos on ' Volksseuchen in früheren Jahrhunderten ' on the Lower Rhine, in the *Histor. Studien und Skizzen*, p. 61* ff.   For Nuremberg see the article of E. Mummenhoff, ' Zur Gesch. der Seuchenhäuser sowie über die sanitären Massregeln und Vorkehrungen gegen die grossen Volkskrankheiten des Mittelalters in Nürnberg ' in the *Festschrift der 65. Versammlung deutscher Naturforscher und Ärzte*, p. 222 ff.

by no means extirpated in Germany at that time. This is learnt from the reports of Paracelsus, Schopff, and others.[1]

In addition to leprosy and to the universal ravages of dysentery and intermittent fever, there came at the turn of the fifteenth century the scourge of syphilis.[2] Known already beforehand, this loathsome complaint now appeared in new forms, and spread to an extent unequalled in the history of disease. The descriptions by contemporaries of the torments and disfigurements suffered by its victims are appalling. ' The unutterable misery which this dreadful disease all over the world, in all classes, and both sexes, has brought to suffering humanity,' writes Valerius Anselm in his ' Berner-chronik,' ' can never be described in words, but also can never be forgotten. For it has such a strange and horrible appearance that no learned doctor will or dares under-take it ; and the patients themselves withdrew to the fields, and they were obliged to have separate huts to live in ; till at length the disease became so powerful and rampant that all (even princes and lords) were obliged to put up with the patients and house them, and it made all sorts of ignorant quacks with no experience of doctoring quite rich men. This one plague (if plagues could help) ought to be enough to humble and tame the pride and voluptuousness of wanton lascivious men.

---

[1] Hirsch, *Pathologie*, ii². 6 ; Haeser, iii³. 87 ; Sprengel, iii. 201 f. On an altar-piece painted in 1516 by Holbein the younger for the convent of St. Catherine at Augsburg three lepers (evidently drawn from living models) are represented kneeling at the feet of St. Elizabeth ; see Virchow and Hessling, 'Das Holbeinsche Aussatzbild' in the *Archiv für pathol. Anatomie* xxiii. 194 f. ; cf. xxii. 190 f.

[2] Fuller details on this repulsive subject are given in Haeser, iii³. 234 ff., and Hirsch, *Pathologie*, ii². 41 ff. ; see also Proksch, *Die Literatur über die venerischen Krankheiten*, Bonn, 1891

But it did not help, and does not help yet. God alone can and must help us!' [1]

'There is no medicine,' complains an unknown poet of Franconia in 1537, 'by which this terrible disease can be controlled, so that its victims are hopeless.' [2] Universal horror was excited by the tremendous spread of this pestilence. It spared 'no sex, no age, no class; the clergy as well as the laity, the great people and the common people were attacked by it, and though the disease, as is usual with epidemics, visited the poor first, it soon passed on to the wealthy classes—even to princes and lords.' [3] 'One person infected another; driven from town and village, men and women, both from the clergy and the laity, roamed about in gangs, covered with ulcers and sores from head to foot, moaning and hopeless. Vain was all known medicine, to save them: their only release was a slow and terrible death.' 'In some cases this disease burnt holes in the body,' says a contemporary, 'eat away the nose and cheeks, and also the throat, so that the victims died of starvation.' [4] Accusations were plentifully hurled at the

---

[1] Fuchs, *Älteste Schriftsteller*, pp. 358–359.   [2] *Ibid.* p. 375.

[3] *Ibid.* p. 433. The enormous contagiousness and spread, and the terrific ravages of syphilis among all classes at that period is only comprehensible in the present day, as was remarked to me by a doctor friend, when it is remembered that for want of all therapeutics—at any rate at the beginning of the epidemic—the disease was left free to develop into its worst stage, and that the generation of that period had not been hereditarily inoculated by the virus, and was not therefore in a certain sense immune as we are in the present age. That the disease in question was really syphilis is proved (1) by the descriptions of the symptoms; (2) by the concurrent statements of immorality being its primary cause; (3) by the later successful use of quicksilver as a remedy, quicksilver being still used as a specific against syphilis. In many cases there may have been leprosy also accompanying the complaint.

[4] Fuchs, *Älteste Schriftsteller*, p. 346; *Archiv für Gesch. von Oberfranken*, xv. ii.

Jews for being the originators of the epidemic through poisoning the fountains ; most people, however, looked upon the dreadful scourge as a righteous judgment of heaven, called down by the moral corruption of Germany.

Paracelsus also attributed the epidemic to luxury and excesses. ' Be it known,' he says, ' that luxury and the worship of Venus were never so powerful as at the time of this visitation. Hence this name (Venus plague) may well be retained, for Venus is the mother of this disease.' And in another place : ' The French disease is not very different from leprosy, for leprosy is brought on by luxury, and then the French disease follows : and that comes through Venus, for she reigns in leprosy.' [1]

The terror of this pestilential disease was universal, especially on account of its infectious nature. Merely touching the hand of a person afflicted with it was enough to communicate it ; even talking to the patients was avoided, for fear of the poison of their breath and exhalations.[2] At the very first the victims of syphilis were expelled from intercourse with other people ; at Prague they lay about in the streets, or under the trees of the Great Circus ; later on they were driven away from the gate of the town where they had settled themselves in stalls. Finally a small house was arranged as a hospital for them. In Switzerland the lepers shunned intercourse with the sufferers from syphilis. By degrees police and medical measures were adopted all over Germany. ' The patients were forbidden to leave their homes, and they were refused admission to bathing-

[1] *Von Ursprung, Ursach und Heilung der Franzosen*, pp. 191–192. Sprengel, iii. 208 ; cf. Sachs, p. 437.
[2] Fuchs, p. 441.

houses, taverns, and even to churches. The canton of
Baden went so far as to banish all victims of syphilis,
and stringently prohibited all syphilitic foreigners from
coming into the country.' [1]

Terror was all the greater, because the skill of the
doctors was powerless at the beginning. At first many
of the doctors would have nothing to do with the
revolting patients. Thereby the actual practice of
healing came into the hands of the barber doctors, the
executioners, artisans, tricksters, and other unscrupulous
people, who without any knowledge of medicine, went
about pretending to cure the miserable victims. For
charlatans and alchemists a golden period now set in.
Many now actually succeeded in solving the great
problem of alchemy, to turn quicksilver [2] into ringing
gold.' [3]

Scarcely had this infectious disease begun to assume
milder forms than fresh plagues visited mankind. Soon
after the Peasants' War different parts of Germany had
suffered severely from famine, from unusual climatic
conditions, and from floods. These disasters were very
generally regarded as divine judgments ; to some they

---

[1] Haeser, iii[3]. 286, 297–298 ; Hasner in the *Prager Medizinische Vierteljahrschrift*, cix. 139. Syphilis was a chief reason of the continual decrease
of the custom of bathing, so essential to the health of the people, which
was so popular in the Middle Ages (see Falk in the *Histor.-polit. Blätter*,
cviii. 811 ff. ; see also Wichner in the *Mitteilungen des Vereins für Gesch.
der Steiermark*, pp. 33, 75 ff., and Kotelmann, *Gesundheitspflege*, p. 63 ff.) ;
cf. Zappert in the *Archiv für österreichische Gesch.* xxi. 137 ff. ; d'Elvert,
p. 84 note, and Kriegk, ii. 34 f. ; this disease also largely influenced the
ruling authorities to abolish bad houses. The fashion of large beards,
and later on of wigs, is closely connected with the spread of syphilis.
Haeser, iii[3]. 316.

[2] As a means against syphilis.

[3] Haeser, iii[3]. 288, 317 ; Simon, *Gesch. der Syphilis*, Hamburg, 1858,
ii. p. 173.

seemed a punishment for the Peasants' War, to others for the Lutheran heresy, to others again for general sinfulness.[1]

' In order, however,' it says in a contemporary memorandum, ' that the poor human creatures in such dire extremity should be cut off from every hope of rescue, there now broke out an unheard-of pestilence, which came over from yonder side of the ocean : it was the English sweat. It carried off thousands and thousands : it killed people before they knew what their illness was. Owing to the novelty of the epidemic and its rapid spread all round about, hearts were thrown into the utmost consternation—nobody felt sure of a to-morrow. Death ensued within twenty-four hours, for the most part even more quickly.' [2]

The ' English sweat ' had first appeared at Hamburg in July 1529, where within twenty-two days it carried off 1000 people. Soon afterwards it broke out in Lübeck, Bremen and Verden. Then Mecklenburg and Pomerania were visited in like manner ; at Rostock most of the professors died of the complaint. Later on the pestilence travelled through Central and Southern Germany, passing finally into Switzerland. How great was the terror it caused is seen, among others, from a Thuringian chronicle. '*Anno* 1528, there was an epidemic of the sweating plague, or English plague, thus named because it came to Germany from England ; many thousands of people died suddenly of it ; it was such a rapid poison that, if anyone only heard it mentioned and worked himself up into a fright, he died of it.' [3]

[1] Hartmann, *M. Alber*, p. 147.   [2] Haeser, iii[3]. 240.
[3] Schnurrer, p. 77; Haeser, iii[3]. 328 f.; Hirsch, *Pathologie*, i[3]. 59 f., and Hecker-Hirsch, *Die grossen Volkskrankheiten des Mittelalters*, Berlin,

As a principal measure against this new disease the steam cure was applied, and in the most senseless manner possible. For full twenty-four hours the sick people, packed up in beds and blankets, were steamed uninterruptedly and, as a contemporary says, ' stewed to death.' As this plague began just at the hottest time of the year it is not surprising that the mortality reached an appalling height. In many places—at Göttingen for instance—it became necessary to bury eight corpses in one grave ; in Dantzic 3000 people are said to have been carried off; in November the death rate was still very high at Augsburg, and within fourteen days out of 3000 patients, 600 died. Innumerable leaflets were distributed recommending the steam cure, and these had a wide circulation, but some of the opinions they put forward were so ridiculous that, wherever the people had still retained mental soundness, they only provoked laughter. A melancholy memorial of the medical superstitions of that time is the little book of medicine ('Arzneibüchlein') of Caspar Kegeler of Leipzig. Without the ' slightest insight into the nature of illness, this book is a preposterous jumble or list of marvellous pills and electuaries concocted out of innumerable ingredients. If only he had seen one sweat fever patient, he would at any rate have realised how impossible it would have been, within twenty-four hours,

1865, p. 274 ff. See also Seitz, *Der Friesel. Historisch-pathologische Untersuchung*, Erlangen, 1845, p. 19 f. ; G. C. F. Lisch, ' Die Schweissucht in Mecklenburg im Jahre 1529, und der fürstliche Leibarzt Profes.or Dr. Rhembertus Giltzheim ' in Lisch, *Jahrbücher des Vereins für mecklenburgische Gesch. und Altertumskunde*, ii. (Schwerin, 1838), pp. 60–83. Concerning the sweating plague of 1529 cf. also Lersch, p. 215 ff. ; Bloos in the *Histor. Studien u. Skizzen*, p. 70* f. For the coming of the plague to Cologne, Dreesen, p. 12 f. according to Weinsberg.

to use even a hundredth part of his boxes and glasses and bottles. The approval with which this medicine book was received by doctors of like insight and opinions is shown by the eight editions which it went through; we cannot dispel the distressing idea that possibly thousands of patients were mismanaged and sacrificed through Kegeler's nostrums.' [1]

After the thirties of the sixteenth century the chroniclers, from year to year, were always writing about plague, pestilence, pestilential diseases, and contagion. Under these terms they included all great epidemics caused by infection.[2] Even contemporaries observed the remarkable fact that this plague never dies out, but recurs annually now here, now there, moves from place to place, from province to province, and comes back again after some years and carries off in large numbers the young people who have grown up meanwhile.[3] If we read through private letters received during the sixteenth century we find that almost every summer accounts of plagues recur. ' *Es stirbt* ' (they are dying) is the technical phrase used. ' Deaths are increasing,' ' the plague is gaining the upper hand '; such and similar expressions, with accounts of particular deaths, occur in all letters of that period.[4]

Flight from the plague-stricken places was the

[1] Hecker-Hirsch, *Die grossen Volkskrankheiten des Mittelalters*, pp. 293 ff., 298 ff., 300–301.

[2] Cf. Schrohe, ' Kurmainz in den Pestjahren 1666–1667 ' (in the *Erläuterungen und Ergänzungen zu Janssens Gesch. des deutschen Volkes*, published by L. Pastor, iii. 5, Freiburg, 1903), 1. See here also for the sanitary measures of the Mayence Electorate since 1526.

[3] Schnurrer, p. 81. For the plague epidemics of the sixteenth century see also Lersch, p. 222 f.

[4] So says Steinhausen, *Gesch. der Briefe*, i. 175–176.

general custom. ' All court retinues, all governing bodies, and especially all the higher educational institutes, moved hither and thither seeking for healthy resorts, and leaving these again immediately if the plague came near them.' Frequently people let themselves be alarmed by the spectre of the plague without ground. Thus, for instance, the senate of the university of Wittenberg on June 15, 1534, ordered the removal of the college to Jena, although there was more anxiety than actual illness in the case.[1] Most of the doctors were helpless and counselless in presence of the epidemic : ' They left the choice and organisation of hygienic measures to the magistrates, and their description to the chronicle-writers, holding fast by the old dogmas, and carefully abstaining from dealing in writing with matters which seemed to go beyond the contents and exposition of the canonical books.' [2] In medical literature the believers in and the deniers of infection stand sharply opposed. The first German doctor who clung firmly to the idea of infection, and laid it down as the principle for all measures against the plague, was Crato von Krafftheim, already often mentioned in these pages.[3] In therapeutic respects there was a general and widespread belief ' in the magic power of precious stones, of the mithridate, and above all of the theriac, on the efficacy of which such high value was set that steps were taken to send a special mission to the East in order to procure the genuine preparation.' [4]

For the year 1541 nearly all the chroniclers record a serious epidemic, which stands out notoriously for its

---

[1] Schnurrer, p. 81 ; Beer, *Krato von Krafftheim*, Vienna, 1862, p. 5.
[2] Opinion of Hecker in Haeser, iii³. 353.   [3] Gillet, i. 68.
[4] Haeser, iii³. 354–356 ; cf. Moehsen, *Beiträge*, p. 129.

extensiveness and its appearance simultaneously in different parts of the empire. ' In the year of Christ, 1541, in the summer,' says a contemporary, ' there broke out on the Rhine stream and in other places a pestilential mortality, which carried off many excellent people. At Strassburg 3300 people died, and more, among whom were many distinguished, excellent and learned persons. In Colmar the deaths were scarcely fewer. At Rheinfelden there were 700. At Basle also a great number.' According to Schadaeus the mortality was so great that the grave-diggers asked for an increase of pay.[1] Of the deaths at Cologne Hermann von Weinsberg reports in his memorials : '*Anno* 1541, the deaths from the pestilence went on in a frightful manner, for although in the year before, 1540, numbers of people had died, the year '41 by far exceeded its predecessor, for many thousands of people died, not only in Cologne, but everywhere in Germany, and this mortality lasted very long, all through the winter to the very end. Sometimes 200 people died in one day. Death spared no one, whether clerical or lay, pastor, chaplain, burgomaster, bailiff, or what not ; so many people died that the courts of justice and the stock exchange were closed. At this time I was living in the Cronen-bursen, and all day long, and often late in the evening, I was constantly crossing the street, where from all the houses they were turning out sick persons and dead ones, which was dreadful to see, and which often filled me with terror when I bethought me how many good friends and neighbours were dying daily ; and so many people fled out of the town that it was left almost empty, and every other house was uninhabited or

[1] Krieger, p. 103 ; cf. Peinlich, i. 368.

closed. Amid all this dying I often had recourse to opening veins which freshens the blood. I used a great deal of incense, white garlic, vinegar, pestilence pills, theriac, and such-like things, constantly fumigated the rooms with juniper and other good perfumes, and our Lord God had mercy on me, so that I remained in good health.'[1]

In the following years the plague went on almost uninterruptedly. In some towns the mortality was quite appalling. At Hamburg in 1547 there were often from seventy to eighty deaths daily among the inhabitants. Of Lübeck, in the year 1548, it is reported that over 16,227 people were carried off, ' young and old, but mostly children and young people, and generally 160 and 170, more or less, in one day, and on August 13 200 people were buried.' In all the churchyards of the ill-fated town there were always large open graves which would hold 100 coffins.[2] At Chur, between June and the beginning of the winter of 1550, over 1300 people died, and at Dortmund in the years 1551 and 1552, 1000 people. Nearly the whole of North Switzerland was devastated. At Zurich the disease (epidemic inflammation of the breast) increased so rapidly that the doctors determined not to visit any patients who needed their help after the second day.[3] In the neighbourhood of Bayreuth the population at this time was

---

[1] Höhlbaum, *Buch Weinsberg*, i. 156; cf. also Dreesen, pp. 3 ff., 48 ff. At Frankfort at that time recipes for preservation against the plague used to be read out from the pulpit. *Zeitschr. für deutsche Kulturgesch.* i. 278.

[2] Cf. Lappenberg, *Hamburger Chroniken*, p. 148 ; H. Paasche in the *Jahrbücher für Nationalökonomie*, N.F. v. 325, and *Archiv für Gesch. der Medizin*, i. 379–380.

[3] A. Heller, *Gesch. der evangelischen Gemeinde in Dortmund*, p. 19 ; *Jahresbericht der naturforschenden Gesells. Graubündens*, N.F. xiv. 21.

reduced by about one-half. At Culmbach, where there had been formerly 800 inhabitants, there were now only seventy-five.[1] In 1552 the plague showed itself also in Styria. In November ' the mortality became so enormous at Graz that the high and low officials ceased their functions, waiting for less dangerous times. These times, however, were not quick in coming. The plague had, indeed, as usually happened, diminished slightly in the depth of winter, but in July " the great mortality and poisonous atmosphere " began to prevail again in Graz, and gained such head from day to day, that the nobles all took flight with their families. The magistrates also repaired to safer places, the provincial delegates going to Judenburg and Schloss Katsch, and later on to Knittelfeld. The provincial excise office was removed to Anger. On July 21 this removal was officially announced in all " five quarters " of the land. The intention had been to remain only a month away from Graz, but the plague lasted for six months and the office was actually still at Anger in March 1554.' [2] At Breslau in 1553 the plague broke out for the sixth time ; in comparison with former ones it was called ' the little plague,' but it attacked 3000 people, of whom a third died.[3]

In 1562 the bubonic plague spread over Germany. In spite of the sanitary precautions, intelligent on the

[1] *Archiv für Oberfranken*, xv. 15.

[2] Peinlich, i. 373-374.

[3] Gillet, i. 68. Concerning the epidemics in Breslau in the years 1542-1543, 1568-1585, and the organisation in connexion with them, cf. Markgraf in *Grätzer, Gohl und Kundmann*, Breslau, 1884, pp. 96 ff., 101 f., 140 f. In the appendix, p. 150 f., there is a list of the medical ordinances and writings issued at Breslau during the plague epidemics. See further Huyskens, *Zeiten der Pest in Münster während der zweiten Hälfte des 16. Jahrhunderts* (Programm, Münster-i.-W., 1901).

whole, taken by the council in this year at Nuremberg, the ravages were terrific. In the mortuary book of the town the deaths are entered accurately day by day ; at the end occurs the following summary, which, in view of the fact that Nuremberg at that time had by no means 40,000 inhabitants, is enough to make one's hair stand on end :

Summa of all the persons who from January 1, *anno* 1562, to the last day of April 1563, came into the Lazaret house .	3349	
Cases of death		1606
Cases of recovery	1671	
Cases of deaths in the town at the above-mentioned time . .		7273
From September 12, 1562, to January 8, 1563, deaths at Werd (Wöhrd)		155
Summa Summarum of all these deaths, and in sixteen months in the town, in the Lazaret and at Werd		9034[1]

The Austrian lands, also, were very severely visited at this time. Reports thence at the end of 1561 say that 'the people are falling like cattle, saving your presence, so that it is heart-rending to see.' 'This terrible mortality lasted on through the following year. In Upper Styria human beings and cattle were carried off in the same way.' [2]

At Basle, in the interval from 1563–1564, more than half the inhabitants were seized with the plague of boils, and a third of them—about 4000, according to Platter's reckoning—were carried off. Strassburg also went through a bad time.[3] By an epidemic which broke out at Freiburg-in-the-Breisgau in 1564, the fourth part of the burghers (according to the state-

---

[1] Solger in the *Deutsche Vierteljahrschrift für öffentliche Gesundheitspflege*, Brunswick, 1870, ii. 73.

[2] Peinlich, i. 377.

[3] Miescher, p. 43 ; cf. Boos, p. 109 ; Krieger, p. 104 f., and Meyer-Ahrens, *Der Stich in den Jahren 1564 und 1565*, Zurich, 1848.

ment of the famous Dr. John Schenck) were carried off.[1] At Rostock and in the neighbourhood, in 1565, there was a fearful plague ; over 9000 people died, seven professors and forty-eight students. In the same year, according to Musculus, Frankfort-on-the-Oder lost about 5000 inhabitants through the plague. In the following year there died at Brunswick 6000 people, at Hanover 4000. The university of Tübingen fled to Esslingen.[2]

The year 1566 was a particularly unhealthy one, because in that year the so-called Hungarian disease (called also headache, heart-burn), which had broken out in the imperial camp at Ofen in 1542, came for the first time into Germany. Home-returning soldiers carried the complaint into Styria and Bohemia, whence it made its entry into Germany itself. ' The illness almost always began between three and four in the afternoon with cold and shivering, followed in fifteen minutes by great heat and unbearable pains in the head, mouth and stomach ; the stomach pain being so intense that the slightest touch from the patients' clothes made them scream out — this was the pathognomic sign of the disease ; other symptoms were unquenchable thirst, a dry tongue, and cracks in the lips. On the second day actual delirium would set in. If swellings appeared on the back of the feet and developed into actual carbuncles, it often became necessary to amputate both feet.[3] From this time the Hungarian disease became a

[1] Maier, *Joh. Schenck*, p. 54.

[2] Chytraeus, *Newe Sachsen-Chronik*, Leipzig, 1598, Part II., p. 194 ; Spieker, *Musculus*, p. 220 f. ; Havemann, ii. 556 ; Schnurrer, p. 112. For the Hamburg bubonic pestilence of 1565 f. see Haeser, *Untersuchungen*, ii. 38.

[3] Peinlich, pp. 380–382 ; Haeser, *Gesch. der Medizin*, iii [3]. 377. For the *Morbus Ungaricus* see also Haeser, *Untersuchungen*, ii. 41 f. ; F. W. Müller in the *Deutsche Klinik*, 1868, No. 26 ; Ludwig Graf Uetterodt,

frequent visitor. 'This malignant fever,' said Dr. John Obendorfer, house-physician to the prince-bishop, in his preface to his 'Kurzer und klarer Bericht von der Natur und Ursachen der ungarischen Krankheit,' published in 1607, 'this malignant fever has now become so common that it comes almost every year, and if we compare it with the pestilence, which does not appear regularly every year, it does not cause much less death than the latter.'[1]

In addition to epidemics Germany was also largely visited by famine at that time. Heartrending descriptions of starvation and want are extant, especially of the misery in Styria in 1570. Bread was made of alder-bark and acorns ; the people were even reduced to eating twigs of trees and vines. ' Numbers of parents were driven to despair because they could not give their children anything to eat, and so they put them out in the streets and ran away from them so as not to see them die of starvation. At Ketmonsdorf a child was found sucking the breast of its mother who was dead of starvation, and another roving about like cattle in the grass to find something eatable. And yet there were abominable people who from love of money closed their well-stocked barns against the poor.'[2]

Things were just as bad in many parts of South Germany. In a ' Song of the Hunger and Death Year, 1571, in the Suabian Land,' it says :

> In fifteen hundred and seventy-one
> A dreadful famine had begun ;
> Full many people fell a prey
> To death, which carried them away.

Zur Gesch. der Heilkunde, Berlin, 1875, p. 445 ff., and T. von Györy, *Morbus Hungaricus*, a medical historical study, Jena, 1901. According to T. von Györy the *Morbus Hungaricus* was the same as *Typhus exanthematicus.*

[1] Lammert, p. 15.   [2] Peinlich, i. 383–384.

This famine gained the upper hand
Over all the German land.
If one man went across the street,
And chanced another man to meet,
They each to other sadly said
Within their homes they had no bread.
Many at night-time wished their bed
Were a supper-table spread.
At the beginning to commence,
Mark you now to what immense
Prices corn had risen then :
On the 3rd of April men
For a malter of rye (the truth I say)
Twelve florins and thirty kreuzer [19s. 10½d.] did pay ;
For a malter of flour florins fifteen [23s. 9d.],
For barley sixteen batzen [2s. 3d.] I ween.
Oats eighteen heller, about two pence.
Peas (unobtainable) but the quart
Four heller, or a half-penny, cost,
Nothing cheap was, anywhere.
Three eggs cost one heller, I declare,
Twenty-eight pfennig [7d.] for a pound of lard,
Thirty-four batzers [1s. 5d.] (O 'twas hard!)
For a slice of salt :
For a faggot of wood you had to give
Two whole florins, as I live,
But for the sum of fifty-six heller
You could buy a measure of wine for your cellar.
The gentry in this dire need
Had in the hospitals agreed
To have bread baked from oats and rye.
Many this bread for their homes did buy.
Three thousand five hundred loaves about,
In one short week were handed out.
For one loaf a dozen pence was paid ;
Three pounds and half a pound it weighed,
And those who took these loaves were bound
Never in taverns to be found.
All who this order disobeyed
The penalty in prison paid.
And will things long remain so bad ?
Sure God won't leave us always sad.
He will not punish us as we deserve.
But in His favour and grace preserve,
And us at all times mercy show,
And His heavenly bread bestow.   Amen.

The years 1574–1577 have acquired a melancholy fame through the universal prevalence of the plague epidemics, which ' scarcely desisted anywhere and raged with extraordinary virulence.' At Trent 6000 people died within six months, in the Upper Inntal also and in the Pustertal the mortality from the same cause was appalling.[1] In Biberach about 500 people died in 1574, and in 1575 and the year after the number of deaths at Württemberg was reckoned to be 30,426.[2] In Styria the doctors complained of the ingratitude of the patients. Some verses, then already in vogue, were revived later on by the celebrated Tyrolese doctor Guarinoni :

> The doctor has three characters :
> ' An angel this ' the first time he appears ;
> Soon after, when he's helped the need,
> ' A demi-god ' he is indeed :
> But when, through him, the patient is quite well
> For thanks, he's called ' a devil out of hell.' [3]

A remarkable instance of the way in which the plague was revived after several years is reported from Freiberg concerning the year 1576. ' In the middle of July a pitter in Freyberg dug up a clay pit near the hospital, into which during the plague of 1564, old rags, oakum and straw from the infected houses had been thrown ; poisonous fumes instantly attacked him, and he was obliged to lie down, and not only he and his family, but many more in the neighbourhood were infected ; and from then till Christmas 1577 there were continuous cases of fatal seizure. The effect of the poison was to throw its victims into a frenzy, and one

---

[1] Sprengel, iii. 246 ; Hirn, i. 482 ; cf. Krieger, p. 107 f.
[2] Cf. Schmid in the *Histor. Jahrb.* xvii. 88.
[3] Pichler, *Guarinoni*, p. 7 ; cf. Peinlich, i. 404.

man in this frantic condition killed his wife with a wooden stick before he died.' [1]

For the eighties the calendar-makers had predicted : ' 1580, an earthquake, a comet, hot weather; 1581 and 1582, inundations, scarcity, famine, pestilence, murder, and incendiarism; from 1584 to 1588, misery, anxiety, and want on account of changes in religious matters : and further scarcity, famine and pestilence ; hence the calendarist concluded with the following rhymes :

> When we come to 88,
> For that year I predicate—
> Unless, meanwhile, the world goes under—
> There will occur a mighty wonder.[2]

These predictions were destined to come true. Influenza spread over many parts of Germany. ' 1580 was illumined by a comet,' it says in the plague-chronicle of Dr. Lebenwaldt, ' then followed a very cold winter, when all the waters were thickly frozen ; swarms of mice destroyed all the field produce, poisonous epidemics crept all over the world with infectious catarrhs, which were called " Bohemian sheep-poison, dry-cough, consumption, sheep's disease, brain disorders." First there had been warm, damp, midday winds, then in the dog-days there were midnight gales. Towards autumn this complaint had spread all over Europe : it began with a dry cough and hoarseness, followed by heavy breathing, with vomiting of foul disordered bile, weakness of the whole body, pains in the limbs, headache, light-headedness, and other serious symptoms, and it carried off a frightful number of people. Those who recovered were left with a cough and chronic hoarseness.' [3]

---

[1] Schnurrer, p. 119.   [2] Peinlich, i. 406–407.

[3] *Ibid.* pp. 407–408; cf. Hirsch, i. 6 and 31, where a minute chronological survey of all the influenza epidemics is given. In Germany this

Concerning the ravages which the 'pestilence' caused in the Grisons in 1581–1582, detailed accounts have been handed down. In Thusis there were 250 deaths, in six villages on the Heinzenberg 800, in Schams 700, in Cazis 150, in Sils 100, in the Rheinwald 748, in the Prättigau, in two villages, 500. 'Total, 3000, young and old, male and female. Mortality also set in at Ems, Vallendas, and in the Lugnez, where, however, it soon began to desist.' [1]

In 1581, in the Lüneburg district, a new epidemic, the so-called *Kriebelkrankheit* (raphania), or spasms, was observed. This complaint was most probably the result of the general lack of corn and of the corruption of corn by blight. The epidemic began with ' a laming of hands and feet, in which the fingers were so rigidly contracted into fists, that even the strongest man could not unlock them ; at the same time the patients broke out into frightful yells, in the middle of which many of them died. Those who survived the fit of yelling would lie with their eyes open and their mouths immovable, and on contraction of the hand, there followed a large bump with intolerable heat, so that the patients called for cold fomentations ; the heat, however, gradually spread to the internal parts, when strong aversion was felt to cold applications. Even if the patients did not succumb to this disease they never recovered their former health, but lost the use of their hands and feet.

complaint appeared first in 1173, and then again in 1387, 1494, 1510, and 1557. In Dortmund in 1580, 2034 people were buried in the Reinoldi churchyard. Heller, *Gesch. der evangelischen Gemeinde*, p. 19 ; see also Gluge, *Die Influenza oder Grippe nach den Quellen historisch-pathologisch dargestellt*, Minden, 1837, pp. 17, 58 f. For the influenza epidemic of 1580 see also Lersch, p. 261 ff.

[1] *Jahresbericht der naturforschenden Gesellsch. Graubündens*, N.F. xiv. 25.

Most of them gave irrational answers, became delirious, lost their memory and hearing, and were afflicted with stammering. Wherever the disease came its ravages were very great, and in two villages it carried off 523 people.' [1]

The year 1582 brought a great pestilence to Bohemia, whence it was carried into Nuremberg by a butcher's journeyman. This man died of the disease. In the hostel where he had lodged two grown-up daughters of the landlord died the following week, and a fortnight later the whole family, parents, children, servants, were all carried off by death. In spite of all the precautions of the town council the epidemic broke out in the town, and was not stamped out till 1583. Two years after another plague followed, which lasted till May 1586 and caused 4703 deaths. [2] In Central Germany, in 1582, Thuringia was severely visited; the number of deaths there is computed at 37,000; many places lost two-thirds of their inhabitants. [3] Basle also was attacked in 1582 by a pestilential disease which committed fearful ravages. By March in the next year it had carried off 1313 people, that is on an average 146 a month. [4] At Frankfort, where in 1582 the bubonic plague appeared, Dr. Strupp drew up in 1583 a ' memorandum of advice how to preserve oneself in health in the midst of the infection '; he recommended taking purgative pills, smelling a musk-apple, chewing a

---

[1] Schnurrer, pp. 137–138 ; cf. Haeser, *Pathologische Untersuchungen*, ii. 93, and Hirsch, ii. 142 f.

[2] Solger in the *Deutsche Vierteljahrschrift für Gesundheitspflege*, ii. 75 f., 79, 81.

[3] Pfeiffer-Ruland, *Pestilentia in nummis*, p. 99 ; cf. also Martin, ' Versuch einer geographischen Darstellung einiger Pestepidemien,' in Petermann's *Geogr. Mitteil.* viii. 261.

[4] Hess, *Bauhin*, p. 41.

little bit of turnip before going out, washing the face with vinegar, drinking sage-, rosemary-, or juniper-wine, and so forth.[1] At Tomils in the Grisons, in the summer of 1584, the plague killed 200 people ; at Schams 150, at Paspels and Almens over 100. A contemporary writes as follows concerning the misery and distress of the years 1585 and 1586 : ' At the beginning of the year (1585) the '' dying '' began, and spread in such a way that in the Grisons mortality was raging in fifty villages. In the district of Disentis 1800 people died, in Lugnez 500, in Thombleschc 400, at Oberhalbstein 1300, at Schweingen 350, at Salux 300. The epidemic lasted here and also at Scharans a year and a half. At Burwein only seven persons were left in eight houses, and at Mons not more than eleven survived. In the four villages 700 people died. At Undervaz out of 550 people only 186 were left. I found the following record everywhere in the churches, and I copied it into my writings : At Davos from July 4 to Martinmas, 174 people died, forty-two recovered. Out of sixty houses eighteen remained empty. In the Brettigouw (I was not there at the time) I heard from numbers of trustworthy people that the plague attacked not only all the villages but also all the farms and houses in the mountains, besides many in the Alps.' The plague also spread its ravages in Tinzen, Mons, Lon, and Thusis. ' That year was a terrible year, and there was also great scarcity of all things : wine, milk, and corn, besides all eatables, went up to tremendous prices, so much so that in the memory of man things had never been so dear in the three cantons.'

' On August 16 (1585) the whole world cracked,

[1] Stricker in the *Zeitschr. für Kulturgesch.* i. 280.

and there was an unheard of amount of thundering and lightning. It rained nearly the whole summer, so that the floods in all countries did great damage. On our Lady's day in August the deluge swept with such force that it carried everything before it, driving along boulders as big as ovens, and it swelled higher and higher ; and an hour before daybreak it burst out with such violence that there was such a roaring and crashing and cracking as if the mountains were all falling in, and incalculable damage was done in Caz, Thusis, and Sils, Fürstno, Rotels, Tomils, and through all the lands to the orchards, meadows, bridges, weirs, fields, and gardens. The Rhine carried away much property of the people at Tusis, besides banks of earth as high as a man. The same disasters happened in the Oberland, in the Rhine valley, in the Brettigouw, in Switzerland, in German and Italian lands. In Ruvis above Ilanz and in Gambolt-schyn the waters submerged some of the houses, and tore them up and carried them away with the occupiers. On October 20 the floods rose again for the third time, with such fury that the bridges which had been rebuilt were again carried away, besides which many pleasure gardens were very greatly damaged. In this year there reigned war, bloodshed, murder, assassination, discord, tumult, misery, hunger, scarcity, pestilence, storms, cold, danger by water and fire, black frost and snow, and all sorts of plagues.

' With pestilence God has visited all the following lands, such as Germany, Austria, Switzerland, the Confederate States, Italy, Bohemia, France, Scotland, &c. In the town of Prague in Bohemia there died 10,000 people. On St. John's Day in the summer there fell heavy snow which spoilt the hemp, so that it had to be taken up and a fresh crop sown. When this second crop had blossomed, there was another great fall of snow, which did much damage to the fruit and other crops, and destroyed the second lot of hemp that had been sown. There was summer in the winter and winter in the summer ; the winter was dry and warm, and the summer was cold and wet.' [1]

The most terrific ravages of the plague befell Breslau in 1585. It broke out there on June 17. In the inner town alone there were sometimes 300 and more deaths in one week. Over 700 people were picked up dead in the streets. ' We are as in a besieged city,' wrote Crato von Krafftheim to his son in Rückerts. ' Nothing is brought to us : neither chickens nor eggs nor any other market produce. One-tenth of the butchers do not slaughter. No corn is brought in to us. So *execrabiles* are the poor Breslauers. The suffering and want are heart-rending.' The total number of victims of the ' great mortality year ' in Breslau amounted to nearly 9000 among 40,000 inhabitants—that is to say, over a fifth of the population. [2]

In the year 1588 raphania broke out among the inhabitants of the Silesian mountains. Caspar Schwenkfeld relates that many of the victims of this complaint went out of their minds and died most distressing deaths. ' When I returned from Basle to my own

[1] *Jahresbericht der naturforschenden Gesellschaft Graubündens*, N.F. xiv. 26–29.

[2] Cf. Gillet, ii. 370 ; Haeser, iii³. 352 ; Markgraf in *Grätzer, Gohl und Kundmann*, p. 102. In comparison Finckenstein recalls to notice, in the *Deutsche Klinik*, 1868, No. 3, that during the strongest cholera epidemic which raged in Breslau in 1866, in the same space of time 4500 people died out of a population of 160,000—*i.e.* not quite the thirtieth part. What, then, are the terrors of cholera compared to a plague of the sixteenth century!

country,' he says, ' I endeavoured to discover the cause of this complaint, and I found it in a certain poison which was contained in the corn. A poisonous dew, or a noxious atmospheric manna had so poisoned the corn that all persons who eat of such bread, especially old people, women and children, died of it. The grains were to such an extent impregnated with it that even when they had been washed they still retained a frothy greasiness ; the flour made from it had also a very nasty smell. Boiled magpies were recommended as the best antidote.' [1]

The last years of the ill-fated century again brought dire calamities. Silesia and Hesse were both visited with raphania. The medical faculty of Marburg recommended at the time a particular raphania-electuary made up of drastic purgatives, such as castoreum, saffron, ginger costus, cummin and cloves ; further a theriaca made of paeonies, mistletoe, castoreum, burnt skulls, theriaca and mithridates ; and a powder of black St. John's berry, devil's bit, benedict roots, laurel leaves, &c.[2]

In the year 1595 most extraordinary climatic conditions prevailed ; cold winds, storms, and rain succeeded each other, so that there was scarcely an interval of summer weather ; spotted typhus spread over all Germany in the following years. At Erfurt, in 1597, no church services could be held as all the clergymen had died. In valleys visited by the plague the memory of those dreadful times is still fresh.[3]

The next year (1596) a famine broke out in North

[1] Sprengel, iii. 270.   [2] Ibid. iii. 271.
[3] Schnurrer, p. 145 ; Pfeiffer-Ruland, *Pestilentia in nummis*, pp. 89, 94, 97.

Germany, and in many places also the raphanin epidemic
returned ; at the same time incendiarism became very
prevalent. In 1597 also the plague was still raging in
the Empire as well as in Austria, where in several towns
it did not even stop in the winter.[1] The loss of human
life was so considerable that in Brandenburg, Saxony,
and Pfalz-Neuburg, it was declared in that year that
' Germany in these last years has lost, by the plague
especially, quite one-third of its population.'[2] The
ravages caused by the epidemics and famines in the
past 100 years had so little abated at the beginning of
the new century, that an historian of the years from 1600
to 1617 called the period : ' Years of misery before the
great war.' ' The persistence of equally unfavourable
conditions in astrological, physical, and social departments added fresh links to the old chain of disease
and death.' In addition to raphania, scurvy, malarial
fever, typhus, the Hungarian disease, red dysentery and
diphtheritis, the bubonic plague carried off countless
victims.[3] In the years 1600 and 1601 some German
districts were severely visited, especially East Prussia
where 18,000 people died, but also Austria.[4] In 1602
the epidemic took a fresh start in numbers of German
provinces. In Kolberg, between Michaelmas and Christmas, there were often sixty deaths a week, not including
the people who died at night and were buried secretly.
At Danzig, up to the end of the year, 16,919 people
died. At Elbing there were sixty burials on August 1,
from forty-five to fifty in each of the following weeks, and

[1] Peinlich, i. 431–432.
[2] Häberlin, xxi. 193 ; see also Stieve, *Akten*, ii. 366 note.
[3] Lammert, p. i. ; Peinlich, i. 461, note : Haeser, iii[3]. 390, 397.
[4] The Markt Althofen, near Friesach, died out almost completely.

in the week after St. Bartholomew's Day, over 400. At
Thorn the deaths from the epidemic were 2000 in number. In the years 1603 and 1604 the epidemics came only
singly into Germany. At the end of 1604 the bubonic
plague was raging so terribly at Frankfort-on-the-Main
that there were not enough people to carry away the
dead bodies. At Müncheberg, near Frankfort-on-the-
Oder, in 1605 the deaths amounted to 112 men, 126
women, fifty young people, 355 children; at Königsberg
1060 people died ; at Luckau in the Niederlausitz three
burgomasters and most of the town councillors died ;
at Anklam in Pomerania 1386 people ; in the province
of Hadeln, 3530 ; in Iglau daily fifteen to twenty people.

In 1606 the Main and Rhine districts were heavily
ravaged. In the village of Damm, near Aschaffenburg,
within the four weeks of September there were about
300 deaths, so that barely 100 inhabitants were left.
' Accordingly in their dire extremity, on the next Friday
before Michaelmas Day (September 29), they prayed and
cried to Almighty God that He would turn away the
great plague, and extinguish all the fires in the hamlets,
and they made a new fire (by rubbing wood), and they
dedicated the afore-mentioned Friday to God, to be
kept in perpetuity as a holy fast day.'

Silesia, Bohemia, Styria, and Moravia also were
sorely afflicted. Many of the patients were killed by
powders and poisoned salves.[1] It is a characteristic
circumstance that whereas the medieval preservatory
methods had been distinguished by their simplicity,
in the sixteenth, and above all in the seventeenth
century, most complicated, often quite horrible and
disgusting, means were used. For instance, a live toad

---

[1] Lammert, pp. 2–12, where the proofs are given.

would be hung up by the feet near to a fire, and a saucer made of wax put under it. In three days the tortured animal would have vomited out all the contents of its stomach—small worms, large flies—into the saucer. These insects, mixed with the wax, were then made into a medicament ' to preserve and cure the plague-infected people.' The powder of dried toads was also used as a plague nostrum. Dried toads, sewed up in bags and hung on the breast, were considered especially efficacious ; even the doctors believed that toads, ' on account of the position of their limbs and the disposition of their pores, acted as a trap to catch everything poisonous that came near them.' Dried toads, softened in vinegar, and laid on plague boils and carbuncles, remained in vogue on into the eighteenth century. In a medicine book of the period there is the following recipe for a toad-preservative. ' Take 3–4 large toads, 7–8 spiders, and as many scorpions, put them all in a tightly closed pot and leave them standing for some time. Then add some virgin wax, shut the pot up again and make a fire round it. When all the ingredients are dissolved, mix them well together and make them into a salve. Put the salve in a silver pot. Anyone who carries this salve about with him may be certain of not being attacked by the plague.' [1]

How senseless the medical art was in regard to these epidemics is shown by a medical pamphlet of Dr. Raimund Minderer, who lived in the middle of the sixteenth century and was a physician of great repute. He recommended the most loathsome, senseless, and

[1] Peinlich, ii. 508–510. Dr. Lieber, in his article ' Die Volksmedizin in Deutschtirol,' gives a similar receipt, from an old manuscript house-book, for a toad-amulet. *Zeitschr. des Deutsch-österreich. Alpenvereins*, xvii. 225–226.

even dangerous means of cure.[1] For instance : 'Hang
live quicksilver, put into a hollowed-out hazel nut,
with Spanish wax, round your throat.' A still better
amulet, according to Minderer, is ' Zenechton,' ' a
plaister made of arsenic (a piece as big as a thaler) sewn
up in dog-leather, and laid on the spot where the heart
is.' If a little ' powder of dried toads is added,' the
plaister will be all the more efficacious, according to
Dr. Minderer.[2] The pamphlet which contained these
nostrums was reprinted in 1633 by the Styrian Estates.[3]
The author, who died in 1621, was constantly summoned
to the courts of princes as a highly prized doctor.[4]

Terrible also was the widespread superstition that
epidemics could be produced by strewing poison about.
In 1542 at Geneva multitudes of men and women were
condemned to lengthy imprisonment, to torture, to
banishment, to the scaffold, and the funeral pile, for
' plague-spreading, sorcery, and for being in league with
Satan.'[5] Proceedings of this sort were frequently repeated. When in 1607 the plague broke out at Franken-
stein in Silesia, no fewer than seventeen people in this
small town were burnt to death for being ' strewers
and scatterers of poison,' and among them was a boy
of fourteen who was beheaded before being burnt.[6]

In the same year the plague found its way into the
outlying habitations of the Spessart. In other parts,
too, its ravages were frightful. At Rüdisborn, near
Windesheim, death carried off all the peasants except-

[1] Minderer, *Medicina militaris*, Augsburg, 1620, p. 66.
[2] *Ibid.* pp. 67–68.   [3] Peinlich, i. 117, 488–489.
[4] *Allgemeine deutsche Biographie*, xxi. 766.
[5] Kampschulte, *Calvin*, p. 426.
[6] See ' Aufzeichnungen des Braunauer Schullehrers M. Bressler '
in the *Zeitschr. für Gesch. Schlesiens*, x. 180.

ing five. At Naumburg-on-the-Saale, from July to September, 2200 people died ; at Zerbst over 1800 ; at Gardelegen also 1800 ; at Gross-Salze-on-the-Elbe 700, nearly half of the inhabitants ; at Wurzen only six houses were spared ; in the parochial district of Lommatsch 1600 people died ; at Hainichen, at the end of the year, there were only six or seven married couples left ; in the town of Patschkau, in Upper Silesia, in 1608 only twenty-two burghers were left alive.[1] In 1609 Switzerland and South Germany suffered especially from the plague. At Basle in the years 1609–1611, according to the detailed reports of Felix Platter, the plague killed 3968 patients out of 6408—*i.e.* 61 per cent. Equally murderous were the ravages of the bubonic plague in Strassburg, where since October 1609 the mortality had increased threefold. ' Up to May 1610 the epidemic remained approximately at the same height ; in June, July, and August it decreased considerably, but only to return in September to its original height, which it maintained till May 1611. From that time till the end of 1613 the rate of mortality was again lower.' Not only at Strassburg, however, but all over the land the bubonic plague continued its ravages ; we read, for instance, in the Thanner chronicle : ' 1609. About this time the dreadful pestilence began again to rage through the whole of Alsatia and the neighbouring districts, and continued also in the following year ; there was great mortality in Ensisheim, Colmar, Ruffach, Seltz, Sennheim. At Thann also one here and another there were laid in the grave, but the town was never shut up.' [2]

In 1611 the whole of Germany, Switzerland again

---

[1] Lammert, pp. 14–19.   [2] Krieger, pp. 111–112.

especially, was ravaged by infectious diseases. At
Zurich the ' great mortality ' rose to such a height that
every day from forty to sixty, or even more, deaths
took place. On September 5 there were 116 deaths,
and on the 16th there were actually 132. Three new
churchyards had to be provided. In like manner the
plague raged all over the country, and in numbers of
villages half the population was carried off. The loss
of lives in town and country was reckoned at 51,200
persons. At Kerenzen, on the lake of Wallenstadt, the
pastor, after the whole parish had been swept away,
entered himself as the last in the book of the dead.
In Thurgau more than half the population—i.e. 33,584
people—fell victims to the plague. It penetrated to the
furthest Alpine valleys, and even animals and birds
became its prey and dropped down dead. The ' black
death,' as the people called it, came also to Constance,
where, between July and November, 1500 people
died. Württemberg, Franconia, and Tyrol were most
heavily visited at that time ; according to the death
registers of the Franconian towns, 20 per cent. of the
inhabitants of these districts were carried off by the
plague. The same was the case in North Germany ;
the people there were overwhelmed with despair. At
Oberbösa, not far from Frankfort, where the plague
slew 188 victims, one of the survivors hanged himself ;
within twenty-four days he had lost his wife and all
his eight children. When in the Saxon villages of
Plotha, Prittitz, and Plenschitz, near Weissenfels, the
plague was followed in 1612 by the ' head-sickness,'
the people became quite frantic, and, if unwatched, laid
suicidal hands on themselves.[1] The height to which the

[1] Lammert, pp. 26 ff., 35. In the following years the plague as a

terror of the people had risen was palpably shown when, in 1613, the plague broke out in the village of Klein-bobritzsch, which had been joined on to Frauenstein ; when the Frauenstein dean, Caspar Hoffmann, according to the duty of his office, visited the sick people in the village, the inhabitants of Frauenstein would not let him come back into the town, so that he was obliged to take up his abode in the open field and carry on there his official work.[1]

Terror of this description was no unusual thing among the Protestants.

Luther was at a loss how to explain the fact ' that in times of epidemic diseases whole populations were seized with abject fear unheard-of in the earlier Catholic times, and that sick people were forsaken and sacrificed by their nearest relations in a most cowardly manner. This circumstance was all the more unpleasant to him as it threw a particularly unfavourable light on the spiritual condition which his teaching had brought about among the people. He and others could not understand how it was that the new teaching, which was far more comforting and reassuring to the con-science than that of the old Church, the teaching that made it so easy for men through firm trust in the imputed righteousness of Christ to obtain direct and unfailing entrance into salvation, should produce an effect entirely different from that which was expected. Luther had already expressed his astonishment in

rule came alone, but it raged with great fierceness. Thus in 1616 the population of Iserlohn was reduced by a plague to only seven young fellows. In the Naumburg district in 1617, an epidemic of red dysentery carried off 1505 people ; in the village of Grochlitz only eleven people survived. Lammert, pp. 46, 47.

[1] Lammert, p. 42.

this respect in 1527 when an epidemic complaint broke out at Wittenberg, and he then took refuge, as indeed he was always wont to do in such cases, in the simplest solution of the problem, viz. that it was Satan who thus filled the hearts of men with fear and trembling at the thought of death, in order thereby to compass the destruction of the Wittenberg university, which he (Satan) detested.' [1]

'Satan' also plays a large part in the memorandum which Luther published in 1527 upon the question ' whether it was right to flee from death.' ' Although I am of opinion,' he says in this document, which gives such a remarkable insight into Wittenberg conditions, ' that all pestilences are sent among mankind by the evil spirits, just as are other plagues, so that they may poison the air, or otherwise breathe out noxious odours, and thus dart their deadly poison into our flesh, nevertheless it is all the same God's judgment and His punishment, which we ought to submit to with patience, and do our best to help our neighbours, even at the risk of our own lives.'

[1] Döllinger, i. 345. The excessive fear of death shown by the Lutherans had already been discussed polemically on the part of the Catholics in 1527. On September 15, 1527, Urban Balduyn wrote from Wittenberg to Stephen Roth at Zwickau : ' Last week, if I am correctly informed, a preacher monk at Leipzig stood up and spoke about the Wittenbergers with their misleading doctrines, and said : " Now you see well how consistently they follow out and act up to their teaching. . . . In the early Christian times people were glad when they died and hastened to meet death, for the doctrine was right at that time. If now these Wittenbergers' doctrine had been right they, too, would have remained at their posts ; but almost all the leading men, who proclaim this teaching abroad, have been the first to take flight. . . . All this must the Wittenbergers suffer from the devil." ' Cf. G. Buchwald, *Zur Wittenberger Stadt- und Universitätsgeschichte in der Reformationszeit*, Leipzig, 1893, p. 6 f. See also Wizel's opinion in the present work, vol. viii. p. 338. [This refers to the German original, vol. viii. of which is not yet translated into English.]

' If therefore one remained in a town when one
firmly believed one could help one's neighbour, or on
the other hand one took precautions when one's help
was not needed, and thus helped everyone to guard
against the poison, death would undoubtedly be more
merciful in such a town. When, however, it happens
that one half of the people are so frightened that they
fly from their neighbours in their need, and another
half are much too foolhardy and take no precautions
at all, but augment the evil, then the devil has his own
way and the mortality may well be great. For by both
parties God and man are highly injured—by the one
through presumption, by the other through cowardly
despair ; then it is the devil who chases and catches
the one that flees, and who also holds fast the one
that stays, so that none escapes from him. Still worse
than these is the class of people who conceal the fact
that they have the complaint, and who go about among
other people, in the belief that if they could infect and
inoculate other people with the poison they would be
freed from it themselves and recover their health ; and
so they go about in the streets and the houses, in the
hope of communicating the disease to others, and by
this means save themselves. And I am fully convinced that it is the devil who is at the bottom of all
this, and that in these ways he makes the wheel go
round. I will also be bold to say that some people are
so desperately wicked that they go about with the
plague on them among their neighbours or into houses,
simply because they wish to spread the epidemic, just
as if the whole matter were a joke, as when out of
roguery one puts lice in anybody's fur or flies in his
room. I know not whether I ought to believe it ;

I do not know which is true, and whether we Germans are human beings or devils ; for verily we come across people beyond all measure gross and wicked, so that the devil is by no means idle. But my advice is that when such people are found they should be collared and taken off to the judges, and should have to answer to the hangman as downright murderers and criminals. What else are such folk than regular assassins in the town ? Just as assassins go about thrusting knives into this person and that, and yet have " done nothing to anyone," so the others infect here a woman, there a child, and have done no harm to anybody ; and they go off laughing as if they had done just the right thing. It would be better to live with wild beasts than with such murderers. I do not know how to preach to these murderers. They care for nothing ; I appeal to the ruling authorities that they should look into the matter and call in help and counsel, not from the doctors, but from the executioner.'

'For thus, through dirt and filth alone, has our pestilence at Wittenberg come about ; the air, God be praised, is still fresh and pure ; but, through sheer foolhardiness and neglect of precaution, some have become poisoned ; and the devil has had his fun out of the terror and flights he has caused. May God restrain him ! Amen.' [1]

---

[1] Collected Works, xxii. 327-336. What Luther says here (p. 340) about the condition of the Wittenberg churchyard is also noteworthy : ' But our churchyard, what is it ?   Four or five streets and two or three market-places ; there is not a commoner or a noisier place in the whole town than is this churchyard, traversed every day, yea, day and night, by men, women, and cattle, to which all the inhabitants have doors and paths leading from their houses, and into which everything is thrown, even perhaps things not fit to be mentioned. Thus all reverence and respect for burial is utterly destroyed, and nobody thinks any more about

Luther had stayed on bravely in Wittenberg in 1527, with Bugenhagen, during the plague, but their example was not followed. When in 1538 rumours of an outbreak of the plague again spread in Wittenberg, the same condition of terror made itself manifest. On October 21 Luther declaimed publicly from the pulpit against such abject trembling and quaking at danger, and soundly rated those who were so frightened at ' an outcry and rumour of pestilence.' ' They ought,' he said, ' to put their trust in the Lord, and each one to go about his business and stay in the town, and if his neighbours needed his help he must not forsake them. We ought not to be so terrified at death when we have been taught about the Word of life and the Lord of life, Who overcame death for us.' [1]

Luther also could not get over his astonishment at the fact that people should be so terror-stricken ' under such a glorious light of the evangel, when they were not so frightened before under the papacy.' He soon, however, found a new explanation for this strange phenomenon. ' The reason,' he said, ' is that under the papacy we trusted in the merits of monks and others. Now, however, each one has to see to it for himself how he believes and how he is to go out of this world.' [2]

That all his exhortations, as well as his own example, were of little avail against the deadly terror of his followers, Luther was to experience anew in the very next years. It was in vain that he urged the people

it than if they were running over a carrion-heap, and even the Turks would not treat the place with such dishonour as we do ; whereas we ought only to be filled with solemn thoughts when we think of death and resurrection, and we ought to respect the saints who are lying there.'

[1] Collected Works, lxi. 419.　　　　　　[2] *Ibid.* pp. 411–412.

from the pulpit to remain at their posts and to tend the sick.[1] 'They all fly,' he was forced to report to Wenceslaus, 'one from the other, and there is scarcely a bleeder or a servitor to be had. I believe it is the devil who has possessed the people with the right pestilence, that they are so disgracefully timid, that brother forsakes brother, and sons their parents, and this is without doubt the reward for contempt of the evangel and for devouring avarice.'[2]

While here the plague is described as a judgment of God, in a letter, written very shortly after, the devil is again brought up in explanation of the facts which are so unpalatable to Luther. 'Here also great want of feeling among relations has been shown, and this has caused me unspeakable distress, and has tried me almost more than I could bear. This is quite a new and remarkable plague of these times, whereby Satan, while visiting only a few with the disease, casts all as it were down to the ground with panic and drives them to flight ; verily this is something monstrous, and an entirely new manifestation under the strong and brightly shining light of the evangel.'[3]

Luther attempted another solution of 'the riddle which tormented him,' when Amsdorf wrote to him that also in the zealous new religionist town of Magdeburg the same cowardly trembling was the rule. 'It is a wonder to me,' he wrote, 'that the more abundantly life in Christ is preached the greater the fear of death becomes with the people, either because while they were under the papacy, from a false hope of life they feared death less, whereas now, when the true hope of

[1] Collected Works, lxiv. 313.   [2] Döllinger, i. 346.
[3] Ibid. i. 346.

life is proclaimed, they feel how weak nature is to believe in the conqueror of death, or else because God tries and tests us through weakness, and allows Satan, while we are thus under the spell of fear, to venture on further and to attack us more strongly. For, so long as we were under the papacy, we were as though stupefied with drink, or drugs, or the like ; . . . we took real death for life, for we did not know what the death and the wrath of God were. Now, however, that the truth is shining, we recognise more clearly the wrath of God, and our nature, awakened from sleep and madness, feels that its strength is powerless to endure death. This is the reason why people are more afraid of death than before. Just as, when we were still under the papacy, we not only did not feel our sins, but believed in all confidence that we were at peace ; now that through recognition of our sinfulness our security has gone from us, we become more frightened than we ought. Then we went to the right quite confidently when we ought to have been trembling; but now we go to the left, all too full of fear, when we ought to be confident. I comfort myself therefore under these circumstances with the thought that Christ will make His strength perfect in weakness. For when we were strong, righteous, and wise under the papacy, Christ's strength was not only not made perfect, but was completely extinguished and unrecognised.' [1]

Exasperated by the cowardliness of his followers, Luther, in a sermon of 1539, gave vent to the following strange utterance : ' Yea, verily, I am fain to pray that God would come down with the pestilence and punish and purge the streets.' Another time he said : ' This

[1] Collected Works, p. 347.

fever in Germany is a healing medicine, for the Germans
would swill and gorge themselves to death if it were
not raging here.   The fever makes them more temperate.' [1]

Luther pèrpetually harks back to the devil as an
explanatory cause of all diseases. ' Oh, the devil is
so mighty and powerful that all diseases, crimes, and
plagues proceed from him!' [2] ' God sends no illness
into the world except through the devil ; for all sorrow
or sickness comes from the devil, not from God.   But
God allows it to happen that it may afflict and punish
us when we despise Him.'   All that belongs to death
is the devil's handiwork and doing, and, vice versa, all
that belongs to life comes from the grace of God and
truth and love, and brings no sadness with it. ' At the
times of pestilence the devil blows into a house, and
what he seizes he carries off.' [3]

Cowardly fear of death and heartless abandonment
of the sick did not only manifest themselves in Luther's
immediate neighbourhood, but to a very great extent
wherever the new, and nominally ' so comforting
doctrines,' had taken root.   If Luther at any rate set
a good personal example, in that he condemned flight
from the plague and bravely took into his own house
the children of a patient who had died of it, this at any
rate cannot be said of most of his colleagues in office.

---

[1] Collected Works, lxiv. 313 ; lxi. 412.
[2] *Ibid.* p. 404 ; cf. p. 414 : ' The doctors only concern themselves
in diseases with *causas naturales*, from what natural causes and from
whence an illness comes, and set about to cure the complaint with
their medicines : and they are right in so doing ; but they do not see
that the devil often hangs an illness about some one's throat for which
there is no *causa naturalis*.' Cf. also the utterance of the Leipzig professor, Dresser, in Döllinger, ii. 417–418.
[3] *Ibid.* lxi. 406.

The times of plague afforded the Protestant clergy the best opportunity ' for competing with their Catholic official predecessors in true evangelical love, and at the same time attaching to themselves inseparably the hearts of many sorely afflicted fellow-creatures. The exact opposite, however, is what happened.[1]

' Is it not a monstrous reproach to them,' wrote George Wizel, ' that those who formerly as followers of Antichrist (to use their own language) did not fear the plague at all, or at any rate very little, now as Christians show such deadly terror of it ? Scarcely anybody visits the sick now ; nobody dares to come near those who are attacked with the plague. Nobody will even look at them from a distance, and everybody is seized with an extraordinary panic. Where now is that faith that can do all things, which we hear so much boasted of ? Where is the love of our neighbour ? Tell me in the name of Christ if ever there has been so little trust, so little love among Christians.' With regard to an infectious complaint which broke out at Nuremberg in 1533, Osiander made the remark : ' Many people become so beside themselves with fear that they say and do all sorts of things which are not seemly in Christians, and at the same time leave undone all sorts of works of love which one Christian is no less bound to do towards another than towards Christ Himself ; and thereby all sorts of offence is occasioned to the weak brethren, and slander accrues to the holy evangel.' [2] Luther himself, who was so indignant at the heartlessness of his followers, advised his colleagues in 1539 to give up the Communion of the Sick. As the chief reason for this he says in his private letters that

---

[1] Kampschulte, *Calvin*, p. 484.   [2] Döllinger, i. 65 : ii. 84, note 6.

'the Communion of the Sick is an intolerable and impossible burden, especially in times of plague.' [1]

In a pamphlet first published in 1578, Michel Eychler, pastor of Wallenrod in Hesse, gives a very sorry account of the behaviour of his colleagues in plague times. ' There are, indeed,' he says, ' some pious servants of Christ who fulfil their duty in an honourable and Christian manner, but most of them are faithless and do not trouble themselves about the duties of their office.' On the other hand, ' whenever it was a question of eating, drinking, money-making, pleasure, &c., then almost every corner was filled with fellows ready to take part.' Faith and love were extinguished. ' And the consequence of all this is that, not by our antagonists, but by our own people, and of our own people I say, of us who make our boast of God and of His Word, it is constantly asked, whether a pastor is bound to visit those who are sick with the plague, especially—looking at the matter in a reasonable way—as it is beyond all measure dangerous and critical.' ' Whereas, then, it shows great hardness of heart and blindness in our own religionists, who boast of the Augsburg Confession and the evangelical truth, to ask such a question,' he has undertaken to write briefly on the subject. Eychler begins by stating the reasons which make it the duty of pastors to visit the sick, and refutes the arguments by which some persons sought to prove that they were not bound to visit the sick in times of plague. Some of these arguments, he says, are interested ones. ' The fourth argument with which they cover and protect themselves is, that they ought not to run the risk of

[1] De Wette, v. 227–228 ; cf. Evers, *Katholisch oder Protestantisch*? Hildesheim, 1881, pp. 408–409.

infection for the sake of their wives and children. The fifth argument, which some people bring forward, is that they are forbidden by the magistrates to go near the plague patients,' on account of the danger of infection. Eychler maintains that the clergy ought not to be affected by such a ' godless order.' ' It is, indeed,' he goes on, ' beyond all comprehension that any pastors should let themselves be bound by such rotten, godless orders, which make human beings act contrary to the Word of God, and leave their poor parishioners unvisited and without consolation in their dangerous sickness. And it is to be bewailed with bitter tears that any pastors should leave their parsonages and go elsewhere, or even go out of the town, the village, or the hamlet, and make their excuse that they attach more importance to the physicians than to the Bible. For the physician says " Get away as fast as you can and be very slow in coming back ; that's the best course during the plague." But the Bible says " A good shepherd lays down his life for the sheep, but a hireling flees." This fleeing of the preachers makes everybody frightened. Thence it follows that parents leave their children, children their parents, husbands their wives and wives their husbands, and brothers and sisters forsake each other. I could cite many examples in proof were it not well enough known already by everybody.' The people reason in this sort of way : ' If the pastor is allowed to look after his own safety and advantage, then they will not forget theirs.' God, so Eychler declares, will severely punish such faithless, undutiful pastors, who run away in this dastardly manner. In the preface which the pastor and superintendent of Nidda, John Pistorius the Elder, the father of the well-known con-

vert, wrote in 1577 to Eychler's publication, there is
the same testimony to the fact that the Protestants ran
away from their plague patients and left them to die
in the most abject despair, without 'nursing, hope, or
comfort.' People were so beside themselves with godless,
uncontrolled fear of the plague that children left their
parents, and husbands and wives each other, and even
pregnant women were forsaken in their extremity.[1]

Complaints like this of the neglect of the plague
patients may be gathered from the most different
Protestant territories. Bernard Werner, preacher at
Schwäbisch Hall, in conjunction with Andrew Osiander,
complains in 1556 in bitter language of the terror of
death which the new religionists showed in times of
plague. He relates how 'the people fled from their
nearest friends, and left them lying about like cats
and dogs.' John Rhodius, pastor at Bischleben, near
Erfurt, blames especially the excessive nervousness of
the laity. He bears witness to the fact that in Thuringia
numbers of Protestant pastors did their duty by the
sick and 'laid down their lives for the sheep.' Nevertheless, in Thuringia also there were some pastors who,
from fear of infection, would administer the Lord's
Supper to the plague patients from the street through
the open window. Why not have the courage to go
into the sick-room ? 'Yes,' we read in Rhodius, 'yes,
say some of the pastors, there is great risk in so doing ;
the wife and children won't have it.'[2]

The want of neighbourly love towards the poor
sick people was also condemned in strong language by

---

[1] Cf. Paulus, 'Die Vernachlässigung der Pestkranken im 16. Jahrhundert' in the *Katholik*, 1895, ii. 280-283.

[2] See Paulus, *l.c.* p. 286.

Professor Tabernaemontanus. ' Since the world began,'
he wrote, ' there has never been greater luxury and
superfluity than at the present time among these last
dregs of the world, when no expense is spared to heap
them up and multiply them daily ; but when money is
wanted for churches, schools and hospitals, or to help
the poor boys, then there is a great outcry and lamenta-
tion that it is a great deal too much, and that everything is too expensive : but God will not let this go
unpunished, and they must not trust to their being
evangelical, as they boast, and think and hope that
their faith will save them ; for that cannot avail, since
they have not the fruits of faith.' [1] ' The fruits of
faith ' were indeed, many of them, of a very peculiar
character in the plague times.

When, after New Year's Day 1576, the plague broke
out in Berlin, the court fled to Küstrin, and then to
Karzig.   At Berlin there was the same want of feeling
shown towards the patients as in other Protestant
towns : ' Each one looked after himself, and nobody
cared about anybody else.'   The conduct of the Berlin
preachers during this time of panic is shown by a letter
of Daniel, dated October 13, 1576 :

' I have heard with astonishment of the way in
which our parsons fight, wrangle and quarrel with one
another.   In St. Nicholas' Church they wanted to fight
with the lighters.   Those of St. Mary pelted each
other with stones on the market-place, and it was hard
work to separate them ; and all this squabbling is about
wretched money—this is the good example which they
set in these times of danger and distress ! Methinks
that our Lord God will not even be so gracious unto

[1] Tabernaemontanus, i. 712.

them as to let them die of the pestilence, but the devil himself will come and carry them off.'[1]

In many places there were neither doctors nor nurses to be had for the poor victims of the plague. In a large number of towns attempts were made to meet the need by instituting special plague doctors, just as special plague preachers were appointed. Amid the general panic it was, as a rule, very difficult to find suitable people for such posts. At Wimpfen-on-the-Neckar it was necessary during the plague epidemic of 1606 to compel the nurses by force to enter the service of the sick. When in this same year, after long continuous rain, a virulent plague broke out at Punitz in the Posen district, the reformed preacher of the place took to flight. The town of Weimar, during the plague of 1607, could not procure either a plague-doctor or a preacher ; the burial of the dead, which was managed by certain old women, was performed so hastily that the corpses often fell out of the coffins, which still further increased the terror of the people. From Brunswick it was reported concerning the plague of 1609 : ' Numbers of hard-hearted, unfeeling people drive their infected servants and pupils out of their houses and leave them to their misery.'[2] At Wittenberg in 1616, after an unusual spell of heat, a sort of fever epidemic broke out with such virulence that in every house there were some sick people ; nobody could be got to nurse them.[3]

---

[1] Moehsen, *Beiträge*, p. 124, note ; cf. p. 149.

[2] Lammert, pp. 10, 13, 16, 23.   For the far from creditable part played by the doctors, see also Gernet, *Medizinalgesch. Hamburgs*, p. 164.

[3] *Deutsche Klinik*, 1868, No. 20.   Concerning the heartlessness of the Elector Palatine Frederick IV, who during the plague of 1596 did not once make inquiries as to the condition of his subjects, see the present work, vol. ix. pp. 213 ff.

In 1572 it became necessary in the Electorate of Saxony to issue stringent orders against the sick-nurses and the sextons, who made a practice of killing and robbing the patients ; their punishment was death by the wheel.[1]

In 1580 the Elector Augustus said, concerning ' quite terrible cases,' that the plague patients were left helpless and alone by their nearest relatives ; they died ' one over the other, without care or comfort.' ' The corpses remained lying in the houses for several days ' ; one would be found in a room, another lying at the door, another in the garden.[2] ' All Christian love had grown cold,' complained the preacher John Schuwardt in 1586, after the death of the Elector ; nobody had any pity for the miserable patients. ' God's threatening and punishing made nobody fear or tremble ; the people had iron foreheads and hearts of stone.'

Very strange opinions concerning the obligations of doctors in times of plague were widely disseminated. The idea prevailed, for instance, that ' the help of the doctors could actually only be demanded by the better class burghers, and it was therefore questionable whether such valuable people ought to expose themselves to the risk of taking infection from the lower classes, who supplied the largest contingent of plague patients, and thus diminish their power of coming to the help of the *honoratiores*.' From multitudes of places evidence is forthcoming to show that ' the regular doctors, and also the barber doctors, were forbidden to visit the

---

[1] Richard, *Licht und Schatten*, p. 320.   See the present work, vol. viii. p. 337.   [Cf. German original, the English translation of which is not yet out].

[2] Richter, *Kirchenordnungen*, ii. 192, 444-445.

plague patients.' In the plague ordinance of the
physician John Böckel, which was drawn up at the
instigation of the Hamburg council and printed in
1597, it says : ' Whereas this illness is well known, and
the *medicus* can give his advice without leaving his
house, and exposing his life by visiting common people
in small pest-stricken tenements, it is fair that he should
be dispensed from personal visits among such people ;
when, however, the gentry or the higher burghers
require the *ordinarius* or any other *medici* in whom,
next to God, they place their trust, neither the ordinary
nor the extraordinary doctor shall refuse their service,
provided they be duly honoured.'

But in order that something at least may be done
for the rest of the people, Böckel proposes that ' one or
more *medici*, itinerants, or barbers should be appointed
to visit and heal the sick ; and that if they come across
any symptoms in the illness which they do not understand, they should consult with the *medicus ordinarius.*'

In like manner it was very generally thought, at
that time, that the preachers also were not bound ' to
visit everybody in all houses, cellars and corners,' and
that it was only obligatory on them to ' respond to the
calls of the gentry and the higher burghers.' [1]

Again and again also we find it said that here and
there ' Protestant patients repudiated the doctors altogether, saying " My God it is Who can well help me
and make me well without medicine." ' [2]   If talk of this

---

[1] Gernet, pp. 161–162.

[2] Peinlich, i. 391. The Protestant preacher Werner Leonhart says
in his pamphlet : *Der geistlich Bysemknopf wider die . . . straff der
Pestilenz* (Nuremberg, 1573) J5a: 'Some of them repudiate the

sort is comprehensible from patients with over-excited nerves, such an excuse goes for nothing with a learned man like the Protestant Benedikt Marti. This man, thoroughly versed in the natural sciences, writes in his ' Theologische Problemen,' published at Bern in 1573 : ' In itself and for itself all medicine is to be condemned ; for illnesses are punishments for sins that have been committed. Therefore it is sinful to use medicine, for it is done chiefly by gluttonous, drunken monks when they are feeling the consequences of their debauches.' [1]

The Protestant people did not all and everywhere share in this opinion of the ' gluttonous, drunken monks.' They still remembered well, in many places, what the convents, slandered by the preachers, abolished by the ruling authorities, or condemned to extinction, had always, above all in times of plague, done for the diminution and relief of human want and misery. Thus from Berlin it was reported that the Franciscan monks there (the last of whom died in 1573) were then, as before, making themselves beloved as doctors, and giving their services benevolently among rich and poor alike.[2]

The decay of the hospitals under the management of the Church had been used as a welcome pretext by the new religionist rulers for abolishing these institutions and completely secularising them. It was not at all taken into account that the unfortunate sick people would come off badly by this change. ' Through the zeal with which war had been waged in many Protestant lands against abuses,. the greatest injury had often been

doctors . . . and say, it is God's punishment, and if He wishes them to live He can well heal them without any medicine.'
[1] Graf, i. 27.   [2] Beer in the *Deutsche Klinik*, 1868, No. 2.

done to existing benevolent institutions. The secularisation of ecclesiastical goods was so thorough-going
that little was left over for charitable purposes.' [1]

We give here a few examples of what went on in
Protestant hospitals. During the epidemic of 1585 a
special lazarette had been erected at Nuremberg, and
a barber had been entrusted with its management.
This man fed the patients when in a high state of fever
on sauerkraut, cod-fish, lentil soup, and buckwheat pap.
Later on a doctor was appointed to look after the
patients, but the conditions in the lazarette did not
improve. ' The steward married, without leave, a dis-
reputable woman, and set up a little tavern business
in his own room ; the sexton's wife let out clothes on
hire, and sold to the patients the sweet wine with which
she was supplied gratis for the use of the hospital ;

[1] *Urtheil von Haeser*, i [3]. 866 ; cf. Weiss, *Apologie des Christentums*
Freiburg, 1884, iv. 692, and the present work, vol. xi. p. 5 f. and pp. 363–
365. In the plague ordinance, drawn up at the instigation of the Hamburg
council in 1597, the physician J. Böckel says : ' A pack of old women were
to serve as sick-nurses ! ' Gernet, *Medizinalgesch. Hamburgs*, p. 161.
The same writer remarks, p. 151 : ' The existing hospitals were scarcely
sufficient at ordinary times, much less during plagues ; the infirmary had
long since been turned into a regular provision institute, and the " Heilige
Geist," which had been rebuilt in 1559, was for the most part used for a
similar purpose at that time. The Ilsaben house, limited to begin with,
had been abolished by the Reformation and also transformed into a
provision institute. Altogether the ruling class of burghers, in numbers
of the towns, and also in Hamburg at the time of the Reformation, had
done much the same as the princes and nobles elsewhere : the convents
and foundations had been confiscated for the benefit of individual classes.
The same thing had happened with us as regards the convents, which had
been turned into benevolent institutions for the daughters of the upper
burgher classes, whereas with a portion of the abundant means that had
become available through their abolition a burgher hospital might well
have been established here as in other places, among others at Bremen.'
The Count Palatine Otto Henry sold hospital property in 1556 in order
to pay off State debts. *Verhandlungen des Vereins für Gesch. der Oberpfalz*,
xxiv. 288.

the inmates drank themselves mad, and all manner of riff-raff who came to the place nominally as visitors carried off wine and bread, so that nothing could prosper in the place. As the barber also fell ill, the convalescent patients profited by the want of supervision to carry on all sorts of irregularities and immorality. The council were at last obliged to interfere and administer punishment in the shape of confinement with bread-and-water diet, imprisonment, banishment from the country, and threats of the executioner.' [1]

At Frankfort-on-the-Main there were heavy complaints in 1618 against the ' retired council ' because it had ' given in to the managers of the hospital and had allowed them year by year to reduce the income of the hospital, so that there were scarcely any provisions left, and it was impossible to get the income restored to its original amount. Moreover, the managers themselves had helped in no slight degree to lessen the funds by the grand banquets and parties which they gave frequently during the year, and also by their insisting that whenever a fat ox or sow was slaughtered the best part was to be sent up to their houses. And even this was not enough, but they must needs take away the beds which had been given to the hospital by God-fearing people for the poor patients to lie on, and had obliged them in a quite unfeeling and un-Christian manner to lie on straw on the ground. They had also hidden away the thirty-six account-books, together with the debt-and alms-book, by which the hospital set great store, and scattered the rest about here and there with their leaves torn out.' [2]

---

[1] Solger in the *Vierteljahrschr. für Gesundheitspflege*, ii. 79–80.
[2] Stricker, p. 130.

A gruesome picture of civilisation is handed down from a Protestant land in 1613. 'In the town of Walkenstein, on the Zschopau (2½ leagues [7½ miles] from Annaberg), the population was considerably diminished in that year by the plague. While this epidemic was spreading terror and despair around, the grave-digger used to steal the clothes from the corpses ; and he also joined with the deacon, Abraham Tränkner, and other associates, in committing thefts in the mortuaries, and carrying on all sorts of iniquity. After the discovery of his evil doings, the grave-digger was tortured on the wheel and burnt to death on July 15, 1615 ; the deacon, however, saved himself by flight.' [1]

This fear of death and heartlessness towards those who were attacked with infectious diseases, never before manifested in such a degree, was perhaps even worse among the Calvinists than among the Lutherans. The behaviour of Calvin and his associates in Geneva is typical in this respect.

When in 1542 Geneva was heavily visited with the plague, the town council had the greatest trouble in procuring a preacher for the plague hospital. Several laymen volunteered help, but among the clergy Pierre Blanchet was the only one who declared himself ready to administer spiritual consolation to the unhappy victims. 'The plague,' wrote Calvin at the time, 'is raging frightfully ; few of the patients are saved. If any mishap befalls Pierre Blanchet, I fear that I shall have to take his place ; for, as you say, as we owe a duty to all our members, we dare not withdraw our help from those who need it most sorely.' It was soon, however, to be seen how much value was

[1] Lammert, p. 42.

to be set on these words.   In the spring of the following
year the plague broke out anew.   On March 30 the
council called on the clerical college to appoint one of
its members ' to look after the poor patients in the
hospital and give them spiritual comfort.'   Besides
Calvin there were six other pastors in Geneva, but not
one of them had the courage to go near the sick people.
In the council's protocol of May 2 the statement of
these ' shepherds of souls ' is entered as follows : ' They
would rather go to the devil or to the gallows than into
the plague hospital.'   Again it was Pierre Blanchet
alone who fulfilled his duty, and in so doing the brave
man met with death on June 1.   The members of the
council decided on the same day that the clergy must
nominate one of their number as spiritual helper to the
poor patients in the plague hospital.   Calvin was to be
excepted in the matter, as they needed his counsel ; ' all
the more therefore were his colleagues urged to choose
one of themselves as a successor to Blanchet.'   Fresh
' helplessness and panic ' seized the clerical college.   They
declared at last that for such a post a man must be
found who was strong and not nervous, and they proposed as a suitable person a foreigner, a Frenchman
from Tours.   The magistrate would not agree to this
proposal.   Then, on June 5, all the six preachers, with
Calvin at the head, appeared at the meeting of the
council to make the public and frank declaration, with
all due formality, that ' not one of them had the courage
to go into the plague hospital, although their office
required of them in good and evil days alike to serve
God and His holy Church.'   They reiterated their proposal to appoint this foreigner, who had the necessary
qualifications, as Blanchet's successor, saying that ' he

would be a great comfort to the poor plague patients.'
It was in vain that the council made counter-proposals.
They readily and repeatedly allowed that their office
required of them a different sort of behaviour, but begged
urgently to be let off, as God had not given them the
gift of courage and strength to go into this said hospital.
Only one of them at last declared himself willing to go
' if the lot should fall on him.' The council, so the
protocol goes on, resolved to ' pray to God that for
the future He would give them a more courageous
spirit,' and informed the pastors that hereafter strict
and entire fulfilment of their official duties would be
required of them ; for this once only consideration
would be exercised and the proposal of the clerical
college adopted. The Frenchman entered on his post
in the hospital, but had to be dismissed later on owing
to his immorality.[1]

' The gift of courage and strength ' which Calvin
and his associates, on their own confession, did not

---

[1] Kampschulte, *Calvin*, pp. 484–487 ; cf. F. Buisson, *Sébastien Castellion.
Sa vie et son œuvre* (1513–1563). *Etude sur les origines du Protestantisme
libéral Français*, Paris, 1892, i. 184–193 ; where the protocols of the council
are given more fully than in Kampschulte. From Buisson, also, we learn
that after all a Geneva pastor, de Geneston, did sacrifice himself in 1545
for the plague patients. The way in which Beza recounts Calvin's
behaviour during the plague is remarkable. In the first edition he says
that while most of the pastors shrank from coming into contact with
infection during the plague, three of them offered their services, viz.
Calvin, Blanchet and Castellion ; he then further relates how lots were
drawn to decide who should go to the hospital : ' Calvinum invitum
Senatus . . . sortiri prohibuerunt ' (*Opp. Calvini*, xxi. 134). The register
of the council shows that the precise opposite happened ; Castellion,
moreover, was not a pastor. In a later edition of 1576 Calvin is presented
as offering himself gladly and voluntarily ; he is determined to go to the
plague hospital : instead of ' invitum ' the text is now : ' licet ultro se
offerentem.' Concerning the truly typical terror of death of the Geneva
preachers in 1564 see Paulus in the *Katholik*, 1895, ii. 284.

possess in the times of plague was present in a high
degree among countless servants of the old, much-
abused Church.

. It is an historical fact that ' in the Catholic times
it was just such ordeals as plagues and epidemics which
served to knit more and more firmly together any
loosening bonds between the clergy and the people,
through the spirit of benevolent love and self-sacrifice
which the Church manifested at such periods ; and
even in the days of greatest degradation the Catholic
clergy, some of them at any rate, had known how to
preserve their ancient repute.' [1] Ever since the new
spirit of the Catholic restoration and reform had penetrated into the German Church, with its quickening,
renovating breath, beautiful flowers had blossomed out
in the garden of Christian loving-kindness.

In Protestant Germany there was an immense
deal of preaching about the uselessness—indeed the
perniciousness—of good works, and at the same time
much complaining that nobody any longer took any
interest in their poor and sick neighbours.[2] In Catholic
Germany with the Church restoration the old spirit of
obedience, humility, self-sacrifice, and willing service
was revived ; that God-like spirit of charity which,
springing from the heart of the Saviour, poured as the
water of life in countless streams over the world, and in
the great times of the Middle Ages completely covered
the earth.

As in the best days of old, so again now, the nursing
of the sick was carried on with exemplary self-sacrifice

[1] Kampschulte, *Calvin*, p. 484.
[2] The most important evidence in this respect is summarised by
Döllinger, ii. 698 ; see also above, p. 98 f.

and in the midst of the greatest perils. Bishops, abbots, clergy, secular and monastic, competed together, in ordinary times as well as in times of plague, in works of Christian love. After the stimulus had been given by the Council of Trent, numbers of German synods busied themselves with the reform of the hospitals.[1] Quite extraordinary services were rendered in this respect by the Würzburg Prince-bishop, Julius Echter of Mespelbrunn. As a veritable 'father of the poor and the sick,' this admirable man, whose name shines in golden letters in the history of the Catholic restoration, 'extended his care and beneficence to all institutions for the poor and the sick, to the hospitals and benevolent foundations of the whole diocese ; he inspected everywhere the condition of the establishments ; wherever through misfortune or dishonesty among the managers loss had been suffered he did his best to remedy it, and where neglect or irregularities had crept in he instituted fresh regulations.' With what indefatigable ardour the Prince-bishop laboured is shown by the hospital ordinances (still in use) of Gerolzhofen, Heidingsfeld, Dettelbach, Arnstein, Münnerstadt, Mellrichstadt, Neustadt, Ebern, Carlstadt, Hassfurt, Iphofen, Königshofen, and Volkach. The hospital ordinance of the last-named place was signed by Julius in 1607, with his own hand and in the following words : 'No one, to my knowledge, has died a bad death who has exercised neighbourly love ; for such an one has many intercessors, and it is impossible that the prayers of many should not be heard.'[2] Contemporaries relate that the Prince-bishop Julius often visited the plague patients in person ; that he nursed many of them with his own

---

[1] Ratzinger, *Armenpflege*, pp. 333, 343.   [2] Buchinger, pp. 243–247.

hands, and thus gained them over to the Catholic faith. As his ' noblest and greatest creation,' Doctor von Gennep mentions the splendid hospital in Würzburg, ' which, under the name of Julius Hospital, was, like the Julius University, instrumental during two centuries in spreading abroad the most priceless deeds of bene- volence, in alleviating the heavy woes of ill-fated human beings, of bestowing health and blessing in abundant measure, and which is still at the present day a distinguished institution, honourably known not only in Lower Franconia but through the whole kingdom of Bavaria, and even in far foreign lands, further even than the German language reaches.' [1]

The Fulda abbot Balthasar von Dernbach also sup- ported the hospitals of his district, and erected a special institution for female patients.   At St. Blaise the abbot Caspar Müller († 1571) restored the ruined hospital; at St. Gall abbot Othmar Kunz († 1577) founded a plague- house.   His successor, Joachim Opfer († 1594), who had received his education at Paris from the Jesuits, under- took personally, with six other priests, the care of the sick during the plague of 1594, and met his death in their service.

How large a number of Catholic priests fell victims to voluntary care of the sick during the plague periods of the sixteenth and seventeenth centuries is known only to Him Who writes down in the Book of Life every cup of water given to a sick person.   But what historical knowledge has handed down fully suffices to prove what treasures the Catholics possessed in times of sickness and need in their priests and monks, who were

---

[1] Buchinger, p. 247 ; cf. Von Wegele, i. 169, and vol. ix. of the present work, pp. 361 ff. and 369.

unhindered by any family ties. In Viersen and in the
Lower Rhine district, in 1606, all the priests of the
Kirchspiel died in the service of the plague patients.
At Constance, from July to November 1611, three
pastors, twelve other priests, and five nuns lost their
lives in nursing the sick.[1]

When in the years 1541–1542 the plague was raging
in Alsace, no fear of death debarred the Barefoot Friars
at Colmar from going to the help of the sick. All the
inmates of the convent there, with the sole exception
of the warden, were attacked by the complaint.[2] At
Bozen, in 1612, twelve Franciscans fell victims to their
active neighbour-love.[3] The chronicler Fortunatus
Huber gives a whole list of martyrs to the love of mankind from among the Franciscan Order. ' Of these
martyrs,' he says, ' I ought indeed to write a separate
book ; for in truth, in all places where the Franciscans
dwell in convents, even indeed where they have only
been sent for, they run, hasten, leap to the bedsides of
the dying and make the difficult way to eternal salvation
easy and sure with their fervent spiritual ministrations.
On the battlefields they stand by the brave and dying
soldiers, pointing out to them piously and disinterestedly
the way of salvation. In times of plague and infectious
illness they care nothing for the risk of death, if only
they can save the souls of the dying. Whole towns,

---

[1] Lammert, pp. 11, 28. See also what H. von Weinsberg says concerning the self-sacrificing labours of the clergy and the Beguins during
the plague of 1553 (Höhlbaum), *Buch Weinsberg*, ii. 43). At Cologne,
later on, the pastor, Caspar Ulenberg, famous as a controversialist († 1617),
showed extreme courage during the ravages of the plague ; although in
feeble health himself, he was indefatigable in administering the consola-
tions of religion to the sick, and while thus employed he caught the
infection.

[2] Rocholl, pp. 85–86.   [3] Lammert, p. 37.

villages, and communities bear attested evidence to the good done (and still being done) by the Franciscans in Germany to the sick, sorrowful, plague-stricken, erring, despairing, suffering, and dying people. How many indeed I know of myself, who through love to God, manifested in holy devotion to their neighbours, soon became inheritors of death, and are now reaping their reward in heaven with all the blessed company of martyrs in the cause of charity ! In them are fulfilled the words of our Redeemer Jesus Christ, " Greater love hath no man than this, that a man lays down his life for his friend." ' [1]

Nobler deeds even of devoted love and heroic self-sacrifice were done by the new Orders, above all by the Jesuits and the Capuchins. Added to these, there was in Germany at the beginning of the seventeenth century yet another organisation, one of those new societies intended exclusively for the care of the sick, ' which by the purity of its aims, and the zeal with which these aims were accomplished, excelled all earlier societies of the kind.' [2] I allude to the society of Brothers of

---

[1] Gaudentius, p. 354.

[2] Haeser, i[3]. 866, 867 ; cf. Haeser, *Geschichte der christlichen Kranken-pflege*, Berlin, 1857, pp. 82, 88, and Uhlhorn, iii. 129 f.   The latter remarks : ' Whereas the old hospital-associations in the Roman Catholic Church, as we shall presently see, underwent remodelling and, under their new organisation adapted to the needs of the time, did such admirable service, those of the Lutheran Church fell into irreparable decay.   A new organisation of voluntary service in works of love, on an evangelical basis, was never taken into consideration.' See also *Handbuch der Kranken-versorgung und Krankenpflege*, published by G. Liebe, P. Jacobsohn, G. Meyer, i. Berlin, 1899.   This first volume begins with the historical development of sick-nursing, by Dr. Dietrich, a Protestant doctor of medicine.   At p. 47 he says : ' The Protestant communities during the first two centuries after the Reformation show little fruitfulness in works of neighbourly love ' (p. 49).   ' The houses for the sick in the Protestant districts were, with few exceptions, very bad, and nothing was done to

Mercy, for whom Prince Karl Eusebius of Liechten-
stein, in 1605, erected at Felsberg in Nether Austria
the first hospital on German ground ; in 1614 the
Emperor Matthias placed a house in Vienna at their
disposal.[1] The members of this Order were bound not
only to nurse the sick but also to keep account of the
patients who had been tended. This was the origin
of the oldest protocol-books of the sick, which have a
high medico-historical interest.[2]

Although sick-nursing, both with the Jesuits and
the Capuchins, was only a secondary object of the
Order, the members of these highly meritorious congregations did quite as good service in the plague periods of
the sixteenth and seventeenth centuries as if they had
been founded exclusively for that purpose. The first
of the Jesuits who laboured in Germany were indefatigable in their attendance on and care for all suffering
people. Claudius Jajus watched through whole nights
by sick-beds ; Nicholas Bobadilla refused the rooms
offered him by Ferdinand I at the court, and took up
his abode in the public sick-house. During the Smal-
caldean war he devoted himself entirely to the care of
the sick and wounded, and was himself once attacked
by the plague, and another time wounded. At Cologne,

improve them.' '. . . Quite otherwise, meanwhile, had the influence
of the Reformation (!) affected the benevolent circle of the Catholic
Church. Here, in the sixteenth and seventeenth centuries, societies for
tending the poor and the sick were organised which, by the purity of their
aims and the zeal with which these aims were accomplished, surpassed
everything of the kind that had been done before' (p. 50). 'The reform
of sick-nursing in the Catholic Church emanated from Spain. . . . From
Spain came the model of the modern hospital and of the nursing organisation which corresponds to modern times.'

[1] Wetzer and Welte's *Kirchenlexikon*, ii². 1333.
[2] Cf. Haas, *Das Krankenmaterial des Spitals der Barmherzigen Brüder
zu Prag vom Jahre 1670 bis auf unsere Zeit*, Prag, 1885.

as at Prague, the first Jesuits gained the love of the people by their self-sacrificing labours at the time of the plague. Cardinal Otto von Truchsess, as well as Duke Albert of Bavaria, praised their undesisting labours in the hospitals and their ' loving-kindness to the lepers.' Bravely they held out everywhere in the perilous atmosphere of the sick-wards, by the bedsides of the dying. This explains the saying ' Luterisch ist gut leben, katholisch gut sterben.' During the Munich plague of 1572 the Jesuits closed their schools, and the Fathers as well as the Brothers nursed the sick by day and by night. When in 1598 the Paderborn canons fled before the plague, the Jesuits remained at their posts, and devoted their attention also to the lepers who had been turned out of the town. ' Who among us are so zealous and indomitable in looking after the sick,' wrote a preacher in 1594, ' as these emissaries of the Antichrist ? ' More eloquent, however, than all other testimonies are the names, in the historical works and annual reports of the Order, of those who lost their lives in voluntary devotion to the care of the sick. Among these, down to the outbreak of the Thirty Years' War, there were no fewer than 121 Fathers.[1] It is a sad,

---

[1] See our present work, vol. viii. pp. 220–223, 242–247, 258–261, 271–273, 316–320 ; vol. ix. pp. 312, 317–318, 319–320, 326–332, 334–337, 342 f., 369–372, 376 ; vol. x. p. 332 f. ; [vol. viii. p. 337 of German original ; the English translation is not yet out], where many other examples are cited, and the proofs given, showing that the Jesuit pupils, above all Guarinoni, behaved as courageously as their masters. At Innsbruck the Jesuits distinguished themselves especially in the plague of 1611. The *Historia Provinciae Societatis Jesu* (Germaniae Superioris Pars iv. auctore F. H. Kropf Dec. viii. 11) relates how the Fathers at that time almost fought for the privilege of administering the Sacrament to the patients in their last hours. At first the Sanctissimum was taken from the distant parish church to the Lazaretto, but the Jesuits soon found themselves obliged to keep it in their own house, because in the

but a true fact, that Protestant authors like Fischart, instead of recognising the self-sacrificing work of the Jesuits in the hospitals, in the service of suffering men and women, scoff at them in the grossest manner.[1]

town all intercourse with people who visited the hospitals was avoided. This it was that first gave rise to the idea that there ought to be a church near the Lazaretto, and Father Köstlan persuaded the burghers to make a vow that they would build a church in that neighbourhood to the honour of the Saints Sebastian, Pirminius and Rochus, the patron saints in deaths from the plague. On September 21, 1611, the magistrate pledged himself most solemnly to see that the church was built. Two months afterwards the epidemic had ceased. Some transactions with the Archduke delayed the laying of the foundation-stone, and the ceremony was postponed till May 24 in the following year, when it was to be performed by the burgomaster—in the documentary statement he is called consul— George Fellengibel. The building was carried on so rapidly that on October 12, 1613, the church ' to the three saints ' was ready to be consecrated by the suffragan bishop and cathedral provost of Brixen, Simon Feuerstein. The funds of the church increased rapidly. Archduke Maximilian presented it with a small government house standing near it ; he also paid for the building of the chief altar, and in 1614 gave an offering of several silver vessels and other church furniture. The small house given by the Archduke was enlarged in order that in times of plague, besides the sexton, a priest, a doctor and a surgeon, to attend the Lazaretto patients, might be lodged in it. In the plague-room set apart in this house the priest kept the garment of wax-cloth which he was obliged always to put on when visiting the patients. Precise rules were written down as to how he was only to go through a small side door into the church, and from the church only by a special sideway into the sick-house. This house is at present set apart for the use of the widows of the pastors of the church of the Three Saints. Concerning the Capuchins see also Pöckl, *Die Kapuziner in Bayern*, Sulzbach, 1826, p. 31 ff. At Memmingen in 1522 the Jesuits devoted themselves indefatigably to the plague patients (seventeen sisters had been carried off, and only nine were left). In 1531 the nuns, who had been tormented in a quite incredible manner, were forced to leave the town for which they had sacrificed themselves at the time of the plague. Gaudentius, pp. 365 f., 369.

[1] See our statements, vol. x. p. 323 ff. ; see also vol. ix. p. 326.

CHAPTER VII

PHILOSOPHY AND THEOLOGY OF THE PROTESTANTS

PHILOSOPHY, resting chiefly on Aristotle, but influenced also in many respects by Plato, and developed into a uniform system—with special regard to theology—by centuries of clear and logical thought from the greatest intellects of medieval times, was the unifying power which, down to the close of the Middle Ages, bound together the various branches of natural science, and connected them all in turn with speculative research into the region of the supernatural. Through the scholastic methods philosophy had developed into a sphere of thought in which jurist and physician, mathematician and astronomer, linguist and historian, had as much right to exercise their intellectual faculties as the speculative theologian and the mystic. Any contradiction between philosophical and theological truth, between reason and revelation, was à *priori* and fundamentally excluded ; for did not both come from God, the absolute Truth, the one Source of all light ? [1] By this it is

---

[1] Thomas Aquinas, *Expositio in librum Boetii de Trinitate*, q. 2, art. 3. '. . . quod dona gratiarum hoc modo naturae adduntur quod eam non tollunt, sed magis perficiunt ; unde et lumen fidei, quod nobis gratis infunditur, non destruit lumen naturalis cognitionis nobis naturaliter inditum.   Quamvis autem naturale lumen mentis humanae sit insufficiens ad manifestationem eorum quae per fidem manifestantur, tamen impossibile est quod ea quae per fidem nobis traduntur divinitus, sint contraria his

not meant that the Catholic learning of the Middle
Ages was a mixture of philosophy and theology, as has
been charged against it by its opponents since the
sixteenth century.[1] The actual essence of scholastic
theology does undoubtedly lie in the close connexion
of philosophy with Church teaching; but philosophy
has not on this account become the authority for
'demonstrating Christianity,' neither in the sense of
any Christian truth being ultimately proved by philosophy, nor in the sense that philosophy has been the
source of new dogmas.[2]

quae per naturam nobis sunt indita; oporteret enim alterum esse falsum :
et cum utrumque sit nobis a Deo, Deus esset nobis auctor falsitatis,
quod est impossibile.' See his exhaustive exposition *De veritate catholicae
fidei contra gentiles*, lib. 1, c. 7 : ' Quamvis . . . veritas fidei christianae
humanae rationis capacitatem excedat, haec tamen, quae ratio naturaliter
indita habet, huic veritati contraria esse non possunt.   Ea enim, quae
naturaliter rationi sunt insita, verissima esse constat, in tantum ut nec ea
esse falsa sit possibile cogitare; nec id quod fide tenetur, quum tam evidenter
divinitus confirmatum sit, fas est credere esse falsum.   Quia igitur solum
falsum vero contrarium est, ut ex eorum definitionibus inspectis manifesto apparet, impossibile est illis principiis, quae ratio naturaliter
cognoscit, praedictam veritatem fidei contrarium esse. . . .' *Summa
theol.*, P. 1, q. 1, art. 8: ' Cum fides infallibili veritati imitatur, impossibile autem sit de vero demonstrari contrarium : manifestum est
probationes, quae contra fidem inducuntur, non esse demonstrationes
sed solubilia argumenta.' This fundamental principle of all Catholic
learning was once more proclaimed by Church authority shortly before
the outbreak of the Protestant disturbances in the Bull issued by Leo X
at the fifth Lateran Council against the New Aristotelians, *Apostolici
Regiminis* of the year 1513 : ' Cum verum vero minime contradicat,
omnem assertionem veritati illuminatae fidei contrariam omnino falsam
esse definimus, et ut aliter dogmatizare non liceat, districtius inhibemus.'

[1] Cf. Denzinger, *Vier Bücher von der religiösen Erkenntnis*, p. 547 f.
[2] Staudenmaier, *Dogmatik*, i. 232, 233 f. : ' The position which Plato
and Aristotle held in this Demonstration was that of welcome witnesses
speaking in the name of a philosophy in harmony with reason.   Not till
reason and philosophy had both had a hearing as well as revelation, tradition, and the Bible, was the decisive syllogism formulated, a syllogism
which thus had for its premises the whole sum of divine and human truth.
Divine and human truth, however, were regarded as standing in such

Learned, speculative doubt was regarded merely as a means for establishing on still deeper foundations that which was already known and firmly held by faith, or as an incentive to further investigation by which to arrive at new and certain conclusions.[1] In the great fundamental matters of all branches of knowledge the technical language, the scientific terminology, the methods, were all similar ; and as regards most of the principal points there were the same opinions, the same unity, clearness and certainty. Thus with clergy and laity alike philosophy stood in high repute, and the struggle of the humanists against the one-sidednesses

relation to each other that the divine formed the basis of the human, and faith, consequently, the basis of scientific knowledge. Hence, however important at that time the thirst for knowledge might be, however high the human mind dared to soar in its speculation, or however deep it plunged, however boldly and confidently it explored the world of nature and the world of spirit, however penetrating and original the investigation, however strong and skilful the dialectics proved, the attitude of mind always remained humble, and the inward vision steadily directed, in pious veneration, to the region of that higher light which illumines mankind in the Gospel, where alone we find the true light, and through which alone our knowledge is raised into all-illuminating science, which, however humble may be the sphere of its working, has as its result the eternal and immortal life, as it is revealed in God. And this was on the whole the great and mighty feature which we connote in the Middle Ages, the impulse of the whole man towards reasonableness and intelligence in God, as well as towards life in Him and in His eternal kingdom, which only for this end He has revealed to us and woven into the finite world.' The spirit of pagan philosophy did not penetrate into Christian theology, but in scholasticism the Aristotelian and Platonic elements appear worked up in such a peculiar manner that an entirely new scientific life is produced. The spirit of Christianity which permeated these (the Aristotelian and Platonic elements) transformed, quickened, and shaped anew and ennobled all things ; and the school-men, says Moehler (*Gesammelte Schriften und Aufsätze* i. 130), can only be robbed of this merit ' by passionate prejudice combined with the grossest ignorance.'

[1] Isolated and transitory rationalistic phenomena, such, for instance, as Abélard, which were combated by the Church theology, are only exceptions which confirm the rule. See Kuhn, *Dogmatik*, i. 413 ff.

and the deteriorations of scholasticism was not able to shake the position of philosophy itself in the spiritual economy of the old Church.[1] Philosophy never stood higher than when it was subservient to theology.

Its fate, however, became very different under the rule of the new doctrine. Luther from the first showed immoderate hatred for Aristotle and the Aristotelian philosophy. In a letter of February 8, 1516, to the Augustine prior, John Lange, at Erfurt,[2] he calls Aristotle ' a comedian who has long mocked the Church with his Greek mask, a Proteus, the cunningest deceiver of spirits, a man whom, if he had not been compact of substantial flesh, people would not have hesitated to regard as the devil.'[3] In 1517, in a disputation held by one Franz Günther, over which he (Luther) presided, he caused theses against Aristotle to be defended. Elsewhere he calls Aristotle ' a great fool, a damned heathen, a senseless word-quibbler, in whom God has punished the ungrateful world.'[4] On May 9, 1518, he writes to Jodocus :[5] ' The Church cannot possibly be reformed unless the canons, the decretals, scholastic

---

[1] ' The philosophical questions of scholasticism may be made to seem ridiculous only by pointing out the most unimportant and trivial instances as typical ones,' says Schlosser, *Vincent de Beauvais*, ii. 14 ; cf. Von Raumer, i. 3 ; see also Moehler, i. 131 ff.

[2] *Luther's Letters*, published by De Wette, i. 15 f.

[3] Letter to Lange, *l.c.* Together with this letter he sent the Aristotelian Jodocus at Eisenach, his teacher, a letter which has not been preserved, ' plenas questionum adversus logicam et philosophiam et theologiam, id est, blasphemiarum et maledictionum contra Aristotelem, Porphyrium, Sententiarios, perdita scilicet studia nostri seculi.'

[4] Cf. G. Th. Strobel, *Neue Beiträge zur Literatur besonders des* 16. *Jahrhunderts*, iv. 1 (1793), 152 ; Döllinger, i. 445. ' If Luther constantly asserts that in the Middle Ages Aristotle was not understood ' (see the letter to Spalatin of January 14, 1518) ' this makes no difference in the nature of his damnatory opinion.' Denzinger, i. 124.

[5] De Wette, i. 108.

theology, philosophy and logic, in their present form, are rooted up, and other studies substituted.' [1]

But if Luther vented his hatred first and chiefly against Aristotle and scholastic philosophy, this was only the expression and the result of his primary attitude towards philosophy in general. 'The name Aristotle was to him the representative and the sum of the whole body of philosophical thought and research, and of the sinister presumption, underlying philosophy, which attempted to grasp things that it was either altogether impossible for man to know, or which were solely objects of faith, to the exclusion of all reasoning.' [2]

This attitude of Luther towards philosophy is most closely connected with his dogmatic views, and the estimate of reason which necessarily resulted from these views. In conformity with his opinions on original sin, as he formulated them in connexion with his doctrine of justification, he denies to fallen man both moral freedom of will and any capacity for knowing the things of God. For temporal things, he says, man's reason is, perhaps, adequate, 'for knowing how to build houses, how to make clothes, how to marry, fight, navigate, and so forth; . . . but in things divine— that is, in things concerning God, to know how to act so as to please God and obtain salvation—in this respect human nature is altogether dense, dull, and blind, and cannot show even so much as a hair's breadth of what these things are. Presumptuous enough indeed she [human nature] is, to go floundering and blundering

---

[1] See I. H. Von Elswich, ' De varia Aristotelis in scholis Protestantium fortuna ' in the edition of Joh. Launoius *De varia Aristotelis in Academia Parisiensi fortuna*, Vitebergae, 1720, 18 ff. ; Denzinger, i. 124 ; Döllinger, i. 475 f. ; Stöckl, *Gesch. der Philosophie*, iii. 482 ff., 512 ff.

[2] Döllinger, i. 445 ; cf. Denzinger, i. 125.

in like a blind horse ; but all that she has to say on the subject is as certainly false and erroneous as it is certain that God exists.'[1] Worse vilifications of reason than Luther uttered are scarcely conceivable.[2] It will suffice here to draw attention to his utterances in the greater commentary to the Epistle to the Galatians (1535) :[3] 'Reason,' he says, ' scorns God, denies His wisdom, justice, mercy, yea, His Godhead itself. She [reason] is always opposed to the true and the good : all her wisdom is only foolishness. In matters of faith she is utterly blind. She does not even rightly recognise and understand moral truths, even such as man's nature, so to say, is born to, as for instance : " What you do not wish to be done to you, that do not do to others." From her very nature she loses herself in pharisaic superstition ; even on the transactions of daily life she cannot pronounce true judgment ; she is the mother of all errors, the source of all that's bad, the plague of man-

[1] *Werke*, published by Walch, xii. 399 ; cf. Staudenmaier, *Zum religiösen Frieden*, i. 225 f. ; Denzinger, i. 125 f. ; *Lutheri Commentarius in epist. ad Galatas*, ii. 20 (ed. Irmischer, Erlangae, 1843, i. 255) : 'Quidquid est in voluntate nostra, est malum, quidquid est in intellectu nostro, est error. Ideo homo in rebus divinis nihil habet, quam tenebras, errores, malitias, et perversitates voluntatis et intellectus.'

[2] A selection of the most vulgar utterances from sermons and from the *Table-talk* is given by F. W. Ph. von Amman, in Winer's *Zeitschr. für wissenschaftliche Theologie*, i. (1829) 5 ff. Wherever, on the other hand, Luther bestows praise on human reason, it is always either a question of its use in purely temporal things, or else it must be acknowledged that in such cases, as in so many other matters, he has not always shown himself consistent ; the genuine Luther and the logical consequence of his system stand revealed in these vituperations against reason, and it is a fruitless undertaking to attempt, as does for instance B. Amman, *l.c.*, with entire misunderstanding of the whole point of view, to prove that ' this virulent and vulgar abuse of this faculty of our minds ' is not so much directed against reason itself, as against ' the quibbling and sophistical intellect.' Cf. Denzinger, i. 127 ff.

[3] See Stöckl, iii. 513 f.

kind.' Hence, according to Luther, it follows that it
is the duty of the Christian 'to strangle this beast,
Reason.'[1] 'Believing men strangle reason and say :
"Look here, Dame Reason! you're a foolish, blind
idiot, you don't understand the least mite of the things
of God, so then don't make a bother with your contradicting, but hold your jaw and be quiet ; and don't
presume to stick yourself up as arbiter of God's Word,
but set yourself to listen to what that Word tells you,
and to believe it." And so the believers strangle this
beast, which the whole world besides cannot strangle, and
thereby they offer the most welcome sacrifice and service
to our Lord God that can ever be presented to Him.'

And just as Luther held reason and faith to be
opposed to each other, so did he regard philosophy
and theology as antagonistic the one to the other ;
he starts from the basis that philosophy, as the knowledge of material things and of what can be learnt by
reason, stands in absolute opposition to the world of
the unseen and the divine. Accordingly, while very
lightly esteeming philosophy in general, he was full
of especial indignation towards every application of
philosophy to religious matters,[2] and called it a devilish

---

[1] See Döllinger, i. 446 ; *Comm. in epist. ad Gal.* iii. 6 (ed. Irmischer,
i. 329 f.). 'Fides rationem mactat et occidit illam bestiam, quam totus
mundus et omnes creaturae occidere non possunt. Sic Abraham eam
occidit fide in verbum Dei. . . . Sic omnes pii, ingredientes cum Abraham
tenebras fidei, mortificant rationem, dicentes : "Tu ratio stulta es, non
sapis quae Dei sunt, itaque ne obstrepas mihi, sed tace, non iudica, sed
audi verbum Dei, et crede." Ita pii fide mactant bestiam majorem
mundo, atque per hoc Deo gratissimum sacrificium et cultum exhibent.'
In like manner Luther emphasises the same opinion from the other side,
stating that there is irreconcilable opposition between faith and reason :
the substance of faith, he says, is to reason 'ridiculum, absurdum,
stultum et impossibile' (*ibid.* p. 328).

[2] He even wished to exclude the formal use of philosophy in religion

crime of the colleges to have set up ' this natural light,' and ascribed to it power to puzzle out divine things and revealed doctrine, to have exalted reason into an instrument fit for the investigation of religious truth, and to have attempted a reconciliation between faith and learning.[1] And thus, in consequence of these

and the training of theologians by means of philosophy. Letter to Spalatin of June 29, 1518 (De Wette, i. 127) : ' You ask me how far I think dialectics useful for true theologians. In my opinion dialectics can only be harmful to theologians. Even if we assume that they are perhaps a useful pastime and exercise for young heads, still in theology, where only faith and higher inspiration are looked for, all syllogisms should be set aside, just as Abraham, when he was going to sacrifice, left his servant and his ass behind.' Staudenmaier, *Zum religiösen Frieden*, i. 228.

[1] Döllinger, i. 444 : ' That was the basic error of the whole system of scholasticism evolved at the universities, and he did not attack and abhor it so much on account of its then decadent condition as for its fundamental principle, viz. the use of human reason in things of religion, which can only be grasped and assimilated by faith. This attitude of repugnance and antagonism grew all the stronger from the frequent reproaches made against him by his opponent that his doctrines, especially those of man's slavish will and of justification, were utterly untenable and senseless from a philosophical standpoint ; and that, without entering into Biblical and traditional opposition grounds, but simply *a priori*, from grounds of pure reason (because the mystery of religion was *above* reason, but could not be *against* it), it was possible for the human mind to become convinced of the faultiness of this system.' Staudenmaier, *Zum religiösen Frieden*, p. 230 : ' The reason why Luther was so fiercely opposed to human reason and to the study of philosophy is easily explained by the fact that he had in himself a distinct feeling and a certain intuitive sense that his doctrine of God as the author of sin, and of man as morally unfree, was condemned by philosophy as the most arrant falsehood.' *Ibid.* p. 228 : ' The connexion in which philosophy stood with the universities in the Middle Ages was sufficient ground for Luther to attack these institutions in his customary manner. Like Wickliffe and Huss, he frequently calls them " inventions of the devil," " workshops of Satan," and so forth. " The high schools of the Pope," he says, ' are the very most abominable whoredom and harlotry of the devil, because they set up Aristotle as a rival light." The " Justiciaries " and " sophists " (*i.e.* the Catholic theologians) he falls foul of above all, because " they do not slay this enemy of God, Reason, but, on the contrary, feed its life." *Comm. in epist. ad Gal.* iii. 6 (ed. Irmischer, i. 331). Because these same people make use of philosophy in religion, he reproaches them

opinions, he fell back on the thesis, which in earlier
times had forthwith been combated and overcome
wherever it turned it, ' that there might be some
things true in theology which were false in philosophy,
and vice versa.' [1] He had so little doubt on this point
that he expressed himself as follows against the Sorbonne which had rejected this thesis : ' The Sorbonne,
the mother of all errors and heresies, has uttered a
thoroughly scandalous pronouncement, in that it has
declared that what is true in theology is also true in
philosophy. By this abominable doctrine the Sorbonne
has plainly declared that the truths of religion are to
be put under the yoke of human reason.' [2]

In his concrete utterances, therefore, this hatred
was directed against philosophy in general, as learning
acquired by reason, and against Aristotle in particular,
as the philosophical authority of the schools, and
against scholastic philosophy. Concerning Aristotle he
spoke in the manner already described above.   The

with mixing up theology and philosophy (*ibid.* i. 384).' Concerning
Luther's attacks on the universities, see our statements, vol. iii. pp. 233–
235 ; vol. iv. p. 355.

[1] Ed. Zeller, *Gesch. der deutschen Philosophie*, p. 29 : ' He is quite in
earnest in the assertion, under which at that time the freethinking Italian
Aristotelians also were wont to conceal their heresies, that things might
be true in theology and false in philosophy ; yes, he did not doubt that
this could be so. . . .' Kuhn, i. 471 : ' The kind of religious consciousness which asserted itself in this manner [as with Luther] was of necessity
hostile to the objective knowledge of religion arrived at through rational
thinking, *i.e.* philosophy. To this consciousness of religion it was not
only a matter of indifference what judgment was passed on it by reason,
whether reason regarded it as allowable and in agreement with itself
or the opposite, but it actually considered it a mark of its genuineness
and purity that it entirely set at nought this contradiction and defied it.'

[2] In a ' Theological Disputation on the question, whether the statement " The Word was made flesh " was true in philosophy.'   January 11,
1541 ; Walch, x. 1398.

greatest philosopher of the Middle Ages, Thomas Aquinas, was in his opinion ' a babbler and a chatterer.' [1] What he has to say against these philosophers, however, applies to philosophy in general.[2] ' If things had gone according to his ideas, philosophy among the Protestants would have had to content itself with a very humble position, and would have played a very small part in affairs.' [3] ' The German Protestants might have been frightened away by Luther from all connexion with philosophy.' [4]

If Luther's views had been carried out with logical consistency they would necessarily have involved the abolition of all philosophy in favour of the immediacy of faith.[5] In reality, however, things shaped themselves otherwise in the Protestant schools, because here, too,

---

[1] Luther's Collected Works, lxii. 116. How little Luther knew about the golden period of scholasticism, and especially about Thomas Aquinas, has been shown by Denifle, *Luther und Lutherthum in der ersten Entwickelung quellenmässig dargestellt*, vol. i. (Maintz, 1904). Denifle's work, so rich in new information, unfortunately did not come out till the present work was already finished, so that an adequate use of it was not possible.

[2] Ed. Zeller, *Gesch. der deutschen Philosophie*, p. 30: ' In his objection to scholasticism he was in agreement with the fathers of recent philosophy ; but the reasons on which this objection was based are in his case altogether those of the antiphilosophic mystic. For him the Middle Ages did not hold too little philosophy, but too much ; not the narrowness and the limitations, but the presumption and the domineering character of its thought, were the chief faults of scholasticism.'

[3] Ed. Zeller, *l.c.* p. 30.

[4] Ed. Zeller, *l.c.* p. 27.

[5] Überweg, *Grundriss der Gesch. der Philosophie*, iii[3]. (1880) 16 ; Möhler, *Gesammelte Schriften und Aufsätze*, i. 260 : ' So long as Luther's and Calvin's teaching was believed to be true there was no poetry, no history, no philosophy, &c., in the Protestant Church ; it is indeed a positive fact that so long as the Protestant community remained Lutheran it had no philosophy, and when it acquired a system of philosophy it was no longer Lutheran. Such is the way in which their faith flies from philosophy, and their philosophy from faith.' See also Schauz, *Apologie des Christentums*, Freiburg, 1898, iii[2]. pp. 563–565.

as in other matters, logical consistency was and had to be sacrificed if the Protestants were to have any learning at all. The founder of a new school philosophy in the Lutheran Church is Melanchthon.

Melanchthon himself only arrived at definite principles in this respect after manifold fluctuations. In his Tübingen days, though disinclined to scholastic philosophy, he appears as a venerator of Aristotle himself. In the year 1518, in the preface and *Postfatio* of the first edition of his Greek grammar he states his intention of publishing, in combination with other scholars, the Aristotelian writings in the original, and thereby bringing the study of the Aristotelian philosophy in Germany for the first time into the right course.[1] All this was changed as soon as he came to Wittenberg. True, in his opening speech on August 29, 1518, he spoke of the restoration of the genuine Aristotelian philosophy as the task which he had set before himself,[2] but soon after, in his first full surrender to Luther's opinions, he remained for a space of time under the influence of Luther's spirit, and allowed himself to be carried away by the same hatred of all philosophy. In a lecture delivered at Wittenberg, in 1520, he repudiated philosophy wholesale as ' pagan abomination.'[3]

' Philosophy,' he said in a pamphlet of 1521, directed against Emser, ' taught at all points the opposite of truth : that man was not a Christian who claimed the title of philosopher.' He laid the blame of atheism on

[1] *Corpus Reformatorum,* i. 26 f. ; cf. A. Richter in the *Neue Jahrbücher für Philologie und Pädagogik,* cii. 478 ; K. Hartfelder, *Philipp Melanchthon als Praeceptor Germaniae,* p. 39 f.

[2] *Corp. Reform.* xi. 15–25 ; cf. Paulsen, p. 73 f. ; Hartfelder, p. 65.

[3] *Corp. Reform.* xi. 34–41.

the metaphysics of Aristotle ; his ethics, he said, were
diametrically opposed to Christ, his whole system of
physics was nothing but empty verbiage which afforded
babbling men matter for disputation.[1] Even in the
first edition of the ' Loci theologici,' of 1521, there are
hostile remarks on philosophy, reason, and Aristotle,
quite in the spirit of Luther.[2]

Melanchthon, however, was soon cured of this blind
hatred, and later on spared no trouble in reviving the
study of Aristotelian philosophy. If one wanted to
oppose the defenders of the old Church in a scientific
manner, it was impossible to do so without philosophy.
' A well-developed system of theological learning and
a regular course of learned study were a *sine qua non*
for a Protestant Church also, and these were unobtainable without the aid of philosophical concepts,'[3] and
Melanchthon accordingly undertook the task of sup-
plying the Protestant schools with a school philosophy.
Of the creation of a new philosophy there could be
no question, as he was not himself an original thinker.
The only thing to be done, therefore, was to choose

---

[1] *Corp. Reform.* i. 286–358. See concerning these utterances *Schmährede
auf die Vernunft und Philosophie,* Paulsen, p. 135 f. See also Hartfelder,
pp. 72–75.

[2] *Corp. Reform.* xxi. 81 f. ' Ut intelligat iuventus . . . quam foede
hallucinati sint ubique in re theologica, qui nobis pro Christi doctrina
Aristotelicas argutias prodidere' (p. 86). 'Et in hoc quidem loco (in the
Frage über die Freiheit des Willens) cum prorsus christiana doctrina a
philosophia et humana ratione dissentiat, tamen sensim irrepsit philosophia in Christianismum, et receptum est impium de libero arbitrio
dogma, et obscurato Christi beneficentia per profanam illam et animalem
rationis nostrae sapientiam. Usurpata est vox liberi arbitrii. . . . Ad-
ditum est e Platonis philosophia vocabulum rationis aeque perniciosum.
Nam perinde atque his posterioribus ecclesiae temporibus Aristotelem
pro Christo sumus amplexi, ita statim post ecclesiae auspicia per Plato-
nicam philosophiam christiana doctrina labefactata est.'

[3] Überweg, *l.c.* p. 17

from among the philosophical authorities of the past,
and now again the lately despised Aristotle stood out
as the one whose system and methods were the best.
' Without this writer,' Melanchthon writes in a letter
to Bernard von Eck, on October 18, 1535, ' not only
can no pure philosophy be attained, but also not even
a correct system of teaching and learning.' [1]   Meanwhile
his mode of adopting the Aristotelian philosophy was
to combine eclectically with it the elements of other
systems also, especially of the Platonic, in order to
construct a system that should be in correspondence
with the dogmatic presuppositions of the new doctrines
and the needs of the new Church.[2]

[1] *Corp. Reform.* ii. 956 : ' Vere indicas plurimum interesse Reipublicae
ut Aristoteles conservetur, et extet in scholis, ac versetur in manibus
discentium.   Nam profecto sine hoc auctore non solum non retineri pura
philosophia, set ne quidem iusta docendi aut discendi ratio ulla poterit.'
Cf. the eulogies of the Aristotelian philosophy in some of Melanchthon's
speeches : ' Unum quoddam philosophiae genus eligendum esse, quod
quam minimum habeat sophistices, et iustam methodum retineat ; talis
est Aristotelis doctrina ' (*ibid.* xi. 282).   ' Plane ita sentio ; magnam
doctrinarum confusionem secuturam esse, si Aristoteles neglectus fuerit,
qui unus ac solus est methodi artifex ' (*ibid.* 349).   With this corresponds
the entire revulsion in his fundamental views.   In direct opposition to
the statement cited from the first edition of the *Loci* against the doctrine
of freedom of will as a falsification of Christianity by philosophy, he
expresses himself in the last version of this work, of 1543, against the
denial of freedom of will, which, he says, is nothing else than the old fatalism
of the Stoics, which must by no means be introduced into the Church
(*ibid.* xi. 650).   On the other hand he now defends the ' libertas voluntatis,
quam Philosophi recte tribuunt homini ' (*ibid.* 654).

[2] Zeller, *Gesch. der deutschen Philosophie*, 33 f. : ' Melanchthon differs
from scholasticism not so much by his general scientific principle as by
the more exact definition and application of this " principle."   All he
does is to oppose another conception to the scholastic conception of
Aristotle and Plato, in the humanistic sense, for scholastic dialectics he
substitutes a simpler system of procedure.   He is at one with the
scholastics, however, in that he is only concerned with a philosophy
which, as regards its essential nature, borrows from the ancients, which
is under the guardianship of positive religion, which is sought after first and

The philosophical writings which Melanchthon produced on this basis were not composed so much in the service of philosophical research as for the purpose of instruction ; they were text-books for young students, and Melanchthon himself called them compilations.[1] Books of this sort he also compiled on Dialectics,[2] Physics,[3] Psychology,[4] and Morals.[5] Besides these

foremost as an auxiliary to theology.' Ritter (*Gesch. der Philosophie*, ix. 515) emphasises ' the unsettled character of Melanchthon's philosophical teaching.' ' He does not strictly adhere to any of its propositions. He puts together side by side a variety of scientific theories, quite unconcerned as to whether they can be reconciled together.' *Ibid.* 496 f. : ' He only feels compelled to differ (as he does in many points) from Aristotle, because in the Church one must teach differently. Of human knowledge in general, as also of his own, he has not much good to say. True, he says, we know little enough, but if we lacked this little, we should lack much indeed. In this sense it was that the reform of Aristotelian philosophy came about, a reform of which the Protestant schools of Germany made their boast.' Concerning Melanchthon's eclectic Aristotelanism cf. also Hartfelder, pp. 177–183.

[1] Zeller says of them (l.c. p. 34) : ' They are also in their way excellent text-books : well arranged, complete, scholarly, of exemplary clearness and lucidity, elegant in style, and admirably adapted to the needs of instruction and the practical application of scholarship.' A full table of contents of the philosophical text-books of Melanchthon is given by A. Richter, ' Melanchthon's Verdienste um den philosophischen Unterricht,' in the *Neue Jahrbücher für Philologie und Pädagogik*, cii. (1870), pp. 456–504. See also Hartfelder, pp. 211–249.

[2] Three forms are to be distinguished : (a) *Compendiaria dialectices ratio*, Lipsiae 1520, etc. ; (b) *Dialectices Phil. Mel. libri quatuor ab auctore ipso de integro in lucem conscripti ac editi*, Hagae, 1528, etc. ; (c) *Erotemata dialectices, continentia fere integram artem, ita scripta, ut juventuti utiliter proponi possint*, Vitebergae, 1547, etc. (In this last form in the *Corp. Reform*, xiii. 513–752.)

[3] *Initia doctrinae physicae, dictata in Academia Vitebergensi*, Viteb. 1549, etc. (*Corp. Reform.* xiii. 5–178.)

[4] *Commentarius de anima*, Viteb. 1540, etc. *Liber de anima, recognitus ab auctore*, Viteb. 1553, etc. (*Corp. Reform.* xiii. 5–178.)

[5] *Philosophiae moralis epitome*, Argent. 1538, etc. (*Corp. Reform.* xvi. 21–164.) *Ethicae doctrinae elementa et enarratio libri quinti Ethicorum*, Viteb. 1550, etc. (*ibid.* pp. 165–276). An older version of Melanchthon's ethics, only distributed in transcripts for the use of the

there are commentaries on some Aristotelian and Ciceronian works.[1]

These text-books of Melanchthon came into use in the Protestant schools everywhere, and for more than half a century they formed the standard for philosophical instruction, after Luther under Melanchthon's influence had at least given in so far as to acknowledge the usefulness of dialectics and rhetoric.[2]

students, and which only came to light a few years ago, when a transcript of it passed out of private hands into the library of the town museum at Nordhausen, is published in the *Philosophische Monatsheft*, xxix. (1893), 129–177. (Cf. H. Heineck, *Die älteste Fassung von Melanchthons Ethik.*) See also *Allgem. Zeitung*, 1893, *Beil.* 17. For the ethical writings see Chr. E. Luthardt, *Melanchthons Arbeiten im Gebiete der Moral* (Programm), Leipzig, 1884.

[1] *In Ethica Aristotelis commentarius*, Viteb. 1529, etc. New edition : *Enarratio aliquot librorum Ethicorum Aristotelis primi, secundi, tertii et quinti*, Viteb. 1545 (*Corp. Reform.* xvi. 277–416). *Commentarii in aliquot politicos libros Aristotelis*, Viteb. 1530 (*ibid.* pp. 417–452). For these commentaries on Aristotle (and for Melanchthon's writings on ethics in general) cf. G. Th. Strobel, *Neue Beiträge*, iv. 1, 151–180 : Melanchthon's *Verdienste um den Aristoteles*. For metaphysics nothing was done by Melanchthon ; even at the beginning of the seventeenth century the Protestants had no text-book on this subject emanating from their own ranks, and when the necessity of including metaphysics in the school curriculum was realised, oddly enough, the *Metaphysica* of the Spanish Jesuit Suarez, which was published in 1605, became 'widely recognised and was used as a text-book among Protestant teachers.' W. Gass, *Gesch. der protestant. Dogmatik*, i. 185. It was only after the impulse had been given by the Catholics that Protestant school philosophy developed in the direction of metaphysics. In 1608 Martini brought out at Helmstädt a text-book entitled *Exercitationes Metaphysicae*.

[2] Cf. Hartfelder, p. 206 f. In the *Unterricht der Visitatoren* (instructions for inspectors) of 1528 and 1538, compiled by Melanchthon and published by Luther for the Saxon schools, it was enjoined that the instruction in grammar should be followed by instruction in dialectics and rhetoric (cf. Löschke, pp. 20 and 118). As regards the manner in which instruction in dialectics was to be given it was attempted, says Löschke (p. 118), in teaching this subject ' to point out at every opportunity the firm basis of the evangelical faith, and, whenever possible, the examples for the explanation of dialectical propositions were taken from the department of religious teaching.' Thus, for instance, Wolfgang Bütner, in hi

As at Wittenberg under the direct agency of Melanchthon himself,[1] so also at the other German Protestant

Dialectica, i.e. art of disputation (Leipzig, 1596), gave a form of definition,
in which all the qualities of a complete definition were exemplified. It is as
follows (Löschke, p. 120) : 'A heretic (*species*) . . . is a proud person (*genus*),
who does not reverence God (*differentia*), . . . who falsifies Holy Scripture
(*proprium*), . . . and who slanders and with terrific tumult misleads and
entangles consciences (*accidens*) . . . in order that he may spread far and
wide his great calumnious outcry (*quantitas*), and gain for himself a special
name and fame (*qualitas*), that he may pull down, destroy and devastate
what God and His Church have built up (*actio*), spit out and strew about
his poison and spleen in all churches and schools without ceasing (*officium*),
animated and stimulated by the devil and by his high and mighty spirit,
to contrive and stir up tumult and misery (*causae*).' ' For the training of
the heart,' Löschke remarks (p. 120), ' such appliances, even though constructed out of religious material, could scarcely be very profitable, but
the pupils were expected to become thoroughly grounded in this labyrinthine
dogmatic system, and thus equipped they could go forth valiantly to the
place of battle, when circumstances called them, to break a lance with
their opponents.' Gass (i. 199) draws special attention to the fact that
' logic was practised for religious and polemical aims ; and the correctness
of the conclusion was taken as a criterion of orthodoxy against the logical
errors of heretics, Romanists or Calvinists.' Balthasar Meisner in his
Philosophia Sobria (Giessen, 1611), besides going through grammatical,
rhetorical and moral questions, examines also (and with preference) the
categories and numbers of metaphysical propositions, and out of every
rule that he discovers he makes an anti-Calvinistic application. Concerning the fate of philosophy in general among the Protestants in the
sixteenth century, Ritter remarks (*Gesch. der Philosophie*, ix. 36 f.) :
'The Protestants were so averse to scholasticism that with it they rejected,
in great measure, philosophy also. A thoroughgoing reform of philosophy
did not enter into their plans. . . . Wherever philosophy attempted to
break through in a free independent course, it was held back and forced
to hide itself. Mystics and theosophists among the Protestants are only
found as separate sectarians. Philosophy could not indeed be wholly
driven out of the schools ; but every effort was made to moderate its
influence, to model it in accordance with theology, and to bring it back,
within the bounds of the sober judgment of healthy human understanding.
This end was always kept in sight, and the text-books of Melanchthon,
which became dominant in the Protestant schools, ministered to it.'

[1] Tholuck, *Gesch. der lutherischen Theologen Wittenbergs*, p. 55 : ' At
Wittenberg, before 1600, philosophical study was confined *solely* to the
Melanchthonian handbooks, and the philosophic culture acquired by this
means can only be rated very low.'

universities through his influence, Aristotelianism, as
expounded in these books, obtained almost universal
dominion.[1] At Leipzig Melanchthon's friend Joachim
Camerarius (1500–1574) laid the foundation for the
study of Aristotelian philosophy. At Tübingen it was
represented by Jacob Scheck (1511–1587), at Altorf by
Philip Scherb († 1605), Ernest Soner (1572–1612),
Michael Pickart (1574–1620), at Rostock by David
Chytraeus (1530–1600), at Jena by Victorin Strigel
(1514–1569). At Helmstädt, where in the university
statutes, set up with the co-operation of Chytraeus in
1576, the Aristotelian writings and the handbooks of
Melanchthon were expressly prescribed [2] as the basis
for philosophical instruction, the first representatives
of Aristotelianism were John Caselius (1533–1613)
and Cornelius Martini (1568–1621),[3] of whom the last
named especially exercised the most determining influence on the direction of philosophical study at
Helmstädt on into the seventeenth century.[4]

So little, however, despite the endeavours of these
academic teachers, did philosophy attain to more
universal repute that the Melanchthonian Henry

---

[1] Cf. Ed. Zeller, *l.c.* pp. 40–44.

[2] Cf. Henke, *Calixtus*, i. 29–31. According to the plan drawn up for
the philosophical faculty, which could not just at the beginning be carried
out in its entirety, ' there were to be, among the ten professors constituting
the faculty, two Aristotelian professors, of whom one was to lecture on the
" Organon " and " Rhetoric " of Aristotle, and the other on his " Physics "
and " Ethics," and to defend them against " misrepresentations or attacks
of the Sophists," and two others, the Dialecticus and Ethicus, who were
only to prepare students for the deeper study of this " *vera et antiqua
philosophia*," especially according to the Melanchthonian handbook.'

[3] Cf. *ibid.* pp. 48 ff., 62 ff.

[4] George Calixtus and Hermann Conring, the most celebrated teachers
of the Helmstädt college, were also introduced to the Aristotelian philosophy by Martini, and remained decided Aristotelians ; cf. Henke, i. 107 ff.;
Zeller, p. 43.

Moller, professor at Wittenberg, actually complained in 1569 of the 'general decline of philosophical studies.'

'How many ministers of churches,' he wrote, 'are there at present in Germany who are not completely ignorant of these sciences, and, what is worse, who do not publicly vouch their aversion to them? The bitter and horrible calumnies with which nearly all the churches in Germany resound, and the coarse, uneducated books scattered broadcast among the people in which philosophy is slandered and distorted for the benefit of the ignorant masses, can have no other result than the complete downfall of learning, the inroad of barbarism into the Church, and boundless licence to insolent innovators to deal at their liking with the Christian doctrines.' [1]   The Lutheran Jacob Scheck ' does not lament without cause,' wrote Perellius in 1576, ' that under the newly arisen light of the Evangel so few people are found who will apply themselves to the highly essential study of Aristotle.' [2] Concerning the complete decline of the study of original sources at the end of the sixteenth century, Solomon Gesner complains as follows in the preface to an epitome of the ' Metaphysics' of the Stagirite, compiled by Versor and published by Zach. Sommer at Wittenberg in 1596 : ' It is a lamentable state of things that in some of the universities, in rooting out scholastic mataeology they have also driven out all sound philosophism as though the abuse damned the use.   Hence it happens that not only the expounders of Aristotle, Greek as well as Latin,

---

[1] *Henr. Molleri Comm. in Malachiam prophetam.* Viteb. 1569 ; Döllinger, ii. 496.

[2] Perellius, *Ein Gespräch von der Jesuiter lehr u. wesen.* Bl. J 2[b].

but Aristotle and Plato themselves, are forced to migrate from lecture halls to private libraries, if, indeed, they are not condemned to exile ; and in place of the study of original authorities, handbooks and abridgements of all sorts are used, which may be taught in elementary schools or read at home.   Hence the prevailing ignorance in physics, ethics, politics, and metaphysics.' [1]

A tremendous stir and fierce contentions were aroused at the universities in the middle of the sixteenth century by the Calvinist Peter Ramus,[2] who violently opposed Aristotelian teaching, dialectics, physics, and metaphysics, and went in for a complete remodelling of scientific and learned education.   In this last respect he contended that ' by special and careful training a boy might be so taught and guided from the seventh year of his age, that at fifteen he would have learnt and digested the whole of philosophy, the Latin language, and all the arts, and would be fit to pass as a philosopher.' [3]

In Germany the Ramistic philosophy gained a large number of adherents, and among them especially two personal pupils of this philosopher, Thomas Freigius (from 1576 to 1582 professor in Altorf) and Franz Fabricius († 1573), the principal for a long term of years of the Düsseldorf gymnasium, who worked continu-

---

[1] Tholuck, *Geist der Lutherischen Theologen Wittenbergs*, p. 56.   Cf. also Elswick, *De varia Aristotelis fortuna*, p. 50 f.   Helmstädt alone, under the above-mentioned teachers, was a seat of study of Aristotle's own works.   ,

[2] Pierre de la Ramée, born in 1515 in the village of Cuthe in Picardy, since 1551 professor in Paris, and murdered in Paris in 1572, after a lengthy residence in foreign parts.

[3] Vormbaum, i. 746.

ously for the spread of the principles of Ramus.[1] John Sturm of Strassburg was also a devotee of this philosophy. Some few, such as the Marburg professor Rudolf Goclenius (1547–1628), sought to connect Aristotle and Ramus. On the whole, however, Ramism met with lively opposition from the academic learned bodies. When Frederick III decided to appoint Ramus as instructor of ethics at Heidelberg, the university, on November 16, 1569, begged the Elector not to substantiate this appointment 'because Ramus was not in agreement with the Aristotelian philosophy (which had now existed for nearly 2000 years, and at all times, as still nowadays, had been considered the best system), but wanted to teach in a new way and method.' His appointment, they urged, 'would produce among the preceptors and pupils discord, quarrelling, factions and all sorts of unpleasantness.'[2]

At the Lutheran universities, because its author was a Calvinist, the philosophy of Ramus was suspected of Calvinism, and branded as worthless. The Elector Christian I of Saxony, in 1588, issued a stringent order to the Wittenberg university to the effect that 'Ramistery was to be altogether avoided and discontinued in public lectures: whoever acted against this command would receive suitable punishment.'[3]

[1] Zeller, p. 48 f. The other representatives of the system of Ramus (Ramism) are enumerated by Brucker (*Hist. crit. philos.* iv. b., 76 f.). See also Elswick, *De varia Aristotelis fortuna*, p. 54 ff.

[2] Winkelmann, i. 311–312.

[3] Grohmann, i. 172–174, and ii. 176. In the Wittenberg inspectoral report of 1585 it was still said : ' In *legendo* let the *Professores phil.* keep to the method of Philip, have also no dispute among each other about Ramistery, for although the *doctrina Rami* be only taught by some private magisters, much disturbance may in time be caused in the academy. . . ' Tholuck, *Geist der Lutherischen Theologen Wittenbergs*, p. 56. ' Although

The Lutheran theologian David Chytraeus, at Rostock, warned the rector Henry Betulius, at Lüneburg, to beware of the hated name of Ramist, and informed him that a complaint concerning his heresy was even then lying before the magistrates.[1]   At Leipzig John Cramer (1530–1602), since he had come forward as a Ramist in 1576, had had a great deal of dissension with the philosophical faculty, but he was protected by the Elector against the university decision in 1582 to remove him from office, and retained at his post until he himself resigned in 1592.[2]

At the university of Helmstädt, where the professor of theology Caspar Pfafrad represented Ramism, the two already mentioned professors of philosophy, Caselius and Cornelius Martini, were the most determined opponents of Ramistic philosophy, but their antagonism did not proceed from grounds of faith, but from their observation that the followers of this philosophy gave up all serious intellectual work, and self-sufficiently depreciated all the old stern Aristotelian school discipline. They saw everywhere how with luxury and demoralisation dislike of work, inordinate contemptuousness, coarseness, and want of taste increased more and more, and the teaching of Ramus seemed to them to give easy sanction to all these

Luther himself had spoken with unjust contempt of Aristotle, still, at the very time when in Saxony other assertions of Luther were rated more highly even than the Gospel, the professors of philosophy, who as followers of Peter Ramus combated the teaching of Aristotle, were treated as enemies of the Lutheran doctrine of justification and deposed from their offices.'   K. A. Menzel, *Neuere Gesch. der Deutschen*, iii. 51.

[1] Döllinger, i. 459.

[2] Cf. G. Voigt, *Über den Ramismus an der Universität Leipzig*, in the report on the transactions of the *Kgl. sächsische Gesellsch. der Wissenschaften* at Leipzig, Philos.-histor. Klasse, xi. (1888) 31–61.

abuses.[1] It is remarkable that those very Lutherans who, as distinguished from the Melanchthonian school, firmly maintained the orthodox Lutheran hostility towards all philosophy and all use of the reason in matters of faith (as, for instance, the Helmstädt professor Daniel Hofmann), joined the Ramist party against Aristotelianism.[2]

Among the Calvinists also there were numbers who disparaged Ramus. Keckermann, for instance, in the years 1599 and 1618, finds fault with his system as a whole because it entirely excludes metaphysics, and also criticises it in detail and calls it confused. The Ramists, he says, 'start with criticism, hence their general mania for innovations.' It is not to his good qualities that Ramus owes the enormous widespread acceptance which he met with in Germany and England (France and Italy meanwhile rejecting him), but to the fact that he avoids the school terminology of the strict dialectics, and goes in for rhetoric and elegance

---

[1] Henke, *Calixtus*, i. 73–77. 'For all the advantages of the former school training, for the solidity and strictness of its methods, for all the practice, effort and exertion which it demanded of the pupils, Ramus had, as he almost confesses himself, nothing else to substitute ; and whilst those who resigned themselves to his guidance lost a comprehensive and in many ways strengthening process of education ; . . . they learnt, on the other hand, at first only to treat with scorn what they did not know, and they became intellectually and morally spoiled by losing the habit of steady work, and acquiring the habit of overestimating desultory dipping into practical knowledge hastily recommended, and to look down self-complacently on the merits of the older training ; a state of things pregnant with harm, as the Ramists began to influence the lower schools and sought to reform them.' *Ibid.* p. 74.

[2] *Ibid.* i. 74 : 'Despisers of philosophy in general were not far removed from men of this sort, who set themselves against the most widely recognised philosophy of their day ; the feeble minimum of philosophy which remained after the Ramist negations was sufficiently small to be considered as nil by the enemies of all philosophy.'

instead ; and further because the peripatetics pursued
study with such terrible earnestness that they were
fain even to echo the dictum of Ammonius : ' The
peripatetic studies demand mule-like drudgery.' [1]   In
like manner spoke Hospinian, professor of the Organon
at Basle, in 1557, concerning the ' Aristoteles-flagel-
lator ' Ramus, and the reasons why he had attracted so
many followers.[2]   Another antagonist of the peripatetic
school philosophy founded by Melanchthon, and one
from a more serious scientific standpoint, arose in
Nicholas Taurellus,[3] since 1580 professor of physics
and medicine at Altorf.   Taurellus, permeated on one

---

[1] Tholuck, *Akademisches Leben*, ii. 4, 5.

[2] *Ibid.* ii. 325.   The Catholic university at Freiburg-in-the-
Breisgau, where Ramus had found entrance, issued in 1590 the strict
injunction that he was to be entirely excluded from the lectures, and that
his name was never to be mentioned unless it was to combat his teaching ;
no student was to have a book by Ramus in his possession.   In 1605 the
university rector boasted of having despatched all the Ramists from
Freiburg.   Schreiber, *Universität Freiburg*, ii. 134, 135.

[3] Nik. Taurellus, born November 26, 1547, at Montpelyard (Montpellier),
died September 28, 1606, at Altorf.   His first work of importance reveals
in its title the tendency of his philosophy : *Philosophiae Triumphus, hoc
est, metaphysica philosophandi methodus, qua divinitus inditis menti notitiis
humanae rationes eo deducuntur, ut firmissimis inde constructis demonstrati-
onibus aperte rei veritas elucescat, et quae diu philosophorum sepulta fuit
auctoritate, philosophia victrix erumpat.   Quaestionibus enim vel sexcentis
ea quibus cum revelata nobis veritate philosophia pugnare videbatur, adeo
vere conciliantur, ut non fidei solum servire dicenda sit, sed ejus esse funda-
mentum* (Basileae, 1573).   Among his later writings the more important
are : *Synopsis Aristotelis Metaphysices ad normam Christianae religionis
explicatae, emendatae et completae* (Hanoviae, 1596) ; *Alpes caesae, hoc est,
Andreae Caesalpini Itali, monstrosa et superba dogmata, discussa et excussa*
(Francofurti, 1597) ; Κοσμολογία.   *Hoc est physicarum et metaphysicarum
discussionum de mundo libri* 2 (Ambergae, 1603) ; *Uranologia* (*ibid.* 1603) ;
*De rerum aeternitate : Nic. Taurelli Metaphysices universalis partes quatuor,
in quibus placita Aristotelis, Vallesii, Piccolominei, Caesalpini, Societatis
Conimbricensis aliorumque discutiuntur, examinantur et refutantur* (Marpurgi,
1604).   See concerning Taurellus Xaver Schmid, *Nik. Taurellus*, Erlangen,
1860, 2nd ed. 1864.

side by the truth of divine revelation, set himself the task of founding a philosophic system in which philosophical truth should be reconciled with religious truth ; philosophy was to serve the purpose of a foundation for theology. In so far as philosophy hitherto had not performed this function, the fault lay not with philosophy as such, but with the philosophers who had obscured the light of philosophy by their own errors, which errors must now be cleared away.[1] In so far as this was the case he combats those authorities in philosophy who have only led her astray, and thus comes into conflict with Aristotelianism, and first of all with that form of it in which among contemporary Italian freethinkers—such as his special butt Caesalpinus (1509–1603)—Averroistic Aristotelianism appears perverted into Pantheism ; but he also combated Aristotle himself. Moreover, in like manner as in the principal question of the relation between reason and faith, philosophy and theology, he had found it necessary to place himself in opposition to the ' reformatory ' principles, so too he saw himself obliged to modify considerably the dogmatic doctrines of the Protestant creeds concerning original sin and grace, since there could not possibly be any reconciliation between the genuine ' reformatory ' views on these matters and the opinions of human reason.[2] The

[1] See Schmid, *Taurellus*, 23 f.

[2] Stöckl, iii. 547 : ' We see what immense pains it cost Taurellus to maintain the truths of philosophy in harmony with his own creed. He finds it indeed impossible to attain this end without antagonising the reform doctrines of original sin and grace, and reducing their bearing within narrower limits. And it is noteworthy that in the struggle he falls, in many respects, from Scylla into Charybdis. His teaching on original sin and redemption is a strange mixture of Lutheranism and Pelagianism. . . . The true mean between the two opposites was unattainable to him from

result was that Taurellus was opposed as well by the
theologians of his own sect as by the representatives of
the Protestant-Aristotelian school philosophy. A Tau-
rellian school was actually formed at Altorf side by side
with the peripatetic Scherbian school. But it did not
have any permanent influence.[1]

At the university of Rostock Eilhard Lubinus (1596–
1621) struck out an independent path, and in connexion
with Neo-Platonism declared evil to be a pure negation,
a *defectus*, but all the same a necessity.[2]

In contradistinction to these different representatives of a learned school philosophy we may mention,
as Protestant mystics, Valentine Weigel (1533–1588),
pastor at Zschopau in Saxony, whose opinion only
became known in wider circles by the publication of
his writings after his death ; and the still better known
Jacob Böhme, to whom the sect of the Weigelians
attached itself and who goes on into the following
period (1575–1624).

But there is also kept up and continued among the
Lutheran theologians a tendency which clings essen-

the standpoint of his own creed. But it is remarkable all the same that
even in those days the maintenance of philosophy from the starting-point
of strict Lutheranism was recognised as an impossibility, and that it was
only through the most extraordinary medley of Lutheran and Pelagian
doctrines that it was thought even in the least degree possible to accomplish this end.' P. 554 f. : ' The doctrinal system of Taurellus is undoubtedly of great interest. This attempt of philosophy to enter into
harmonious relations with the " reformatory " creeds, to win back the
field snatched away from it, without coming into open antagonism with
theology, is a phenomenon which is very instructive as regards a knowledge of the then conditions, and of the relations of the newly arisen
dogmatic teaching to philosophy.'

[1] Schmid, *Taurellus*, p. 18 f.

[2] *Phosphorus de prima causa et natura mali*, Rostockii, 1596. Dorner,
p. 527. Tholuck, *Akademisches Leben*, ii. 5 f. 109. G. Frank, *Gesch. der
protestantischen Theologie*, i. 345 f.

tially to the logical outcome of the Lutheran principles, and which keeps up hostility against reason and philosophy.[1]   The leading figure in this respect is the Helmstädt theologian, Daniel Hofmann (1538–1611),[2] who caused a great sensation by his strife with the philosophers of that place, Caselius and Martini.   In theses ' De Deo et Christi tum persona tum officio,' which he had printed in 1598 and caused to be publicly defended under his presidency, Hofmann declared his rejection of all philosophical study, as injurious to theology, and of all exercise of the reason in matters of faith.[3]   A colloquy with his adversaries had only the effect of making him reiterate his opinions in still more immoderate terms.[4]   The end of it was that Hofmann, after his opponents had complained of him to the government, was compelled by the decision of Duke

---

[1] See above, p. 136.

[2] Cf. Ernst Schlee, *Der Streit des Daniel Hofmann über das Verhältniss der Philosophie zur Theologie*, Marburg, 1862.

[3] He made therein the assertions : ' Quod quanto magis excoleretur ratio humana philosophicis istis studiis, tanto armatior hostis prodiret, et quo seipsam armaret impensius, eo theologiam invaderet atrocius et errores jungeret speciosius, Ipsum lumen rationis naturaliter et carnaliter adversari Deo et summis mandatis ejus, imo esse inimicitiam adversus Deum praecipue in divinis et spiritualibus rebus : nec excipiendam philosophiam in mente Platonis et Aristotelis : philosophiam depraedatricem esse haeresim et hostem theologiae, opus carnis, Pelagianismi ream.' Denzinger, i. 134.   He also repeats in these theses Luther's rejection of the *abominabilis sententia* of the Sorbonne (see above, p. 124). Henke, *Calixtus*, i. 70.   Schlee, p. 15 ff.

[4] In the most unmistakable manner he now declared : ' Non abusum se philosophiae tantum istis assertionibus petere, sed etiam de vero, veriore et verissimo usu philosophiae intelligere, adeo ut philosophia, quando in officio sit in recto usu contraria sit theologiae.' Denzinger, i. 134.   He also defended his views in two publications of 1600 : *Pro duplici veritate Lutheri a philosophia impugnata et ad pudendorum locum ablegata* ; and : *Super quaestione num syllogismus rationis locum habeat in regno fidei.*   Henke, p. 71.

Henry Julius of Brunswick, in 1601, to make an apology
to the government, and was removed from the university ; he was not allowed to return to Helmstädt till
1603, when he received permission again to deliver
lectures.[1] His anti - philosophical tendency was
handed on in Helmstädt, after 1617, by John Angelus
von Werdenhagen (1581–1652), who had been appointed
to the chair of ethics in 1616, and who was dismissed
in 1618 on account of his opinions, and later on attached
himself to Jacob Böhme.[2] In like manner Wenzes-
laus Schilling, as student or private tutor in the philosophical faculty, in 1616, aired sundry opinions
similar to Hofmann's, and was excluded from the
faculty.[3]

To these opponents of philosophy on theological
principles, there joined themselves later on some whose
antagonism was the result of pure fanaticism against
philosophy. Thus Carlstadt, after teaching scholastic
philosophy at Wittenberg in the early years after 1505
of the sixteenth century, and publishing a few scholastic
writings, which it must be said do not reflect much credit
on his knowledge and capacity in the domain of philosophy,[4] in 1517, first of all entered the list with Luther
against scholastics and for Augustinism, and declared
himself opposed to all use of philosophy, and also of
logic in theology,[5] and then, developing further in this

---

[1] Henke, pp. 72, 99 ff.   Schlee, pp. 16–42.
[2] Henke, pp. 242–352.   Schlee, pp. 46–48.
[3] Henke, p. 45 f.
[4] See respecting these G. Bauch, Andreas Karlstadt als ' Scholastiker '
in the *Zeitschr. für Kirchengesch.* xviii. (1898) 37–57.
[5] He wrote as follows to Spalatin in 1518 on the question, in what
points logic was necessary for theology: 'Tibi respondeo : in nullo locorum,
quia Christus non indiget figmentis humanis. Hominum scientia et
sapientia hujus mundi est apud Deum stultitia et expolianda est anima

direction, went finally to such lengths that he told the
students they had better stay at home and work in
the fields, for the Bible says : " In the sweat of thy
brow thou shalt eat bread " ; learning was of no use ;
the spirit was all in all.'

This mentality made itself felt in other ways.   In
many places the preachers declared war against all
philosophical studies.   Thus the Leipzig university, after
being Protestantised in 1539, complained to Duke
Henry : ' The preachers do all in their power from the
pulpit to make the students and the whole college
hated by the people ; they abuse and pour contempt on
philosophical and humanistic studies, calling them pagan
and devilish, and they vilify the magisters and doctors
to the people as ignorant asses, who understand nothing
of the Holy Scriptures, and cannot even themselves put
together three words of Latin.' [1]

With philosophy, thanks to Luther's procedure,
speculative theology also was for a time set aside, in fact
if not in name, for without speculation any deeper grasp
of revelation, any seriously scientific theology, is an
impossibility.

' A young man,' said Luther, ' should avoid the
philosophy and theology of the schools as he would
shun the death of his soul.   The Gospels are not so dark

philosophicis praestigiis, quae Christum videre vult.   Dicit enim Apostolus :
Curate ne quis vos depraedetur per inanem fallaciam.   Et sapiens ait :
Odibilis est Deo omnis Sophista.   Propterea existimo Dialecticam non
esse necessariam Theologiae.'   Elswick, *De varia Aristotelis fortuna*,
p. 30.   Elswick remarks here that at the Leipzig Disputation the despised
logic avenged itself brilliantly, when Carlstadt, according to a statement
of Zwingli, presented the spectacle of a recruit who was provided with
weapons but did not understand how to use them.

[1] Winer, *De facult. evangel. in Universitate Lipsie originibus*, Lipsiae,
1839, p. 23.

but that a child can understand them. How, I ask,
were the Christians taught at the time of the martyrs,
when there was no such philosophy and school-theo-
rising ?   How did Christ Himself teach ?   St. Agnes
was a theologian (*theologa*) of thirteen years old, likewise Lucia and Anastasia ; where did they get their
learning ? ' [1]

Scholastic theology, however, was not, as might have
been expected, replaced by a simple catechismal faith,
a peaceful, childlike conception of Christianity, independent of all scientific and learned illumination, but on
the contrary there ensued a destructive, demolishing,
calumniating, controversial theology, such as had not
been known since the days of Arius.   Luther's whole
activity in the first period of his labours was of an almost
exclusively agitating, demolishing, destructive nature.[2]

[1] Döllinger, i. 482 f.   Döllinger comments on the above : ' And so the
whole of speculative theology was abolished and set aside as not only
superfluous, but as an altogether injurious study.   Historic, traditional
theology, the whole body of patristic study, could not expect a more
favourable judgment and fate from a system which began by insisting
that the whole chain of traditional and dogmatical consciousness, the
whole existing course of doctrinal development, should be given up as
altogether false.'

[2] See our remarks, vol. iii. pp. 87 ff., 106 f., 125, 205 ff., 232 ff., 264 ff.,
332 ff. ; vol. iv. p. 102 ff.   See Döllinger in Hortig's *Handbuch der Kirchengeschichte*, ii. 2, 920 : ' Polemics among the Protestants, even after the
first life and death battle was over, retained that acrid, quarrelsome,
detestable, sordid sophistry which is peculiar to every sect opposed to
the Church.   In order to be convinced of the great difference between
Catholic and Protestant dogmatising one has but to compare with each
other, for instance, Bellarmin's *Kontroversen* and the *Locos theologicos*
of Gerhard.   Hence all those endless perversions and misrepresentations
of Catholic doctrine, so that full half of all Catholic defence writings had
to deal solely with the repudiation of such dishonourable attacks ; hence
that multitude of groundless accusations, which were heaped up against
the Catholics, that ransacking of all the centuries of Church history in
order to use the failings of individual popes, bishops, clergy and monks,
the misdoings and errors of single theologians as weapons against the

With the same passionate virulence which he had ex-
pended on the doctrines and fabric of the old Church,
he now entered the field against all new religionists
who did not blindly and unconditionally submit to his
doctrinal authority : against Carlstadt, Oecolampadius,
Zwingli, the Anabaptists. In the year 1525 complete
anarchy already prevailed in the domain of religion.
Between Lutherans and Zwinglians, who fought each
other for life and death, one attempt after another was
made at reconciliation ; but each in turn failed, and then
fresh quarrels followed. After long years of contention
concerning the Eucharist, Luther himself did not know
in the end what Melanchthon thought on the subject :
' For he (Philippus) did not call it by another name,
regarded it indeed as an objectionable ceremony ; he
had not seen him partake of it for a long time.' [1]

From out the ever-swelling flood of controversial
theology, the first written creeds of Protestantism are
seen emerging like islands in a stormy sea : the Augsburg
Confession (1530) with its various emendations ; the
Wittenberg Concord (1536) ; the Frankfort Recess
(1558) ; the Württemberg Creed (1559) ; the Heidelberg
Catechism (1563) ; the Torgau Book (1576) ; the Bergen
Book (1577) ; the Formula of Concord (1580).[2]

However zealously Luther, conformably to his principles,[3] had antagonised all theology of the schools, he

whole body ; hence, finally, the presence in almost every theological book
of attacks, often of the most far-fetched nature, against the doctrine and
discipline of the Church. All this shows up the error in the struggle against
the truth.'

[1] See present work, vol. v. pp. 542, 543.

[2] *Ibid.* vol. v. p. 252 ff. and note xviii. in Appendix (p. 555), 537 ff. ;
and vol. iv. pp. 46 ff., 74 ff., 314 ff. ; vol. viii. p. 405 ff.

[3] As the formation of a Protestant school-philosophy was contrary to
these principles, had the latter been generally regarded ' there would not

was never able to gather up his collective teaching in one comprehensive work, and as little did he succeed in hindering the development on the Protestant side of a school-theology in some measure similar to the old one, or in preventing the various novel systems of doctrine from drifting in part, though with completely changed meanings, into the terminology of the old Church learning.   The extensive literature of creed formularies which sprung out of the religious contentions contains much of dialectical acumen and mental discipline which their authors had brought with them from earlier times, and also shows an extensive knowledge of Holy Writ, even though their knowledge is mixed up with arbitrary interpretation.

The great master in the art of combining, adapting, comparing, as also of manipulating the theological phraseology transported from the old Church, was Melanchthon, 'the organising spirit of the German Reformation.'[1]   Just as it was he who laid the foundations of Protestantism in philosophy, so he too gave

---

have been any science of the faith in Protestantism, not even a creed or dogma ; for the interpretation of Scripture, the grasp and understanding of its contents, is by no means possible in a purely supernatural way without the exercise of reason and without reasonable judgment.   As, however, an absolute separation of revealed religion from reason is contrary to the nature of things, we do not find such a divorce practically carried out, but only a combination of the two differing from the combinations that had hitherto been known.'   Kuhn, i. 473 f.

[1] This is what Dorner (p. 272) calls him.   For his theology see Herrlinger, *Die Theologie Melanchthons in ihrer geschichtlichen Entwickelung*, Gotha, 1879, and also Tollin in *Beilage zur Allgem. Zeitung*, 1879, No. 11, and Schürer's *Theolog. Literatur-Zeitung* (1879), p. 520 f.   For a characterisation of Melanchthon see also the (somewhat excessively) panegyric work of Ellinger, *Phil. Melanchthon. Ein Lebensbild*, Berlin, 1902, and the short but deeply penetrating study by O. Klopp, *Phil. Melanchthon*, Berlin, 1897.   Further Melanchthon literature may be found in the *Histor. Jahrbuch*, xviii. 686 f.

the German Protestants their first connected dogmatic system, in his 'Loci communes rerum theologicarum seu hypotyposes theologicae,' commonly cited as 'Loci theologici' or 'Loci communes,' which appeared in their first form in the Wittenberg edition in 1521. The history of this work, with the essential alterations in regard to the dogmatic matter which it underwent in 1535 and 1543, gives the best insight into the fluctuations and changes in the views of its author.[1] This book, which is an outcome of lectures on the Epistle to the Romans, attempts in its first form to give a systematic presentation of the principal articles of Christian doctrine.[2] This first edition of the 'Loci' is, however, by no means a complete presentment of *Dogma*. The teaching about God, the unity of God, the Trinity, the Creation, the Incarnation, are not dealt with; as to these mysteries of the Godhead, says Melanchthon, we had better worship them than try to investigate them. The scholastic disputations about them have all proved

---

[1] Staubenmaier, *Dogmatik*, i. 270. 'The continual changes he made in the actual substance proceeded as well from the indecision of his own mind, as from the power which Luther exercised over him to an almost tyrannical extent. Thus there came into existence a dogmatic work concerning which, later on, as regards the alterations and re-alterations he made in it, a veritable literary history could be written' (*Versuch einer Literaturgeschichte von Philipp Melanchthons 'Locis theologicis*,' by H. Th. Strobel, Altorf and Nuremberg, 1776). The *Loci* in their three different forms, with bibliographical notes on the further versions of each, are in vol. xxi. of the *Corpus Reformatorum*. Concerning the latest version of Melanchthon's *Loci*, edited by Kolde (Leipzig, 1900) see Schürer's *Theolog. Literatur-Zeitung*, 1901, p. 15 ; *ibid.* 1902, p. 695 f. ; concerning Römer, *Die Entwickelung des Glaubensbegriffs bei Melanchthon*, Bonn, 1902.

[2] 'Ut intelligat juventus, et quae sint in scripturis potissimum requirenda, et quam foede hallucinati sint ubique in re theologica qui nobis pro Christi doctrina Aristotelicas argutias prodidere.' *Corp. Reform.* xxi. 82.

fruitless, and have only obscured the Evangel and the good works of Christ. On the other hand, we cannot be Christians if we are not acquainted with the remaining articles, on the might of sin, on law and on grace ; for it is by these that Christ first becomes known. Thus Melanchthon intends in his work to present the substance of these doctrines, which also forms the subject of the Epistle to the Romans ; [1] that is to say, doctrines which are insisted on in Luther's new teaching, whereas the fundamental dogmas of Christianity are set aside as things which have no practical interest.[2]

[1] *Corp. Reform.* pp. 83–85.

[2] Kuhn, i. 475 f. ' We see from this how the overweening tendency of the reformers towards a subjectively practical Christianity caused a segregation of dogmatic matter which was inadmissible from the standpoint of objective philosophy. We see further that this tendency essentially reacted against the objective character of Christian doctrine, and would only allow of subjectively practical knowledge. Can this be wondered at when the reformers declared themselves opposed to philosophy and its application to the Christian truth on the ground that it obscured and imperilled the latter ? Here consciousness of the difference between religious faith and objective knowledge, between dogma and its explanation is not yet apparent, or rather the one is confounded with the other. But the reason of this is not that these men did not know how to distinguish the two from each other, but that for subjective reasons, from the standpoint which had been taken up for the Christian religion, the distinction was not admissible. For one thing the conception of Christian truth had ceased to be an objective one, a conception in harmony with objective knowledge, with reason and philosophy; next, all actually objective dogma was rejected, and all that was retained was a faith determined by actual dogmatic consciousness, which is of an essentially subjective nature. Hence the antagonism to scholasticism was still kept up even where, as with Melanchthon in the later editions of the *Loci*, Christian doctrine had in great measure recoiled from the irrationalistic standpoint of opposition to human reason. It was contrary to the Reformation principle to recognise any dogma which had been formulated through the medium of objective understanding and which had its warrant in the authority of the Church ; the reformers insisted always on a subjective faith, which had its support in the Bible alone, and was arrived at by subjective interpretation of Scripture, and hence also by the subjective understanding.

In the first text of the ' Loci ' Melanchthon adheres
in every respect, in the principal matters as also in the
treatment of special articles of faith, to the standpoint of
Luther.   Luther therefore could never sufficiently praise
the book ; all the Fathers put together, he said, were
nothing compared to it ; it was the very best book next
to the writings of the Apostles, and worthy to be included
in the Canon.[1]   Meanwhile Melanchthon himself since
1530 had given up recommending the book for reading,
because he thought much in it was still too crude and
needed alteration.   The revised version of 1535 became
almost an entirely different book.   A characteristic
difference between this edition and the former one is
above all that the subject-matter is now no longer
confined to anthropological and soteriological dogmas,
and that the points of doctrine which were left out
before are now included, and thus a complete scheme of
Dogmatics is given.   These additional articles, however,
are treated very briefly in proportion to the whole,
' more in the form of simple statement than as a
dogmatic treatise.' [2]   The other essential difference is
that Melanchthon has now abandoned his former
strictly Lutheran position in the matters of sin and
freedom of will, and that accordingly his teaching

[1] See *Corp. Reform.* xxi. 78 ; Franck, *Gesch. der protestantische Theologie*,
i. 27 f.

[2] W. Gass (i. 38) explains the subsequent completion of the dogmatic
system as the result not of scholarly theological interest, but of the
necessity for averting, by definite explanation, the threatened danger
that these basic dogmas of Christianity, which Melanchthon did not
wish to see shaken, might be lost sight of by the followers of the new
doctrines (*ibid.*).   On the earlier omission there now followed a simple
acceptance, as in the case of the Augsburg Confession. This precedent
was to take away from Melanchthon's successors the liberty of examining
into the Trinity and the Person of Christ, and to hold private opinions on
these points.'

on the powers of men, on freedom, and on man's
participation in the work of salvation has become quite
different,[1] and correspondingly also the character of
his theology in general in its relation to philosophy and
reason, as well as in its relation to the theology of the
part which before he had treated depreciatingly, but
now called in to his support whenever it suited him.
The third version ' goes somewhat further in the same
direction, and approaches still nearer, both in form and
substance, to the Catholic standpoint.'[2] Thus in its
second and third versions the book can actually be
described as a treatise on dogmatic, which it was not
in its first form.[3]

So far as the influence of Melanchthon and his school
extended, this work of his served as a convenient basis
and guide for dogmatic study and lecturing. As with
the Sentences of Lombard in the Middle Ages, so
now the ' Loci ' of Melanchthon were made the subject
of much comment by his co-religionists, and also, in

[1] Kuhn, i. 479.   See also our statements, vol. vii. p. 56 ff.
[2] Kuhn, i. 470 f.
[3] Gass, i. 45 f.   ' If now we study our *Loci theologici* again as a whole,
not, however, in the first, but in the third edition, we shall scarcely
recognise it.   Tone, attitude, language, have become quite different,
and the bulk has increased threefold, not to mention the changes in particular doctrines.   The condition of things had so altered, meanwhile,
that the Church was now completely severed from the papacy and firmly
established on an independent footing ; but dogmatic controversy had
begun within it, and it needed therefore rather the systematisation of
accepted dogmas than outward championship.   Hence we find no more
polemics against the schoolmen, many of whom are mentioned with
respect, no more bitter attacks against false philosophy.   The close but
vivacious reasoning on certain essential theological points, the irregular
but strongly coloured sketches, have expanded into a full-bodied manual
of dogmatic theology, whose author has fallen in with the requirements
of systematic teaching. . . . In short, we have before us the selfsame
Melanchthon who heads the list of dogmatic theologians in the narrower
sense.

scholastic fashion, by those theologians who in dogmatic
controversial questions took an opposite position, while
as regards form and arrangement they adhered to
this model.[1]   All further dogmatic text-books produced
in the sixteenth century bore the same relation to that
of Melanchthon.   The most important of these were the
manuals of Victorin Strigel,[2] Nicholas Selnekker,[3] and,
above all, Martin Chemnitz.[4]   In this first period of
Protestant theology, Chemnitz, next to Melanchthon,
stands out as by far the most important writer on dogma,
as well for his speculative powers as for his knowledge of the older Catholic theology and its scholastic
conception ; and accordingly he often met with great
regard among the champions of Catholic doctrine.   His
' Loci theologici,' his principal dogmatic work, besides
various treatises on special dogmatic questions, is
regarded on the Protestant side as a book ' which had
rendered quite remarkable service to the Lutheran
Church,'[5] and ' which even now may pass muster as
a standard dogmatic work for the Lutheran Church.[6]
With the closest adherence, however, to the text of
Melanchthon, he did not represent the standpoint of the
master in the questions under controversy among the

---

[1] Gass, i. 50 f. ; Kuhn, i. 481.

[2] *V. Strigelii Loci theologici, quibus loci communes Melanchthonis
illustrantur*, ed. a Chr. Pezelio, 4 vols.   Neap. Nemet. 1581-1584.   (From
the lectures which he delivered at Jena and Leipzig down to his banishment from Leipzig in 1567.)

[3] *Nic. Selneckerii Institutiones Christianae religionis*, Francofurti ad M.
1573-1579.

[4] *M. Chemnitii Loci theologici post autoris obitum cura Polyc. Leyseri.*
Francofurti ad M. 1591, and other additions.   See concerning Chemnitz
the Monographs of Pressel (Elberfeld, 1862) ; Lentz (Gotha, 1866) ; Hachfeld (Leipzig, 1867) ; as also Herzog's *Realenzyklopädie*, iii. 796-804.

[5] Hachfeld, *M. Chemnitz*, p. 41.

[6] Kurtz, *Kirchengeschichte*, ii[11]. 138.

Lutherans, but that of the Formula of Concord, and thus 'he forms an important turning-point in the development of Protestant theology.' [1]   Under this category come also the dogmatic compendiums of the Tübingen theologians Heerbrand [2] and Hafenreffer,[3] who conformed even too closely to the method of Melanchthon's 'Loci,' thus giving practical assent to the Formula of Concord.

Didactic writings of this kind and the controversial writings which resulted from the dissensions among the Protestants in the sixteenth century produced that particular type of Protestant scholasticism, the full development of which in scholastic form belongs to the seventeenth century.   After the authority, first of the Pope, and then of Luther, had been thrown overboard, the same men who had repudiated the old scholasticism as empty formalism, began to outbid each other in the most unedifying subtleties and word-splittings about

[1] Gass, i. 52.   On the character of this work Gass remarks (i. 70): 'His adherence to the text of Melanchthon moderated the tone of his polemics, and his circumspection caused him to deal very cautiously in the use of Luther's writings.   We recognise the learned author of the *Examen concilii Tridentini*.   The study of the history of dogmas, at first very fragmentary, must now be made serviceable in a comprehensive manner to the study of dogma itself, and Chemnitz is the first who, under the title of *Certamina*, gives us the whole history of ancient heresies, with the contributions of the Fathers and the school-men on the subject.   The historical part is usually introduced by a collection of Biblical names and texts referring to the question, and a clear statement of the point at issue. These three features, added to the order of treatment established by Melanchthon, give a sufficient idea of the work.'

[2] *J. Heerbrandi Compendium theologicum*, Tubingae, 1573, etc.   In the attempts of the Tübingen theologians to win the Greek Church over to Protestantism this work played a part ; in 1577 it was sent to Constantinople in a Greek translation made by Martin Crusius ; cf. Hefele, *Beiträge zur Kirchengeschichte*, i. 458.

[3] Matth. Hafenreffer, *Loci theologici sive compendium theologicum*, Tübingae, 1601, etc.

separate points of doctrine which they had wrested
from the more or less connected system left by the
first religious innovators, and which they now set up
in a one-sided manner as foundation-stones of the new
doctrine.   Thus the Antinomians John Agricola and
Nicholas von Amsdorf, the defenders of good works
George Major and Justus Menius, the less extreme
Antinomians Andrew Musculus, Poach and Otto.
Andrew Osiander, Franz Stancarus, Brenz, Christopher
Binder, Martin Chemnitz, and numerous other theologians, exhausted their strength in examinations, as
contradictory as they were subtle, into the doctrine of
the person and the two natures of Christ,[1] as also on
the work of redemption and its appropriation by faith
in justification.   The books of these Protestant teachers
are chiefly distinguished as disconnected scholasticism
altogether out of joint, and playing with the venerable
school expressions as with feather balls.   All compact,
well-knit, scholastic method is completely wanting.[2]

Melanchthon himself, the father of Protestant dogmatic theology, did not get much thanks for his trouble.
Nobody had more antagonism to bear than he; no one
suffered a harder fate on account of his serious addiction
to learning; no one at the end of his life spoke more

---

[1] Brenz in his pamphlet *De personali unione duarum naturarum in
Christo* (1561), and in various succeeding writings, combated especially
against the Swiss theologian Bullinger, the doctrine of the ubiquity of
the body of Christ.   See also the present work, vol. vii. p. 77 ff.   'In
part opposition to this *Suabian Christology* (Dorner, p. 357), Chemnitz
presented the doctrine of the *communicatio idiomatum* in his book *De
duabus naturis in Christo* (1570).

[2] See concerning the Protestant scholasticism the opinion of Hefele
in Wetzer and Wette's *Kirchenlexicon*, i[2]. 822 f.   Staudenmaier pronounces
on this Protestant scholasticism (*Dogmatik*, i. 271) that it was only distinguished from the old scholasticism by being ' quite soulless,' and was
further spoiled by polemics.

hopelessly concerning the new theology, and indeed the whole of the new doctrine, than did Melanchthon. Amsdorf denounced him as a snake whom Luther had nourished in his bosom ; Agricola preached against him in Berlin as a heretic ; [1] the Suabian theologians accused him of having attacked the Christian doctrine of the dignity of man and of having torn asunder the two natures of Christ ; Nicholas Gallus asserted that he had adulterated Luther's doctrine of the slavish will ; most of the Lutherans accused him of having betrayed the cause of the Lutherans to the papists ; Schnepf, who had joined the Flacians, wanted to force him into public recantation. Melanchthon, on his part, had fallen out egregiously with Wenzel Link, Osiander, Didymus, and Brenz, and had called his Lutheran opponents, in a letter to Philip of Hesse in 1558, ' downright idolatrous sophistical bloodhounds.' [2] The new theology settled down into a war of all against all.

The first of the different controversies among the Lutherans was the Antinomian controversy, in which John Agricola,[3] who in 1527 had already taken umbrage because Melanchthon in his ' Unterricht der Visitatoren ' enjoined the preachers to preach the law to the people, had since 1537, as professor at Wittenberg, polemised afresh against the law, until at length, after Luther himself had written against him, he came in 1541 to a conciliatory explanation.

At Königsberg since 1549, alarmed by its practical results, Andrew Osiander had been combating the

---

[1] See our remarks, vol. vii. p. 56.

[2] Döllinger, i. 416–417 ; see our remarks, vol. vii. p. 139.

[3] Cf. G. Kawerau, *Johann Agricola of Eisleben*, Berlin, 1881 ; *ibid.* ' Briefe und Urkunden zur Geschichte des antinomistischen Streites,' in the *Zeitschrift für Kirchengeschichte*, iv. (1880) 299–342 u. 437–465.

Lutheran doctrine of justification.[1] To the Lutheran conception of justification as the effect of a legal sentence (an *actus forensis*) he opposed the idea of justification as effected in man by the indwelling of Christ, and by the communication of the essential righteousness of Christ. He met with much antagonism especially from Melanchthon, Flacius Illyricus, John Apinus, Joachim Westphal and Joachim Mörlin,[2] while Brenz, in a memorandum to Duke Albert of Prussia, spoke in his favour. After Osiander's death in 1552, the court preacher Funk became the leader of the Osiandrites, until his opponents succeeded in influencing the Duke, formerly well disposed to Osiandrism, in the opposite direction ; whereupon the matter was brought to a close in 1566 by the execution of the court preacher and the forcible extermination of Osiandrism.[3]

From the Osiandrist there branched out the Stancarist controversy, Franz Stancarus going the length, in opposition to Osiander, of asserting that Christ was only the Mediator and Redeemer of mankind through His human nature.

The dissensions which ensued revealed clearly the cleft which, in a manner no longer to be disguised, divided the so-called ' Philipists ' from the consistent followers of the genuine Lutheran principles. To this connexion belongs also the Majorist controversy.[4] The Wittenberg professor, George Major, in agreement with the later doctrine of Melanchthon, had, since 1551, opposed to the Lutheran doctrine of justification the

---

[1] See our remarks, vol. vii. pp. 11, 12.
[2] *Ibid.* vol. vii. p. 12 f. ; Franck, i. 150–156.
[3] *Ibid.* vol. vii. p. 300 ff.
[4] *Ibid.* vol. vii. p. 17 f.

doctrine that good works are necessary to salvation, and
that nobody can be saved without good works.   Justus
Menius, superintendent in Gotha, ranged himself on
Major's side.   Both were fiercely attacked as heretics
by the strict Lutherans, such as Flacius Illyricus,
Nicholas von Amsdorf, John Wigand, Joachim
Mörlin, Alexius Praetorius.   Amsdorf, in a pamphlet
published in 1559, definitely asserted that good works
were prejudicial to salvation.   This opposition against
Majorism was reinforced by the new Antinomianism
represented by Andrew Musculus, Poach, and Otto.[1]

Next followed the synergist and Flacian controversies.   Synergism—that is to say, a certain co-operation
of free will with grace in the process of conversion—
had been championed in 1555 by a pupil of Melanchthon, John Pfeffinger at Leipzig, in his ' Quaestiones
de libertate voluntatis humanae ' ; Pfeffinger was in
sympathy with Melanchthon and with the Leipzig
Interim, but in opposition to Luther.   Amsdorf and
Flacius rose up against him in defence of the Lutheran
teaching.   In the further course of the development
the Melanchthonian Victorin Strigel at Jena and
Flacius, as heads of the movement, stood opposed to
each other, their mutual antagonism being especially
marked in the disputation of Weimar organised by Duke
Frederick of Saxony in 1560.[2]   Strigel held firmly to
the still more cautious propositions of Melanchthon,
who acknowledged as little as possible the doctrine of
predestination, recognising human freedom (*liberum
arbitrium*) in everyday matters, but insisting on the
impotence of men in spiritual things, while at the same

[1] Dorner, pp. 341, 343.
[2] See our remarks, vol. vii. pp. 143–148.

time he taught the doctrine of the universality of the promise of grace. He was above all concerned to safeguard the existence of a moral nature in man, by the co-operation of which the work of grace was accomplished : the Holy Ghost he insisted did not operate in men as though they were lifeless blocks and stones ; a certain synergy (co-operation) must be attributed to the human will. Flacius, on the other hand, defended the doctrine of non-freedom of the will to the uttermost, clinging firmly to the proposition that original sin was no *accident*, but the *substance* of fallen man. ' Original sin ' he declared ' was a substance, for otherwise holiness also would not be a substance ; the soul was by nature a mirror or image of Satan, it was original sin (*peccatum originale*), although not thus disfigured without God's ordinance.' [1] It was utter demonism, this doctrine of the substantial bedevilment of human nature, which was thus introduced into the doctrine of grace. Flacius's unqualified proclamation of this doctrine removed him still further from his former friends, and thus out of the synergic controversy there proceeded the Flacianist controversy, in which the champions of strict Lutheranism, Wigand and Hesshus, came forward as decided opponents of Flacius, and denounced his doctrines as Manicheism,[2] till in 1575 Flacius died, while simultaneously the persecution of his followers in the Mansfeld district (under Cyriacus Spangenberg) was raging.[3]

[1] Dorner, p. 363.

[2] See our remarks, vol. viii. p. 177 f.

[3] *Ibid.* vol. viii. p. 171 ff.   Gass (i. 60 f.) remarks concerning the fate of Flacius : ' A logical clinging to the Word which startled even his confederates implied a destiny to which Flacius hastened. After all the angry and violent proceedings of the contending sects the Lutheran party was, on the whole, victorious, but its victory required a victim, and Flacius suffered for the sins of many.'

Finally, there were the crypto-Calvinistic controversies concerning the doctrines of the Lord's Supper
between the orthodox Lutherans and the Philipists.[1]

The entire course of those dissensions shows confusion without parallel. One error begat another
according as this or that point was more strongly
emphasised by Luther, or mixed with Zwinglian or
Calvinistic views. The whole history of Protestant
theology from the Augsburg Confession (1530) to the
Formula of Concord (1580) presents a picture of continuous discord and bitterest civil strife.

In the chaos of this hurly-burly it is scarcely possible
to discover any scientific progress, any clearing up of
ideas, any harmonious synthesis.[2] It is a perpetual
swinging backwards and forwards between untenable
extremes; a battle between errors, whose roots may be
largely traced back to heresies of earlier times; a process
of self-laceration among those who, one and all, pretended that they possessed the true Word of God, but

[1] See our remarks, vol. viii. 172–177; 182–197.

[2] Dorner attempts the following grouping (pp. 334–336): 'The six
principal controversies in question form three connected pairs, and by
them the Lutheran Church of the period was most deeply stirred. These
three pairs are as follows: the Antinomian and the Majorist controversy,
the Osiandrist and the Stancarist, the Synergist and the Flacian.' 'At
the first glance,' he remarks further on, 'they present a picture of the
most hopeless confusion, especially as the parties concerned cross and
recross in manifold variety. Thus the so-called Gnesio-Lutherans are
partly with Melanchthon against Osiander, partly against Melanchthon
on account of his conciliatory attitude towards the reformers; at the
same time they are both to a great extent on the reformed and Calvinistic
side, as they both represent the primary absolute predestination doctrine
against Melanchthon's doctrine of free-will. . . . In all these questions
it is always a middle position, a formulation of doctrine excluding the
extreme, which, as in the Formula of Concord, though not throughout
equally satisfying, obtains Church sanction.'

who were for the most part united only in their hatred
of the old Church.

In all the stages of its development this theology
bears the stamp of a fanaticism which not only attacks
its opponents with arguments and pamphlets, but
drives them from the pulpit, throws them into prison,
sends them into exile, and even sometimes to the scaffold,[1]
as happened to the court preacher of Duke Albert of
Prussia.[2]

Among those men also who, on behalf of peace,
helped to draw up the Torgau Book (1576),[3] the Bergen
Book (1577),[4] and the Formula of Concord (1580),[5]
there reigned the same spirit of mutual mistrust, dislike
and hatred. They spoke most ill of each other : James
Andreä, the father of the whole work of unification,
called his fellow-worker Selnekker ' a desperate scoun-
drel, a good-for-nothing villain, a hangdog thief.' [6]

One does not get a favourable impression of the
scientific and scholarly value of this theological work
of pacification when one finds the Saxon theologians
who took part in it, most of them former pupils of
Melanchthon, sacrificing the whole of his doctrines,
while Martin Chemnitz boasts of ' having for ever
extinguished the memory of Melanchthon.' [7] And now
the theologians who had made away with the patchwork
system that Melanchthon had so laboriously pieced
together, had a task similar to his before them in
harmonising, comparing, modifying, touching up, and
even distorting, the new conflicting doctrines that had

---

[1] See our remarks, vol. vi. p. 334 f. ; vol. vii. pp. 11–73, 144 ff., 273 ff. ;
vol. viii. p. 148 ff.

[2] Vol. vii. p. 304 ; and above, p. 155. [3] Vol. viii. p. 405 ff.
[4] Vol. viii. p. 413 ff. [5] Vol. viii. p. 426 f.
[6] Vol. viii. p. 414, note 1. [7] Vol. viii. p. 406 f.

sprung up meanwhile ; and it cannot be said that their
decisions were at all points essentially determined by
inward truth ; rather was it outward policy or necessity which brought the disputants unwillingly to
agreement.[1]

The Formula of Concord itself only served to embitter
the dissensions among the Protestants ; ' above all the
cleft between the Lutherans and Calvinists was so
greatly deepened and widened that it seemed inevitable
but that war and bloodshed must soon follow.' [2]

In this work of unifying Protestant theology no
slight service was rendered by the Catholic controversialists and apologists, and also and especially by the
Tridentine Council and the Roman Catechism, in that
these opposed to the hurly-burly and confusion of the
new teaching the settled, uniform system of a theology
harmonious and consistent in all its parts, and thereby

[1] Dorner (pp. 370–371) puts this very well ; he says : ' However many
the imperfections of the Formula of Concord, and however far from
praiseworthy the means towards its accomplishment may often have
been, there was nevertheless a sort of historical necessity at the bottom
of its construction. The Lutheran Church had indeed its common as well
as its ecumenical symbols, at any rate the Augustana with its apology,
but in their limited field and their original scope the most approved of them
could not supply rules for decision in all the discussions that had arisen
later on, and so by degrees, one after another, all the more important
towns and provinces of Germany sought to satisfy their desire for unity
by formulating separate confessions of faith. The practical incentive
to this course was given by the doctrinal obligations imposed on the clergy
and by the ordination tests. . . . But this in itself, in the divided state of
Germany, and considering the attitude of imperial authority towards the
Reformation, must have led to endless sectarian splitting up of the
Lutheran Church had not the growing tendency to particularism been
opposed by a counteracting element which was able to keep the Lutherans
together in one body, and to preserve for the Lutheran Church, as also
for the development of its teaching, the style of a great Church.'
[2] *Beiträge zur evangelischen Konkordie*, pp. 49–50 ; see our remarks,
vol. viii. pp. 430–438.

made manifest to the dissentient theologians the defects and the glaring discords which Protestantism presented both in its formal and material principles (*i.e.* private judgment and Bible only). The sharply defined terminology and the wealth of speculative matter which they offered stood here also in very good stead. The only creative and inventive originality which the Protestant fusion (or reunion) theologians displayed was in the production of fresh errors awkwardly combined and in reciprocal anathematising. At the religious conferences, when they stood face to face with well-schooled theologians of the old Church, whenever the disputation assumed a strictly scientific form, they were almost always compelled to give in or to have recourse to unproved statements, asseverations, accusations and calumnies.[1] The transactions which they carried on among themselves were generally still more tumultuous—*e.g.* the Heidelberg disputation in 1584, on which occasion the Lutheran John Marbach opposed the Calvinist James Grynaeus. The students who attended the conference made known their theological proclivities by stamping in the presence of the Court Palatine, and when Grynaeus left the chair, to go home with his friends Zanchius, Widebram and Tossanus, they were hissed, hooted and jeered at by the students.[2]

In the Saxon electorate itself, the victory of ' pure Lutheranism ' over the Calvinising efforts was by no means a final one. After the accession of the Elector Christian I (1586), and under the Chancellor Krell, there followed again a reign of Calvinism, which lasted till

[1] See our remarks, vol. vi. p. 147 ff. ; vol. vii. p. 29.
[2] *Ibid.* vol. ix. p. 96 ff.

after the death of the Elector (1591), when it was
forcibly eradicated, and the dominion of the Formula
of Concord firmly established by the Church Visitation
of 1592.[1]

Among the schools of Lutheran orthodoxy,[2] Wittenberg, since the separation of the Melanchthonians,
had held the first rank.   Here worked, at the end of
the sixteenth and the beginning of the seventeenth century, three theologians hailing from Suabia : Polycarp
Leiser the Elder (since 1576 ; he migrated to Brunswick
under Krell, and returned to Wittenberg in 1592 ; † 1610),
Aegidius Hunnius (since 1592 ; formerly professor at
Marburg, 1576–1592 ; † 1608), and Leonard Hutter or
Hütter (Hutterus ; † 1616), the most influential dogmatist of Wittenberg in the seventeenth century.   The
best known work of the latter is the dogmatic compendium [3] which went through a series of editions after 1610,
was translated into German and other languages and
extensively commented on.   This Compendium, which
came into use as a school-book in place of the suppressed ' Loci ' of Melanchthon, presents the Lutheran
system of faith ' without over many explanations, in the
form most convenient for committing to memory.' [4]

---

[1] See our remarks, vol. ix. pp. 149–168

[2] Cf. Tholuck, *Akademisches Leben*, ii. 15–152 ; Gass, i. 246–300 ;
Dorner, pp. 524–531.   Concerning Wittenberg specially see also Tholuck,
Geist der Lutherischen Theologen.

[3] *L. Hutteri Compendium locorum theologicorum, ex Scriptura s. et
Libro Concordiae collectum*, Wittenbergae, 1610.

[4] Dorner, p. 530.   Cf. Gass, i. 253 : ' What Hutter justly aimed at,
that he achieved, and the reward of achievement did not escape him.
The faith had to be learnt, and for faithful instruction and vivid impression
his book was the right one.   To short questions—for the plan of the
Compendium is catechetical—there follow concise answers written in
straightforward, precise language, and progressing in suitable gradation
from easy to more difficult.   True, Hutter's answers are mostly passages

After this text-book Hutter wrote a comprehensive dogmatic work, which was not published till after his death in 1619,[1] but the importance of which for the history of Protestant dogmatics was second to that of the Compendium.[2] Among his other writings the best known are the 'Concordia Concors' (Wittenberg, 1614), directed against Hospinian's 'Concordia Discors,' and the controversial pamphlet against Calvinism, 'Calvinista aulico-politicus' (Wittenberg, 1614).[3] Hunnius had devoted himself as dogmatist to some special points of controversy, especially to the defence of the doctrine of ubiquity, and the Lutheran doctrine of predestination.[4] Indeed, most of the theologians of Wittenberg were arch-models of Lutheran scholastic and dogmatism, though there were some some few representatives of a more moderate tendency. As a group of men who, ' without founding immoderate pre-

from the Concordia and the Augustana, and where these are not adequate he has recourse to Chemnitz, sometimes even to Melanchthon (ubi quidem ille ὀρθοδοξίαν tenuit), while among contemporary authorities he values especially his distinguished colleague Aegidius Hunnius ; but the great self-reliance and symmetry of his method give to the whole work the impress of independence. Moreover his teaching is imparted with such simplicity and strength of conviction that any doubts or misgivings that may be stirred up in the pupils' young minds are only aroused to be at once repulsed.'

[1] *Loci communes theologici ex s. Scriptura diligenter eruti, veterum patrum testimoniis passim roborati, et conformati ad methodum locorum Melanchthonis*, Vitebergae, 1619, in fol., and again in two later editions.

[2] Dorner, p. 530 f. : ' In his greater work he proceeds in a more thoroughly dogmatic spirit, but with less attention to system and sound exegesis. The chief endeavour of the learned and acute polemist is to triumph over Melanchthon and the Reformed.'

[3] See our remarks, vol. x. pp. 315–317.

[4] *Bekenntniss von der Person Christi* (1577) ; *Libelli IV de persona Christi ejusque ad dexteram sedentis divina majestate* (1585) ; *Articuli de providentia Dei et praedestinatione seu electione filiorum Dei ad salutem* (1595) ; *De libero arbitrio* (1598).

tensions on the possession of the Cathedra Lutheri, were
yet firm adherents of the doctrinal standard established
through the " Formulae Concordia," and who by their
mildness, tolerance, practical earnestness and solicitude
for the Church were to serve as models for later times,'
a recent Protestant scholar [1] mentions in contrast to
such ' blind zealots ' [2] as Hunnius and Hutter, and in
addition to Leiser, a number of younger professors, of
whom the following, with their labours, fall partly
within our own period : Balthasar Meisner, since 1611
professor of ethics at Wittenberg, since 1613 professor
of theology († 1626),[3] among whose writings the
' Philosophia sobria,' 1611, a work on the misuse of
philosophy in learning, was studied down to the thir-
teenth century ; Wolfgang Franz, since 1605 († 1628),[4]
who besides his activity as exegetist was author of an
important work on dogmatic polemics, ' Disputationes
de articulis Augustanae Confessionis ' (1609), in which
he dealt chiefly with Socinianism ; James Martini, since
1602 professor of logic, with a salary of only 120
florins, appointed professor of theology first in 1623
(† 1649).[5]

The university of Jena, which could not attain to
any higher importance during the theological dissensions of the second half of the sixteenth century, was
raised at the beginning of the seventeenth century by
the great dogmatician John Gerhard ' to one of the
first centres of Lutheranism.' [6]   Gerhard, ' the pearl of
the orthodox Lutherans of that period,' [7] the greatest

[1] Tholuck, Akademisches Leben, ii. 142.
[2] Tholuck, Geist der lutherischen Theologen, p. 4.
[3] Ibid. pp. 14–37.   [4] Ibid. pp. 37–40.   [5] Ibid. pp. 40–42.
[6] Gass. i. 247.
[7] Tholuck, Geist der lutherischen Theologen, p. 50.

dogmatician of the Lutheran Church,[1] 'the arch-theologian of his century,'[2] 'the venerable leader of historic-dogmatic erudition,'[3] born at Quedlinburg in 1582, studied at Wittenberg and Jena, became superintendent at Heldburg in 1606, superintendent-general at Coburg in 1615, was appointed professor of theology at Jena in 1616, and died there in 1637.[4] His chief dogmatic work consists of the nine volumes of the 'Loci theologici,' published during the years 1610–1622, which in virtue both of their comprehensive scope and their contents form the chief compendium of Lutheran dogmatics.[5] Gerhard's great polemical work against the Catholic Church, the four-volumed 'Confessio

---

[1] Dorner, p. 530.   [2] Frank, p. 371.   [3] Gass, i. 259.

[4] See concerning him Herzog's *Realenzyklopädie*, vi. 554–561.

[5] *Loci communes theologici cum pro adstruenda veritate, tum pro destruenda quorumvis contradicentium falsitate solide et copiose explicati*, Jenae, 1610–1622. Several times reprinted ; the best edition is that of Joh. Friedrich Cotta, in 20 quarto volumes, published at Tübingen, 1767–1781. Gerhard's work, says Dorner (p. 530), 'is distinguished for its pious tone, for great patristic and scholastic learning, for wealth of ideas, and finally for precision of thought and skill in dogmatic criticism and apologetics. It has exercised a permanent influence on the consolidation of Lutheran doctrinal opinions, it was the principal agent in guiding the so-called "Book-keeper of Catholic Orthodoxy," Quenstedt, and still to-day forms a mine of dogmatic knowledge.' Gass, p. 261 f. : 'Gerhard is by no means a mere collector of materials and authorities, although uncommonly industrious in this respect, for from Justin the Martyr down to the schoolman Biel, he marshals out all the better-known ecclesiastical writers (often uncritically, it stands to reason). Unfortunately he lacked the better methods of dogmatic history of which Chemnitz was the pioneer ; instead of giving surveys and connected proofs, he falls easily into mere narrative, and mangles his materials by dividing them into the orthodox and the heretical. But in the reference section of the *Loci* he holds an equal balance between the exposition of the dogma and its demonstration, and on the exegetic argument, which his precursors often treated very lightly, Gerhard expends the greatest labour. The uniformity of treatment, the indefatigableness with which, from the initial statement of his thesis down to the refutation of objection, he meets his opponents at every point, distinguish his work and caused it to be prized above all others by the

Catholica,' belongs to the last years of his life (1634–1637). His exegetic works will be mentioned later on. Among his works of edification written for the advancement of practical Christianity the 'Meditationes sacrae' (1606) had a specially wide circulation, and have gone through countless editions and translations, down to the present day ; this book, however, is made up out of the treasures of the Catholic past in the departments of Christian morality, asceticism and mysticism, and is based, as Gerhard himself owns, especially on Augustine, Anselm, Bernard and Tauler.

With Gerhard two other theological professors of the same Christian name, John Himmel and John Major, formed at Jena the 'Johannine Triad,' as they were called.[1]

Further, Tübingen stands in the first rank among the universities which represented orthodoxy in strict conformity with the Concord : 'As the Württemberg Church is the one which stood most loyally by the Saxon Church in the consolidation of Lutheran doctrine, which supplied Wittenberg with teachers, and in the Formula of Concord erected a barrier against crypto-Calvinism, so, too, the Tübingen faculty, in its staff of

Roman controversialists. His own Church, with but few exceptions, gave him nothing but admiration ; but in the next century the reproach was raised that it was Gerhard who had introduced the scholastic element into Protestant theology.' J. Kunze (in Herzog's *Realenzyklopädie*, vi. 559) further draws special attention to the fact that 'the attitude regularly adopted by him was one of opposition to Rome,' and says that this, combined with the other characteristics of his work, makes it clear ' how this work has come to rank as the actual apex and keystone of the dogmatic development which Melanchthon began in the Lutheran Church,' and how ' it held for so long an authoritative position.' Concerning Gerhard's theology see Gass, i. 262–300.

[1] Cf Tholuck, *Akademisches Leben*, i. 137.

instructors, was from the beginning of the century onwards the chief stronghold of orthodox faith according to the Formula of Concord.'[1]   Here worked James Andreä (1562–1590), the dogmaticians James Heerbrand (who, originally a pupil of Melanchthon, came later to this point of view, 1565–1600) and Matthias Hafenreffer (1592–1619),[2] Stephen Gerlach (1578–1612),[3] John George Sigwart (1587–1618), Andrew Osiander (1607–1627). By a fierce spirit of passionate controversy the divines of the ensuing period, such as Luke Osiander the Younger (1619–1638) and Thummius (1618–1630), are distinguished as theologians ' to whom the Holy Spirit appeared rather in the form of a raven than in that of a dove.'[4]

Strassburg, also, which in the age of the Reformation had been a centre of the reformed theology, where Calvin, Bucer, Capito and others had worked, changed its views under the influence exercised by John Marbach, after his victory over Zanchi in 1561, and in the course of the seventeenth century ' became a hotbed of the strictest Lutheran ardour.'[5]

In the first battles and in the struggle concerning the introduction of the Formula of Concord, Melchior Speckler and John Pappus stood on the side of Marbach as Lutheran champions against John Sturm.[6] The most noteworthy of the theologians, however, belong to the later period of the century.

In Hesse the university of Giessen, founded in

[1] Tholuck, ii. 132.   [2] See above, pp. 151, 152.
[3] This man had before played a part as Mission preacher at Constantinople (since 1573) in the attempts made by James Andreä and the Tübingen philologist, Martin Crusius, to win over the Greek Church to Protestantism.   Cf. Hefele, *Beiträge zur Kirchengeschichte*, i. 446 ff.
[4] Tholuck, ii. 133.   [5] *Ibid.* p. 125.   [6] Frank, i. 266 ff.

1607, became the seat of the Lutheran theologians after their eviction from the Calvinised town of Marburg (1605), and when in 1625 Marburg was made Lutheran again the Giessen college was transplanted there and remained there till 1650. The most important theologians in the first period are John Winckelmann († 1626), Balthasar Mentzer († 1627), and Christopher Helvicus († 1617).

In Greifswald, James Runge († 1597) and Frederick Runge, who had come from Melanchthon's school, had adopted a position of compromise at the end of the sixteenth century, and had brought about the initiatory steps in the rejection of the Formula of Concord in Pomerania. Since, however, in 1593 the three chief tenets of this Formula—those of the Lord's Supper, the Person of Christ, and Predestination—had obtained symbolic sanction,[1] 'redhot hatred of Calvinism became characteristic of the Pomeranian Church. The most influential of the academic representatives of the new Wittenberg orthodoxy was Bartholomew Krakewitz († 1642), who came forward 'full of zeal for the university, for the rights of the clergy, against the papists (even the presence of a hostile garrison could not restrain him from preaching against the Pope as Antichrist), and against the Calvinists.'[2] It was through him that, in 1623, the obligations of the Formula Concordiae were also removed from the statutes of the Faculties.

Rostock, under the moderating influence of David Chytraeus, Melanchthon's friend, who laboured at the university there for close on fifty years (1551–1600), was, in the sixteenth century, 'the nursery-ground of

---

[1] Tholuck, *Akademisches Leben*, ii. 44.   [2] *Ibid*. ii. 45.

Melanchthon's humanism.'   Even after he had accepted
the Formula of Concord, among whose authors he was,
Chytraeus remained ' free from the rabid zeal of several
of his associates.' [1]   The ' more practical Biblical spirit '
which he had introduced among the faculty remained
influential with its members during nearly the whole of
the seventeenth century.   Among the theologians who in
the sixteenth century and at the beginning of the seventeenth worked with and after Chytraeus in this spirit,
belong Simon Pauli (1560–1591), Bacmeister (1562–1608),
Paul Tarnov (1604–1637), and his nephew John Tarnov
(1614–1629), ' an exegetist with whom the Lutheran
Church, at that period, had none who could stand
beside him.' [2]   To these belongs, after 1615, John
Quistorp the Elder.   Side by side with them, however,
(1609–1624) there is a group of Lutheran zealots, headed
by Affelmann, who is described by Tholuck as ' a controversialist full of acumen and dialectical skill, but
full also of the coarsest virulence of contemporary
polemics.' [3]

In Leipzig also ' there prevailed on the whole a comparatively milder tone ' ; [4] ' down to the end of the
century the theologians are almost all quiet men whose
attitude towards the budding Calixtinian and practical
tendency of the age is one of aloofness rather than
combativeness, and who, moreover, are not altogether
unfavourable to the practical tendency.' [5]   A chief

---

[1] Tholuck, *Akademisches Leben*, p. 100 f.   Among his numerous writings
the two speeches on theological study are specially noteworthy : ' Oratio
de studio theologiae recte inchoando,' Vitebergae, 1577, and ' Oratio de
studio theologiae exercitiis verae pietatis et virtutis potius quam con-
tentionibus et rixis disputationum colendo,' Vitebergae, 1581. Often
reprinted.

[2] *Ibid.* i. 103.   [3] *Ibid.* p. 104.
[4] Dorner, p. 529.   [5] Tholuck, p. 84.

representative of this tendency was one Höpfner, who had become famous as the author of a work on justification.

At the university of Helmstädt, founded in 1576, the theological tendency took a line of its own.[1] While the philosophy represented at the university was dominated by Melanchthonian humanism, the first theologians then, who had been appointed through the instrumentality of Chemnitz, held strictly Lutheran opinions. The most important of these men were Timotheus Kirchner (formerly, since 1568, professor at Jena, in 1579 dismissed from the Helmstädt professorship, † 1584), joint author with Selnekker and Chemnitz of the 'Apology of the Book of Concord' (Dresden, 1584).[2] With him worked Daniel Hofmann († 1611), specially known through his controversies with the philosophers of the place,[3] Basilius Sattler (later on consistorial councillor and court preacher at Wolfenbüttel; † 1624), and, since 1577, Tilmann Hesshus († 1588). In the direction represented by Hofmann and Hesshus, their pupil Kaspar Pfafrad worked also since 1593 (he died in 1622),[4] whilst the other younger theologians, Lorenz Scheurle († 1613), Henry Boethius († 1622), and John von Fuchte († 1622), approached more closely to the humanistic tendency of Caselius.[5] The actual significance, however, of the Helmstädt theological faculty only begins when George Calixtus was appointed to a professorship there in 1614. He exercised a dominating influence over the university and determined its spirit, and his influence, radiating thence, made

---

[1] See Henke, *Calixtus*, 2 vols.; Halle, 1853–1856.
[2] Frank, i. 254–256.　　　[3] See above, p. 141.
[4] Henke, i. 75.　　　[5] *Ibid.* i. 54.

itself felt, especially in the university of Königsberg. The controversies that arose from his teaching and the actual scope of his work belong, however, to the following period.

At Altorf, in conformity with the prevalent tendency of Nuremberg, where the Formula of Concord was persistently rejected, Philippism, even with a distinct tendency to Calvinism, as with Moritz Heiling († 1595) and Dürnhofer († 1594), continued to be generally prevalent during the sixteenth century and down to 1620. The Lutheran creed during this period was only represented at the university by Schopper (1598–1616), supported by his pupil Saubert († 1646 as pastor at Nuremberg), and the Nuremberg pastor John Schröder (1611–1621). The Lutheran tendency gained the upper hand for a time (1614–1626) through George König, who, however, while outwardly professing the tendency, came under suspicion of being in secret conspiracy with the Socinians.[1] After the third decade of the century the influence of Helmstädt, embodied in Cornelius Martini and Calixtus, begins to make itself felt, until the Calixtian tendency gains the ascendancy.

Outside the universities the following men, among others, became known as representatives of Lutheran theology : James Reineccius, rector at Hamburg since 1613 ; at Coburg, where Gerhard also held office for a time as superintendent-general (1615–1616), Meysart since 1616, and Fink from 1616–1631 ; at Weimar, as superintendent-general, Albert Grawer († 1617), ' a genuine pupil of Aegidius Hunnius, one of the most disputatious of theologians (*theologus disputax*), who, as

―――――――――

[1] Tholuck, ii. 18 f.

shield and sword of Lutheranism, taught with a sharp tongue, always ready with an *absurdum est, falsum est, nescit quid loquatur* ; who at the prince's table made fun of Gerhard's writings, an implacable enemy of the Calvinists as long as there was any breath in him ; a man thoroughly versed in the language of the schools.' [1] This man also came forward as literary opponent to the Rostock philosopher Lubinus. Finally, Conrad Schlüsselburg, superintendent in Stralsund († 1619), ' a man of the hardest denominational conviction (*lutheranissimus theologus*)' ; [2] the perfect type of a Lutheran controversial theologian. ' Even as a student he accused the Wittenberg professors Peucer, Cruciger and Pezel of having apostatised from Luther's doctrine. When, on going up for his Master's degree, he was called over the coals for his language by Peucer, he told him to his face that he considered him a fanatical sacramentarian and a contemner of the *communicatio idiomatum realis.* Put under house-arrest by the provost, he repeated his accusation before the convention of professors. Then Peucer became beyond measure enraged, and was about to give the Flacian rascal and young whipper-snapper, who had scarcely left his mother's apron-strings, a box on the ears. The old G. Major interposed, and said kindly : ' My dear son Conrad, leave the Flacians to themselves and stay you with us, your preceptors.' This admonition failing to pacify the youth, he was sentenced to perpetual exclusion by the senate, ' propter seditiosas obtrectationes atque criminationes et propter injurias, calumnias, mendacia contra veritatem et hanc docentes in perpetuum ' (1568), and the injunction was sent to Jena, Königsberg

---

[1] Frank, i. 346.   [2] *Ibid.* i. 247.

and Leipzig. On an appeal from the culprit to the later Wittenbergers Mylius and Leiser, he was set free (1586) and restored to his former position with the words : ' Whosoever, on account of this period of exclusion shall hold *Conradum Schlüsselburgium pro infami* and shall revile him, such an one will plainly show that he is not rightly in accord with the pure doctrine of the Augsburg Confession, for none should ignore that infamy attaches not to the exclusion but to its cause.' In later times Schlüsselburg was always among those *qui stant in proelio in die Domini,* so that Chemnitz ascribed to him a *natura rixatrix, criminatrix et turbatrix.* He called Melanchthon a scandalous apostate, Strigel a Vertumnus and Ecebolista, Pezel his ' late deceptor,' and himself an Anti-Calvinista.[1] His principal work is the comprehensive ' Catalogus haereticorum ' (13 vols., 1597–1601), in which he attacks all the opponents of the strict Lutheran persuasion since the so-called Reformation ; ' his heretics are, for instance, the Antitrinitarians, the new Manichaeans (Flacians), the Calvinists, Antinomians, Synergists, Osianderists, Majorists, Jesuits, Stancarists, Stenkfeldians, Servetians, Anabaptists, Adiaphorists, and Interimists.' [2]

On the side of the reformed Zwingli is only promi-

---

[1] Frank, i. 247.

[2] Döllinger in Hortig's *Handbuch der Kirchengeschichte,* ii. 2, 926. Gass (i. 249) classifies all those dogmatisers who represented the type of Lutheranism which the Formula of Concord had restored in two sets : (1) such as were ' right believers and dogmaticians from religious grounds,' and (2) such as were ' religious only on the ground of the dogma and within the limits of the dogma.' The first class is known by its more lenient attitude towards people of a different way of thinking ; the second ' shine by learning and acumen, but by such acumen as becomes a weapon of inveterate stubbornness. The zeal for the House of the Lord devours them, but they alone know where this House is, and they alone can point the way to its entrance.'

nent in the history of Protestant dogmatics through his strongly rationalistic doctrine of the Lord's Supper and the theological controversies which clustered round it. He, no more than Luther, ever composed any coherent and genuine dogmatic work. His chief work in this connexion is the 'Kommentar von der wahren und falschen Religion.'

The first dogmatic work which is of a systematic character, and which had a determining and fundamental influence on the development of scientific dogmatics among the reformed religionists, is Calvin's 'Institutio Cristianae Religionis,' published first at Basel, 1536; revised in 1539, and again revised in the final principal edition of 1559.[1]

Chief among the contemporary theologians in Germany and Switzerland who worked with Calvin at the

[1] Concerning this work, of which Frank (i. 74) writes that it resembles 'a high-vaulted, sombre cathedral, in which the solemnity of religion fills the soul with devotional awe,' Staudenmaier (*Dogmatik*, i. 272) pronounces the following apt judgment : 'As in many other instances, so too here, Calvin shows much keener judgment, far better method, and much greater dialectical skill than Melanchthon ; but his whole system (like his own spirit) is so obfuscated by the dark shadow of absolute belief in predestination, a belief which militates both against the human and the Christian spirit, and cannot either hold its own scientifically, that it excites an emotional conflict which the author has no chance of allaying save by intimidation and terror. The Calvinistic theology, in so far as it is dominated by the doctrine of Predestination, is a system of terrorising woven out of and consistently worked out by the finest sophisms, a system the like of which can only be found in the political domain—the terrorism of the French Republic. For the rest it deserves the reproach (equally incurred by Lutheran dogmatics) of not being based on the Bible but on views which it has itself foisted on the Bible. Aspects, finally, in which Calvin remained at one with Catholicism are at least better discussed here than in the dogmatic work of Melanchthon ; the chief question remains, what amount of good Calvin's talents might have accomplished if he had not allowed himself to be led away from the whole conception of Christian truth into ways of error by the false light of the doctrine of Predestination.'

preparation of the 'Dogmatik' are, Andrew Hyperius in Marburg († 1564),[1] a man of peaceful spirit, in spite of his leaning towards Calvin; Wolfgang Musculus at Bern († 1563) ;[2] Benedict Aretius in Marburg and Bern († 1574),[3] Henry Bullinger at Zurich († 1575),[4] who, first of all a Zwinglian and a follower of Zwingli at Zurich, joint author of the ' Confessio Helvetica prior ' of 1536, approached gradually nearer and nearer to Calvinism and co-operated substantially in uniting the Swiss reformed religionists on a Calvinistic basis, from which standpoint he composed, in 1566, the ' Confessio Helvetica posterior,' which he sent to the Elector Frederick III ; and finally the Italian Peter Martyr Vermigli (Vermilius, † 1562), who worked with Bullinger at Zurich.[5] All these theologians are partly Calvin's collaborators, too near their great model to show any advance in spirit or doctrine. All they did was to put into shape the materials at hand, and to help in watching over the interests in the maintenance and defence of which the reformed theologians were to strengthen their position. Not one of them came near even to the purity of Calvinistic thought ; their freedom from the restraints of formulae allowed them, as in Lutheranism,

---

[1] *Methodus theologiae*, Basileae, 1567 ff. Gass calls him (i. 131) ' precious for his simplicity and correctness of language.' Here also should be mentioned his methodological treatise, *De recte formando theologiae studio*, Basileae, 1556.

[2] *Loci communes theologici*, Bernae, 1573.

[3] *Examen theologicum*, Bernae, 1584 et 1598, and *Theologiae problemata seu loci communes*, Genevae, 1599.

[4] *Compendiam christianae religionis e puro Dei verbo depromptum*, Basileae, 1556.

[5] *Loci communes theologici*, in two volumes, compiled after his death from his writings and published by J. Grynaeus, Basle, 1580.

to expand their material according   to necessity into learned and polemical completeness.[1]

The first town in Germany to become a seminary for the reformed theology [2] was Heidelberg, where, after the Protestantisation of the university in 1559, and, above all, after Calvinism had been established in the land, there were men at work who ' effected the transition of Philippism into Calvinism.' [3]   These men were Caspar Olevianus († 1587) and Zacharias Ursinus († 1583), the authors of the Heidelberg Catechism (1562); further, the Frenchman Boquin († 1582), and the Italian Tremellius († 1580) and Zanchius (before at Strassburg, where he made way for the Lutheran Marbach,[4] † 1590). The termination of the short period of Lutheranism in the land under Ludwig VI (1576–1583) caused these professors to leave the country ; some of them went to Neustadt on the Haardt, where, at the *Gymnasium illustre*, Franz Junius and Daniel Jossanus worked in these years side by side with Zanchius and Ursinus. After Ludwig' VI's death, however, Heidelberg (after 1583) became again the ' metropolis of the German reformed theology.' [5]   Here taught David Pareus (1584–1622),[6] Daniel Tossanus (1586–1602), Henry Alting (1612–1622), Paul Tossanus, a son of Daniel Tossanus ; also, in the philosophical faculty, the Aristotelian Bartholomew Keckermann (1592 to 1602 ;   after 1602, in his

---

[1] Gass, i. 130.

[2] Succinct statistics of the reformed scholars in Germany and Switzerland, in Dorner, pp. 434–441 note ; see also Tholuck, *Akademisches Leben*, ii. 246–377.

[3] Tholuck, p. 265.   [4] See above, p. 167.

[5] Tholuck, ii. 266.   The Lutheran professors, John Marbach and Schopper, were dismissed ; see our remarks, vol. ix. p. 97 ff.

[6] *Irenicon sive de unione et synodo evangelicorum concilianda* (1614).

native city Danzig, where he died in 1609, at the age of thirty-eight), who was active in various departments, and who, in addition to a number of philosophical writings,[1] also compiled a ' Systema theologiae ' (1607) which contains ' the most original and sagacious deductions.' [2]

At the high school of Herborn, founded in 1584, the following men were regarded as shining lights : Olevian (1584–1587, the former Heidelberg professor) and John Piscator (1584–1625 ; also formerly, 1574–1576, at Heidelberg), a Ramist in philosophy, chiefly active as exegetist ; George Pasor (1615–1626), the philologist Matthias Martinus of Bremen (who died at Bremen in 1630) ; [3] later on, John Henry Alsted (from 1619, † 1638 at Weissenburg in Transylvania), Nethenius (since 1669), John Melchior (since 1682).

In comparison with Heidelberg and Herborn, the universities of Marburg, Frankfort-on-the-Oder and Duisburg are of less importance. At Marburg, which, to the end of the sixteenth century, represented Philippism (one of the most notable theologians of this tendency was Andrew Hyperius, 1542–1564),[4] but where also with the theologians of this tendency more or less inclined to the reformed standpoint, strict Lutherans also worked (such as Aegidius Hunnius, 1574–1592, before he came to Wittenberg), we may mention

---

[1] *Praecognita logica* (1599) ; *Praecognita philosophiae* (1608), *Rhetorica ecclesiastica* (1600), *Systeme der Ethik, Politik, Ökonomie, Physik, Astronomie*, and others.

[2] Tholuck, ii. 266, who sums up his opinion of Keckermann as follows : ' A man of such versatile activity, combined with constructive originality, theology has seldom possessed.'

[3] *Christianae doctrinae summa capita*, Herbornae, 1603 ; *Summula s. theologiae*, Bremae, 1610.

[4] His *Opuscula theologica* in two volumes, Basle, 1570 and 1581.

George Sohn (1574–1584 ; later on, 1584–1590, at Heidelberg) ;[1] more pronounced Calvinistic doctrine was taught later on, after the Dordrecht Synod, by Eglin (professor at Marburg since 1606), George Cruciger, John Heine, and John Crocius († 1659), ' the most important theologian of Marburg,'[2] the champion of the reformed system of doctrine against Catholics, Lutherans, and Weigelians. At Frankfort-on-the-Oder, in its first period of Protestantism, Andrew Musculus, joint author of the Formula of Concord (1547–1581), was an especially active representative of strict Lutheranism. Among his colleagues, Heidenreich († 1617) and Christopher Pelargus (since 1591, † 1633), starting from the Philippist standpoint, approached nearer and nearer to Calvinism. The latter repudiated all his earlier Calvinistic writings, and altered his dogmatic compendia[3] in the second edition (1616) in favour of the reformed standpoint. He was in consequence fiercely attacked by his former Lutheran friends, as, for instance, by Daniel Cramer in Stettin. Schlüsselburg wrote a controversial treatise against him under the title : ' Antwort auf die Schmähekarten des grossen Heuchlers und unbeständigen, wetterwendischen, Ecebolisten und nunmehr erkannten Calvinisten D. Chr. Pelargi' (Rostock, 1616), and drew in it the parallel : ' Just as the stork or Adebar spends the summer with us because then he picks up dainty morsels and good fodder, but at the approach of the hard, cold winter flies off to far-distant places, so this Pelargus, the stork, in like manner used his beak for a

---

[1] *Synopsis corporis doctrinae Ph. Melanchthonis* (1588), *Exegesis praecipuorum articulorum confessionis* (1591).

[2] Dorner, p. 436.   [3] *Compendium theologicum,* Francof. 1603.

time in the summer when there was no danger,
punished and damned the unbelieving Sacramentarians
with bad names, but, now that he has to use his beak in
the hard, cold winter of persecution, the stork will not
give voice.'[1] His altered second edition also involved
him in a controversy with the Wittenberg Lutheran
Balduin,[2] and the provost Simon Gedicke, in Berlin,
wrote his 'Pelargus Apostata' against him (Leipzig,
1617). In consequence of the Elector John Sigismund
of Brandenburg's adoption of the reformed creed, the
theological faculty, till then Lutheran, was changed
and filled with teachers who more decidedly represented
the reformed standpoint; John Berg (after 1616),
Wolfgang Crell (after 1618), Gregory Franck (1617–
1651). 'Nevertheless, with the sole exception of Crell,
an outspoken Supralapsarian, the attitude of the
faculty, especially of Pelargus, was more unionist than
Calvinist. Pelargus remains, even after the second
edition of his "Compendium theologicum," in which he
entirely adopts Calvin's doctrine of the Lord's Supper,
Lutheran pastor and superintendent-general; he
ordains—and, moreover, with the willing assistance of
the other Lutheran clergy—Lutheran and reformed
candidates, and the faculty bestows the degree of Doctor
on Lutheran and reformed theologians.'[3] Later on

---

[1] Frank, i. 314 f.

[2] Gass, i. 302. Gass remarks in order to describe his position more
exactly: 'He is an example rather of Lutheranism expanded, than of
Lutheranism denied. . . . A reformed colouring is on the whole unmistakable. . . . His standpoint is part reformed, part Lutheran, and
he bases himself on the older stadium of Lutheran theology which precedes
his confessional splits. This position makes him syncretistic, while in
the instructional method he adopts the school forms, now coming into
vogue, of the casual method' (p. 302 f.).

[3] Tholuck, *Akademisches Leben*, ii. 254.

Christopher Becmann, as well as some conciliation theologians (1676–1717), represented strict Calvinism. The university of Duisburg does not come into our period as it was not opened till 1656. At the academic gymnasium at Bremen, founded by Christopher Pezel in 1584, the theological workers were (after 1610) the rector, Matthias Martinius, already mentioned in connexion with Heidelberg ; Louis Crocius, after 1610 († 1655) ; Isselburg after 1612 ; Pierius after 1612 ; at the academic gymnasium founded at Steinfurt, in the first period of its existence, Conrad Vorstius till his departure for Leyden, in 1610, and the metaphysician Timpler.

In Switzerland the seminaries of reformed theology were Basle, Bern, Zurich, Lausanne and Geneva. At Basle, till the beginning of the seventeenth century, the theologians were John James Grynaeus (after 1575; 1584 ' lent to the Count Palatine at Heidelberg,' since 1586 ' *antistes* ' (rector) at Basle, † 1617) ; John Buxtorf the Elder (1590–1629) ; as dogmatician, especially Amandus Polanus von Polansdorf, a native of Silesia (1596–1610), ' a Ramistic Aristotelian, who spread abroad his opinions on all the points of his creed in " systems " and in theses,' and Wolleb (1618–1629),[1] whose theological compendium[2] gained great repute, and was used also in England and Germany as a manual.[3] A remarkably ' mongrel ' attitude was taken up by Simon Sulzer (1532–1585), who, as a reformed

---

[1] Gass, i. 396 f. *Syntagma theologiae christianae*, Hanoviae, 1610 et 1624 ; Genevae, 1612. *Sylloge thesium theologicarum ad methodi leges conscriptarum*, Basileae, 1610. For his theology see Gass, i. 397–404.

[2] *Compendium theologiae Christianae*, Basileae, 1626, which, according to Dorner, p. 439, is ' classical in its conciseness, clearness, and acumen.'

[3] Tholuck, ii. 326.

theologian inclining to Lutheranism, officiated also as reformed ' *antistes* ' in Basle (after 1553) and as Lutheran superintendent in the upper margraviate of Baden.[1] Bern, after Wolfgang Musculus (1549–1563)[2] and Benedikt Aretius (1563–1574),[3] down to the second half of the seventeenth century, had no theologians worth mention. In view of ' the stepmotherly behaviour of the government towards learning and the eminently practical character of the Bernese people,' important services to learning were not to be expected there.[4] At Zurich, where the older professors Bibliander, Pellican, Louis Lavater, Gualter had represented a more practical Biblical tendency, Peter Martyr Vermigli (since 1556) had brought the stricter predestination into vogue.[5] As the most eminent theologians of the ensuing period we may mention Henry Bullinger (*antistes* since 1534, † 1575),[6] William Stucki the Elder (1563–1607), Rudolf Hospinian, the opponent of the Formula of Concord (†1626), Caspar Waser (1561–1626), John James Breitinger (*antistes* since 1613).

It is a noteworthy fact that it was the Calvinists who took the most trouble to construct a complete system of Protestant scholastics.[7] In confirmation of

---

[1] Tholuck, ii. 321. [2] *Loci communes s. theologiae* (1563).

[3] *Problemata theologica* (1578). [4] Tholuck, ii. 340.

[5] His antagonist Bibliander in 1560, while allowed to retain his salary, was dismissed from his post as teacher, nominally on account of age and physical and mental debility, but in reality for opposing the Calvinistic tenet of predestination and ' quia morosius coepit praelegere et vellicare D. Martyrem.' See Tholuck, ii. 359 ; Frank, i. 176.

[6] *De Scripturae s. auctoritate, certitudine, firmitate et absoluta perfectione*, Turici, 1538.

[7] Dorner, p. 443. ' The scholastic method, going back to Aristotle, seemed indeed at first somewhat suspicious, as it threatened danger to the practical interests of religion. But the desirability—one might say the necessity—for firmly securing the possession that had been won, worked with

this we may particularly notice, besides the books of
the Dutch theologians (Macovius and others), which
specially expounded these methods, the handbook of
John Henry Alsted at Herborn.[1] In Switzerland,
also, owing to the influence of Dutch, French and
English scholarship, the philosophy of Ramus met with
little acceptance ; most of the reformed theologians
went back to Aristotle and the scholastic method, and
were less concerned to deal with further religious innovations than to shape into a methodical system the
opinions and doctrines already in vogue.   In the main,
however, the Swiss colleges took less part in the
construction of this new Protestant scholasticism than
did those of Germany.[2]   The fight against it carried on
by Coccejus from Bremen belongs to the following
period.

A war of polemics of a more systematised nature
and more scientific form against the Catholic Church
and doctrine, side by side with which, however, the
tumultuous polemics of purely popular literature of

irresistible force towards the adoption of a method which was better fitted
than any other to direct the scientific impulse rather to the systematisation
and defence of existing dogma as an unchangeable asset, than to the
examination of the contents of dogma.'   In Dorner's opinion ' it was
chiefly the superficiality of Ramus which served to obtain for Aristotle
sole dominion in evangelical scholastics also, without distinction of creeds,
and to inaugurate a new scholastic age ' (p. 444).

[1] *Theologia scholastica, exhibens locos comm. theolog. methodo scholastica*,
Hanov. 1618.

[2] Tholuck, *Akademisches Leben*, ii. 318 : ' The practical tendency of
the national character scarcely allowed the school-theology to gain
dominion.   When towards the end of the century the baptists appealed
to the Church " not to tolerate the *theologia scholastica* any longer in the
schools," they were answered by a memorandum of the Bern clergy :
" This, however, is quite a misunderstanding ; what, to speak correctly, is
called *theologia scholastica*, has no place either in our, or in other, reformed schools, and it is therefore quite unnecessary even to allude to it." '

abuse set going by Luther, went on with undiminished
virulence,[1] was inaugurated by Martin Chemnitz with
his 'Examen Concilii Tridentini.' Before this Chemnitz had issued a controversial work entitled 'Theologiae
Jesuitarum praecipua capita' (Leipzig, 1562), against
the treatise of the Jesuits of Cologne (1560), 'Doctrina
de praecipuis doctrinae coelestis capitibus,' which had
been written as an attack on the catechism of John
Monheim in Düsseldorf, entitled 'Doctrina coelestis.'
Catholic answers to the pamphlet of Chemnitz came
from John Alber at Ingolstadt, and then from the
Portuguese theologian Diego (James) Payva de
Andrada, who was present as a theologian at the Council
of Trent.[2]

Instead of replying to his last opponent personally,
it occurred to Chemnitz to put his answer in the form
of a comprehensive 'Examination of the Council of
Trent,' 'Examen Concilii Tridentini,' which is an attack
on the whole Catholic system of doctrine based on the
Tridentine decrees, and in which Andrada is only considered secondarily as interpreter of the latter. The
work appeared in four parts in the years 1565–1573.[3]

---

[1] See our remarks, vol. x. pp. 228–255. For the Protestant polemics
directed specially against the Jesuits see *ibid*. pp. 323–402.

[2] *Orthodoxarum explicationum libri decem, in quibus omnia fere de
religione capita, quae his temporibus ab haereticis in controversiam
vocantur, aperte et dilucide explicantur*, Coloniae, 1564.

[3] The full title, according to later editions, is : *Examinis Concilii
Tridentini, per Martinum Chemnizium scripti, opus integrum : quatuor
partes, in quibus praecipuorum capitum totius doctrinae papisticae firma et
solida refutatio, tum ex sacrae Scripturae fontibus, tum ex orthodoxorum
Patrum consensu, collecta est, uno volumine complectens. Ad veritatis
Christianae et anti-christianae falsitatis cognitionem perquam utile et
necessarium*, vol. i. 1565 ; ii. 1566 ; iii. and iv. 1573. Often reprinted ;
latest edition by Preuss, Berlin, 1861. A German translation was published in 1576 by the preacher George Nigrinus in Giessen. An extensive

The first volume deals with traditions, Holy Scripture, original sin, concupiscence, the conception of the Virgin Mary, the works of the unbelievers, justification, faith and good works ; the second treats of the Sacraments ; the third of virginity, of the celibacy of priests, of purgatory, of the invocation and veneration of the Saints ; the fourth volume of the relics of Saints, images, and indulgences, fasts and festivals. Chemnitz goes through all the different decrees of the Council, and after giving the text of each, he set about to refute it, with great display of exegetical, historical and patristic knowledge.   His plan is to show that Luther's teaching is that of the Bible and of the past, and thus to prove the error of the Catholics.   And to this end this valiant champion of the ' pure evangel,' like his other associates, in his treatment of the doctrine of justification and of other articles of the faith, as also of the cult and discipline of the Catholic Church (rejected by the Protestants in consequence of their new doctrine of justification) and of the veneration of the saints, does not scruple first of all to distort the Catholic teaching in an absurd manner, and in opposition to the plain text of the Tridentine decrees, in order to be able to fight them effectually.   On this work of Chemnitz all later Protestant polemics, down to our time, are based.[1]

With still greater fierceness the polemical contest

---

summary of the work is given by H. Hachfeld in his *Monographie über M. Chemnitz* (Leipzig, 1867), pp. 253–491, which for the rest is characterised by blind hatred and utter want of understanding of Catholicism, and a corresponding coarseness of tone.

[1] On the Catholic side Andrada wrote a counter-treatise, which appeared after his death in 1577 : *Defensio Tridentinae fidei Catholicae, quinque libris comprehensa, adversus calumnias haereticorum et praesertim Martini Chemnitii*, Lisbonae, 1578, Coloniae, 1580.   Another came from Jodocus

was carried on by Conrad Schlüsselburg, who snapped and snarled in all directions.[1] The most important Lutheran controversialist against the Catholics after Chemnitz is John Gerhard with his ' Confessio catholica,' the tendency of which is seen from the title.[2] Against Bellarmin also, who, at the beginning of the seventeenth century, was combated as the most dreaded Catholic champion in a number of counter-pamphlets, Gerhard directed a special pamphlet.[3]

With no less passionateness, however, than they fought against the Catholics, the adherents of both the Protestant creeds fought each other.[4] Every pronounced follower of one or the other party felt called upon to show his colours by fighting his opponents. Men who showed a spirit of compromise, even if they did not go so far as Pelargus,[5] were treated as apostates by their own co-religionists. Such was the view taken by the strict Lutherans of Melanchthon himself, the ' Praeceptor Germaniae,' to whom, nevertheless, the Lutheran Church in the sixteenth century owed all that she possessed of scholarly culture.[6] Flacius attacks

Ravenstein : *Propugnaculum Concilii Tridentini*, Lovanii, 1577. Bellarmin also, in his great work *Disputationes de controversiis christianae fidei adversus hujus temporis haereticos*, Romae, 1581, comments on Chemnitz.

[1] See above, p. 172.

[2] *Confessio Catholica, in qua doctrina catholica et evangelica, quam ecclesiae Augustanae confessioni addictae profitentur, ex Romano-Catholicorum scriptorum suffragiis confirmatur*, 4 vols., Irenae, 1634–1637.

[3] *Bellarminus ὀρθοδοξίας testis etc.*, Jena, 1631–1633.

[4] Concerning the spirit and tone in which this was done see our remarks, vol. x. pp. 256–322.

[5] See above, p. 178.

[6] The Flacian Joachim Mörlin († 1571) said in a public speech : ' We should not be able to construct a syllogism if Melanchthon had not taught us how to do so. He is our preceptor, and we needs must call him a preceptor. When, however, we came to *locum de Coena Domini, de*

him for the Catholic, Hesshus for the Calvinist element
in his teaching.   This last zealot for pure Lutheranism
took it very much to heart that it was from a pupil
of Melanchthon that he received his doctor's degree.[1]
His like-minded comrade, John Wigand, was such a
desperate controversialist that, despising Neminists,
'Silentarians' and turncoats, he regarded theological
pugilism as the mark of the children of God.[2]   The
campaign against the Calvinist doctrine of the Lord's
Supper had been carried on since 1552 with great
fierceness in a series of controversial pamphlets by the
Hamburg preacher (later superintendent), Joachim
Westphal († 1574),[3] the most passionate opponent
of the reformed creeds, of whom Melanchthon said
that he raged *corporaliter*, and whom Melanchthon's
pupils called a coarse, uncouth blockhead and bear.
Calvin's saying about Luther's apes was applied
first to him : ' Westphal and the other never-resting
Saxons incessantly cry down the reformed religionists
as heretics, false prophets, wolves, Sacrament twisters,
who were more hateful to them than even the papists.'[4]
Aegidius Hunnius wrote against the Calvinistic
doctrine of predestination.[5]   In a more popular form

libero arbitrio, de justificatione hominis, de interimisticis actionibus,
then let the devil praise thee, Philip ; I will do so nevermore.'   Frank,
i. 98.

[1] Frank, p. 97.   [2] *Ibid.* p. 97.

[3] *Farrago confusanearum et inter se dissidentium opinionum de Coena
Domini ex Sacramentariorum libris congesta* (1552) ; *Recta fides de Coena
Domini* (1553).   For his further works belonging hereto, especially the
controversial writings exchanged directly with Calvin, and the whole
course of the controversy, see Dorner, p. 400 ff.

[4] Frank, i. 99.

[5] *Articulus de providentia Dei et aeterna praedestinatione seu electione
filiorum Dei ad salutem* (1595).   *De libero arbitrio* (1598).   Cf. Dorner,
p. 369 f.

Philip Nicolai at Hamburg († 1608) entered the lists against this same doctrine ; [1] this writer called 'the Calvinistic Lord God, who hurled so many hundred thousands of men, at his own caprice, into the abyss of hell, and who drove desperate villains to all sorts of sin and shame, a bellowing ox and . . . a wanton, lascivious, lewd, depraved, cunning, deceitful and bloodthirsty Moloch, an abomination of devastation in holy places, a hellish Behemoth, an accursed Leviathan and devil incarnate, fit for Calicut in India ; and he called the Holy Ghost of the Calvinists an advocate of sin and an enemy of man.' [2]

To the question, ' Do you then fully believe that the Calvinists teach and worship the devil incarnate instead of the true and living God ? ' Nicolai in the same treatise answers : ' I believe this from the bottom of my heart, and declare it as a positive truth. I will not gainsay Luther in the very least in this respect, but accept as a true statement what he said of these factious spirits in his short creed of the Lord's Supper, namely, that they have " indevilled, bedevilled and throughdevilled hearts." ' [3]   To the Lutheran opponent of Calvinist predestination, Luther's book, ' De servo arbitrio ' must have been rather an awkward business ; but even here they found a way of escape.[4]

[1] *Kurzer Bericht von der Calvinisten Gott und ihrer Religion*, Frankfort 1597.

[2] Frank, i. 280 f. ; cf. Döllinger, i. 496 f.

[3] Tholuck, *Das kirchliche Leben des* 17. *Jahrhunderts*, pp. 48–49.

[4] Frank, i. 281 : ' When Luther's book on the slavish will was held up in defence of absolute predestination, this hellish bawling was silenced either by bringing forward a later retractation of Luther's, or by the answer that Luther in this book had not argued *simpliciter* but only *secundum quid*, in order to show that the clever human reason, if left to itself, must be reduced to absurdity.   This was publicly contradicted by Schlüsselburg,

Among the Wittenberg theologians, after the setting up of the Lutherans' symbol of doctrine, there were none who did not come forward with controversial writings against the Calvinists.[1] 'A treatise, or at least a disputation, against Calvinists and papists was at that time, no less than a magister's diploma, part of the outfit of an efficient student of theology.'[2]

Polycarp Leiser the Elder, whom Tholuck includes among those theologians who 'with perfect loyalty to the standard of doctrine established by the Formula of Concord, by their gentleness, patience, practical zeal and care for the Church should have served as models for later times,'[3] wrote the notorious treatise : 'Ob wie und warum man lieber mit den Papisten Kennschaft haben und gleichsam mehr Vertrauen zu ihnen tragen soll denn mit und zu den Calvinisten.'[4] Hutter was praised by his friends as Malleus Calvinistarum and Redonatus Lutherus.[5] On the other side the theologians directed their attacks chiefly against the Formula of

who exculpated Luther by saying that he (Luther) " because Calvinus at that time had not yet uttered forth his nonsense, spoke more confidently " (*securius*).   And although Luther in his book *Contra Erasmum* had used hard words, these were not nearly so coarse as those of the Zwinglians, who write that God is the cause of sin. . .' (*Antwort auf die Schmähekarten Pelargi*, Rostock, 1616.)

[1] Franz, *Syntagma controversiarum orthodoxae ecclesiae cum gente Calviniana* (1612).   Meisner, *De Calvinismo fugiendo* (1614).   Leiser, ii. *Harmonia Calvinianorum et Photinianorum* (1614).   Iac. Martin, *Collegium anticalvinianum* (1642).   See Tholuck, *Geist der lutherischen Theologie*, p. 115.

[2] Tholuck, *l.c.* p. 115 f.

[3] Tholuck, *Akademisches Leben*, ii. 142.

[4] In his *Dreyfache Erklärung des Catechismi Lutheri*, Dresden, 1602, the treatise was published anew by Hoe von Hoenegg, 1620.   See Tholuck, *Geist der lutherischen Theologie*, p. 115 f.

[5] Hutter, *Calvinista aulico-politicus* (1614) ; see above, p. 163.   A *Calvinista aulico-politicus alter* was written, with the co-operation of Hutter (1614), by the like-minded Dresden chief court preacher, Hoe von Hoenegg.

Concord. This controversy was carried on with especial zeal at Neustadt-on-the-Haardt by the reformed theologians who had been driven out of Heidelberg during the Lutheran episode of 1576–1583.[1] The principal pamphlet in this connexion is 'Admonitio Neostadiensis,' written by Ursinus in 1581. In Switzerland Rudolf Hospinian, of Zurich, assumed a more irritable sectarian tone [2] in his 'Concordia Discors,' written against the Formula of Concord.[3] The polemics in these writings were aimed especially against the Lutheran doctrine of ubiquity. In their tone the polemics of the reformed theologians against the Lutherans differ from those of the Lutherans in that 'while sharper weapons are used in them, there is less of the *rabies theologica* than of sarcasm and scorn, which descend to actual frivolity.' [4]

The aims of the anti-Catholic polemics—polemics indeed of the coarsest nature—were also served throughout by the Protestant Church History which Flacius introduced with the 'Magdeburg Centuries.' [5] From any sort of historical or scholastic sense the authors of such a work, to whom history is a mere fighting-ground for their passionate hatred against the Catholic Church and the papacy, are far removed. By means of these 'Centuries,' moreover, the need of a Church History on the Protestant side seemed to have been satisfied for a long period to come. The spirit of the 'Centuries' acted decisively on the publications which followed; for the rest, all that Protestantism produced in this

---

[1] See above, p. 175.   [2] Dorner, p. 439.

[3] *Concordia discors seu de origine et progressu Formulae Concordiae Bergensis*, Turici, 1607.

[4] Tholuck, *Kirchliches Leben*, p. 262.

[5] See our remarks, vol. x. p. 7 ff., and above, vol. xiii. p. 458.

respect in the seventeenth century shows on the whole
' a barren and unedifying character.' [1]

But if Luther was antagonistic to the speculative
theology of medieval scholasticism, he quite as much
abhorred the positive historical theology of the Fathers
of the Church.   Concerning the latter he constantly
expressed himself in the most condemnatory terms.
St. Thomas Aquinas and St. Chrysostom he called ' idle
prattlers,' and described the latter as an ' ambitious,
haughty man,' calling his golden eloquence ' a sack full
of words with nothing behind them.'   St. Cyprian, he
said, was a feeble Theologus ; St. Basil was utterly good
for nothing, he was a monk, and he wouldn't give a
hair for him ; Origen he had already placed under the
ban ; and as for Gregory the Great, the devil had misled him with a childish heresy.   St. Augustine also he
would not trust, because he had been mixed up with
the foolery of monkism, and had also often erred.   St.
Jerome, he said, should only be read for the sake of
history ; of the faith, and of the right and true Church
and way of life there was not a single word in his
writings. [2]   In his ' Table-talk ' he calls all the Fathers

---

[1] Gass, i. 168.

[2] Döllinger, i. 485.   See also Richard Simon, *Histoire critique des principaux commentateurs du Nouveau Testament*, Rotterdam, 1693, p. 685 :
' Luther méprise la plupart des Pères, surtout Origene et St. Jérôme,
auxquels même il dit souvent des injures sans en avoir d'autre raison, que
parce qu'il les trouvoit fort éloignez de ses sentimens.   Il a osé avancer
ce paradoxe, qui est une preuve évidente de son entêtement, qu'il n'y a
point de plus impertinents ou de plus ridicules Commentateurs de l'Ecriture
parmi les anciens Ecrivains Ecclésiastiques, qu'Origène et Jérôme (Luth.
De serv. arbit. adv. Erasm. fol. 196).   Cum inter ecclesiasticos scriptores
nulli fere sint, qui ineptius et absurdius divinas litteras tractarint, quam
Origenes et Hieronymus.'   For Luther's depreciatory sayings about the
Fathers of the Church see also Holzhei, *Die Inspiration der Heiligen
Schrift*, Munich, 1895, p. 30 f.

of the Church pumps from which before his (Luther's) time Christians drank foul, stinking water, instead of drawing from the pure fountain of the Scriptures.

A scientific, patristic system on such a basis was an impossibility. Luther and his pupils went on the plan of abusing everything in order to lower the standing of the Holy Fathers, as compared with that of the Holy Scriptures, and put a stop, as far as possible, to the study of the Fathers,[1] and put themselves in their place. It was especially those controversial tilts against the Catholics which obliged them to look out passages from the Fathers, and, putting their own interpretations on them, to use them as weapons of defence or attack. Older theologians of the first Lutheran generation looked on meanwhile with distress at the tendency growing up among the younger ones to busy themselves with the writings of the Fathers ; they saw in this a temptation of Satan, who sought thereby to undermine the authority of Luther.[2]

When, later on, Protestantism diverged further and further from the original teaching of Luther, the theologians began again to associate themselves with the Holy Fathers, but at first only in a detached, unhistorical manner, just so far as it suited their subjective views.

---

[1] Thus even Melanchthon himself in his first period, when he was still an obedient mouthpiece of Luther, in the first edition of his *Loci theologici* could find nothing better to say of the ecclesiastical theology, in order to show it up as quite worthless in contrast to the Holy Scriptures, than the following (*Corp. Reform.* xxi. 83) : ' Ex Origene si tollas inconcinnas allegorias et philosophicarum sententiarum silvam, quantulum erit reliquum ? Et tamen hunc auctorem magno consensu sequuntur Graeci, et ex Latinis qui videntur esse columnae, Ambrosius et Hieronymus. Post hos fere quo quisque recentior est, eo est insincerior, degeneravitque tandem disciplina christiana in scholasticas nugas, de quibus dubites, impiae magis sint, an stultae.'

[2] Döllinger, i. 453.

In this fashion the great controversialist Chemnitz made extensive use of patristic passages, torn from their context and arbitrarily interpreted, which he marshalled as pretended allies against the Tridentinum. The same policy was, later on, even more ostentatiously carried out by Gerhard.

In these proceedings there was no question whatever of historic sense or objective insight into the spirit of the Christian past and its teachings ; as far as that goes the truest insight into the actual circumstances, and possibly also the greatest amount of honesty, was manifested on Luther's side.

Learned researches in the domain of patrology—*i.e.* into the lives and writings of the Fathers—were not carried on by the Protestants till the following period, and in the second half also of the seventeenth century the reformed theologians (especially the Anglicans) had a larger share in the work than the Lutherans. Among the latter, John Gerhard made the first start with his ' Patrologie,' which was not published till a long while after his death.[1]

Like the patristic writings, the canon law was also neglected and set aside.[2] In place of it there came a chaos of hundreds of different Church ordinances,

---

[1] *Patrologia, sive de primitivae ecclesiae christianae doctorum vita ac lucubrationibus opusculum posthumum*, Jenae, 1653. For the further literature see O. Bardenhewer, *Patrologie*, Freiburg, 1901, p. 9.

[2] ' On the side of the Protestant theologians the study of ecclesiastical law was wholly neglected. One result of this was the utter incapacity of the theologians (who, with absolutely unimportant exceptions, had no legal training whatever) to get an accurate grasp of matters of Church law, and another, that the government of the Church fell into the hands of secular jurists, who then, and down to the present day, formed everywhere the majority in the consistories, or at any rate were Presidents and controlled the decisions. This further explains how it was that canon law was

statutes, territorial constitutions, of which scarcely two ever harmonised with each other, and which chopped and changed according to the arbitrary wills of the princes, a chaos out of which no sort of scientific system could be shaped.

Moral theology, for a long space of time, was treated by the Lutherans, after the precedent of Melanchthon, not as an independent department, but only as a branch of dogmatics, in connexion with the dogmatic system.[1] It is also only natural that under the dominating influence of the Lutheran doctrine of justification, interest in the problems of moral theology, wherever any such interest existed, should retreat far into the background.[2] The current statement that it was

almost solely represented by the juridical faculties, and that it was only practised by jurists, that the number of the theologians who have written on the subject of canon law is small as compared with the jurists, and also that the works of theologians have been on the whole without influence on the development of law.' Schulte, *Quellen*, III. ii. 289–290.

[1] Melanchthon's ethical writings (see above, p. 129) only relate to moral philosophy and have nothing to do with theology.

[2] Henke (*Calixtus*, i. 508) expends himself in grandiloquent phrases on the ' moral impulses ' which were influential in Luther's Reformation, on the moral indignation anent the forgetfulness . . . of true personal penitence and conversion, on the false confidence in ' a Church making penance easy,' and then expounds in the same breath the separateness of the purely divine action of justification from the after progress, conditioned on morality, of the work of sanctification ; he had as it were pledged himself to almost exclusive acceptance of the former (the purely divine action) and thereby excluded himself from the latter, and therewith also from ethics.' Gass (i. 173) speaks still more strongly : ' The Reformation had engendered its religious faith from a moral basis, and on this faith attempt was now made to build up Protestant morality. But the faith of the Protestants was indissolubly bound up with the rejection of good works—that is to say, on a negative, and, from the moral standpoint, an apparently contradictory basis, and this anomaly could not forthwith be overcome by reinstating under some new title what had been abjured at the outset. " Doing " or action or works can have no separate independent foothold by the side of the faith, of which it should be the outcome and

Calixtus who made the first attempt to treat moral theology independently is not altogether correct. Isolated attempts of this sort occur, it is true, in the sixteenth century. Attention has been drawn to the treatise of Thomas Venatorius at Nuremberg († 1551) on Christian virtue,[1] and to the text-book of Paul von Eitzen in Schleswig († 1598) ;[2] these solitary attempts, however, remained without further influence, and soon passed into oblivion. It was actually true that ' more than sixty years after the issue of Paul von Eitzen's' works it was *a new thing* for a Lutheran theologian to turn his attention to the subject of ethics, and such a one would then still be regarded as an innovator by those who made it a matter of conscience to want to hear of nothing but faith and the doctrine of faith alone.'[3] In spite, therefore, of these unimportant precursors, the further development of moral theology

result, because its justification and readoption would have made it a second condition of salvation. Good works and law were, however, the two only names with which, at that period, a system of ethics could have been connected ; both are denied, and with them there is an end of ethics, and this collapse of ethics is justified, if it only stands for the energy and the confidence with which Protestantism, averse to halved principles or dualism of principle, made the Christian life flow only from the one source of faith and grace.' Thus Protestantism, says Gass finally, ' has neither injured the ethical nature of its consciousness, nor passed sentence *a priori* and for ever against the formation of a separate moral system.'

[1] *De virtute christiana libri tres*, Norimbergae, 1529. See J. C. G. Schwarz, ' Thomas Venatorius und die ersten Anfänge der protestantischen Ethik im Zusammenhage mit der Entwicklung der Rechtfertigungslehre ' in the *Theol. Studien und Kritiken*, 1850, pp. 79–142.

[2] *Ethicae doctrinae libri quatuor conscripti in usum studiosae iuventutis*, 2 vols., Vitebergae, 1571–1573 ; three more editions down to 1588. See L. Pelt, ' Die christliche Ethik in der lutherischen Kirche von Calixtus,' in the *Theolog. Studien und Kritiken*, 1848, pp. 271–319.

[3] Henke, *Calixtus*, i. 513 f.

as an independent branch is actually associated with the text-book of Calixtus.[1]

It is somewhat remarkable that the reformed theologians should have given more special attention to the systematising of moral theology than the Lutherans, for, looking at the matter in its logical consequence, the doctrine of predestination is even more calculated to do away with ethics than the Lutheran doctrine of justification. In addition to the inconsistency with its own principles which is common to all forms of the older Protestantism, the well-grounded fear of the results likely to follow from hurling the doctrine of predestination, without an antidote, among the people may well be adduced as a chief explanation of this phenomenon: with the Swiss the more practical tendency of the nation may also be taken into account. Here (in Switzerland) the history of the special systematising of morals begin with the 'Ethica Christiana' of Lambert Danäus, at Geneva (1577).

There are no German works of this kind belonging to the period which immediately follows : the grandest and most important representative of German mysticism and asceticism among the Lutherans was John Arndt († 1621 as superintendent-general at Celle) with his four books 'Vour wahren Christentum' (1695 ff.) and the 'Paradies Gärtlein,' which are written in a spirit essentially influenced by the Catholic mystics of the Middle Ages (Thomas à Kempis, Tauler). For his efforts to institute a living system of Christianity among his fellow-believers he was attacked and slandered in the grossest manner by Lutheran zealots, such as Deneke in Brunswick and Corvinus in Danzig.

[1] *Epitome theologiae moralis* (1634).   See Henke, i. 514–526.

His most violent opponent was Luke Osiander at Tübingen,[1] who accused him of a most remarkable mixture of heresies : namely, papism, monachism, enthusiasm, Pelagianism, Calvinism, Schwenkfeldianism, Flacianism and Weigelianism.   His book, Osiander said, was a ' book of hell ' ; he had plagiarised from Weigel's books, and ' from the stinking, unhealthy streams of those who had lived in the thick darkness of popery.'[2] With Arndt we must especially couple the name of John Gerhard, whose literary first-fruits in this connexion have already been mentioned earlier in these pages.[3]

In the domain of exegesis, as was to be expected in view of the principle that had been established, a literally comprehensive literature was produced.[4] The usual Protestant estimate of this literature and of its inner substance and scientific value corresponds as little as possible to facts.   ' To the illusions which are spread abroad concerning the motive springs, and the development of the Reformation belongs also the idea that this religious movement had been partly accompanied, partly followed by a fundamental and scientific study of the Holy Scriptures, based on exact knowledge and comparison of original Greek and Hebrew texts. How little this was the case is learnt from a glance at the mass of contemporary Protestant theological, exegetical and polemical writings.'[5]   On the one hand the study of

---

[1] *Theologisches Bedenken und christliche Erinnerung, welcher Gestalt J. Arndten genanntes wahres Christentum angesehen und zu achten sei*, Tübingen, 1624.

[2] Franck, i. 362.   [3] See above, p. 166.

[4] See, in general, Gottlob Wilhelm Meyer, *Gesch. der Schrifterklärung*, ii. and iii. Göttingen, 1303 f.

[5] Döllinger, i. 454.

Biblical languages and of Biblical knowledge had certainly no need to wait for the Reformation to be grounded and quickened anew ; for it had been carried on in earnest in the German high schools and elsewhere in the Catholic world before Luther's time.[1]

' Here also Luther proceeded in his usual manner ; he knew how far he might dare to go in his writings, and what he could force on the belief of that portion of the people which had now placed its unwavering confidence in him. He knew well, moreover, how to avail himself of the Catholic Biblical works, and the Bible editions which had so far appeared ; he knew well what the Catholic universities, professors and monks had already done for the study of Holy Scripture, and the Bible languages ; he knew well what extraordinary pains had been taken, what an enormous amount of collaboration had gone on, in Spain over the Complutensian Polyglot ; he knew well that at most of the Catholic universities there were Chairs of the Hebrew language.' ' But in the writings intended for the people, in which he was above all concerned to kindle and feed the hatred and contempt of the people against the Church and the clergy, and then, again, clever calculator that he was, to tickle German vanity, and to press German national prejudice into the service of his cause,

---

[1] See Döllinger, i. 457 f. ; Alzog, *Kirchengeschichte*, i[10]. (1882), 128–132 ; also Tholuck, *Akademisches Leben*, i. 102 f. In the Innsbruck *Zeitschr. für Katholische Theologie*, 1898, pp. 165–172. (From the theological lectures of the Catholic university of Leipzig), J. R. Zenner reprints two chapters of a rare incunable (*Officii misse sacrique canonis expositio . . . in alma universitate Lipezensi edita*, Reutlingen, 1483), which are a concrete example (for the university of Leipzig) of ' what was taught and how it was taught ' ; to be taken to heart by those ' who are still labouring under the delusion that it was the Reformation which first raised the Bible into proper estimation.'

he told the people that " hitherto, at the instigation
of the devil, the knowledge and use of the Biblical
languages had been suppressed in every way, in order
that the evangel might not come to the light of day ; in
Germany alone, in this country favoured before all
others by God, had the Biblical languages, and through
these the evangel, now first been preserved." ' [1]   As
little therefore as it was true that Luther and his associates had the task of first starting the scientific study
of the Bible, so little also in conformity with facts was
the assertion that it was through their labours that
a knowledge of the Bible, grounded on original texts,
had become general among the preachers of the new
faith.   Attention has been drawn to the fact that in
Protestant Germany it was in 1586 or 1587, at Wittenberg, that a Hebrew Bible was first printed, while of the
earlier Hebrew Bibles printed elsewhere, the edition of
Sebastian Münster, which appeared at Basle in 1536, was
the only one whieh had much circulation in Germany,
and that editions of the Greek New Testament, did not
appear at Leipzig before 1542, and again in 1563, while
the editions of the Erasmian New Testament printed
at Basle, Hagenau and Strassburg only found their
way to Germany in a comparatively small number of
copies ; in the face of these facts it is scarcely possible
to believe that more than one out of twenty preachers
and candidates possessed Greek New Testaments, not
to speak of Hebrew Old Testaments.   Here lies the
explanation of Melanchthon's frequent complaints that
' the sources of learning were so grievously neglected.'
Not only the laity but the preachers also contented
themselves with Luther's German translation, and con-

---

[1] Döllinger, i. 456 f., 459.

structed on it their Biblical evidence, though they did
not omit occasionally to point the people to the two
languages, through the knowledge of which the true
teaching of Christ and the Apostles after a long night of
darkness had now again come to light, and also to draw
their attention to the voluntary darkness in which,
in this respect, the papists still continued.[1]

The manner and method itself in which, according
to Luther's example, the Protestants conducted their
exegesis is anything but scientific, and nothing corresponds less to the facts than the notion that the
reformers and their coadjutors, true to their principle
of ' the Bible only,' made Scripture as it stands the basis
of their dogmatising.

Exactly the opposite is the case : their exegesis is
throughout under the dominating influence of their
a priori dogmatic assumptions, laid down independently
of exegesis, and their sole after-task was to justify their
assumptions by corresponding twisting and distortion
of Biblical words. ' Whereas Luther and Melanchthon,'
says a Protestant theologian,[2] ' compelled " dogmatics "
to go to Scripture alone, or to Scripture in the first
place, for its proofs, it was, above all, desirable a new
exegesis should be produced ; that need, however, was
not yet felt, or rather, it should be said, the reformers
allowed a system of exegesis to be forced on them un-
awares by polemics, a system which was almost worse
than none ; and this caused the most pernicious results as
regards " dogmatics." The dogmatic theologian blindly
accepted the lead of polemics ; every text useful in
polemics was set down as a striking proof from Scrip-

---

[1] Döllinger, i. 455, 456.
[2] Planck, *Einleitung in die theolog. Wissenschaften*, ii. 516.

ture.   Thus a number of doubtful proofs were adduced,
and the ease with which this could be done further led
to increase the evil.   This was the weak side which our
dogma retained all too long.' [1]

The Church ordinance of the Elector Augustus of
Saxony of 1580 limits the scope of exegetical study at
the university expressly to dogmatic-polemical interest
on the one hand, and to the deductions of practical consequences on the other hand.   ' The professors,' it says,
' shall not waste their time over *opinionibus doctorum
ecclesiæ*, or other unnecessary subtleties, but shall devote
all their attention and energies to explaining the actual
signification of every passage of Holy Writ, in the
simplest way possible, to their pupils, and to showing

---

[1] On this Staudenmeier remarks (*Dogmatik*, i. 272): ' If we penetrate
to the inner meaning of what Planck says concerning the " dogmatic "
of his Church at the time of its commencement, we find that he proves in
it a ὕστερον πρότερον, in that he quite correctly refers to the topsy-turvi-
ness in the situation, for when the Protestant theologians wanted to deduce
their dogma from the Bible as the sole source, instead of effecting this by
explanation of the Bible, they set up a system of " dogmatics " created
beforehand by the spirit of polemics which ruled their exegesis, and by this
arrangement they departed from the principle of making doctrines of
faith dependent on Scripture and on Scripture alone.'   See also Richard
Simon, *Histoire critique du Vieux Testament*, Amsterdam, 1685, p. 427 :
' Sous le prétexte de ne suivre que la pure parole de Dieu, ils ont bien plus
souvent suivi les conséquences qu'ils ont prétendu tirer immédiatement
de l'Ecriture, que cette pure parole de Dieu ; et c'est ce qui fait que bien
qu'ils soient tous d'accord entre eux pour leur premier principe, leurs
sentimens sont néanmoins très différens.   Cependant ils osent assurer que
l'Ecriture est d'elle-même claire et facile à entendre.   En quoi ils font
bien voir qu'ils se trompent, puisqu'ils tirent des conséquences si différentes
d'un seul et même principe qu'ils supposent être évident.'   F. Paulsen,
p. 147 : ' The innovators built their Church, as they pretended, on the
pure Word of God, *i.e.* also ultimately on philology; which philology indeed
consisted practically in arbitrary interpretation of already established
theological propositions.'   How small a part linguistic knowledge, which
ought to have been the chief arbiter in questions of form, played among
the students is shown by the continuous complaints of Melanchthon ;
ibid. p. 138.

them how these may be used either for the confirmation of our Church doctrine or the refutation of errors or false doctrine, or for consolation, or for admonition and warning against sin.'[1] All scholastic and scientific considerations are thus excluded by statute.

Another remarkable characteristic is the way in which Luther himself subjected the Biblical canon to his own subjective judgment, and allowed himself to pass the most depreciatory sentences on those books of the Bible which were diametrically opposed to his subjective opinions. From this standpoint of criticism he not only rejected the whole Deutero-canonical books of the Old Testament, but he also placed the proto-canonical books of the Old Testament, in so far as these do not speak directly of the Messiah to come, and of salvation by the grace of God, below the level of truly divine writings of equal rank with New Testament Scriptures ; and he was indeed not far short of rejecting the Old Testament Scriptures after the manner of the Gnostics. He denies to them direct divine inspiration. ' Moses and the prophets preached,' he says, ' but we do not hear in them God Himself. For Moses received the law from the angels, and his commandments are therefore of lesser authority. When I hear Moses ordering good works, I listen to him as to one who is proclaiming the commands or repeating the speech of an emperor or a prince. But this is not the same as

---

[1] Tholuck, *Kirchliches Leben*, p. 71. He remarks on this : ' Thus in the Lutheran commentaries also, linguistic and historical explanation consists only of passing remarks, on which follows immediately the *usus dogmaticus, elenchthicus et practicus.*' ' Lutheran exposition is not characterised by historical illustration from the conditions of the times and of its writers, and in this respect is essentially different from that of the reformed theologians.'

to hear God Himself. For when God Himself speaks
to men, they can hear nothing but promises of grace,
mercy and all goodness.'[1] But the New Testament
also had to submit in the same way to the sovereign
judgment of his subjective standpoint. 'You must
distinguish the books correctly, and judge them all separately. St. John's Gospel, and St. Paul's Epistles,
especially the Epistle to the Romans, and Peter's
first Epistle are the true pith and marrow of all the
books. For in these you will not find much about the
works and miracles of Christ ; but you will find told in
a masterly way how faith in Christ overcomes sin,
death and hell, and gives life, righteousness and salvation, which is the true kernel of the Gospels. To sum up,
St. John's Gospel and his first Epistle, Paul's Epistles,
especially those to the Romans, Galatians, and Ephesians,
and Peter's first Epistle, are the books which will show
you Christ and teach all that is necessary for you to
know, and to give you salvation, even though you
should nevermore see or hear of any other book or
teaching. Therefore St. James's Epistle is a thoroughly
straw-epistle as compared to these, for it has no evangelical character about it.'[2] And of the Apocalypse
he says in the preface to it : 'Finally let each one
think about it as his spirit prompts him. My spirit
cannot penetrate into this book. . . . I keep to the
books which present Christ to me plainly and clearly.'
It is obvious that Luther applies here the same
principle which is made to hold good (only with more
consistency) in modern rationalistic criticism, a principle which must logically involve the fundamental

---

[1] Walch, vii. 2044 ; Kuhn, i. 114 f.
[2] In the preface to the New Testament of 1542, Walch, xiv. 105.

rejection of the last remnant of old Protestant faith.

After the living authority of the Church has been rejected, the principle of arbitrary subjective individual authority (although the full scope of this principle is not yet recognised) takes its place ; first of all it is the subjective authority of the founders of the new faith that is to be decisive ; the canon is made up arbitrarily by a process of subjective selection ; certain parts of the Bible which harmonise best with individual pre-assumptions are put in the foreground, while others are rejected, and a third set, which the authorities can neither exactly make use of nor dare take on themselves to reject altogether, are put on one side with unconcealed depreciation. How such a proceeding can be reconciled with the pretended deep veneration for the revealed Word of God is only one of the many unsolved problems which the so-called Reformation presents to the unprejudiced observer. With exactly the same subjective arbitrariness the authorities then go on to explain those texts which they consider worthy of exposition. The whole method of old-Protestant exegesis is admirably characterised by the well-known distich of a later Protestant theologian, Samuel Wexenfels, according to whom the Bible is a book in which each one may seek his own dogmas and accordingly finds them there, because he is resolved to find them :

> Hic liber est, in quo sua quaerit dogmata quisque,
> Invenit et pariter dogmata quisque sua.

Luther is himself the standing prototype of Protestant exegesis, pursued on this method, ' in his manner unsurpassed.' [1] Among his exegetical writings may be

[1] So Kurz, *Kirchengeschichte*, ii [11]. 138.

mentioned in the Old Testament department the commentaries on Genesis [1] and on the Psalms,[2] and on New Testament ground, besides explanations of single passages in other books, the two commentaries on the Epistle to the Galatians, the shorter one of 1519, and, above all, as one of Luther's principal works, the larger commentary of 1535, compiled from his lectures.[3]

What has been said above concerning the Protestant exegesis of the sixteenth century is specially applicable to Luther ; it was he, indeed, who stamped this character on it. ' Luther as expounder of the Bible is one of the most remarkable, and, indeed, one of the most enigmatical, phenomena in the department of religious psychology. It is a revelation into the inner workings of this powerful mind when we find the same man who bases his whole right and his calling to found a new Church in opposition to the old one on his interpretation of Scripture, the man who, Bible in hand, tells his Catholic adversaries a hundred times over that they are incapable of getting away from the evidence of Biblical truth which he has brought to light, and who calls them deliberate, hardened sinners against the Holy Ghost, stiffnecked blockheads, who recognise the purity of his doctrine and nevertheless dispute it, when this man starts again and again from the assumption that we must first form for ourselves a distinct conception of the work of Christ, and of the appropriation

---

[1] ' Enarrationes in Genesin,' in the Erlangen edition of the Latin works of Luther, vols. i.-xi. See also Zöckler, *Luther als Ausleger des Alten Testament, gewürdigt auf Grund seines grösseren Genesiskommentars,* Greifswald, 1884 ; published before in *Evangel. Kirchenzeitung,* 1884.

[2] Erlangen edition of the Latin works, vols. xiv.-xx.

[3] *Neue Ausgabe des grösseren Kommentars* (Commentarius in epistolam S. Pauli ad Galatas), prepared by Irmischer, 3 vols., Erlangen, 1843-1844 ; the third volume contains also the smaller commentary of 1519.

by man of the redemption, as a standard of doctrine
to which contradicting texts must be made to conform
by hook and by crook.'[1] A crushing judgment on the
unscientific character of Luther's whole exegetical work
is passed by a French scholar.[2]

But in all the learned exegesis which occurs here and
there, in the commentary on Genesis especially, Luther
stands in the same position of dependence on Nicholas
of Lyra, as is expressed in the well-known couplet :

> ' Si Lyra non lyrasset,
> Lutherus non saltasset.'[3]
> Had Lyra not played his lyre
> Luther could never have danced.

---

[1] Döllinger, iii. 156 f., 158–173. Döllinger brings forward examples
to throw light on the relation in which Luther's Bible exposition stood to
his theory of justification.

[2] Rich. Simon, *Histoire critique du Vieux Testament*, p. 432 ; Luther
' n'a le plus souvent consulté que les préjugés dont il était rempli. . . .
Il mêle dans ses commentaires des questions de théologie et une infinité
d'autres choses mal-à-propos ; de sorte que ce sont plutôt des leçons de
théologie et des disputes, que de véritables commentaires. C'est ce
qu'on peut voir dans son explication sur le livre de la Genèse, où il y a un
grand nombre de digressions peu judicieuses. Il a cru qu'en faisant des
leçons de morale, et qu'en criant fortement contre ceux qui n'étaient pas
de son sentiment, il apportait de grands éclaircissements à la Parole de
Dieu.' P. 433 : ' Comme il n'était pas tout-à-fait capable de faire des
commentaires sur l'Ecriture selon le sens littéral et grammatical, il s'est
le plus souvent étendu sur des questions et des remarques inutiles. Il
a suivi cette méthode dans l'explication qu'il a donnée de quelques
Psaumes sous le titre de *Operationes in Psalmos*.' Concerning these Psalm
commentaries, the French writer goes on to say : ' Tout cet ouvrage est
rempli d'allégories et de fausses maximes.' P. 434 : Luther expounded
Scripture ' plutôt selon les faux préjugés dont il étoit entêté, que selon la
vérité du texte.' *Histoire critique des principaux commentateurs du Nouveau
Testament*, Rotterdam, 1693, p. 684 : ' Cet homme était si rempli de ses
préjugés, qu'il revoyait plutôt ses livres pour debiter avec plus de liberté
ses nouveautez, que pour produire quelque chose de plus exact sur le texte
de l'Ecriture. Ayant une fois pris party, il ne songea qu'à l'appuyer,
et comme l'Epitre aux Galates luy paroissoit favorable pour son dessein,
il s'y arrêta d'avantage que sur le reste du Nouveau Testament.'

[3] Zöckler also, inclined as he is to ascribe to the commentary on

Moreover, these exegetical writings of Luther are brimful of polemics ; the larger commentary on the Galatians consists only of dogmatic-polemical disquisitions on the doctrine of justification, and the want of scientific force in the argument is made up for, as in all his other polemical writings, by the violence of his abuse of his opponents, which he always finds opportunities for introducing.[1] ' What shall I say,' writes Ulrich

Genesis the greatest possible importance, allows that in the above couplet there is, as regards Luther's Biblical translation and Old Testament exegesis, an element of truth which the reformer himself would hardly have questioned. Respecting the commentary on Genesis, however, it is true to the fullest extent.   But he considers that this dependence was ' of no blind, uncritical nature.'   *Evangel. Kirchenzeitung*, 1884, p. 212.

[1] What Luther was capable of doing in this respect, not only in his ' popular' writings, but in those also which lay claim to a learned character, may be seen from a small selection of passages from the larger commentary on the Epistle to the Galatians, i. 173 f. (ed. Irmischer): ' Papa non solum miscuit legem cum evangelio, sed meras leges, et eas tantum ceremoniales, ex evangelio fecit, confudit politica et ecclesiastica, quae vere satanica et infernalis confusio est.'   P. 183 : ' Damnanda est igitur perniciosa et impia opinio papistarum qui tribuunt operi operato meritum gratiae et remissionis peccatorum.'   P. 184 f. : ' Haec est theologia regni antichristiani, quam ideo commemoro . . . ut palam fiat, quam longe aberraverint a veritate caeci isti et caecorum duces, et quam ista sua impia et blasphema doctrina non solum obscuraverint, sed simpliciter sustulerint evangelium et Christum obruerint. . . . Talia monstrosa portenta et horribiles blasphemiae debebant proponi Turcis et Judaeis, non ecclesiae Christi.   Et ea res satis ostendit papam cum suis episcopis, doctoribus, monachis etc. neque habuisse ullam cognitionem aut curam rerum sacrarum, neque sollicitos fuisse pro salute deserti et miserabiliter discerpti gregis.   Nam si vel per nebulam vidissent, quid Paulus vocet peccatum, quid gratiam, tales abominationes et impias nugas non obtrusissent populo christiano.'   P. 223 : ' Quid quaeso papistae aliud sunt, cum optimi sunt, quam vastatores regni Christi, et exstructores regni diaboli, peccati, irae Dei et mortis aeternae ? '   P. 267 : ' Abominationes et blasphemiae regni papistici sunt inaestimabiles, et tamen sophistae caeci et indurati, etiamnum in tanta luce veritatis, perseverant in impiis et vanissimis illis suis opinionibus.'   P. 301. ' . . . Contra papistas, Judaeos nostros, quorum abominationes et larvas impugnamus et damnamus doctrina nostra, ut Christi beneficia et gloriam illustremus.'   Vol. ii. 8 : ' Pereant sophistae cum sua maledicta glossa, et damnetur vox ista: fides formata.'

Zasius respecting the nature of the Lutheran exegesis to Bonifacius Amerbach, ' about this Luther, who in his shamelessness has turned the whole of the Sacred Scriptures, the Old and New Testaments, from the first chapter of Genesis to the end, into nothing but threats and maledictions against the Pope, the bishops and priests, as though through all the centuries God had nothing else to do than to thunder anathemas against the priests ? ' [1]

More was done for the exegesis of the New Testament by Melanchthon. Among the works which he produced in this connexion we may speciallly mention the commentaries on the Epistle to the Romans (1532, 1540, 1558), and on the Gospel of St. John, 1546. Melanchthon, at any rate, possessed the qualifications necessary for exegesis, above all the linguistic knowledge, in

According to ii. 164, it is one of the necessary qualifications of a man well-pleasing to God that he should hate the Pope and 'fanatics.' ii. 176 : ' Sic Satan horribiliter lusit in mortibus animarum per papam, ideoque papatus est verissima carnificina conscientiarum et ipsissimum diaboli regnum.' ii. 207 f. : ' Proferimus sententiam contra decreta, traditiones et leges papae, quod non solum sint infirma, egena et inutilia ad justitiam elementa, sed exsecrabilia, maledicta et diabolica, etc., quia blasphemant gratiam, evertunt evangelium, fidem abolent, Christum tollunt, etc.' iii. 108 : ' Nos maledicimus et damnamus traditiones humanas de missis, ordinibus, votis, cultibus, operibus et omnibus abominationibus papae et haereticorum, tamquam sordes diaboli.' i. 149 is the superlatively naive statement, peculiarly illustrative of Luther's mental condition, that if the Pope would accept his (Luther's) doctrine of justification he would not only carry him on his hands, but even kiss his feet ; ' quia vero hoc impetrare non possumus, vicissim superbimus in Deo ultra omnem modum, neque omnibus angelis in coelo, neque Petro aut Paulo, neque centum caesaribus, neque mille papis, neque toti mundo latum digitum cessuri.' Because the Pope rejected his teaching, ' ideo superbia nostra contra papam maxime est necessaria, et nisi sic superbiremus et contemneremus in Spiritu Sancto ipsum cum sua doctrina et diabolum mendacii patrem in eo loquentem, nullo modo retinere possemus articulum justitiae fidei.'

[1] See present work, vol. iii. p. 213.

a higher degree than Luther. His commentaries consequently bear a more scholarly stamp than those of the latter, and go more into the actual explanation of the text, which, with Luther, is only made to serve as a rallying point for his dogmatic-polemical utterances. As a philologist also Melanchthon devotes more attention to the formal side of exposition, often, perhaps, with one-sided emphasis of rhetorical aspects.[1] It is noteworthy that with regard to the Biblical canon he has more respect than Luther for tradition, and does not, like the latter, set up his own subjective opinions as supreme arbiter.[2] With regard to the material side of his exposition, Melanchthon's exegesis is also under the dominant influence of dogma. The text of Scripture is regularly ' and with wearisome monotony,' brought back to dogmatic and moral *loci* : ' the study of Scripture serves chiefly the object of bringing forward proofs for points of dogma, and that not only in the sense of mechanical accumulation of *dicta probantia*, but also as showing a systematic development of the Scriptural text up to the definiteness of the dogmatic and ethical doctrine.'[3] Neither does the ' refined ' Melanchthon shrink in his commentaries from coarse attacks on the Catholics on most unsuitable occasions.[4]

Another important labourer in the field of exegesis

---

[1] The keen-eyed critic, Richard Simon, says (*Hist. crit. des principaux Commentateurs du Nouv. Test.* p. 695) with regard to Melanchthon's commentaries : ' On y voit toujours cet esprit de rhéteur et de déclamateur, qui paroît dans tous ses livres. Il y fait de longues analyses, exposant ces Epîtres de la même manière qu'il expliquoit dans les écoles les oraisons de Cicéron, comme si cet Apôtre avoit suivi les règles de la Rhétorique.'

[2] See Herrlinger, p. 359 f.

[3] Herrlinger, pp. 371, 372.

[4] Instances are cited by G. W. Meyer, *Gesch. der Schrifterklärung*, i. 385 f., 393 f.

among the Lutheran theologians was John Brenz, whose commentaries on most of the Biblical books, of the Old Testament especially, in the edition of his collected works (Tübingen, 1576 ff.) fill four folio volumes. He was reckoned as the first exegetist of his day next to Luther and Melanchthon.[1] Luther wrote eulogistic prefaces to several of his works, and in the preface to his commentary on the prophet Amos (1530) actually paid him the compliment of saying : ' I think so highly of your writings, that my own books altogether stink in my nostrils when I compare them with yours, and such as yours.' [2]

The most notable of the remaining Lutheran exegetists issued from Melanchthon's school : prominent names among these are Victorin Strigel ; [3] Joachim Camerarius, who, as professor of the Greek and Latin languages at Leipzig († 1574), wrote ' Notationes ' to the books of the New Testament, in which, as a philologist, he gave special attention to linguistic explanation ; [4] David Chytraeus, at Rostock, who, in the years 1556-1599, published commentaries on most of the Old

---

[1] G. W. Meyer, p. 431.   A. Lang, *Der Evangelienkommentar Martin Butzers und die Grundsätze seiner Theologie*, Leipzig, 1900.

[2] Meyer, p. 426.

[3] *Hypomnemata in omnes Psalmos Davidis*, Lipsiae, 1562.   *Hypomnemata in omnes libros Novi Testamenti, ibid.* 1564.

[4] *Notatio figurarum sermonis in libris quatuor evangeliorum, ibid.* 1572. *Notatio figurarum orationis . . . in apostolicis scriptis, ibid.* 1572.   G. W. Meyer, ii. 509 : ' Camerarius thought it more in accordance with his office of teacher to insert short remarks on the words and phrases used in the New Testament, on the construction and the different figures of speech, than to indulge in dogmatic and polemical digressions, or to plunge into the depths of allegorical and tropological explanations.   It may therefore be justly said of him that in view of the great carefulness with which he stuck to this plan almost throughout, he ranks first among his contemporaries as a purely grammatical expounder.'

Testament and on several of the New Testament books ; [1]
Esrom Rüdinger, the stepson of Camerarius, who later on,
after having been for a time professor of the Greek
language at Wittenberg, joined the Bohemian Brotherhood in Moravia,[2] author of a paraphrase of the Psalms ; [3]
and finally, and above all, Flacius Illyricus and Martin
Chemnitz.

Flacius, as author of two greater works, takes a
distinguished place in the history of Protestant exegesis.
His ' Clavis Scripturae Sacrae ' [4] is intended to lay the
scholastic foundation of exegesis ; the first part, in the
form of an alphabetical dictionary, gives the meaning of
Bible words and phrases ; the second part deals with
Biblical hermeneutics.   In accordance with the theory
here worked out, he follows up this dictionary with his
' Glossa Compendiaria,' [5] an exegetical handbook to
the New Testament, in which he gives the Greek text
accompanied by the Latin translation of Erasmus,
and also his own explanations.   His aim, in this work,
as he himself explains, was to meet the want of a practical, usable commentary, which, in a compact and short
form, would help to the understanding of the text
as contrasted with all the discursive commentaries
which, up till then, had been produced by his religious
party.   ' It was only a pity that this all too dogmatical
and polemical author, in the execution of the glossary,
not seldom lost sight entirely of the ideal which he had

[1] His *Opera exegetica* (on the Old Testament) collected in 2 vols.
Wittenberg, 1590-1592, and Leipzig, 1598 f.

[2] See G. W. Meyer, iii. 405 f.

[3] *Libri Psalmorum paraphrasis latina*, Gorlicii, 1580-1581.

[4] *Clavis Scripturae sacrae, seu de sermone sacrarum literarum*, 2 vols.,
Basle, 1567.

[5] *Glossa compendiaria in Novum Testamentum, ibid.* 1570.

set before him ; for though it cannot be denied that in
many places the grammatical meaning is very well given
and with admirable brevity, and that the Biblical ideas
are very well worked out, the scope and coherency of
the book as carefully considered as the survey of different
parts of chapters is facilitated by short tables of contents,
it is also equally true that the author soon digressed from
his purpose of writing a compendiary glossary which
should be confined to the simple presentation of the
literal sense, and strayed too far into fuller explanation
of points which seemed to him of more importance, and
emphasises his own favourite opinions much more
definitely than the author whom he is explaining had
emphasised them, and ended by allowing free course
to his strong polemical bias at every opportunity, now
against the members of the Roman Church, now
against the followers of Calvin, now against individuals
of his own party with whom he had fallen out, and above
all against the Synergists. Hence there is scarcely need
of proof to show that all the worth and usefulness of
what, in many respects, is a valuable work is not a
little diminished.' [1]

[1] G. W. Meyer, ii. 503 f. : Richard Simon brings out still more sharply
the contrast between the plan conceived and the execution thereof (*Hist.
crit. des Commentateurs*, p. 702) : ' Sa Glose n'est pas si abrégée qu'elle ne
soit sujette à la plupart des défauts qu'il a repris dans les autres avec
tant de sévérité. En quoy il est beaucoup plus blâmable qu'eux, puis
que s'étant proposé de ne donner que des Scolies pour faire entendre le texte
du Nouveau Testament il se jette souvent sur des controverses de Théologie.
Il veut qu'on ne trouve dans un commentaire que ce qui sert précisément
à entendre la parole de Dieu, afin qu'on la puisse distinguer de celle des
hommes : et néanmoins il fait venir partout les préjugez de sa doctrine.
Il s'emporte avec excès contre ceux qu'il nomme Papistes. Si quelque
ancien Père, ou quelque nouveau Commentateur luy paroissent éloignez
du véritable sens, il les redresse avec des termes injurieux.' ' Il est bien
difficile,' says Simon further, ' qu'un Protestant, quelque bon sens qu'il

After the publication in 1537 of a ' Gospel Harmony ' [1]
by Andrew Osiander (famous later on for the controversial agitation connected with his name),[2] Martin
Chemnitz undertook a comprehensive work of this kind.
He left it unfinished, however, and it was carried on
by Polycarp Leiser, and finally completed by John
Gerhard.[3] This work of Chemnitz also exhibits the
sound erudition of the author,[4] but shares nevertheless
in a high degree the usual defect of Lutheran commentaries, of indulging *con amore* in discursive dogmatic
explanations and in polemical sallies, now against the
Catholics, now against the Calvinists.

Other prominent representatives of Lutheran or-
thodoxy, after the Formula of Concord, were Aegidius
Hunnius, Luke Osiander and Matthias Hoe von
Hoenegg, and John Tarnov : these men, however,
' in their endeavours to give zealous support to the
Church system sanctioned by the Formula of Concord,
erred, if possible, even more than their precursors since
Luther, in subordinating their exegesis to their dog-

---

ait, soit exemt de cet esprit de party qui domine dans la plupart de
leurs livres, et qui devoit être banni entièrement de la glosse d'Illyricus,
puisqu'il s'est proposé de ne dire que ce qui faisoit à son sujet.'

[1] See above, p. 154 f.

[2] *Harmonia historiae evangelicae, graece et latine, in quatuor libros
distributa, una cum libro annotationum*, Basle, 1537, often reprinted.

[3] The work of Chemnitz with Leiser's continuation appeared first
in 1593 ; the work of Gerhard, under the title *Harmonia Evangelistarum
Chemnitio-Lyseriana a Jo. Gerhard continuata et iusto commentario illustrata*,
Jena, 1626–1627.   The work appeared complete under the title *Harmonia
quatuor Evangelistarum, a theologis celeberrimis Martino Chemnitio primum
inchoata, a Polycarpo Lysero post continuata, atque a D. Joanne Gerhardo
tandem felicissime absoluta*, at Geneva, 1628 and 1641, at Frankfort and
Hamburg, 1652, and again at Hamburg in 1704.   G. W. Meyer, iii. 424 f.

[4] Richard Simon, p. 717 : ' On voit que ce Protestant s'était appliqué
avec soin à l'étude des Livres Sacrez, et qu'il n'avoit pas même négligé
celle des Pères et des autres Ecrivains Ecclésiastiques.'

matic ideas.'[1] Aegidius Hunnius wrote commentaries on the Gospels of Matthew and John, and on most of the Epistles of the Apostle Paul, and also on the first twenty-one chapters of Genesis.[2]

Polycarp Leiser earned his title of exegetist not only by his continuation of the Chemnitzian 'Gospel-Harmony,' but also by a six-volumed commentary on Genesis,[3] in which 'almost entirely disregarding what was necessary for grammatical explanation, he sought to insert his whole orthodox Lutheran dogmatics into the Book of Genesis, and with the weapons he borrowed from this book to combat now Calvin and his followers, now the Pope and the Roman Church, now the anti-Trinitarians.'[4] Lucas Osiander and Matthias Hoe von Hoenegg wrote a commentary on the Apocalypse which was prized in its day.[5]

---

[1] G. W. Meyer, iii. 407. Gass also (i. 157) does not dispute the justice of the assertion that ' the Protestant explanation of Scripture from Flacius down to the Pietist period had moved little or not at all from the same position, so far at least as concerns the spirit and the truth of the understanding of Scripture ' ; ' for these go backwards ' ; it would be unjust, however, to say this of the whole field of Bible study.

[2] Collected in vols. iii. and iv. of the *Opera latina Aeg. Hunnii*, Vitebergae, 1608 ; later editions of his exegetical works were published by J. S. Frustking under the titles : *Thesaurus apostolicus, ibid.* 1705, and *Thesaurus evangelicus, ibid.* 1706. Meyer (iii. 408 f.) criticises him as follows : ' In his exposition of Matthew and John he confined himself to a short and meagre development of the sense and a short description of the historical circumstances, he was utterly poor in grammatical remarks, but all the richer, on the other hand, in the coarsest dogmatic interpretations and digressions ; . . . he used his exegesis, as occasion allowed, in order to defend his theological system now against the reformed theologians, now against the Catholics.' Richard Simon, p. 708, says : 'Ce sont plutôt des leçons de théologie, que de véritables commentaires parce qu'il s'étend plus sur les disputes qui regardent la Religion, que sur les paroles de son texte, qu'il ne laisse pas néanmoins d'éclaircir.'

[3] Leipzig, 1604 ff. [4] G. W. Meyer, iii. 409.

[5] Leipzig, 1610–1640.

John Tarnov, of Rostock, was an exception among the Lutheran exegetists of his time in that he had more understanding of what exegesis should be, and was a more original writer than his contemporaries : [1] among his works the ' Exercitationes biblicae ' and the commentary on the Minor Prophets were the most famous.[2] Tarnov went on the avowed plan of improving the actual work of exegesis which his co-religionists had disregarded. ' It is quite a common thing,' he said in the preface to the first edition of his ' Exercitationes ' of 1619, ' for theologians to neglect the fundamental text of the Bible, indeed the Bible itself.' [3] He stirred up great opposition, because, holding firmly to his basic principles, he dared ' recklessly to set aside expositions which had been defended by the first men of the Church—by Luther, by Chemnitz, by Hunnius,' and actually to mention these theologians by name ; this caused the Jena theologians to send a manifesto to the Rostock faculty ' demanding the suppression of the great names that had been blamed, failing which they

[1] G. W. Meyer, iii. 422.

[2] *Exercitationum biblicarum libri quatuor, in quibus verus et genuinus sensus locorum scripturae multorum ex verbo Dei textuque authentico diligentius inquiritur ac defenditur*, Rostock, 1819 ; 2nd ed., 1627. *Commentarius in prophetas minores*, published by J. Benedict Carzov, Frankfort and Leipzig, 1688 and 1766.

[3] Tholuck, *Geist der lutherischen Theologie*, p. 153 f. In a letter of the year 1619 Tarnov wrote : ' I intend publishing a commentary on the minor prophets, and while engaged on this, I also expound other Biblical texts, ' ut ita, si fieri possit ad biblia Deique verbum, extra quae proh dolor, hodie plerique theologiae dant operam, studiosam juventutem reducam, quae nunc maximam partem studio perverso antequam sciat thesin et biblia legerit, tantum in controversiis et homiliis ab illis bono fine editis, tota est . . . ego primum id ago ut firmem ex verbo Dei eoque in textu authentico lecto et recte intellecto nostros ; alii videant, qui sunt majoribus donis praediti et ipsos haeresiarchos refutent.' Tholuck, *Melanchthons Leben*, ii. 103.

threatened to lodge a petition with the Mecklenburg government itself.'[1] Paul Tarnov, uncle of John, took up his nephew's cause in a letter to the Jena faculty; John Tarnov, however, in order to avoid the suppression of the contemplated second edition of his work, was obliged to yield so far to his opponent as to omit the names.[2] Gerhard, before embarking on the continuation of the Chemnitz-Leiser ' Gospel Harmony,' had published commentaries on the Passion and on the Resurrection and Ascension of Christ.[3]

More was done on the whole in the sixteenth and seventeenth centuries for the actual scientific study and understanding of Holy Scripture among the reformed theologians than among the Lutherans. At Zurich the first exegetical lectures were delivered under the name of ' Prophecy '; they were instituted in 1523, and the students and clergy were obliged to take part in them. ' The Bible occupies a very prominent place,' we read in a college ordinance, ' it has been studied with great diligence of late years, according to its arrangement. All the time that used to be spent daily on the recitation of the canonical hours, an hour or more, is now devoted to the Bible. A youngster reads a whole chapter or half one, as directed by the time-table for the day. But he reads it in the Latin version of Jerome. Then the Hebrew lecturer— *i.e.* professor (Bibliander et Pellican)—reads the same chapter and explains it from the same language's peculiarities. Then this chapter is read for the third

[1] Tholuck, *Geist der lutherischen Theologen*, pp. 153, 155.

[2] *Ibid.* pp. 155–160.

[3] *Commentarius in harmoniam historiae evangelicae de passione Christi*, and *Commentarius in harmoniam hist. evang. de resurrectione et ascensione Christi*, both at Jena in 1617.

time in Greek, as the Seventy interpreters expounded
it (by Zwingli) ; and, finally, it is all explained in Latin
most carefully to those able to follow and to the learned.
Afterwards the minister of the Word explains it in
German from the pulpit to the common people,' for
the improvement of the faithful : prayer opens and
closes this discourse.[1]

The promoters of the study of the Hebrew language
in these earlier years were Konrad Pellican and Sebastian
Münster.   For exegesis itself, after the previous labours
of Zwingli, Oecolampadius, Bucer, and others, Calvin
with his penetrating insight was the admired and unequalled model for the theologians of this creed.   In
the whole learned exegetical work of this religious
party, however, the Swiss[2] and Dutch theologians had
a far greater share than the Germans, whose exegetical
work is small in comparison with their dogmatic controversies.   Among the German reformed theologians
the following are the most eminent as regards exegetical
services : (1) John Piscator, professor at Heidelberg,
and, after 1584, at Herborn, where he died in 1625 ;
author of a German translation of the Bible,[3] the
so-called Straf-mich-Gott-Bibel (May-God-punish-me-
Bible), after his own translation of Mark viii. 12 : ' If a

---

[1] Tholuck, *Akademisches Leben*, ii. 358.

[2] As promoters of the study of Oriental languages the two John
Buxtorfs, father and son (the elder, 1590–1629, the younger 1647–1664),
gained especial renown.   With the names of these two scholars, the elder
of whom published a *Lexicon Hebraeo-Chaldaicum* in 1607 and a *Thesaurus grammaticus linguae sanctae hebraeae* in 1609, there was associated the
controversy on the age of vowel signs and accents, the Buxtorfs defending
the position that they were primordial and inspired.

[3] *Biblia, das ist : Alle Bücher der Heiligen Schrift des Alten und Neuen
Testaments. 'Aus Hebreischer und Griechischer spraach . . . jetzund aufs
new verteuscht durch Joh. Piscator,'* Herborn, 1602, and often reprinted.

sign is given to this generation, may God punish me,'
which was introduced at Bern and other places into use
in the churches ; he also wrote commentaries on all
the books of the Old and New Testaments.   (2) David
Pareus,   who   roused   great   opposition   among   the
Lutherans by his edition of the Lutheran Bible with
Calvinistic notes (the Neustädt Bible, Neustädt-on-the-
Haardt, 1587), in which James Andreä, of Tübingen,
' found sixteen dreadful errors, and therefore warned
the public against this piece of arch-villainy and
this   devilish   knavery.' [1]   (3) The   Italian   Emanuel
Tremellius († 1580), as professor at Heidelberg, translated, in conjunction with his son-in-law Francis
Junius, the Old Testament from Hebrew into Latin, [2]
and the New Testament from the Syrian. [3]   (4) Christopher Pelargus, at Frankfort-on-the-Oder, wrote commentaries on Matthew and John, and on the Acts of the
Apostles, which are distinguished above other Protestant
works by minute regard to the patristic expounders. [4]

Among the subjects of the university lectures, down
to the second half of the seventeenth century, we find
no mention anywhere, except at Helmstädt, of Church
history and moral theology. [5]   At Wittenberg, when in
1533 the theological faculty received its new statutes,
there were three professors of theology, with the pastor

[1] Franck, i. 308.
[2] *Testamenti veteris Biblia sacra, sive Libri canonici, priscae Judaeorum
ecclesiae a Deo traditi, Latini recens ex Hebraeo facti, brevibusque scholiis
illustrati ab Immanuele Tremellio et Francisco Junio*, first in five parts
(Frankfort-on-the-Main, 1575–1579), and as a whole in two vols. . . . 1579.
[3] First in his edition of the *Syrian New Testament*, Geneva, 1569, and
often reprinted ; also appended to many later editions of the Old Testament
of Tremellius-Junius.
[4] See Richard Simon, *Hist. crit. des Commentaires*, p. 709 f.
[5] Tholuck, *Kirchliches Leben*, p. 72.

of Wittenberg as a fourth lecturer. According to these
statutes the two first professors were to lecture regularly
for an hour four times a week, the one on a book of the
Old, the other on a book of the New, Testament, to
wit : out of the Old Testament, on the Psalms, Genesis
and Isaiah, out of the New Testament on the Epistles of
Paul to the Romans and the Galatians, and the Gospel
of St. John ; and besides this, from time to time from
St. Augustine's book ' De spiritu et litera.' The third
professor was to lecture twice a week on the remaining
Epistles of Paul, and the Epistles of Peter and John, and
to preach twice ; the pastor likewise was to lecture
twice a week for an hour on the Gospel of Matthew, the
Book of Deuteronomy, and sometimes on one of the
Minor Prophets. This was the whole theology curriculum ; the sentences of Lombard, it was expressly stated,
were to be given up.[1] Moreover, the list of lectures
at Wittenberg in 1561 includes neither homiletics nor
hermeneutics, pastoral theology, morality, Church history, &c. The theological faculty consisted altogether
of six professors—*i.e.* four professors of theology, and
besides these the professors of the Greek and Hebrew
tongues.[2] These between them lectured every week
four hours on Melanchthon's ' Loci ' and ' Examen,'
six hours on the Epistles of Paul, two hours on the
Gospels, four hours on the Minor Prophets, one hour on
the elements of the Hebrew language, with exposition
of either the Psalms or the Proverbs. The study of
theology could scarcely have been carried on with more
moderation. Out of the lectures of the ten professors
who worked in the philosophical faculty, only three

---

[1] Paulsen, p. 152 f. ; cf. Bruchmüller, p. 31 f.
[2] Tholuck, *Akademisches Leben*, i. 57.

hours a week were devoted to actual philosophy, two to the rules of dialectics, and one to ethics. In the juridical faculty there were six professors, in the medical, from 1548 to 1566, only two ; it was not till 1566 that a third was added.[1]

According to the Church ordinance of the Elector Augustus of 1580, the following theological staff was arranged for Wittenberg : ' Two professors for the Old Testament, viz. one for the Pentateuch and one for the Prophets ; two for the New Testament, one for the Epistles of Paul, especially those to the Romans and the Galatians, the other for the Epistles of Paul to Timothy and Titus, and also for the " Loci communes " of Melanchthon.' [2] With few exceptions, the theological faculties at the rest of the universities, all through the seventeenth century, were not only not stronger but as a rule even weaker. Marburg, according to the statute of 1529, had only two theologians ; later on there were three, and in 1674, temporarily, four. For Tübingen the ordinance of Duke Christopher of 1557 decreed three theological professors ; the statutes of 1601 and the Ordinance of 1606 raised the number to four ; but this fourth, the rector, was only required, as an extra-ordinarian, to lecture two hours a week. In like manner for Giessen, Heidelberg, Strassburg, Jena, Altorf, Greifs-wald, Kiel, Herborn, the rule was only three ordinaries for theology, and even this small number was not always fully made up.[3] Heidelberg, in 1605, had for its

---

[1] Strobel, *Neue Beiträge zur Literatur*, i. 123–136. The catalogue of the theological lectures at Wittenberg in 1561 ; also Tholuck, *Akademisches Leben*, i. 98, who also gives catalogues of other colleges in the sixteenth and seventeenth centuries.

[2] *Ibid. Akademisches Leben*, i. 57, and *ibid. Kirchliches Leben*.

[3] *Ibid. Akademisches Leben*, i. 57, and 155 f., note 73.

whole number only sixteen professors : one theologian
lectured on the Old and the New Testament and on the
' Loci communes.' [1]   Such figures as these do not say
much for the status of learning—especially as regards
theology—at Wittenberg, even though the number of
students there had risen to 1500 in 1582, and in 1613
actually to 3000, and though the theological faculty
in the Lutheran controversies generally decided the
question.

The whole interest of academic theological instruction, as carried on in the sixteenth century, was con-
centrated on Bible study and the ' Loci communes.'
Theoretically, the methodological writings of Hyperius,
Hutter, Meisner, Gerhard, and others dealt with the
organisation and pursuit of theological study.[2]   In the
plan of study as developed in these writings for the
schools of the Lutheran creed, ' one-sided attention to
polemics and the setting aside of historical interests
is still evident.'   Knowledge of the Bible, complete
familiarity with its substance and text, is the first and
last consideration ;   hence during the first years cursory
and halting reading goes on side by side, and fills up an
important part of the day.   In the second and third
years the theological student has to work at the dogmatic articles till he has gained complete mastery over
them.   To the exegetic studies succeeds forthwith the
study of the ' Loci ' in the form fixed by the Church, for
as these make up the substance of theology, the study
of theology is in the main nothing else than the propping
up with Biblical texts of doctrinal propositions already

[1] Hautz, *Gesch. der Universität Heidelberg*, ii. 138–139.
[2] Hyperius, *De recte formando theologiae studio* (1556).   Gerhard,
Methodus studii theologici (1620).

imposed by the Church. Dogma thus stands in close proximity to the Bible : the bridge connecting them is too short and narrow to allow of an independent survey being taken of either independently of the other.

Herewith the student steps on to polemical ground. He has to arm himself on all sides in order to be a match for the Calvinists no less than for the Romanists ; for Jesuits and Calvinists, as Meisner puts it, ' conduct the *agmina adversariorum.* . . . Finally, in the fourth or fifth year, after the polemical art has been mastered, comes the turn of Church history. . . . Thus only from the safe heights of the citadel of dogmatic creed, and only with eyes sharpened to spy out all that is hostile, is it advisable to survey the historic development of Christianity.   Now first is the student, fully armed and secured against error, allowed to enter on the wide field of literature ; he may now read the Fathers of the Church, and even the school-men, although these *philosophiam cum theologia in unum chaos miscuerunt* [mix up philosophy with theology in one and the same chaos]. Above all, he is admonished to read the writings of Luther, especially those of his last fully enlightened period.' [1]

Meanwhile, as regards Church history, even a slight study of it within the narrow limits of the above-mentioned theories, remained, as a rule, only a pious wish. As we have already said, Helmstädt was the only university in the curriculum of which Church history had a place from the beginning ; by the statute of 1576 this branch of study was connected with the professorship of the New Testament ; it was not till 1650 that it

[1] Gass, i. 226–228.

acquired an independent position.[1] In the academic
course of the other universities it had no place. It
was considered that it was quite sufficiently taught
in the lectures on World history, which was at that
time treated as the history of the four monarchies.
The slight interest that was felt at that time in
Church history, as such, is shown also by the lack
of any literary productions of note on this subject
since the Magdeburg Centuries ; and even those owe
their existence only to a polemical and not to any
historical interest. ' Perfectly satisfied as well with the
form of faith as expressed in the symbols as in the manifestation of life in the Church, the theologians felt no
need to go back to the ecclesiastical past, except for
the sake of polemics against their adversaries.'[2] Moral
theology, in spite of the occasional literary work
devoted to it in earlier years,[3] did not obtain admission
to the academic curriculum till after the appearance of
the ' Theologia Moralis ' of Calixtus ; and it appears
not to have been taught regularly, even at Helmstädt,
till toward the second half of the seventeenth century.[4]
Homiletic theology ' was seldom presented in a learned
manner, but all the more practically therefore *in con-
cionatoriis.*' In this respect also Helmstädt was in
advance of the age, for the first statutes of 1576 made
the third professor there responsible for homiletic
exercises, whereas at the other universities, though
homiletics were not wholly left out, they were not the
business of any special professor.[5] Catechising was
completely lacking in the group of lectures, and this was

---

[1] Tholuck, *Akademisches Leben,* i. 115 ; Henke, *Calixtus,* i. 31 f.
[2] Tholuck, i. 114.   [3] See above, p. 193.
[4] Tholuck, i. 112.   [5] *Ibid.* p. 118.

the case in general even to the end of the seventeenth century.[1] It is, however, specially noteworthy that in the further course of development at the Protestant universities the study of exegesis, which at the first either wholly ousted all other kinds of theology or else drove it into the background as a secondary matter, fell itself into extreme decline, so that in the second half of the seventeenth century it happened in many years that there were no exegetical lectures at all, while the study of controversies became ever more and more the principal subject of academic instruction.[2]

Of the pride and presumption which the manner of treating theology at Wittenberg produced in the students, Luther himself had already had occasion to complain. ' There are a number of students here,' he said in his exposition of the 26th Psalm,[3] who, when they have been one year at Wittenberg, are so brimful of knowledge that they set themselves up as being more learned than I am. When they go into the country among other people then their learning breaks out like a waterspout, and seems to weigh a whole hundred-weight, but if you put it on a scale you will find it as light as a dram ; this comes from their self-conceit, when they have only learnt one or two words, or perhaps only heard one word. As we see, worse luck nowadays, they bring up such a multitude of ranters that we have enough to do to keep them quiet. When they have only heard us once they flatter themselves that they know everything, and they know and understand a great deal more than those who have preached to them.'

[1] Tholuck, p. 119 f.
[2] *Ibid*. pp. 104–107 ; *Kirchliches Leben*, p. 71 f.
[3] Walch, v. 434 ; Döllinger, i. 400.

With the growth of conceit the slackening of study naturally goes hand in hand. How greatly, even in the period immediately following Luther, the study of the Holy Scriptures was neglected by the students of theology is seen from the complaint of the Wittenberg professor, Paul Krell : ' Contempt for the Divine Word is now so great that even the students of theology neglect its careful study and contemplation, as though they had had enough of it ; when they have read a chapter or two here and there they think they have swallowed the whole sum of divine wisdom at one gulp.' [1] Balthasar Meisner, addressing the theologians at the funeral of Hutter, said : ' Most of you want nowadays to be your own teachers, and you consider it a disgrace to sit among the learners. The museum is your proper place, you say, the lectures are for the novices.' [2]

Added to this there prevailed contempt for theological study in general, and consequently there was a great lack of theological students, especially from the higher ranks of society, concerning which complaints were loud and numerous. ' At the three schools at Eisleben,' wrote Cyriacus Spangenberg in 1570, ' there are about a thousand boys, and here in the valley of Mansfeld and at Heckstatt we have a few hundreds. Do you think thirty of them will become preachers ? Alas ! if there were but ten for certain ! But verily these would not fill all the

---

[1] Döllinger, *ibid.*

[2] Tholuck, *Akademisches Leben*, i. 130.   In *Kirchliches Leben*, p. 112 f., Tholuck gives examples of the total ignorance which, in the sixteenth and at the beginning of the seventeenth century, was often found among the Lutheran clergy.   The same was the case with the reformed clergy, p. 270 f.

pastorates.' [1] ' It has, alas ! almost come to this,' wrote
George Lauterbeck in 1563, ' that parents, especially
rich ones, are ashamed to keep their children at the
study of Holy Scripture for fear they should become
learned enough to have the charge of churches and
schools ; they prefer their studying law, or medicine,
or becoming traders and merchants.' [2] In like manner
Wigand said in 1571 : ' No position in the world is
more despised that that of the clergy. Many, therefore, shrink from it, and it is considered ignominious to
become a preacher or a theologian. Young men who
have a little means and are able to prolong their studies,
want to rise to higher and more profitable positions.
The ministers of the Divine Word are regarded as a
degenerate race, which cannot lift itself higher and get
into easy circumstances, such as are open to everybody,
and which philosophers, doctors of medicine, jurists,
burghers, peasants, nobles and commoners can fill just
as well as a theologian.' [3] Andrew Musculus, the
zealous representative of Lutheranism in Frankfort-on-
the-Oder, who, in his different writings, made numerous
complaints of the religious decline among the Lutherans,[4]
writes in August 1557, concerning the contempt of
theological study : ' The office of preacher has become
so mean a thing among us Lutherans that nowadays
there are no parents to be found who will consent to
their children's entering it ; they rather deter them
from it. If anyone questions the truth of this, let him
show me one nobleman, one notable and well-to-do
burgher, who keeps his sons to such studies ; they must
all be jurists or merchants, and it would grieve the

[1] Ehespiegel, p. 84[b].   [2] Döllinger, i. 464.
[3] *Ibid.* p. 466.   [4] *Ibid.* ii. 393 f.

VOL. XIV.   Q

parents sorely if any of their children entered on the beggarly office of preacher. And as to any princes nowadays, as used to happen in the devil's name in the days of the Papacy, entering the service of the Church of Christ, they would think it better never to have been born, and their parents would wish they had been drowned in the first bath. That this is true experience shows. The princes and lords do their part in this respect ; in order that we may be rid of the Word all the sooner, they tear both His coats off the Lord Christ, and snatch all the Church goods for themselves, if this has not been done already, and matins is no longer sung.' ' Up till now we have had in the towns and in the country wealthy ministers of the Church, because numbers of learned people came to us from the abbeys and convents and served the Church ; also many handi-craftsmen, who had first studied to a certain extent, were ready to take Church offices in the country. Now, however, such people are no longer to be had, and they are gradually dying out, and no young men will fill their place ; tell me, ye princes, lords and noblemen, where will they come from now ? Are they to be sought for and found in the universities ; there they are not. We have here four or five high schools in which God's Word is taught, but this I know, that if you took twenty or thirty preachers away from them to set over the churches, as far as possible, you would have nearly the whole lot of them, and would scarcely leave any in. This, I aver, means that the Word itself is driven out. Personally, however, I am convinced that since the evangel is thus despised by us and degraded to the rank of a lackey, God will put an end to the world.' [1]

[1] Döllinger, ii. 410–412.

The chief reason theological studies were so detested, wrote the theologian George Major in 1564, lay in the needy and despised condition of the scholars of divinity ; the second in the religious disturbances and doctrinal controversies, amid which it seemed impossible to attain to a firm theological conviction. One no longer knew on which of the contending sides the true doctrine was to be found. From this state of uncertainty, out of which even good people eager for learning could not extricate themselves, there arose first disgust and contempt, then anger and vexation of spirit against the Church dogmas, and finally mockery of religion and epicurean blasphemy.[1]

' What is going to come of it all,' asked the Lutheran Melchior von Ossa, ' which party are the poor, simple lay folk to believe in, or how shall the poor laity protect themselves ; to what schools shall pious, respectable, God-fearing people send their children ? For every different preacher among the schismatics insists on having his own doctrines taught in the schools and churches under him, and they call in the help of the secular rulers to coerce the people into their own way of thinking. What are war, sedition and outward want compared to such schism and discord ? No enmity is fiercer and rabider than that which divides religious parties ; hide and cover it as much as one may, odious distrust ensues.'[2]

' Not the least of the evils of our worse than iron age,' wrote Andrew Hyperius, one of the most prominent theologians of the university of Marburg, ' is that only a very small minority of young men take up the study

---

[1] Döllinger, ii. 170–171 ; see also *ibid.* 463.

[2] Von Langenn, *Melchior von Ossa*, pp. 155–156, 195.

of theology in earnest ; the majority, when they have
made a little progress, and roused expectation about
themselves, give it all up and turn to other subjects.'
Hyperius attributes this to the unceasing religious dissensions, ' originators of which are now found in greater
numbers than in any other century,' and to the utter
contempt in which the clerical estate stood.   ' To such
a pass had things come that godless men think themselves justified in oppressing and injuring an individual
for the sole reason that he has devoted himself to
the study of theology.   In many districts there are
numbers of churches without any preacher, and the
people live like cattle without any Christian instruction.
Only two generations before the ministers of churches
took great pains to educate young people for the clerical
estate ; at the present day, however, this zeal had grown
cold and there were but few who troubled themselves
about the matter.' [1]   In like manner the conditions of
the seventies in the sixteenth century are described by
the superintendent Christopher Fischer († 1597 as
superintendent-general at Celle) : ' Nobody helps to
keep up the office of preacher ; on the contrary, it is
robbed of that with which it was endowed of old.
Schools go to the ground, young people are not brought
up as plants of God ; parents prefer training their
children for merchandise, shopkeeping, or any lucrative
business.   And, although some parents allow their
children to study, they will not have them devote
themselves to theology ; they will not educate parsons
who are offensive (an eyesore) to everyone.   Preachers
are so scantily provided for that they can scarcely ward
off starvation.   If they die they leave behind them

---

[1] Döllinger, ii. 220–222 ; see also i. 469.

wives and children who are soon after driven to beggary. Therefore everybody shuns the profession, and all prefer to learn a handicraft rather than become a butt for scorn and derision, and suffer want into the bargain.' [1]

If it had not been for the constant supply which flowed in to the clerical profession from the large families of children, so common among the preachers, the dearth of the latter would soon have made itself felt in a much more serious manner.[2]

Of 'free investigation' there was nowhere any question. At Helmstädt all the professors were obliged to subscribe in the most unqualified manner to the Articles of Faith embodied in the *Corpus doctrinae*, and it was enjoined that proceedings must forthwith be instituted against any professor who taught otherwise, or even associated himself with those who taught differently. The professors of each faculty were obliged, before proposing any new colleagues for special appointments, to test them as to whether they agreed with the method of teaching prescribed in the statutes. Even the medical professors were directed to such inspired persons as Hippocrates, Galen, and Avicenna, as to infallible authorities, and were warned against the

---

[1] Döllinger, ii. 310 ; see also similar utterances of other theologians on the contempt of theological study, pp. 325, 349, 561, 563–564.

[2] *Ibid.* i. 437. The reference to the ' clerical aftergrowth from the families of the clergy in which, in some cases, the succession was carried on in Levitical fashion through centuries,' is the only important testimony, besides a list of the few names of noble descent which occur among the Pro-testant theologians of the sixteenth century, which Tholuck (*Akademisches Leben*, i. 168 f.) opposes to the mass of evidence collected by Döllinger in proof of the contempt shown for theological study and the lack of students of theology. ' The facts, he is forced to own, are in some measure true enough.' It was not till the seventeenth century, under altered conditions, that any traces can be found of an oversupply of candidates.

innovations of empirics.[1] The whole scientific and
scholastic life had to adapt itself to the dominant
theological tendency of the moment, or else suspicion,
coercion and persecution followed.[2]

The Protestantism of the sixteenth century certainly
exhibited the most varying tendencies side by side,
though by no means in a free competition of forces, with
the weapons of the spirit. With isolated exceptions of
greater tolerance of mind, we find everywhere the
opinions which are exactly in harmony with those of the
territorial prince of the day, striving their utmost to
suppress all differing views. The theory of the absolute
Church authority of the secular powers was in itself
enough to make a system of tolerance impossible on the
Protestant side. ' Historically speaking, nothing is
more unjust than the assertion that the Reformation
was a movement for freedom of conscience. Exactly
the opposite is the truth. For themselves, indeed,
Lutherans and Calvinists, just like all men at all times,
demanded freedom of conscience, but to grant this
freedom to others when they themselves were the
stronger party, did not occur to them.'[3] This applies
not only to the behaviour of Protestants towards
Catholics, but also to the reciprocal behaviour of the
different Protestant religious or theological parties
towards each other. From the very first religious life
among the Protestants was influenced by the hopeless
contradiction that on the one hand Luther imposed it
as a sacred duty on every individual, in all matters of
faith, to set aside every authority, above all that of the

---

[1] Henke, *Universität Helmstädt*, pp. 32–35 ; Calixtus, i. 26–29.
[2] Henke, *Universtät Helmstädt*, p. 57 ; Calixtus, i. 47.
[3] Döllinger, *Kirche und Kirchen*, Munich, 1861, p. 68.

Church, and to follow only his own judgment, while on the other hand the reformed theologians gave the secular princes power over the religion of their land and their subjects, and insisted that it was the right and the duty of the ruler to establish the ' pure evangel ' and the new Church, and to keep out all strange doctrine. ' Luther never attempted to solve this contradiction. In practice he was content that the princes should have supreme control over religion, doctrine and Church, and that it was their right and their duty to suppress every religious creed which differed from their own.' [1] The carrying out of this principle naturally concerns not only the practical organisation of Church matters and systems in the different territories, but also the pursuit of theological learning. ' The view of the question taken by the reformed theologians, of course, naturally was that the princes would let themselves be guided by the advice of the theologians ; that above all they should follow the counsel of the theological faculties in all questions of doctrine.' But these faculties changed and changed again, and whenever the territorial prince made up his mind to alter the religion of his territory, the old professors were removed and new ones appointed.[2]

Moreover, antagonism had also grown up among the Protestant universities, and one reproached the other with being the fosterer and begetter of false doctrine. If any particular university came under the charge of heterodoxy from the dominant party, the professors of the other universities, as well as the preachers in the towns and in the country, strove zealously by pamphlets, and by sermons from the professor's chair or the

---

[1] Döllinger, *Kirche und Kirchen*, p. 52 f.   [2] *Ibid.* p. 56.

pulpit, to warn the public against attendance at the condemned university. Wittenberg itself, but lately regarded as the birthplace of a new revelation and of the newly awakened Church of Christ, in 1567 was declared to be a ' stinking cesspool of the devil ' ; it was preached that a mother had far better murder her son than send him to Wittenberg, or, indeed, to any university.[1]

Censorship of the press, as it was carried on in the Protestant territories, took good care that no views which were not in agreement with those of the party dominant at the time in the particular district should find public expression. The reformed theologians had been the first who had called in the arm of secular authorities against writings that displeased them, not only indeed against Catholic writings but also against Protestant publications of different party tendencies. When the controversy on the Lord's Supper was started at Wittenberg, the utmost precautions were taken to suppress the writings of the Swiss Reformed theologians and of the German preachers who shared the latter's views. At the instigation of Luther and Melanchthon there was issued, in 1528, by the Elector John of Saxony, an edict to the following effect : ' Books and pamphlets (of the Anabaptists, Sacramentarians, &c.) must not be allowed to be bought or sold or read, and anyone who is aware of such being done by anybody, whether a stranger or an acquaintance, must give information to you or to the magistrates of the place, in order that the offender may be taken up and in due time punished according to his offence ; also those

[1] Döllinger, *Reformation*, i. 469 f. ; see also the present work, vol. vii. p. 277.

who are aware of such breaches of the orders laid down
herein, and do not give information, shall be punished
by loss of life and property.'   Orders of this sort did not
only apply to booksellers and to the spread of objectionable writings among the laity, but were intended also
for the preachers.   Thus the Margrave John of the
Neumark Brandenburg forbad the clergy of his land
to make any use whatever of the writings of the
Zwinglians and the Calvinists, just as elsewhere the
reading of the writings of Catholic theologians was
expressly forbidden ; and so also with the Church
agenda of the Duke of Brunswick of 1594.   In Saxony
no books were allowed to be published without the
sanction of the theological faculty and the four deans ;
this decree was used by the party dominant at the time
being to suppress first the writings of the Philipists and
then of the Flacians, when distasteful to them.   Where-
ever the prince, according to old Byzantine fashion,
thought himself a theologian, he managed the censorship
in person.   Thus, in 1585, the zealous Lutheran Duke
Louis of Württemberg boasted that ' he took good care
not to let any pamphlet of his theologians get into
print which had not been first read and approved of,'
and a few years later he assured the Ingoldstadt theologian Gregory of Valentine that ' his councillors and
servants knew well that the controversial writings of his
theologians were never published until they had been
read and sanctioned by him.' [1] At Helmstädt the order
was reiterated in an inspectoral-recess of January 18,
1603, that manuscripts before being printed must be
sent up to the court for inspection, and afterwards
straight to the dean and the printer, so that the author

[1] Döllinger, *Reformation*, i. 495–499, 503.

could not possibly insert any additions.[1] Violation of the orders of the censorship was everywhere to be severely punished. In addition to the action of the princes with regard to the censorship, the preachers in the Protestant towns were continually beseeching the magistrates to suppress the writings of all the opposing parties.[2] In the party divisions among the Lutherans, it fell out also that in Lutheran Germany the sharpness of the weapons which Luther and his associates forged against their adversaries was turned against the very persons who justly regarded themselves as Luther's most orthodox disciples. Of this the Flacian Matthäus Judex complains in his pamphlet ' Von der rechtmässigen Über-wachung der Presse '(1566), which in this respect is worthy of note. ' It is political tyranny,' he says, ' when the secular magistrates and their courts arrogate to themselves all rights over the press both native and foreign, and without asking the Church—in spite, indeed, of the Church's objections—issue public decrees that the theologians under their jurisdiction are not to publish anything without their consent, and that no home or foreign publications are to be used without their approval, so that even the Holy Ghost and His minister are not allowed the rightful and necessary freedom for safeguarding the spread of truth, and for the suppression and warding off of error, of corruption, of doctrine, and of vice.' Faithful preachers and theologians, he says, ' are deposed and banished simply because they will not submit to this enslavement of the press ; he himself had defied it, for when a pamphlet of his had lain a whole year at the court, he finally had it printed himself without leave. It is also, however,

---

[1] Henke, *Calixtus*, i. 93 f.   [2] Döllinger, i. 500–502.

striking as regards this pamphlet that Judex himself gets constantly involved in the most palpable contradictions. He considers it, for instance, quite in the right order of things that the writings of the Catholics, the Calvinists and the Anabaptists should be suppressed; a sharp censorship must be carried on, and everything forbidden which is contrary to the pure doctrine; 'but the secular authorities must herein be entirely guided by the opinions of the preachers, and must do no more than lend a helping hand to preachers; altogether the secular potentates, in matters of conscience, must submit themselves to the preachers.' But how the secular potentates were to discover in the party fights of the Lutherans who were the orthodox Lutherans, is a question on which Judex does not touch. He makes it, however, a matter of conscience for scholars and preachers, those of his own party of course, not to submit to the censorship of the secular magistrates.[1]

Under such conditions, and while the leading theologians, especially among the Lutherans, became more and more factious and presumptuous, the decay of theological study caused also, more or less, a decline in the other branches of learning. Complaints on this score begin to make themselves heard even in the first years after the introduction of the religious innovations, not only from Erasmus and other humanists,[2] but also among the leaders of Protestantism itself, especially from Melanchthon, in whose letters and speeches, from 1522 till his death, laments on the decay of all the fine arts and all learning never cease. The theologians, or, as he said, the pseudo-theologians, by which the new

---

[1] Döllinger, *Reformation*, i. 506-510.   [2] *Ibid*. p. 437 ff.

theologians of Wittenberg origin, not the old scholastic ones, are meant, have driven away the Muses with their barbarous wrangling. ' It is only too true,' he writes on July 22, 1522, to Eobanus Hessus, ' that poetry is neglected by the young ; this signifies, if I am not mistaken in everything, the impending collapse of literature and learning ; we shall leave behind us a generation which knows less than that of Scotus.' In a letter to the same friend in April 1523, he exclaims : ' Good God ! are these men theologians whose wisdom consists in the contempt of learning ? Must it not be that out of this there will come a still stupider and more godless kind of sophistry ? ' In his public speeches also, after 1524, the want of interest shown by the students in art, science and learning, and especially in the study of Greek, forms a standing subject of complaint.[1] In his preface to Luther's book on the schools of the year, 1524, he says : ' Those preachers who from their pulpits everywhere, nowadays, set the inexperienced young against study ought to have their tongues cut out.' [2] This state of things continued for a long time in the after-Reformation period : the scholastic inferiority of Protestantism lasted on so long as the causes of it, which were an integral part of its nature, lasted—i.e. so long as the religious opinions of the sixteenth century still retained any authority in the Protestant religious communities.[3] Added to the inherent incapacity of Protestantism under its given

---

[1] Paulsen, pp. 136–138.

[2] Döllinger, i. 441.

[3] Further evidence of this occurs in Joh. Gottfried Eichhorn, *Geschichte der Literatur*, ii. 2. 593 ff. ; iii. 1. 267 f., 320 f. ; Döllinger, i. 492–495. See also Lisch, *Jahrbücher*, v. 160–161 ; Schanz, *Apologie des Christentums*, iii. 563–565.

assumption to do anything itself in this direction, there
was the ' laughable bigotry,' as the Protestant Eichhorn
said,[1] ' with which the Protestants despised improvements in learning when they originated with the
Catholic Church.' A typical example of this is the
objection to the Gregorian Calendar (1582), to the
adoption of which the Protestants did not agree until
the eighteenth century. The Tübingen senate, for
instance, protested against it because the new calendar
was ' manifestly compiled with a view to furthering the
idolatrous popish system,' and added : ' We hold the
Pope to be an abominable, raging bear-wolf. Satan
has been driven out of the Christian Church, and we
will not have him smuggled in again by his vicegerent
the Pope.' [2]

With the unity of the faith, the unity and coherence
of learning were also split up ; with the loss of inter-
national unity the hitherto free movement of theology,
as also of the other branches of study, was lost also.
Only the princes and their court theologians were free
within their territory ; all the rest, professors as well as
pupils, were slaves within the same region.

' We meanwhile,' complains the ' Treuherzige Ver-
mahnung der pfälzischen Kirchen,' ' tear each other's
hair, and the young men study nothing else with the
evangelicals than how best the Lutherans may fight
the Calvinists and the Calvinists the Lutherans. This,
God have mercy on us ! makes up the whole of the
theology of the evangelicals in our days.' [3]

---

[1] *Gesch. der Literatur*, ii. 2, 597 f.
[2] Schanz, iii. 292 f.   See our remarks, vol. x. p. 62.
[3] Goldast, *Politische Reichshändel*, p. 902.

CHAPTER VIII

THEOLOGY AND PHILOSOPHY OF THE CATHOLICS

THE history of Catholic theology during the period of the Church schism falls into two epochs, separated from each other by the Council of Trent.

The theologians of the first period were compelled, in the nature of things, to make it their first business to secure for the traditional articles of the faith the firm support of unimpeachable proofs. The assertions of the innovators on the saving grace of faith alone, and on universal priesthood, together with their attacks on the Church doctrines of justification and grace, transubstantiation, indulgence, the Pope's primacy, purgatory, the veneration of saints, and so forth, made it necessary that these questions should be more deeply investigated, and that the disputed points should be established on a positive theological basis derived from the immediate sources of revelation. In the fulfilment of this task, fortunately for scholasticism in Germany which had in part degenerated into mere dialectics, the speculative theories of the earlier school-men, modified, of course, by the conditions of the time, were largely borrowed from.[1]

[1] Besides the remarkable statements of Usingen in Paulus (Usingen, p. 20), see also the corresponding remarks of Eck, who in the course of his own development clearly reflects both the condition of theology at the beginning of the century, and its revolutionised state after the split

It was part of the conditions of this period that the defenders of the old faith, in contradistinction to the earlier method of procedure, turned aside from the works handed down by commentators, and produced original, independent, theological writings.[1] If in this sense the theology of that period had undeniably a positive character, it was nevertheless chiefly polemico-apologetical ; controversial writings were its preponderating feature ; the other branches of theological learning were as much in the background as was philosophy. Even Erasmus complained that nobody read or bought anything but publications for or against Luther. The great spiritual conflict engaged all attention and energy.

It is a prejudice still widely prevalent that the incessant attacks of the religious innovators were only met by the Catholics with half measures of resistance. Exactly the opposite is the truth. The number of meritorious scholars, who in those difficult times held high the Catholic banner, is very considerable. Even leaving out of account the Dutch [2] representatives who in a certain sense belong to Germany, we can point

in the Church. ' God,' says Eck, ' has permitted these heresies to grow up in order to rouse the theologians from indolence, and from wasting their time in unprofitable controversial questions, and from talking of nothing else in theological books than relativities, formalities, universals, distinction of different phases in the same moment, and other theological chaff. So much water of philosophy, not to say sophistry, has been poured by the theologians into the wine of theology, that the latter has lost its original flavour by admixture of senseless and thorny questions.' *De primatu*, i. 1 ; see also *Omnia opera Schatzgeri*, Ingolst. 1543, fol. 7ᵇ.

[1] See Heinrich, *Dogmatische Theologie*, i. 111, and Linsenmann in the *Tübinger Theol. Quartalschr.* 1866, p. 572.

[2] See concerning these F. J. Holzwarth, *Abfall der Niederlande*, i. Schaffhausen, 1865–1872, 115 ff., and Werner, *Gesch. der apolog. und polem. Literatur*, v. 270 ff.

to at least two hundred writers [1] both among the secular and the regular clergy, and even among the laity—
and this solely during the period down to the conclusion of the Council of Trent—who in German-speaking
districts, and under the most unfavourable conditions
imaginable, valiantly and fearlessly carried on the defence of the old faith and of the existing organisations
of Church and society.[2]   The life and the work of
most of these men is little known, their services to
the Church, to learning, and to language are very inade-
quately prized ; their names and memories indeed have

---

[1] Enough here to mention the following names : the jurist, John
Bossinger (author of the following pamphlet : *Ist denn keine Salbe mehr
in Gilead, und will S. Sebald nicht mehr helfen ?* Mainz, 1549 ; see Wetzer
und Welte's *Kirchenlexikon*, ii[2]. 1130) ; the jurist, Conrad Braun (see below,
p. 297) ; the industrious Adam Walasser, a native of Ulm (cf. *Katholik*,
1895, ii. 453–467) ; the Alsatian school-man, Jerome Gebweiler (Paulus,
Kathol. Schriftsteller, p. 551) ; Nicholas Mameranus (see Rübsam in the
Historisches Jahrbuch, x. 525 f.) ; Kaspar Querhamer, president of the
council at Hall († 1557 ; cf. *Histor.-polit. Blätter*, cxii. 22–37) ; the states-
man, Christoph von Schwarzenburg († 1538 ; see *ibid.* cxi. 10–33 ; cxii.
130 ff.) ; the humanist and school-man, Matthias Bredenbach (cf. the
interesting treatise of R. Heinrichs, Frankfort, 1890) ; and *Katholik*,
1893, i. 345 ff. ; see also above, p. 145) ; John Albert von Wimpfen,
Wolfgang Hermann, John Atrocianus, Roth von Schreckenstein (cf.
Paulus, *Kathol. Schriftsteller*, s.v.) ; as well as the Swiss writers, Compar
Valentin and Joachim Grüdt (*ibid. Nachtrag*, pp. 214, 215–216).   For
Compar see also, now, Kluser, *Der Landschreiber Valentin Compar von
Uri und sein Streit mit Zwingli*, Altdorf, 1894.   It is noteworthy that a
Leipzig shoemaker named Conrad Bockshirn was the author of an anti-
Lutheran pamphlet : *Eine krefftige Erweisung des freyen willens, und
annennung bey Gott der christlichen guten Werk*, Leipzig, 1534.   A copy
of this rare treatise is in the Royal Library at Berlin.

[2] See Falk, *Corp. Catholic.* p. 450 ff. and Paulus, *Kathol. Schriftsteller*,
p. 544 ff.   Besides these two valuable compilations I also used * Meuser,
Die antireformatorischen Schriftsteller des 16. *Jahrhunderts*, 2 vols. MS.
Germ. fol. 977 u. 978 *der kgl. Bibliothek zu Berlin.*   This, too, should be the
place for reference to the important contributions supplied by Friedensburg
to the *Zeitschr. für Kirchengesch.* vol. xvi. from the correspondence of the
Catholic scholars of Germany in the Reformation period.

had to suffer largely, though without any grounds, from the hatred and odium with which they have been pursued by their enemies.[1] It is only the most recent investigations which have at all cleared up matters in this respect.

Altogether it is evident that ' the old Catholic culture did not leave Luther's opponents without counsel and without weapons against all those new assertions so entirely contradictory to the spirit of theology, and that the very dogmas through which the Council of Trent refuted the heresies had, for the most part, been already clearly and sharply stated by the theologians at the beginning of the Reformation.' [2]

It is difficult in the great spiritual campaign, to decide where the palm belongs, to the secular or the monastic clergy ; so much, however, is certain, that the ' Orders ' produced more literary champions than is generally supposed. Even the Augustinian Eremites, to whom Luther belonged, and from out whose midst numbers of disorderly monks swelled the ranks of the innovators, can point to scholars of their own who entered the list zealously in defence of the old faith. Besides the Munich prior Wolfgang Cäppelmair, all too early snatched away by death in 1546, the provincial of the Rheno-Suabian province, Conrad Treger († 1542), and the Würzburg prior Siegfried († 1562),[3] Bartholomew Usingen and John Hoffmeister are especially deserving of notice.

[1] See Wedewer, *Dietenberger*, p. 2.
[2] Otto, *Cochlaeus*, p. 132 ; cf. Paulus, *Hoffmeister*, p. 261.
[3] See concerning the above-named Paulus, *Hoffmeister*, pp. 136 f., 145 f., and *Kathol. Schriftsteller*, pp. 549, 559, 561, as also *Katholik*, 1899, i. 419–447, 511–534 for Conrad Treger. For Cäppelmair see Reinhard-stöttner, *Forschungen*, ii. 75 f.

Bartholomew Arnoldi von Usingen, Luther's preceptor and for many years professor of philosophy at the University of Erfurt, resolved, when already advanced in years, to enter the Augustinian Order, ' in order to be able to serve God better.' Luther's attempts to win over the old professor to his side failed : Usingen remained unmoved and, under the most difficult circumstances, true to the old Church. For this he fell a victim to the hardest calumniations. After he had taken up the office of cathedral preacher at Erfurt in 1522, he defended with indefatigable ardour the doctrines attacked by the innovators. And now the persecution of this courageous defender of the old faith increased and multiplied ; often, on his way home from preaching, Usingen was pelted with mud and stones ; for a time he was in danger of life from the infuriated mob. But he did not waver ; on the contrary, he entered the lists for the old Church with pen and paper. With vigour and activity astounding in an old man of sixty, he published in a short time a whole series of polemical writings ; he was never in doubt as to answers to a single one of his assailants.

In these controversial writings of the Erfurt period Usingen had already expounded the doctrine of justification with great distinctness ; soon after his banishment from the above-named town he produced a special treatise on this important subject. From a theological point of view his expositions are of high interest ; the doctrine of justification was set forth by him in the same spirit and the same words as later on by the Council of Trent.

For the last years of his life Usingen found a place of refuge at Würzburg, where he laboured with blessed results both as inspector of convents and as preacher. In spite of his advanced age he even then produced a series of apologetic writings on purgatory, the veneration of saints, and the erroneous doctrines of the Anabaptists. In 1530 he took part in the Augsburg Diet, and in the following year criticised Melanchthon's Apology of the Augsburg Confession. On September 9, 1532, God called the brave combatant to Himself.[1]

Still more important was the work done by John Hoffmeister.

Born at Oberndorf on the Neckar, three leagues from Rottweil, he came early to Colmar, where he joined the Augustinian Order, and then went to Mayence and Freiburg for his further education. He next received ordination as a priest, and in 1533 became prior of the Augustinian Convent at Colmar, where he worked under the most difficult circumstances. Nine years later came the appointment of this distinguished monk to be provincial of Rheinland-Schwaben, and in 1546 his nomination by the general of the Order, Seripando, to the vicar-generalship over the whole of Germany. As such he endeavoured to carry out in his province the reform of the Order which had been decided on at the General Council at Rome in 1539. In 1545 Hoffmeister shone at the Diet of Worms and in 1546 at the Religious Conference at Ratisbon, both as collocutor and as pulpit orator. King Ferdinand I was his most zealous listener. At Whitsuntide 1547

---

[1] Cf. Paulus, *Der Augustiner Barthol. Arnoldi von Usingen*, pp. 1 ff., 15 ff., 27 ff., 42 ff., 105 ff. ; cf. *Polemica de ss. eucharistiae sacramento inter Bartholomaeum Arnoldi de Usingen O.E.S.A. eiusque Olim in universitate Erphurdiana discipulum Martinum Lutherum anno* 1530 manuscript. ' *De sacramentis ecclesiae* ' *extracta ac introductione variisque commentariis necnon imagine illustrata a Dominico Fr. X. P. Duijustee*, Herbip. 1903.

Hoffmeister also held another provincial chapter at Hagenau ; on his return from there he was attacked by a malignant fever, of which he died at Günzburg on August 21, 1547, when barely thirty-eight years old. He was deeply mourned by all friends of true reform. It is very remarkable that in the space of his comparatively short life he found time, in addition to his labours as member of an Order and as preacher, to produce more than twenty theological works.

His first literary achievement is the collection of dialogues belonging to the year 1538. In these he discusses nearly all the disputed doctrines of the time, and shows how in most of the points the innovators were not only at variance with but often even sharply opposed to each other, and not seldom in their writings defended the Catholic faith. Soon after the publication of the Latin dialogues, Hoffmeister wrote a pamphlet in German on the Council and the Smalcaldian Articles. which was addressed to the common people. While the diligent Augustinian monk in his other writings was on the whole very moderate, in this popular treatise he indulged in more vehement language. Anyhow he could say, like another Catholic protagonist (Dietenberger) : ' Since Luther has been so abusive, I have paid him back in his own coin.' In the following period Hoffmeister edited a work of his friend Anhauser on the Holy Sacrifice of the Mass, and treated the same subject in a pamphlet which shows not only sincere piety, but also thorough theological knowledge. The peace-making efforts of Charles V incited him to publish a work on the Augsburg Confession, in which he aimed at showing on what basis a union of the separated religious parties might be effected. The different articles of the creed above-mentioned are carefully tested and examined to see how far they accord with or differ from the old Church doctrines. In this, as in his other treatises, Hoffmeister shows great erudition; not only the works of the Fathers of the Church and the schoolmen, but also the principal writings of the innovators and the Catholic counter-writings, are familiar to him. Again and again in these pages he shows up the contradictions which exist between the Augsburg Confession and other new-religionist writings. Even though the learned Augustinian at that time indulged in the deceptive hope of an understanding between Protestants and Catholics, he kept far aloof in his theological explanations from all double meanings and equivocations, such as the men of the middle course often had recourse to. 'His dogmatic standpoint is strictly Catholic; only on the basis of Catholic dogmas (with the abolition of course of many abuses) could the lost unity, in his opinion, be restored.' At the end of his work he says : ' If the reader thinks that I have stated the matter correctly, then let him with me return heartfelt thanks to God the Lord, the distributor of all good ; if not, then let him pray God for forgiveness for me, who have always sought the welfare of the Church, to which I would have this book dedicated. To err is human; if anyone therefore points out any error to me, I shall be thankful for the service he has rendered. I have done my best, and what I have received from the free bounty of the Lord, I have joyfully given for the welfare of his Bride. If any ungracious word has escaped towards anybody, may I be forgiven for it ; it is not given to everybody always to control his feelings. We see the unity of the Church ;

we love the Church, to the Church we have wholly
surrendered ourselves. May she be ever preserved for
us in prosperity and continue fruitful in the Holy Ghost
through her eternal Bridegroom Jesus Christ, to whom
be glory and honour for ever and ever.' [1]

No less indefatigable than Hoffmeister in the defence of the Catholic cause was Augustine Marius.
A member at first of the Order of Canons Regular
at Ulm, he entered in 1511 the University of Vienna,
where in 1520 he obtained the degree of doctor of
Theology. In the following year he became cathedral
preacher at Ratisbon, and in 1522 he was nominated
by the Freising Bishop Philip to be his coadjutor.
Marius fulfilled this office 'with exemplary diligence
and apostolic zeal, proclaimed the Word of God with
holy enthusiasm, and opposed the innovations by
word and pen with ardour and decision, so that through
his zeal and his watchfulness the diocese of Freising
remained safe from the dangers of erroneous teaching
and heresy.' With equal indefatigableness, if not with
the same results, Marius defended the doctrines of the
old Church at Basle, where he migrated in 1526. After
the Catholic religion had been violently suppressed in
that town, the dauntless man took up the office of

[1] Paulus, *Hoffmeister*, pp. 72 f., 89 f., 109 f., 110 f.   Here (p. 280 ff.)
it is convincingly shown, as opposed to the opinion of A. v. Druffel, that
Hoffmeister was no follower of the compromising, half Lutheran ' Justi-
ficationists.'   The utterly unhistorical manner in which G. Bossert (*Joh.
Hoffmeister*, Barmen, 1892) tries to stamp Hoffmeister as an immoral
person and makes him die in a state of despair, is triumphantly refuted
by Paulus in the *Histor.-polit. Blätter*, cxi. (1893) 589 f.   See also Paulus,
Luthers Lebensende (*Erläut. u. Ergänz. zu Janssens Gesch. des deutschen
Volkes*, edited by L. Pastor, Freiburg, 1898, i. 1), p. 9 ff., where Bossert
is refuted.   About Hoffmeister's writings see also Falk, *Bibelstudien*,
Mayence, 1901, p. 193 f.

cathedral preacher and coadjutor bishop at Würzburg, from which place he attended the Augsburg Diet and took part in the refutation of the Augsburg Confession. Marius carried on the laborious work of a coadjutor bishop till his death on November 25, 1543. In the second period of his life, also, he found time for the production of numerous writings dealing with the Church doctrines of the most holy Sacrament of the Altar and of the predestination of mankind. In earlier years Marius had written a Defence of the Holy Sacrifice of the Mass and a refutation of the tenets of the Anabaptists. Besides these there is mention of works by him on the invocation of the saints and on free will.[1]

To the Canons Regular of St. Augustine belonged also Kilian Leib, prior of the Abbey of Rebdorf, near Eichstätt (†1553). Active also as an historian,[2] this man not only opposed the Lutheran innovation in his sermons, but also wrote several pamphlets on celibacy and on the causes of heresy.[3]

From the Order of Carmelites we have as a polemical author, besides Alexander Candidus (Blanckardt, †1555 as Dean of the Cologne Theological Faculty),[4] the highly meritorious Eberhard Billick, born about 1500 at Cologne, died in 1557. Billick early devoted himself to study, entered the Carmelite Order, and soon

---

[1] Fuller details occur in Renninger, ' Die Weihbischöfe von Würzburg ' in the *Archiv für Unter-Franken*, xviii., Würzburg, 1865, iii. 158 ; cf. Wiedermann, *Eck*, pp. 412–417.

[2] See present work, vol. xiii. p. 440.

[3] Suttner, *Bibl. Eystett.* Eichstätt, 1866, p. 10 ff. ; Werner, iv. 49, 182 f. ; Hefele-Hergenröther, *Konziliengesch.* ix. 844 ; Wetzer und Welte's *Kirchenlexikon*, vii[2]. 1643 f. Unprinted writings of K. Leib are mentioned by * Meuser (see above, p. 240 n. 2).

[4] Hartzheim, p. 14. Postina, *Billick, passim.*

became a chief pillar of the Latin Church in the Lower Rhine district. That with all his sincere loyalty to the old Church he did not shut his eyes to the prevalent abuses in it is shown by his synodial speech in 1526. As prior of the convent and professor of the University of Cologne Billick, during his whole life, threw the full weight of his position and his learning into the scale whenever it was a question of defending the faith of his fathers. He also took a personal part in other important transactions. In 1540 he attended the religious conference at Worms. Two years later he was chosen at Aix-la-Chapelle to be provincial of the Dutch Carmelite province. After the Elector Hermann, Archbishop of Cologne, had openly declared his leaning towards the new doctrines, Billick was one of the first and most eager opponents of the attempt to Protestantise the archbishopric of Cologne. His activity during this decisive period was quite extraordinary. In the name of the delegates of the secondary clergy and of the University he drew up a memorandum against the appointment of Bucer, in which he proved himself a skilful and acute controversialist. This piece of writing is undoubtedly composed in the violent tone customary at that time in controversy ; but it shows up the weaknesses of the Bucerian system and its contradictions to the Gospel, in a masterly way. At the end of March, 1545, Billick published another fierce pamphlet against the Protestantism which was invading Cologne. But it was not only as an author that Billick was active in the defence of the old Faith ; he worked also for the cause through sermons, exhortations and counsels. The conversion of Thauer was due mainly to his instrumentality. Billick was also kept busily employed on missions to the Emperor and to different diets in the same interest. In 1546 he took part in the second religious conference at Ratisbon. At Cologne, where he encouraged the introduction of the Jesuits, Billick occupied till his death an important position. He was moreover indefatigably active in the service of his own convent; in spite of the storminess of the times he managed that the cloisters of the same should be adorned with costly pictures. His labours were recognised by the highest ecclesiastical authorities; the Archbishop of Cologne destined him for his auxiliary bishop and vicar-general in pontificalibus, and Pope Paul IV bestowed on him the title of Bishop of Cyrene. But the indefatigable man died before his consecration in 1557.[1]

Several of the Cistercians laboured also zealously in defence of the Catholic cause. Of such were the abbots Paul Amnicola (Bachmann, †1535 at the convent of Zell near Meissen) and Wolfgang Mayer at Alderspach in Bavaria.[2] The first of these belongs to the earliest combatants against Luther, and in his sharply worded, often needlessly coarse writings, frequently made use of the German language; Peter Blomevenna (†at Cologne in 1536), on the contrary,

[1] See Meuser in *Dieringer's Zeitschr. für Kathol. Theologie*, ii. (1884), 62–67, and my article in Wetzer and Welte's *Kirchenlexikon*, ii³. 836 ff. For the Cologne Carmelite, Burkhard Billick, whose works are not printed, see Hartzheim, p. 40, A. Postina, *Der Karmelit Eberhard Billick* (*Erläut. u. Ergänz. zu Janssens Geschichte des deutschen Volkes*, published by L. Pastor, Freiburg, 1901).

[2] Floss in Wetzer and Welte's *Kirchenlexikon*, i². 1829 f. Paulus, *Kathol. Schriftsteller*, p. 555 ; Werner, *Gesch. der apolog. und polem. Literatur*, iv. 49 ; Steph. Wiest, *De Wolfgango Mario . . . Programma historico-theologicum*, Ingolstadii, 1788 f. Paulus, 'Wolfgang Mayer' in the *Histor. Jahrbuch*, xv. 575 to 588.

wrote in Latin, but his works were promptly translated
into German. Like Blomevenna, John Justus Lands-
berger also belonged to the Carthusian Order. This
man, who died at Cologne in 1539 in the fame of holiness,
was chiefly active as an ascetic writer, but he was also
author of some popular books in defence of the Church,
such as the dialogue between a Lutheran soldier and a
monk on cloister life.[1]

A band of stalwart fighters for the Catholic cause
was supplied by the Order of St. Benedict, Henry
von Schleinitz, Florian Trefler von Benediktbeuren,
Wolfgang Sedel, John Chrysostomi Hirschbeck zu
Scheyern and Nicholas Buchner, abbot of Zwiefalten.[2]
The learned Nicholas Ellenbog (†1543 at Ottobeuren)
belongs also to this group; his controversial writings,
sometimes very violent, in defence of the monastic life,
were never printed, nor were his other works on the
veneration of the saints, the most holy Sacrament of
the altar, and the invocation of souls in purgatory.
Ellenbog was also the author of a very comprehensive
exposition of the Passion of Christ as well as of explanations of some of the Psalms and of the Rule of
St. Benedict.[3]

The activity of the above-named monks was far

---

[1] Kessel in Wetzer and Welte's *Kirchenlexikon*, ii². 921–923 ; vi.
1699–1700 ; for Blomevenna see also the present work, vol. i. p. 100.

[2] Further literature concerning the above named will be found in
Paulus, *Kathol. Schriftsteller*, p. 555. See also our remarks, vol. ix. p. 335,
note 5, and Kobolt, pp. 626 f., 697 f. For W. Sedel see Paulus in the
Histor.-Blätter, cxiii. 165 ff. ; P. Lindner, *Die Äbte und Mönche der Benedik-
tiner Abtei Tegernsee*, i. Munich, 1897, 96 ff. ; Fr. Roth in the *Beiträge zur
deutschen Kirchengesch.* vi. (1901) 97 ff. and Riezler, vi. 367.

[3] See L. Geiger in the *Österreich. Vierteljahrschrift für kathol. Theol.*
1870, pp. 45–112, 181–208 ; 1871, pp. 443–459, a very good and exhaustive work. See also the present work, vol. i. p. 105.

exceeded by the disciples of St. Francis, who, next to
the Dominicans, were the chief combatants against the
religious innovations in the first days of the Church
split ; everywhere, in Bavaria, in Franconia and in the
Palatinate, in the Rhinelands, in Alsatia, in the Breisgau
and in Suabia they stood in the vanguard of the Catholic
champions. With true insight Luther recognised in
them his most serious opponents : accordingly he
ordered his followers to direct their weapons first and
foremost at them.[1] In 1520 the Franciscan, Augustine
von Alfeld, had already written a special treatise defending the divine right of the Primacy against the
attacks of Luther. The latter first made no answer to
the ' Leipzig ox,' but changed his mind afterwards and
produced the pamphlet, ' Von dem Bapsthum zu Rom
wider den hochberühmten Romanisten zu Leipzig.'
Alfeld answered in another pamphlet, which appeared
also in 1520, and in which he complained of Luther for
calling him a ' donkey, ox, monkey, frog, heretic, liar,
hog, and for loading him with all sorts of slander and
abuse.' [2] Other Franciscans also began tolerably early
to write against Luther, as for instance, Bernhard von
Jüterbogk, and later on Kaspar Meckenlör, Kaspar
Sager and Jacob Schwederich.[3] It was a Franciscan,
Nicholas Ferber, named Herborn, after his birthplace,
who valiantly opposed the powerful Landgrave Philip

---

[1] Paulus, *Schatzgeyer*, p. 139 ; see Lemmens, *Niedersächsische Franciskaner Klöster im Mittelalter*, Hildsheim, 1896, p. 41 f.

[2] Floss in Wetzer und Welte's *Kirchenlexikon*, i². 1682 f., and especially
L. Lemmens, *Peter Augustin von Alfeld* († 1532) *ein Franciskaner aus den
ersten Jahren der Glaubensspaltung (Erläut. und Ergänz. zu Janssens
Gesch. des deutschen Volkes*, published by L. Pastor, Freiburg, 1898), i. 4.

[3] Paulus, *Kathol. Schriftsteller*, pp. 545, 550, 558–559, and Appendix,
218.   Falk, *Corp. Cath.* p. 461.   See also Woker, p. 37 f.

in Hesse. Driven out of his native place Herborn betook himself to the archdiocese of Cologne, became guardian at Brühl, cathedral preacher at Cologne, and finally commissary general of his Order; as such he died in 1535. He was zealously active as a writer. His principal work is the ' Handbuch gegen die neuen Irrlehren.' [1] Another Franciscan distinguished as a defender of the Catholic cause is Henry Helmesius of Halberstadt. He had entered the Order in the province of Cologne, and had been for a long time a much-applauded cathedral preacher in the archiepiscopal metropolis. The great persecution of the Saxon Franciscans drove this ardent enthusiast for the Church back to his home, where he continued to work energetically under the most difficult circumstances. He was twice elected provincial and he also came forward against Luther with his pen. His strongly polemical writings show him to have been well versed in the Holy Scripture. In vehement language Helmesius complains of the consequences of the new doctrines. Luther, he says, has profaned and despoiled the Church; he has promised freedom, but he has made the yoke of the poor man heavier, and doubled his bondage. Instead of truth he has given us error; instead of peace, disturbances; instead of unity, strife throughout the land. The Lutheran teaching about faith has had the worst results. ' The lords are destitute

---

[1] Besides Wetzer and Welte's *Kirchenlexikon,* iv². 1348 f. see also * Meuser, ii. 36 f. ; Nebe in the *Denkschrift des theol. Seminars zu Herborn,* 1868 ; Krafft, *Aufzeichnungen Bullingers,* Elberfeld, 1870, p. 81 ; *Histor. Jahrbuch,* 1892, p. 194 f. and *Sitzungsberichte der Wiener Akademie,* cviii. 826 f. See also the present work, vol. v. p. 85 ff. and L. Schmitt, *Der Kölner Theologe Nikolaus Stagefyr und der Franziskaner Nikolaus Herborn,* Freiburg, 1896, ii. 464 f. ; 1892, ii. 465 f.

of virtue, yea verily full of transgression ; the rich no longer give alms, on the contrary they rob the poor. The priests are devoid of sanctity, they are lovers of horses and women ; the men are without chaste love, the women without shame, the wives without piety, the young women without modesty. The world is full of anarchy and strife.[1] Another Catholic champion, a contemporary of Helmesius and a member of the same Order, was the Erfurt guardian, Conrad Kling, who alone during the general apostasy, maintained the Catholic worship in its integrity at Erfurt. The writings of this brave man did not appear till after his death in 1556. Chief among these are his theological treatises (' *Loci* communes theologici ') in which he discusses the points of dispute between Catholics and Protestants in relation to Melanchthon's work of the same name.[2]

The Minorite, John Heller, († 1536 at Brühl) fought the Anabaptists. In connexion with him was the provincial of the Cologne province, John von Deventer, a doughty controversialist.[3] The two writers, Franciscus Polygranus and Antonius König-stein, of the Order of St. Francis, also belong by birth and vocation to the Rhenish provinces.[4] Honourable mention is also due to the Franciscan, Ludolf Naaman, of Schleswig.[5]

Comprehensive labours as exegetical writer, con-

[1] Woker, p. 38 ; cf. Wetzer und Welte's *Kirchenlexikon*, v². 1572.

[2] Wetzer und Welte's *Kirchenlexikon*, iii². 552 ; cf. Werner, *Gesch. der apolog. und polem. Literatur*, iv. 48, 57, 234, 251 ; Gaudentius, p. 15 f. and Paulus in the *Katholik*, 1894, i. 146 ff.

[3] Wetzer and Welte's *Kirchenlexikon*, v². 1751 ; vi. 1650. Hartzheim, p. 56.

[4] See Gaudentius, pp. 14–15, 63, 319.

[5] See K. Flebbe, *Ludolf Naaman, der Gründer des Schleswiger Gymnasiums*, Flensburg, 1885, and Paulus in the *Katholik*, 1901, i. 327 f.

troversialist and pulpit orator, were carried on by the Franciscan, John Bihl, a man as greatly distinguished for zeal and courage as for learning and virtue. A native of Suabia, like so many other champions of the Church against the Lutheran innovation, he was sent in 1528 by his superiors to Mayence to fill the post of preacher at the Franciscan Church there. He held this office till 1539 when the cathedral pulpit was assigned to him.

This worthy son of St. Francis did not bear in vain the name of the earnest preacher of repentance, John the Baptist. Like another John for nearly thirty years he made his voice resound in the Metropolis of the Catholic Rhinelands ' admonishing men earnestly to repent, while by his blameless life he set them a good example.' [1]

With all the unyielding firmness of his religious standpoint, Wild was full of gentleness and love of peace. He could not endure the fierce polemics which were then the order of the day. Although he very frequently entered the lists for the disputed articles of faith he never allowed himself to be carried away into passionate attacks on his opponents, still less to slander and vilification.[2] ' In my preaching,' he was able to write in 1550 to the Archbishop of Mayence, ' I have ever striven, as my congregation without doubt will testify, to give to the common men, in the midst of all the disputed points of our holy religion, a well-grounded, Christian and consistent instruction, without abuse or

---

[1] H. Pantaleon, *Deutscher Nation Heldenbuch*, Part 3, Basle, 1578, p. 358.

[2] It is noteworthy that in the numerous writings of this monk Luther is never mentioned.

contempt of any one, and to direct the hearts of my people towards peace, love and unity amongst themselves and towards all others.'

This conciliatory spirit was especially manifested by him on the outbreak of the Smalcaldian war. The sight of the fatherland so piteously rent asunder filled his soul with pain and grief. In consequence of the religious wars, he lamented, ' Germany had become a laughing stock to her neighbours.' ' Each one wants to get a morsel from us '; the Germans are obliged to submit to the most bitter scorn. ' Ha, these are the proud Germans, who help to destroy all countries, to mix themselves up in all wars, but are now reduced to destroying each other. Is it not a pitiful thing that strangers and foreigners should know such things about us and repeat them with mockery ? God have pity on us, God forgive all those who have in any way been the cause that we cannot and will not come to an understanding. I myself have always striven for this end. I would always gladly have helped to peace and unity.' Even now he again exhorts his hearers to pray fervently for peace and unity. He could not himself, he said, encourage war. ' If it was against the Turks that we were to put full strength I would gladly join in singing and blowing the war trumpet and diligently would I exhort to the fight. But I will not bring myself to stir up Christians against Christians, although indeed I see and read, though with great amazement, how some preachers abominably and venomously instigate their congregatious to war, even against their God-given rulers.'

The ' abominable and venomous instigations ' of the then preachers, their ' slandering and abusing,' is more than once most severely condemned by this admirable friar. 'What is more common nowadays,' he says, 'than this dreadful habit of abusing and vilifying which actually goes on between Christians? Nobody is spared, either clergy or laity, either Pope or emperor. People are not even satisfied with emitting venom in that way with their tongues. No! Writers, painters, printers must needs add their help. And this, forsooth, is Christian! Yea verily, none are busier in this way than those who set up for being the best Christians. And in no place does all this go on more energetically than in the pulpit. This, then, is evangelical preaching, to let our people go on unreproved and unpunished in all sorts of wantonness, crime, insolence, disobedience, and to think of nothing but raging and screaming at the absent. To punish sins is the duty of a preacher; slandering and abusing is a disgrace, and fit for none but liars and mountebanks.'

What were the principles by which Wild was guided in his actions is best seen from a memorial speech delivered by him in 1552 on the occasion of Mayence falling a prey to rough soldiery. From fear of the 'princely incendiary,' Albert of Brandenburg-Kulmbach, the whole of the clergy had taken flight. The brave Franciscan alone remained fearlessly at his post, striving persistently to comfort and hearten the terror-stricken people. For some weeks, indeed, he was obliged to give over his beloved pulpit to Lutheran preachers; he succeeded, however, by his manly conduct in inspiring even the wild margrave of Brandenburg with respect and reverence. After the withdrawal of the enemy Wild delivered a splendid address, containing, as it were, the programme of all his preaching.

'What has lately been uttered here,' he said to his numerous crowd of hearers, 'about monks and priests, cowls and shaven heads, will not, I hope, injure my past sermons in your minds, nor make them seem to you less to be trusted. Methinks I can preach Christ and the truth as well in a cowl and with a shaven head as in any other garb. Therefore I have no reason for shame and fear on account of the sermons which I have preached. Although I wear a cowl and have a tonsure my conscience bears me witness, and I know before God I speak the truth, that I have not, knowingly or with intention, taught anything contrary to Scripture. I have at all times delighted to search out the Scriptures and their true meaning, and I shall continue so to do. God's grace and His mercy, manifested to us through Christ, I have ever preached, and I shall do so still. The Word of God and the Gospel of Christ I have proclaimed, but in such a way that no man can make it a cloak for his wickedness; I shall go on doing so, for thus I am taught by St. Peter and St. Paul. I have always pointed to faith in Christ as the anchor of hope; not, however, to an idle faith, but to a true, living, powerful and active faith, which works through love; yea verily, in addition to faith I have also taught you the fear of God, and the love and all that belongs to a Christian life; I shall continue to do so, for thus have Peter and Paul and Christ instructed me. All my sermons have been aimed at the improvement of life; they will be so still. Ranting in the pulpit I have never been capable of, nor am inclined to it now.

' I know not either of what use it is, it does not seem to me much of an art. Wherever Scripture has not corresponded with our preaching and living, there I have dealt out punishment, but with discretion and on both sides, for I see and find imperfections on both sides ; I shall continue the same system. Such has been hitherto my mode of teaching ; I hope nobody will find fault with it, for I do not know how to alter it. I have felt obliged to speak thus at length at this fresh epoch in my preaching, in order that you may see that everything which monks and priests preach is not after all quite so bad as some people make out. Let such people come across a poor modest country priest, or a poor insignificant monk hidden away in his monastery ; in the pride of their ranting abilities they at once offer advice as to the right way of preaching the Gospel. For I call no other preaching right preaching than that which aims at improvement.'

Only a short period of further usefulness was, alas, to be granted to the distinguished theologian. The indefatigable monk, who did not yet number sixty years, had grown old before his time through all the great strains on his energies. He died on September 8, 1554.[1]

When Protestantism began also to spread from Saxony into Silesia, the Schweidnitz Minorite, Michael Hildebrant, stood out against it. Since the middle of the thirties he had been defending the old Church against the preachers of heresy in a series of pamphlets

---

[1] See besides the literature summarised by Falk (*Corp. Cath.* pp. 454-455) the work by N. Paulus, *Joh. Wild, ein Mainzer Domprediger des* 16. *Jahrhunderts*, which appeared in 1893 as the third number of the *Verein der Görres-Gesellschaft* for 1893. Here, too, in the Appendix 2 are fuller details about Wild's writings in the Index of prohibited works. Of Wild's well-nigh innumerable sermons Jocham published a yearly series (2 vols., Ratisbon, 1841-1842). Concerning Wild see also Falk, *Bibelstudien*, pp. 185 ff., 196 ff.

with as much zeal as skill.[1]   The chapter of the Order
of the Austrian Franciscan province had already,
in 1522, appointed no fewer than thirty controversial
preachers to refute the Lutheran heresies publicly, and
to explain and defend the disputed points of the faith.
Amongst the numbers who in the above-named province fought by word and by writing against the innovations the following stand out prominently : Father
Anselm of Vienna, Father Medardus of Kirchen, Father
Ambrose of Rohrbach, Father Thomas of Salzburg,
Father Francis of Schwaz, Father George of Amberg,
Father Michael of Bruneck, Father Christopher of
Baden, Father Dionysius of Rain, Father John Camers,
and many others.[2]   Bavaria also has a goodly
number of authors to show belonging to this same
province of the Order : the Bamberger Franciscan of
the stricter observance, John Link and Wolfgang
Schmilkhofer, whose polemical treatises have unfortunately never been printed, John Albert (cathedral
preacher and guardian at Ratisbon), John Wiezler
(† 1554 at Munich) [3] and, most important of all, Kaspar
Schatzgeyer (born 1463 at Landshut, † 1527 at Munich).

Schatzgeyer began his higher studies at Ingolstadt,
entered the Franciscan Order at Landshut, and became
later guardian at Munich, Ingolstadt and Nuremberg, and was repeatedly elected provincial.   Mild in

---

[1] It is to Soffner's credit to have revived the memory of this almost
entirely forgotten champion in his book, *Der Minorit Fr. M. Hillebrant*,
Breslau, 1885.   Soffner has also given an account of another distinguished
defender of the old church in Silesia : *Seb. Schlemmer, Domherr und
Domprediger in Breslau*, Breslau, 1888.

[2] Gaudentius, p. 19 f.   Aschbach, *Universität Wien*, ii. 175 ff. ; iii. 11.

[3] Paulus, *Kathol. Schriftsteller*, pp. 545, 555, 561–562.   The polemical
tracts of Link are preserved in the Cod. germ. 4364 of the Court library
at Munich.   Concerning Wiezler see Paulus in the *Katholik*, 1894, i. 40 ff.

character he strove at the commencement of the schism
to work for conciliatory measures, but soon realised the
hopelessness of such efforts. With quite extraordinary
ardour he then entered the lists for the old faith and
wielded his pen indefatigably in its defence, in spite
of the overwhelming business connected with his
Order. In the course of a few years he issued more
than twenty publications, directed especially against
Luther, Osiander and John von Schwarzenberg. The
last is the object of attack in his pamphlet entitled
' Fürhaltung 30 Artikel, so in gegenwärtigen Ver-
wirrung auf die Bahn gebracht und durch einen neuen
Beschwörer der alten Schlange gerechtfertigt werden,'
a work distinguished by its popular tone. Schatzgeyer
did not shut his eyes to the many abuses in Church life
at that period, but he knew well how to distinguish
between reformation and revolution.[1]

Among the Franciscans of the South German
province who shared with Schatzgeyer the pen and
paper fight against the religious innovations, special
notice is due to the learned and eloquent Daniel
Agricola and to John Findling. The latter, styled also
Apobolymaeus, made it his business, both by writing
and preaching, to warn the people against the new
errors of doctrine. In a German tract entitled ' An-
zaigung zwayer falschen Zungen des Luthers,' Findling deals with the attitude of the Wittenbergers
towards the Peasant War ; in a popular, often very

---

[1] See * Meuser, ii. 421 f. ; von Druffel in the *Sitzungsberichte der Münchener Akademie*, 1890, ii. 397 ff., and on the other hand *Passauer Monats-
schrift*, 1893, p. 681 ff. ; Werner, *Gesch. der apolog. und polem. Literatur*, iv.
48, 133, 142, 168; *Histor.-polit. Blätter*, lxxix. 201 f., and especially the
valuable monograph of N. Paulus, Freiburg, 1898.

coarse manner, he shows how Luther first stirred up
the peasants to rebellion, in order afterwards to condemn them mercilessly. In other writings Findling
also shows up forcefully and minutely the countless
contradictions of which Luther was guilty.[1]

A man better known than all who have been
mentioned is Thomas Murner, one of the most inveterate
combatants both against Luther and against Zwingli.
So much has already been said by us of this author,
who was as prolific as he was a powerful writer, and
who handled the German language with masterly skill,[2]
that a brief mention is all that is necessary here.

More numerous perhaps, quite as admirable at any
rate, were the Catholic champions belonging to the
Order of St. Dominic.[3] Tetzel's coming forward
against Luther is as it were a typical example. Here,
too, the Rhenish Order distinguished itself before all
others. In Cologne alone seven Dominicans became
valiant fighters for the old faith, which they defended in
their writings, with blessed results. These seven were
James von Hochstraten (†1527), Conrad Cöllin (†1536),
Bernhard von Luxemburg (†1535), John Pesselius,
Tilmann Smeling, John Host and John Slotanus.
Hochstraten produced no fewer than six works against
the religious innovators ; a comparison of the teaching
of Luther with that of St. Augustine, a defence of the
Catholic veneration of Saints, a treatise on purgatory,
and three pamphlets against the Lutheran doctrine of

---

[1] Paulus, *Schatzgeyer*, pp. 137–139.

[2] See our remarks, vol. iii. p. 147 ff. ; vol. iv. p. 149 ff. ; vol. v. p. 133 ;
vol. xi. pp. 331–345 ; vol. xii. p. 59 ff. ; see also Eubel, p. 68 ff.

[3] See Paulus, *Die deutschen Dominicaner im Kampfe gegen Luther*
(1518–1563), *Erläut. und Ergänz. zu Janssens Geschichte des deutschen
Volkes*, published by L. Pastor, iv. 1 and 2, Freiburg, 1903.

justification. Slotanus wrote especially against the doctrines of the Anabaptists.[1]   John Host came from the duchy of Berg,[2] Matthias Sittardus from Aix-la-Chapelle,[3] and William Hammer from Neuss.   .

Of the life of Hammer little is known. He studied at Cologne, worked at Ulm, later at Colmar, and died at an advanced age in the convent of Gotteszell, near Schwäbisch-Gmünd. Hammer was still alive in 1554, when his ' Kommentare zu Genesis ' was published. This is a thoroughly unique work. The text is almost exclusively explained by passages from the old classical authors ; here and there, with apposite mention of individual religious teachers, he attacks the innovators with great decision.[4]

South Germany was the sphere of John Fabri. Born at Heilbronn in Württemberg, in 1504, he joined the Preaching Order in 1520. To what persecutions a Catholic priest was exposed at that time he was soon to experience. At Augsburg the new-religionist magistrate

---

[1] Besides Wetzer and Welte's *Kirchenlexikon*, ii². 433 ; vi². 1158, see especially Quétif, ii. 71, 130, 135 f., 175 f. ; Werner, *Gesch. der apolog. und polem. Literatur*, iv. 46, 120 f., 212 ; Lämmer, *Vortrident. Theologie*, p. 17 f., and Weiss in the *Histor.-polit. Blätter*, lxxix. 196.   Concerning Cöllin see the present work, vol. iii. pp. 54–56, and the *Innsbrucker Zeitschr. für katholische Theologie*, 1896, p. 47 f. ; concerning Hochstraten see our remarks, vol. iii. pp. 54 f., 56 f. ; see also Cremans, *De J. Hochstrati vita et scriptis*, Bonnae, 1869, * Meuser, ii. 55 ff., and Paulus in the *Katholik*, 1897, ii. 160 ff. and 1902, i. 22 f.   Concerning Bernh. v. Luxemburg, see Paulus, *ibid.* 1897, ii. 166 ff. ; Joh. Pesselius, *ibid.* 1896 ; ii. 475 ff. ; Tilmann Smeling, *ibid.* 1897 ; ii. 237 f. ; Joh. Slotanus, *ibid.* 238 ff. ; Paulus, *Deutsche Dominikaner, passim.*

[2] J. Host von Romberg, see Paulus in the *Katholik*, 1895, ii. 481 ff. ; 1896, i. 473 f. ; 1897, i. 188 ff. ; 1901, ii. 187 ff.

[3] Quétif, ii. 88, 215 ; Lammertz in Dieringer's *Kathol. Zeitschr. für Wissenschaft und Kunst*, Jahrg. 2 (1845), ii. 306–321, and Paulus in the *Histor.-polit. Blätter*, cxvi. 237 f., 329 f.   Four still unprinted sermons of Sittardus preached at Innsbruck, 1563, are in the Munich *Cod. germ.* p. 943.

[4] Paulus in the *Histor.-polit. Blätter*, cviii. 428 ff. ; Paulus, *Deutsche Dominikaner*, p. 181 ff.

forbade him to preach ; at Wimpfen his life was actually
in danger. In 1540 he was at Colmar as preacher,
later on at Freiburg in the Breisgau, Schlettstadt and
Augsburg, where his labours had great results. Almost all
his writings are in the German language, as, for instance,
his Catechism, his book of Confession and a Prayer-book.
The treatise ' Ob die Heilige Schrift zum Schaden der
Menschen gebraucht werden kann ' (' Whether the Holy
Scriptures can be used to the injury of Mankind ') was
the outcome of his sermons. The reopening of the
Council of Trent in 1551 gave rise to a short pamphlet
written for the occasion. Other works of his were
directed against the Anabaptists ; the question of the
primacy he discussed in a small popular treatise in
which he enumerates the successive popes and em-
perors. In Latin writings he stood up for the presence
of Peter at Rome, and for the Catholic doctrine of
faith. Through a work published in German, ' Der
rechte Weg, den der Gläubige wandeln soll, damit er selig
werde ' (' The right Way in which a Believer should walk
in order to be saved '), he became entangled in a controversy with Flacius Illyricus, from which he came out
victorious. His comprehensive work on the Holy Sacrifice of the Mass, dedicated to King Ferdinand, had a
very wide circulation. Connected with this work was
an exposition of the prophet Joel, an admonition,
' An das edle Bayernland wider das Lästerbuch eines
Sektenmeisters,' and defence of his work on the Holy
Mass, directed against Flacius Illyricus. A further
work was cut short by his death. In the prime of
manhood the valiant champion was carried away on
February 27, 1558.[1]

[1] Paulus, ' Joh. Fabri ' in the *Katholik*, 1892, i. 17 ff., 108 ff. ; cf. 1893,
ii. 221 ff., and Paulus, *Deutsche Dominikaner*, p. 232 ff.

Prominent among the remaining Dominicans who worked in South Germany at the defence of the old faith are, the prior of Rottweil, George Neudorfer, who came forward against Ambrose Blarer, John Faber of Augsburg, and Balthasar Werlin at Colmar, the probable author of the interesting publication, 'Wider die Verderblichkeit der Colloquia.' [1]

The above names do not complete the list of Catholic champions belonging to the Dominican Order. Honourable notice is above all due to Michael Vehe, the author of one of the first German Catholic hymn-books († 1539). He belonged to the number of those Catholic theologians who were commissioned by Charles V to refute the Augsburg Confession, and in 1534 he took part in the Leipzig religious conference. Before this Vehe had already produced several writings against the religious innovators, such as a short treatise on the Holy Communion in one kind, and a refutation of Bugenhagen's pamphlet 'Wider die Kelchdiebe.' This last work is remarkable for its popular tone, its irony, and its masterly language. On the whole Vehe was entirely averse to impassioned polemics, and in his other writings he displayed the greatest moderation ; as, for instance, in the admirable treatise which he published in 1532, 'Wie unterschiederlicher Weise Gott und seine auserwählten Heiligen von uns Christen sollen verehrt werden.' Of striking significance also are his Latin treatises which appeared three years later, and in which he most carefully explains the doctrines of the Church and of the general councils, as well as those of justification, faith

---

[1] Falk, *Corp. Cath.* p. 460 ; Paulus, *Katholische Schriftsteller*, p. 561 ; and Paulus, ' Joh. Faber und sein Gutachten über Luther,' in the *Histor. Jahrbuch*, xvii. 39 f.

and good works. Although these works belong to the best apologetic writings which were then published in Germany in defence of the old faith, they remained, nevertheless, unnoticed for a long time.[1] Similar obscurity was also for a long time the fate of Bartholomew Kleindienst, who entered the Preaching Order at Augsburg at the beginning of 1550 and died in 1560. Shortly afterwards his 'Rechtcatholisch und evangelisch Ermahnung an seine liben Deutschen' was published; it is addressed especially to those Christians 'who are weak in the faith, or also erring and doubtful, but at the same time sincere-hearted.'[2]

Vehe's pupil, John Dietenberger, was one of the best Catholic champions Germany can boast of in the first half of the sixteenth century.[3] Born in 1475 at Frankfort-on-the-Main, he entered the Dominican convent there at an early age and obtained a doctor's degree at Mayence in 1515. The confidence of the brother members gained for him repeatedly the post of prior of the Order at Frankfort and Coblentz; he delivered theological lectures at Coblentz and Mayence; in 1530 at the Augsburg Diet he was one of the twenty confutators of the Augsburg Confession. After the year

---

[1] Concerning Vehe see especially Paulus in the *Histor.-polit. Blätter*, cx. (1892), 469 ff. See also *Katholik*, 1855, ii. 366 f., and Paulus, *Deutsche Dominikaner*, p. 215 f. * Meuser, ii. 535.

[2] See Paulus in the *Histor.-polit. Blätter*, cix. 485 ff. Paulus has not noticed the 'Triplex ratio qua fratres praedicatores sui ordinis provinciam superioris Germaniae facile et optime reformare valeant, rev. patribus eiusdem ordinis Gamundiae ad celebrandum provinciale capitulum congregatis proposita per Frid. Barth. Klaindinst 1558' bei (A. Dressel), *Vier Dokumente aus Römischen Archiven*, Leipzig, 1843, pp. 69–90.

[3] For what follows see the excellent monograph of H. Wedewer, and the criticism of it by Janssen in the *Histor.-polit. Blätter*, ciii. 54 ff. See also Paulus, *Deutsche Dominikaner*, p. 186 f.

1532 he worked as professor of exegesis at the college of Mayence, where he died on September 4, 1537. Not less than twenty-two printed and two unprinted writings of Dietenberger have been preserved. In all of them he shows himself both a learned and ready controversialist, defending the articles of faith attacked by the innovators with the same weapons which they used : with plentiful proofs, *i.e.*, from Holy Writ. In another fashion also he fought his opponents with their own weapons, viz. by writing little tracts which were distributed in many thousands of copies. To these belong the following treatises : ' Obe die Christen mügen durch iere guten Werk das Hymelreich verdienen ' ; ' Dass Jungfrauen die Klöster nümer götlich verlassen mögen ' ; ' Von Menschenlehr ' ; ' Obe der Gelaub allein selig mache ' ; ' Wie man Gotes Heiligen in dem Hymmelanruffen soll ' ; ' Ob St. Peter zu Rom gewesen sei ' ; and so forth.

There are few writings of that period in which the different Church doctrines are so admirably and intelligibly set forth for the people as in those tracts of Dietenberger. Occasionally, too, he makes use of verse, as, for instance, in his treatise on the veneration of saints, where the following lines occur :

> We men must pray to God alone,
>   And only ask the Saints to stand
> As mediators at His throne,
>   And grace and mercy from His hand
> Receive for us that grace we need,
> And none but God gives it indeed ;
> It helps much when Saints for us plead. . . .
> He that the Saints invokes and God,
> Or honours in his especial need,
> Above all invokes and honours God,
> In whom he has all hope
> As in the only one that can help him.

What he says about the monastic life and the different degrees of members of Orders is especially edifying; for instance : ' We see in the Passion of Christ three kinds of crosses—the first, that of the Redeemer, the second, that of the redeemed, and the third, that of the condemned. The first is borne by the perfected saints, who rejoice in the Cross and in suffering, who yearn for more of it, who count all suffering as gain. The second is carried by others who do not rejoice in it quite in the same way as the first, but who carry it patiently in the hope of eternal reward, who overcome themselves, who do violence to themselves in order to take possession of the kingdom of Heaven. What a blessed thing it was for the converted thief that he was nailed to the cross so that he could not get down from it, a temptation to which otherwise he might easily have yielded ! And just so it is with the members of monastic orders and the vows, the solitude, the obedience, the fasts, the self-mortification, &c., to which their condition compels them, and which force them to overcome temptation and to remain steadfast. The third cross, finally, is borne by many and brings no reward ; it has nothing to do with Orders or vows, but it is the cross of those who have made ill use of good—that is to say, have, through their own fault, turned that which should have been a means of salvation into poison.'

' It is untrue, however,' Dietenberger goes on in an apostrophe to Luther, ' if you assert that the monastic condition is dangerous ; it is not the condition, but the abuse of the grace, the abuse of the good it confers, which is dangerous. The same may be said of the evangel and of all that is good : it may be abused. We see this in all conditions. How often there is

great contradiction between the life of the individual
and the excellence and elevation of his condition ! Why
do you fall foul of the monastic state for that which it
has in common with all other states ? Why do you not
rather deduce the admirableness of the monastic state
from the pious lives and exemplary conduct of the good
monks, instead of concluding from the bad conduct of
a few that the condition itself is dangerous ? Was
the chalice of the Lord dangerous because a Judas
drank out of it ? The wickedness of individual monks
does not originate with the Order, but comes from their
own hearts which abuse what is good. As little as the
whole company of the Apostles is to be abused because
of the wickedness of Judas, so little is the monastic
state to be reproached on account of the vices of the
few who have fallen off.' [1]

Dietenberger's refutation of the Augsburg Creed,
which appeared in 1532, is a quite admirable production. He heads it with a detailed account of the Church
and its authority, thus avoiding the fault of many other
Catholic theologians who, before dealing with this
principal point, lose themselves entirely in comparatively unimportant details of doctrine.[2]

Dietenberger's numerous and profound polemical
writings were crowned by the two principal works of his
life, his interpretation of the Old and New Testaments,
and his Catechism, which was a masterpiece for subject-
matter, style and form. His object in compiling the
latter was to enable every individual to stand up for his
faith ; but the work ' has no trace or flavour of hatred
against the holders of other creeds ; it is written in the

---

[1] Wedewer, *Dietenberger*, p. 304 ff.
[2] *Ibid.* pp. 141–142.

calmest and most exalted language, it is the most loving code of instruction on the duties of pious Christians, entirely free from rancour and polemics. It bears noble testimony to the fact that, if Dietenberger sometimes wrote sharply and fiercely against the new doctrines, it was not out of hatred and ill-will, but because he thought that the conditions of the time " against our own and the Christian Church's customary use " required such outspoken language. In this work, however, where he is not writing to combat the enemy, but to instruct the faithful children of the Church, we find throughout the language of a heart redolent of love.' [1] A special feature of this Catechism is that, side by side with the Commandments, the corresponding transgressions are enumerated, whereby greater completeness is achieved.

The subdivisions of this Catechism into Faith, God's Commandments, Prayer and Sacraments correspond to the chief primitive catechetical Articles of the Church ; they go back either altogether or in part to the other catechisms of the sixteenth century ; for instance, to those of Wizel, John Fabri, Gropper, Michael Helding and John von Maltitz (bishop of Meissen, 1538–1549). The catechism of the latter, a work of great importance in the history of civilisation, is specially intended for the Christian home ; the instructions given in it on the duties of rulers and subjects, on passive resistance, on the relations between natural, ecclesiastical and imperial law, on contracts, usury, the education of school children, &c. &c., must be described as admirable. [2]

[1] Wedewer, pp. 207–208.
[2] Fuller details occur in Moufang, *Katholische Katechismen des* 16. *Jahrhunderts*, pp. 1 ff., 107 ff., 135 ff., 243 ff., 365 f., 415 f., 467 f.

An intimate friend of Dietenberger was Ambrosius Pelargus. Born at Nidda in Hesse, in 1493, he entered the Dominican Order at Frankfort, and went, in 1519, to the Heidelberg university. Only a few years later the young monk defended at Basle, in a manner as illuminating as it was thorough, the Holy Sacrifice of the Mass against the attacks of the innovators, and was in consequence drawn into a controversy with Oecolampadius. From 1529 to 1533 Pelargus worked at Freiburg in the Breisgau. Here he wrote several small pamphlets, which refuted especially the views of the Anabaptists. Against Brenz he directed a treatise on the punishment of heretics. In 1537 he migrated to Treves, where, until his death, he laboured with blessed results both at the university of the place and as cathedral preacher. In 1540 he took part in the religious convention at Worms, and in 1546 and 1551 in the Council of Trent.[1]

The Dominicans mentioned so far belong to the so-called German province. In the Saxon province also a number of disciples of St. Dominic worked with their pens against the religious innovators. Among them are Hermann Rab, Peter Rauch von Ansbach, Cornelius von Sneek,[2] Augustin von Getelen,[3] and, above all, John Mensing, provincial of the Saxon province, later on suffragan of Halberstadt († about

[1] See Paulus in the *Histor.-polit. Blätter*, cx. 1–14, 81–97. See also the present work, vol. ix. p. 333. Concerning Pelargus at the Council of Trent, Ehses writes in the *Zeitschrift Pastor bonus*, 1897, p. 322 f. See now also Paulus, *Dominikaner*, p. 190 f.

[2] See Paulus in the *Innsbrucker Zeitschrift für Katholische Theologie*, 1901, p. 401 f., and *Deutsche Dominikaner*, pp. 49, 67 f.

[3] Quétif, ii. 82 f. Paulus, *Katholische Schriftsteller*, pp. 557, 560, and Appendix, p. 215. See also Wrede, *Einführung der Reformation im Lüneburgischen*, Göttingen, 1887, pp. 112, 121, 142 f., and *Innsbrucker Zeitschr. für Katholische Theologie*, 1901, 412 f.

1541). This learned monk had already come forward with an apologetic pamphlet in 1523 ; three years later he published a series of treatises on the sacrificial character of the Holy Mass. His pamphlet, on the authority of the Church, published in 1528, is an admirable and thoroughly popular production. To the same year belongs a refutation by him of the ' senseless ' doctrine of Amsdorf, that faith alone without any good works was sufficient for man's salvation. This treatise also was distinguished both for its clearness and for its popular language. By desire of the Elector Joachim I of Brandenburg, Mensing came, in 1529, to Frankfort-on-the-Oder, where he worked with blessed results as preacher and as university professor. In the suite of the above-named prince Mensing attended the Diet of Augsburg in 1530 ; he opposed the Apology of Melanchthon in two pamphlets, in one of which he dealt with the doctrine of original sin, and in the other with justification by faith. ' I would gladly,' he says in the preface to the first pamphlet, ' if it were not injurious to Christianity in general, speak in milder and more courteous language ; whereas, however, the adversaries with their lies, make out all pious doctrines, together with the whole of Christianity, to be Pelagianism, and therefore heresy, as their Apology shows, I cannot, must not, spare them. I must call things by their right names, and think more of sparing the many holy men than the Lutherans, who stick at no falsehoods.' [1]

The above list of names, which might easily be

---

[1] See * Meuser, ii. 267 f., as well as Paulus in the *Katholik*, 1893, ii. 21 ff., 120 ff., and *Deutsche Dominikaner*, p. 16 ff. A. Warko, *Joh. Mensing's Lehre von der Erbsünde und Rechtfertigung*, with an introductory notice on Mensing's life and writings, Breslau, 1903. See also Paulus in the *Katholik*, 1904, i. 154 ff.

lengthened, shows plainly the great importance of the monastic Orders to the Church as regards learning. These names are also a refutation of the fable about the degradation of the monasteries at the time of the Church schism. But from the ranks of the secular clergy also at that time numbers of scholars engaged in the theological campaign. At Erfurt, where Luther himself studied, the university at once split into two parties. On the anti-Lutheran side stood Jodocus Truttvetter, one of the most eminent of German theologians. It was only his death, in 1519, which prevented this learned investigator from sharing in the literary contest which soon reached a great height at Erfurt. What part the Augustinian Usingen took in it at once became evident. Most noteworthy among his fellow-combatants was the humanist, John Femelius, who, with true understanding of the times, tried his skill in popular polemics. In his treatise on the veneration of the Saints he aimed at placing the simple lay folk, ' who had not been long accustomed to the Scripture,' in a position to form for themselves in the confusion of opinions a calm and correct judgment. He admonishes them ' not to judge so confidently and presumptuously as heretofore in this great matter '; and above all not to let themselves be led astray by the vociferation of the preachers. All the arguments which down to this time they had brought forward at Erfurt were insufficient and sophistical ; they con- sisted only of ' hectoring, howling and storming.' By means of a few imitations of their favourite argu- ments, he tried to make this understood. With St. Paul, he said, to whom they were so fond of appealing, they were as much in harmony ' as a bellowing ox with a young nightingale.' Coarse, dull blockheads they were, ' who twisted what was perfectly true into the worst meaning, and pronounced a fool's judgment in matters which they did not in the least understand.' [1]

While at the Erfurt university the conflict between Catholics and Protestants went on for a longer time ; the college at Basle first and that of Tübingen in 1535 were wrested from the Catholics by force. All the more important was it, therefore, that Duke George of Saxony preserved the Catholic character of the university of Leipzig, and thus retained a bulwark of the Church in North Germany. But it was also equally important that Prince George, permeated with a sense of the significance of the literary contest against the Wittenbergers, himself took up the championship of the Church with the hottest zeal. To the end of his life he continued to surround himself with a number of Catholic scholars, who were also kept busily occupied in writing against Luther.[2]

The humanist Hieronymus Emser, born, in 1478, of a distinguished noble family, had been in Prince George's service since 1504.[3] At first Emser had been

[1] Kampschulte, *Erfurt*, ii. 162–163 ; cf. Döllinger, *Reformation*, i. 611, and Paulus, *Usingen*, p. 38 f.

[2] See *Histor.-polit. Blätter*. xlvi. 462.

[3] Cf. J. J. Müller in the *Unschuld. Nachrichten*, 1720, 1721 and 1726 ; Waldau, *Emsers Leben und Schriften*, Ansbach, 1783 ; Erhard in Ersch-Gruber (section 1), xxxiv. 161–167 ; Aschbach, *Kirchenlexikon*, ii. 576 f. ; *Allgemeine Deutsche Biographie*, vi. 98 ff. ; Wetzer und Welte's *Kirchenlexikon*, iv [2] 479 ff. ; Enders, *Luther und Emser, ihre Streitschriften aus dem Jahre* 1521, Halle, 1889–1891, vols. i. and ii. ; P. Mosen, *H. Emser, der Vorkampfer Roms gegen die Reformation*, Leipziger Dissert. Halle, 1890 ; Kawerau, *H. Emser*, Halle, 1898. I take this opportunity for reiterating the wish expressed by Paulus (*Histor. Jahrbuch*. xix. 639) that on the part of the Catholics a literary memorial should at last be raised to the indefatigable Emser.

on friendly terms with Luther, but in 1519 he came
into angry collision with him in consequence of having,
in an official letter to the provost of Leitmeritz,
John Zack, touched on Luther's sorest point, viz. his
behaviour to the Hussite Bohemians. The Wittenberg
doctor burst out in his most violent manner against the
' he-goat ' Emser in a special pamphlet. Emser was
not slow in answering. In November 1519 he had
already completed his article of defence. ' So then,'
he writes here, ' no writing can go forth from you into
the world that is not charged with cynical blood, and
armed as it were with the teeth of a bloodhound ?
Belial is your father, the father of all insolent monks.
This inflammatory mocking spirit in your writings is
not the Spirit of Christ ; it can only produce fresh
schism and vexation in the Church.' The adherents of
Luther considered themselves so greatly injured by this
pamphlet that they had it publicly burnt. But they
were soon to realise that Emser was not annihilated by
this proceeding. At the beginning of 1521 he appeared
again on the arena of battle with the pamphlet ' Wider
das unchristliche Buch Martini Luthers Augustiners an
den teutschen Adel.' [1] Luther had received the first
sheet of this publication ' through treachery ' ; this
was enough to set him at work on a counter-pamphlet
' An den Bock zu Leipzig.' The latter retaliated with
the leaflet ' An den Stier zu Wittenberg,' which called
forth Luther's tract ' Auf des Bocks zu Leipzig
Antwort.' Emser replied in ' Auf des Stiers zu Wittenberg wütende Replika.' When Luther fired off at his
' ass,' Emser, another special pamphlet defending

---

[1] For the incisive admonition in this address to the German nation
see the present work, vol. iii. p. 128 ff.

himself against Emser's attack on his Address to the German nobility, Emser retorted with a 'Quadruplika.' Luther now thought of handing over to Amsdorf the task of defending him; but he changed his mind, and again set himself to tackle his dangerous adversary,[1] who, however, was at once ready with an answer. In 1522 Emser wrote a pamphlet against Carlstadt, in reference to the Wittenberg iconoclastic riots, and also translated several anti-Lutheran treatises into German. In 1523 he published his writing, 'Verwarnung wider den falsch genannten ekklesiasten und wahrhaffen Erzketzer Martin Luther,' which he dedicated to the Emperor, and in which he specially discusses his opponent's doctrine of justification and his strange theories about the sacrament of marriage.[2] In the following year Emser defended against Zwingli the age of the canon of the Mass and the substance of the prayers in it. The Peasant War gave him an incentive to fresh treatises, in which, sometimes in constrained, sometimes unconstrained, language, he attacked Luther most bitterly. In all probability the satiric piece 'Bockspiel Martin Luthers' comes also from the pen of Emser,[3] who to his death, which occurred the following year, 1527, was indefatigable in his literary attacks on the religious innovators.

The weight which Emser, through his writings, threw into the scale against Luther is not to be under-

---

[1] The Protestant Maurenbrecher (*Kathol. Reformation*, i. 175) remarks : 'Luther pretended indeed to despise Emser's attacks, but they wounded him more than he was willing to allow.'

[2] See present work, vol. iii. pp. 257, 345, 351.

[3] See Janssen in the *Katholik*, 1889, i. 134 ; also our remarks, vol. xi. pp. 58–69.

valued.   His mastery of form is recognised even by his
fiercest opponents.   In German prose he was surpassed
by few of his contemporaries.[1]   The innumerable
leaflets of the indefatigable controversialist contributed enormously to the enlightenment of the people.
Sharply and mercilessly, however, as Emser fought
against Luther and his followers,[2] he did not deny the
necessity for the abolition of clerical abuses, but he
wanted these to be remedied in a regular manner through

[1] So says Mosen, p. 21, who, as a rule, generally seeks to depreciate his
heroes.

[2] Kawerau (*Emser*, ii.) says : ' Emser has insisted that the audacity and
bluntness of his speech was a Suabian characteristic of his, and in very
truth it must be averred of him that in all his contests he preserved this
characteristic, that as a downright honest fellow he was free from all shifti-
ness and unstraightforwardness ; in his personal confessions his open-
heartedness was astounding, in combat his bluntness was unqualified.
Only seldom do we find him belying this frankness of manner.'   Kawerau's
article ends with the following summing up : ' In the circle of men who
in Albertine Saxony led the campaign against the Reformation—among
which figured Hieronymus Dungersheim, of Ochsenfart, professor of
theology ; Augustine Alfeld, the Franciscan at Leipzig ; Joh. Koss, licentiate ; Paul Bachmann (Ammicola), the Zeller abbot ; Francis Arnoldi,
pastor at Cologne, near Meissen ; Wolfgang Wulffer, chaplain at Briersnitz,
near Dresden—Hieronymus Emser was undoubtedly by far the most
important ; neither by retort nor by contemptuous disdain on the
Lutheran side could this most indefatigable champion of the Catholic
cause be reduced to silence.   In fertile productiveness in this literary
campaign the ex-Dominican, Peter Sylvius, alone equalled him, but Emser
was the superior in language and demeanour, despite all his exasperation
and bitterness against Luther.   His successor, John Cochlaeus, who, after
him, since the beginning of 1528, had been theological adviser to Duke
George, was his sole superior in humanistic and theological culture, and
in polemical skill.   Until the advent of Luther, Emser's life gives the
impression of desultoriness and aimlessness ; he is without any great
life purpose.   ' Humanistic and theological interests draw him hither and
thither, but nowhere does any absorbing task enchain him, apart from
his Benno studies, which transitorily lay serious claim to his energies.
Then Luther appears and supplies him with a vocation, to which, when
already ageing and failing in health, he devotes his whole strength.
He has now an ideal for which to fight ; his life acquires earnestness of
purpose and a deeper meaning.'

the legitimately appointed ways and means. With all his might, therefore, he fought against the innovators, who with the abuses would have destroyed the cause itself. ' We must reform, but not destroy,' he said in his ' Apologetikon ' against Zwingl ; ' we must venerate the Saints and not despise them ; the priesthood must become better, but it must continue to exist. Away with unnecessary pomp in dress ! Alms must be given to the poor. Would that the prelates might feed their sheep, and not devour them, and the ecclesiastical posts fall into the hands of virtue and wisdom, and not into those of avarice and birthright. Let the preachers exhort to prayer and not to persecution, to forgiveness and not to cursing.' [1]

Even more energetic than himself in the literary campaign was Emser's friend, John Cochlaeus.[2] Ever

[1] See Mosen, pp. 55 f., 58, and Kawerau, *Emser*, p. 85 ff. See also vol. iii. p. 332, of the present work.

[2] As unfortunately, owing to the suffering condition of Dr. Otto, a continuation of his work on Cochlaeus is not to be expected, a monograph on the polemical labours of this Catholic champion, the most important one, decidedly, next to Eck, is a thing much to be desired. The Dissertation of U. de Weldige-Cremer, *De Joannis Cochlaei vita* (Monasterii, 1865), is not sufficient. Gess (*Joh. Cochlaeus*, Berlin, 1886) has only given contributions ; on sixty-two pages an author like Cochlaeus cannot be dealt with adequately. The wish expressed above for an exhaustive account of the polemical work of Cochlaeus was not satisfied by M. Spahn's *J. Cochlaeus, Ein Lebensbild aus der Zeit der Kirchenspaltung*, Berlin, 1898, a work in many respects very immature. Schlecht, who in the *Histor. Jahrbuch*, xix. 938, recognises Spahn's merits on the literary historical side, says aptly in this respect that Spahn contributes less towards the appreciation of the Cochlaean theology than does Lämmer, who is not quoted by Spahn, in his *Vortridentinische Theologie*, published in 1858. Cochlaeus, so Spahn rightly insists, *l.c.*, was something more than a ' Landsknecht of theology ' (Spahn, p. 336), a ' base spirit ' (p. 329), whom ' the greatness of the opponents alone has raised to distinction ' (p. 300), ' without his ever having attained to an actual understanding of the Reformation idea ' (p. 72). Many of Spahn's criticisms—for instance, that Cochlaeus, ' as a theological writer was nothing more

since the latter, in 1522, had fought Luther in his

than a denier of Protestant doctrines ' (p. 300), that ' most of his writings are utterly worthless ' (p. 227)—can only be explained on the assumption that the writer had not acquired sufficient theological knowledge. It is also a bad feature of this work that Spahn, to put it mildly, shows a Janus face ; side by side with thoroughly Catholic passages there are others in which the youthful author ' cannot renounce the Protestant professors and teachers whose conception and treatment he follows more lovingly than critically in his appreciation of the Reformation.' S. Ehses in the *Römische Quartalschr.* xii. 457. Consequently Spahn sets up a much higher standard for the hero of his book than for his hero's opponent, and actually works himself up to ' a certain sort of admiration for the personality and the work of Luther.' The remarks made in this respect by so competent and thoughtful a critic as Ehses (*ibid.* p. 456 f.) are so excellent that they deserve a place here. ' It is certainly true,' says Ehses, ' that there is something Titanic in the action of a man who sets about with defiant grip to overthrow a world-commanding edifice which has stood through many centuries ; no doubt in such an operation we behold gigantic blows struck, which lesser spirits and weaker hands would not be equal to. But for all this Luther is not " the greatest German of his time," as Spahn calls him at p. 84 ; for if destructive power can in its way be called great, true greatness must be measured by that which a man reconstructs in place of what he has destroyed. Moreover, the reiterated assertion that Cochlaeus, in the somewhat narrow scope of his polemics, did not arrive at a full understanding of the aims and endeavours of Luther and Melanchthon, as well as the low estimate of the effects which the writings of Cochlaeus had on his opponents, were the outcome of a sort of fanatical admiration for the violent, uncontrolled proceedings of Luther and his friends, who, as though blindfold, hurled thrust after thrust with ever-increasing recklessness at the Pope and the Catholic Church. That Cochlaeus did clearly and accurately seize on the salient features in the war of annihilation planned against Rome is repeatedly asserted by Spahn. When, however, the latter demands of the man who stood in the fiercest heat of the battle a scientific diagnosis or statement of all the different views of all the multitudinous opponents, with their up and down heaving and swaying and their ever-increasing contradictions, he sets a task which even now, after 300 years, historians and theologians find difficult, if not impossible, to accomplish. And is it indeed such an altogether crushing, overwhelming " flash of inspiration " when Luther, in answer to Cochlaeus's appeal to the great Fathers of the Church, says : " Let them brag on happily about their old Fathers, have we not on our side our Father in Heaven who is high above all Fathers in the Church ? " And is it not almost a naive imputation on the reader when Spahn, p. 81, actually sees a great victory of Luther over Cochlaeus in the fact that Cochlaeus did not answer a thoroughly just reproach from Luther ? As Luther traced his

treatise on the Holy Sacraments,[1] scarcely a year
passed without his lifting up his voice against the
religious innovator. The style of Cochlaeus's polemical
writings is thoroughly rhetorical. ' It is as though, for
his excitable, stormy spirit, the calm, scientific investigation of controversial points, which keeps strictly
within the limits of its subject and only proceeds step
by step in its development, were too circumscribed,
tedious and wearisome ; again and again, whenever
opportunity offers, he relieves the pain and oppression
of his heart by longer or shorter descriptions of the
conditions of the time, by apostrophes to Luther, by
exhortations, warnings and vehement invective. He
does not even despise petty witticisms.' ' Thanks to

doctrine to the direct revelation of God, Cochlaeus asked him for proofs
in the shape of signs and miracles. Spahn considers Luther's assertion
appropriate from his (Luther's) point of view, but thinks the retort of
Cochlaeus " nonsensical," and so comes to the conclusion that " Luther
shows right judgment in leaving the questioner without an answer." Also,
what Spahn says in the section *Cochlaeus als Polemiker* (p. 217) concerning
Cochlaeus's idea of the relation between Holy Scripture and the authority
of the Church, in spite of many unassailable propositions, smacks somewhat of Protestant views, and rather suggests that the Holy Scriptures are
a book of absolute data, completely independent of the interpretation and
authorisation of the Church. How otherwise could Spahn make it a
reproach against Cochlaeus (p. 214) that he is averse to the assumption of
a " condition of lordship," as Spahn puts it, of the Church over Holy
Scripture ? And how could he (p. 216) speak with a certain amount of
warmth of the " reverential admiration for Holy Scripture " which John
von Wessel had discovered in the writings of Rupert von Deutz, " an
admiration which led him himself into contradiction with the Church " ?
Neither must we leave unanswered the inaccurate assertion (p. 31) that
the right of existence of the temporal power of the Pope rests on the
faithful acceptation of the false Constantinian donation.'

[1] It is known that Cochlaeus, like so many others, had at first greeted
the advent of Luther with joy, because he expected the initiation of a
veritable reform. How a complete change gradually came over his mind
is shown by Dittrich in the *Histor. Jahrb.* x. 110 f. with reference to a
treatise of Kolde. See, now, also Spahn, *Cochlaeus*, p. 62 f., and also the
criticism of Schlecht in the *Histor. Jahrb.* xix. 938.

his theological training, Cochlaeus never wavered in his judgment of the often startlingly new and paradoxical teaching of Luther; his clearsightedness and the philosophic culture of his intellect enabled him to seize at once the particular point on which the whole hinged ; his great familiarity with the Scriptures supplied him at every turn with abundance of passages which hit the enemy hard, and the many-sided culture he had acquired enabled him to illustrate his propositions from manifold domains of learning and to clothe them with a certain amount of taste.'

This bright side has undoubtedly its corresponding shadows : frequent repetitions, dragging in of things which are foreign to the subject, vehemence and hardness of expression, sometimes also hastiness and want of polish. ' Cochlaeus worked very rapidly and, as it seems, with feverish excitement.' [1] As a Christian, as a theologian, as a German, he felt the devastations of the politico-religious revolution most deeply, and set to work, accordingly, with his whole might to stem the flood of Lutheranism. ' Luther's storm-showers of tracts and leaflets, written in hot haste and issuing forth in greater and greater abundance to mislead the people, must, he felt, be met with as swift a counter-storm, if all was not to be lost. It is from this point of view that most of the writings of Cochlaeus must be judged. As little as the Lutheran books are they learned disquisitions for professional theologians ; they are merely leaflets and tracts for the enlightenment and guidance of those among the educated classes, clergy

[1] Otto, *Cochlaeus*, pp. 126, 130 ; cf. Aschbach, *Kirchenlexikon*, ii. 123. Gess also (p. 58) admits that there is ' a relatively important skilfulness of form in almost all his writings.'

as well as laity (and there were many such at that time) who were most keenly interested in theological matters.' [1]

So great was the zeal of Cochlaeus that he actually refused an advantageous post at Rome, in order to give his whole strength to the defence of the old Church in his native land. At Frankfort, where he was dean of the ' Liebfrauenstift,' his writings had made him so detested by the new-religionist burghers that he found himself compelled, in 1525, to leave the town. He went to Mayence, and, not feeling safe there either, on to Cologne. The following year he received from the Pope, Clement VII., a canonry at St. Victor, near Mayence, but he had already been summoned to Dresden by Duke George of Saxony as successor to Emser. Here he continued in the most confidential relations to the territorial sovereign until the death of the noble Duke in 1539.[2] The literary activity of Cochlaeus in his new abode was very wide-spread. He not only wrote articles of defence against Luther for Duke George, and gave his name to treatises which proceeded from the Duke, but he also brought out a series of original works. In 1529 he published his virulent pamphlet against the ' Seven-headed ' Luther. The innumerable contradictions in which the latter was involved are here summed up: in the doctrine of the Lord's Supper alone Cochlaeus, in a special pamphlet, pointed out sixty-four cases of flagrant changes of opinion. The tone is vehement throughout, but it must be remembered that Cochlaeus had been

---

[1] Otto, *Cochlaeus*, p. 131.

[2] Gess, pp. 27, 34, 36. Spahn, pp. 133 ff., 174 ff., 246 ff. Since July or August 1535, Cochlaeus had had his residence at Meissen, where Duke George had provided him with a canonry. Otto, *Cochlaeus*, p. 252 ff.

goaded into anger by the Wittenbergers by abusive names, such as ' Kochlöffel,' ' Rotzlöffel,' ' Ginlöffel,' &c.[1] Concerning the aim of this pamphlet, he says himself that he compiled it from the Latin and German writings of Luther, first, for the sake of the Catholic preachers, in order that they might be able to answer the Lutherans, and put them to shame through Luther's own writings without lengthy searching and trouble ; and, secondly, on account of the foreign nations, so that the scholars who did not understand German should have a short way at any future Council by which to learn how and what Luther wrote in German, and might thus be able to condemn him as a wicked rogue out of his own mouth.[2]

To this same year, 1529, belongs the little work ' 25 Ursachen, unter Einer Gestalt das Sacrament den Laien zu reichen ' (' Twenty-five Reasons for giving the Sacrament to the Laity in one Form '). In 1530 Cochlaeus took part at Augsburg in the Constitution of the Confession,[3] after which he again devoted himself to the publication of pamphlets, greater and smaller, against the religious innovators. Transubstantiation, the Mass, and Original Sin were the chief among the disputed doctrines which he dealt with. Besides Luther, Cochlaeus now directed his attacks against the literary mouthpiece of the new religionists, Philip Melanchthon. As in the ' Seven-headed Luther,' so now in his ' Philippics ' he shows up mercilessly the contradictions and inconsistencies of Melanchthon.

---

[1] Werner, *Gesch. der apolog. und polem. Literatur*, iv. 54.   Gess, p. 38. Cochlaeus also showed up Luther's contradictions in other writings. See Werner, iv. 173 f. ; Weldige-Cremer, p. 60.

[2] Cochlaeus, *Historia M. Luthers, deutsch durch J. Ch. Hüber*, p. 431.

[3] See Ficker, xxii. f., xxix. xxx. xlv. xlviii. lvi. f., xcii. f.

He gives expression here to the opinion that the open attacks and vilifications of Luther are not so bad as the ' snakelike cunning and hypocrisy of Melanchthon.' The three first Philippics were finished in 1531 ; shortly after followed the fourth, but the whole work could not be published till 1534, as Cochlaeus was short of money. In the same year he and others published also a justification of the veneration of Saints. In the ensuing years he wrote several more pamphlets dealing especially with the question of assembling a Council.[1]

The death of his patron Duke George and the suppression of the Catholic Church in Saxony obliged Cochlaeus, in 1539, to resume once more his wanderer's staff. He first went to Breslau, where he was a canon. Then he took part in the religious conferences at Hagenau, Worms and Ratisbon, though without playing any important *rôle*. He did not think much of attempts of this sort at unification. ' With the Lutherans,' he wrote, ' concordiality means opening up a greater schism.' In 1543 he accepted an invitation from Bishop Moritz of Hutten, to Eichstätt, and in 1546 accompanied the bishop to the religious conference at Ratisbon. During this time also he was indefatigable with his pen. In 1543 he published his pamphlet against Bullinger, ' On the authority of the Canonical Books and of the Church,' which is considered one of his best and most thoughtful works. On Bullinger's replying to this, Cochlaeus brought out a

---

[1] Cf. Lämmer, *Vortrid. Theologie*, p. 56 ff. Werner, iv. 101, 154, 229 ff. Weldige-Cremer, p. 58 ff. For the polemics of Cochlaeus against Melanchthon see also Spahn, pp. 165, 168 ff., 184 ff. According to Spahn (p. 168) the fourth Philippic was not written till the year 1531. Cochlaeus wrote a fifth Philippic in 1540 and a sixth in 1543, both of which were printed in 1544, *ibid.* pp. 278, 298.

counter-reply in 1544, in which he dealt chiefly with the question concerning the sources of the Catholic doctrines. Two years later he came forward with a treatise against Melanchthon and the Protestant collocutors at the Ratisbon religious conference; in 1548 and 1549 he sojourned in Mayence. In the summer of this last year he went back to Breslau physically broken and in want of rest. He died there on the 10th of January, 1552.[1]

Considering what a restless and unsettled life he had, the indefatigable literary activity of Cochlaeus deserves the highest praise.[2] Not only his zeal and his power of work, but also his self-sacrificing devotion were calculated to excite admiration. Like so many other Catholic champions he was obliged personally to defray the cost of publishing his works. He complains repeatedly of this state of things.[3] Thus on November 20, 1540, he writes from Worms to a friend staying in Rome: ' For twenty years past nothing has been so fatal to us Catholics in our contest with the heretics as the great untrustworthiness and indifference of the printers, as well as the want of money : untrustworthiness, I say, because they make the grossest mistakes in printing; indifference because they would not sell or circulate anything; want of money, because the publishers, nearly all of them at the service of the Lutherans, would only work for us in return for heavy payment. If your Grace will not believe me, then ask

---

[1] See Gess, pp. 47–57 ; Werner, pp. 231, 234 ; Spahn, p. 310 ff.

[2] A complete list of his writings from 1522 to 1550 is given by Spahn with bibliographical accuracy, p. 341 f. For the work of Cochlaeus, as historian, see vol. xiii. p. 455.

[3] See Gess, p. 41, and vol. iii. p. 106, of the present work. See also Spahn, pp. 258 f., 266, 270.

the rest who are present here, especially Eck, Nausea and Mensing, who have published a good many writings at their own expense. Under these circumstances, as I could not conveniently publish at Cologne or at Mayence, Strassburg, Leipzig, and Augsburg, I was obliged to apply to a relation who, later on, founded a printing establishment. In the course of four or five years I spent over 1000 florins in the business. So long as the pious Duke George was alive this expenditure did not distress me. But after his death, this printer, whose name was Nicolaus Wolrab, was thrown into a vile prison at Leipzig by the Lutheran Duke Henry, and the books of Wizel and Nausea which were then in his printing house were all pitched into the water. If the arch-Lutheran Duchess, who hoped to win Wolrab over to the new doctrine, had not come to the prisoner's rescue he would either have been punished with death or with imprisonment for life. In this extremity the unhappy man went over to Lutheranism, for which he now works against the grain. I was then obliged to address myself to another relative who lived at Dresden, and who had been bookbinder and bookseller under Duke George, and who now, by my advice, removed with his wife and family to Mayence, and bought up Wolrab's types, in order to print for me and other Catholic writers.' Cochlaeus then began begging for help for the support of this publisher—he is the well-known Franz Beham—and this all the more zealously ' as the " ecclesiastical dignitaries " do not trouble themselves in the least about such matters ! ' [1]

Among those who warmly appreciated the services of Cochlaeus we note especially the noble-minded

---

[1] Bellesheim, *Gesch. der Kathol. Kirche in Irland*, ii. 692 f. ; see Widmann, *Mainzer Presse*, p. 3. See also below, p. 297 f.

Cardinal Reginald Pole. ' I was always of opinion,'
he wrote, ' that your writings deserved not only the
goodwill but also the strong support of all whose duty
it is to protect and maintain religion and learning ; for
you are pre-eminently the one who has resisted the
onslaughts of the opponents in those districts where
the greatest danger prevailed.' [1]

George Wizel, another man much tossed about by
the storms of the period, received also, like Cochlaeus,
hospitable harbourage from Duke George.[2] A student
of the Erfurt humanist school, Wizel had sat at the feet
of Luther and Melanchthon at Wittenberg. Although
he had received priest's orders from the Bishop
Adolf of Merseburg, he soon joined the new Church,
having been strongly influenced by the writings of
Erasmus. He married, and became a Lutheran preacher
in Thuringia. Here he became aware of the deep moral
degradation of the new-religionists. Ardent study of
the Church Fathers brought him nearer again to the
Catholic Church ; outward misfortunes also, hostilities
and suspicions, added their influence. It became more
and more clear to him that Luther had not aimed at the
removal of Church abuses but at a Church schism. In

---

[1] *Reg. Poli Epist. ed. Quirini*, III. 1 ; see also the despatch of Campeggio to Sadolet in Balan, *Mon. ref. Luth.* pp. 520–521.

[2] See Kampschulte, *De G. Wicelio*, Bonnae, 1856 ; Döllinger, *Reformation*, p. 121 ff. ; Pastor, *Reunionsbestrebungen*, p. 140 ff. ; G. Schmidt, *G.
Wizel*, Vienna, 1876 ; Reusch's *Theolog. Literaturblatt*, 1877, p. 179 ff. ;
Falk in the *Katholik*, 1891, i. 129 ff. ; *Briegers Zeitschr.* ii. 386 ff. ; Kawerau
in Herzog's *Real-Enzyklopädie*, xxvii[2]. 241 ff. ; Paulus in Wetzer und
Welte's *Kirchenlexikon*, xii[2]. 1726 f. The catechetical works of Wizel are
dealt with by Moufang in the *Katholik*, 1877, lvii. 159 ff. ; 1880, ii. 646 ;
and *Katechismen*, Preface, p. 1 f., 107 ff., 407 ff. That the catalogue of
Wizel's writings given by Räss, i. 146 ff., is incomplete has been remarked
by Kampschulte in Reusch's *Literaturblatt*, ii. 274. For the writings of
Wizel printed at Mayence see Falk, *Bibelstudien*, pp. 188 f., 190 ff.

the latter he would not take part.   In 1531 he resigned
his pastorate at Niemegk and returned with his wife
and children to his home at Vacha, where he had to
fight with crushing poverty.   His endeavours to obtain
a professorship at Erfurt were shipwrecked at the last
moment through his opposition to Luther.   Wizel had
come forward openly against the teaching of the latter
with a defence of good works, which appeared in 1532.
This was followed in the next years by ' Ein unüber-
windlicher, gründlicher Bericht was die Rechtfertigung
in Paulo sei,' ' Verklärung des neunden Artikels unsers
heiligen Glaubens die Kirche Gottes betreffend,' and
' Evangelium M. Luthers,' and also a defence of his
renunciation of the new doctrine.

In 1533 Wizel was appointed pastor of the very
small community at Eisleben.   In this almost wholly
Lutheran town he had to suffer the most bitter persecutions.   ' At Vacha the dogs had growled at him, here
the wolves fell upon him.'   In spite of all difficulties,
however, he went on unweariedly with his literary
labours, and told hard truths to the religious innovators.
With the rest of the defenders of the Church he would
not even then make common cause, but preferred to
stand in the middle between the combatants, or above
them.   When in 1538 the Catholic Count of Mansfeld
died, Wizel was again obliged to change his place of
abode.   He went to Dresden, and entered the service
of Duke George.   He had already, a year before this,
published a theological pamphlet at Leipzig—' Weg
zur Eintracht der Kirche '—which, with all its defects,
still bears honourable testimony to the noble spirit
which animated Wizel and to his love for Church and
Fatherland.   He addresses himself here to the Pope,

the Emperor, and all the bishops and princes, and implores them to restore unity to the Church on the foundation of the Apostles, the Holy Scriptures, and the Fathers of the Church. A council must be called and both parties given a hearing at it. Lutherans as well as Catholics must listen to his reproaches. The Catholics, he said, were wrong in that they defended not only the use but also the misuse; the Lutherans in that they set aside both *use* and *misuse*, and persisted in schism. Both parties must yield something if unity was to be brought about. Wizel then makes his suggestions through twenty-eight chapters, in which he handles the principal points of dispute. From the Catholics he demands the abandonment of scholastic expressions and of Aristotelian methods, as well as the abolition of numerous abuses in clerical life. Marriage of priests and communion in both kinds may be allowed, and the confiscated Church goods given up. The Lutherans are admonished not to interfere with the dogmas of the old Church, to abstain from schism, and after the attendant abuses have been done away with, to restore the right of excommunication, confession, ordination of priests and confirmation. He also exacts from the new-religionists toleration of monasteries, at the same time saying that the latter must be diminished in number and reformed.[1]

Entry into the service of Duke George gave Wizel forthwith the opportunity to test the practical value of his peaceful conciliatory plans. In order to give a firm basis to the transactions at the Leipzig religious conference which had been organised by Duke George, he drew up a fresh eirenicon, in which he laid down

[1] Pastor, *Reunionsbestrebungen*, pp. 145 f., 162 f.

the form of the apostolic Church as ' norm.' This
work, which appeared at Mayence in the years 1540 and
1541, is entitled ' Typus ecclesiae prioris : Anzeigung,
wie die heilige Kyrche Gottes inwendig siben und mehr
hundert Yaren nach unseres Herrn Auffart gestelt
gewesen sey ' (' Demonstration of the inner constitution
of the Church of God for seven hundred and more
years after the Ascension of our Lord.')

In this treatise Wizel endeavoured to show that
' the condition of our dear Mother, the holy, universal,
and Christian Church, was best when it was most similar
and most in conformity with the first and the oldest
Churches.' He therefore took into consideration ' first
of all the antiquity, then the reform, and finally the
unification of individual doctrines and customs.' The
seven Sacraments he wished to retain, also the Holy Mass,
with the removal of the new additions. Monkhood
he also praised as recommended by the Fathers ; but
he blamed the monks of his time who ' had taken possession of the most fruitful and the pleasantest places,'
and who adhered more to Aristotle than to Augustine.
Against the robbers of convent goods he spoke very
severely : ' An enemy of God and of the Church is he
who thinks to root out the *monastica*, an enemy of
Christ and of the Roman Empire is he who takes to
himself and makes his own the property of the
convents.' He also stands up for the Church
festivals, and complains of their abolition by the
Lutherans. As regards the feast days, he says the
Catholics had inordinately increased the number of
these, but the Lutherans had reduced it far too much.
As to the Councils, he only recognises the authority
of the first four. Those ceremonies and usages which

had already obtained in the Apostolic Church are by no means to be abolished, as Luther would wish done. Hence he defends the vigils, the canonical hours, the use of the sign of the cross, the pilgrimages. He is, nevertheless, very far from overestimating the value of these ceremonies ; on the contrary he says expressly that ' much more depends on the Christian life than on all ceremonies and observances.' The pith of the whole work is that Wizel proposed to take the disciplinary and dogmatic constitution of the Church as it was in the eighth century, as the starting-point for the efforts of unification. To the contending theologians on both sides he recommends a return to this Apostolic Church.

The Leipzig religious conference ended, like all other attempts of the kind, without any result. Nevertheless, Wizel did not give up his pacific endeavours. In popular as well as in learned books he still sought to propagate his ideas.[1]

When Duke George died, Wizel nourished the hope of finding a patron for his plans in the Duke's successor, Joachim II, of Brandenburg ; and, in fact, this prince did consult him in the working out of the new Church ordinance ; but Wizel soon came to see that his well-intended proposals for reconciliation when put into practice only benefited the new Church organisation. He therefore left Berlin, where Protestantism had obtained dominion, and went to Fulda, to the abbot John, who was also bent on bringing about peace. He remained there till 1554, restlessly active all the time, and

---

[1] See Pastor, *Reunionsbestrebungen*, p. 150 ff., where there is a table of contents of the *Drei Gesprächbüchlein* (1539), (not yet properly appreciated), which aptly describes the standpoint of the peacemaker, Wizel.

trying his hand at nearly every branch of theological literature. In 1554 he removed to Mayence, to escape from the persecutions of the Fulda Lutherans. ' From my enemies,' he complained bitterly a year later, ' I have received everywhere, instead of a reasonable answer to my writings, only the most violent abuse, and instead of an appropriate refutation, only hostile persecution. Personal advantage and gain my writings have never brought me, but they have fastened on me the bitterest hatred of the whole Lutheran world ; so much so, that I am scarcely safe anywhere, not even in my own house, and I cannot go a journey anywhere without exposure to the greatest danger.' [1] With strained attention he then followed the course of the Emperor Charles V's efforts as peacemaker. When the latter, in 1548, tried to bridge over the schism by means of his Interim, Wizel believed himself near the goal of his hopes. The violent opposition of the Lutherans to the Interim incited him to a defence of the Imperial plan. In spite of the events of the years that followed, Wizel, till his death at Mayence, in 1573, held on stubbornly to the deceptive hope of the possibility of coming to an understanding with the Protestants. Even in the last years of his life he defended the ' Royal way ' of a middle course, recommended the most extraordinary concessions to the new-religionists, and expressed himself in bitter terms against the Catholic theologians of the Council of Trent.[2] In the new epoch which set in with the above-mentioned Church assembly, and the activity

---

[1] Döllinger, i. 29.
[2] See Kampschulte, *De G. Wicelio*, pp. 29, 31 f., where there are fuller details concerning Wizel's *Via regia* ; see also Kawerau in Herzog's *Real-enzyklopädie*, xvii[2]. 249 f.

of the Jesuits, a compromising theology on Wizel's plan was out of the question.

Other Catholic champions in the territory of Duke George, besides Emser, Cochlaeus and Wizel, and who also, by encouragement of the Duke, worked actively with their pens against the new-religionists, were the monks already mentioned, Alfeld and Amnicola ; further Franz Arnoldi, pastor at Cologne, near Meissen ; the Leipzig theological professor, Hieronymus Dungersheim ; the Leipzig licentiate, John Koss ; Wolfgang Wulffer, chaplain at Briessnitz, near Dresden ; the Meissen bishop John von Schleinitz and his successor, John von Maltitz ; [1] and finally Peter Sylvius. The latter is among the earliest and the most zealous of Luther's opponents. Sylvius also had hard battles to fight with the unfavourableness of the times. His first piece of polemical writing, in 1525, he was obliged to have printed at his own expense at Dresden. As he did not count on being able to sell the book he resolved to distribute it gratis, and leave his other writings unprinted. Against all expectation, however, it happened that 'people bought the pamphlet gladly.' Besides this he received 'from certain God-fearing people and prelates, clergy and also laymen,' contributions of money towards 'printing his little books.' Fiercely, and at times immoderately, Sylvius opposed the new doctrines in these publications. After he had been presented with a chaplaincy at Rochlitz by Duke

---

[1] For the above named see the 'Literaturangaben' in Falk, *Corp. Cath.* pp. 450, 453, 457, and Paulus, *Katholische Schriftsteller*, p. 562. For H. Dungersheim see the 'Literaturangaben' in Falk, p. 453, and Brieger, *Theolog. Promotionen*, pp. 54–55.

George, in 1528, he went on with the same hot zeal,
bringing out tract after tract against the innovators.
Even now there were still great difficulties to be overcome in publishing these writings. In one of his last
polemical pamphlets Sylvius himself said : ' I have
published these eight-and-twenty booklets at my own
expense, though with some help from Christian gentlemen, and those same farthings which I have spared
from my body [my bodily wants] I wished, like the
poor widow with her mite, to lay in the treasury of
God's Church, never looking for any temporal profit
or renown.   Rather, indeed, have I daily awaited,
though undismayed, the inhuman, ferocious slandering
of the Lutherans. And although for the last five years,
owing to the serious illness which, God knows, has
attacked me, quite innocent though I have been like
a young child in my simplicity—it was brought on by
poison given me three times in quick succession—
I could not travel about, or see about my books, but
was kept closely shut up, nevertheless I have had one
book after another printed, so long as I received a
penny from my priestly office, although all my days I
have expected death rather than life. And, moreover,
no Lutheran person can dare to say of me, as is their
wont, that I have been moved to write against this
Luther on account of rich benefices promised to me by
the clergy ; for up to the present day I have had no
residence of my own in any Church benefice, where, in
my weak old days, I could lay my head comfortably,
or where I might safely collect together the books which
are scattered in so many places, or shut up in casks,
except that a secular but right Christian prince (may

God reward him !) has granted me a clerical benefice
in a village, albeit without a residence.' [1]

The above writers constituted the ducal ' Georgische
Canzley und Schmiden ' (chancellery and forge) which
caused much vexation and indignation to the Lutheranly minded.[2] Great beyond measure, therefore, was
the rejoicing in these circles when Duke George died,
on April 17, 1539, and his Lutheranly minded
brother Henry succeeded him. The whole land and
also the university of Leipzig was Protestantised
by force ; all who would not conform were granted
liberty to go away ' to wander forth into misery,'
as the bishop John of Meissen complained to the
Emperor. In the same year, Joachim II of Brandenburg also went over to Protestantism, and thereby
North Germany was as good as lost to the Church.
His father, Joachim I, firmly convinced of the truth
of the Catholic religion, had preserved his subjects
from heretical teaching, and had also taken various
Catholic writers under his protection ; for instance,
Wolfgang Redorfer († 1559),[3] Peter Rauch, John
Mensing, and above all Conrad Wimpina. The latter,
who was professor of theology at Frankfort-on-the-Oder
(† 1531), took part in the refutation of the Augsburg
Confession, and published a larger work under the
title ' Kurzgefasste Sectengeschichte ' ('Anacephalaeosis
Sectarum '). In the introduction he complains that the
new heretical teachers are always asking for proofs
and refutation, but they put aside unread all books

[1] See Paulus in the *Katholik*, 1893, i. 49 ff., and J. K. Seidemann in
the *Archiv für Literaturgeschichte*, iv. 177 f. ; v. 6 ff., 287 ff.

[2] Haussmann, *Lebensbeschreibung Laz. Spenglers*, Nuremberg, 1741,
pp. 367–368. See *Histor.-polit. Blätter*, xlvi. 464–465.

[3] See Lämmer, *Vortrid. Theologie*, pp. 32, 35, and Ficker, xlvii.

written against them under the pretext that it is ' all
only scholastic stuff, and a theology tainted with the
venom of logic, and corrupted by the dregs of philosophy.'
Wimpina's work falls into three parts. In the first he
gives a complete survey of all the earlier sects from the
time of the Apostles down to his own day, in order to
show that the new heretics were only reviving errors
which had long ago been rejected by the Church, and he
combines with this survey the refutation of a number
of assertions of Luther, which, the latter declared, the
Paris theological faculty had been unable to upset.
A great number of controversial points, especially the
doctrine of justification, were skilfully treated by him.
Wimpina also contended with Luther for a just judgment concerning the Aristotelian philosophy. The
second part begins with combating the Lutheran
doctrines on monastic vows and celibacy ; then follows
an explanation of priesthood, the Sacrifice of the Mass,
the Eucharist, confession, the veneration of Saints and
relics, accompanied with constant, often very violent,
polemics against the new heretical teachers. The
third part also, which deals with destiny, providence,
predestination, and lucky chance, is polemical in
character. The section on predestination is, in great
measure, directed against Melanchthon.[1]

   Earlier even than Wimpina, the Frauenburg canon
Tiedemann Giese (later bishop of Kulm, then of Con-

----

[1] See Mittermüller in the *Katholik*, 1869, i. 641–682 ; ii. 1–21, 129–166,
257–286, 385–403 ; cf. Lämmer, p. 30 f. ; Kawerau in Herzog's *Realenzyklopädie*, xvii[2]. 195–199. Also Brieger, *Theologische Promotionen*,
ix. 46, 51. Müller in the *Theolog. Studien und Kritiken*, 1893, lxvi.
83–125 ; 1894, 339 f. Lauch, *Geschichte des Leipziger Früh-Human-
ismus*, Leipzig, 1899. Paulus in Wetzer und Welte's *Kirchenlexikon*, xii[2].
1682 f.

stance, † 1550) [1] had come forward publicly with a
pamphlet, in which, with classical calm, clearness and
confidence, he subjected the Lutheran doctrine of
justification to a process of critical analysis, mild in
form but annihilating in substance. It was by his
friend Copernicus that Giese, himself shrinking from
publicity, was persuaded to bring out this masterly
treatise, which, among all the contemporary apologies
of the Catholic dogma, can at any rate claim, if
not to have been the first, at least to have been
the one which most decisively and fundamentally
recognised and set forth the kernel of the Lutheran
doctrine of justification. With exemplary calm and
dignity, in a style and form throughout noble and
conciliatory, and with exclusive reference to Holy
Scripture, Giese separates truth from error.[2]

Besides these men, North Germany can also boast
of many other valiant defenders of the old faith. In
Magdeburg, Wolfgang Schindler distinguished himself
in this respect ; in Rostock, the rector of the university,
John Kruse, and the theology professor, Bartoldus
Moller ; the latter, after his banishment from Rostock,
found refuge at Hamburg, where he continued the fight
against the innovators. At Warburg and Münster,
Otto Beckmann defended the old faith against Protestant attacks ; in Dortmund, Jacob Schopper.[3]

The Rhenish lands also have a goodly number of

[1] See Hipler, *Ermländische Literaturgeschichte*, p. 100 ff. ; *Allgemeine
deutsche Biographie*, ix. 151 ff. ; and Prowe, i. 2, 26, 176 f. Here the year
of death is erroneously given as 1549.

[2] Giese's pamphlet, which had reached the position of unique rarity,
was again made generally accessible by Hipler in *Spicileg. Cop.* p. 5 ff.

[3] See Falk, *Corp. Cath.* p. 461, and Paulus, *Katholische Schriftsteller*,
pp. 546, 554, 556, 559.

Catholic writers to show. That numbers of monks worked here for the defence of the Church has just been stated above. But there was no lack also of champions outside the ranks of the monastic Orders, such as the renowned jurisprudent Conrad Braun, assessor, and for two years president, of the Kammergericht at Spires, later on canon at Freising, and chancellor to Cardinal Otto von Augsburg († 1563). The bitterest persecutions and hostilities on the part of the sectaries could not intimidate this courageous man. In the Imperial chamber as well as in various writings he fought most zealously against the innovators.[1]

At Mayence, which in that stormy period served as a place of refuge for many banished ecclesiastical princes and monks,[2] in addition to Nausea, Cochlaeus, Dietenberger and Wizel there worked for a time. The ancient episcopal town had been of the highest importance since the 'forties as a Catholic publishing centre. Until 1539 Leipzig had been the starting point of the polemico-theological literature of the adherents of the old faith; after the forcible suppression of every Catholic sign of life by Duke Henry, Mayence had taken its place. There, in the cradle of the printing art, Franz Beham placed his press at the exclusive service of the literature of Catholicism. Thanks to the industry of its owner, and the efforts of Cochlaeus, the new publishing house soon reached a flourishing condition. By 1553 it had already issued ninety works. The list of authors contains names of the best repute : Cochlaeus, Nausea, Michael Helding, John Wild, Wizel, John Hoffmeister, Conrad

---

[1] See the careful article of Paulus in the *Histor. Jahrbuch*, xiv. 517–548.
[2] See Falk in the *Katholik*, 1888, i. 81 ff.

Thamer, Cornelius Loos, Bishop Cromer, Cardinal Hosius, and others.[1]

In the Treves district the controversialist Bartholomew Latomus († 1570), and at Aix-la-Chapelle the provost William Insulanus († 1556), became authors of publications on the Holy Eucharist and on Grace.[2]

A considerable number of Catholic theologians came from the ranks of the secular clergy of sacred Cologne. Only the most prominent ones need be mentioned here : Ortwin Gratius and Arnold von Tungern, professors at the university, and known in the Reuchlin controversy,[3] and the controversialists, Arnold Haldrein, Jacob Horst and Matthias Cremer.[4] All these, however, are outshone by John Gropper.[5] His contemporaries, without exception, praise the admirable virtues and the profound learning of this man, who devoted his whole strength to stem the storm-flood of the new doctrines, and to whom

[1] Widmann, *Mainzer Presse*, vi. 72 ff.   Concerning M. Helding see Wetzer und Welte's *Kirchenlexikon*, x[1]. 121 f. ; Moufang, *Katechismen*, p. 365 ff. ; Aschbach, *Kirchenlexikon*, iii. 211 ff. ; and above all, Paulus in the *Katholik*, 1894, ii. 410 f., 481 f.

[2] See Marx, *Erzstift Trier*, ii. 499 ; v. Bianco, p. 747 f. ; and ** Memser, ii. 193 f. (for Insulanus).

[3] See the present work, vol. i. pp. 96 f., 98, 104 ; vol. iii. p. 54 ; Wetzer und Welte's *Kirchenlexikon*, v. 1036 f. ; Widmann, *Mainzer Presse*, p. 16 f. ; Reichling, *O. Gratius*, Heiligenstadt, 1884.

[4] Wetzer und Welte's *Kirchenlexikon*, iii[2]. 1173–1174 ; v. 1460.   Paulus, *Katholische Schriftsteller*, p. 552, and Appendix, p. 216.   Macco in the *Zeitschrift, Aus Aachens Vorzeit*, 13 Jahrg.

[5] The literature about Gropper is summarised in Pastor, *Reunionsbestrebungen*, p. 166 note 1.   See also Dittrich's Monograph on *G. Contarini*, Braunsberg, 1885.   Besides these there are the important Roman documents which Schwarz has published in the *Histor. Jahrbuch*, vii. 392 ff., 594 ff.   Jostes (*Daniel von Soest*, Paderborn, 1888) supposes Gropper to be identical with Daniel von Soest, the author of the satirical writings, *Gemeine Beicht, Dialogon and Apologeticon*, which formed a polemical apologetic of the Catholic faith.   Janssen (vol. xii. p. 71, n. 3, of the present work) is inclined to agree with this assumption.

it was in great measure due that Cologne retained her
honourable title of ' Faithful daughter of the Roman
Church.'   Born at Soest, in Westphalia, on February
24, 1503, John Gropper in 1525, had obtained the
doctorate in law at Cologne, and in the following year
had become keeper of the seal of the archbishopric.
As such he accompanied Archbishop Hermann, in 1530,
to the Augsburg Diet, where he acted mildly and for-
bearingly in the spirit of toleration and conciliation.
The Erasmian party at the court of the Elector soon
grew fond of this finely cultured man, and tried in
every way to support him. Gropper was enrolled
in the special court service of the Archbishop, whose
most influential counsellor he soon became. When,
in 1536, a great provincial council assembled in the
Rhenish metropolis, the formulation of the resolutions
was entrusted to him.   He was besides commissioned to
compile a small handbook of Christian doctrine.   This
work, which grew to be a complete system of Dogmatic,
of more than 500 folio pages, appeared in print in
1538 at the same time as the Canons of the Provincial
Council.   The object of the Canons was to do away with
the worst of the ecclesiastical abuses, that of the dogmatic manual to provide an antidote against the continually
widening spread of heretical teaching.   There can be
no doubt that the Dogmatic of Gropper, though in the
main soundly Catholic, is not free from theological
errors.   What makes it of special importance is the
peculiar character of the conciliatory doctrine of justification which he set forth, and which in several points
came very near to the Protestant version of this doctrine.
Gropper, by his exposition of this doctrine placed himself in the ranks of those mediating theologians who

hoped to bring about a reconciliation between the Protestants and the Church by partial surrender and compromise.

The father of this middle party is Erasmus of Rotterdam. After long wavering and hesitating, he at last, in 1524, attacked Luther in the heart of his errors, viz. in that doctrine which is utterly subversive of all human dignity, the non-freedom of the will; [1] at the same time he had not yet openly joined the ranks of the defenders of the old Church ; then, as before, he endeavoured to maintain a middle position. As both parties rejected his ambiguous proposals towards reconciliation he withdrew, deeply offended, and devoted himself to the publication of Church Fathers. At the Augsburg Diet, also, the learned scholar, who was averse to all appearance in public, did not show himself, although numbers of very distinguished men wished for his presence there. It was not till the later years of his life that Erasmus came forward in public again, with schemes for reconciliation. The renowned humanist had thus embarked on a sphere in which, owing to his theological standpoint, he could not achieve any results. His ideal in theology was the utmost possible elasticity, breadth of interpretation and indefiniteness. There was nothing he so greatly detested as a speculative basis in theological doctrine, a distinct and sharply outlined conception, the practice of systematising and deducing in dogmatics and morals. Hence his ingrained hostility towards scholastics. At a period when many fundamental doctrines of faith were being

---

[1] Concerning the controversy between Erasmus and Luther see K. A. Menzel, i. 143 f. ; Köstlin, *Luther*, i². 688 f. ; Drummond, ii. 200 f. ; Döllinger, iii. 25 f. ; and Riffel (who goes most into detail), ii. 250–298.

questioned he made the proposal, in all seriousness, not to attempt the settlement of disputed points at a council, but to postpone it 'till such time as we should see God, without a glass, face to face'! A man who represented such views as these, who had quite lost the definite conception of the Church, had no platform whatever for a compromise or a reconciliation between the great conflicting ideas of the day.[1] Any adoption of his proposals would certainly have made the confusion still greater ; for the unity which he wanted could only be bought at the price of indefiniteness.[2] Men of sound and thorough theological culture like Albertus Pius of Carpi rightly therefore declared themselves openly against the new 'true theology of Erasmus.'[3] If, however, his peace-making efforts found not a few adherents, this is primarily explained by the conditions of the time, which made reconciliation at any price seem desirable ; and also by the circumstance that men deficiently trained in theology and autodidacticians, like Julius Pflug (later on Bishop of Naumburg), took part in the solution of the great problems of the day.

The influence which Erasmus exercised on scholars like Pflug and Wizel, who inclined towards conciliatory endeavours, is by no means to be lightly estimated ; in all essential points these men are dependent on him.[4] The same applies to Gropper. The semi-Lutheran

[1] See Kerker, ' Erasmus und sein theologischer Standpunkt,' in the *Tübinger Theolog. Quartalschrift*, 1859, pp. 531–566. See also A. Richter, *Erasmus-Studien*, Dresden, 1891.

[2] See Pastor, *Reunionsbestrebungen*, pp. 133–134.

[3] See present work, vol. iii. p. 15 ff.

[4] Concerning Pflug see Pastor, *Reunionsbestrebungen*, p. 136 f. ; Aschbach, *Kirchenlexikon*, iv. 530 ; and Beutel, *Über den Ursprung des Augsburger Interims*, Dresden, 1888.

doctrine of justification which he professed was held also in similar form by Erasmus. This attempt to remodel the dogma of justification partly in the sense of the religious innovators was soon to attain to the greatest importance. During the religious conference of Worms, Gropper and the Imperial secretary Velt-wyck carried on transactions with Bucer and Capito. The result of these strictly private discussions was the ' Ratisbon Book.' This publication was based on the transactions of the religious conference. During the course of the latter Gropper went to the utmost limits of concession ; he even exceeded them. At one moment it seemed as if the work of unification was about to succeed. On May 2, 1541, a formula respecting the doctrine of justification, drawn up by both parties, was accepted. This document, however, was such a mongrel production that no party was actually satisfied with it. The semi-Lutheran doctrine of justification was adopted in it, and Protestant and Catholic elements were mixed in the strangest manner. This ' extraor-dinary medley of opposite views ' [1] soon became dis-tasteful to its actual originators. Melanchthon was by no means satisfied with it. Gropper and Pflug represented to the Emperor that the formula needed further working up in order to make it harmonise with the Catholic Church. By this action the middle party showed itself to be incapable of effecting a real reunion. No wonder that the first apparent success was the signal for the immediate downfall of the whole party.

Nevertheless we must beware of pronouncing too

[1] Vetter, *Die Religionsverhandlungen auf dem Reichstage zu Regensburg*, Jena, 1889, p. 15.

severe a judgment on men who, like Gropper at Ratisbon, accepted the semi-Lutheran doctrine of justification. The Council had not yet pronounced on this question, which was little considered by the old theologians. It was a period of transition, of uncertainty, of unclearness. At such times much was held to be possible. Gropper and his fellow-thinkers erred undoubtedly, but they erred with the best intentions.[1] In exculpation of Gropper, it must also be remembered that he was no scholastically trained theologian. 'In my youth,' he writes, 'I studied jurisprudence. The Bible and the Holy Fathers I did not begin to study till 1530, when discussions on religious questions were going on at the Diet at Augsburg, and then only privately without a teacher.'[2]

If it cannot be denied that Gropper, at Ratisbon, overstepped the limits of the permissible in his concessions to the innovators, his adhesion to the old Church was nevertheless beyond all doubt sublime. When the Council of Trent defined a single formal cause of justification as Catholic doctrine, he submitted to it with the most complete readiness.[3] At Cologne, however, he was actually the saviour of the old faith. Scarcely had the unholy Archbishop Hermann, at the end of 1542, summoned Bucer to his court and initiated the attempt to Protestantise his archbishopric, than Gropper stood up against him 'with the most resolute opposition.' In 1544 he published, first in German and then in Latin, a refutation of the

[1] Pastor, *Reunionsbestrebungen*, pp. 250, 269 f. Concerning Gropper's work at Ratisbon see also Dittrich in the *Histor. Jahrb.* xiii. 196 f.

[2] Pastor, *Reunionsbestrebungen*, vii. 412 ; x. 404.

[3] Müller, *Epist. ad Pflugium*, Lipsiae, 1802, p. 114 f. See Döllinger, iii. 311.

archiepiscopal Reformation book compiled by Bucer and Melanchthon, in which he contrasted the new doctrines, section by section, with the old Catholic ones. Even on the Protestant side it is admitted that " The whole controversial literature of the years 1543–1547 has no work of equal importance to show on the part of the opponents of the Archbishop.' [1] In the ensuing years Gropper in all ways incessantly opposed the innovators. His great work, ' Von wahrer, wesentlicher und bleibender Gegenwärtigkert des Leibes und Blutes Christi im hochwürdigsten heiligsten Sakrament des Altars und von der Communion unter einer Gestalt ' (1548), was connected with a controversial pamphlet against Bucer. In addition to these publications this active scholar also produced catechetical works, equally with the object of opposing the innovators. As the Protestants sought everywhere to spread their doctrines by means of popular pamphlets, catechisms, postilles and agents, it was the duty of the Catholics, he thought, to do the same in order not to lose hold of the common people and the young generation. In these works it was advisable to keep as close as possible to the actual words of Scripture and to tradition, which had always a stronger influence on the people than the words of the authors.

At Cologne, where, owing to the excommunication of the Archbishop Hermann, Gropper felt that the worst danger was averted, he energetically promoted the labours of the Jesuits. In his native town of Soest he accomplished, in 1548, the restoration of the Catholic church. Three years later he accompanied the new Archbishop

---

[1] Brieger in Ersch und Gruber's *Enzyklopädie*, xcii. 235.

Adolf von Schauenburg to the Council of Trent, where he delivered an address on the misuse of Appellations. At the instigation of Adolf, Gropper, who meanwhile had become provost at Bonn, and archdeacon of the archbishopric, drew up a memorandum in which he showed that only a general council would be able to settle the religious schism. Religious conferences, he said, only made the antagonists more stubborn, besides which a common basis for disputation was wanting, as also a competent judge.

High distinction was destined to befall this exemplary theologian in the evening of his life. On December 18, 1555, the Pope Paul IV raised him to the dignity of cardinal. The modest scholar, however, refused the purple. When four years later he appeared in Rome, probably in order to prevent the consecration of the unworthy archbishop John Gebhard, of Mansfeld, he was accorded the most honourable reception by the Pope. He had already been ailing in health on the journey, and he was taken ill again at Rome, and died there on March 14, 1559. His last days were clouded by the hostility of personal opponents. He defended himself so effectually against accusations of erroneous beliefs that came from this direction, that Pius IV, in the Consistory, bewailed his death in a long speech, and pronounced severe blame on his calumniators.[1]

In Alsatia, Michael Buchinger laboured as preacher, and in the writings of this excellent man it is specially to be noticed that he defended the veneration of images, the command to fast, and the most holy Sacrament of the altar.[2]

---

[1] Schwarz in the *Histor. Jahrbuch*, vii. 596 f.
[2] Paulus in the *Katholik*, 1892, ii. 203 ff.

To South Germany, likewise, belongs the work of the famous John Heigerlin, styled Faber.[1]   The son of a smith (hence his Latin name Faber), born in 1478 at Leutkirch in the Allgäu, he studied theology and jurisprudence at Freiburg in the Breisgau, became pastor at Lindau, and in 1518 vicar-general to the Bishop of Constance. With Erasmus and numerous other humanists, also with Oecolampadius and Zwingli, Faber stood in the most active intercourse. The unworthy traffic in indulgences of the Franciscan Samson was opposed with the utmost zeal by ' that man of distinguished talent, learning and piety,' who also boldly drew attention to the abuses at the Roman Court. It cannot, therefore, seem surprising that he should at first have viewed with favourable eyes the advent of Luther ; when, however, the latter broke openly with the Church, Faber assumed a decidedly hostile attitude towards him.

In the autumn of 1521 he made a journey to Rome, where, with the assistance of Cardinal Schinner, he completed a work against Luther's new dogmas. It was dedicated to Pope Hadrian VI, and was published in 1522 in the Eternal City. Backed by his extensive reading, Faber here assails Luther's pamphlet ' Von

---

[1] See Kettner, *De J. Fabri vita scriptisque*, Lipsiae, 1737 ; R. Roth, *Geschichte der Reichsstadt Leutkirch*, i. (1870) 200 ; ii. 90 ff. ; Wetzer und Welte's *Kirchenlexikon*, iv². 1172 ff. ; Herzog's *Realenzyklopädie*, iv². 475 ff. ; Kopallik, *Regesten der Erzbischöfe Wien*, ii. 11 f. ; and Nagl-Zeidler, p. 602 f. Horawitz intended writing a monograph on Faber, but only the first sheets of it appeared (*Separatabdruck aus den Sitzungsberichten der Wiener Akademie*, Wien, 1884) ; for the criticism of which cf. Wahl in the *Tübinger Theolog. Quartalschr.* lxviii. 337 ff.   See also Kink, i. 243 ff. ; Wiedemann, ii. 1 ff. ; and *Zeitschrift für Gesch. des Oberrheins*, viii. (1893) 17 ff.   The statement again repeated by Horawitz that Faber entered the Dominican Order is certainly incorrect ; see Denis, p. 266 f., and Wiedemann, *Reformation*, ii. 25, note 2.

dem Papestum in Rom.' ' The wrath of Hutten and
the repeated editions of the work show that Faber
hit more than one sore point.' His publication, in
which the Primacy and the secular dominion of the
Pope are defended, and the abolition of abuses in a
legitimate manner insisted on, ' contributed largely
towards separating the reform party in Germany from
the revolutionary party.' [1]

Luther was greatly incensed ; he called Faber
' an arch-fool, a donkey's head, a whoremonger,' and
commissioned Justus Jonas to refute him. In 1523
Jonas had already finished this task, quite in the style
of Luther. Faber, on the title-page of this book, is
called ' Patron of the whores.' The only other task
that Jonas attempted was a defence of the marriage
of priests. Chastity, he said, was impossible, because
contrary to nature. The abusive language of Jonas
did not hinder the spread of Faber's pamphlet, the new
editions of which had a furious sale. Faber was now
attacked also by Zwingli ; in 1523 he came forward
against him at the Zurich disputation. In the same
year King Ferdinand I appointed him his councillor.
Thenceforth the career of this highly gifted man became extensively ramified. ' Indefatigably, with word
and writing, in colloquies, by sermons, and in public
transactions, and by personal influence on princes and
towns in Germany, and in Switzerland,' he fought against
the new religionists. In 1526 he took part in the Baden
religious conference, and attended the Diet at Spires.
In 1527 he was working in England under commission
of King Ferdinand. In 1529 he appeared at the Diet
of Spires ; in 1530 at that of Augsburg, where he took

[1] Höfler, *Adrian VI*, p. 363.

a prominent part in the refutation of the Confession ; he was at that period so overburdened with work that he had no time for rest at night.[1] In the same year he became Bishop of Vienna, at which town he died on May 21, 1541, after a thorny but enormously fruitful career of activity.

In addition to his numerous official occupations and travels Faber found time also in his later years to write pamphlets against the innovators. How carefully and thoroughly he studied the works of the adversaries, especially those of Luther, is seen from the abundant quotations in his literary remains preserved in the Vienna Court library.[2]

In 1528 he submitted Luther's 'Instructions to the Saxon Inspectors' to severe criticism. In the same year he published a pamphlet against the Moravian Anabaptists, defended against Oecolampadius the invocation of Saints, and wrote a comparison between the doctrines of Huss and those of Luther.[3] In 1530 he published a collection of a multitude of Luther's contradictions, and in 1535 defended against Luther the Mass and the priesthood, while, in 1536, he brought out a special treatise on faith and good works, dedicated to Ferdinand I. At the same time he drew up a memorandum on the council question, intended for Pope Paul III, in which he emphasised above all the necessity for the Catholics to put themselves in a position to refute the doctrines of the seceders from the faith on the ground of their

[1] See *Ficker*, pp. xxiv f., xxviii–xxix, xl, xlii f., xlv, xlviii, lxxii f., lxxxii f., xciii.

[2] *Ibid.* p. xxiv.

[3] See Werner, iv. 170 f., 204, 222 ; Kettner, *De J. Fabri vita scriptisque*, p. 31.

own writings, and insisted that the really poor and needy champions of the Church in Germany should be supported by the Curia, and supplied with the necessary means for attending the Council.   Four years later, on the occasion of the Worms religious conference, Faber drew up a memorandum by which he hoped to prevent the recurrence of the faults made by the Catholics in earlier transactions.[1]   How much the indefatigable Vienna bishop did for the Church during the storms of that revolutionary period will not be fully known until the story of his life is told from original sources.   It was with good ground that the friends of innovation looked on him as ' one of their most active and, by reason of his influential position, most dangerous enemies.   His contemporaries and fellow-believers praise him as the model of a Catholic bishop, as an ornament of the Church, as a man distinguished for learning, wisdom, and purity of morals.' [2]   ' What Cochlaeus is for Saxony,' wrote Alexander in 1532, ' Eck for the Danubeland, Nausea for the Rhineland, Ber [3] for Switzerland, that John Faber is for the lands of the Roman King.' [4]

In the closest bonds of friendship with Faber stood Frederic Nausea, his successor to the episcopal chair at Vienna.[5]   Born in 1480 at Waischenfeld, in the

[1] See *Nuntiaturberichte*, ii. 13 f., and Pastor, *Reunionsbestrebungen*, pp. 103, 199.

[2] See Herzog's *Realenzyklopädie*, iv². 475.

[3] Concerning Ludwig Ver see *Sitzungsberichte der Wiener Akademie*, cviii. 811 f. ; Vischer, *Gesch. der Universität Basel*, Basel, 1860 ; Fiala in Wetzer und Welte's *Kirchenlexikon*, ii². 492 f., and *Nuntiaturberichte*, i. 2, 63.

[4] Lämmer, *Mon. Vat.* p. 119.   See also the report of Vergerius of June 13, 1533, in the *Nuntiaturberichte*, i. 95.

[5] Besides the monograph of Metzner see also the supplementary contributions of Falk in the *Geschichteblätter der mittelrheinischen Bistümer*, i. 190 ff., and the *Katholik*, 1889, i. 314 ; as well as Döllinger, *Beiträge*,

Bamberg district, a son of the wheelwright Grau (hence
the Latinised family name of Nausea), he devoted himself at Leipzig to the higher branches of study, and went
afterwards to Pavia and Padua, where philology, theology and jurisprudence were cultivated. In 1524 he
travelled through Germany, Hungary and Italy as
secretary to the legate Lorenz Campeggio ; two years
later he was to have entered on the post of pastor at
the Bartholomew foundation at Frankfort-on-the-Main,
but found himself compelled to fly from the Protestant
town. He then betook himself to Mayence, where he
became unweariedly active in the Catholic cause.
Through his friend Faber he came into closer relations with King Ferdinand, who appointed him royal
preacher and court counsellor at Vienna. Here he soon
developed even greater activity ·than at Mayence.
Next to literary work it was the office of preacher
which made most claim on him. In 1538 he became
coadjutor, and in 1541 successor, to his friend Faber.
As bishop of Vienna he drew up for Ferdinand I a
memorandum on the question of Church reunion, and
took part also in the transactions of the Council of
Trent. He died at Trent on February 6, 1552.

The number of Nausea's publications is enormous.
They belong in part to philology and jurisprudence
and in part to theology. Most of them were printed
by Quentel at Cologne. Of his theological works those
that stand out pre-eminently are the sermons circulated in many thousands of copies. By means of these
he preserved thousands of people in the old Church,

iii. 152 ff., and *Histor.-Jahrbuch*, viii. 1 ff. ; Kopalik, *Regesten der Erzdiözese*
Wien, ii. 29 f. ; Nagl-Zeidler, p. 603 ; M. Eymer, *Fr. Nausea, ein Kirchen-
fürst und Pädagoge*, Leitmeritz, 1899.

and brought as many back to it.[1]   A master of exegesis,
he handles the Holy Scriptures with admirable bravery ;
clearly and precisely he presents to sight the Catholic
teaching on faith and duty, and is able with dialectical
skill to meet all objections victoriously.   He exhibits
herein an ascetic training which fills the reader with
veneration.   His teaching is profusely illustrated by
examples from the history of the world, the Church
and the Saints.   As a rule, he avoids anything akin to
rhetoric and ornament.[2]

Nausea also rendered important service by his
Catholic catechism.   He had already compiled this at
Mayence, but could not get it published till 1543.
Excessive pressure of business and work, failing health
and want of the necessary means for publication, were
the causes of this long delay.   Besides which, in order
to make his book as complete and trustworthy as
possible, he had submitted it to a number of cardinals
for examination ; for he wished to produce a work
which might possibly be adopted and recommended
by the forthcoming Council of Trent as a general text-
book, and thus meet a widely felt want.   Although
this hope was not fulfilled, Nausea's Catechism, a folio
volume of 654 pages, met with such high approval in
clerical circles that during the lifetime of its author
it went through several editions in Germany and elsewhere.[3]

While Nausea in his Catechism speaks against
Communion in both forms, later on, in his work on the

[1] See Lämmer, *Mon. Vat.* pp. 96, 99.   On his tombstone Nausea is
represented preaching ; see Denis, p. 392.

[2] Metzner, p. 103.

[3] Moufang, ' Die Mainzer Katechismen ' in the *Katholik*, 1877, Jahrg. 57,
pp. 627–633.

Council, he advocated the maintenance of the usage in the hope by this means of more easily winning back seceders to the Church. He also thought it right, in view of the many and gross scandals which made the clerical condition contemptible and led to a distressing dearth of priests, to put it to the Pope's conscience whether the obligatory character of celibacy should not be abolished.

More fruitful in blessings, however, than any such proposals was his agitation for the reform of the clergy. One reason among others for the decay of morals he found to be the neglect of the study of the Church Fathers. He therefore again and again most urgently recommended the works of the Holy Fathers, as well as those of the great scholars of the Middle Ages, to the notice of his contemporaries.[1]

The Bavarian theologians distinguished themselves even more than those of the Rhinelands in the first half of the sixteenth century. Here, too, the secular clergy can boast of admirable representatives of the old doctrines: individuals among them rendered services of quite remarkable importance. This applies above all to the 'Deutsche Theologie' of Bertold Pirstinger (1508–1525 bishop of Chiemsee), which was printed at Munich in 1528. 'To the praise of God,' says the author, ' for the service of the Christian Church, for the help of the German nation, and for the salutary instruction of us miserable people, I have herewith undertaken to collect from writings and teachers, above all from the books of St. Augustine, and put together in this treatise all that is in conformity with the truth and serviceable to the foundation of Christian

[1] Metzner, pp. 80, 102.

faith, in the hope that my readers may get out of it good counsel and information as to how and what they ought finally to believe as truth.' He had no desire, he said, to dispute with those who felt envy towards the priesthood, or dislike of good works or disinclination to God's service. Such people the devil never left out of his ' carding comb.' To those, however, who had erred from the way of truth not out of wickedness but from want of understanding, to these pious people God sent help in time of temptation. Such a help, Bertold hoped, his book would be to the Germans who were misled by the Lutheran heresies. No doubt the book would be abused, slandered, ridiculed, rejected and condemned by the opponents. None the less had he, ' as a servant who owed God his Lord a hundred measures of wheat or a hundred tankards of oil, endeavoured to compress the following opinions into a hundred chapters.' In those he not only deals with the disputed points of faith and works, Scripture and Church authority, nature and grace, sacraments, purgatory, indulgence, hierarchy, vows, but also with the doctrines of the most Holy Trinity, the Incarnation of God, as well as cosmological and Church-law questions of all sorts. This work of Bertold, characterised by genuine religious fervour and sound scholarship, and which may be described as a complete system of dogmatics, belongs to the most interesting productions of Catholic literature at that period in Germany.[1]

With Bertold Pirstinger we may group John

---

[1] See Maurenbrecher, *Kathol. Reformation*, i. 248 ; Lämmer, *Vortrid. Theologie*, pp. 29–30 ; *Histor.-polit. Blätter*, vii. 113 ff. ; Scheeben, i. 444 ; Heinrich, *Dogmatik*, i. 103, note 2.

Altensteig, pastor at Mindelheim; John Haner, cathedral preacher at Bamberg; Lorenz Hochwart and
Paul Hirschbeck, both preachers at Ratisbon; John
Freyberger, canon at Freising; Leonhard Haller,
Bishop-designate at Eichstätt; Matthias Kretz, preacher
at Augsburg and Munich;[1] finally the Ingolstadt professors George Hauer († 1536), Nicholas Apel († 1545),
Leonard Marstaller († 1546), George Theander,[2] and at
their head John Eck.

This renowned champion of the Catholic cause was
a man of distinguished and rare endowments. For his
scholarship and for the work he accomplished he deserves the first rank among the theologians who were
active in Bavaria.[3] He was born on November 13,
1486, in the Suabian village of Eck, in somewhat
needy circumstances. Michael Maier, 'an honest
peasant,' was his father; but later on he generally
called himself only John von Eck, after his native
place, or simply John Eck, in Latin Johannes Eckius
(Eccius). At the age of eight an uncle, Martin Maier,
pastor at Rottenburg, 'took him away from the
domestic hearth' and set him to study, and his
talents developed with amazing rapidity. In three
years he had completed his humanistic studies, and
in another three years his philosophical studies. At
the age of fourteen (January 1501) he took the degree
of doctor of philosophy, when not quite twenty-four

---

[1] For the above-named see Kobolt, pp. 232, 330 f., 382 ff.; Paulus,
Katholische Schriftsteller, pp. 546, 550–554; *Histor.-polit. Blätter*, cxi. 30.
Concerning Kretz specially, Paulus in the *Histor.-polit. Blätter*, cxiv.
(1894) 1 ff. 'Zwölf Briefe von Johann Haner, meist an Aleander gerichtet,
einzelne an Vergerio, Kard. Sancho und Paul III,' published at Friedensburg in the *Beiträge zur bayrischen Kirchengesch.* v.

[2] See Paulus, *Katholische Schriftsteller*, pp. 546, 552, 555, 560.

[3] Opinion of Riezler, vi. 359 f.; see also iv. 56 f., 304 f.

(October 22, 1510) that of doctor of theology, and at the time of his ordination as priest (December 13, 1508), ' in spite of his youth and impecuniosity,' he stood already in the friendliest relations with the most important scholars of the day.[1]

Eck was a man of marvellously versatile talents. He was interested in everything, in the most difficult questions of scholasticism as well as in mystic theology, in speculative problems as well as in all the positive knowledge of his time. He entered with the keenest enthusiasm into the newly revived humanist studies.[2] The speeches and sermons of his first priest's years are overladen with quotations from the classics.[3] In Hebrew, the study of which he began at Freiburg, he strove still in his later years to perfect himself. At Bologna he copied old inscriptions, at Vienna and Melk he examined manuscripts of older scholars. For his edition of Dionysius the Areopagite he procured an old manuscript from Ratisbon ; against Luther he made use of an unprinted collection of canons anterior to Gratian.

In the question of the improvement of the calendar he was as able in the name of the Ingolstadt university to make his opinion carry weight as he also did in the department of jurisprudence. Even the customs and the history of the Tartars excited his attention ; he translated a ' Traktat von baiden Sarmatien und andern anstossenden Landen in Asia und Europa wunderparlich zu hören.' [4]

---

[1] Wiedemann, *Dr. Johann Eck*, pp. 8, 27, 29.

[2] See present work, vol. i. p. 74, and Wiedemann, pp. 3 f., 36, 43, 495.

[3] Even in theological writings he makes use of evidence from the poets. *De poenitentia*, i. 7.

[4] Fuller details occur in Wiedemann, pp. 23, 60, 71, 74, 457, 488, 500.

Eck also developed a wealth of scholastic activity in other directions after he had obtained at Ingolstadt, at the end of 1510, a fixed post as professor of theology and pro-chancellor of the university. At Freiburg, where he had taken his doctor's degree, he had not succeeded, in spite of his fitness, in obtaining a similar post.

As a young professor at Ingolstadt Eck at first adhered entirely to the late scholastic tendency. He based his lectures on the subtlest of all the great scholastics, Duns Scotus, although he also showed signs of being influenced by Gerson. His first great theological work dealt with the difficult question of predestination. He delighted at that time in putting forward hazardous theses,[1] the defence of which was more a matter of intellectual gymnastics, of readiness in fighting, than of the truth of the cause. At the disputations therefore, especially at those of Bologna in the year 1515 and at Vienna in 1516, he succeeded, in addition to his other distinctions, in acquiring the renown of a skilled disputator and an important theologian. Nevertheless Eck, even at that time, felt the deficiencies of the declining scholastics. His first work,[2] was directed against a tendency to old-fashionedness at the university of Freiburg. The commentaries on Peter Hispanus (Pope John XXI), as also on the logical, psychological and natural philosophical writings of Aristotle, which he brought out in quick succession in the years 1517–1520, were intended, in accordance with the sentiments of the ducal government, to serve

---

[1] Examples are given in Wiedemann, p. 65. See the ' Thesenzettel ' in the *Disputatio Viennae habita*.

[2] *Bursa pavonis. Logices exercitamenta.*

the purpose of a reform of philosophical studies at Ingolstadt.[1]

A complete revolution took place in Eck's scholastic activity after, almost by chance, he had become involved in a controversy with Luther. If hitherto he had only pursued theoretical ends in his scholasticism, he now resolved to put his knowledge to practical use in order to take part in the burning questions of the day. His travels now no longer had a purely scientific aim. Three times he made his appearance in Rome : twice in relation to the Bull against Luther, and a third time as ambassador of his prince. A visit to King Henry VIII of England and his theologians was undoubtedly connected with apologetic efforts.[2] As Eck at Leipzig was the champion against Luther and Carlstadt, so in 1526 he appeared at Baden as the opponent of Zwingli's followers. He mixed himself up, unbidden, in the religious controversies at Ulm. ' So long as I live,' he wrote, ' I shall be the enemy of all heretics, schismatics and apostates from our holy faith, and shall fight them to my utmost powers.' The repute of the indefatigable combatant was already at this time very great. On his journey to Baden the town council of Constance solicited his help in the religious disturbances of the place ; at Memmingen the oppressed Catholic clergy appealed to his science. At the Diet at Augsburg in 1530 he developed such wonderful activity that Cardinal Campeggio was moved to report to Rome, ' For the continuous works that he has accomplished, and is still accomplishing, I consider him worthy of a bishop's chair.' At the colloquies at

---

[1] Wiedemann, p. 33.
[2] *Ibid*. pp. 30, 139, 184, 185.

Worms in 1540 and at Ratisbon in 1541 he was the principal speaker on the Catholic side. During the last day, half of the friends of the Interim gave way before his clearness and firmness of principle. Even in his last illness he was busy as an author. At length, on February 10, 1543, death snatched the pen from his hand.[1]

Eck's polemical works, by their number alone, give evidence of the zeal and power of work of their author. At the time of his first battles with Luther, from August 1518 to the end of 1519, he brought out no less than thirteen smaller publications, ten of which referred to the Leipzig disputation.[2] Many of his later works were also in like manner written for occasions. In many of them some work or other of an opponent is analysed and refuted—as, for instance, in the ' Verlegung der Disputation zu Bern ' in 1528, and the ' Ableinung der Verantwurtung Burgermeisters und Rats der Stat Costentz ' in 1527. Others were written with the object of discussing the religious conditions in favour of the Catholics, as in ' Ein Sendbrief an eine

[1] Wiedemann, pp. 206, 258, 260, 262, 266, 352. Concerning Eck's appearance at Ratisbon see the present work, vol. vi. p. 160; and also Dittrich, *Contarini*, Braunsberg, 1885; and the same writer's *Miscellanea Ratisbonensia*, Brunsbergae, 1892 ; for Eck's work at the Augsburg Diet of 1530 and his share in the confutation of the Augsburg Confession see Ficker, pp. xxvii, xxxii f., xxxv f., xcviii.   Eck und Adelmann, see Thurnhofer, *Bernhard Adelmann*, p. 54 f.

[2] ' At the greater Leipzig disputation,' says Riezler (iv. 59), ' which was carried on between Eck, Carlstadt, and Luther from June 27 to July 15, 1519, Eck was at an advantage—perhaps also in scholarship and skill— but certainly from the fact that he knew exactly what he believed and what he wanted, while Luther was not yet clear about his aims, and it was through the disputation itself that the process of religious fermentation was hastened on in his consciousness.

fromme Eidgenossenschaft.' Others, again,[1] were intended to ward off attacks on his person.

Of still greater importance are those works in which
particular controversial points are discussed and the
Catholic doctrines systematically established. The first
and most comprehensive work of this class deals with
the doctrine of the supremacy of the Pope. The
choice of the subject was determined by Luther's
pamphlet ' Von der Gewalt des Papstes,' and the
importance of the question. ' Just as great masters in
the arts of painting and sculpture bestow especial
care on the delineation of the head, so I, in taking up
my pen against Luther's heresies, have begun with the
head—that is to say, with the authority of the Church
and the Pope. For if once this truth were triumphantly proved, all the attacks of the unworthy must
fall to the ground.' [2] Like the subject, so too the
method of treatment was determined with regard to the
opponents. Special consideration was bestowed on, the
humanists, ' who think, forsooth, to ascend from the
school of Diomedes and Priscian into the school of
Christ.' [3] With the speculative utterances of scholasticism nothing was to be gained from those grammar theologians. ' When these men see that Luther only quotes
from Holy Scripture and from the Fathers, they are at
once caught. I will therefore refute Luther's pamphlet

---

[1] *Schutzred Kindlicher Unschuld wider den Catechisten Andre Hosander
und sein Schmachbüchlein* (1540). In the *Replica Io. Eckii adversus
scripta secunda Buceri apostatae* (1543) there is an ' Expurgatio Eckii a
mendaci infamatione, quia adhuc vivit Eckius.' By these two publications we are accurately instructed concerning the career of the author.

[2] *De poenitentia*, Ingolstadii, 1522, dedicatio.

[3] *De primatu*, i. 1.

with perfectly clear evidence from the Christian faith, and prove our doctrines out of the Holy Scriptures, the statements of holy Fathers and the decrees of sacred Councils, setting aside later authors to whom Luther, in his presumption, attaches no importance.' So then in the first book of this work the passages in Holy Scripture relating to the precedence of St. Peter are discussed, the explanations of the Fathers are brought forward, those of Luther refuted. The second book presents the doctrines of the Fathers and the Councils on the same subject, and adds at the end a few reasons for a monarchical constitution of the Church. The third book refutes Luther's theory that the Primacy is of purely human origin. The work bears witness to the voluminousness of Eck's reading and refutes Luther's assertions. It was unavoidable in the then condition of criticism that Eck should borrow (especially from Gratian) many texts that were not genuine.[1] Frequently, meanwhile, where contemporary research had already raised doubts, as with regard to the Donation of Constantine, Eck entertains the same critical scruples.[2] Of historical interest are the author's judgment on the Constance synod, his remarks on the abuses at the Roman Curia, his complaints of the secularisation of the bishops.[3]

[1] See Hergenröther in the continuation of Hefele's *Konziliengesch.* ix. 104 ff., 130.

[2] Instabit diversarius, hanc (donationem) esse inanem paleam sine grano, quam Dantes Florentinus et Laurentius Valla diu triturarunt, multi praeterea ex jureconsultis dubitant an sit facta, ut Leopoldus Bebenburgius . . . explicat ; et qui credunt eam esse factam, adhuc dubitant an valuerit. . . . At utcunque sit, tantae dubietatis pelagum hic non expiscabimur. Quia ut Card. Cusanus inquit, ista quaestio non est soluta hactenus, nec solvetur verisimiliter unquam.' *De primatu*, ii. 16.

[3] *De primatu*, i. 43 ; iii. 6, 49, 50. For the proposals for reform which Eck made at Rome in 1523, see *Histor. Jahrbuch*, 1884, p. 371 f.

In exactly the same way Eck defended the Catholic doctrines of purgatory (1523–1530), of penitence (1522–1523), of veneration of images (1522), of the Holy Mass (1526). Speculative theories are dealt with as much as possible, and the principal stress laid on the positive proof of Catholic teaching from Scripture and tradition.

A smaller popular publication of Eck, however, his so-called ' Handbüchlein ' which he opposed to Melanchthon's ' Loci communes,' had an incomparably larger circulation than the longer work intended chiefly for scholars.[1] This book, published at the wish of Cardinal Campeggio, deals with all the controversial points between Catholics and new-religionists, with the burning questions of the authority of councils and popes, of sacraments and justification, as well as with the objections of the Protestants to annates and the lawfulness of the Turkish war. The plan of the book is as follows. At the head of each chapter the Catholic doctrine is summed up in the thesis form. Then comes the proof by means of passages from the Fathers and from Scripture, and the refutation of objections from opponents ; and at the end the results and the positive contents of the whole are once more surveyed and summed up. The warm approval which the little book met with is seen from the numerous editions it went through.

[1] *Enchiridion locorum communium adversus Lutheranos* (Landshut, 1525, German translation, s.l. 1530. We make use of that of 1565). This little book, says Eck in the preface to the edition of 1529, he published by the advice of Cardinal Campeggio : ' quo occupatiores, quibus non vacat grandia heroum volumina revolvere, in promptu et brevi (ut aiunt) manu haberent, quo haereticis occurrerent.' At the same time it was to be a ' summarium credendorum ' for the ' simpliciores,' ' ne a pseudoapostolis subverterentur.' Wiedemann, p. 536. With Eck's ' short and apt ' treatment in his *Enchiridion* on the relation of inspired writing to Church tradition and doctrinal authority, cf. Holzhey, p. 149 f.

Again in 1525 four fresh editions appeared, including
one in London and one in Cracow.   In the following
year it went through one fresh edition both at Cologne
and Rostock, and through three others besides ; on the
whole it is reckoned that there were fifty editions up
to 1600, amongst them eight at Cologne, nine at Ingolstadt, five at Paris, four at Lyons, and three at
Antwerp.   It was dedicated to Henry VIII. of England,
whose book against Luther Eck had defended in a
special pamphlet in 1523.   In 1530 Eck began to have
his works against Luther reprinted in a collective form.[1]

Eck also did work of much value against the new-
religionists by means of his sermons.   Owing to the
dearth of such works on the Catholic side, the Protestant homilies were also read among the Catholics,
and ignorant priests used to take from these the
materials for their addresses ; [2] the Dukes William and
Louis of Bavaria had therefore enlisted the services of
the renowned apologist to do away with this anomaly.
Eck's explanations of the Sunday and feast day Gospels
and his sermons on the sacraments met with so much
approval that the German version of them went through
four editions between 1530 and 1583, and of the Latin
translation seventeen editions had been called for by
1579,[3] independently of the version in Eck's collected
works.   As these homilies are not addressed immediately to the people, but to unlearned priests ' who

[1] Wiedemann, pp. 528 ff., 586 f.
[2] ' Nam dum schismatici acervos, imo montes homiliarum emiserint,
contra catholici rarenter sermones ad plebem ediderunt, adeo ut inquisiti
tam ex clero quam laicis hunc fucum praetexerint : emisse quidem se
et legisse Lutheri et aliorum homilias, quia catholicorum non extarent
venales.'   Homiliarius, dedicatio.
[3] Wiedemann, pp. 573–580, 597–611, 613.

cannot swim without cork,'[1] there is care given to
rhetorical flourishes, and more to clear and substantial
explanation. A fifth part of Eck's sermons[2] gives
explanations of the Ten Commandments, and is interesting because in explaining the moral law Eck often
goes into detail, which makes it possible to get an
insight into the casuistry of that period.[3]

That Eck in his polemical writings hit on the right
method is shown by the results. ' Hear me, you
apostate,' he exclaims to Bucer ; ' does not Eck make
use of the words of Scripture and of the Fathers ?

[1] This circumstance explains why it is that here and there in the
text reference is given to other works where fuller information may be
found. In the funeral oration at the burial of the Emperor Maximilian
(unnoticed by Wiedemann. It is in *Homiliarius*, Ingolstadii, 1536, tom.
iv. fol. 272 f.) there occurs one reference to Thomas à Kempis, probably
to the *Imitation* (fol. 273ᵃ), so that Eck seems to have considered à
Kempis as the author of this famous book.

[2] Not noticed by Wiedemann and Schneid. The title is, *Der Fünft und
letst | Tail Christenlicher Predig von den | zehen Gebotten, wie die zu halten,
und | wie die übertretten werden, Zu | wolfart den frumen Chri- | sten des
alten glau- | bens. | Durch doctor Johan Eck | Vicecancellier zu In- |
Goldstat. | Getruckt zu Ingoldstadt, durch | Georgen Krapffen. | MDXXXIX.*

[3] Among other things Eck deals with the questions of usury and
interest, to which he devotes four whole sermons (26–29, fol. 1ᵇ–lixᶜ.).
In the decision of disputed points Eck tries to hold a middle position ;
he will neither ' allow consciences to be too elastic and put bolsters or
pillows under the elbows of sinners,' nor will he ' condemn a whole multitude as criminals ' (fol. xxviᶜ.). For when anything is ' a common usage
in the land, and the habitual practice of people who are accounted respectable and pious, God-fearing and of a good conscience, and is an ancient
and traditional custom, that thing must not be looked upon as a sin or
an injustice.' ' It is not always necessary for people to go by the safe
road, though it may be advisable. What I mean is, that when there are
different and contradictory opinions as to what is sinful, it is not necessary
always to choose the safer way, for he does not sin who chooses another
way ' (fol. xxviiiᵃ.). Concerning Eck and the Church law against taking
interest see also Schneid in the *Histor.-polit. Blätter*, cviii. 321 ff., 473 ff.,
570 ff., 659 ff., 789 ff., where, however, Janssen's account in the present
work is omitted.

Why do you not reply to him concerning his writings on the Primacy of Peter, on penitence, on the Mass, on purgatory, on so many of his homilies, on so much of all sorts ?   At Wittenberg they bragged before the Leipzig Disputation : " Eck will not be a match for Carlstadt and Luther, for he will quote from his Scotus, Occam, Thomas, and so forth, while the others will back themselves up with Augustine and Cyprian." But what did the Catholic Duke George of Saxony say to me ? " I see that you too bring forward the Church Fathers and the Holy Scriptures, and more happily than your opponents." ' [1]

His opponents were only successful in killing his argument by silence.[2] His personality, however, was not passed over in silence. It was said of him that he only persisted on the Catholic side from interested motives ; an ironical remark of the dread adversary at Ratisbon was interpreted as signifying that he had formally offered his services to the Protestants. He was further accused of covetousness, of ambition, of drunkenness and of immorality. ' The new Christians,' he himself complains, ' are eager to hurl their scorn at all representatives of the good cause, to slander and ridicule them in lampoons and caricatures. Amid such bitter persecutions the Catholics must say with Christ : " Let them alone ; they are blind leaders of the blind." [3] Eck, for the most part, was silent under such attacks.

---

[1] Wiedemann, p. 275 (from Eck's *Apologia*).

[2] Eck, however, did not remain quite unanswered. ' As the Dialogue [*Eckius dedolatus*, an undignified piece of buffoonery] is the satirical monument of Eck's first important appearance at the Leipzig Disputation of 1519, so the *Oratio* [a similar production] celebrates in similar vein his last [?] appearance at the Augsburg Diet of 1530 ; it is an answer to Eck's 404 articles.' ' Eckius dedolatus,' published by S. Szamatólski, in Latin, in the *Literaturdenkmäler des* 15. *und* 16. *Jahrhunderts*, II. xi.

[3] ' Neochristiani nihil prius habent, quam omnes bonos cujuscumque

Sometimes, however, he felt called upon to defend himself. Against the charges of avarice and ambition he made known that he had refused more than one canonry. ' Your [Osiander's] slandering tongue accuses me of avarice. You do me injustice. I shall remain a schoolmaster to the end of my days. I may tell you, moreover, that I have been offered cathedral canonries at Cologne, Augsburg, Trent, Liège and Ratisbon ; I prefer, however, to remain at my studies.' [1]

In answer to the charge of immorality he asks with the greatest *sangfroid* if it is likely that an impecunious man who at the age of fourteen had already obtained the doctor's degree of philosophy, to whom at eighteen the educational and moral supervision of a number of youngsters was entrusted, whom so many distinguished men had honoured with their friendship, could at the same time have been leading a life of sin, as his enemies reproached him with having done. ' Were the prelates, the nobles and the burghers who entrusted their nephews and sons to my care, blind from love for me ? ' [2]

' Who has ever seen me drink too much, even when I have been somewhat merry in the company of my

ordinis eludere, calumniari, scriptis et imaginibus subsannare.   In hujusmodi pessimis contumeliis dicere debent catholici cum Christo : Sinite illos, caeci enim sunt et duces caecorum.   Alias tamen in universum curae et cordi esse cuique debet, ut nomen bonum habeat.'   Hom. I. de S. Petr. et Paul. *Homiliarius de Sanctis*, fol. 135[d].

[1] Wiedemann, p. 376.

[2] *Ibid.* p. 379.   It would not be quite inconsistent with the utterances above if Eck had at one time been guilty of moral error, as seems to be pretty clear from the funeral orations of his friends.   See *Tres orationes funebres in exequiis Io. Eckii Ingolstadii habitae*, Ingolstadii, 1543, B[3], B[4], C[7].   In the first speech John Salicetus says at any rate of the opponent who reproaches Eck with ' luxum ' : ' scimus et nos quam *sobrie et caste* vivant (the opponents)—they ought not therefore to look at the straw in their neighbour's eye. . . . Vos autem, patres amplissimi, quos ut veros Christianos etiam de iis, quorum vita non admodum *integra et sceleris pura est*, pie sentire scio, cum amicis . . . deflete (Eck).   On the

friends and guests ? The arduous work I have done, the many lectures to my pupils, the many sermons to the people, the many books that have been written by me with my own hand, bear witness to my sobriety.' [1]

Eck, on the testimony of his own writings, was a man of vivacious spirits, of jovial, and at the same time, firm character, and of inexhaustible capacity for and love of work. Even Catholics—as, for instance, S. Pallavicini—have complained of the bitter tone of his writings which, they opine, drove Luther even more obstinately back upon his errors. It must, however, be acknowledged that it was not he who first adopted the acrid tone.[2] But even these accusers do ample justice to Eck's scholarship.[3] For Cochlaeus Eck was *par excellence* ' the highly learned and deeply grounded

other hand the second orator, George Flach, speaks of Eck's *innocentissima vita*—of his *morum claritate*.   The third, however, Michael Wagner, says : Labilis est humana natura, et ut ad casum facilis, sic facile post casum assurgit ; nihil aliud (crede mihi) communis ille inimicus (the devil), in *vulnerando pugile nostro effecit*, quam quod sibi solertiorem cautioremque hostem vendicavit.   *Eckii peccata novimus* sicut et Regii prophetae Davidis, novimus autem et quaesitam medicinam, frequentia jejunia, lachrimas amarissimas, saepe repetitam confessionem. . . . Quis hoc pacto non consequeretur misericordiam ?   Quis hisce medicinis pristinae *sanitati non* restitueretur ? ' If, therefore, Eck was not quite irreproachable as regards moral purity, the same evidence at any rate shows that he did serious penance.   That his opponents exaggerated Eck's trespasses in immoderate measure is undoubted.   That he was guilty of gross excesses Eck denies, but he confesses that he was a sinner.

[1] Wiedemann, p. 377.

[2] ' Malui tamen modestiam servare theologicam,' he says in his *Defensio contra amarulentas Andr. Bodenstein invectiones*, ' quam mulier-cularum more rixari, scommatibusque aculeatis et injuriis maledicum referire, quod non existimem viri boni esse, vel inferre vel referre injuriam. . . . Id tamen imprimis curandum, cum de mysteriis sacratissimae fidei nostrae agitur.' See Wiedemann, p. 93.

[3] Pallavicini, *Istoria del Conc. di Trento*, l. i. c. 6, Milano, 1745, i. 64. ' Echio . . . uomo eccellente per dottrina et per eloquenza, come rendono palese le sue opere date alla stampa. . . . E questa [la contraddizione] dal Echio sarebbesi potuta far meno acerba. . . . Forse i contradditori, col dichiararlo Eretico primo del tempo, il fecero diventare.'

theologian.' Cardinal Pole honoured him with the title of ' Achilles of the Catholics.' [1]

When John Eck entered into eternal rest there were dwelling on German soil members of the Order of Jesuits from whom the most energetic opposition to Protestantism was to proceed. With the advent of the Jesuits and the comprehensive definitions of Church doctrine through the Council of Trent, a new epoch begins for Catholic theology ; a fresh and genuinely Catholic spirit penetrates into all countries, even into the grievously devastated land of Germany.

The significance of the Council in theological respects can scarcely be overestimated ; its dogmatic decisions are expressed with admirable clearness, precision and wisdom ; numbers of its decrees are models of doctrinal teaching in the Church. From out the mist and fog of human opinions rises the divine fabric of Catholic faith in fresh purity and beauty, strong and uniform, the astonishment even of the enemies of the Church.[2] The dogmatic connexion with the apostolic past was re-established at all the contested points ; error and truth were severed to a nicety ; all hazy, unclean, compromising theology had the ground cut from under it.[3] All Catholics felt themselves

---

[1] Wiedemann, p. 424. That Eck was the most dangerous and the readiest of Luther's opponents is generally acknowledged by modern Protestant historians ; see Maurenbrecher, *Katholische Reformation*, i. 175 ; Günther, *P. Apian*, p. 88 ; Ficker, p. xxxii. See also Menzel's statement in the *Histor.-polit. Blätter*, lxix. 813, and Gess, *Cochlaeus*, p. 28.

[2] See present work, vol. viii. p. 263 ff.

[3] Here belong the endeavours of G. Cassander, for which see Fritzer's *De Cassandri eiusque sociorum studiis irenicis*, Monast. 1865, and Deschrevel, *Hist. du Seminaire de Bruges*, Bruges, 1891, p. 385 ff. See also my article on Cassander in Wetzer und Welte's *Kirchenlexikon*, 11[2], 2020.

again united ; new life streamed through the old Church.

Immediately after the conclusion of the Council a time of prosperity begins for Catholic theology, a time ' which for abundance and variety of work has not its like in the history of the Church.' The actual greatness of this period consists in the fact that ' all matters of theology were worked at with the most intimate connexion and interdependence. The exegesis of that period is no mere philological critical performance, but it presses into its service the attainments both of the school-men and the Fathers, for the deeper under-standing and fuller establishment of Catholic doctrine ; it was in this very combination of scholastic culture and sound exegetical-historical knowledge that the strength of the great controversialists lay. The best scholastic theologians did not confine themselves to one-sided speculation, but further developed the scholastic tradition on the basis of Scripture and the Fathers. And the most eminent patristic theologians on their side used scholasticism as a clue to the under-standing of the holy Fathers, just as numbers of theo-logians were actively engaged at the same time in all or several of these departments.[1]

In this general prosperity Germany had also her share. A survey of the theological literature which then grew up leaves no doubt that at that time also polemics and controversy held predominance. A dif-ference, however, is plainly recognisable in this depart-ment as compared with the foregoing periods ; polemics and controversy become more systematic and are carried on in great style, whereby they attain to higher

[1] Scheeben, *Dogmatik*, i. 446.

perfection. The chief merit is here due to the Order of the Society of Jesus. The numerous polemical and controversial writers of the pre-Tridentine period achieved great things ; but they lacked a centre, they fought singly and therefore obtained no decisive results. It was the Jesuits who first organised a systematic opposition to Protestantism, who came forward methodically, uniformly, compactly, in support of the old faith. Their colleges and schools soon sprang up in all the districts of Catholic Germany, and were not only focuses of Church life, but also strongholds of ecclesiastical learning ; whereas on the part of the Protestants the flood of polemical literature was still continually rising. The Jesuits also turned their energies chiefly to controversy and polemics. In this department they produced a larger number of champions than all the rest of the Orders put together.[1]

The first leading representative of Jesuit polemics in Germany, Gregory of Valentia, is of Spanish origin, but nearly twenty-three years of his best work belong to Germany, and nearly all his writings came out in Germany. Born in 1551 at Medina del Campo, this intellectually gifted man worked from 1575 as teacher of scholastic theology at Dillingen and Ingolstadt. He was rightly regarded as one of the first theologians of his day, equally great in the field of scholastic and positive as in that of polemical theology.[2] The most important of his controversial writings is that which appeared at Ingolstadt in 1585, entitled ' Analyse des

---

[1] Hurter, *Nomenclator lit.* p. 163.   A complete list of Catholic polemists is as little contemplated for this period as for the previous one.   Such a list would require a work to itself.

[2] See Scheeben, i. 451 ; Hurter, p. 151 f. ; de Backer, iii. 1264 f. ; Verdière, ii. 166 f., 519 f.

katholischen Glaubens.'   The object of this work was
to show that the Catholic creed alone was able to prove
itself the true one, and that the infallible authority of
the Church, embodied in the Pope, was the absolutely
requisite protector and guardian of the true Christian
faith.   ' Christian doctrine,' says Valentia, ' contains
much dogma and truth that is beyond the comprehension of human reason ; therefore the credibility of
this teaching must be secured and supported in a
manner which fully makes up for the want of rationalistic evidence ; the believing Christian must know why
he believes that which he accepts in faith.   An absolutely adequate ground for his religious opinions can
only exist when there is an authority on the strength
of which that which is believed rests with unconditional
certainty.   This infallible doctrinal authority in matters of faith cannot be a purely human one, although
its representatives, according to divine ordinance, are
human, for the latter, in order that they may pronounce
and decide with perfect truth, must be inspired by God.
This God-inspired authority must always be present
in the Church and must at all times be accessible to
inquiry ; hence it must always and through all time be
kept up and continued in the Church, and that Church
will be the true one which can show the living presence
of a doctrinal authority instituted and guided by God.
This can only be done by the Catholic Church which
has for its head the Pope, and possesses in him the
living embodiment of this infallible doctrinal authority.
Whenever the Pope speaks *ex cathedra* on matters of
faith, his pronouncement is to be recognised as an
infallible decision, and all the faithful must submit

themselves to it.'[1] The strictly theological thought-process developed here is substantially the same as that which, with greater or less minuteness and exactitude, recurs in all the controversialists of the Jesuit Order.

On the whole no fewer than twenty-six controversial pamphlets of Gregory of Valentia have been preserved; they appeared in a collected form in 1591. As soon as he received information that a polemical work by a Protestant theologian was in the press, he exerted himself to obtain the proof-sheets of it in order, simultaneously with the attack, to be able to bring out an answer and defence. For his readiness in combat Gregory was greatly detested by the Protestants; his criticism of the doctrine of the Lord's Supper called forth a whole deluge of fierce counter-pamphlets.[2] Sometimes indeed—as, for instance, in his polemics against the Württemberg theologian Heerbrand—the fiery Spaniard went too far in his mode of expressing himself, by which he drew on him the reproaches of Canisius.[3] The latter, of an exceptionally gentle nature, and the most striking contrast to Luther, was not only an enemy of all hard and bitter polemics, but

---

[1] Werner, *Gesch. der Kathol. Theologie*, p. 6.

[2] See Werner, *Suarez*, i. 49 f.

[3] See present work, vol. x. p. 159 f. The Spanish Jesuit, Hieronymus Nadal, who had done such good service to the German Jesuits by his repeated ' visitations,' earnestly enjoined the choleric theological professors of the Ingolstadt College, Pisan and Peltan, that they should by no means yield one jot of Catholic truth, but that they must be discreet in the extreme in disputing with their official colleagues and other scholars. ' They ought to show such moderation and such calmness of behaviour, as rather to fall under suspicion of negligence and superficiality than to give the slightest occasion for controversy.' *Monumenta Paedagogica Societatis Jesu, quae primam Rationem Studiorum anno 1586 editam praecessere. Edd. Caecilius Gomez Rodeles S.J., Marianus Lecina S.J. etc.*, Matriti, 1901, p. 784.

in the first years of his activity averse even to any directly hostile measures against the innovators. ' Not to dispute, but to endure, to build up more by deeds than by words,' this was his principle. Later on, indeed, after more accurate acquaintance with German conditions, even the mild Canisius saw the necessity for direct defence, and actually proposed to found a kind of college of authors among the German Jesuits.[1] In a work, begun by command of Pope Pius V, he expressed himself in an outspoken manner against the Magdeburg Centuriators. He wished to show up the dishonourableness and preposterousness of the treatment which they had accorded certain great figures of primitive Christianity. Accordingly in 1571 he issued the Latin treatise on John the Baptist, and in 1577 the one ' Über Maria, die unvergleichliche Jungfrau und hochheilige Gottesmutter.' In 1583 he combined both these works in one massive folio volume, under the title ' Entstellungen des Wortes Gottes.' The second part, which deals with Mary, is especially valuable ; Canisius has here expounded his original scheme of refuting the Centuriators, so as to set forth the whole Catholic doctrine concerning Mary and the worship of Mary, and to defend it against all the errors and misrepresentations that the course of centuries had brought forth. In this work Canisius displayed astonishing knowledge of theological literature from the times of the Fathers down to his own day ; the learned scholar William Sirleti, director of the Vatican Library at Rome, had contributed a number of hitherto unprinted writings from Greek Fathers and Church writers. Cardinal

---

[1] See present work, vol. viii. pp. 236, 240. See Nagl-Zeidler, p. 603 f., where the latest Canisian literature is catalogued.

Hosius, himself a great scholar, was highly delighted with the book ; for the period of the religious schism it is indeed unique of its kind.[1]

Most of the polemists of the Society of Jesus lived in Bavaria, where the Order had powerful patrons in the Dukes William V and Maximilian I. The greater number of the works of these controversialists were written and printed at Ingolstadt, and then at Dillingen and Cologne. The most exhaustive work in defence of the Catholic faith against the attacks of the Protestants, the ' Disputations ' of Bellarmin, distinguished by great scholarship and by a dignified tone free from all calumniation of opponents, appeared first at Ingolstadt in the years 1581–1592, in three folio volumes.

Of a large number of polemists of the Jesuit Order who were active in Germany the following stand out prominently : Hermann Thyraeus of Neuss († 1591), the Spaniard Alphonso Pisanus († 1598), Hieronymus Torres († 1611), Theodore Anton Peltanus of Liège († 1584), the Lotharingian John Moquet († 1642), Matthias Mayrhofer of Landshut († 1641), Jacob Keller († 1631), and Sebastian Heiss of Augsburg († 1614). The latter, who was professor at Ingolstadt from 1599 to 1613, was distinguished by rare endowments, many-sided culture, and extraordinarily extensive reading. In his controversial writings he dealt with the Church doctrines on the Eucharist and the Sacrifice of the Mass.[2]

Able controversialists also came forward in the

---

[1] Riess, *Canisius*, pp. 420–447. Braunsberger in the *Zeitschr. für Kathol. Theologie*, 1890, pp. 738–739. Scheeben, iii. 478.

[2] See concerning the above-named Hurter and de Backer. Concerning Mayrhofer and Keller see also the present work, vol. x. pp. 479 f., 386 f., 387–393.

Jesuits, John Spitznaes († 1609), Jacob Crusius of Bamberg († 1617), Emmeran Welser († 1618), and John Hammer of Goslar († 1606), author of the pamphlet, combated by many Protestants, ' Prädi-kanten-Latein, das ist drei Fragen, allen genannten evangelischen Prädikanten von vielen Katholischen oftermals aufgegeben, aber nie bishero gründlich beantwortet, jetzo auf's neue in Reimen verfasst ; 1. Ob es wahr sei, dass der Papst von Gotteswort abgefallen und dasselbe unterdrückt habe ?   2. Ob die genannten Evangelischen katholisch seien ?   3. Ob jemals Einer durchs neue Evangelium selig geworden ? ' [1]

Those hitherto mentioned are far surpassed by George Scherer, Jacob Gretser and Adam Tanner.

George Scherer, who has been most vilely calum-niated by the Protestants,[2] came from Schwaz in Tyrol.   He entered the Jesuit Order in 1559, and for forty years he carried on truly apostolic labours, which were especially beneficial to the Austrian lands. He died in 1605.[3] His very numerous controversial writings appeared in 1599, collected in two volumes in the Moravian Praemonstratensian convent at Bruck. In these writings the author shows a skill in the manage-ment of the German language which is by no means insignificant for that period. This applies especially to a treatise ' Merk- und Kennzeichen der wahren und falschen Kirchen,' and to another in which ' Zwölf Ursachen der Bekehrung vom Luthertum zum Chris-tentum ' are expounded. ' No other faith,' he says in

---

[1] Hurter, p. 166.
[2] See the present work, vol. x. p. 332.
[3] See *Katholik*, 1864, ii. 35 f. ; Hurter, p. 164 f. ; de Backer, ii. 606 f. ; Nagl-Zeidler, p. 608 f.

conclusion, ' no other Church has hitherto stood more firmly and persistently under such manifold persecutions. We find here God's Word unmutilated, pure and sound, without falsification, with all the well-grounded explanations and commentaries of the holy Fathers and teachers. Through this faith our forefathers became pious, God-fearing and conscientious, and through it they were also blessed by God Almighty in things spiritual and temporal. In this Church and faith there is the true harmony and unity, *one* heart, *one* soul, in all the faithful ; here are the rightly ordained priesthood, the true Sacrament of the Altar, the true absolution and forgiveness of sins. Here is the quite undivided, seamless robe of the Christian religion. Here are the pillars and foundation of the truth ; here is the school of the Holy Ghost in which all truth is learnt.'

Scherer understands admirably how to adapt himself to the comprehension of the people ; here and there, it is true, his mode of expression corresponds all too much with the spirit of the bitter polemics of the period. This, for instance, is the case with his controversial treatise against the Württemberg theologians Osiander, Otzinder and Heerbrand.

Like other controversialists of his time Scherer endeavoured to show, one by one, that the doctrines of the new-religionists were nothing more than revivals of errors that had long ago been put down. This was the purpose of the treatise, published in Vienna in 1588, ' Der lutherische Bettlermantel.' ' The attacks of the Protestants on the doctrines, usages and institutions of the Church which they have rejected,' he says here, ' are only a repetition of those old heretical opinions

which the Church condemned in the patristic age.
They say with Aërius that prayers, vigils, sacrifices for
the dead are useless, and that fasting is good for
nothing; they say with Simon Magus and Eunomius
that faith alone is necessary to salvation, and that
works are unimportant; in their rejection of the
chrysom at baptism and confirmation the Novatians
and the Donatists forestalled them; in the rejection of
the veneration of Saints they are following Vigilantius;
Jovinian in his day denied that virginity was preferable
to marriage; that Scripture recognises no difference
between bishops and presbyters is a heresy of the
already mentioned old Aërius; in their hatred of the
Pope and the Roman Chair the Protestants are only
reiterating the abuses uttered by the Petilians and the
Novatians. The Lutheran doctrine of original sin is
Manicheism; the doctrine of the ubiquity of the
heavenly body of Christ is Eutychian; the assertion that
Christ is only present in the Sacrament at the moment
of partaking of it is an ancient heresy, against which,
in their time, Gregory of Nyssa and Cyril of Alexandria
both wrote.[1]

Adam Tanner, pupil of Gregory of Valentia, was
also a son of the land of Tyrol. Side by side with his
long years of tuitional labour this highly eminent
theologian[2] found time for extensive literary work.
Of his controversial writings, beside the report on the
Ratisbon religious conference of 1601, and a pamphlet
on the principle of faith, by far the most noteworthy
is his 'Anatomie der Augsburger Konfession.' This
treatise falls into two parts. In the first part he

[1] Werner, *Gesch. der Kathol. Theologie*, pp. 15–16.
[2] See the opinion of Scheeben in the *Katholik*, 1867, i. 162.

brings forward ten reasons to prove that the Confession ought to be rejected. In the second part, again on the strength of ten reasons, he shows that the Church of the above-named Confession is not the true one. The arguments of the opponents are very exhaustively refuted. Tanner has an eye especially on the work of the Protestant theologian James Heilbrunner.

Tanner's importance as controversialist is very highly estimated ; to many, indeed, he ranks as the first Catholic polemical writer in Germany at that period.[1]

James Gretser, ' possibly the most learned among the Jesuits of his time,' was also a pupil of Gregory of Valentia.[2] Born in 1562 at Markdorf, in the diocese of Constance, he early entered the Society of Jesus, and studied at Ingolstadt, where in 1588 he became professor of philosophy, and in 1592 professor of theology. Apart from a few interruptions, necessitated by his literary labours, he went on teaching at Ingolstadt till 1616, when his enfeebled health obliged him to retire. He died in 1625. Although his instructional work of so many years' standing was for the most part devoted to scholastic philosophy and theology, his immensely numerous writings (seventeen folio volumes)[3] are chiefly concerned with positive branches of knowledge : archæological and historical investigations, the publication of documents of historic importance, and above all polemical disquisitions. The mere list of his Pro-

[1] Hurter, p. 254 f. ; cf. Verdière, ii. 250 ; de Backer, ii. 1050 ff.

[2] Werner, *Suarez*, i. 50. See concerning Gretser, Hurter, p. 279 f. ; Verdière, ii. 230 f., 327 ; Wetzer und Welte's *Kirchenlexikon*, v[2]. 1199–1200. See also the present work, vol. x. pp. 343–345, and vol. xiii. p. 337 f.

[3] Ratisbon, 1734–1741. Cf. de Backer, i. 2254–2279, and Sommervogel, iii. 1763 ff., who reckons up 229 printed and 39 manuscript works by Gretser.

testant opponents is enough to show how indefatigably active Gretser was.   There are extant controversialist writings from his pen against Junius, Danaeus, Hospinian, Dresser, Marbach, Melchior Volk, James Heilbrunner, Zäemann, Molineus, Daniel Cramer, Samuel Huber, Goldast, Leonard Hutter, Mornay, Aegidius Hunnius, Andrew Libavius, Simon Stein, Gabriel Lermaeus, Cambilhon, Andrew Lonner, John Forster, John James Huldreich, Ernest Zephyrius, John Pappus, Thomas Wegelin, Mark Beumler, Hasenmüller and Leiser.   In all these writings Gretser displays perfection of scholarship and masterly acumen, and the materials, collected from the most different directions, give evidence of unequalled industry and indefatigableness. The literary fruitfulness of the author and his power of work inspire admiration and astonishment.   Unfortunately, however, we cannot give unqualified praise to Gretser's polemical action.   A rough, unsophisticated character to start with, he too often answered the abuse of his opponents in the same tone.   His brother in the Order, Conrad Vetter, went even further than Gretser in this respect.[1]   Happily this armed style of polemics, descending to the lowest depths of coarse popular tone, became by no means generally prevalent among the Jesuits—a fact due to the influence of the penetrating admonitions of the blessed Canisius and other members of the Society.[2]

How difficult it must have been for the Jesuits and other Catholic controversialists to preserve moderation, a glance at the antagonistic literature will show.   It is no exaggeration when a modern historian describes

---

[1] See the present work, vol. x. p. 149 f.
[2] See above, p. 327 f., and present work, vol. viii. p. 237, note 1.

the latter as ' a sea of deliberate lies, systematic calumniation, brutality and baseness.' [1]   ' The Antichrist at
Rome ' and the ' bestial swinish *Jesuwider wärtigen* '
were the principal butts of these combatants.

Onslaughts from the Protestants, no less violent in
character, had to be endured by a number of controversialists who by the grace of God had been led back
to the old Church.   These men were loudly accused of
the most scandalous treachery, and so monstrous was
the provocation to which they were subjected that
they were driven to self-defence.   For a long time their
memory and reputation suffered under the attacks of
that period, and it is only by the latest critical research
that they have been exculpated.   When we look more
closely into the life of these converts we cannot in truth
doubt the honourableness of their character and the
purity of their motives.   ' Against their proofs and
arguments the opponents have nothing substantial to
bring forward.   In religious and theological culture
they stand high above their adversaries ; in popularity
of style and linguistic skill they equal them in great
measure.   Their bitterness and coarseness only goes
the length of that of their accusers and persecutors :
it is only the echo of what the latter have cried out
in the wood.   The vivisection of Lutheranism which
these converts performed on Luther's own writings
were simply defence measures, and all that is repulsive
in them is taken from the writings of Luther and of his
followers.' [2]

At the same time it cannot be denied that indi-

---

[1] Dr. Cardauns in his recension of vol. v. (German) of the present
work in the *Köln. Volkszeitung*, 1886, No. 287, 3. Blatt.

[2] A. Baumgartner in the *Stimmen aus Maria-Laach*, xxxi. 553.

viduals among the Catholics did adopt a tone which was altogether unsuitable.

To the number of these controversialists belong Frederick Staphylus, James Rabe, John Nas, Sebastian Flasch, and John Pistorius. In all these writers we plainly see the influence of the new epoch which began with the Council of Trent and the advent of the Jesuits. The same is the case with the controversialists George Eder, Jodocus Lorichius, Andrew Erstenberger, John Paul Windeck, Caspar Schoppe, Andrew Forner and Aegidius Albertinus.[1] Like Albertinus, Andrew Fabricius († 1581) was also for a time in Bavarian service. He is the author of a work on the Augsburg Confession, which is remarkable for its learning and acumen ; in it he shows that all the various doctrines in which this Protestant confession differs from the teaching of the Church had been borrowed earlier from heresies, long ago condemned, and he also shows up the deviations of the later editions of the Confession printed at Wittenberg, from the official copies handed in to the Emperor Charles V. ' This work, in its scope, method and contents, rises above the average, and hits a vulnerable spot, for, over and above sub-

---

[1] The most important polemical works of the above-named writers have already been discussed in vols. ix. and x. of the present work. See also Riezler, vi. 369 f., 383 f. Concerning Eder see also Weidemann, *Reformation*, ii. 143 ff., and Paulus in the *Histor.-polit. Blätter*, cxv. (1895) 13 ff., 81 f. ; for Pistorius see Hurter, p. 167 f., and *Histor. Jahrbuch*, xxiv. 755 f. For Jodocus Lorichius see Ehses in the *Festschrift zum 1100-jährigen Jubiläum des deutschen Campo Santo in Rom*, Freiburg, 1897, 242 ff. For Albertinus see K. v. Reinhardstöttner in the *Jahrbuch für Münchener Gesch.* ii. (1888) 13–87 ; and the same author in the *Forschungen zur Kultur und Literaturgeschichte Bayerns*, ii. (1894) 86–118 ; Riezler, vi. 344 f. ; Paulus in the *Histor.-polit. Blätter*, cxxxiii. (1904) 589 ff., 646 ff. For the style of Albertinus see the *Programm* of Himmler, Munich, 1902.

stantial refutation, it aims at showing how, up till then, the reform dogmatics had been subject to flux and change.'[1] Against the innovators, whose dogma was so fluctuating and changeable, Fabricius calls for the severest measures, even for recourse to the power of arms.[2] The same position was maintained by the Munich canon Dobereiner and by Maximilian's tutor, John Baptist Fickler, a number of whose sharp-toned controversial writings are extant.[3]

Contemporaneously with the above named the religious innovator Johann zum Wege (latinised A Via), Bavarian court preacher, also developed brisk literary activity. He translated the ' Confessio ' of Cardinal Hosius and the ' Lives of the Saints ' by Surius, and by commission of Duke Albert V compiled, for distribution among the people, a work entitled ' Christliche Lehr und Ermanung, wie man jetzschwebende Irrthumm durchs Wort Gottes erkennen und fliehen sol ' (Munich, 1569). This was followed the next year by a defence of the Catholic doctrines of the Holy Eucharist, the Mass, and the veneration of Saints.[4]

Rudolf Clenck, a secular priest, who acted for a time as lecturer on theology at Ingolstadt, came before the public with writings on celibacy, justification, confession and marriage. A long and important career of tuitional labour was enjoyed by Peter Stevart,

---

[1] Kellner in the *Allgemeine deutsche Biographie,* vi. 503.

[2] See Wetzer und Welte's *Kirchenlexikon,* iv². 1191, and the present work, vol. v. p. 216.

[3] See Föringer in the *Allgemeine deutsche Biographie*, vi. 775 f. ; see also the present work, vol. x. pp. 216, 217.

[4] See Streber in Wetzer und Welte's *Kirchenlexikon*, vi². 1780 f., where, however, there lacks any allusion to the notice on *Zum Wege* collected by Falk in the *Zeitschr. für Kathol. Theologie,* ii. 802 f. See, now, the article by Roth in the *Histor. Jahrbuch,* xvi. 565–575.

from whose pen a defence of the Jesuit Order is extant.[1]

The controversialist Oswald Fischer, styled Arnsperger († 1568 as suffragan of Freising), was also a professor at this same university. Contemporaneous with him was the scholar and convert Martin Eisengrein († 1578), author of numerous polemical tracts, based on deep study of the Fathers, besides controversial sermons, which were printed separately and had a wide circulation. Eisengrein was the means of winning for the Church the Saxon Caspar Franck. This man, of whom death all too early deprived science († 1584, aged 41), ' belongs to the more important of the scholars who were the pride of the university of Ingolstadt in the sixteenth century, and his numerous polemical writings give evidence of earnest study, especially in the department of patristics.' Special notice is also due to his simple and full account of the reasons of his conversion.[2]

Jacob Feucht, as learned as he was eloquent, since 1572 suffragan bishop of Bamberg, enjoyed only a short period of activity at Ingolstadt. In consequence of a pamphlet which he published in 1572 under the title, ' Christlicher Bericht, wie ein Christ auf die 37 Hauptartikel des wahren christlichen Glaubens antworten soll,' he became involved in a long controversy with Osiander. Of Feucht's admirable sermons, which

---

[1] See Hurter, 9 *a*, 327, as well as the present work, vol. x. pp. 208–213. Concerning Rudolf Clenck see the excellent article of L. Pfleger in the *Histor.-polit. Blätter*, cxxxii. 45 ff., 90 ff.

[2] See Wetzer und Welte's *Kirchenlexikon*, iv². 341 f. (see here, too, for John Eisengrein, author of several valued ascetic works) and 1683 f. ; as well as Räss, ii. 20 f., *Allgemeine deutsche Biographie*, vii. 272 f., and Paulus in the *Histor.-polit. Blätter*, cxxiv. (1899) 545 ff., 617 ff. Concerning Fischer see Prantl, ii. 491, and Kobolt, p. 225.

were largely polemical in character, we shall speak
further on.[1]

The men so far enumerated, the number of whom
might easily be multiplied, are witnesses to the services
rendered the Catholic cause by Bavaria,[2] and, above
all, by Ingolstadt, in those difficult times. The university of Ingolstadt, in the second half of the sixteenth
century, appears in the light of the actual centre of
Catholic efforts and operations in Germany.[3] Nowhere
else was sacred learning so zealously pursued. Here
a series of eminent Protestant laymen and clergy
received their first instigation to return to the bosom
of the Church ; here most of the Catholic defence
writings originated and were printed. In rivalry with
the university of Ingolstadt was that of Dillingen,
where the controversialist Alphonso Pisanus, and for
a time also the Netherlander William Lindanus, gave
instruction. Among the numerous polemical writings
of Lindanus, his defence of celibacy against Chemnitz
and his ' Evangelische Rüstkammer ' stand out prominently.[4]

The same importance which Ingolstadt acquired
for the South of Germany, was gained for the Rhine
and Main districts by Cologne and Würzburg.

---

[1] Below in the chapter on Sermons.

[2] Among other Bavarian champions of the Catholic Church may be
mentioned George Lauter and Albert Hunger (Hurter, p. 170), as also the
Bamberg suffragan bishop, Frederick Forner, whose works are minutely
described by Wittmann in the *Histor.-polit. Blätter*, lxxxvi. 565 ff., 656 ff.
See also *Berichte des Histor. Vereins für Oberfranken*, xxxiv. 147 ff., and
Von Reinhardstöttner, ' Volkschriftsteller der Gegenreformation in
Altbayern ' in the *Forschungen zur Kultur- und Literaturgesch. Bayerns*, ii.
(1894) 46–109.

[3] Kampschulte in *Reuschs Literaturbl.* ii. 912 ; cf. Ranke, *Päpste*, ii[6]. 22.

[4] Concerning Lindanus see Hurter, p. 62 f.

An eminent worker at the colleges of both these towns was Franz Coster, who belonged to the Society of Jesus for full sixty-seven years (1552–1619). This saintly man did lasting service both by his ascetic writings and his polemical works. His famous ' Handbuch der Kontroversen' appeared first at Cologne in 1585, went through several editions in the following years, was translated into various languages, and provoked not a few Protestant counter-publications. In 1591 the renowned Jesuit Nicholas Serarius entered the Würzburg theological faculty ; he was, however, removed to Mayence in 1597. The exegetic writings, still to be mentioned, as well as the polemical writings of this important scholar were all produced here. Among the latter the violent controversial pamphlet ' Luthers Nachlicht ' is specially noticeable ; the author here aims at answering the question ' whether Dr. Martin Luther was the man through whom the devil began this wondrous game.' ' And to this,' writes Serarius, ' I answer briefly and roundly, yes, that is the truth and nothing else. And this is what I am going to prove in the name of God with these following thirty arguments, proofs and conclusions.'

When Serarius went to Mayence, the Netherlander Martin Becanus came to Würzburg, where he lectured with great success on dogmatic-polemical theology. He too was called (in 1601) to Mayence, and he died in 1624 at Vienna, where he held at the time the post of father confessor to the Emperor Ferdinand II. In numerous writings, distinguished by brevity and clearness, he defended the old Church against Calvinistic, Anglican and Lutheran theologians. His ' Handbuch der Kontroversen,' of which he published an abridgment, is distinguished by the clearness of its method.[1] Two very able works were written by Balthasar Hager. The first of these, ' Kleiner Wegweiser zum wahren Glauben,' is in the German language ; the other, in Latin, draws a comparison between the Augsburg Confession and the Council of Trent and the Word of God.[2]

Other men who distinguished themselves as controversialists are the Würzburg professors Peter Röstius, Christopher Marianus, Maximilian Sandaeus,[3] and Adam Contzen.

The latter, born in 1573 at Montjoie, near Aix-la-Chapelle, professor of theology at Würzburg and Mainz, was distinguished not only as a teacher but also as author, spiritual adviser to princes, Christian politician, and national economist († 1635). In two learned pamphlets he undertook to defend the first controversialist of that period against the attacks of the Heidelberg professor David Pareus ; in his letter of thanks Bellarmin dwelt eulogistically on the ' extent of piety and learning, the felicitous style, the penetration, the mature judgment, the nervous force,' which his champion had exhibited.

---

[1] Concerning the above named see the statements of Ruland, p. 6 ff. ; see also Von Wegele, i. 275 f., and concerning Becanus, also the present work, vol. ix. p. 463, note 1, vol. x. p. 205 ff., as also O. Happel, *Katholisches und protestantisches Christentum nach der Auffassung der alten Katholischen Polemik insbesondere des Martinus Becanus* (Dissertation), Würzburg, 1898. In addition to the writings of Serarius and Becanus see also Falk, *Bibelstudien*, pp. 206 ff., 210 ff.

[2] ' In quo opusculo,' says Ruland (p. 58), ' prima—ut ita dicam—inveni lineamenta Theologiae Symbolicae, quam nostris diebus miratur orbis in Opere Symbolico Moehleri.'

[3] With the exception of Marianus, all members of the Society of Jesus ; cf. Ruland, p. 34 f. Concerning Peter Röstius see also Werner, *Suarez*, i. 63.

Contzen had accepted the principle of his teacher
Serarius that it was right not only to pray for those of
a different faith, but also to study with a view to their
benefit.   Accordingly he made the development of the
new religion the object of his most ardent study.   This
stood him in good stead when, in 1617, the so-called
Reformation jubilee was celebrated by incessant attacks
on the Catholics.   He brought out at that time a publication under the somewhat curious title ' Frohlocken
über Frohlocken, evangelisches Jubiläum, fromme
Thränen aller Römisch-Katholischen ' ; the book bears
the motto ' Am Himmel ist *eine* Sonne, auf Erden
eine Kirche ; in dieser lebt *ein* Christus und *ein* Glaube.'
Few works of that period show such a thorough knowledge of the whole development of Protestantism,
such vigour and movement in style as are met with
here.   Contzen was not only a controversialist but
also a peacemaker.   With the utmost lucidity he
defended the principles according to which alone it
would be possible to effect a union between the divided
creeds.   Since truth is *one* and can be proved absolutely, he lays down the condition : ' Acceptance of the
decisions of the Council of Trent.'   Against the ' Monita
Secreta ' which appeared in 1612, this ever-ready man
defended his Order in a ' dialogue ' in a manner as
thorough as it was witty.[1]

Besides Contzen, the Rhenish lands can boast of a
further group of defenders of the Catholic faith in the
second half of the sixteenth century.   We confine
ourselves here to the most important of these, viz. the
Jesuits Peter Michael Brillmacher († 1595), Henry
Blissemius († 1586) ; Jodocus Coccius, canon at Jülich

[1] Brischar, *A. Contzen*, pp. 18, 22 ff., 29 ff., 57 f., 61

(† 1618) ; Franz Agricola, pastor at Rödingen near Jülich, later on at Villard († 1624) ; Cornelius Loos († 1595) ; Theodore Graminaeus ; John Nopel, auxiliary bishop at Cologne († 1605) ; Justus Calvinus Baronius of Xanten ; John Magirus of Koblentz († 1609) ; Tilmann Bredenbach († 1587) ;[1] and Caspar Ulenberg († 1617).[2] This excellent man, born at Lippstadt in 1549, was won over to the Catholic Church in 1572, at Cologne, by the auxiliary bishop John Nopel, known as a controversialist, and by Gerwin Calenius. Three years later he entered the priesthood, became pastor at Kaiserswerth, and then of St. Kunibert at Cologne. Here he completed his principal work, ' Erhebliche und wichtige Ursachen, warumb die altgleubige Catholische Christen bei dem alten waren Christenthumb bis in ihren Tod bestendiglich verharren ; warumb auch alle die, so sich bey diesen Zeiten unterm Namen des Evangelii haben verführen lassen, von der Newerung abstehen und sich widerumb zum selbigen alten Christenthumb wenden sollen.' As his reason for writing this work, which appeared in 1589 in a German and a Latin edition, Ulenberg

---

[1] In addition to Hurter, *Nomenclator lit.*, see also concerning F. Agricola the careful article by Floss in Wetzer und Welte's *Kirchenlexikon*, i[2]. 353 f., and concerning Coccius see Räss, viii. 500.

[2] See Räss, ii. 550 ff. ; Panzer, *Gesch. der Kathol. Bibelübersetzungen*, p. 140 ff., and the *Biography* by Meshovius (Cologne, 1638), which is prefixed in an abridged form to the new edition of Ulenberg's *Zweiundzwanzig Beweggründe*. Here (p. xxviii f.) the remaining writings of this admirable man are enumerated. See also, now, the article by Kleffner in Wetzer und Welte's *Kirchenlexikon*, xii[2]. 185 f., and that in the *Kathol. Seelsorger*, 1899, No. 5. Cologne also was of great importance as the publishing centre of Catholic writings. Among foreign theologians, who by the writings they had printed there gained great influence on the intellectual tendency of the learned world of Cologne, Ennen (iv. 726) mentions Jacob Pamelius, Stephen Lindius, Melchior Canus, John Hessels and John Lindanus.

says in the preface he feels strongly moved by his gratitude for the great grace of conversion which the eternal mercy had granted him, to work with all his might for the conversion of his erring brethren. This aim the author has eminently accomplished. The repose, the scholarship and the directness of purpose with which he has utilised a wealth of material, as well as the concise, intelligible, and impressive character of his style, correspond in the most admirable manner to the needs of the time.

As in the Rhinelands, in Franconia and in Bavaria, so too in Austria the Jesuit Order supplied the greatest number of and the most distinguished polemical writers. First on the list we must again place Henry Blissemius, who died in 1586 in the capital of Styria. Then come the Spaniard Peter Ximenez, whose tracts and speeches were published at Graz in the years 1589–1594, the Englishman William Wright, and the Augsburg convert Christopher Mayer.[1] Wright and Mayer were both removed to Vienna in the last years of their lives. Mayer († 1626) is credited, even by enemies of the Order, with great scholarship, and with moderation towards those professing other creeds.[2] His ' Acht Glaubenskontroversen ' appeared first at Cologne in 1622, and went through numerous editions. It is said that John Hoffer, who had been commissioned by the Elector of Saxony and the Leipzig university to write a refutation of this pamphlet of Mayer, was won over by it to the Catholic truth ; Hoffer, later on, entered the Society of Jesus and proved one of the most active defenders of the Church.[3]

[1] Krones, *Universität Graz*, p. 379.
[2] Mayer, *Kultur in Niederösterreich*, p. 189, note 64.
[3] Stoeger, *Script. prov. Austr. Soc. Jesu*, Viennae, 1853, p. 222.   Wurzbach, *Biogr. Lexikon*, xviii. 96 f.

For a certain length of time the convert John Zehender worked in the Austrian lands, and in 1601 he published, in dialogue form, his reasons for returning to the Church.[1]

In speaking of the polemical activity of the Jesuits and converts in the period after the Council of Trent, the literary labours of the members of the old Order must not be overlooked ; and if these fall considerably into the background as compared with the fulness of youthful power displayed by the Society of Jesus, there were nevertheless not wanting among them able defenders of the old faith.   The services of a John Nas would have done credit to the Order of the Jesuits. In connexion with him we may mention as members of the Franciscan Order, Michael Anisius, George Eckhart, John Francis Kemminger, Marquard Leo, and others.[2] Of the Dominicans we may mention John Andrew Coppenstein and Antony Rescius ; of the Benedictines, Bernard Rubenus.[3]

The survey of the polemists of the post-Tridentine period would be incomplete if special mention were not made of two men of extraordinary intellectual power, who carried on work of the highest significance in an ecclesiastical principality further removed from the great world-market, Stanislaus Hosius and Martin Cromer. To these two bishops Ermland owes its religious and scholastic renovation, and to them also Braunsberg owes the glory of having gained for the

[1] Räss, iii. 5 f.   Here, too, there is mention of another dialogue by Zehender, somewhat coarser in tone.

[2] Concerning the last-named see Gaudentius ; for the remainder see present work, vol. x. pp. 88 ff., 93 ff., 135 ff., and Nagl-Zeidler, p. 605 f.

[3] Cf. Echard, ii. 350, 449 f. ; Hurter, p. 166.   Concerning Rescius see Renninger, *Weihbischöfe*, p. 171 ff.

Catholic Church in the north-east an importance similar to that which Ingolstadt won for the south.

Fulfilled with the conviction that as a bishop he ought in every way to make a stand against the enemies of the Church, Hosius, in spite of his many official duties, was also unremittingly active with his pen. Most of his polemical writings appeared in Germany at Cologne, and at Dillingen, where they exercised great influence. Thus, for instance, the 'Dialog über den Laienkelch, die Priesterehe und die Liturgie in der Landessprache,' the treatise 'Von dem ausdrücklichen Worte Gottes,' and the admirable refutation of the Suabian religious innovator John Brenz, to which Canisius wrote a beautiful preface.[1]

But all these publications were eclipsed by a complete work published at Mayence in 1557, in which Hosius, in juxtaposition to the Augsburg Confession, gives a systematic presentment of the whole body of Catholic doctrine, a presentment 'so thoroughgoing as regards its contents' that its importance cannot be highly enough estimated. The feeling that in this work, constructed on the basis of Scripture, furnished throughout with the choicest passages from the Fathers, distinguished by pure Latinity, exhaustive contents, dignity and warmth of style, Hosius had excelled the writers of the opposition, soon began to find expression in Catholic as well as in Protestant circles, and the appellations, 'pillar of the Church, a second Augustine, death of Luther, hammer of the heretics, idol of the papists,' by which on both sides the bishop of Ermland was designated, 'owe their origin chiefly to the incisive influence of his "Confessio." In literary respects also

[1] Cf. *Canisii Epistulae*, ii. 894–898.

this book had an almost unheard-of success among Catholic writings; even in the author's lifetime the original passed through about thirty editions in the most celebrated printing presses of all European countries, while numbers of translations of the work appeared in German, Polish, French, Italian, English, Scotch, Dutch, Moravian, and even in Arabic and Armenian.' [1]

Next to Hosius it was his successor in the episcopal chair of Ermland, Martin Cromer (1579–1589), who in difficult times was a bulwark of the old faith in the north-east. His 'Vier Gespräche über die wahre und falsche Religion' appeared in a German translation at Dillingen in 1560, and forms a refutation of the objections of the innovators, distinguished alike for popular and easily intelligible style, and for their thoroughness and aptness. At the end of the conversations the author expresses himself in a very noteworthy manner on the authority of the Holy See. ' In doctrinal controversies,' he says, ' there is a way of settling matters which is still older and simpler than councils. It is the way of the statutes and dogmas of the Chair of Peter, to whose care and guidance Christ entrusted His sheep in an especial manner and in preference of the other apostles, whom He appointed as the foundation and visible head of His Church. The popes, his successors, have, it is true, in individual cases, like Peter in denying the Lord, wavered in their love, but never in their faith. Whereas councils are not

---

[1] Hipler, *Predigten von Hosius und Cromer*, p. 8, and Wetzer und Welte's *Kirchenlexikon*, vi². 297. See also Eichhorn, *Hosius*, i. 219 ff., 285 ff. ; ii. 257 ff., 460 f., 556 f. Concerning the controversial sermons of Hosius see below, the chapter on preaching.

always practicable, the saving doctrine must be sought for at the Chair of Peter, against which the gates of hell cannot prevail.'

In 1560 Cromer came forward with a treatise on celibacy, which was printed at Cologne ; ten years later his famous Catecheses appeared in Latin, German and Polish. Whereas the Roman catechism 'was rather large and not to be had in every market or in these parts,' we read in the preface, he had brought out, ' for the benefit and use both of the priests and of other ordinary Christians of this bishopric, a few short but very vigorous and well-grounded instructions and admonitions, called Catecheses, relating above all to those points and articles which had been constantly in use among Christian believers from ancient times down to the present day, but were now almost all of them attacked by the enemies of the Church, such as the holy Sacraments, the holy Sacrifice of the Mass, and the prayer which is intended for the souls of deceased believers in Christ.' [1] Written in a genuinely popular style, this piece of controversial writing, coming from a period of the heaviest oppression of the German Church, is a beautiful testimony to the dignity and mildness with which the best and most influential champions of the old faith behaved towards the polemics of their opponents.

As in polemics and controversy, so in all other branches of theology and in the department of theological instruction, the Jesuits, after the conclusion of

---

[1] Hipler, *Predigten und Katechesen von Hosius und Cromer*, pp. 87 ff., 96–97 ; see Eichhorn, *M. Cromer*, Braunsberg, 1868 ; and Hipler in the *Zeitschr. für Gesch. Ermland*, Jahrg. 1891, pp. 145–290.

the Council of Trent, had stood in the first ranks. Their Order produced an almost inexhaustible number of workers ; by reason of its astoundingly rapid and universal spread its sphere was by no means confined to one country, but it was able as occasion demanded to reinforce the spiritual energies of other lands also. And in like manner all the various developments of learning in foreign parts were forthwith turned to account by him. The very great importance of this was seen pre-eminently in the field of theological instruction, where the Jesuits had their eyes especially on the revival of scholastic learning. There was the utmost need of help in this respect in Germany, for the old theological learning had almost entirely collapsed during the storms of the last decades. Even at Cologne, where at least the old methods of study had been fundamentally maintained, the theological faculty had seriously declined ; for a time the lectures had been quite abolished. Things were no better elsewhere. At Ingolstadt, after Eck's death, Marstaller was the sole professor of theology. After his decease the faculty from 1546 to 1548 had been completely orphaned. Similar conditions prevailed at Vienna and Freiburg.[1] It needed the united, vigorous organisation of the Jesuit Order and the indefatigable zeal of its members to bring about a change under such circumstances. At Ingolstadt the Jesuits first gained a firm footing as teachers of theology ; Claude Jajus had already, in 1544, given temporary help there with theological lectures. In November 1549 there appeared at the college of Ingolstadt one of the ablest

[1] See present work, vol. xiii. pp. 235, 245 ; Wetzer und Welte's *Kirchenlexikon*, vii[2]. 910 ; Prantl, i. 187 ; Aschbach, *Wiener Universität*, iii. 88.

men whom the young Order had to show—the Netherlander Peter Canisius. The annalist of the university
rightly calls him a genius, an incomparable scholar,
a distinguished philosopher, a profound theologian, a
diligent teacher, a great orator and preacher.[1] Simultaneously with Canisius, though only for a short time,
the Jesuits Jajus and Salmeron began holding theological lectures. From the year 1556, in uninterrupted
succession, members of the Society acted as professors
of the theological faculty, in which the Order placed
now half, now the greater proportion of the regular
professors.[2] In the ensuing period Jesuits were seen
in the theological professional pulpits at Prague,
Cologne, Treves and Vienna.[3]

The same was the case at the newly founded colleges
at Dillingen, Graz and Würzburg. Everywhere fresh
life now sprang up in the theological faculties. It was
a circumstance of extreme importance that the Jesuits,
at all the theological schools at which they worked,
brought back into vogue the old scholastic methods.
Germany indeed offered no very favourable ground for
this kind of learning. The religious dissensions stood
in the foreground and laid claim on the best energies.[4]

[1] Mederer, i. 227 ; cf. ii. 150.   [2] Prantl, i. 306.

[3] Concerning the labours of Peter Canisius at the Vienna university,
where he acted as professor of the theological faculty from 1553 to 1556,
see *Nachträge zu Aschbach*, i. 1. 128–156. At Vienna, where Protestantism
had acquired great influence at the university, the exertions of Canisius
‘ did not for a long time succeed in establishing for the Order the dominating
position which it had rapidly acquired at other universities without especial
strain ; here (at Vienna) neither in the time of Canisius nor during the half-
century following did the Order possess more than the two chairs granted by
Ferdinand in the theological faculty ; and it was actually obliged to defend
this position against a formidable rival.’ Aschbach, p. 140. In 1556
Canisius returned to Ingolstadt.

[4] See above, p. 241 f. ; and Werner, *Gesch. der Kathol. Theologie*, p. 44 f.

The old tradition had been broken through, and scholastics had to be introduced afresh from abroad. Hence in the ensuing period it was chiefly to foreigners that the university authorities entrusted scholastic professorships. Among these foreigners there were men of pre-eminent importance. Just as a few decades later the learned Spaniard Roderick de Arriaga shone at Prague, the Italian Francesco Amici at Graz and Vienna, so from the year 1575 Gregory of Valentia was a distinguished teacher of scholastic theology at Dillingen and Ingolstadt. In addition to him the Belgian Becanus, mentioned already above among the polemists, also won great renown as a theological teacher. He was admired for the lucidity, the distinctness and the conciseness of his theological expositions. After Becanus had taught philosophy for four years at Würzburg, he lectured on scholastic theology for twenty-two years at Würzburg, Mayence and Vienna. Like him the controversialists Max Sandaeus (since 1605 professor at Würzburg and then at Vienna) and Francis Coster did lasting service to Germany by their instructional labours. Both these men, however, were surpassed in importance by the Spaniard Alfonsus Pisanus, who taught theology at Dillingen and Ingolstadt for a number of years and published several of his works in Germany. The Belgian John Couvillon, after a six years' career as teacher at the university of Ingolstadt, was sent by Duke Albert V, in 1562, as theologian to the Church Assembly of Trent.[1]

At Ingolstadt and, since 1594, at Vienna also there were three chairs of scholastic theology; at Dillingen, and indeed at most of the Jesuit universities, at least two.

[1] Mederer, i. 273, 304. Concerning the theologians mentioned in the text, see above, p. 345 f. ; concerning Amici, Krones, *Universität Graz.*

In course of time native Germans, pupils of the German college at Rome or of the rising university of Ingolstadt, were able to enter the list of teachers. Henry Blissemius from Cologne, who had studied in the Germanicum, became teacher of scholastic theology at Prague and Graz after the year 1556. Michael Eisele from Gmünd in Suabia, also a pupil of the German college, came to Ingolstadt as teacher of philosophy in 1585, and was afterwards, from 1590 till his death in 1613, professor of scholastic theology at Ingolstadt, Dillingen, Munich and Constance. He left behind him a theological tract on the doctrine of grace.

Among the most important theologians whom Ingolstadt at that time produced, are the famous controversialists Nas, Gretser and Tanner.[1]

Tanner gave instruction in turn in the different theological branches at Ingolstadt and Munich, and was then for fifteen years teacher of scholastic theology at Ingolstadt, until he succeeded Becanus at the university of Vienna. Besides his numerous controversial writings he left behind two dogmatic works, one of them a text-book on scholastic theology, which places him side by side with the most eminent foreign theologians of the period, and guarantees him a name of honour for all future times.[2] The Jesuit controversialists Brillmacher and Keller also worked as teachers of theology at the different German universities.

If by means of these men scholasticism in Germany was raised to a higher level, this happened in a manner which from the first clearly showed the difference between the later and the older scholastics. This

---

[1] See above, pp. 323 f. and 338 ff.   [2] See Scheeben, i. 452.

older scholasticism was nothing else than the classical exposition and demonstration of the Church system of doctrines. It started from the truths of revelation, which it accepted as incontestably true, endeavoured by syllogisms to unfold the contents of these truths, to define more exactly both the dogmas and the errors opposed to the dogmas, to expound the reciprocal relations of the various truths of the faith as well as the consequences following from these truths, to interpret revealed truth by means of natural science, and to lay bare the nothingness of heretical objections. On the other hand it did not fall within the department of this scholasticism to go back first to the sources of revelation, to Scripture and to the works of the Fathers, for proofs of the truths which the Catholic Church recognised as revealed.[1] There were at all times ecclesiastical scholars, who devoted themselves by preference to the investigation of these sources of revelation, the *doctores biblici*, as they have often been called in contradistinction to the scholastics, the *doctores sententiarii*. Moreover the greatest among these scholastics, such as Thomas Aquinas, were also distinguished by profound Scriptural research as well as by familiarity with the Fathers. In the scholastic lectures and writings, however, all was dominated by theological speculation, and when in the sixteenth century the religious innovators busied themselves chiefly in ransacking the sources of revelation in order to make use of them according to their own ideas, the natural consequence was that on the Catholic side also the study of positive theology came to be pursued with increased zeal.

[1] Kleutgen, *Theologie der Vorzeit*, iii. 24 ff., 95 ff.

This tendency had already begun to develop in the polemists of the pre-Tridentine period, and it now progressed rapidly. It was not only that men of such distinguished scholarly importance as Gretser or Serarius gave themselves up as authors almost exclusively to the cultivation of positive theology, but the actual representatives of scholasticism, Valentia, Tanner, Becanus, and so forth, took to prefacing the speculative statements of the different dogmas with exhaustive and solid evidences taken from the Holy Scriptures, the patristic teachings, and the councils, and they continually came back upon these proofs in their expositions. Yet another difference from the older scholasticism became evident. There were now such a number and such a variety of errors for the theologians to elucidate and to combat, that on the whole there was neither time nor strength left to waste on the trifling disputations which had delighted the former school-men.

But the most important change effected was that, during the process of resuscitating scholastics in Germany, the old text-book of Peter Lombard was forced out of the schools. In spite of the great veneration in which, till then, the works of St. Thomas had been held by the whole Church, down to the end of the fifteenth century, there seems to have been no thought of making them replace the Sentences, as the basis of theological school instruction. At the end of the fifteenth century lectures on St. Thomas were given at Cologne ; at the beginning of the sixteenth century the same was done at the universities of Leipzig and Rostock. Cajetan was the first who in the years 1507–1522 compiled a complete commentary on the

'Summa Theologica' of Aquinas; other celebrated school-men from abroad followed his example. When the Dominican Conrad Cöllin of Ulm, in 1507, was appointed professor of scholastic theology at the convent of his Order at Heidelberg, in addition to his lectures on the Master of Sentences, he began an exposition of the 'Summa' of St. Thomas. He met with so much sympathy in this work that on his removal to Cologne he was urged to publish it both by the Heidelberg convent and by his former general of the Order Cajetan. His commentary on one part of the 'Summa' appeared at Cologne in 1512. He is also credited with having left behind him commentaries on the other sections of the 'Summa' at any rate in manuscript.[1] But these intentions were not fully carried out.

In all the German colleges the Sentences of Lombard were still assigned the first place. Even Peter Soto, in the years 1550–1555, gave lectures on them at Dillingen; at the new seminary in Eichstätt, in 1565, the exposition of Lombard was enjoined; a like decree was included in the statutes for the university of Würzburg in 1587. In Germany, as well as abroad by renowned Dominican theologians, commentaries on the four books of the 'Sentences' appeared continuously.[2] The Jesuits, however, were enjoined to hold by St. Thomas; at the Roman college since 1556 the Spaniard Jacob Ledesma had introduced the 'Summa' of Aquinas, and after him

[1] Hartzheim, p. 63 ; cf. Wetzer und Welte's *Kirchenlexikon*, vii². 821.

[2] The Cologne Carmelite, Albert Clumparts († 1585), published a lengthy work on Peter Lombard ; his countryman and fellow Carmelite, John Billick (1576 ; † 1563), the Carmelite Caspar von Barenstein († 1576), and others, also left behind them commentaries on the *Sentences*. Concerning John Billick see the Monograph of Dr. Postina on Eberhard Billick in the *Erläut. und Ergänz. zu Janssens Geschichte des deutschen Volkes*, published by L. Pastor, ii. Heft 2 and 3. Freiburg, 1901, *passim*.

Francis Toletus continued to comment on it.[1]   Peter
Canisius wrote on September 29, 1550, to St. Ignatius
from Ingolstadt : ' The study of theology has fallen into
decay in this college ; in order to reinstate it we have
planned a new course of lectures, which is to have for
its object the " Summa " of St. Thomas.'   Soon afterwards, on April 30, 1551, Canisius recommended the
study of St. Thomas to a young Cologne scholar.[2]
Wherever the Jesuits had gained a firm footing in the
colleges they endeavoured to substitute St. Thomas
for Peter Lombard. ' We have to thank the Jesuits
for being the first to refer the post-Tridentine theology
of Catholic Germany back again to St. Thomas Aquinas,
and for having in general connected it again with the
old traditions of the great medieval schools.' [3]

The study of theology could not but gain in every
respect by this close connexion with the great Aquinas.
The 'Summa' of St. Thomas was above all distinguished
by great order and completeness, and comprised in
systematic sequence the whole sum of revealed doctrine,
speculative as well as practical.   With depth of thought
it combined brevity and simplicity of presentment and
admirable purity of doctrine.   In all these points Peter
Lombard was behind Aquinas.[4]

In the memorandum on the reform of the theological
faculty of Cologne,[5] which the director of the Jesuit
college of Cologne drew up in 1570 by order of the

---

[1] In the oldest curriculum of this college, which passed as model for
all the other Jesuit institutes, the Summa of St. Thomas was already
prescribed in 1566.   Pachtler, *Ratio stud.* i. 197.

[2] *Canisii Epistulae,* i. 336, 366.

[3] Werner, *Gesch. der Kathol. Theologie*, p. 45.

[4] Kleutgen, *Theologie der Vorzeit*, iii. 90 ff.

[5] See Bianco, *Die alte Universität Köln*, i. 335.

magistrate, he made the proposal that, apart from the traditional exposition of the ' Sentences ' of Lombard, the Dominican prior Dietrich von Herzogenbusch should lecture for an hour daily on the ' Summa ' of St. Thomas. ' It is scarcely possible to say,' he goes on, ' how useful this would be for candidates of theology. It would also be extraordinarily pleasing to the Pope, for he sets high value on St. Thomas.' At Ingolstadt the ' Summa ' had already been introduced before the advent of Gregory of Valentia. With a certain amount of solemnity the annals [1] of 1575 state that ' This year the professors of theology began the theological course according to St. Thomas.' Their example was soon followed at Würzburg and Mayence, and before the end of the century theology was taught according to St. Thomas at all the German Jesuit universities.

There were three scholars who stood out prominently as the agents in bringing about this change : Gregory of Valentia, Arriaga, and Becanus. The first of these wrote a commentary on the ' Summa ' of St. Thomas, which numbers no less than four folio volumes, and which had a large circulation. In this work, which appeared at Ingolstadt in 1611, Gregory follows most closely the great Aquinas, only differing from him in that, in correspondence with the conditions of the age, he treats the strong patristic evidence in greater detail. Still more exhaustive is the work of Arriaga, which fills eight folio volumes, is compiled in a positive, scholastic manner, and throws the discussion of controversies entirely into the background. The ' Scholastic Theology ' of Becanus is far more concise than the works of

---

[1] Mederer, ii. 26 ; cf. the plan of study of March 1575 in Prantl, *Gesch. der Universität Ingolstadt*, ii. 295.

both the other theologians, though for the rest it bears the same character.

The transformation which scholasticism underwent in the process of its revival in Germany proved of quite especial service to two branches of theological knowledge. Biblical study now came prominently into the foreground. That the taste for Scriptural research had not disappeared even at the time of the worst disturbances in Germany is shown by Hittorp's edition of the ' Vulgate,' printed at Cologne in 1530—quite an extraordinary achievement for that period—which ' fulfils in the highest measure the requirements of a learned and critical edition of the traditional text.' [1] The compiler, Gobelinus Laridius, with expert linguistic regard to the original Hebrew and Greek texts, had compared not less than fifteen of the oldest manuscripts accessible to him with the earlier editions of the Bible.

In the ensuing period, the drastic prescriptions of the Council of Trent, and its decree that at all the higher schools (those of the convents not excepted) explanatory lectures should be given on the Holy Scriptures, had a great influence on Biblical studies. Everywhere commentators of note now came forward, and great zeal was also manifested for the study of Biblical languages. The Jesuit Peltanus also compiled a work of importance for dogmatics, in which he gave a detailed explanation and defence of the decisions of the Council with regard to the Holy Scriptures.

As regards the original text as well as the understanding of the Scriptures, the German Carthusian, Peter Carbo († 1590), did good service by his learned

---

[1] Kaulen, *Gesch. der Vulgata*, Mayence, 1868, p. 361. For another edition of 1539 cf. Hartzheim, p. 37.

writings, published at Prague. Peter Stevart [1] of Liège, who had completed his theological training at Ingolstadt, had been professor of exegesis since 1575, regent of the new seminary at Eichstätt since 1581, then from 1584 to 1619 academic instructor, and for many years Rector Magnificus at Ingolstadt, left behind him a considerable number of commentaries on the letters of St. Paul and St. James.[2]

Great renown as an exegetist, and that even with the Protestants, was gained by Andrew Masius, secretary to the archbishop of Lund and bishop of Constance, John von Weeze, who since 1558 had been councillor in the service of Duke William of Cleves († 1573). Besides his participation in the compilation of the great Polyglot Bible printed by Plantin, we must above all mention his edition of the Book of Joshua, which appeared in 1574. The exegesis of Masius is characterised both by the endeavour to reproduce exactly the literal meaning of the sacred text, and by severe criticism of the old and new Jewish Bible expounders.[3]

Still more important are the exegetical works of the Jesuit Nicholas Serarius, a Lotharingian, who from childhood up had been educated in Germany, and who worked exclusively at German universities († 1609). Baronius calls this marvellously industrious man (his collected works fill sixteen folio volumes) 'the light of the Church of Germany.' After lecturing on philosophy

---

[1] He had also a benefice in the Apostles' Church at Cologne ; † 1626 as provost and vicar-general at Liège. Hartzheim, p. 283. Mederer, ii. 240.

[2] For the commentary of Peter Stevart on the Epistle of St. James (Ingolstadt, 1591) see *Katholik*, 1903, i. 191 f

[3] Cf. Hurter, p. 22 f. Lossen, *Briefe von A. Masius*, Leipzig, 1886, pp. xix–xx. Reusch, *Index*, i. 571 ; ii. 1273.

and scholastic theology at Würzburg, Serarius occupied for twenty years, partly there and partly at Mayence, the post of professor of exegesis. In addition to his valuable works in the field of local history and his numerous other writings, he wrote commentaries on all the historical books of the ancient and also on the Catholic epistles of the New Testament. In these he shows himself equally able as philologist and as theologian, only in the explanation of the historical books he displays a certain amount of prolixity. The part of his work which was most valued is the prologues (Prolegomena) which he prefixed to the different commentaries, and which in 1602 he published in a separate volume at Cologne; in this volume nearly all the questions relating to introduction to the Holy Scriptures are dealt with in an admirable manner.[1]

A contemporary of Serarius and a member of the same order was Martin Antony Delrio, born of Spanish parents who had migrated to Antwerp. He began by embracing a juridical career, in which he attained to the rank of procurator-general. In 1580 he entered the Jesuit Order, taught theology at Douay, Liège and Graz, and died in 1608. Justin Lipsius calls him 'the wonder of his age.' In the last period of his life Delrio occupied himself largely with exegetical work, the fruits of which appeared in his explanations of Genesis, the Song of Solomon, and Lamentations.[2]

Attention was now also given to moral theology; special works were written on the subject, and special courses of lectures also held.

[1] See de Backer, iii. 761–766 ; Ruland, pp. 13–21 ; *Katholik* (1864), ii. 162 f.   Hurter, pp. 196–198 ; *Zeitschr. für katholische Theologie*, xxiii. 366 f.   See also vol. xiii. p. 460.

[2] Hurter, p. 191 f. ; Krones, p. 377.

In the stormy, disturbed times prior to the Council of Trent, the work of defence had made such claim on all the strength of the Catholics, that there was little time or energy for cultivating theology, in spite of its importance in the practical ministry of religion. Among the small number of scholars who at that time studied this branch of learning, the Dominican Conrad Cöllin, who in 1523 came forward with a special work on moral theology, again calls for notice. A still more complete effort of this sort appears in the 'Handbuch der Pastoral Theologie' of the learned Peter Binsfeld († 1598), coadjutor bishop of Treves, a pupil of the German college at Rome.

The Jesuits Balthasar Hagel [1] and Paul Laymann were at that time highly honoured as teachers of moral theology. 'In the judgment of cases of conscience Hagel was so remarkably able that copies of his "Lectures to Students" were eagerly sought after, and the most difficult questions were brought to him from abroad.[2] Still greater repute was enjoyed by Laymann, who in the years 1609–1625 lectured on moral theology at Munich, and afterwards on canon law at Dillingen.[3] His 'Moraltheologie' appeared first in 1625 at Munich in four volumes. This work placed him at the head of German moralists : what Tanner among the German

---

[1] Born at Murnau (Bavaria), a Jesuit since 1572, teacher of dogmatics for many years at Ingolstadt. He died in 1616. Long before Laymann he compiled a practical handbook of morality : *Scholae theologiae, in quibus casuum conscientiae cognoscendorum brevis ac certa methodus traditur. Libri tres,* Ingolstadii traditi anno 1606. Cf. De Backer, ii. 6 ; Sommervogel, iv. 18–19.

[2] Mederer, ii. 216.

[3] Concerning Laymann, Binsfeld, and Delrio, see the present work (German), vol. viii. *passim.* (The English translation of vol. viii. is not yet out.)

Jesuits had done for dogmatics, that Laymann did for morals. A marked feature of this work is that its casuistical matter is arranged on a basis borrowed from Thomas Aquinas, and by its reference to ecclesiastical and civil law it has acquired an essentially juridical character. Special traits of Laymann are his sobriety of judgment and his striving after all-round thoroughness in his propositions.

Laymann was also distinguished as a canonist: his commentaries on the Decretals are still prized at the present day. Besides him a number of other Jesuits did good service by canonistical work; as, for instance, Peter Thyraeus, Serarius, Gretser and Moquet. Side by side with these may be mentioned Rudolf Clenck, John Richard Ossanaeus, Peter Binsfeld, Cornelius Schulting, Friedrich Martini, and, above all, Henry Canisius. The latter, a learned layman and a relative of the renowned Peter Canisius, had held the chair of canon law at Ingolstadt from 1590 till his death in 1610, and left behind him a number of canonical writings.[1] He gained even greater renown by the publication of numerous unprinted works of patristic and medieval times.

The careful editing of patristic and other memorable ecclesiastical works was indeed the chief way in which the newly awakened theological zeal showed itself in Germany. In 1538 there appeared in two folio volumes a collection of Councils compiled by the Franciscan Peter Crabbe. Later on, in 1567, the Carthusian Laurence Surius, known as an historian, published a new and complete collection in four folio volumes. The

---

[1] See Schulte, *Quellen*, iii. 1. 127–131, 134–135. Here, too (p. 124 f.), is a list of the few canonical works of the pre-Tridentine period.

Cologne canon and professor, Severin Binius, whose
‘ Collectio Conciliorum ’ appeared at Cologne in 1606,
surpassed all his predecessors.[1]   Surius further prepared
an edition of the works of Pope Leo the Great, while
Binius brought out a revised text of the Church histories
of Eusebius, Socrates, Theodoret, Sozomenus and Evag-
rius.[2]   Surius also translated many of the writings of
Faber, Gropper and Staphylus, and compiled a large
collection of Lives of the Saints ; this last work is indeed
wanting in critical insight, but all the same it brought
much usable material to light.[3]

In this department also the Jesuits soon assumed
the lead.   In the forefront stood the first provincial
of the Order for South Germany and Austria, Peter
Canisius.   The literary activity of this extraordinary
man extends over more than fifty years, from 1543 to
1596.[4]   He began his career in 1543, at Cologne, as a
youth of twenty-two, with a critical edition of the
works of the Dominican mystic John Tauler, for which,
in especial, the Dominican nunnery of St. Gertrude at
Cologne had supplied him with valuable manuscripts ;
various writings of Tauler and his like-minded associates
were first published here.[5]   In 1546 followed the works

---

[1] Hefele, *Konziliengesch.* i². 75.

[2] See Werner, *Gesch. der Kathol. Theologie*, pp. 39–40.   In correction of
Werner it must be said that the first printed collection of conciliar acts
was compiled by the Paris canon, Jacob Merlin, in 1523.   Hefele, i². 74.

[3] Wattenbach, *Deutschlands Geschichtsquellen*, i⁴. 9.

[4] Concerning the numerous writings of Canisius see Alegambe, *Bibl.
Script. Soc. Jesu*, Antverpiae, 1643, pp. 374–377.   De Backer, i. 1046–1067 ;
iii. 2054–2055.   Sommervogel, iv. 617–688 ; viii. 1974–1983.   O. Braunsberger in the *Zeitschr. für katholische Theologie*, 1890, pp. 720–744. Paulus
(*l.c.*), 1902, pp. 574–583.   *Canisii Epistulae*, ii. 883–901 ; iii. 772–800.

[5] *Canisii Epistulae*, i. 79–93.   The Tauler edition is also of value
because among the many thousands of writings which the members of the
Society of Jesus have published since their first foundation it is far and
away the first.

of Cyril of Alexandria in Latin, in two folio volumes. As the dedicatory preface of the first volume indicates, Cyril is presented as a model for the German bishops. Canisius next published the sermons and homilies of Leo the Great as witness from Christian antiquity against the innovators. In relation with this is his handy edition of selected letters and other writings of St. Jerome, arranged for school use, first published in 1602, and afterwards in about forty fresh editions. With this may be classed, further, the translation of the Martyrologium, enriched with many additions, which Adam Walasser brought out first in 1562 at Dillingen, under the direction and with the active co-operation of Canisius.[1] For the edition of St. Cyprian by Erasmus, Canisius had already collected nearly 1000 variants, when he learnt that another scholar was engaged in preparing a new edition of this Church Father.[2]

The principal work of Canisius is his Catechism, spread over the whole Catholic world, and which he himself arranged in five different editions, two German and three Latin.[3] This was followed by his pamphlet (already mentioned) against the Magdeburg Centuriators, by the Latin 'Remarks' on the Gospel of Sundays and festivals, intended primarily for the use of the priests, which was repeatedly reprinted in two quarto volumes, by the German lives of German and Swiss Saints—St. Beatus, Fridolin, Ursus and Victor, Mauritius, Ida von

[1] The book was frequently reprinted later on. We must especially notice in it the cordial praise, bubbling up from a genuine German heart, of the 'great and saintly Emperor Carolus.' The chancellor Gerson also comes in for praise. (*Canisii Epistulae*, iii. 795.)

[2] *Canisii Epistulae*, ii. 781–782.

[3] Besides the present work, vol. viii. pp. 277–292, see now **Braunsberger,** *Entstehung und erste Entwickelung der Katechismen des sel. Petrus Canisius* Freiburg, 1890.

Toggenburg, St. Nikolaus von der Flüe—published in smaller and larger volumes, and finally, not to mention other works, by a series of Latin and German devotional books; of one of the latter, 'Manuale Catholicorum,' more than thirty editions in different languages are known.

With counsel, as well as with practical help, moreover, Canisius took part also in the scholastic labours of others; for instance, in 1556, at Ingolstadt, he prepared a new edition, adapted to German needs, of the Latin grammar by his fellow Jesuit Hannibal Codrettus; occupied himself in 1557, and for some years after, in editing the writings of Hosius and Martin Cromer, which were published at Antwerp, Cologne and Paris; translated into German in 1559 two Latin pamphlets of Hosius; in 1562 supplied the theologian of the Trent Council, Didakus Payva de Andrada, with contributions for his admirable publication 'Orthodoxae Explicationes,' which appeared first at Venice in 1564; busied himself in making accessible to the Germans, through a Cologne printer, the celebrated work on justification (1572) by the Spanish Franciscan, Andrew of Vega, who had also been one of the theologians at the Council of Trent, edited in 1578 a new version of St. Epiphanius, and in 1580 urged his Roman superior of the Order to make the learned Father Francis Turrian have his works newly revised, cleared from all eccentricities and brought into publicity.[1]   He also took an active part

---

[1] *Io. Alph. de Polanco S.J., Vita Ignatii Loiolae et rerum Societatis Jesu Historia*, vi. Matriti, 1898, p. 411.   *Canisii Epistulae*, i. 592, note 2; ii. 424, 453, 888, 897–899; iii. 242, 292, 424, 453.   Paulus in the *Histor.-polit. Blätter*, 1898, i. 765.   Unprinted letters of Canisius to Mercurian, Augsburg, January 24, and to Manareus, Dillingen, November 20, 1580, most kindly contributed by P. Braunsberger.

in bringing out a complete edition of the ' Councils ' which the Jesuits at Cologne were preparing. On November 8, 1561, he thanked Father Salmeron for the memoranda of advice which he had sent from Rome, and promised him to write to Cologne and say that they were by no means to grudge the costs necessary for the authors.

It was indeed a matter of heartfelt rejoicing to this man, so keenly zealous for the welfare of souls, that the mission reports, written in Spanish and in Italian, which flowed into Rome from India, Japan, and other countries, were being translated into good Latin and printed in Germany.[1] During the last period of the Church assembly of Trent (1562–1563), by means of numerous parcels of books sent from Augsburg, he brought to the knowledge of the Fathers of the Council all the theological novelties of the Frankfort book-fair, above all the newest Protestant writings.[2] At the same time he addressed urgent requests to Trent and to Rome, especially to the cardinals Hosius and Truchsess, begging that they would instigate the Catholic scholars to take up their pens and defend the Church in learned writings.[3] A few years earlier, in 1560, he had already gained from the Emperor printing privileges for three presses.[4]

Besides Canisius, his brothers of the Order, Theodore Peltanus and Gretser, as well as Peter Stevart, already mentioned as exegetist, distinguished themselves by patristic writings. Peltanus was born in the neighbour-

---

[1] *Canisii Epistulae*, iii. 303, 344, 580.
[2] *Ibid.* iii. 240, 322, 326, 363, 374, 393, 396, 409, 428, 485, 489, 492, 530, 575.
[3] *Ibid.* iii. 30, 31, 296, 372, 392.
[4] *Ibid.* ii. 678.

hood of Liège, but he, like Canisius, passed as a German. From 1556 till his death in 1584 he was occupied with scholastic work, partly at Ingolstadt where he was professor for ten years, and partly at Ausgburg. Gretser contributed the materials for the principal work of Henry Canisius, the celebrated ' Antiquae Lectiones,' which fill six quarto volumes.[1]

3.

Philosophy in Germany, at the beginning of the sixteenth century, still moved almost in the same grooves as at the close of the Middle Ages. United in the great fundamental principles,[2] fiercely at feud on individual points, the opinions of Thomists, Scotists, Occamists, stood opposed to one another. With the keenest interest men plunged into minute questions of metaphysics and logic, and spent on problems, the answer to which could have no other interest than that of a solved riddle, the most astonishing industry and acumen. According to an approximate estimate, ' which is certainly not an exaggerated one,' in the depart-ment of logic alone, in the period from 1480 to 1520, the printed works, older and newer, averaged from fifteen to eighteen a year.[3] True, this calculation includes the whole of cultivated Europe. But Germany was not behind other nations in zeal. A philosophical compen-dium by Usingen, after having already passed through several editions, went through another reprint of 2000 copies, and at the end of eleven years, after the

---

[1] Werner, *Gesch. der Kathol. Theologie*, pp. 40–42 ; Medcrer, ii. 6 ; Sommervogel, iii. 1744 ff., and above, p. 460 f.

[2] See above, p. 116.

[3] Prantl, *Gesch. der Logik im Abendlande*, iv. 173.

death of the author, another edition was called for, as
there was not a single copy left in the book-market.[1]

Even in theology, disquisitions of purely theological
character were allowed undue space. Disregarding
the needs of practical life, ' just as though these were
sleeping the sleep of Endymion,' [2] even the divinity
scholars, at any rate in their disputations, busied themselves more with philosophical speculations than with
actual theological arguments. After the split in the
Church this failing was generally recognised by all
theologians of insight, and the justness of the complaints on this score is shown by a glance at the syllabus
for Eck's Vienna disputation of 1516.[3]

On Aristotle, indeed, they were not so dependent
as Luther had reproached his own scholastic opponents
with being. They knew very well that even ' the
Philosopher ' had frequently erred, and they said so
openly.[4] Nevertheless, in the main and on the whole

---

[1] Paulus, *Der Augustiner Barth. Arnoldi von Usingen*, p. 2.

[2] Eck, *De primatu*, i. 1.

[3] As regards the Incarnation, for instance, Eck goes into the question :
whether the persons of the Father and the Holy Ghost could have become
' man '—whether the same human nature could be taken on at the same
time by two divine persons—whether at least by several divine persons *non
primo unionem terminantibus*—whether the Eternal Word could also
take on an irrational nature—whether a rational creature could assume a
created nature.   Questions, all of them, which could not be answered
so well from theological evidences as from pure grounds of reason, and which
must in so far be called philosophical questions.

[4] ' Quamvis Aristoteles habitus sit inter philosophos tamquam princeps,
non tamen sua scripta undecunque quadrant veritati, nec philosophia
infudit se uni homini tota et nihil reliquit aliis. . . . Sicut ergo ipse
ingressus est labores suorum magistrorum, et invenit eos quandoque
errasse, sic alii ingressi sunt suos labores et invenerunt, eum non solum
errasse, verum etiam sibi ipsi clarissime contradixisse.' Usingen in
Paulus, p. 6. Quotations from older scholastics in Schneid, *Aristoteles
in der Scholastik*, Eiehstätt, 1875, p. 81 ff.

they held firmly by Aristotle as the basis of a rational philosophy.

The attacks against Aristotle which had proceeded in Italy from the humanists met with no response in Germany for a long time. Rudolf Agricola in his writings [1] had, indeed, to some extent, followed similar tendencies, and like Laurentius Valla, had attempted to replace strict logic by a kind of rhetoric.[2] For the rest, however, the shallow attacks of the Italians were not once honoured with a refutation.[3] Not till the younger school of German humanists began to exercise their influence at the universities was the old scholastic method driven into the background.[4]

But, however resolutely the reform proposals of the humanists were rejected, there was no blindness as regards the imperfections of contemporary philosophy. The theologians had already been at work at a reform of study before the outbreak of the war with the religious innovators 'awoke them from their sleep,' and compelled them to turn their attention to tasks of more real import. To the well-known opponent of Luther, John Eck, as a renovator of philosophic study, prominent significance attaches.[5] When the Bavarian government was desirous of instituting a fresh organisation of study at the university of Ingolstadt, the ducal commissioners entrusted Eck with the compilation of new philosophical text-books. In an astonishingly short time Eck completed his commentaries on Aristotle's

---

[1] *De inventione dialectica.*

[2] Prantl, *Gesch. der Logik*, iv. 167 f.

[3] ' Putrescat ille quidem (Valla) inscitia sua, cum doctis omnibus ludibrio habeatur.' Eck in Prantl, *Gesch. der Logik*, iv. 288.

[4] See present work, vol. iii. p. 26 f.

[5] Prantl, *Gesch. der Logik*, iv. 284 f.

writings on logic and physics, and on Peter Hispanus.
' He made it his aim to clear away the useless chaff
of sophisms and endless logical disquisitions,' and
' to go back to the pure, unadulterated philosophy of
Aristotle.' [1]   A new translation of the ' Stagirite ' by
Argyropulus was made by Eck the basis of his commentary, and the original Greek text often brought
forward in explanation for more than half a century,
the ' Cursus Eccianus,' continued to be at Ingolstadt
the text-book of philosophical lectures.

In addition to Eck, several other literary opponents
of the religious innovators had distinguished themselves
as authors in the domain of philosophy ; as, for instance,
Usingen, Cochlaeus and Wimpina. The imaginative
Murner had also compiled a compendium of logic, in
which, as a help to memory, he had connected all the
different dogmas of logic with the emblems of fifty-one
playing-cards.[2]

After the Council of Trent the reform of scholastic
theology was soon followed by the remodelling of
philosophy. Aristotle was still firmly adhered to in
spite of the attacks of a Patrizzi, a Ramus, and so forth,
but in the explanation of the ' Philosopher ' an attempt
was made to keep free from those faults which, in the
latest commentators, none blamed more severely •than
these very founders of the new scholasticism ; above all
the tendency to useless subtleties and tastelessness of
style. It is to Spain and Italy that we owe the most

[1] *In summulas Petri Hisp.* dedicatio.

[2] On the title-page of this *Logica memorativa* the logician is depicted
as a hunter, whose equipment symbolises the different parts of logic.
Thus the hunting-knife is the syllogism, the hunter's legs are *praedicabilia*
and *praedicamenta*, his hounds are *veritas* and *falsitas*, the object of the
chase, a hare, is *problema*, and so forth.   Prantl, *Gesch. der Logik*, iv. 294.

important works of the new tendency. But in Germany also confessional polemics and apologetics had not so entirely absorbed all interest as to leave none over for pure scientific questions of philosophy. Works of important scholastic value did not indeed appear. A few commentaries on Aristotle, written by German Jesuits, remained unprinted owing to the unfavourableness of the times, or for other reasons.[1] But then, as before, a thorough philosophical training was required in those who devoted themselves to the higher studies.[2] The Jesuits especially, to whom fell a large share of the work of reviving ecclesiastical learning in Germany, pressed urgently for the reform of philosophy also. Thus in 1555, in his reform proposals for the university of Ingolstadt, Canisius had already expressed the wish that Aristotelian dialectics, which had been disgracefully neglected for so many years, might be reinstated, and that the lectures on this subject, attendance at which had formerly been a necessary step to a Master's degree, should be re-established.[3] ' For the lectures on Aristotle,' he had written at another time, ' you must both stir up the unwilling and excite in them a zeal for disputations.'[4] The confraters of Bl. Canisius shared his zeal. Accordingly in 1558, at Ingolstadt, where the study of Aristotle had been confined to extracts

---

[1] De Backer, *s.v. Baumann*, Coscan.

[2] ' Cursum [philosophicum] vero audient integrum omnes, qui gradum aliquem in philosophia suscepturi sunt, quive theologiae ac medicinae studiis operam dabunt.' Ducal ordinance for Ingolstadt, 1572. Mederer, iv. 336.

[3] ' Redeat in scholam dialectica Aristotelis, tot annis turpiter intermissa, et lectiones magistrandis necessariae compleantur.' Pachtler, ii. 355.

[4] ' Ad Aristotelis lectiones etiam repugnantes provocabitis, in disputandi fervore confirmabitis.' Canisius, *Brief an die Scholastiker S. J. in Köln*, Febr. 25, 1548. Pachtler, ii. 135.

from his writings, Hermes Halbpaur began himself to deal with the text of the philosopher, and to expound it to the students.[1]   What strenuous exertions were made to appropriate the achievements of the German Southern reformers of ecclesiastical learning is best seen by the surprisingly large number of reprints of the most eminent foreign philosophical works.   Of the thirty-four editions of the logic of Fonseca, the ' Portuguese Aristotle,' half were printed in German towns. A similar work by Cardinal Toledo was published nine times at Cologne, and thirteen times in foreign towns. The statistics are the same as regards the Aristotelian commentaries by the Jesuits of Coimbra, the works of Pereyra, Lorinus, and others.[2]   Altogether the study of philosophy was pushed aside at that time by other more engrossing interests.   The more important men, for instance, of the Jesuit Order, Laymann, Gretser, Serarius, Forer, were all of them for a time employed as professors of logic, though it was seldom that a man of talent remained all his life at this work and devoted his whole energies to it.   Most of them, after a few years, turned their attention to theology, especially to apologetics, or to practical life.   Philosophic study was regarded as a preparation for higher branches, and was intended to train the mind to grasp philosophic questions sharply and clearly, and to accustom it to weigh accurately the pros and cons.[3]

[1]   *Canisii Epistulae,* ii. 390, note 2.

[2]   Sommervogel, *s.v.* Fonseca, Toledo, &c.

[3]   Leibniz also, in this sense, spoke favourably of Aristotle's logic : ' I am of opinion that an inferior head, with the help and the practice of this logic, will have the advantage over the best head, just as a child with a ruler can draw straighter lines than the greatest master without one.' *Brief an G. Wagner,* Pesch, *Instit. logic.* i. 72.

Special value was therefore laid on the disputations, those exercises ‘ which are the best means for developing intellectual acumen.’ [1]   With what ardour pupils and professors engaged in them is seen from the immense number of so-called theses and disputations which were printed. In the case of the more important of these exercises, in which the pupils displayed their skill in intellectual combat in the presence of outsiders, the professors were in the habit of summing up and developing the propositions in shorter or longer treatises. These theses, of which an immense quantity appeared yearly at Dillingen and Ingolstadt, were generally taken from Aristotle, and either comprised the main contents of one of the logical or physical treatises of the Stagyrite, or else summed up his views on some controversial point, or dealt with different difficult questions of philosophy.[2]   Publications of this sort have naturally no important value for the promotion of learning.

Like the Society of Jesus, the other Orders also held firmly by the Aristotelian philosophy.[3] For their disputations they chose by preference matter more nearly connected with practical life. To the sphere of practical philosophy belongs also the single great philosophical

---

[1] ‘ Scholastica exercitia, quibus ad excitanda ingenia nihil est aptius.’ *Edikt des Herzogs von Bayern von* 1572.   Mederer, iv. 337.

[2] A great number of such disputations are summarised by Rixner, *Geschichte der Philosophie bei den Katholiken in Altbayern, bayrisch Schwaben und bayrisch Franken*, Munich, 1835, p. 18 ff.   An idea of this literature may be gained from the five disputations in the works of Gretser (xvi. 549 f.).   The theological ‘ theses ’ of the Fathers Alfonsus Pisanus and Theodore Peltanus enjoyed such a great reputation after 1563, that orders for them came from many parts of Germany to Ingolstadt. *Epistolae P. Hieronymi Nadal*, ii. Matriti, 1899, 492.

[3] Ziegelbauer, ii. 280 ; iv. 290, 301.

work of Catholic Germany of that period, namely, Adam Contzen's ' Zehn Bücher Politik.'

Machiavelli's doctrines of statecraft, with their degradation of Christianity and of religion, and their practical godlessness, did not find acceptance in Italy only. In France, says a pamphlet from the circle of the reformers, there were many statesmen who read Machiavelli more eagerly than did the priests their breviaries or the Turks their Alcoran.[1] The much-travelled Jesuit Ribadeneira [2] said that this teacher of corruption had so many disciples everywhere, that there were such a multitude of so-called ' politicians ' who, while professing faith in the name of Christians, persecuted Christ, that their number was incalculable, and incalculable also the harm which they did to the State.

' At the present day,' says also Contzen, ' the execrable race of pseudo-politicians, at whose head Machiavelli carried the torch which set so many kingdoms in flames, has grown mighty, and in many places all too mighty. To Machiavelli religion is a means to State ends ; he praises vice and error when they are serviceable to dominion ; justice, according to him, must yield to usefulness. What else does he make of a prince than a ruthless criminal, a crafty hypocrite ? [3]

One reason for the extensive spread of Machiavellism was to be found, according to Catholic writers, in the heresies of the sixteenth century, in the religious anarchy, in the unsatisfactory inconsistencies and in-

---

[1] *Commentariorum de regno aut quovis principatu recte et tranquille administrando libri tres*, Argentorati, 1611, pp. 6, 15.

[2] *Princeps christianus adv. N. Machiavellum ceterosque huius temporis politicos*, Moguntiae, 1603, Praefatio.

[3] *Politicor.* i. 1.

consequence of Protestantism. ' Whereas some ' (of
the ' atheists ' or ' pseudo-politicians '), says Contzen,
' amid such manifold variety of religious creeds cannot
decide on any one in particular, they reject all religion.' [1]
' Atheists ' became a common appellation by which
to designate the ' politicians.' [2] ' Although nowadays,'
says Lessius,[3] ' there are many people who altogether
deny the Godhead, they are nevertheless not known
everywhere as deniers of God. For they hide their
secret in silence from fear of the laws, and only speak
of it in a confidential circle. Occasion for this evil is
above all given by the heresies of our century, which
almost all lead to atheism. For if once people have
apostatised from the Catholic religion, they have nothing substantial left in which the spirit can find rest.
And so it happens that just the most talented among
the heretics fall into doubt on the most important points
of religion, and either cease to believe in any God at
all, or else lapse into a state of wavering in which they
are ready to take up with any religion which is the
most to their advantage. These people we call politicians, because for them the object of all religion is the
State.' [4]

---

[1] *Politicor*. ii. 14 : ' Atheorum tamen seu pseudopoliticorum duplex
est sententia de republica gubernanda. Quidam enim palam omnem
non modo religionem, verum etiam superstitionem de medio tollunt. . . .
dum enim in tam magna religionum varietate nullam eligere possunt,
omni carent.'

[2] ' (Athei) dicuntur etiam synecdochica denominatione Politici . . .
et signate Machiavellistae.' G. Voetius, *Sel. disp. theol.* i. Ultrajecti,
1648, 117.

[3] *De numine eiusque providentia. Opuscula*, Lugduni, 1651, p. 215.
Cf. G. Voetius, ' De atheismo,' in his *Opera*, i. 115–226.

[4] ' Simultaneously with the appearance of the evangel in France,'
says also the Calvinistic pamphlet mentioned above, p. 378 n 1. (*Widmung
an Fr. v. Hastings und Eduard Bacon*), ' Satan stirred up mockers and wits

After several foreign works against the ' politicians ' had been reprinted in Germany, Contzen set himself to compile an independent work in which, with constant reference to Machiavelli, he aimed at showing the nature of 'true, genuine statesmanship, which had for its basis the laws of God, for its builder healthy reason, for its equipment true cleverness, religiousness and virtue.' He endeavoured to show how the system of the Florentines was in opposition not only to the laws of God but also to natural cleverness, and could never produce anything lasting. As the foundation of his view of the State he begins by showing that the State is not the work of chance and of blind destiny, but a creation of God, whose providence is continually watching over the nations and deciding their fate. The aim of all statecraft lies in the wellbeing of the community and of individuals through the exercise of virtue and religion. Among the means to this end, to the discussion of which Contzen then proceeds, he dwells with special delight on the education of the young. The conditions which lead to the greatness and the power of a people, the faults which bring on the inner dissolution of the State, are dealt with in the following books. A treatise on war concludes the work, which, in spite of individual defects, is nevertheless a worthy presentation of great Christian ideas of a State.

who in merry jest fell foul of all the principles of religion and politics. Gradually this jesting turned to sober earnest, and out of words there grew up deeds.'

CHAPTER IX

TRANSLATION OF THE HOLY SCRIPTURES INTO THE
GERMAN LANGUAGE BY CATHOLICS AND PROTESTANTS

' WHAT the sun is in the firmament,' so taught the
German theologian Caspar Schatzgeyer at the beginning
of the sixteenth century, ' that the Holy Scriptures are
in the heaven of the Church ; the Church writers, on the
other hand, the Fathers and the theologians, are to be
compared to the stars. We must therefore study the
Bible more than other writings.' [1] In agreement with
this it says at the end of a Koberger Vulgate of 1477 :
' The Holy Scriptures excel all the learning of the
world. For all other sciences treat of the creatures,
but the Scriptures teach us to know the Creator. All
believers should watch zealously and exert themselves
unremittingly to understand the contents of these most
useful and exalted writings, and to retain them in the
memory. Holy Scripture is that beautiful garden of
Paradise in which the leaves of the commandments
grow green, the branches of evangelical counsel sprout,
the flowers of good examples blossom ; where the
rivulets of parables bubble, the nests of promises are
hidden, the music of the Psalms delights us ! '

These words admirably describe the attitude which

---

[1] ' Sacra scriptura principali et praecipuo studio est amplectenda,
et in ea animus excolendus. In fonte enim potius quam in rivulis potan-
dum est.' Schatzgeyer, *Opera*, p. 325ᵃ.

the Church in the Middle Ages held with regard to Holy
Scripture. That the Bible at that time was a book
lying under a bank is an unhistorical assertion. ' Facts
loudly proclaim the opposite. The book of the Holy
Scriptures was the most widely circulated book in the
Middle Ages, and had the most tremendous influence
on the life of the nations.' [1] First and foremost the
study of the Bible was urgently enjoined on the priests.
A ' Seelsorgehandbuch ' ('Handbook for the Care of
Souls') of the year 1514 described the Bible as the
chief source for sermons ; [2] the study of it was recommended by Trithemius as the surest means of
preserving the priestly spirit.[3] The ' Book of Ecclesiastical Law ' gives a list of those Fathers and Councils
who encouraged the study of the Scriptures.[4] The
Breviary and the Missal, which are for the most part
made up of words from Holy Scripture, at any rate kept
the priests constantly in official touch with the Book of
books. To what extent the Bible, above all the Gospels,
served as the actual source of pious contemplation for
all the monastic orders and all who devoted themselves
to a life of prayer is sufficiently seen from Thomas à
Kempis, who, in agreement with the Fathers, compares
the Word of Christ with the Eucharist, the body of
Christ, and declares that without the Eucharist and the
Holy Scriptures, his food and his light, life would be

[1] Opinion of Michael, *Gesch. der deutschen Volkes*, iii. (1903) 223. See
Holzhey, *Inspiration*, iii., and J. Hoffmann, *Die Heilige Schrift, ein Volkes-
und Schulbuch in der Vergangenheit*, Kempten, 1902.

[2] *Katholik*, 1889, ii. 176.

[3] Trithemius, *De sacerdotum vita instituenda*, c. 4.

[4] *Dist.* 36, 38. ' Ignorantia mater cunctorum errorum maxime in
sacerdotibus vitanda est, qui docendi officium in populis susceperunt.
Sacerdotes enim legere sanctas scripturas admonet Paulus apostolus.'
C. i. *dist*. 38.

unbearable to him.[1] If a monk would attain to perfection, said Trithemius, let him learn to go through the
text of the story of the Passion with frequent medita-
tion. 'Let him picture to himself the different scenes
in the passion of Christ, as though he had been present
at them ; let him imagine to himself that he is accompanying Christ on His way to the Cross, that he sees
Him and hears Him speak, in order that thus he may
become inflamed with love for the Redeemer.[2] How
abundantly also all these exhortations to the study of
Scripture bore fruit at that time is shown by the fact
that down to the year 1501 not less than 124, in the
following century over 400, editions of the Latin
Vulgate were published,[3] apart from the 186 editions
of the Mass-book, the 173 editions of the Breviary,
and the numerous other printed works which related
to Holy Scripture or served to explain it.

The laity were kept up in the knowledge of Scripture
by the sermons, attendance at which was stringently
insisted on.[4] The whole scheme of decoration of the
churches, the sculpture on the walls, the priestly garments, and all the vessels and utensils for the service
of God, as Geiler von Kaisersberg[5] pointed out, re-

---

[1] *Imitatio Christi*, iv. 11. The comparison between *Corpus Christi*
and *verbum Christi* goes back as far as to N. Hilarius (in *Ps.* 127, note 110)
and to Pseudo-Augustinus (Serm. 300 ; Migne, *Patr. lat.* xxxix. 2319).
Among contemporaries, Silv. Prierias, for one, treats of it. *Katholik*,
1889, ii. 176.

[2] Trithemius, *De triplici regione claustralium*, regio 2, art. 8.

[3] W. A. Copinger, ' The first half-century of the Latin Bible ' (*Histor.-
polit. Blätter*, cx. [1892] 849). Copinger considers thirteen of these editions,
L. Delisle twelve more of them, as doubtful ; the remaining ninety-nine
belong certainly to the fifteenth century.

[4] See present work, vol. i. p. 38 ff.

[5] *Christenlich bilger* (Strassburg, 1512), fol. 127. Joh. Müller (*Quellenschriften und Gesch. des deutsch-sprachlichen Unterrichts bis zur Mitte des*

minded the congregation of the law of God, the life of
the Redeemer and his prototypes in the Old Testament.

The desire to possess the Holy Scriptures in the
mother tongue is already met with on German soil
in the time of Charlemagne ; and, strange to say, it is
just the earliest translators of the Middle Ages who
have come nearest to perfection in this task.

The fragments of the Gospel of St. Matthew which
came from the convent Monsee are pre-eminently an
achievement of the eighth century. The Germanising
of Tatian's Gospel harmony, which dates from the
ninth century, keeps so closely to the Latin text that
one cannot help regretting the loss of old German
forms of speech which make such a faithful transposi-
tion possible. The poetical paraphrases of the Gospels,
the 'Heliand' (Saviour) with their perfect fusion of the
Christian and the Germanic spirit, Otfried's Gospel
harmony with its tender thoughtful piety, afford as
honourable a testimony to the ninth century as do the
translation of the Psalms by the St. Gall monk Notker
(† 1022), and that of the Song of Solomon by the
abbot Williram for the eleventh century ; and if the

16. *Jahrhunderts*, Gotha, 1882) remarks (p. 339) : ' They acted in the Middle
Ages according to the saying of Gregory the Great, that pictures were the
books of the unlearned and ignorant ; the whole available church space,
when the necessary means and artists could be procured, was made into
an open book of sacred history and legends, with special profusion of
decorative paintings. The widely circulated *Biblia pauperum* . . . in
which the types and symbols of the Old Covenant were painted side by
side with the corresponding facts or persons of the New Testament, and
explained by Bible texts or by rhymes, supplied much that was useful in
the way of motives and copies. The great quantity of pictorial Bibles
and Bible stories in poetry and prose, and of other fifteenth century
religious works, either manuscript or printed, and illustrated with
woodcuts, were also, like the artistic pictures and images on the walls of
churches, intended for domestic and instructional use.'

fragments of Gospel translations from this last period have excited less admiration on the part of antiquarian investigators, it was only because the imperfect knowledge of Latin at that date hindered the translators from producing exemplary work.

When, however, in the middle of the twelfth century literature passed into the hands of the laity, then, to judge from the number of manuscripts preserved,[1] the interest in Biblical translations declined. Only a few Psalters and one German Gospel have come down to us from the flourishing period of German literature.

But in the fourteenth century, when secular poetry was degenerating and becoming insipid, a reaction set in, and literary activity turned once more to

> The best adventurer's treasure,
> Which ever to my ears gave pleasure.[2]

Of the period from 1300 to 1500 there are 203 Biblical manuscripts known at the present day. Many of them, it is true, contain only one or the other of the books of the Bible, but sixteen of them comprise, or did formerly comprise, the whole of the Scriptures; ten of them contain the whole of the Old Testament, eight contain the Gospels, another eight contain the whole New Testament, and one of them the four Gospels and the Acts of the Apostles.[3] Down to the end of the fifteenth century the interest in German translations of the Holy Scriptures seems to have gone on increasing; for out of these manuscripts seventy-five belong to the fourteenth and 128 to the fifteenth century.

The texts of these German translations, especially

---

[1] Much has been lost; see Michael, iii. 224.
[2] *Prolog der Wenzelbibel*, Walther, p. 295.
[3] Walther, p. 709 f.

at the beginning of the reawakening interest, differ greatly one from the other. Attempts of the sort were made in numbers of different places, without the various translators knowing what each of them was doing. In the fifteenth century the impulse to new productions flagged, and people became content with copying translations already made.

As regards the value of the work done, the second period of translation is far behind the first early German period. Men of like culture with a Notker or a Williram turned their energies in later times to other tasks ; the difficult work of Germanising the Scriptures was relegated to somewhat unskilful hands. Many indeed of the translators of the fourteenth and fifteenth centuries displayed very great facility of language, but it was only seldom that the mastery of the mother tongue was combined with an adequate knowledge of Latin. Too often the work betrayed the hand of a pupil. When the original was not clearly written, the translator often failed to decipher it correctly.[1] Latin words of this sort resembling each other in sound are confounded in the strangest manner.[2] Another time the want of

[1] Thus, for instance, a translator of the fourteenth century, read Ps. lxvii. 22 ' in deliciis (pleasures) suis ' instead of ' in delictis ' (faults) and translated it ' in iren wollusten ' (in their lusts) ; Proverbs xxv. 24 he read ' in angulo dogmatis ' instead of ' domatis ' (of a house), (' in dem Winkel des Lehrer's ') (in the corner of the teacher). Walther, p. 63. A century later another translator read Job xv. 2, ' jumentum ' (a beast of burden) instead of ' in ventum ' (to the wind), ' in somno ' (in sleep) instead of ' insomnem ' (sleepless) (Esther vi. 1). Walther, p. 341 f.

[2] ' Instruxerunt *aciem* contra Israel ' (1 Kings iv. 2) = ' Sy richten die Spitz gegen israhel' (they direct the point against Israel). Is. xxi. 8, ' super *speculam* (watch-tower) Domini ego sum ' = ' ich bin über den Spiegel des Herren ' (I am above the mirror of the Lord). ' Praepositus ' in medieval Latin means ' Provost.' Hence 2 Maccabees iv. 27, ' Sostratus, qui arci erat praepositus ' (set over the castle) is translated : ' Der do was ein Probst in der Höhe ' (He who was a provost on high). Walther, p. 45.

archaeological knowledge led to the strangest mistakes.[1] Some translators were so conscientious as to leave standing in the middle of the Latin text the words which they were unable to puzzle out;[2] others, when they were not clear about the meaning, placed the Latin phrase by the side of the German, or left a gap in the manuscript to be filled up later on. Others were less careful and circumspect, and made a complete hash of their translation.[3]

Again, the difficulty of turning Latin construction into idiomatic German is not completely overcome in the older translations. Even an otherwise extremely skilful translator of the fourteenth century still retains in many places modes of construction which can only be understood as literal reproductions of old classical language.[4] Side by side with these are other translations the author of which has shown the most complete

---

[1] Ps. lxxvii. 12 : ' In campo Taneos ' (on the field of Tanis in Egypt) is read ' in capotaneos ' and translated ' among the captains.' ' Decapoli ' (of the ten cities) is understood as ' de Capoli ' and rendered ' of Capoli ' (Matt. iv. 25). Instead of ' insigne Castorum ' the translator reads ' in signis castrorum ' ; ' he who was in the sign of the hostels.' Walther, p. 63. The mistakes mentioned in this and the preceding notes are repeated, with numbers of others, in the translation which is the basis of the first German Bible that was printed.

[2] ' Habent vinger *senos* ' (1 Chron. xx. 6). Walther, p. 341.

[3] ' Irreprehensibilis ' (unblamable) becomes ' incomprehensible ' ; ' solium ' (throne) is translated ' Sohle ' (sole of a shoe) ; ' nulla ratione,' ' durch keine Vernunft.' Walther, p. 342.

[4] ' Sic ergo orante Esdra, implorante eo et flente ' is rendered in the so-called second class of translations as ' also darumbe petende Esdra, vnd flehende got, vnd weynende ' (' Thus Esdras, praying and imploring God, and weeping '). And actually where the Latin text does not make use of the absolute participle construction, the translator chooses it : ' cum haec omnia habeam, nihil me habere puto ' : ' Das alles habende, nichcz wene ich mich zu haben ' (' This all having nothing ween I myself to have ') (Esther v. 13). In like manner he uses occasionally the accusative with infinitive : ' Worumb leidest du nit, mich zu sein von meinen sünden reine ? ' (Job x. 14). Walther, pp. 332, 338.

mastery of the mother tongue, and has ' with relatively astounding perfection ' accomplished his purpose ' to produce a genuinely German Bible ' ; ' truly exemplary is the skill with which he so frequently hits on the best, or at any rate on a very excellent, German equivalent.' [1]

The medieval translations are done from the Latin Vulgate. Only one Psalter, the oldest manuscript of which bears the date 1386, is translated from the Hebrew Psalter of St. Jerome. However little St. Jerome succeeded in Christian antiquity in dislodging or supplanting the earlier and long domiciled translation of the Psalms, so little also could a similar attempt meet with success in the Middle Ages. The original text was continually altered more and more in correspondence with the familiar diction of the Vulgate until the early form could no longer be recognised.[2]

The extensive circulation of the German Bible was bound to increase still further when the art of printing provided so easy a means for publication.   Few towns,[3] it is true, took part in publication : in South Germany,

[1] Walther, pp. 353–355, 497, 512.

[2] *Ibid.* p. 600 f.

[3] The different printed editions, according to the series catalogued by Walther, are : (i) High German Bibles in the edition of: 1. Mentel (Strassburg), 1466 ; 2. Eggestein (Strassburg), about 1470 ; 3. Pflanzmann (Augsburg), about 1473 ; 4. Zainer (Augsburg), about 1473 ; 5. The Swiss Bible (Basle ?) ; 6 (perhaps 7). Zainer (Augsburg), 1477 ; 7 (perhaps 6). Sorg (Augsburg), 1477 ; 8. Sorg (Augsburg), 1480 ; 9. Koberger (Nuremberg), 1483 ; 10. Grüninger (Strassburg), 1485 ; 11 and 12. Schönsperger (Augsburg), 1487, 1490 ; 13. H. Otmar (Augsburg), 1507 ; 14. S. Otmar (Augsburg), 1518. (ii) Low German : 1 and 2. Cologne Bible by Quentel, about 1480 ; 3. Lübeck Bible by Arndes, 1494 ; 4. Halberstadt Bible by Trutebul, 1522.   That the edition of Mentel is the first printed Bible is also shown by K. Biltz, *Neue Beiträge zur Gesch. der deutschen Sprache und Literatur*, Berlin, 1891, 97 f.

Strassburg with three editions, Nuremberg and a Swiss town with one edition, and Augsburg with eight, were the only contributors. Still new reprints followed one another pretty quickly. Twice over, the same year, or near about the same year, produced two editions ; the editions of Zainer, Sorg, Schönsperger, had to be printed a second time. Less eagerness for the Holy Scriptures in German was shown in North Germany, where only four editions came out at lengthy intervals. The rapid spread of translation is also borne witness to by contemporaries, and is confirmed by the comparatively large number of works of this kind still preserved. Thus of Koberger's edition of 1483 there are still fifty-eight copies extant, of the first Mentel edition twenty-eight, of the earliest edition, that of 1518, ten. If with these figures we compare the statement, accidentally preserved, that out of 4000 printed copies of a translation of a breviary only eight are now to be found in the libraries,[1] the strong language of a Sebastian Brant concerning the spread of the German Bibles [2] can no longer cause such great surprise.

As, meanwhile, since the fourteenth century, scholars of theological and linguistic culture made very little use of the German Bible, the putting it in print remained at first a mere matter of book-dealers' speculation. Mentel had printed a translation belonging to the fourteenth century, the language of which was already antiquated in his time, and the text not exactly of the first quality. Eggestein simply took for his edition Mentel's printed copy, and reproduced it with such faithfulness that every page of his copies begins with

---

[1] Walther, p. 613.
[2] See present work, vol. i. p. 301.

the same word as the corresponding page in Mentel.
If in the new print there was no room left on a page
for the last word, the word was left out. The absur-
dities in Mentel's translation occur again in the second
Bible ; the corrections are few. As Eggestein acted in
the case of Mentel's Bible, so Pflanzmann at Augsburg
dealt with Eggestein : a few of the mistakes he improved,
but for the rest he multiplied faults in his edition by
making fresh ones. And this was the way in which
all the later printers proceeded.[1] The servility with
which this copying was executed is seen from the fact
that a whole series of flagrant perversions of texts runs
through all the editions.[2] The fourth edition of Zainer
at Augsburg in 1473 and the ninth of Koberger at
Nuremberg in 1483 show important revisions of the
text. The woodcuts with which Koberger illustrated
his edition were taken by him from the Cologne Bible.
It is to be regretted that he did not also make better
use of the text of this Low German translation for his
own German Bible.

In Lower Germany, where the Brethren of the
Common Life promoted the reading of pious books in

[1] The 2nd Bible was printed from the 1st, the 4th from the 2nd,
the 5th and 6th from the 4th, the 7th and 8th from the 5th. The 9th is
the basis for the 11th and 12th, the 13th for the 14th. Walther, pp. 14 f.
35, 41, 98, 112.

[2] As, for instance, the mistakes cited above at p. 386, note 1. All the
editions from the 4th to the 12th leave out at John vi. 63 the word ' flesh,'
and print, ' aber das ist nit nütz ' (' It is the Spirit that quickeneth but *that*
profiteth nothing '). These same Bibles print Ephes. iv. 13 : ' des *altars*
Christi ' instead of ' des alters Christi' (' altar ' instead of ' age '). It is
not till the 13th edition that this fault is corrected (Walther, p. 112).
From the 2nd to the 8th Bible a whole line was left out at 1 Ezra viii. 10.
Not till the 9th edition was it replaced. In all the editions before the
9th at Judges xix. 16, the proper name ' Jemini ' had been read as
' gemini ' and translated ' twins.' (Walther, p. 107.)

the language of the country, the manuscript version of the Bible in Low German had had such wide circulation that at least twenty-five of these manuscripts are still to be seen at the present day.   It was of much higher value than the High German translations.[1]   When Quentel at Cologne, about the year 1480, was thinking of printing the Holy Scriptures in Low German, the 'help and counsel of a number of learned scholars' was solicited, and with the help of the High German and the Delft Bible, and an extremely good Low German manuscript a comparatively excellent work was produced.   There are two editions of this translation : one which gives the Psalms in the Cologne Low German, and the remaining books in West-Low-German, the Dutch dialect, and a second, which makes use of the Nether-Saxon language.   The two other Low German works, the Lübeck Bible of 1494, and the Halberstadt one of 1522, are also well executed.   Both make use in most of the sections of the labours of their precursors.   The Cologne and Lübeck editions, in all difficult passages, supplement the text with glossaries, taken for the most part from Nicholas von Lyra.

From what quarters the translations of the Middle Ages come, and what aims they serve, is very often not clearly explained.   That heretical sects also made use of the German Bible is undoubted ; that the translation into German was first instigated by heretics cannot be proved.[2]

[1] See Walther, p. 651.

[2] The reasons adduced by Keller and Haupt in proof of Waldensian origin have been ably demolished by Jostes (*Die Waldenser und die vorlutherische deutsche Bibelübersetzung*, Münster, 1885) and by Walther's *Untersuchungen* (p. 55 f.).   If Walther frequently discovers in the readers and translators of the German Bible something akin to the spirit of the

Concerning the aims and purposes of the translators, only vague indications are usually found in the
prefaces and final remarks of the manuscripts and prints.
Thus, for instance, a German translation of the Book of
Job says that ' the honourable and wise Hans Sättelin '
caused this book to be written, ' To the praise and honour
of the high and Holy Trinity in Unity, God the Father,
Son, and Holy Ghost, and for the glory and delight
of the highly laudable Virgin Mary and all the Saints.' [1]
' In honour of the chaste maiden the work is prepared,
1470, by the hand of Perchtoldi Furtmeyr Yluminist.' [2]
One manuscript only gives more detailed information

Reformation, his arguments are largely the result of an erroneous conception of Catholic dogma and Catholic life (see pp. 649, 689 f.). Whether,
indeed, individual manuscripts are connected with Hussite and Waldensian endeavour later research can alone decide.   Jostes (' Die Waldenser-
bibeln ' and ' Meister Johannes Rellach,' in the *Histor. Jahrbuch*, xv. [1894]
771–795) goes against Walther, who, although he sees the untenableness
of Keller and Haupt's defence of their hypothesis, nevertheless does not
assume a wholly unequivocal attitude towards them, but rather seeks
' to procure them admission through a little back door '—examines anew
Walther's arguments in favour of the Waldensian origin of some few
German Bible translations.   Next, on the strength of the preface of a
German manuscript Bible of Nuremberg, he starts the theory that the monk
John Rellach (probably a Dominican), belonging to the diocese of
Constance, is not, as Walther thinks, merely the copyist or the editor of
a still existing older translation, but that the translation circulated by
the pre-Lutheran Bible printing press, on the handwritten testimony of
the Nuremberg manuscript and the correlated Wolfenbüttel manuscript,
is his own work published after 1450.   G. Grupp (' Die deutsche
Bibelübersetzung des Mittelalters,' in the *Histor.-polit. Blätter*, cxv. [1895]
931–940) agrees with Jostes.   On the other hand H. Haupt, in the
Zeitschr. für Kirchengesch. xvii. (1897) 280 f., says that ' Jostes' Polemik is
done very smartly, but not convincingly;' and we must abide by the decision
which Walther arrived at in a thoroughly thoughtful and intelligent
manner, that Rellach was not the original author, but only the editor of the
translation of the Bible translation ascribed to him by Jostes.   Nestle also
(*Urtext und Übersetzungen der Bibel*, p. 127) firmly defends the probability
of the Waldensian origin against Jostes.

[1] Walther, p. 130.   [2] *Ibid.* p. 320.

as to how 'the Master came to take in hand this
Germanising of the Holy Scriptures.' In Rome, so
we are told by Leonard Eutychius, archbishop of
Mitylene—'when 1400 and fifty years were counted
after the birth of Christ' (!)—the melancholy news was
proclaimed of how Constantinople had been taken by
the Turks, 'the Church of Sophia turned into a cattle-
shed,' and the costly library 'in which Jews and Pagans,
Tartars and Turks, and all sorts of learned people had
read the books of the Bible, destroyed and spoilt; and
when, after an affecting sermon on the downfall of the
imperial city, we Brothers and students at Rome were
feeling very sad, Brother John Rellach began thus:
"With the help of God we will not despair nor give
way on this account. The ship of St. Peter will have
many and many shocks, but it will not go down for all
that. If the Greek books have been destroyed, we
Christians will make the Latin books into German, so
that the laity may be all the better strengthened and
confirmed in the Christian faith." Therefore, whereas
God the Lord had helped me safely home from Rome
into the bishopric of Constance, I undertook the seventh
book of the Bible.' Rellach, however, does not seem
to have got on very far with his work at that time.
First of all he set out on travels 'over the Haring-See'
(Herring=North Sea) to Trondheim, Upsala, Finland,
to see if he could not 'stir up Christendom by a description of the misery in the fallen imperial city. But
nobody would take it to heart, either the clergy or the
laity.' The Master was very disconsolate, and said:
'Lord God, come to my help, what shall I do now?
And I went back to my home in the bishopric of Constance. There I found that the students had begun at

Strassburg and at Basle, at Spires and Worms, to turn the Bible into German.' They fell upon Rellach with the question : ' Master, how goes it with that Plan ? ' whereupon Rellach answers : ' Let me only take up my pen ! No one should praise his own power.' [1]

That the object was to serve the laity and the unlearned by translating the Bible is especially emphasised in the prologue to the Cologne Bible. It is also stated there what particular lay people the translators had specially in view, viz. ' Above all cloistered children,' that is, people in convents. With the exception of the lay brothers and sisters, all, even the unlearned members of Orders, were bound to attend the Church prayers, and as these prayers were mostly made up from passages of the Holy Scriptures, it was especially desirable that they should have some means to help them to the understanding of their daily prayers. A large number of the manuscripts that have been preserved comes also from the convents for women.' [2] According to remarks written in some of the copies a Psalter seems to have been a not unfrequent gift to persons entering convents.[3] Sometimes also German translations of the sacred books were presented to convents or to churches, because there they were most easily accessible for general use. A Psalter, according to a remark on the first page, was presented to the altar of St. Anna, ' in order that every good person may seek herein his soul's salvation.' [4]

But portions of the Holy Scriptures or complete

---

[1] Walther, p. 149 f. See the ' Original Text über Rellach bei Jostes ' in the *Histor. Jahrbuch*, xv. 793–795 ; see also *ibid*. p. 783 f.

[2] Walther, pp. 137, 311, 315, and so forth.

[3] *Ibid*. pp. 594, 624, 698, 730.

[4] *Ibid*. p. 683 ; cf. p. 698.

manuscripts also formed part of the private possessions of the laity. Princely personages and distinguished gentlemen would order for themselves, or receive as wedding presents, copies splendidly got up.[1] Psalters were found in the possession of burgher-folk before the invention of printing. 'This book belongs to Master Casper's wife and her children,' is inscribed in a manuscript of the second half of the fourteenth century; 'This book belongs to my dear mother, Ursula of Freiberg,' is inscribed in a Psalm book finished in 1442, and similar allusions to the owners may be read in many of the copies.[2]

Besides statements of this sort concerning owners and translators, we find in some of the manuscripts notes which show that the people were not all in agreement concerning the translation of the Scriptures into the language of the country. Thus a writer of a period not exactly known complains that many people 'have fallen foul of me, and cried out against me in many ways, because that I, after the pattern of good and highly learned people, have turned some parts of Holy Scripture into German, although many holy and wise men, priests and laymen, must be well-pleased that the Holy Scriptures are truthfully rendered into German.' [3]

The attitude of the ecclesiastical authorities towards the translation of the Holy Scriptures into popular languages was from the very first quite clear in its dogmatic principle. Christ had instituted the College of Apostles as an organ for proclaiming His teaching, an organ which was to be continually kept going by

---

[1] Walther, p. 322 ; cf. p. 413.
[2] *Ibid*. pp. 684, 593, 729 ff.
[3] *Ibid*. p. 594 ; cf. p. 649.

legitimately appointed successors to the Apostles, which
would last till the end of the times, and would be
kept safe against errors in faith by divine protection.
The sources of the faith were to be found not only
in Holy Scripture but in everything which this
magisterium prescribes as the doctrine of Christ, the
so-called tradition, and without the evidence of tradition it is impossible to decide whether a book belongs
to the canon of Holy Scripture or whether the books of
the canon are really the Word of God. Of its being
the duty of all people to read the Scriptures, of any right
belonging to individuals to regard all that they found
in the sacred books as the teaching of Christ, they had
no notion whatever.

In addition to the influence of dogma, certain
experiences with regard to Scriptural research served
to determine the action of the ecclesiastical authorities
in this respect. It had come to light in the course of
the centuries that all heretics appealed to the Scriptures.
It was known that ' by false exposition of the Gospel
of Christ a gospel of man's '[1] invention might be produced ; that a guide in the interpretation of this the
most difficult of all books was indispensable. It was
also considered that there was no contradiction in
regarding the Holy Scriptures as ' the holiest of all
non-sacramental things,' and at the same time thinking
it possible that the reading of Scripture might be
dangerous and injurious for many people.[2]

---

[1] ' Grande periculum est in Ecclesia loqui, ne forte interpretatione
perversa de evangelio Christi hominis fiat evangelium aut, quod peius
est, diaboli.' St. Jerome, In epist. ad Gal., ed. Martianay, iv. 231.

[2] See concerning the attitude of the Catholic Church towards the
reading of the Bible in the language of the people : Bellarmin, De verbo
Dei, ii. 15, 16 ; Benedict XIV. De syn. dioec. vi. 10 ; Fontana, Constitutio

From opinions of this sort there resulted the practical rule that the Bible-reading of the laity must be subject to the guidance of the Church. It should be recommended to those who were likely to derive benefit from it; forbidden, or limited, where injury was to be feared.

In the legislation of the Church, which was generally binding, limitation of Bible-reading first occurs after the Council of Trent; actual inhibition in the matter never happened. Persons who had sufficient culture to be able at least to understand the Latin text were not kept away from the Scriptures by the general law of the Church.

It was, moreover, not till after the end of the twelfth century that individual legislation occupied itself with the translations of the Bible. At Metz, men and women, in defiance of the priests, had gathered together in private conventicles in which the Holy Scriptures had been read, and where even women had presumed to come forward as preachers. The bishop considered the matter of sufficient importance to justify his appealing to Innocent III for instructions as to procedure. The Pope answered with the utmost discretion. He praised the desire to become acquainted with the Holy Scriptures; on the other hand, the presumption with which these people separated themselves from the other Christians and exercised the office of preacher without ordination incurred his displeasure. No proceedings, however, must be taken against the Bible-readers of Metz till they expressly withdrew their obedience from

' *Unigenitus*,' iii. 688 f. ; Malou, *Das Bibellesen in der Volkssprache*, the German by Stoeveken, Schaffhausen, 1849 ; Wiseman, *Vermischte Schriften*, vol. iii. Part ii. p. 1 ff. ; Michael, iii. 231 f.

their ecclesiastical superiors.[1]   In the following century
the proceedings of the sects in France provoked the most
severe inhibitions from several councils, while in Spain
the secular government was several times driven to like
measures.   Wickliffe's greatly falsified translation of
the Bible caused the secular authorities in England to
inhibit the book ; a council held at Oxford in 1408
prohibited the use of all English Bibles which should be
published after Wickliffe's time without approbation.[2]
For Germany, up to the beginning of the fifteenth
century, there comes first under consideration a decree
of the papal legate Guido of Palestrina, of the year
1202, which makes the possession of German and
French books ' on the Holy Scriptures ' dependent on
the approbation of the bishop.[3]

When in the fourteenth century the errors of the
Beghardi led to the interference of the Inquisition,
Charles IV issued an edict from Lucca on June 17, 1369,
against ' vicious, erring German writings tainted with
the leprosy of heresy, in which the name of our Lord
Jesus Christ and the glorious Virgin His mother Mary
were slandered, the universal faith of Christians depreciated, cursed or calumniated.'   Incidentally there occurs
in this edict the statement that the laity ' according
to the canonical statutes must not make use of books

[1] *Innocentii III. Epistolae*, ii. 141, 142, 235.

[2] Bender, ' Joh. Wicliff als Bibelübersetzer,' in the *Katholik*, lxv.
(1884) 292 ff.

[3] *Aub. Miraei opp. dipl.* i. Lovanii, 1723, 564.   *Libri de divinis scrip-*
turis are not in the first place Bible translations, but theological books
in general.   See Nicol. de Lyra, Prologus primus in postillam bibliae :
scriptura quae proprie theologia dicitur, cum ipsa sola sit textus huius
scientiae.   Thus *Scriptura* is often synonymous with *theologia*.   See
now Michael, iii. 233.

on the Holy Scriptures written in the dialect of the land.' [1]

All these regulations had for their *raison d'être* the existence of abuses, and could not have any validity in countries and under conditions where abuses were not to be feared. In Wickliffe's time Charles IV's daughter Queen Anne possessed the Gospel in German, Bohemian, and English, and after her death her zeal for the Holy Scriptures was eulogised by the Archbishop Arundel.[2] In Germany, in 1386, Otto von Passau ' recommended that the writings of the Old and the New Testament should be read plentifully with reverence and earnestness, either in German or in Latin, in the case of those who understand Latin.' [3] The Brethren of the Common Life were especially active in the dissemination of religious writings in the mother tongue, and they endeavoured at least to make known among the laity those portions of the Scriptures which were easier to understand.

Altogether there were a good many people who did not like to see German books, especially Germanised Bibles, in the hands of the laity. The Brethren of the Common Life had to maintain their ground against numbers of opponents.[4] But everywhere it is only individuals among the clergy who are described as

---

[1] Mosheim, *De Beghardis et beguinabus*, Lipsiae, 1790, pp. 368–375. Concerning Libri de S. Scriptura see note 3. The *Canonicæ sanctiones* are probably the prohibitions of the older French councils. The council of Toulouse (1229) especially, which contains the first Bible prohibition (c. 14) was regarded as the legal source for the proceedings of the Inquisition.

[2] *Katholik*, lxv. (1884) 293. We shall not therefore agree with Walther (p. 616) in thinking it possible that Charles IV's edict ' hindered a member of his family from having a translation of the Bible in the language of the land.'

[3] Walther, p. 737.

[4] Jostes in the *Histor. Jahrbuch*, 1890, pp. 1–22, 709–717.

antagonists. It is expressly added that other clerics were in sympathy with the translations into the mother tongue. Both views, however, appear to have been regarded merely as private opinions, of which, *per se,* neither could claim the sanction of greater orthodoxy. The clerical authorities only committed themselves to an opinion so far as not to put any obstacle in the way of the Brethren of the Common Life. Archbishop Bertold of Mayence also, in his edicts about books of 1485 and 1486,[1] only wanted to proceed against the abuse of reading translations. 'Unintelligent, presumptuous and ignorant people,' says the edict, had taken upon themselves to translate theological and juridical works into German, and that indeed in such a manner that even learned people said they could scarcely understand their books. Whereas the falsification of the text of a book, especially in the case of the Holy Scriptures, is fraught with great dangers, he herewith issues this decree, which, in spite of severe language against the bad translations, did not prohibit German Bibles, but only insisted on their having the approbation of a censorship.

Towards the close of the fifteenth century clear-sighted men began to incline more to the opinions of those who considered the general circulation of the Scriptures harmful rather than useful. Geiler von Kaisersberg speaks of persons who 'talk unbecomingly and jokingly of the Holy Scriptures, and say, for instance, that they are like a wax nose which can be

---

[1] Gudenus, *Cod. dipl.* iv. 469 f. *Archiv für Gesch. des deutsch. Buchhandels*, ix. 238 f. In the writings of Gudenus, iv. 474, the archbishop wishes for extension of the decrees to his suffragan bishoprics. Whether this was effected cannot be decided.

turned and twisted about.' [1] He takes up the cudgels
against the people 'who falsify the Scriptures by
forced interpretations contrary to the sense of Holy
Writ.' By arbitrary interpretation of this sort ' all the
bad people defend their own evil condition : wanton
monks uphold their resistance to reform, the clergy
their accumulation of benefices, the laity their perjury
and the violation of clerical immunity.' [2]

The substitute which Luther offered the German
people for the shattered ecclesiastical organisation, the
discarded ecclesiastical learning, the abolished Sacraments, the impoverished Church service, and ruined
Christian art, consisted chiefly in the ' unadulterated
Word of God '—i.e. in his own translation of the Bible—
and in the ' new evangelical ' preaching connected with
it.   He reiterated these two phrases so continuously
and with such stirring and overwhelming eloquence
that he succeeded, in many parts of Germany, in
establishing the conviction, which lasted through centuries, that it was he who had ' first dug the Bible up
from under a bank,' and handed out the Book of Life
to the people thirsting for religious instruction. [3]

Independent research has established the complete
untenableness of those assertions : neither before nor
after the invention of printing was the Bible ' under the
bank ' ; Luther is by no means the first Bible translator among the Germans, even if it be allowed that

---

[1] *Narrenschiff*, No. xi. (Argent. 1511, v. *V.*).

[2] *Ibid*. No. ciii. (xxxii. *Z.*).

[3] ' The *Biblia* was unknown to the people under the papacy.'   *Luther's
Table-talk*, published by Irmischer, i. 85.   See Falk on the *Kettenbücher*
(Bibles on the chain) in the *Histor.-polit. Blätter*, cxii. 324 ff.   Concerning
the spread of the Bible before Luther see the evidence adduced against
Walther by Grupp in the *Histor.-polit. Blätter*, cxv. (1895) 935 ff.

his translation surpassed previous ones in linguistic respects, and had an incomparably larger circulation.

Before the year 1521 Luther had already attempted to translate single portions of the Bible. The first manuscript which he himself made over to the press in 1517 contains a translation and an exposition of the penitential Psalms. Then followed, extending to 1521, the Lord's Prayer, the Prayer of King Manasseh, the Ten Commandments, the Magnificat with the prayer of King Solomon, a few Psalms and evangelical passages. It was during his concealment at the Wartburg that he first set about making a complete translation of the whole Bible from the original text. On December 18, 1521, he informed his friend John Lang, who in the summer of that year had published a translation of the Gospel of St. Matthew, that he intended translating the New Testament : ' this is wanted by our people (the Wittenberg friends, especially Melanchthon) : do you also go on with the work you have begun ; would that every town had its translator of the Bible, would that this book might occupy the tongues, hands, eyes and ears of all the world ! ' [1]   The New Testament, as the easier work, was undertaken before the Old Testament.[2]   In January 1522 he acknowledges to his friend Amsdorf : ' I shall endeavour to translate the Bible, although I may have undertaken a task exceeding my powers. I now see for the first time what translating means, and why the work has not been undertaken by any one whose name was made known. The Old

___

[1] De Wette, ii. 115–116 ; Enders, iii. 256.

[2] Concerning Luther's defective linguistic knowledge see Köstlin, i[2]. 115, and Hopf, *Bibelübersetzung*, pp. 41, 45.

Testament, however, I shall not touch if you are not at hand to help me.' [1]

In spite of all difficulties and of all Luther's many other occupations, the work in the Wartburg ' went on with astounding rapidity.' Three months had not gone by before the first copy of the translation of the New Testament was ready. The Erasmian edition and the Vulgate had served as basis.[2] Whether Luther also made use of an older German translation is a disputed point.[3]

On his return to Wittenberg Luther at once began, with the help of Melanchthon, to improve the first rough manuscript ; friends in distant places, like Spalatin, were also taken into counsel on individual points.   It

[1] De Wette, ii. 123 ; Enders, iii. 271.

[2] See Schott, *Bibelübersetzung*, p. 31 ; Hopf, *Bibelübersetzung*, p. 48 f., and Krafft (see note 5), p. 9.

[3] The following Protestants were of opinion that Luther had helped himself by the use of the medieval German translation : Hopf (p. 23 ff. note 52), Geffcken (*Bilderkatechismus des* 15. *Jahrhunderts*, p. 6 f.), Krafft (*Über die deutsche Bibel von Luther*, Bonn, 1883), Haupt (*Die deutsche Bibelübersetzung*, Würzburg, 1885, p. 48, note 3), and Keller (*Die Waldenser*, &c. pp. 52 ff., 62) ; against this opinion see W. Walther, *Luther's Bibelübersetzung kein Plagiat*, Erlangen, 1891. Walther himself, however, is obliged to agree with Krafft that ' there was already a large supply of available Biblical matter at hand which Luther was able to turn to account.' He says further that, ' nowadays the Geffcken-Krafft theory has gained the victory, because one party considers it proved, and the other party dare not combat it.'   How doubtful the whole question is, is shown by the fact that an investigator like Walther felt it incumbent on him to write a special treatise against Krafft's treatise, while even Panzer declared the refutation of those who asserted that Luther had used these earlier translations to be quite superfluous.   It is not mentioned by Walther that so enthusiastic a worshipper of Luther as Kolde wrote as lately as in 1889 (*Luther*, ii. 33) : ' It is possible, indeed very probable, that later on he may have compared his work with earlier translations, but at the Wartburg itself he was without the means to do so.'   A statement of Luther, lately made known by Loesche (*Anal. Luth.* p. 281), seems at first sight to favour the assumption that Luther was acquainted with the Bible of the Middle Ages, but it affords no convincing proof.

might have been expected that the printing of so difficult and important a work would not have been started
until the whole translation was completed. Luther,
however, proceeded otherwise. Piece by piece his
manuscript went up to the printing press, while he was
still at work with the rest. Three presses were kept
going at the same time. Whereas this translation of
the Holy Scriptures was to ' help the cause of polemics
against the Church,' the work was interlarded with
inimical remarks, and great care was taken to keep to
the style of the common people. Possibly in order
to secure its admission among Catholics also, the first
edition appeared anonymously under the title ' Das
Newe Testament. Deutzsch, Vuittemberg,' in folio,
price 1½ gulden. This version, called from the time of
its appearing ' The September Bible,' which Lucas
Cranach illustrated with numerous woodcuts, went
through another greatly improved edition in 1522,
so great was the demand for it. The printer and
publisher, who now first revealed his name, was
Melchior Lotther. Further editions and reprints soon
followed.[1]

Encouraged by his great success, Luther forthwith
set to work on the Old Testament ; in this undertaking
he made use of a Hebrew text which had appeared at
Brescia in 1494, but he could not do without the Vul-

[1] See Panzer, *Gesch. der Bibelübersetzung Luthers*, p. 35 ff. ; Nestle, in
Herzog's *Realenzyklopädie*, Artikel ' Bibelübersetzungen ' in *Urtext und
Übersetzungen der Bibel*, p. 130 ff. See also Nestle, ' Die erste Lutherbibel
mit Verszählung ' (the Heidelberg edition, 1568), in the *Zentralblatt für
Bibliotekswesen*, 20 Jahrg. (1903), pp. 273–277. Concerning Lotther see
Serapeum, 1851, p. 335 f. The ' gulden ' then in circulation in Ernestine
Saxony was equal to 20 good groschens, in present money 4 marks, 20
pfennigs. Grimm, *Bibelübersetzung*, p. 9, note 1. *Neudruck der September-
bibel in den deutschen Drucken älterer Zeit*, i. Berlin, 1883.

gate and the Septuaginta also.[1] In spite of arduous
study he did not succeed, as he confessed later on, in
becoming ' a grammatical and accurate Hebraist.' [2]
No wonder that he was now glad of help from learned
friends ; besides Melanchthon, Aurogallus, and two
other Hebraists, Bernard Ziegler and John Förster,
were his special assistants. The printing and the improvement of the manuscript again went on side by
side. In 1523 there appeared the five Books of Moses
under the general title, misleading to purchasers :
' Das Alte Testament. Deutsch, M. Luther, Vuittem-

[1] The Latin translations of Santes Pagninus and of Seb. Münster, and
the commentaries of Nicholas von Lyra, and especially the *glossa ordinaria*
were also consulted ; see Herzog's *Realenzyklopädie*, iii. 550.

[2] Luther's knowledge of Hebrew is exemplified by his smaller
edition (manual, as distinct from *desk* edition) of the Hebrew
Bible now in Berlin (see *Stimmen aus Maria-Laach*, 1895, i. 105 f.).
Luther's heirs bought in 1593 their grandfather's *Ebreische Biebell* from
Joachim Friedrich von Brandenburg, the administrator of Magdeburg,
as the book ' which he (Luther) had constantly carried about, and also used
at that time when he was translating the Bible into German, and with his
own hand and great industry wrote out the Hebrew roots and other things
necessary for the good of Christendom, from which it may often be
ascertained why this or that had been thus translated, whereby the
enemies of the Holy Evangel could be powerfully refuted, both among
the papists and Calvinists, who in venomous and cunning manner against
their own consciences comment on and abuse this precious work and
industry of our dear grandfather at rest in God.' Later examination of
this Lutheran Bible has shown that the marginal glosses are for the most
part not the work of the reformer, but of a German Jew who was in possession of the book before Luther. In the Luther anniversary, 1883, an
eminent scholar based a whole treatise, in honour of the Reformer, on
the marginal glosses of the Berlin Bible. The latest critique of the
Lutheran hand Bible ends with the sentence : ' Take it all in all, we do not
find in this costly Bible version of this great man all that we expected.
Hebrew was not his strong point—accordingly he kept to the text of the
Vulgate and the Septuagint, without doubt to the advantage of his beautiful
German translation of the Bible. He gave the Greek text the preference
over the Masoretic. This gives us food for reflection ! ' (*Alt-testamentliche
Untersuchungen von Dr. Johann Bachmann*. 1. Buch, Berlin, 1894, p. 101 ff.
Appendix iv

berg.' In the preface the translator confessed to having
profited by help in his work, from whatever quarter
he could get it. In the ensuing years there appeared
' Der andere Theil des Alten Testamentes' (the historical
Books of Joshua to Esther) as well as the third part
(the Book of Job, the Psalms, Proverbs, Ecclesiastes,
and the Song of Solomon).[1] But then followed a long
pause. It was not till February 1527 that Luther
announced the resumption of the work. He is now
going to begin the Prophets : ' this will be a work
worthy of the utmost gratitude with which this barbarous and in reality bestial nation (the Germans) has
treated me ; at the same time I shall let fly at the
fanatical spirits.' [2] The translation of the Prophets,
in which Cruciger, Aurogallus and Förster helped,
proceeded very slowly and with many interruptions.
Controversial and libellous pamphlets sometimes claimed
Luther's whole attention. It was not till 1532 that the
whole work appeared under the title ' Die Propheten
alle deutsch ' ; single books had been published beforehand. The same thing happened with the deutero-
canonical books, which Luther called Apocrypha ; in
the case of these he often confounded the task of
the translator with that of the editor, critic, and
expounder.[3]

Meanwhile the desire to have the whole Bible
translated in the spirit of the new teaching led to the
so-called combined Bibles, in which that which Luther
had not yet translated was contributed by other hands.
The first work of this kind was published at Zurich

[1] Panzer, *Gesch. der Bibelübersetzung Luthers*, pp. 146 ff., 158 ff.
[2] De Wette, iii. 161.
[3] Opinion of Grimm in the *Theolog. Studien u. Kritiken*, lvi. (1883) 376.

in the years 1525–1529, in six folio volumes.[1] Luther's
translation of the collective Bible appeared as a whole
first in 1534, under the title : ' Biblia, das ist die ganze
Heilige Schrift, Deutsch. Mart. Luth. Wittemberg.
Begnadet mit Kurfürstlicher zu Sachsen freiheit. Ge-
druckt durch Hans Lufft, 1534.' [2]

The circulation of the Luther Bible, which was
illustrated with numbers of woodcuts, was extraordinarily large.[3] In nearly all the new editions, but
especially in the chief edition of 1541, improvements
were made. In this indefatigable work of revision
also, Luther obtained the help of numerous friends
who excelled him in linguistic knowledge. Mathesius,
who was living in Luther's house in the years 1540 and
1541, tells of the gathering together of ' the best people
who were within reach, who met weekly for a few hours
before the evening meal in the doctor's convent,
namely, Dr. John Bugenhagen, Dr. Justus Jonas, Dr.
Cruciger, Dr. Melanchthon, and Matthew Aurogallus.
George Rörer, the co-rector, was also of the number ;
frequently foreign doctors and scholars came to help in
this great work, as, for instance, Dr. Bernard Ziegler

---

[1] Concerning other combined Bibles see Herzog's *Realenzyklopädie*,
iii. 350 ; cf. Panzer, p. 261 ff.

[2] Hans Lufft, who set up a printing press at Wittenberg in 1524, became
henceforth the principal printer of Bibles, which, however, he did not,
like Lotther, print on his own account, but for a society of Wittenberg
booksellers. See Grimm, *Bibelübersetzung*, p. 11, note 1. See also Brieger's
Zeitschrift, i. 161.

[3] Panzer, pp. 300 ff., 343 ff. Herzog's *Realenzyklopädie*, iii. 549 f.
In 1534 there already appeared at Lübeck a Low German translation of
the Lutheran Bible, done under the direction of Bugenhagen. The
best Low German edition of the Luther Bible came out at Goslar in 1624 ;
see Krafft, p. 23, and K. W. Schaub, concerning the Low German translations of the Lutheran New Testament which appeared in print in the
sixteenth century, Halle, 1889.

and Dr. Forstemius. Then when the Doctor had gone through the Bibles already published, and had informed himself of Jews and foreign linguists and of old Germans, what were the right words to use (as, for instance, he would have a sheep cut up in order that a German butcher might tell him the names of all the different parts of the animal), Dr. Martin Luther would come into the consistory with his old Latin and new German Bibles, added to which he always had the Hebrew text. Herr Philippus (Melanchthon) would bring with him the Greek text, Dr. Cruciger the Hebrew and the Chaldaic Bibles, the professors had with them their Rabbis, Dr. Pommer had also a Latin text of his own, with which he was very familiar. Each one of them, beforehand, had worked up the text, on which consultation was to be held, and compared the Greek, Latin, and Jewish interpretations. Then the President proposed a text and took the votes, and heard what each one had to say respecting the quality of the language, or the interpretation of the ancient doctors.' [1]

This constant process of improving shows more plainly than all else how little Luther himself was convinced' of the absolute perfection of his work. And the persistent consultation of expert linguists proves that this translation of the Bible was by no means the work of Luther alone, and that its linguistic merits as compared with previous translations were not exclusively due to him.

All the same, however, Luther's deserts as regard the development of the German language are great. We must nevertheless be careful to distinguish sharply between the sound and form of words on the one hand

---

[1] Hopf, *Bibelübersetzung*, pp. 66–67.

and syntax and style on the other. In the last respect
no one of any insight will wish to dispute the service
which Luther has rendered. He rightly made it his
chief endeavour to shape his language from out the
rich storehouse of popular phraseology. 'We must
not, as the donkeys do,' he said, ' ask of the letters in
the Latin language how we are to speak German, but
we must ask the mothers in their houses, the children
in the streets, the common people in the market-place,
and we must watch their lips and learn how they talk,
and be guided by them in translating, and then they
will understand us and know that we are speaking
German to them.'

The force and expressiveness of the popular speech
was hit off by Luther in a masterly manner in his
Bible translations. In this respect his work surpasses
all that went before. But it is quite another matter
as regards the significance of Luther's work for the
formation of the language in the proper sense of
the word. His followers in this respect allowed
themselves   limitless   exaggerations.   John Clajus
(† 1592 as preacher at Bendeleben in Thuringia)
explains Luther's language as divine inspiration.
' As the Holy Ghost,' he says in his grammar,
' spoke pure Hebrew through Moses, and Greek through
the Apostles, so He spoke pure German through his
chosen instrument Martin Luther. It would not otherwise have been possible for a man to speak so accurately,
so subtly and with such originality without anybody's
help and guidance, seeing that our language is considered so difficult and so at variance with all grammatical rules.' [1]   Even later on it was also maintained

---

[1] See Wülcker in the *Germania, Vierteljahrschrift für deutsche Alter-
thumskunde*, xxviii. (1883) 191.   Schott, *Bibelübersetzung*, p. 134.

that Luther had been the creator of the new High
German language of literature.[1] This, however, is by
no means the case.

' Certain it is that no new language came through
Luther : he made use of an already current book-
language which had developed in Central and South
Germany through the official intercourse of princely
and municipal chanceries. This was the language of
the imperial chancery which had become crystallised
at the end of the fourteenth century in Bohemia,
under and after the rule of the Luxemburgers, and by
the adoption of Mid-German elements had become
adapted to a means of communication between the
North and the South. On the model of this imperial
language of the imperial chancery the Mid-German
chanceries—the eastern ones first of all—soon began to
form their language, and thus towards the end of the
fifteenth century there grew up gradually a firmer
basis for a common German language (" Gemeines

---

[1] ' Luther invented the New High German, and indeed in *one* day, at
one stroke, he created it.'   So spoke the Berlin university professor, H. von
Treitschke, in a lecture on November 7, 1883. See *Berliner Germania*, 1883,
No. 264, 2 Bl. where the following extract is given from an article ' Luther
und Heine ' : ' With regard to Luther's translation of the Bible Heine
says : " Luther not only gave us freedom of movement, but also the means
of movement ; to the spirit, namely, he gave a body. To thought he
gave the word. He created the German language. And he did this inas-
much as with the wonderful power that God had given him, he translated
the Bible out of a dead language which was as good as buried into another
language which had not yet come to life." '   Riehm wrote in 1884 (*Theolog.
Studien und Kritiken*, Jahrg. 57, i. 348) : ' Luther is avowedly recognised [!]
by our greatest German philologists as the actual creator of the new High
German language of literature.'   Meanwhile, anybody who has only a
slight conception of the nature of language knows that even the greatest
genius and master of language is not capable of creating a language : no
human being can do this. The more thoughtful investigation of later
times has condemned wholesale the views of those who on this point still
cling to the Luther legend.

Deutsch "). From the public chanceries this language penetrated into private circles, became first the language of law courts and of business, and later on, and only very slowly, the language of scholars and educated persons.' [1]

Luther himself has often acknowledged that the language of the chanceries had been for him a model of the highest importance. 'I have no particular, special German language of my own,' he said, 'but I use the common German language so that both the Upper and Lower lands may understand me. I write according to the speech of the Saxon chancery, which is used by all the princes and kings in Germany ; the Emperor Maximilian and the Elector Frederick have fused all the different modes of German speech in the Roman empire into a uniform language of books and writing.' [2]

If, however, Luther was by no means the creator of New High German, and also not the first who raised the chancery language to the language of literature, he did at any rate 'help on, by his Bible translation, the development and crystallisation of that written language

---

[1] Burdach, *Einigung der neuhochdeutschen Schriftsprache*, pp. 1–2. See Wülcker in the *Zeitschr. des Vereins für thüringische Geschichte*, N.F. i. 349 ff. *Germania*, xxviii. 191 ff. See also Kauffmann, *Gesch. der Schwäbischen Mundart*, Strassburg, 1890. Appendix : *Die Schriftsprache*, p. 287 ff. Franz Jelinek (*Die Sprache der Wenzelbibel, Programm der k. k. Oberrealschule in Görz*, 1898–1899, Görz, 1899) 'comes to the conclusion that the Bible in the Vienna Court library, translated in 1390 for King Wenzel IV of Bohemia, is written in the mixture of South and Mid-German, which was in use at the court chancelleries of Charles IV and Wenzel IV, and which formed the basis of the chancery language of the Saxon courts, and hence, also, of the Lutheran translation of the Bible.' *Deutsche Literaturzeitung*, 1901, No. 8, Sp. 455.

[2] Collected works, lxii. 313. See besides Wülcker, p. 203 f. ; Opitz, *Die Sprache Luthers*, Halle, 1869, p. 30 f. ; Dannehl, *Niederdeutsche Sprache und Literatur*, Berlin, 1875, p. 11 f., and present work, vol. i. p. 304.

which, in spite of all variations and digressions, was uniform in its exterior conformation.' [1]

But in this respect also we must be careful not to overestimate his influence. Later investigations have accurately shown where and when the effects of his language had their limits, and how the current of its influence was interrupted not only by foreign counter-streams but also by itself. In this connexion exhaustive research has established first of all that Luther's language was actually never fixed and final. In the first period of his literary career he was still essentially under the influence of the dialect of his Thuringian home ; then when he began to adopt the chancery language he had a tremendous struggle before he was able to master it ; with advancing years he freed himself more and more from his native speech and improved the language of his own writings, chiefly his translation of the Bible. ' How, I ask, could a language which in itself is an eternal growing, be a rule for the time which was still groping in darkness and uncertainty after the proper German of literature ? How could contradictions be harmonised, uncertainties settled, by an authority itself full of contradictions and uncertainties ? ' [2] Besides all this there is another point to be considered. The numerous reprints of the Lutheran translation of the Bible showed, on the whole, very little regard for Luther's style of writing. The Frank-

---

[1] Burdach, *Einigung der neuhochdeutschen Schriftsprache*, p. 6. Karl von Bahder (*Grundlagen des neuhochdeutschen Lautsystems*, Strassburg, 1890, p. 60, note 1) draws attention to the fact that the Meissen speech does not first come into notice through having been used by Luther, but dates from an older period.

[2] Burdach, pp. 7–8. See Hopf, *Bibelübersetzung*, p. 230 ff. ; Opitz, p. 7 ff., and Karl von Bahder, p. 62.

fort and Nuremberg printers were guilty of much arbitrariness with respect to the genuine Wittenberg editions. In the seventeenth century also alterations were made in them, ' though not of so thorough-going a nature as to bring the diction of the Bible into correspondence with the progress of the living speech. Which then, in this case, was the true Lutheran German ? Of course always that of the Bible accessible at the moment. How in this wild confusion of German speech could unity, symmetry, harmony, be effected through the language of the Bible alone ? ' [1]

It is a fact of still greater importance that the

---

[1] Burdach, p. 8. Kluge (*Von Luther bis Lessing*, Strassburg, 1888) is completely silent as to the fact that the chancery language was persistently regarded by Luther as having a standard value. E. Schröder in the *Gött. Gel. Anz.* 1888, p. 284. Here, on the other hand, we are reminded of certain evidences ' which come from good Protestant quarters, and from their systematic connexion are free from all suspicion of partiality : in 1531 the Silesian Fabian Frangk, in his *Orthographei*, mentions the chancery of Maximilian and Luther's writings in the same breath, whereby he certainly does not mean to set down Luther as an accepted model of speech, but all the same gives expression to tendencies which turned also in that direction. In 1578 the Augsburg gymnasium rector Hieronymus Wolf, a Lutheran, and educated at Wittenberg, is altogether silent about Luther, and recognises only the authority of the imperial chancery.' See Müller, *Quellenschriften*, p. 94. A very severe sentence on Kluge's *Von Luther bis Lessing*, and therewith on the traditional Protestant overestimate of Luther's influence on the language of literature, is passed by Roethe in the *Histor. Zeitschr.* lxix. (1892) 523 f. ' Only in general let it be remarked that Luther's importance as regards the German literary language is exaggerated in the most one-sided manner. For this end an incredibly distorted picture is drawn of the position occupied by the mother tongue in the German Middle Ages ; Kluge dates its origin in the sixteenth century, no prominence is anywhere given to the fact that the Middle German speech had acquired a leading part already before Luther ; that in South Germany, especially in the town chancelleries, there were strong leanings to a universal language, above all that this South German common speech was nearer, in important things, to our present literary speech than was the language of Luther. Strong as was the impulse which Luther gave to the birth of our literary speech, his is only one formative element among many others of equal value.'

language of the man who had upset the religious unity
of the German nation, was inevitably bound to excite
antagonism among those who did not wish to know
anything about his new teaching. In the confusion
of the first period it seemed, however, as though
Lutheran German would be adopted by the Catholics
also, for Emser and Dietenberger gave it the preference
in their translations of the Bible. Later on, however,
the adherents of the old Church opposed fierce resistance to the ' heretical German.' [1] The grammarian
Laurentius Albertus was altogether hostile to the
German of Luther ; in vehement language he let fly at
' the stuttering barbarians who through un-German
Bible translations have made the Word of God, which
can only retain its normal purity in the Latin speech,
quite unintelligible ; individuals to whom the genuine
High German is, as it were, quite unknown had presumed
to explain to the purer-speaking Germans—i.e. the South
Germans—the nature and true properties of the German
language.' [2]

[1] ' The introduction of the grammar of Clajus into Catholic schools,
[on which Kluge also (pp. 38 and 127) lays so great stress] proves very little :
it was not indeed till the second half of the seventeenth century, when
Luther's German was already antiquated, that this grammar was extensively used.' Burdach, p. 9. See Dannehl, p. 13. Moreover, later
investigation on the ground already touched here will have many more
corrections to make. Thus, for instance, I find in Jostes (Daniel von
Soest, p. 393, note 2) the following interesting remark : ' A scholarly account
of the struggle between the High German language of literature and the
Low Saxon dialects will show in general what these texts prove in the
case of a single town, that it was the clergy of the old faith who first, and
the Protestant Estates who last gave up the dialect.' See also Histor.-
polit. Blätter, cii. 552.

[2] Cited from Burdach, p. 10. In reformed Switzerland also ' Luther's
authority was by no means recognised in the sixteenth century. There
were indeed three distinct kinds of literary language : Mid-German, South
German, and Swiss. In 1570 a grammarian still describes the German of

The new-religionists themselves stirred up opposition to the Lutheran German by the zeal with which they frequently strove, with the language, to force the new faith also on the Catholics. In this way Luther's translation itself caused a counter-stream which could not fail to arrest the development of a uniform language.[1]

As in the matter of religion, so, too, as regards language, Germany at the beginning of the seventeenth

Augsburg as the most elegant of languages. It was not till the end of the century that Luther's canon penetrated through the whole of Switzerland.' Paul, *Grundriss der germanischen Philologie*, Strassburg, 1891, i. 542.

[1] E. Schröder remarks in an exhaustive critique, in which he rejects the assertions in Kluge's ' *Von Luther bis Lessing*' (*Gött. Gel. Anz.* 1888) : ' The development of our New High German common language is carried on by Luther also, in the main and on the whole, in the same grammatical paths as were struck by the literary language of Upper Saxony and Silesia in the fourteenth and fifteenth centuries. What is due to Luther is that he recognised with more certainty than others the adaptability of this book-dialect to a common language, and that by his work and by its success he was the most effectual promoter of the unity of the German language. He shaped this language into a fuller and more expressive instrument as regards vocabulary and syntax than any German written language had ever been before. It is well to observe that those Upper Saxons and Silesians who furnish us with the most important proofs of the repute of Lutheran German saw in Luther, at the same time, the classicist of narrower literary language of their native land. But without the strong support which, in its essential points, and especially as contrasted with the Alemannic Mid and Lower Franconian, and Low Saxon, this language had in the chancery language, apart from the significant circumstance that throughout the whole seventeenth century the centre of literary development lay in Silesia, and next in Upper Saxony, the final victory of " Lutheran German " would have been doubtful. Highly as I rate the personal share of the reformer in the work of unifying the language, it seems to me nevertheless that in the literature of the seventeenth century the Lutheran language stood far more in the background than the grammarians, who had not yet arrived at distinguishing between grammar and orthography, would allow. I hold it indeed to be probable that the often intolerant bragging of Protestants about the " German of Luther," here and there contributed to impede and make difficult the progress of the common language.'

century was altogether disunited. This fact can be proved by quite unequivocal evidence from different parts of the country.[1] To the time, then, of the deepest degradation of the German people belong those renewed efforts towards the elevation and unification of the German book-language which, after hard labour and by the united endeavours of Catholics and Protestants, were finally to lead to the desired goal. Impartial research shows, therefore, that the unification of the new High German language of literature would have come about even without Luther.[2]

[1] See Burdach, p. 16 ff. This investigator, against whose data C. Franke also ('Grundzüge der Schriftsprache Luthers,' in the *Neues Lausitzscher Magazin*, lxiv. Görlitz, 1888, 306) has nothing to oppose, remarks : ' About the year 1600 the German people had at any rate not attained to a uniform written language capable of embodying a cultivated national literature.' And a statement such as Rudolf von Raumer makes in his *Unterricht im Deutschen* (4th edit. p. 31): ' Thus as early as 1600 Luther's language had become the book-language both of the Catholics and the Protestants ' is fundamentally false, although it corresponds with the traditional idea, and has been repeatedly, and variously, uttered by Rückert and others. If Luther's language had really been the general book-language in the North and in the South there would then have been a uniform language of literature. That there was no such language it is quite needless to demonstrate, for to anyone who examines only a dozen printed books from different parts of Germany in 1600 the matter is as clear as daylight.

[2] We may be permitted here to refer again to the statement of such an authority as Wilmanns, who, in his lecture ' Die Arbeit an der Sprache ' (Bonn, 1890) said: 'Luther's position in the history of our literary language is much disputed. The idea that we owe to him the uniformity of our written language is not for a moment to be entertained. This unity would have come without him. For the movement which led to it had long been astir, and it was not even Luther, moreover, who brought it to a climax. But that Luther and the Reformation, on the other hand, did materially hasten on the movement, and determined [or more correctly helped to determine] the actual form which the language of literature assumed, is equally certain.' How inaccurate it is to make a period of literary style begin with Luther, is insisted on by Schröder, p. 271. See also Burdach in Zarncke's *Zentralblatt*, 1896, No. 4, in the criticism of the article of A. Berger, ' Die Kulturaufgabe der Reformation,' and ' M. Luther in Kulturgeschichlicher Darstellung,' in the *Histor.-polit. Blätter*,

Luther's efforts to bring the diction of his translation of the Bible into the closest possible correspondence
with the language of the common people led of itself
to coarse, clumsy, unsuitable expressions. By freeing
himself from the stiff, traditional style he undoubtedly
helped on the extraordinarily wide circulation of his
translation, but he not seldom sank into platitude and
impaired the dignity of the Holy Scriptures. Even
enthusiastic admirers of the Bible translator said,
' Nobody who has been instructed in an impartial
and thorough manner will attempt to defend all
the phraseology of the Lutheran Bible. Some of it
is altogether ignoble and could easily have been
avoided.' [1]

There is no lack, moreover, of mistakes, careless-
nesses (for instance, Ezekiel xli. 20 is missing), and
flagrant inaccuracies in this highly renowned work.
' Undoubted perversions of the words and ideas of
the original text occur not only in the more difficult

cxiii. (1894) 145 f.   In the latter place the ' Rathsannalen des Görlitzer
Burgomeister Joh. Hass' (published in the *Scriptores rerum Lusaticarum*,
Görlitz, 1850) are discussed.   Hass, however, was full of aversion towards
Luther, he would not and did not need to learn of him.   On the other
hand, Schmid (*Histor. Jahrbuch*, xvii. 89) aptly remarks, that it should be
observed that the model of the Latin language in the middle schools
had a decidedly advantageous influence on the development of the German
language.   Among the princes the love of foreign travel led to contempt for
the mother tongue (see our remarks, vol. viii. [German] p. 209, note 3).
(The English translation of vol. viii. is not yet out.)

[1] Hopf, *Bibelübersetzung*, p. 271.   De Lagarde (*Die revidierte Lutherbibel*)
remarks (pp. 2–3): ' To offer to the people for their edification something
written in the sixteenth century seems to me the height of folly.   In
proportion as it is characteristically sixteenth century writing, and not
an echo of earlier times, it bristles with *foulnesses* ; Mathesius, Meyfart,
and, up to a certain point, though least of all, Luther, when they write
well, write older German than that of their period, and therefore as regards
all that pleases in their style they are not at all personally responsible.'

books of the Old Testament, but also here and there in the easier portions.' [1]

But it is a still heavier charge against Luther that ' on principle' he deals very freely with the sacred text. Thus, for instance, he always uses the word *Gemeinde* (congregation) instead of *Kirche* (church), only using the latter word in the Old Testament in the case of the heathen temples and the illegal sanctuaries of the Israelites. Further he violates the sacred text for polemical purposes against the old Church, and does not even disdain the introduction of offensive witticisms. [2]

But his worst offence is that he does not resist the temptation arbitrarily and intentionally to falsify a large number of passages in support of his new doctrine of justification. [3] He ' knew the people of the period, he knew that of the thousands who professed his doctrines

[1] Hopf, *Bibelübersetzung*, p. 221 ; see pp. 176 f., 180, 204, 288. Bunsen calls Luther's translation ' the most inaccurate rendering, even if it bears marks of great genius ' ; ' *three thousand passages* in it,' he says, ' need correction.' Nippold, *Bunsen*, iii. Leipzig, 1871, 483.

[2] Cf. Riehm, ' Luther als Bibelübersetzer ' in the *Theolog. Studien und Kritiken*, lvii. (1884) 306, 312–313 ; cf. Hopf, p. 87. ' When Luther,' says Riehm, ' uses the word " Pfaffen " (priest) for priests of idols and sooth-sayers, when a ritualistic injunction (Lev. xxi. 5) given to the priests is rendered by him : ' He shall also make no *Platte* (plate, for tonsure) on his head,' and when the text Baruch vi. 30 : ' Priests sit in their temples, having their garments rent, and their heads and beards shaven and nothing on their heads,' is rendered by him : ' The priests sit in their temples in wide surplices (Chorröcken), shave their beards and wear plates (tonsures), sit with bare heads, howling and screaming before their idols '—then the translator's intention is clear to all eyes.

[3] ' The only preacher,' says Döllinger (*Kirche und Kirchen*, pp. 469–470), ' of whom it is known that he dealt frankly with his parishioners on this point is the Prussian preacher Ehrenström, who emigrated to America ; he had taught his congregation Greek, and then shown them how Luther had everywhere translated falsely (Wangemann's *Preuss. Kirchengesch.* iii. 132). On the other hand, Palmer (*Homiletik*, p. 303) most emphatically admonishes all preachers never to tell the people that this or that passage of Luther is falsely translated ; this is a secret on which absolute silence must be kept ; the utmost that may be acknowledged is that the translation is not clear.'

not one would take the trouble to compare the new translation critically with the original text, that on the contrary the preachers of his party in all their sermons and catechisings would far prefer to abide exclusively by his translation and to present every Bible passage to the people in this garb.' [1]

It was the Epistles of St. Paul especially which Luther tried to make serviceable to his purpose. In this intentional perversion of the apostolic language he helped himself chiefly by the insertion of the little modifying words ' allein ' and ' nur ' (alone and only). Thus Rom. iv. 15 now read : ' The law worketh *only* wrath,' and Rom. iii. 20 : ' For by the law *only* is the knowledge of sin.'

The most serious falsification was committed by Luther through the interpolation of the little word ' alone ' at Rom. iii. 28 : ' Therefore we conclude that a man is justified by faith *alone* without the deeds of the law.' The arbitrariness which came into play here had already been blamed by his contemporaries. The way in which he defended himself against this reproach is immensely characteristic of Luther. ' If,' wrote he, ' your new papist makes much ado about the word *sola*, alone, just say straight out to him : Doctor Martin Luther *will* have it so, and says, papist and donkey are one and the same thing ; thus I will and am deter-mined to have it ; my will is the reason.' Further he attempted to prove that the word ' alone ' gives the meaning of the Apostle. Luther then concludes with the words : ' And I repent me that I did not add thereto the words *all*, thus : without *all* works, *all* law, so that it may be spoken out with a full, round sound. Thus,

---

[1] Döllinger, *Reformation*, iii. 139.

therefore, it shall remain in my New Testament, and though all Pope-donkeys should go raving mad they will not alter my decision.' [1]

We cannot regard as anything but a 'palpable falsification' the turn which Luther has given to Rom. iii. 23–26, a passage of such great dogmatic importance, and which contradicts his whole system.

ENGLISH REVISED VERSION, 1881

Rom. iii. 23 : For all have sinned, and fall short of the glory of God ; (24) being justified freely by his grace through the redemption that is in Christ Jesus : (25) whom God set forth *to be* a propitiation, through faith, by his blood, to shew his righteousness, because of the passing over of the sins done aforetime, in the forbearance of God ; (26) for the shewing, *I say*, of his righteousness at this present season ; that he might himself be just, and the justifier of him that hath faith in Jesus.

LUTHER'S VERSION

23. For all are sinners and are short of the glory they should have in God : (24) and they are justified without merit by his grace through the redemption accomplished by Christ Jesus, (25) whom God has set forth to be a seat of grace (Gnadenstuel) through faith in his blood, that *he may present the righteousness which is acceptable to him*, forgiving the sins which had remained till then under divine forbearance, (26) that *he might in his season offer* (darbieten) *the righteousness which is acceptable to him*, that he might himself *alone* be just and the justifier of him that is of the faith in Jesus.

On the same principles Luther mistranslates Acts xiii. 38–39.

REVISED VERSION

(38) Be it known unto you therefore, brethren, that through this man is proclaimed unto you remission of sins : (39) and by him every one that believeth is justified from all things, from which ye could not be justified by the law of Moses.

LUTHER'S VERSION

Be it known unto you therefore, dear brethren, that through this man is proclaimed unto you remissions of sins, and of all things of which you could not be justified in the law of Moses. *But whosoever believeth in this* (man), *he is just* (Wer aber an diesen gleubet, der ist gerecht).[2]

---

[1] Walch, xxi. 314 f., 327 ; cf. Döllinger, *Reformation*, iii. 141–142, and (Klopp) *Studien über Katholizismus und Protestantismus*, p. 65 ff.

[2] See Döllinger, iii. 148. P. de Lagarde (*Die revidierte Lutherbibel des*

In his glosses and his Bible exposition Luther went on the same system which he had pursued in translating the sacred text.

In a certain sense the way in which in his glosses he was able ' to turn all sorts of irrelevant utterances of Scripture into weapons against the doctrine of works, and salvation by works,' and into recommendations of the faith which makes everything superfluous except the trust in grace alone, is worthy of admiration. Let the explanation of Matt. xxvi. 10 serve as an example. To the passage about the Magdalen : ' She hath wrought a good work upon Me,' Luther adds the marginal gloss, ' Thus one sees that faith alone makes the work

Halleschen Waisenhauses) remarks (pp. 24–25) : ' The " Revisionskommission " has not taken sufficient notice of what Döllinger (*Reformation*, pp. 139–156) has to say on Luther's translation, although Janssen (ii[3]. 198) had pointed it out. It may also be mentioned that Paulsen in his recent history of higher education in Germany (p. 147) quotes and approves Döllinger's criticism ; it shows that even a non-Catholic writer, provided he be unprejudiced and conscientious, is able to see the facts as they are : in the present case the facts are very simple. The committee of revisers has indeed suppressed the *nur* (only) slipped by Luther into Rom. iii. 20, and has substituted in Rom. viii. 3, " for the sake of sin " in lieu of " through sin." But in Rom. iv. 15, the revisers retain a *nur* and iii. 28 an *allein* (alone), although the original ignores these words so useful to Protestant dogmatics. Luther has told us his mind on the *allein* in his answer to contemporary fault-finders : " Dr. Martin Luther will have it so, and says : Papist and ass is the same thing : *sic volo, sic jubeo, stet pro ratione voluntas.*" (Walch, xxi. 314.) Readers not at home in Luther's writings are directed to his pamphlet *Against Papacy in Rome, founded by the Devil* (published 1545) in various places, but notably to folio N of the first impression, and to the wretched illustration of the papacy contrived by Lucas Cranach under Luther's direction, also published in 1545 : for lovers of truth the said illustration should be reproduced in photo-lithography (Janssen, ii[8]. 281). De Lagarde here quotes the alterations indicated in one text, then he concludes : Herr Leopold Witte, in his *Life of Tholuck*, p. 89, remarks that as early as 1839 Tholuck had drawn the revisers' attention to the dogmatic importance of the Aorist suppressed by Luther : possibly this statement will open the revisers' eyes.'

good. For all reason has condemned this work, as the
Apostles themselves did also. For those works are the
best of which we do not know how good they are.'
To the saying of Christ : ' So that the world may know
that I love the Father, and as the Father gave me com-
mandment even so I do,' Luther gives the explanation :
' The world must learn that Christ alone does the
will of the Father *for us.*' [1]

All the falsifications however, all the glosses inspired
by sectarian bias, were not able to remodel the whole
of the Scriptures in the spirit of the new teaching.
There still remained numbers of passages in which ' that
which Luther abominated, namely, righteousness based
on works, or a share of works in righteousness, is taught.'
He therefore gave the instructions that ' in all places
of Holy Scripture in which the righteousness of works
seems to be enjoined, the only answer was to do like
the Apostle in the Epistle to the Hebrews and always
prefix the word *faith,* and then refer everything that was
attributed to works to faith instead ; for instance,
when Christ says : " Give alms and all will be well with
you," the explanation is : Give alms in faith and all is
well with you, not through the almsgiving, but through
your faith.' [2]

Other passages contradicting his system Luther
managed to get rid of by establishing as the chief
principle of his Biblical exposition that all must be
explained ' for Christ,' *i.e.* according to Luther's
doctrine that faith alone could save.[3] In the utilisa-
tion of other texts this strange exegetist made himself

[1] See Döllinger, iii. 153 f., where numbers of other instances are given.
[2] *Ibid.* iii. 159.
[3] Wedewer, *Dietenberger,* p. 155 ; Döllinger, iii. 157, 167.

very much at home ; he simply gave them the meaning which corresponded best with his own system. Thus on one occasion, in quoting the saying of St. Paul at Rom. xi. he allowed himself no fewer than three falsifications all at once.[1]   There was no exaggeration in what the famous jurist Ulrich Zasius wrote : ' Luther twists and turns the Holy Scriptures to such an extent that he upsets all connexion in them, and veils the whole Bible in darkness. With insolent shamelessness he explains the whole of the Scriptures, both the Old and the New Testament, from the first chapter of Genesis to the end, into nothing but threats and cursings against the popes, bishops and priests, as though through all the centuries God had had no other occupation than to thunder at the priests.[2]

Part of the Scriptures, however, could not in any way, either by falsification or by senseless explanation, be brought into harmony with the new teaching, namely, the Epistle of St. James. More strongly and more unequivocally than here, it could not be said that through works man was justified before God. Melanchthon, nevertheless, made an attempt to reconcile St. James with the new doctrine. Luther, however, was not satisfied : ' The two are diametrically opposed : faith makes righteous, and faith does not make righteous ; if any man can rhyme these together,

[1] ' What the Apostle says of the Jews and heathen, Luther applies to all Christians, as though the latter with regard to good works, notwith-standing their Christian faith, were no better than the unbelieving ; hence instead of the apostolic words, he puts in " us all," namely, all Christians ; then he inserts the words " and know that no one can be justified by good works," and finally he makes the addition : " und allein aus Gnaden rechtfertige " (and justifies by faith alone).'   Döllinger, iii. 160.

[2] Döllinger, i. 188 ; cf. 491 f. concerning Luther's want of sincerity respecting the study of the Bible in the Church.

I will put my biretta on him and let myself be christened fool.' [1] There was, therefore, nothing left for Luther but to call the Epistle an 'epistle of straw,' and to denounce St. James as a fool.[2]

The father of innovation spoke with equal contempt of other portions of the Scriptures. The Pentateuch is to him 'only the *Sachsenspiegel* [Saxon code of laws] of the Jews, which is no longer binding on us.' The Book of Ecclesiastes 'has neither boot nor spur, it rides only in socks, like myself when I was still in the convent.' The letter to the Hebrews was rejected by Luther because it did not come from any of the Apostles, and equally so the Book of Revelation, which he considered neither 'apostolic nor prophetic': 'Let each one think of it according as his mind inclines; my mind cannot make anything out of this book.' [3]

It cannot be a matter of surprise that the adherents of the old faith should have taken up arms against a 'tendency work,' the falsified text of which gave an impetus to the spread of the new doctrines, whose prefaces and glosses attacked the Church and damaged the repute of the Holy Scriptures. The prohibitive

[1] Döllinger, iii. 335, 358.

[2] This Luther did before the Wittenberg students. *Opera exeget. lat.* (Erl. edition) v. 227. Later on, in the preface to his New Testament, Luther left out the passage against the 'epistle of straw.' However, he still allowed himself, verbally, to make the strongest attacks on the Epistle of St. James (see Loesche, *Anal. Luth.* p. 296). Walther, in the *Theolog. Studien und Kritiken*, lxvi. (1893) 596 ff., has drawn attention to several manuscript marginal notes of Luther on this part of the Holy Scriptures. 'No wonder,' says Walther, 'that Richter did not dare to publish these remarks of Luther without comments which might excuse them, and that Walch said openly, "Luther makes use of expressions against the Epistle of St. James which are opposed to its divine character, and therefore doubtful."'

[3] See present work, vol. iii. pp. 240–242. See also Holzhey, *Inspiration der Heiligen Schrift*, pp. 133–135.

edicts issued in the Duchy of Saxony, in Austria and in the Mark of Brandenburg against the Lutheran translation of the Bible were fully justified;[1] they were, however, regarded by the new-religionists as unheard-of proceedings. Hieronymus Emser, accordingly, wrote a treatise entitled ' Auss was Grund und Ursach Luthers Dolmetschung über das neue Testament dem gemeinen Man billig verboten worden sey, mit scheynbarlicher Anzeigung, wie, wo und an welchen Stellen, Luther den Text vorkert und ungetreulich gehandelt, oder mit falschen Glosen und Vorreden auss der alten Christelichen Ban auf seyn Vorteyl und Whan geführt hab.' 1523.[2]

Luther, says Emser, ' has in many places confused, stultified and perverted the old trustworthy text of the Christian Church to its great disadvantage, and also poisoned it with heretical glosses and prefaces '; more than 1400 passages need improvement.[3] A principal charge made by Emser is that Luther ' almost every-where forces the Scriptures on to the question of faith

---

[1] See present work, vol. iii. p. 241 f.

[2] Panzer, *Gesch. der Kathol. Bibelübersetzungen*, p. 16. On the reverse side of the title-page of Emser's pamphlet are the following verses :

> Go forth, my book, with God for guide,
> Let not thy journey ill betide ;
> Fear not, fear not the devil's children—
> They may revile thee, they cannot hinder.
> But should'st thou meet a Christian friend,
> To him my greeting warm extend,
> And eke my service, and him tell
> Through God I him admonish well
> Firm in the ancient faith to stand ;
> God never will let go his hand,
> Nor His own faithful ones neglect ;
> St. Peter's ship can ne'er be wrecked,
> Although in patience it must bide
> Awhile. Farewell : forth on thy journey ride.

[3] Kawerau (*Emser*, pp. 61–63) would like to make Emser's criticisms on Luther's translation—and he only instances those on the Epistle to the Galatians—appear in the light of paltry fault-finding.

and works, even when neither faith nor works are
thought of.' However just this criticism may have
been, Luther was so little disturbed by it that in later
editions he altered still other passages in the same
sense.[1] It was with perfect truth that John Dietenberger said : ' As regards the Holy Scriptures, to which
Luther is constantly appealing, there is nobody who
" adds to and takes from them" more than he does.
He rejects from the Bible whatever he wills ; he adds
to it whatever confirms his errors.' [2]

' That Luther falsified the writings of the Old and
the New Covenant and remodelled them with his false
translation,' wrote George Wizel in 1548, ' is so certain
that it cannot be denied. The Germans will not believe
it ; one day, however, I know that they will believe
me, but not till all hope of salvation is lost.' [3] Twelve
years earlier George Wizel had already come forward
with an exhaustive and learned review of the Lutheran
translation of the Old Testament.[4] ' Here you see
brought to light, diligent reader,' says the preface,
' not only how in so many hundreds of places of the
Holy Scriptures the new German translation of the
Hebrew and Greek are contrary to the truth, but also
how many passages are dark and difficult to understand.' In the preface addressed to Bishop Melchior
Zobel of Würzburg, Wizel explains the reason and aim
of his work : ' Whereas the Wittenberg translation has

---

[1] See Hopf, p. 106 f., and Riehm, p. 314.

[2] Wedewer, *Dietenberger*, p. 315.

[3] Döllinger, *Reformation*, i. 121.

[4] *Annotationes in sacras literas*, first published at Leipzig in 1536,
then again in 1555 and 1557 at Mayence. I make use of the last edition.
The value of this work is also recognised by Panzer, pp. 30, 32 ; Hopf,
p. 132, and Herzog, *Realenzyklopädie*, xvii. 246. That Luther had regard
to several of Wizel's corrections is shown by Riehm, p. 301.

the reputation of being a most exact rendering of the
Hebrew truth, and is therefore gladly welcomed by
everyone, I have at length been moved not only by
its immoderate fame, but far more by the danger and
injury it brings to the common people, to look through
this said translation and compare it with the Hebrew,
in order that I may advise and warn against it not only
my own friends, lords and patrons, but also all Germans,
my brothers in Christ. Those who have stubborn,
blinded hearts may preach against me, bark, rail and
write as much as they like, but they will gain nothing.
I arm myself with patience every day in this wearisome,
hard battle with heresy ; but henceforth, now that this
work of mine has come to light in this dear land, and
that the enemy's fortune and might are increasing,
I must arm myself more strongly. I must not be
disturbed by any amount of wanton words of mockery.
Slander and abuse will come in plenty. For how else
should such people be able to answer me ? He, this
Luther, says that he has weighed every word before he
has uttered it, and translated with all diligence and
fidelity. But this does not satisfy us. I well believe
that he has considered and weighed, but who knows
whether the scales were true ? If the scales were right
then it is to be feared that the balance user may have
cheated. Let other people also weigh and consider.
What is then found right, let that be right.'

Although other Catholic writers, such as Hieronymus
Dungersheim [1] and Kilian Leib [2] showed up the faults
and falsifications of the Lutheran translation of the

---

[1] Concerning the treatises of this scholar not mentioned by Panzer,
see *Meuser (see above, p. 240 n.[2]), i. 351.

[2] *De sacrae scripturae dissonis translationibus*, s. l. 1542.

Bible the circulation of the work was not thereby
hindered. 'Everybody nowadays wants to read the
Bible, the Holy Scriptures,' wrote Caspar Querhamer
in 1535; 'whether it is a good thing, God knows; I
will not pronounce judgment. . . . Luther and others
have Germanised them, but their translations are not
always correct. Now it is desirable, since everybody
will have a German Bible, that the prelates should
set to work to have the Bible translated into German,
and made accessible to the people, by means of a
learned committee.' [1]

A learned committee was not formed, but the
adherents of the old faith persisted in opposing the
Lutheran translation with Catholic ones.[2]

Here, too, Emser was again the first to come forward.
In 1527 there appeared 'Das naw Testament nach
Lawt der christlichen Kirchen bewerten Text corrigiert
un wiederumb zurecht gebracht.' The title shows at
once that this was no independent translation. The
publisher openly acknowledges that he has only attempted to combine together, in the orthodox Church
sense, a collection of older and newer translations. No
secret is made of the 'new translation' having been
used; but Luther's name is not mentioned.[3] This

[1] See Paulus in the *Histor.-polit. Blätter*, cxii. 28 f.   Emser had already
proposed the same thing ; see Kawerau, p. 65.

[2] The edition of the New Testament in German, published by J.
Beringer in 1526, as Panzer remarks, p. 6, note 3, does not belong here, as
it is a mere reprint of Luther's New Testament.   Concerning this edition
see also *Serapeum*, 1854, p. 333 f.   Concerning some Catholic translations
of single portions of Holy Scripture, of the years 1522–1524, by C. Amman,
Otmar Nachtigall, and Nicholas Krumpach, see Wetzer und Welte's
Kirchenlexikon, ii². 754 f.

[3] See Mosen (*H. Emser*, p. 47), who says that Emser is naturally not
responsible for the title of the second edition, published after his death,
which is : *Das New Testament so Emser säliger verdeutscht.*   To what

work, which was undertaken at the instigation of Duke George of Saxony, was eagerly read, as is shown by the many new editions it went through.[1]

How great and universal the interest in Holy Scripture was at that time (an interest of which Luther took the best advantage) is shown by the circumstance that already in 1534 the Dominican John Dietenberger published a translation of the whole Bible. He, too, made diligent use of Luther's work, in so far as this could be done without detriment to accuracy and orthodoxy. Dietenberger makes no more secret of this than did Emser. ' Whereas nowadays,' he writes, ' so many people are being misled by false Bibles, and soon nobody will any longer know whom or what he is to believe, several devout, pious Christians, both of high and low degree, have often exhorted and earnestly begged that for their comfort and salvation the newly Germanised Bible might be looked through, and that all that was not in accordance with the faith

extent Emser utilised the Lutheran translation is shown by Panzer's summary in *Katholische Bibelübersetzungen*, p. 42 ff. See also Kawerau, *Emser*, p. 67 ff. Emser's New Testament, says Kawerau (p. 70), ' is a revision of the Lutheran text according to the Vulgate and according to Catholic interpretation of the Scriptures. The Greek text is only so far considered that in a series of cases attention is drawn in the margin to its deviations ' ; p. 72 : If Emser ' had himself claimed to be a "translator" his work would have deserved the accusation, now and then still brought against it to-day, of being plagiarism. [For instance, Kluge.] But this he never pretended to be, only an emendator of the Lutheran translation. Hence this accusation must be rejected as unjust.' It was only Luther himself who could raise this charge ' with a certain amount of moral right.' See also B. Lindmeyr, *Der Wortschatz in Luthers, Emsers und Ecks Übersetzung des Neuen Testamentes. Ein Beitrag zur Geschichte der neuhochdeutschen Schriftsprache*, Strassburg, 1899.

[1] On October 28, 1529, Cochlaeus, Emser's successor in his post with Duke George, sent the fifth edition of the Emser New Testament to the Princess Margaret of Anhalt ; see the letter of Cochlaeus to the Princess in Kawerau's *Emser*, p. 74 f.

and with the trustworthy old Latin Bible might be removed, and a German Bible be prepared free from all errors, and in accordance with the Latin Bible.'

It was Dietenberger's intention to give a faithful translation of the Vulgate, avoiding both the linguistic harshness and faults of the old, and the dogmatic errors of the new Lutheran translation. This aim, on the whole, he accomplished.[1] Far less successful, on the other hand, was the stiff translation which the renowned John Eck published at Ingolstadt in 1537. In this case also it was a prince, Duke William IV of Bavaria, who gave the impulse to the work.[2] Eck's translation went through two editions in the sixteenth and four in the seventeenth century, while Dietenberger's had a wider circulation than any other Catholic Bible in the German language. Forty editions of the whole work and over twenty of the New Testament, the Psalter and the Book of Sirach can be identified. 'Some of these were very handsomely got up, in order that externally also they might stand comparison with the Lutheran translation.'[3] For the use of the Low German-speaking district the Carmelite Alexander Blanckardt published at Cologne, in 1547, a German translation of the whole of the Holy Scriptures, corrected according

[1] See Wedewer, *Dietenberger*, pp. 164, 174. For Dietenberger's translation of the Bible see also Falk, *Bibelstudien*, pp. 165 ff., 221 f.

[2] Panzer, *Katholische Bibelübersetzungen*, p. 117 ff. Wiedemann, *Eck*, p. 615 ff. Concerning Eck's ignorance of the original language see Hopf, p. 47. Cf. G. Keferstein, *Der Lautstand in den Bibelübersetzungen von Emser und Eck. Jenaische Dissertation*, 1888 ; Von Bahder, *Neuhochdeutsches Lautsystem*, p. 9 f. ; Lindmeyr, in the pamphlet cited above (p. 428, n. 3), shows that Eck is independent in the Old Testament, and that in the New Testament he works from the foundation aid by Emser, the 'honourable and admirable man,' not, however, from the original edition but from a copy or a reprint revised by Dietenberger.

[3] Wedewer, *Dietenberger*, p. 197.

to the Vulgate.   In the dedication to the Utrecht bishop, George von Egmont, Blanckardt says that his work was suggested by the petition of many good people, and the injunction of the doctors and magisters of Holy Scripture at Cologne, that the German Bibles, which were so false and incorrect, might be compared with the unfalsified Latin text.[1]

Emser, as well as Dietenberger and Eck, was fully conscious of the great danger, in an age torn with religious dissensions and filled with heresies, of putting the Bible into the hands of the common people ; it was only the necessity for counteracting the Lutheran Bible translations which caused these very justifiable scruples to retreat into the background. Emser says in his epilogue to his New Testament : ' Although I am not yet quite certain in my own mind whether it is good or bad to Germanise the Bible and give it to the common people, for the Scriptures are a whirlpool in which many even of the most highly learned are drowned ; those who want to go through the door of Scripture must needs stoop very low so as not to knock their heads.   Therefore every layman had better concern himself more about godly living than about the Scriptures, which are only commended to the scholars.' Dietenberger mentions particularly as the reason which induced him to make his translation that he wished that ' no one of our party should henceforth have any cause to complain that the evangel or the Word of God was kept back from him or refused him, and that all pious Christians should be better able to detect the falsity of Luther's translation and guard themselves against it.'   Eck speaks still more emphatically.   ' It

[1] Streber in Wetzer und Welte's *Kirchenlexikon,* ii[2]. 899.

cannot be useful, good or salutary,' he writes, ' that the
Holy Scriptures, the Biblical books, should be translated into a common vernacular language, but, on the
contrary, it is dangerous and harmful. For thereby
the common people may easily be puffed up with pride,
and become self-satisfied, because they think themselves
able to deal with the mysteries and the difficult passages
of the Scriptures according to their own assumed
conceits.'   In other matters nobody presumes to think
he can find the right way without learning ; why, then,
should it be different in the case of the Scriptures which
are still more difficult and obscure ?   Inexpert laymen
could not but fall into many errors and heresies in this
way.   It was only because he felt that a translation
of the Bible was now necessary, because the common
people were bewildered by numbers of false renderings
and no longer knew exactly which was the genuine
text of the Bible or what was human invention, that he
had been moved to comply with the injunction of his
Duke.[1]

The translation and general reading of the Bible
was strongly advocated by George Wizel in his ' Annotationes ' which appeared in 1536.   Nothing on earth,
he said, was better than ' a faithful translation of the
Holy Bible, because this book was the source of all
our faith, doctrine, worship and conduct.'   If St.
Jerome had been alive he would certainly have helped

---

[1] The Duke also settled the plan which Eck was to follow in his translation.   ' I am to translate the Bible anew according to the literal meaning
as it is chanted, read, and accepted by the Holy Latin Churches, and not
to trouble myself as to how it reads in Hebrew, Greek, or Chaldean (for
the rabbis themselves do not agree in their understanding and interpretation of the Scriptures), but to keep to the reading of our Latin Churches.'
Wiedemann, *Eck*, p. 617.

in the work.   Even Luther with his German translation had done good, though he had himself lessened his merits by mixing the good with an incalculable amount of bad, so that among all translators he was found to be the most inaccurate.   That the Latin text was corrupt there was no doubt whatever.   Wizel, accordingly, protests most emphatically against the enemies of languages and arts who say that people should be content with the ordinary edition and not read or countenance any fresh versions.   This was quite wrong. The great teachers of the Church had also gone back to the Hebrew text.   ' Why should not we do the same, above all at this time, in the midst of such sects, such sophists and fanatics ?   Since, then, our holy ancestors had used the Hebrew truth side by side with St. Jerome's translation, it was not forbidden us to do likewise.'   The study of languages did not make heretics, as some were crying out, but this ignorance of language made great donkeys ; ' it is the evil spirit that makes heretics, and not the Scriptures.'   Neither Emser nor Dietenberger could regard the reading of the German Bible as wrong, as they had helped in the translation as far as they were able.   ' But I would, nevertheless, give the following advice to a studious Christian, namely, that rather than he should entirely avoid Bible reading he should use the present German version, with the precaution that he proceed warily with the passages indicated.   Moreover I would indeed recommend him to go on reading and believing in the name of the Lord, but that at the same time he should not put away from him *virgulam censoriam* [criticism]—that is to say, that he should also seek out those who can tell him when anything is wrongly

translated.   Others, indeed, ought to do this, but since
nobody will, I feel myself called and impelled to do
it myself.   If I have not displayed great art herein,
I have at any rate shown fidelity and faith, and
pointed out to my neighbour the way in which I mean
to go myself.'

The Augustinian John Hoffmeister spoke even
more clearly and justly than Wizel on the value and
the reading of the Holy Scriptures.   ' Whereas the holy
Prophets, Apostles and Evangelists,' he says, ' did not
write by human cleverness, but by the inspiration of the
Spirit, we must not read the Holy Scriptures as the
writings of the heathen or the worldly-wise, with only
slight attention and, so to say, superficially, but with
great reverence, with diligence and special seriousness,
remembering always that the manner of our soul's
salvation is contained and revealed in the Holy
Scriptures.'

Notwithstanding this, however, the Scriptures cannot be regarded as the one only source of faith, and first
and foremost because all that Christ and the Apostles
taught is not contained in them.   Side by side with
the Scriptures, therefore, the traditions of the Church
must be consulted.   But, even if the Scriptures did
contain all the necessary articles of faith, they would
still not suffice in themselves for a source of faith.   For
who can tell us what books are to be included among the
Holy Scriptures ?   Only the God-inspired and directed
Church.[1]

In like manner spoke the Dominican John Mensing.
' Not that we despise or undervalue the Holy Scriptures,' he says, ' or wish to make them seem con-

[1] Paulus, *Hoffmeister*, pp. 262–264.

temptible to anybody : with all due reverence we
firmly believe all that is contained in the canonical
writings of the Old and New Testaments.   But we are
not so fully convinced that these writings contain all
that is necessary as to regard as human invention all
that the Church teaches us outside the Scriptures, for the
Scriptures themselves enjoin us to obey the teaching of
the Church and the Fathers.'   Besides which it is only
from the mouth of the Church that we can learn which
books were written by the inspiration of the Holy Spirit.
' Where stands it written that we must put our faith in
the Gospels of Matthew, John or the others ?   How
absurdly you are acting in opposition to your own
doctrine ! '   As it is from the Church that we learn
which books contain the Word of God, so, too, it is the
Church which informs us as to the true meaning of the
Holy Scriptures.   The opponents say, indeed, that
Scripture is so clear that everybody can understand it
without outside help.   ' But if the heretics think the
Scriptures are so clear, why do they make so many
books in order to bring Scripture down to their understanding ?   If Scripture is so plain, clear and easy to
understand, why then are they all so much in disagree-
ment about this one phrase, " This is My Body " ? ' [1]

How far removed the Catholics were from anything
like depreciation of the Scriptures is shown by a statement of Canisius.   ' Without the Word of God which
He has revealed to us,' says the latter, ' we should
lead the most wretched existence in our pilgrimage
through this world : as sheep without shepherds, a
prey to devouring wolves ; as little children without
bread, perishing with hunger, we should all be ruined.

[1] *Katholik*, 1893, ii. 31.

God's Word, as the Scriptures reveal it, is the knowledge of salvation, a shining light in a dark place ; it
is the hidden mystery, the heavenly manna, gold pure
and refined, the learning of the saints, the teaching of
the Spirit and the Truth.   All those who rightly use
this sealed book become the pupils of God, children
of the Spirit, wise and righteous, the friends and inheritors of God.' [1]

At the Council of Trent,[2] in 1546, the opinions about
the translations of the Bible were still very diverse.
Among the abuses respecting the Holy Scriptures which
the Council of Trent was to remedy, the translation of
Scripture into the vernacular was not included.   When
Cardinal Pacheco proposed this subject also for discussion, he met with strong opposition, especially from
Cardinal Madruzzo.   Opinions on this question were
very divided.   Some of the Fathers insisted that translations into all the popular languages should be undertaken by the Council, and that these translations should
be considered authentic in the respective lands.[3]   Others
thought that the prohibition of translations would be
more advisable.   On account of the differences in
opinion and in the conditions of different countries, it
was considered best for the present not to discuss
Pacheco's proposal at all.   It was thought that a recom-

---

[1] *De Verbi Dei corruptelis i. Praemonitio ad lectorem.*   To the court
preacher of Ferdinand I, Bishop Urban von Gurk, Canisius recommended,
as a preparation for his preaching, first and foremost the study of the
Holy Scriptures (*Canisii Epistulae*, ii. 332).

[2] Theiner, *Acta Conc. Trid.* i. 64 f.

[3] *Ibid.* 83.   Le Plat, *Monumenta ad Conc. Trid. pert.* iii. 399 : ' Valde
discussum fuit a Patribus, an ipsa S. Scriptura verti deberet in linguam
vernaculam, nonnullis id enixe petentibus, atque ut a s. Synodo decretum
fieri deberet, multis rationibus contendentibus, ne praesertim qui linguam
latinam ignorant, lectione s. Scripturarum carerent.'

mendation of the translations by the Council would have
no practical result in Spain and France, because the
Governments of these countries objected so strongly
to seeing the Bible in the hands of the people.   In
Germany, Poland, Italy, on the other hand, prohibition
of the translations already made would lead to great
difficulties.[1]

It was in harmony with these opinions that later on
the fourth rule of the Tridentine Index neither generally forbade nor generally allowed translations into
the vernacular, but made the matter dependent on the
bishop's decision.   In Germany, where Emser's, Eck's
and Dietenberger's translations had become domiciled,
the episcopal sanction was held to be generally extended
to all believers.[2]

The polemics against the Lutheran Bible were still
kept up by the Catholics in the period after the Council
of Trent.   In his pamphlet published in 1561, under
the title ' Christlicher Gegenbericht an den gottseligen

[1] Hispaniarum enim Galliaeque regna anne recipient unquam s. libros
verti in linguam vernaculam ? Certe non. Tum quia regiis edictis adeo id
prohibitum sub gravissimis poenis est, quod magis saecularem potentiam,
quam permissionem concilii pertimescent, tum etiam quod jam diu
experientia didicerunt, quantum scandali, damni impietas et mala versio
hujusmodi in illis regnis attulit. Anne vero Germani, Itali, Poloni, et
reliquae nationes negativam [the prohibition of the translations] suscipient ?
Certe etiam non.   Quum e converso in plurimis locis harum nationum
aedificationem instructionemque dictam versionem afferre perspexerunt.'
' Expediret igitur magis unamquamque nationem in suis institutis circa
hoc relinquere, ut ubi bonum esset concederetur, ubi malum prohiberetur.'
Massarelli in Theiner, p. 67.

[2] See Serarius, *Proleg. bibl.* c. 20, q. 3 ; Tanner, *Theol.* iii. 319 (*De fide
disp.* i. q. 5, dub. 2, note 88) : ' Ipso usu in Germania obtentum esse videtur,
ut bibliorum germanicorum lectio per se illicita non censeatur, si modo
ea versio ab aliquo catholico interprete profecta sit.' ' Quo fit, ut recentior
illa observatio Indicis ad reg. 4, Clementis VIII auctoritate edita, . . . in
Germania locum non habeat.'   Cf. Gretser, *Defensio Controvers. Bellarmini*,
ii. 15 (*Opera*, viii. 415).

gemeinen Laien vom rechten, wahren Verstande des
göttlichen Wortes, von Verdolmetschung der deutschen
Bibel und der Einigkeit der lutherischen Prädikanten ' ;
the convert Frederick Staphylus criticised minutely the
falsifications of the Lutheran translation, and said concerning the Bible-reading of the Protestants : ' Every
layman, forsooth, is to take up the Bible with un-
washed hands, yea, verily to ride booted and spurred
into the midst of the Scriptures without any preparation to show him how and in what sense they are to
be rightly understood.' This, says Staphylus, would be
just the same as if ' the common people were to drive
out the doctors and apothecaries from the chemists'
shops and dispense the medicines themselves.' [1]

The Ingolstadt theologian Frederick Traub published in 1578 a treatise entitled ' Nothwendige Avisa
oder Warnung vor des Luthers Teutschen Bibel, so an
unzählbarlichen Orten offentlich gefälscht, derhalben
von keinem Christen, so um seiner Seele Heil nicht
muthwilliglich betrogen werden will, gelesen werden
kann oder soll.' [2]

The Jesuits Gretser, Keller and Holzhai show, in
exhaustive disquisitions, in how many places Luther has
translated falsely.[3] The same purpose was fulfilled by
an extensive work of the Ehingen provost, Melchior
Zanger, which appeared in 1605 under the title ' Verit-

---

[1] See present work, vol. x. p. 80.

[2] According to Hopf (p. 135) Traub only repeats the criticisms of
Emser, and combats also such passages as Luther has altered.

[3] See Hurter, p. 300 ; Wedewer, *Dietenberger*, pp. 154–155. The
convert J. L. Holler says in his account of his conversion, printed in 1654,
that it was the arbitrariness with which Luther treated the Bible that led
him into the Catholic Church.   The catalogue drawn up by Holler of
Luther's falsifications of the New Testament was reprinted by Räss,
vii. 99 f.

able and manifest proof in what way Martin Luther falsified the Holy Scriptures both of the Old and the New Testament, translating them in different places contrary to the sense of all the chief languages and of the whole Catholic Church, with interpolations, irregular remarks, suppression of whole books, verses and words, &c., dangerously falsified and perverted, whereby the highly honoured German nation of our dear Fatherland has been lamentably misled and deceived.'

A decade later the excellent Cologne pastor, Caspar Ulenberg,[1] by command of the Elector Ferdinand of Bavaria, began a new Catholic translation, which was revised by the Cologne theological faculty. It was not published till 1630. Ulenberg tells us himself on what principles he proceeded in this work : Conscientious adhesion to the text (approved by the Church) of the edition of Sixtus V, nevertheless with observance of the freedom which St. Jerome and other well-known exegetists allowed themselves, so that not necessarily the precise word, but the idea, should be translated ; secondly, expansive explanation of what the Scriptural text only gives briefly and obscurely ; and, finally, faithful rendering of that interpretation which the Holy Fathers have received from the Church and the Church from the Holy Ghost.[2]

If not free from faults, Ulenberg's work is nevertheless a valuable contribution ; it marks a decided stage of progress in comparison with previous translations. The outward success was also proportionately greater. The Ulenberg translation, in its first form, went through twenty-two editions ; later on, after revision by

---

[1] See above, p. 111, note 1, and 347 f.
[2] Panzer, *Katholische Bibelübersetzungen*, p. 147.

the Mayence theologians, it appeared under the title
' Catholic or Mayence Bible,' and in so many fresh
editions that in this form it may be regarded as the
actual German Bible of the Catholics.

How right and wise the principles of the old Church
are with respect to the Holy Scriptures is plainly shown
by a glance into the opposite camp.

Unhallowed confusion and unbounded obscuration of
learning were the necessary consequences of universal
Bible-reading.   Cochlaeus relates that ' even tailors and
shoemakers, yea, verily women and laymen of all sorts,
who had only learnt to read a little, read Luther's
translation of the New Testament with the highest
enthusiasm ; some of them carried it about in their
bosoms and learnt it by heart.   And in this way within
a few months they gained so much skill and experience
that they had no scruples in disputing about the faith
and the Gospel even with magisters and doctors of the
Holy Scriptures ; poor wretched women like Argula von
Grumbach presumed to challenge the licentiates, the
doctors and whole universities to disputations.' [1]   People
holding opinions of the most diverse kind sought
and found confirmation of their views in the Bible.
Luther insisted that ' there was no plainer book written
on earth than the Holy Scriptures,' and that they only
allowed of one interpretation.   Nevertheless multitudes
of new-religionists deduced the most contradictory
doctrines from this ' plain ' Book.   The Anabaptists, as
well as Zwingli and Calvin, were led by their Bible
studies to conclusions very many of which were in
direct contradiction to Luther's opinions.   Luther in

---

[1] Hopf, p. 59.   Concerning A. von Grumbach see present work, vol. ii.
(German original, 13th and 14th ed.) p. 300, note 2.

such cases generally helped himself out of the difficulty
by declaring that those who found doctrines differing
from his own in the Bible were of the devil. The
Swiss, he said, had not got a subtle devil, but a coarse,
substantial one.

Catholic writers lost no time in showing up in the
true light Luther's statement as to the great clearness
of the Bible. ' If our opponents,' writes the Augustinian John Hoffmeister, ' say there is no need of the
Church to enlighten us as to the true meaning of the
Bible, that the Bible is so clear and simple that everybody can understand it without outside help, we may
well be allowed to ask how long this has been the case.
If the Holy Scriptures have always been so easy and
plain for all to understand, how comes it that the
preachers of the New Evangel have only so lately come
to the true understanding of them ? Or did they
perhaps knowingly deceive the people in earlier times ?
And if Scripture is so clear, why then is it understood
so differently by different people, one way by the
Lutherans, another way by the Zwinglians, and still
another way by the Anabaptists ?   And this, moreover,
not in accessory matters, but in essential points which
relate to important articles of the faith and of the holy
Sacraments ! ' Concerning the arbitrary manner in
which the new-religionists proceeded in the interpretation of Holy Scripture, Hoffmeister remarks : ' In
these our dangerous times it happens that each one
invents for him or herself special opinions and beliefs,
and then pretends to find confirmation for them in the
Bible. The result is that there are as many beliefs, or
rather misbeliefs, as there are subtle and erring heads.
Thus Luther tells the Zwinglians—and the Zwinglians

in their turn tell him—that they have not found their opinions and doctrines in the Holy Scriptures or taken them out of them, but that they have put them into them, so that they make themselves masters of the Scriptures and no pupils.' [1]

Telling evidence for the truth of this statement is abundantly supplied by the history of the sixteenth and seventeenth centuries. As the Lutherans abolished the ancient Church on grounds of the Scriptures, so the Calvinists abolished Lutheranism on similar grounds. When, in 1613, the Elector John Sigismund of Brandenburg went over to Calvinism, he said in his confession of faith that he was following the Holy Scriptures. ' This Empress Holy Scripture must rule and govern, and all others, let them call themselves what they will, must be subject and obedient to her, be it the Pope, Luther, Augustine, Paul, or an angel from heaven.' Hence the saying about the Bible :

Hic liber est, in quo sua quaerit dogmata quisque,
Invenit et pariter dogmata quisque sua.' [2]

Luther's opinion that ' there was no clearer book on earth than the Bible ' early met with frequent contradiction from the new-religionists themselves. In 1539 the well-known Sebastian Franck published a pamphlet in which he dwelt emphatically on the difficulty and obscurity of the Bible. It was a book sealed with seven seals, he said ; the seven seals were seven wicked spirits (human fear, human reason, under-

---

[1] Paulus, *Hoffmeister*, pp. 264–265. See in this connexion the utterances of K. Schwenkfeld in Döllinger, i. 271, and in the same place Wizel's complaint concerning the arbitrary treatment of Holy Scripture by the new-religionist preachers.

[2] See present work, vol. x. pp. 303, 304.

standing, opinion, obstinacy, art and worldliness).
Each one of these seals formed a separate obstacle to
the pure understanding of the Scriptures. ' The Bible,'
says Franck, ' is to us a fast-closed hunting-book, from
which we suck nothing but poison, error, lies, darkness
and heresy; because we seat ourselves on it and read this
seven-sealed book through boards, and only gape at it
from outside like fools and monkeys, and imagine to
ourselves and speculate that this, that, and the other
is in it ; so it happens that in the light we still grope
blindly. On the other hand, God has purposely veiled
the Scriptures, His Word, in this language so difficult to
understand. Just as God set a flaming sword to guard
the tree of life, though He did not wish to shut us out
from life, but in order that we might not live for ever in
this desert waste, this darkness, this mortuary and den
of murderers, so, too, God has sealed His Book of life,
Christ and art with seven seals, so that the sows may not
also break into the rose-garden and paradise, and come
to the truth, yea, to the book and tree of life, without
any repentance, living still in their unbelief, which is not
the appointed way that God has ordained ; and therefore
I say God has a special way, and a hidden language of
parables, allegories, enigmatical and suchlike talk, just
as Pythagoras used to talk with his pupils, so that his
words might not be picked up and wasted by dogs and
swine, so that His Word may remain a secret, with His
own people in the school of Christ.' [1]

Not a few Protestants also circulated strong opinions
on the dangers and the abuses of the study of the Bible,
which, according to Luther, was to be the sole source of
knowledge respecting the Christian faith. The Witten-

[1] Erbkam, *Gesch. der protestant. Sekten*, Hamburg, 1848, pp. 295–296.

berg professor Paul Krell uttered in 1560 an emphatic
warning that ' people should not go to the Bible-readings
without having first prepared themselves for them by
studying the writings and instructions of Melanchthon ;
for he himself had found from experience that without
this preparation the study of the Bible was useless ;
or else, as was now happening to the great injury and
detriment of the Church, they would be obliged to
swallow the whole apparatus of Biblical learning which
evil-minded, envious, restless men, under the pretext of
piety and religion, had fabricated for the gratification
of their wild passions and raging lusts.   Herein, indeed,
lay the cause of the terrible religious fighting of the
day ; under the cloak of religion the most despicable
intriguers had placed their tongues at the service of
the great, and they twisted and turned religion according to the pleasure of their patrons.' [1]   The Protestant
satirist Fischart spoke out still more strongly. Holy
Scripture, he says, is nothing but a conjuror's bag—

> ' Wherewith a monkey game they play,
> Each dealing with it his own way,

in consequence of which the common people do not
know what to think or do.' [2]

The confusion in the Protestant camp was still further
augmented by the disputes concerning the texts of
Luther's translations.   Luther had scarcely breathed
his last when these dissensions began.[3]   In 1546

---

[1] Döllinger, *Reformation*, ii. 561.

[2] See present work, vol. xi. pp. 375–376.

[3] Luther had foreseen this ; see Loesche, *Anal. Luth.* p. 304.   The
Zurich Bible also did not escape the fate of arbitrary alteration.   Mezger
(p. 144) says that after the death of the printer Christopher Froschauer,
' Bible printing became more a booksellers' speculation.'   Not only did

Luther's pupil and friend, George Rörer, had published Luther's translation in a new edition. In the 'conclusion' Rörer explained that 'according to the injunction of the dear lord and father Luther,' he had occasionally altered words, sometimes even whole phrases and sentences, especially in Romans and in the First Epistle to the Corinthians, which alterations 'God-fearing men would be well pleased with.' Exactly the opposite was the case. The 'God-fearing men' complained of inroads on another man's property, mutilation of the true bequest, falsification in the interest of the teaching of Melanchthon. The excitement in the strictly Lutheran circles was still greater when, in the years 1548 and 1550, altered editions of the Lutheran Bible appeared, and 'the men who were so zealous for the improvement of the Bible did not shrink from the pious fraud of publishing copies of the edition of 1550 with fresh title-pages, bearing the date 1545, in order that the simple-minded readers might be more easily deceived, and might take this new edition to be identical with the last that had been printed under Luther's supervision.' [1]   When the editions of the ensuing years were found to contain still greater alterations on the text of 1545, the excitement of the strict Lutherans became more and more intense.   'In some of the copies,' wrote George Cölestin, 'words are changed, in some the whole sense, in some paragraphs, in some whole chapters, in some the Prophets, in some the Psalms.   In some copies

there gradually creep in ' a great quantity of mistakes in printing, which were always reprinted, and also always multiplied, but also numbers of arbitrary alterations were introduced into the translation.'

[1] Schott, *Bibelübersetzung*, pp. 153–154. See Herzog's *Realenzyklopädie*, iii. 549 ; Hopf, p. 313 f. ; and *Stimmen aus Maria-Laach*, 1895, i. 106.

whole sentences and fine adages are altered and perverted, in some beautiful words of consolation are quite
left out.   In some the prefaces are changed or left out
and new ones substituted,' and so forth.   This is the way
that ' after Luther's death his Bibles are treated.   If
this had been winked at all along, what sort of a Bible
should our dear children and descendants have in the
end ?   What would become of all Luther's struggles,
entreaties, prayers, admonitions, punishments ? '   In
his memorandum on the falsification of 2 Corinthians iii.,
Cölestin says, ' the new version is full of offence.'   When
the simple-minded Christians begin to observe that this
chapter of St. Paul is wrongly rendered, they will begin
to have doubts about the whole work.   On the other
hand, if we ourselves begin correcting Luther and
instructing him by altering his Biblical text, what will
the popish calumniators not do ?   And who among the
popish laity will not be strengthened in the conviction
that the whole Lutheran Bible is a falsified work ?
Furthermore, the papists will be confirmed in their
calumnious assertion that ' the Lutherans appeal to the
Bible, but that they have no uniform standard, for
no one version coincides with another.'   ' It will also be
said that the Scriptures are so obscure that Luther
himself did not rightly understand them, and still less
was he able rightly to translate them, and that this was
palpably true, as the Lutherans themselves constantly
altered Luther's version.' [1]

The Wittenberg professor, Paul Krell, defended the

[1] J. C. Bertram, *Historische Abhandlung von Unterdrückung der letzten Änderungen Lutheri im teutschen Neuen Testament, bei J. S. Semler* ;
Richard Simon's *Kritische Historie der Übersetzungen des Neuen Testamentes*, part 2.   Translated from the French by H. M. A. Cramer, Halle,
1780, pp. 300 f., 333 ff.

genuineness of the Wittenberg Bibles printed after Luther's death, and fiercely reviled those who fell foul of those editions. In the end the secular authorities also mixed themselves up in this theological strife. The Elector Augustus of Saxony forbade any further printing of the Bible, and ordered an exact revision of it to be made. For this purpose Luther's hand edition, preserved in the Jena library, was made use of. According to the injunctions of the Formula of Concord the Elector issued the following command to the Wittenbergers : ' Whereas it is considered that the edition of the year 1545 coincides the most accurately with the version of the Herr Luther, a printed copy of the Bible shall be taken and corrected according to the edition of 1545, and the Bible shall be printed according to this said correct copy, and in no other way.' But the work of printing had no sooner begun than it was interrupted, because complaints arose that ' if at Wittenberg they had set in hand something new with the Bible, and erased and interpolated as they liked, the book would again be printed falsely and incorrectly.' After a new revision, executed by Mirus and Glaser, orders were again sent to Wittenberg that they were to go on with the printing of the Bible. Finally, in 1581, there appeared the new translation, which professed to have kept as closely as possible to the edition of 1545, but which nevertheless contained many deviations therefrom.[1]

The edition of 1581 ' was to serve as the standard text for all future reprints ; however, outside the Saxon Electorate no one cared for the will of the Elector.' [2]

---

[1] Schott, p. 157 f.   [2] Grimm, p. 39.

The controversy concerning the Lutheran translation of the Bible went on raging with undiminished
fury among the new-religionists. When, in 1587, the
Heidelberg theologian David Pareus came forward
with another fresh edition of the Lutheran Bible, the
Tübingen divinity scholar James Andreä issued a
warning pamphlet, in which he denounced this Bible
as ' a highly punishable, false, and thoroughly devilish
piece of villainy.' For, said he, ' not only had Luther's
prefaces been for the most part omitted, and replaced
by other admonitions which were diametrically opposed
to Luther's wholesome doctrines, but also the false,
heretical and damnable Calvinistic errors had been here
and there most cunningly and mischievously woven into
the principal Christian doctrines ; and whereas Luther's
name was printed on it, so that it might be called
Luther's Bible and be sold as such, this proceeding was
nothing else than falsification of foreign books, con-
cocting false letters, erasing of seals, and might be
summed up as a piece of arch-villainy which ought to be
punished with the gallows by the Christian authorities,
while the falsified Bible ought to be burnt in the fire.' [1]

The orthodox Lutherans were also thrown into
great perturbation by a version of the Bible edited by
the court preacher Salmuth with Calvinistic glosses, the
printing of which began in 1590. It was only through
the circumstance of the Elector Christian's death in 1591,
in consequence of his drunken habits, that this edition
was suppressed. The Lutherans, however, were not
left at rest in this matter. Fresh agitation was caused
by a Bible which appeared at Herborn in 1595. Against
this ' German Bible, interlarded with Calvinistic poison,'

[1] K. A. Menzel, v. 171. See Schott, p. 161, and Hagemann, p. 148.

the Wittenberg theologians forthwith issued ' a true-hearted, necessary and earnest warning to all the evangelical Churches of the German nation.' [1]

The early enthusiasm of the new-religionists for the Lutheran Bible lapsed largely later on into the opposite feeling of indifference. Luther himself in 1540 had expressed anxiety in this respect : ' I am afraid,' he said, ' that people will not read the Bible much, for they are almost tired of it, and no one thinks much about it.' On another occasion he said : ' It has given us labour enough, but it will be little regarded by our people. Our opponents read the translation more than do our own followers.' [2] After Luther's death things were no different in this respect. Paul Krell spoke in 1560 of the general aversion to Bible reading, and the celebrated Marburg theologian Andrew Hyperius expressed his astonishment in 1581 ' that everybody wanted to be called Christian, and yet they were all utterly indolent and indifferent about reading or hearing the Holy Scriptures. Only a very few people had a Bible in the house, and among these few there was seldom one person who had really read the Bible two or three times through in his life ; moreover, there prevailed everywhere a condition of immorality, a contempt of all the restraints of religion and respectability, such as was grievous to behold. Hyperius, accordingly, urged on the authorities that they ought to insist by means of strict legislation that every householder should read, or have read, a few chapters of the Bible every day

---

[1] See Schott, p. 162. A new Bible was published by the reformed Joh. Piscator at Herborn in 1602 ff. See Hagemann, p. 151, and Mezger, p. 285 f.

[2] Loesche, *Anal. Luth.* pp. 82, 251 ; cf. 281.

in his house, and should examine his household in the
portion which had been read. The secular rulers, he
insisted, must not delay in this matter, and they must
make and enforce a law to this effect, so that the people
might acquire a more thorough knowledge of the doctrines of the faith, and that their morals, which in these
unhallowed times were so corrupt and abominable,
might be improved.' [1] ' Although in the present day,'
wrote later on Sigismund Evenius, ' the Bible is printed
in such a convenient and beautiful form, in such fine,
pleasant type, on such beautiful, clean paper, and sold
at such a low price, nevertheless the stinginess and the
devilish greed of gold, and the unreasonable, thought-
less, nay, unchristian, expenditure of worldly goods is
so great among us that, while we spend hundreds and
thousands of thalers on stately buildings, on costly
clothing, and other feminine adornment, and also on
grand entertainments, all purses are fastened close with
iron chains when it is a question of spending one or, at
the outside, a couple of thalers on the acquisition of our
highest and more than golden treasure, and of making
it accessible to our ignorant children.' [2]

[1] Döllinger, *Reformation*, ii. 220, 561.
[2] Evenius, pp. 37–38. For the meagre circulation of the Bible in
Württemberg, where not even every preacher had a German Bible, see
Schnurrer, pp. 178–179. In Brandenburg, at the time of the inspection
in 1600, it was found that some of the village pastors had no Bibles. The
same state of things is recorded in the Nassau Church ordinance of 1609 ;
see Tholuck, *Kirchliches Leben*, p. 112. From this may be concluded how
many among the people possessed Bibles ! ' It must necessarily cause
surprise,' says Löschke (p. 85), ' to see that the place occupied by the Bible
in the schools was an extremely limited one. When, however, we study
the school-plan drawn up by Luther and Melanchthon, it becomes evident
that the reformers themselves did much too little to satisfy this need of
the people which they fully recognised ; nearly the whole of school-time
was devoted to the study of languages, and only a few hours to instruction

in Christianity in general, still fewer to the study of the Holy Scriptures. By the people—so it was said—the German Bible was read diligently, but in the schools it was seldom to be found.' Among the reasons why the Bible was so little read by the young, George Lauterbeck, in an admonitory pamphlet which appeared at Eisleben in 1554, pointed out the following : ' In the first place the young were frightened off by the numerous divisions and sects in Christianity ; this plague of schism and dissension had come to such a pitch that there were scarcely two people to be found holding the same opinions ; each and every one had his own fancies, and the worst of it was that each appealed to the Holy Scriptures.' ' The Divine Holy Scriptures are lying prostrate, despised and reviled ; nobody wants to learn from them, and we ought to be ashamed of ourselves as Christians.' Löschke, pp. 85–86.   ' A *German* Bible in *Latin* schools, in which the pupils were punished if they spoke a word of German to each other—what a contradiction this would be indeed ! The Bible was deficient in the old-fashioned garb which alone was respected.' ' Bible reading outside school-time was recommended by most of the school ordinances, by many of them very urgently ' (p. 87 ff.).

CHAPTER X

PREACHING BY CATHOLICS AND PROTESTANTS

AFTER the spread of the new doctrines and sects there arose a number of eloquent preachers equipped with thorough and comprehensive theological learning, who treated dogmatic truths and moral laws with clearness and insight, and who, out of the fulness of joy in their own faith, sought by their oratory to influence the beliefs and the lives of their hearers. Prominent among these, in the sixteenth century, were Frederick Nausea, cathedral preacher at Mayence, court preacher to King Ferdinand I, and bishop of Vienna; Michael Helding, suffragan bishop of Mayence and bishop of Merseburg; Leonard Haller, suffragan bishop of Eichstätt; James Feucht and John Ertlin, auxiliary bishops of Bamberg; John Nas, bishop of Brixen, and Stanislaus Hosius, bishop of Ermland; the Franciscans John Wild and Michael Anisius; the celebrated Augustinian John Hoffmeister, the Dominicans John Fabri and Ambrose Storch (Pelargus); the Benedictines Quirinus Rest and Wolfgang Sedelius; the Jesuits Peter Canisius, George Scherer and Jeremias Drexel; the secular priests George Wizel, Michael Buchinger, John Rasser and Martin Eisengrein.[1]

---

[1] The 914 pages of sermons of the sixteenth century, published by Von Brischar in the first volume of his most meritorious work, *Die*

The first rank among the above named, as well with regard to the significance as to the number of their works, is undoubtedly occupied by Wild, Scherer and Feucht—all three equally distinguished by a vigorous, pithy style, and by the manly independence of spirit with which they showed up the heavy abuses and crimes among clerical and secular rulers, and took up the cudgels for the poor and the oppressed.

The Franciscan John Wild, since 1539 cathedral preacher at Mayence,[1] published his sermons in a number of treatises, in which he explained separate books of the Old and the New Testament, expounded the truths of the faith fundamentally and clearly, in-stilled the laws of morality in simple, fervent language, and introduced his readers to the whole of Catholic Church life, especially the solemnities of the Church festivals.[2] For holders of other opinions he entertained neither anger nor hatred. When, in 1552, on the con-

---

Katholischen Kanzelredner seit den drei letzten Jahrhunderten, are, as the preface, vii–viii, rightly says, free from coarseness and bad taste. ' Numbers of preachers distinguish themselves by thorough knowledge and profitable application of the Holy Scriptures and the works of the Church Fathers, by making apt use of the maxims, by the way in which they illustrate their subject through examples from profane, Church and Scripture history, by intelligent observation of nature, by the introduction of beautiful similes, symbols and allegories, for which indeed our age has lost almost all interest and understanding, although in earlier times they played an important part.' ' All that was interesting and instructive, these preachers, the best of them at least, made use of, in order to illustrate their subjects on all sides, and to make them intelligible and attractive to their congregations. In this respect, and especially also as regards tenderness, sincerity and depth of religious feeling and beauty of thought, we moderns have much to learn from them.' ** Concerning Hoffmeister as preacher see the admirable monograph of Paulus, pp. 38–68. For Eck's work as preacher, see above, p. 321. Concerning John Rasser see Pfleger's excellent articles in the *Strassburg Diözesanblatt,* 1902, pp. 146 f., 182 f. Concerning Drexel see Riezler, vi. 375 f.

[1] See above, p. 524.   [2] Brischar, i. 243–381.

quest of the town by the Margrave Albert von Brandenburg-Kulmbach, he was driven for a time from his
office, and reviled in the most outrageous manner by
the Lutheran preachers who had possessed themselves
of his pulpit, he showed no resentment, and on his
restoration spoke with the greatest moderation of past
events.   From the very first he chose the Holy Scriptures as the subject of his addresses.   ' I have always,
hitherto, been careful,' he declared in 1552, ' to have
a right basis for my preaching, and I shall go on doing
the same.   Each one of us can build most securely
when he first looks round for a good foundation ; people
will be less inclined to doubt the teaching presented to
them when they see that it is not reared on insecure
ground.   What, however, can be more stable, more
certain, more unfailing than the Holy Scriptures ?   But
these writings must be read with true understanding.
And this true understanding of the Scriptures is not
what each individual derives from his own inner consciousness, or what this, that, or the other spirit
breathes into him, but it is that which the Holy Ghost
has given from the beginning, and in which the
universal, holy Christian Church has uniformly and
harmoniously abided from the time of the Apostles.'

In his synodal sermons of 1549, Wild pointed out
to the bishops and abbots assembled at the synods
at Mayence how little care had been bestowed on the
training of efficient preachers.   ' There is nothing that
the Church can dispense with less than the office of
pastor and preacher, and yet there is nothing that is
thought less about.   In all other matters more care and
attention is given, and we may well wonder whence
comes this criminal neglect and what the leaders of the

Church are thinking about. Now we excuse ourselves
by saying that nobody wants to fill this office, that the
young men will no longer study for a clerical profession,
for abbeys and convents ; above all, that they will not
study theology. This is indeed very true ; that there is
a dearth of candidates all the world sees and knows.
But whose is the fault ? Most certainly theirs who in
the first place let all study go to the ground, and
secondly allow so much genius, so many promising,
studious young people to be wasted, and who offer no
advantages, no fit means of subsistence to scholars.
' Owing to the gross and penal neglect of the prelates,
some of whom have now been many years in the
Church, it has come to this, that there are not only no
magisters from whom the young *clerici* can learn their
business, no doctors of divinity from whom the priests
can get instruction in theology and the Scriptures, but
also the school-men have nothing more than a name
without the thing. What wonder, then, is it that there
is a dearth of learned people ? ' ' By their souls' salvation,' he implored the prelates to attend to their
business, and to make efforts for the training of efficient
preachers. ' Do not let avarice overmaster you in
this matter, do not let self-seeking be the cause that
the Church is robbed of good shepherds and learned
preachers. The Church goods are then best spent—and
to this end they were mostly given—when they serve
for the glory of God, the use of the Church, and the
salvation of souls.' [1]

The Jesuit George Scherer († 1605), who was

---

[1] Kehrein, ii. 114 f. Brischar, i. 306 ff. *Ein Verzeichnis der Predigt-
werke Wilds*, in Kehrein, i. 52. With the complaints of Wild, cf. those of
the Augustinian Hoffmeister in Paulus, p. 39 ff.

indefatigable as theological writer and pulpit orator, published a number of sermons of dogmatic, moral and polemical contents. For lectures of the last sort he laid down in one of his postilles the following 'Christian rule' for preachers : 'Moderation must be observed in attacking and exposing the heretics, whom a Christian preacher should rather endeavour to persuade with right arguments than to vex with many words of scolding and reviling. The archangel Michael would not even vilify the devil, as the Apostle Jude writes in his epistle.' This also was the opinion of Gregory of Nazianzen : not with words of slander and abuse must the antagonists be answered, 'but after the example of the mild and peaceable Lord Christ.' 'In railing, vituperating, abusing, reviling and blaspheming we Catholic preachers must knock under to the sectarian preachers, as it is known to everyone that in this unhallowed art they are powerful masters and far outdo the devil himself. In the presentation of the Catholic faith preachers must excel both in discretion and moderation, especially when dealing with unbelievers and sects.' [1] 'There is no art in slandering and blaspheming, but there is art in preaching the Word of God simply and heartily, in proclaiming the truth with lofty courage, in preserving the same moderation

---

[1] Scherer's *Postill oder Auslegungen der Sonntäglichen Evangelien* (Ursel edition of 1622), Bl. iiii[b].–v.   Cf. Brischar, ii. 6.   ** John Hoffmeister also only embarked reluctantly on religious polemics in the pulpit.   From the very first he chose the Holy Scriptures as the subject of his religious addresses.   ' If here and there some passage of Scripture affords him the opportunity of combating the innovators,' says Paulus (pp. 52–53), ' he does it generally with a few brief words and with dignity and propriety. Only very seldom does he indulge in utterances which would not be tolerated in a preacher to-day.   Hoffmeister was of opinion that the pulpit was not the proper place for slandering and reviling.

towards high and low, in not sparing sins where they are open to the sight, but in reproving them fearlessly whenever the occasion arises.' Such an occasion, for instance, Scherer seized in a discourse at the funeral of a Benedictine monk at Vienna in 1583. He reminded his hearers of the judgment of God on grand prelates who neglected their duties, who lived in pomp and splendour, in gluttony and drinking, who spent or squandered the Church goods for their own benefit, and so ' set a most atrocious and terrible example not only to their fellow-prelates, but also to all the clergy and laity, to believers and unbelievers, to Catholics and sectarians.' 'Furthermore there are prelates who act tyrannically towards their brothers, who, at their caprice, beat, torture, imprison and chain them with fetters ; who maintain no morality and discipline in the convents, who allow everything to go to the bad, punish no vice, shut their eyes to offences, let their pastoral staffs lie idle, and never think of grinding, sharpening and polishing them up.' Others, again, concern themselves little or nothing about the schools, dislike the liberal arts, cannot bear learned people about them, because perhaps they themselves are stupid and ignorant. These people are the cause that, instead of learning and education, nothing but barbarism, pedantry and gross ignorance prevail everywhere. In former times there was no place where study was pursued so zealously as in the convents, where the best and most admirable libraries were found. Nowadays, owing to the ignorance and negligence of some of the prelates, there is often less study in the convents than anywhere else. What few books are still left in the libraries are devoured by mice and moths, buried in dust and

dirt. Since, then, such overseers prefer the darkness
of ignorance to the light of knowledge, it is easy
to reckon that in this state of mind they will not
greatly shine and distinguish themselves, but will go
from darkness to darkness (St. Matt. xxii. 25).' [1]

Equally fearless and outspoken in his zeal against
the abuses and crimes in clerical and secular governments was the Bamberg coadjutor-bishop James
Feucht, a man universally revered by the people for his
apologetic and polemical works, and a true apostle of
the diocese († 1580). Openly before all the people he
scourged ' " the benefice-hunters," who only want the
wool and the milk of the sheep, but who do not trouble
themselves about the sheep themselves, but appoint
hirelings to look after them, to whom they give a
slender portion of their income.' ' Great,' he says, ' is
the responsibility of the bishops who let themselves be
misled by their election capitulations into bestowing
the best pastorates on people ' (on canons of noble
birth, most of them not ordained to priests' Orders)
' who are only on the look out for a lucrative income
without wishing or being able to fulfil the duties connected with it.' ' To some of our indolent bishops
worldly pomp is more important than spiritual rule.
For intelligent people enough has been said to convince
them. In some bishoprics, indeed, religion is in such a
tumble-down condition that it is pitiful to behold. The
bishops wink at it all, just as though they were not
bishops and bound to answer before God.' For the
protection of the people he raised his voice against
' the usurers, flayers and fleecers ' among the ruling
authorities with whom ' upright administration of jus-

[1] Brischar, ii. 123–29.

tice was a rarity.' ' They will not protect and safeguard
the poor widows and orphans as they do the rich. For
the rich, or, as St. James says, for those who wear fine
clothing and have gold rings on their fingers, who use
silver beakers or who can fork out a few gold pieces, lawsuits, even though without a shadow of right in them,
must be settled as quickly as possible in favour of
the wealthy suitors. But the lawsuits of the poor, who
cannot afford to bribe, are allowed to drag on for weeks,
months, even for years. Neither burgomaster nor
councillors have time to think about these. Such cases
neither a burgomaster nor a councillor will take up.
And so, even if their case be the most righteous, the
poor must either submit to losing it or watch its being
spun out to their heavy cost.' ' If the great lords who
are idle all the week through, take it into their heads
to go out hunting or fishing or birdcatching, whole
parishes are summoned to attend on pain of bodily
punishment or fines. Whoever can carry a spear must
sally forth and spend half or the whole of the day, like
an unreasoning brute, scampering through wood and
field, up hill and down hill, without having had any
food or drink, and without having attended divine
service. Is it a question of building a new castle, or
treasure-house or hostel, in this or the other village,
then the people must do service with horse and
waggon and hand labour, till their heartstrings crack,
till the blood oozes out under their nails, and they can
no longer bend or stoop any more.' [1]

Feucht's principal work, ' Grosse Katholische Pos-

---

[1] Feucht, *Sammlung von Predigten*, Cologne, 1574, p. 142 ff. *Grosse
Postille*, Cologne, 1577 and 1578, i[a]. 78, and ii[a]. 31 ff. ; see what he says
about the court folk, ii[a]. 59.

tille,' which appeared first at Cologne in the years 1577 and 1578 in two folio volumes, and then in repeated fresh editions, takes a place of the first rank as regards scholastic knowledge and popular style among the very numerous postille books of the sixteenth century; it characterises the coadjutor-bishop as one of the best German prose writers of that time. His successor the coadjutor-bishop John Ertlin, himself a pulpit orator of sound scholarship and refined feeling, gave an extract from the ' Grosse Postille ' with special respect to sermons on controverted doctrines. ' Wise discretion and a mild and gentle spirit ' would not be found wanting in them, he said, ' whereas with the postilles of the sectarians the opposite was the case.' In the prescriptions which Feucht gave for preaching he said, they must not let a passion for condemnation frighten people off from conversion and from the Catholic faith ; in quite orthodox Catholic places they should not preach about heresies.[1]

The Lenten sermons which the Ermland bishop Stanislaus Hosius [2] composed in 1553, in defence of the Catholic teaching and Church practices, are distinguished alike by their contents and by their clear, concise style, free from all passionateness. ' Whereas our office,' the first sermon begins, ' requires of us that we should proclaim the Word of God to you, I have come to you not with grand words or with lofty wisdom, for I count myself as knowing nothing among you save

[1] Fuller details on Feucht's different works on preaching are given by P. Wittmann, ' Jakob Feucht,' in the *Histor.-polit. Blätter*, lxxxix. 572–582, especially by J. Metzner and John Ertlin, Bamberg, 1886, pp. 36–56, 63–64. ' Eine Anzahl Predigten von Feucht und Ertlin,' in Brischar, i. 544–675.

[2] See above, p. 349.

Jesus Christ and Him crucified.' All our sermons 'must proclaim nothing else save Jesus Christ and Him crucified, to the Jews a stumbling-block, to the Greeks foolishness, but to us who are called the power of God and a divine wisdom.' 'Him also not only unto you, but to all your parents and forefathers of the time when they accepted the faith of the Lord Christ, they have preached with all diligence in the Christian Church.' On the showing of the doctors of the Church, Hosius points out how falsely the new-religionists had attributed to the Catholics a perverted doctrine of salvation by works. 'Nothing else has ever been taught in the Church but that works are only well-pleasing to God, that works are only rewarded by God, when they are done in the faith of our Mediator, our Lord Jesus Christ. Any works done outside of the faith, let them be as excellent and praiseworthy as possible, cannot gain for us eternal life.' 'From this it is obvious how shameless those people are who dare to say that up till now it has been taught in the Catholic Church that our sins are forgiven us, and that we gain the kingdom of heaven by the merit of our own works and not by the merits of Christ. If only they would mention by name anyone who has written like this, anyone who has taught that the works which are done outside of Christ, and directed elsewhere than to Christ, could win for us forgiveness of sins or eternal life. But they cannot name any, because also all the monks write and teach the opposite, that only *those* works are acceptable to God and serviceable to us, which proceed from the Lord Christ and are directed to the Lord Christ. This was the doctrine read by the children and women thirty years ago, at the time when the new sect came into Prussia and spread there.'

With equal ability Hosius deals with the significance
of the Church ceremonial and the Church year, with
confession, communion in one kind, the opponents of
Christ and the most holy Sacrament of the Altar, the
imitation of the Holy Virgin and true penitence and
conversion. Of abuse and vilification of the new-
religionists, after the manner of the Protestant
preachers against the Catholics, there is not the
slightest trace in Hosius.[1]

The same propriety, decency and skill which the
publisher of these sermons praised in the Ermland bishop
abound also in the sermons of the convert Martin
Eisengrein († 1578 as vice-chancellor of the university
of Ingolstadt).[2]

Frederick Nausea, bishop in Vienna since 1541, a
man of powerful eloquence, showed himself in many of
his homiletic and apologetic writings one of the most
thorough dogmaticians and exegetists, and also a perfect master of dialectics.[3] Clearly and vigorously he
sets forth the Catholic teaching on faith and duty,
refutes triumphantly the objections of the opponents,
and brings forward in illustration of his subject a multitude of examples from the history of the world, the
Church and the Saints. He avoided anything in the
shape of rhetorical ornament, as he himself declares,
and ' for two reasons.' ' First, because all my preaching
is nothing of my own, but is all gathered together from
the Holy, Divine Scriptures, and it is sure and certain
that this same Holy Scripture does not need to be

---

[1] F. Hipler, *Die deutschen Predigten und Katechesen der ermländischen
Bischöfe Hosius und Kromer*, pp. 14–20, 33–41.

[2] See the sermons printed in Brischar, i. 435–543.

[3] See above, p. 309 ff.

adorned and embellished with high-flying, flowery, elegant human words and phrases. The word of truth is in itself, and through its divine simplicity, strong, powerful, lovely, friendly, gracious and eloquent enough, and does not need our daubing and embellishing. Secondly, the great and wonderful height and depth of things divine, which are dealt with in these sermons, on account of their greatness and their difficulty, do not allow of any special adornment, whether of words or phrases, such as may well be used for the improvement of oratory in all sorts of human, secular and worldly matters.' [1]

On the whole it may be said of the many hundreds of Catholic sermons printed in the sixteenth century, that they are free from eccentricities, bad taste and coarsenesses. But that much of the preaching of the time was marred by these characteristics is evident from the warnings of George Scherer that ' Preachers must not be buffoons, and tellers of tales and fables, but they must treat God's Word with becoming gravity

[1] J. Metzner, *Friedrich Nausea*, p. 103. Fuller details concerning Nausea's sermons are given at p. 31 ff. At Vienna Nausea preached every Sunday and feast day in the cathedral of St. Stephen. The schoolmaster Wolfgang Schmeltzl says, in his *Lobspruch der Stadt Wien*, of the year 1548 :

> With joy to the temple did I repair,
> A reverent congregation there
> To hear God's Word had gathered ;

> A crowd of many thousand men,
> And Bishop Nausea preached to them,
> As at all times the shepherd good
> Himself gave to his sheep their food.

See Pastor, *Die kirchlichen Reunionsbestrebungen während der Regierung Karls V*, p. 281 ff. ' Would God,' wrote an ecclesiastical prince, ' that there were in Germany forty preachers like Nausea ! One might then hope, according to the view of the Roman King and of many other knowing people, for a tremendous return of converts to the fold.' Pastor, p. 282.

and dignity. There is no harm in occasionally
refreshing and stimulating apathetic listeners with an
amusing story or a saying brought in opportunely ;
but to make a practice of telling obscene tales and all
sorts of tomfoolery in order to attract people and get
an imposing audience, this is absolutely forbidden ;
such proceedings belong not to the pulpit, but to other
places.' Further, ' the preachers, in their sermons,
must not soar high and bring in all sorts of subtle,
recondite matters,' but must address themselves to the
understanding of the common people ; ' to be ostenta-
tious, to philosophise largely, or to be always bringing
in Latin, Greek or Hebrew without any necessity,
this is not for edification, for the common people carry
nothing of it home with them, or at the best only say
that their pastor has preached a powerful sermon,
but if one asks them what the pastor said, they answer,
' I don't know, I could not understand it.' [1] George
Wizel in 1539, in a letter to John von Maltitz, bishop
of Meissen, drew attention as follows to improprieties
of this sort. ' Some preachers frequently introduce
such wretched stuff, such irrelevant subjects, such
useless phantasies, that intelligent hearers are made
quite ill with listening to them. Such men as these,
who quote not only from the Scriptures but also from
the most ancient Fathers, dispute and argue in the
pulpit just as if they were in college.'

' It is in part undoubtedly true,' he says in the
same letter with regard to the preachers of the new
Evangel and their sympathetic reception among the

---

[1] Postill (see above, p. 455 ff.), Bl. 6. Brischar, ii. 9–10. ** Concerning
deterioration in the nature of sermons at the close of the Middle Ages, see
present work, vol. i. p. 41 f.

people, ' that in our days the holy office of preaching
has been somewhat exalted, but would God it might
produce better fruits! Everybody wishes for good
preachers. The wish is praiseworthy, but the choice
of preachers often proves deceptive because everybody
does not know how to judge between good and bad
preachers. For it is verily not a question of fine
sounding speech, but of spirit, understanding and
innocency of life. Still less is it a matter of mocking
and scolding, which is best done by senseless people.
The unlearned laymen want to meddle here too much,
and there is too much desire to give way to them and
to comply with their wishes, which cannot end in good.
With burning tears in our eyes we grieve before God
that nowadays scarcely any sermon is tolerated—I will
not say praised—unless it says what everybody likes
to hear. The preacher may be worldly and of carnal
behaviour, but if he artfully cloaks himself with the
dear Gospel, he is regarded as another Peter or Paul.
If his sermon is couched in worldly, common speech,
if it cringes to the people, snarls at the clergy, stirs to
apostasy, blows the trumpet of freedom, does nothing
but console, promises great things, holds out novelties,
it is praised as the true word in all the streets and
extolled in every house. But if a preacher is somewhat
serious, restrains himself, is self-denying and lives in a
priestly manner, then he must be a Pharisee, and if his
preaching is about penance, repentance, absolution,
the fruits of penance, new birth, new life, good works,
the service of God, baptismal vows, obedience to divine
commands, the discipline of the Church, contempt of
the world, patience under persecution, warfare with
the flesh, the Last Judgment, and so forth, he is popish

and lacerates the consciences of dear, pious men.
Thus this new world can scarcely endure to hear the
old evangelical doctrines.' 'Especially in the great
towns, those preachers hold the first place who best
rebuke the priests, monks and nuns, and without
cessation, and without distinction can ridicule, abuse
and condemn almost everything that used to be held
in the Church some hundred years ago.' [1]

2.

In the Church system of the new-religionists the
sermon was considered the principal element and the
central point of public divine service ; it was therefore
all the more disastrous that, from the first, preaching
assumed a polemical character, and preachers looked
upon religious polemics as their chief task.[2]

It was Luther who stamped this character on
preaching. With all the force of eloquence that was
his he constantly delivered sermons with a view to

---

[1] Kehrein, i. 39–41.

[2] ' Polemising in the pulpit, useless and unfruitful for the most part
as it was, was the favourite hobby-horse of most of the preachers of that
period. At the beginning they fought against living opponents, Calvinists,
Catholics, Jews, Turks, Majorists, and so on. Finally they brought into
pulpit discussion heresies to which no one was any longer inclined, and
they preached, for instance, against Patripassians, Valentinians, Mace-
donians, &c., and by this never-ending pulpit fulmination against the
ancient heretics, which filled the air with dissensions, they did far more
harm than good, for the audiences, instead of receiving the edification
they sought and hoped for, were most of them puzzled and bewildered.'
Schuler, i. 150, and the examples, pp. 269–279. ' They polemised in
the pulpits and thereby left out of sight the chief object of preaching,
Christian edification.' ' This fruitless polemising was regarded as the
chief matter in the religious addresses, and it was considered a sort of
honour to overwhelm the opponents with words of slander and abuse.
Thus melancholy was the outlook as regards the edification of the congregation.' Schenk, pp. 17, 32, 42.

slandering the Catholic Church and its worship, and he insisted that his preachers should ' virulently condemn the papacy and its followers, just like the devil and his kingdom,' that they should curse 'the Pope and his kingdom, blaspheme and abuse it, and never hold their jaws, but preach against it without ceasing,' even if some say that ' all we are capable of is to damn, abuse and vilify the Pope and his followers.' [1] In this way he trained up a race of preachers of whom he himself complained : even those ' who set up for being the best ' knew nothing—very few of them excepted—of the fact that the knowledge of Christ and of His Father alone was eternal life.' ' Pope, monks and nuns, they might all scold as they liked.' [2]

Consciously and systematically the preachers set about to denounce every single Catholic doctrine and religious usage as ' an abomination of idolatry and blasphemy,' and to fill the people with abhorrence of ' the popish synagogue of the devil and the satellites of Satan.' Unceasingly the Catholic doctrines were misrepresented in the most outrageous manner, and the papacy cried down as ' the common work of all the devils.' [3] In the same vulgar language which Fischart

[1] Collected Works, xxiii. 57 ; xxxvi. 410.   ** Cf. also vol. v. p. 94 f. of the present work, and Paulus, *Hoffmeister*, p. 53.

[2] See Döllinger, i. 305. In a school consecration sermon of 1609, John Asseburg at Tangermünde ' described the custom of a Catholic Church or school consecration ; he called the consecrating bishop a *Weibisch-kopf* (woman's head), and he changed the Latin appellation Suffraganeus into Saufraganeus ' (Pohlmann, pp. 295–296), with the remark : ' If in the pulpit before the audience seeking edification they allowed themselves such wretched and feeble facetiousnesses, how must they have talked at social gatherings, in banqueting halls and at public meetings ! '

[3] In our third to the ninth volume we have quoted a number of such sermons, and given passages from them.

used in his 'Bienenkorb,' [1] preachers like John Lauch
and Fabian Heyden mocked and derided from the
pulpit the Holy Mass and its different ceremonies.[2]
One preacher tried to prove from the 'Rosenkranz'
that among the Catholics the number of idols amounted
to 140 ; another declared that even organ-pipes were
sometimes worshipped by them ; a third said that in
the papacy there were not four, but five, six, even seven
gospels.[3] For the comfort of the believers, however,
with all these proclamations of 'popish, more than
heathenish abomination' it was always announced
anew that the downfall of the papacy was at hand.
'The soul will go out of the Roman Antichrist before
his complete downfall,' so preached, for instance, Luke
Osiander in 1589. 'He is putting forth his last strength
now through papal scribes.' 'The Pope exalts himself
above God, for he allows his feet to be kissed.'[4]

In contrast to disunited Protestantism, split up into
countless sects, 'the unity of faith among the Catholics
constantly stared the evangelicals in the face' to the
great annoyance of the preachers. But this 'unity of
faith among the Catholics,' the Tübingen provost and
chancellor James Andreä explained in one of his sermons,
was no mark of the true Church, for among the Jews
also there reigned similar unity : 'Why indeed should
the devil make them disunited ? They, no less than
the Jews, served his will in everything. Therefore the
Jews also find protection under him and live in peace
with one another.' [5]

---

[1] See our remarks, vol. x. pp. 40–51.
[2] See Diefenbach, *Die lutherische Kanzel*, pp. 78, 104–106.
[3] *Ibid.* pp. 83, 100 ff.
[4] *Sieben Predigten*, Tübingen, 1589, pp. 1, 12.
[5] Schuier, i. 273.

It was not only, however, against the Catholics that
the new-religionists polemised ; in a like impassioned
manner, rather indeed even more virulently, they
strove to settle from the pulpit all the innumerable
points of controversy which had arisen in Protestantism.
All the different combatants appealed alike to the
Word of God, and according to their individual interpretation of it denounced their opponents as ' abortions
of the devil ' and handed them over ' to Satan.' Thus,
for instance, in 1567 the Jena professors said that
' Flacius and his colleagues in their pulpits had preached
of nothing else than Synergists, Adiaphorists, Schwenk-
feldians, Majorites, Antinomians, Philipists, Calvinists,
Schwegists, and such like innumerable eccentric sects
whom they only named in order to damn them. Meanwhile the common people have been listening to the
novel and unusual style of preaching and have forgotten
their catechism, and because they do not understand
these strange sects the Churches are left empty and
deserted, God's Word is set aside, and the sermons are
only listened to as a fairy tale, or a fresh piece of news
would be, and afterwards discussed with laughter in
the beer and wine shops ; from all which there has
resulted so much mischief, discontent and uproar that
the ruling authorities have had enough to do to keep
peace.' [1] In a ' Christliche Klagewort ' of 1605 a

[1] Heppe, *Gesch. des deutschen Protestantismus*, i. 75. ' In nearly all
sermons the preachers let fly at the Calvinists and Sacramentarians,
and in all funeral sermons it was stated as something creditable and
worthy of imitation that the departed detested the Calvinists from the
bottom of his heart, and fought against them.' Schuler, i. 123. The
famous Königsberg preacher, Sebastian Artomedes, in his sermons on
the Last Supper (1590), described the Calvinists as ' raging army of the
devil ' ; 'he packed these sophists, distorters and dancers off to the devil.'
' The miserable pagan Ovid was a better theologian than our Calvinists ;

Protestant says : ' The great majority of the preachers
have become so incensed with anger and hatred, that
there is no town, scarcely even a village, where the
chief part of the sermon on Sundays and high festivals
is not taken up with slandering and bedevilling, or at
any rate with all sorts of subtle disputations which the
masses of the people cannot understand, and which are
only ridiculed by them, or else which give occasion for
disputing and quarrelling among the young.' There
is common complaining of ' the wildness, the disputa-
tiousness, the unruliness and general viciousness of the
young, and it is manifest to the sight of all ; but those
who complain are themselves chiefly to blame because
they cashier and send to the devil everybody who will
not dance exactly to their piping, and they teach the
young to do the same. And every tenth word they
utter is " devil," whereby they do unutterable harm and
mischief. And if the princely lords and councillors
attempt to put a bit in their mouths and to forbid this
slandering and abusing from public pulpits, the whole
lot of them cry out that the authorities are trying to
stop the reign of the Holy Spirit, and that they (the
preachers) cannot desist from exercising their office of
Christian punishment. Hence, then, between preachers
and rulers and their councillors there is no less quarrelling and strife than among the preachers themselves,
and everybody can hear everywhere with what honourable titles they load each other, so that it is verily a
shame and disgrace that all this should go on openly
before the eyes of the common people.' ' What sort of
respect,' the ' Klagewort ' goes on, ' can the people

if these villains are not villains, then turnips are not turnips '
(pp. 274–277).

have for the preachers, teachers, superintendents and other Church ministers when they hear and read how these gentlemen slang and bedevil each other and drag each other in the mud ? There is nothing too abominable for them to say and write about each other.' [1]

Not less injurious in its effect on the people than the never-ending pulpit polemics was the constant insistence in sermons innumerable on the doctrine of faith alone as opposed to good works. There were actually preachers high in esteem who did not scruple

[1] See our remarks, vol. x. pp. 256–280, where there are fuller proofs of the truth of the state of things described in the *Klagewort*. Other *Klageworte* (Lamentations) of Protestants on the prevalent polemical nature of the sermons are discussed by Döllinger, ii. 700–704, where reference is made in the notes to several utterances in this same volume. Concerning the effects of pulpit polemics, Döllinger says (ii. 699) : ' In all directions we find attention drawn to the influx of cursing, swearing, and blaspheming among the people after the Reformation, as to a strongly marked feature of the age. The writings during the whole period from 1525 to the end of the century are full of complaints on this score.' ' This state of things was partly a result of the general religious deterioration and decay, partly also due to the method introduced by Luther and the reformers of representing everything hitherto held sacred by the people, or (like the Mass) regarded as the central point of divine worship, as a network of Satanic abomination, and of the terrible curses and anathemas, the bitter scorn and mockery, with which the people were deluged year in, year out from the pulpit, and which were hurled at everything that had till then been hedged round with religious sanctity. The controversies carried on between Zwinglians, Melanchthonians, and Calvinists on the one hand and Lutherans on the other, about the Lord's Supper and the Person of Christ, and the means used to stir up all the passions of the people and to turn them into weapons in this fight, the disputations that went on in drinking taverns and in family life on religious controversial questions—all this put together naturally produced that deadening of all finer religious feeling, that growing spirit of coarse familiarity and contempt, which was manifestly taking the place of the former reverential awe, and which led the people, in moments of passion and even in ordinary conversation, to abuse and desecrate even the Person of the Redeemer and all the holy things which their minds and ears were accustomed to associate with the cursings of the preachers.'

openly to declare the doctrine, ' Good works are injurious to salvation.' [1]   Like the Wittenberg castle
preacher George Major, the Lutheran jurist Melchior
von Ossa also ascribed to sermons of this sort the fact
that ' the people were becoming altogether coarse and
wanton, so that there was neither loyalty, honour nor
faith left among the masses, but only wickedness and
vice, rampant everywhere.' ' Many of the preachers,'
he says in another place, ' and the greater number in
the villages, only tickle the ears of the people with the
preaching of grace, and take away their faith in good
earnest works, commanded by God, so that these
good works become quite hateful to the people.' ' It
is plain to sight how coarse, bold and insolent the
people are being made in this way.' [2]

The result of this sort of preaching was that the
people, as the preachers times innumerable complained,
' do not want to hear anything more about Christian
law and good works.' ' When they are told,' wrote
George Major, from long experience, in 1553 and 1558,
' that through grace alone, without any works of our
own, we are justified and saved by faith only, they
won't listen to anything about law and good works ;
they are hostile to all sermons on these matters and
will not put up with them. The majority of mankind
have now become Epicureans, they believe in no divine
punishment, laugh at all reminders of a future judgment and eternal punishment, and regard them as
fables.' [3] For ' zealous preachers,' said the Meissen

---

[1] See our remarks, vol. vii. p. 18 ff.
[2] Von Langenn, *M. v. Ossa*, pp. 114, 155.
[3] Döllinger, ii. 167, 172 ; iii. 493 ff.

superintendent Gregory Strigenicius in his sermons
on the Book of Jonah, 'the people do not care.' It
has come to this that when punishment is inflicted
for vices, especially for gross ones such as gluttony
and drunkenness, adultery and so on, even those who
pretend to be good Christians look angry and show
disapproval, and either deride such necessary punishment and mock the preachers, or else become bitterly
inimical towards them. Hence it is 'nowadays a
special preachers' complaint: the longer we preach
the worse the people become.' [1]   Only 'a small handful,'
said Hartmann Braun, pastor at Grünberg in Hesse,
in 1610, 'go to church.' During divine service 'most
of them run about in the fields; some loaf about outside
the public halls, buying and selling, and quarrelling
with each other; others sit in the taverns, others in
harlots' houses, others crouch and hide in corners to
gamble; . . . they curse and swear like very devils'
children, and declare they'll do away with all preaching
about law.   O Germany, what great misfortunes
must befall thee for all this!' [2]   'These mocking-birds
and wild finches, the Epicurean and Sadducean swinish
folk,' he said in another place, 'have their own special
language.' The one says 'Quid Bibel? Babel. What
are the five books of Moses to me? Had I only five
fine villages!' Another says 'What for should I
sing the Psalms? Had I only palms and salmon!
What is the Litany? A wretched priest's howling.'
Another: 'What is God? I'd rather have gold.'
Another: 'The resurrection of the dead is a knavish

---

[1] Strigenicius, *Jonas*, pp. 33*b*, 59*b*, 342.

[2] *Der Christen Kirchgang*, Giessen, 1610, Bl. D 2*b*.   Cf. Diefenbach,
p. 56, and the *Klagerufe anderer Prediger*, p. 38 ff.   ** For Braun's *Wetter-
predigten*, see Niedner, *Zeitschrift für histor. Theol.* xliv. 422.

delirium.' Another : ' *Gestorben, gar verdorben* ; eat, drink and make merry ; after death there is no more pleasure.' 'Hell is planted with turnips ; catch what you can, what you catch you have ; where a profit is to be made there is no cause for shame ; be just to no man and get rich.' 'Such talk and more of it the devils' children and hell firebrands carry on together.'[1]

In order to attract the people to church and enchain their attention, the preachers filled their sermons with all sorts of ' strange and wonderful matter,' with fables and old wives' tales.[2] ' The people,' George Rollenhagen complained in 1595, ' will scarcely listen to any sermons or read any postilles which are not patched up with wonderful stories, fables and parables like a beggar's cloak. '[3]

' Wonderful stories ' of this sort abound especially in the sermons ' Von den heiligen Engeln und vom Teufel,' which the Wittenberg preacher Sebastian Fröschel published in 1563. He relates, among other things, how the devil constantly stole the butter out of the butter tub of the superintendent's wife, till at last Bugenhagen seated himself on the tub, and punished the devil so effectually that he never wished to come again.[4]   The preacher Sebastian Artomedes at Königs-

---

[1] *Proverbium Christi :* Where the carcase is the eagles flock together. Giessen, 1609, pp. 34–36.

[2] The following is not an isolated complaint : ' Plenus est sermo insipidis historiolis, vel potius fabellis anilibus ad usus homileticos maximam partem accommodatis.' Schmidt, p. 67.

[3] Preface to the *Froschmäuseler*. The people, wrote Nicholas Selnekker, are only attentive to the sermons when ' something wonderful, strange, or controversial is preached.' ' Those who preach simply and plainly are of no account.' Döllinger, ii. 347.

[4] ** Frösche, *Von den heiligen Engeln. Vom Teufel. Und der Menschen Seele. Drey Sermon*, Wittenberg, 1563, K. S.   See Schuler, i. 130, note.

berg, in a sermon on the Lord's Supper, preached in 1590, told how the theologian Carlstadt had been put an end to by the devil. The preacher Karl Sauerborn described to his congregation how ' wonderfully and visibly ' the devil had repeatedly appeared to a Protestant prince, now as a dog, now as a cat, ' which talked with a human voice.' [1] Another favourite theme for sermons was ' the wonderful and terrible arts of witches.' [2]

' The people,' said Hartmut Eisel in a sermon of 1562, ' are so unaccustomed to the pure, simple food of the gospel, and have grown so weary of it and disgusted with it that, with the exception of a few godly old wives and young women, they cannot be got to go to church, unless the preachers relate to them all sorts of wonderful tales of rare apparitions in heaven and earth, of blood-rain, abortions, enchanters, and devil's brides, bodily appearances of the devil, and so forth ; then they prick up their ears and listen, but just in the same way as if they were listening to tales of the marvels of the Venusberg ; they are not improved by what they hear, and only laugh about it on the tavern benches. They come again the following Sunday only to hear more of this ear-tickling, blood-curdling stuff ; and if the preacher fails in the supply and cannot give them any more tales, they say, " The parson's an old dunce, he has outpreached himself," and the church soon becomes empty and deserted.' [3]

All the latest news, all the town gossip, was frequently woven into the sermons, as well as the personal

---

[1] See our remarks, vol. xii. p. 372 ff.

[2] The subject of witches is dealt with more fully in vol. viii. (German) of this work. (The English translation of vol. viii. is not yet out.)

[3] *Histor.-polit. Blätter*, ci. 182–183.

experiences, happy or unhappy, of the preachers themselves ; one special theme was the everlasting complaints as to insufficient remuneration.[1]

' I will not worry you with my complaints and
grievances,' said the pastor Melchior Hamberger in his
Whitsunday sermon in 1561, ' although, as you your-
selves well know, with a sick wife and seven children
I cannot even afford dry bread ; I will not speak to you
about myself and my wife nor entertain you with other
worldly details, but I will preach to you of the Holy
Ghost, who should dwell in us all, so that it may not be
said of me as is said of so many other preachers : " When
the people come out of church, instead of having heard
about the holy Evangel, they have often heard little
else than strange and ridiculous tales, or at any rate
only about unspiritual, worldly matters." ' [2] Professor
John Mülmann at Leipzig in his sermons on the
' Melancholische Trauergeist und Herzfresser,' enumerated the different means to be used against ' constipation of the bowels which was the chief cause of
melancholy.' [3] Martin Bohemus, preacher at Lauben
in the Oberlausitz, delivered no less than twenty-three
sermons on the human body : on the head, the hair, the
skin, the flesh, the bones, the veins, the eyes, ears and
nose, the fingers and nails, the stomach and the navel,
the spleen and the bladder. He added two sermons
on the human soul, what it was, whether every man
had a soul of his own, how many souls each one had,

---

[1] Tholuck, *Kirchliches Leben*, i. 140–141.

[2] *Pfingstpredig*, Leipzig, 1561, p. 2. The Lutheran pastor at Langen-
prozelten once, in 1551, held himself and his wife up as models for the
congregation, but his wife at once gave him publicly the lie. *Archiv
des histor. Vereins für Unterfranken*, Heft xix. 2. pp. 123–124.

[3] *Flagellum Antimelancholicum*, Leipzig, 1618, p. 27.

and in what part of the body it dwelt. [1] In connexion
with St. Matthew x. 30, Andrew Schopp, pastor at
Wernigerode, preached as follows : ' First, as to the
origin, nature, form and natural characteristics of our
hair ; secondly, as to the right use of human hair ;
thirdly, as to the memories, warnings, admonitions
and consolation which proceed from the hair; fourthly,
how to treat and use it in a Christian manner.' [2]

Another degenerate type of preaching consisted in
those prolix addresses, dealing partly with single books
of Scripture, partly with other matter of all sorts, and
which, while professing a practical aim, not seldom

[1] Bohemus in the second and third part of the *Theologica contemplatio·*
The sermons on the body comprise 455 pages, those on the soul 41 pages.

[2] Tholuck, *Kirchliches Leben*, p. 136. Concerning other extraordinary
sermons see Schenk, pp. 36–38, 70 ; Diefenbach, *Die lutherische Kanzel*,
pp. 153–182. ** Carpzov preached through a whole year on Christ as
our true hand-worker, showing in special sermons how He was the best
cloth-maker, the best lantern-maker, the best upholsterer. Dietrich
called Christ the best chimney-sweep, dealing first with the chimney-
sweep, secondly with the way of getting rid of soot, thirdly with the
broom. Kahnis, p. 114. In an *Adlerspredigt* (Tübingen, 1590. Complete
title in Goedeke, ii. 387) the pastor, Thomas Birk, at Untertürkheim, in
Württemberg, discussed as follows the passage ' Where the carcase is,
there will the eagles be gathered together.' ' Why Christ was called a
carcase,' and refuted the objection that the Holy Lord's Supper was not
to be called a carcase. He added to his sermon a sacred Eagle-song, to
be sung to seven melodies. Christians, he said, should be diligent in
attending the Lord's Supper :

> Because the eternal God,
> The heavenly carcase and soul's food,
> Has therein before us placed
> In a mysterious way.
>
> .   .   .   .   .
>
> Although in cuckoo fashion
> The children of the world set little
> Store by this most gracious meal
>
> .   .   .   .   .
>
> When they should visit the church
> They hide and drink instead their field and eke their house.

digressed into the most extraordinary expositions, and by their length and prosiness could only have a wearisome effect on the listeners.[1]

To this class belong in part the 171 sermons which James Stöcker, dean at the town church of Jena, preached in the years 1609–1612 on the Book of Jesus Sirach : they cover 1100 printed folio pages.[2] Infinitely more discursive is the Meissen cathedral preacher Gregory Strigenicius in his 100 sermons on the Flood, which he published in 1613 and which cover 1480 folio pages. Eighteen pages are occupied with the description of the ' entry of the irrational creatures ' into the ark, ' all the wonderful and strange things that occurred during this entry,' why God allowed ' this entry to take place publicly,' and ' how it came to pass that the irrational creatures placed themselves in position so obediently.'[3] Not till the ninety-fourth sermon does he come to the point of : ' When the flood came and how it gained the upper hand.'[4]

The ninety-first sermon is of special interest from the point of view of contemporary history, as it discusses the low esteem in which the married clergy and their families were held in the parishes.

---

[1] Falling asleep in church was the natural consequence of such preaching, and naps during sermon time were such common occurrences that Major, in the funeral sermon on J. Gerhard, said : ' This great man was never seen to be asleep in church ' (Tholuck, *Kirchliches Leben*, p. 144). In 1616, at Arnstadt, the proposal was made to appoint a special official for the purpose of waking up sleepers in church. (*Neue Beiträge von alten und neuen theologischen Sachen* [1750], p. 447.) These ' awakeners ' were armed with sticks (cf. *Altenburger Kirchenordnung vom Jahre* 1705, p. 21). In the church ordinance of Hall, says Brenz, in 1526, ' in the afternoon there were more people asleep than awake in church.'

[2] *Spiegel christlicher Hausszucht Jesus Sirachs*, &c., Jhena, 1616.

[3] *Diluvium*, pp. 586b–605.

[4] Pp. 664–669.

Luther had repeatedly complained that ' the Church ministers who live in the married state are despised, the clergy have become a curse, a scourge, a mockery, and a bane to all people.[1] The jurists would not recognise the marriages of priests as valid, nor their children as legitimate and lawful heirs.[2] In 1573 the Elector John George of Brandenburg was obliged to issue the following command : ' The wedded wives and the children of pastors and clergymen shall be entitled to the same rights and liberties as the children of other married couples.' The conjugal state was allowed to the clergy as well as to the laity, and was therefore true wedlock. Therefore ' the wedded wives, and the children of the clergy and the pastors, were entitled to enjoy inheritance, succession, heritage and rights of heirship, and all other privileges and liberties bestowed by the constitution of the land as well as other people.' [3]

Nevertheless the Protestant people still retained to a great extent their dislike of married priests (*beweibte Priester*) ; many parents were very reluctant to let their daughters marry preachers, and even among the wives of preachers doubts sometimes arose as to whether their marriage was valid. Hence Strigenicius took care to praise those families which, like Noah and his sons, had entered into a marriage bond. Noah, he said, was ' a preacher of the pure religion,' the ' race of parsons ' had been just as much detested in his time as it was now. ' The preachers and the ministers of the Divine Word are still despised, and no name is more mocked and ridiculed than that of priest. Many

---

[1] See the numerous utterances of Luther on the contempt of the preachers in Döllinger, i. 312 ff.

[2] See our remarks above, p. 4, 5 f.   [3] Mylius, i[a]. 302.

people imagine that the priests are not so good and honourable as other people, and not worthy mates for the children of respectable people. Many think it a great disgrace that they should be expected to be friends with preachers and ministers of God's Word, and to give them one of their children in marriage. Hence some of our squires, burghers and peasants have the audacity to say: " It would be an everlasting disgrace on my friends, if I were to give my daughter to a preacher." Now, however, they could see plainly from the history of Noah and his sons that the priests and preachers had always had lawful wives.' ' It will be a source of great comfort to all wives of priests to know that even if they are despised by the world, they are nevertheless living in a holy estate and order.' ' It is comforting also for those who are friends with the ministers of the Church. The devil often puts all sorts of ideas into the minds of pious parents, but in opposition to this they should observe that the marriage of priests is well pleasing to God, and that in the sin-flood the only people he wished to save were the children and wives of priests, through whom the whole human race was to be again renewed and propagated.' Noah, as a preacher of righteousness, was ' mocked and ridiculed by the world ; his children must have been looked on only as children of priests by the children of the world ; he and his belongings must have been a bye-word to everybody,' but God showed him such high honour that out of respect for him, instead of deputing the angels, His heavenly court attendants, to close the door of the ark for him, He Himself became personally Noah's ' attendant and door-keeper, and waited on him Himself.' ' That indeed was something wonderful and high and great, and not to be lightly esteemed that the Lord, the eternal Son of God, Himself took this charge upon Him and shut the door behind Noah. Such a door-keeper was never before or after heard of by anyone.' [1]

Before his sermons on the Flood, Gregory Strigenicius had treated the history of the prophet Jonah in 122 sermons. In 1595 he dedicated these to three dukes of Saxony, with instructions to the estate of princes in which, among other things, he says : 'Under the papacy it was taught, forsooth, that no prince could die in a state of salvation and attain to heaven.' [2] Two editions of the work appeared in 1602, and a third in 1619, covering 918 folio pages. The explanation of the passage 'But the Lord sent out a great wind into the sea, and there was a mighty tempest in the sea ' (Jonah i. 4) covers nearly eighty folio pages.[3] Seven folio pages are filled with the discussion of 'What Jonah did during his three days in the whale's belly.' [4] To the five words, 'Unto Jonah son of Amittai ' four sermons are devoted.

Cyriacus Spangenberg preached whole sermons on the titles, the greatness and the signatures of the Apostles.[5] It was by no means rare for preachers to spend a whole hour on one single name, and to dwell on the origin, the native land, the age, the manner of life, the residence, &c., of the person in question. In

---

[1] *Diluvium,* pp. 636–641, 647.

[2] Strigenicius, *Jonas* ; Vorrede, Bl. A 2ᵇ.   At Bl. 35ᵇ it says, 'If Luther had not stood up against Rome, in fifty years all the secular chiefs would have become ecclesiastics.'

[3] Bl. 79–120. *Ein wahrhaftiger Bericht,* concerning a storm, which on July 5, 1582, devastated the village of Rockhausen, takes 4½ folio pages. Bl. 95ᵃ–97ᵇ.

[4] Bl. 249–252ᵇ.   [5] Schmidt, *Gesch. der Predigt,* p. 64.

like manner they often discussed landscapes, mountains, rivers and gardens.[1] John Matthesius, pastor at Joachimsthal, delivered sixteen mine sermons, 'in which he spoke of all sorts of mining work and metals, their nature and quality, and how they could be turned to profit and use, with excellent and instructive explanations of all that is said in Holy Scripture about metals, and how the Holy Ghost has symbolised the articles of our Christian faith in metals and mining work.'[2] James Herrenschmidt, preacher at Öttingen, explained, in 1610, in his Whitsuntide sermon, why the Holy Ghost had appeared to 'all Christians for their necessary instruction' in the shape of a dove. 'First,' he said, 'the dove is a sort of bird that is not always spreading out his shining wings like a proud, painted peacock, or always swimming in the water and delights like a mad goose, or always hurrying after prey like a devouring raven, but it sits always on a simple little twig and there it often coos the whole day long. Such is the nature and way of the lovely winged dove, the Holy Ghost.' In heaven, he told his audience, 'the buildings are adorned with beautiful pearls, the rooms are artistically gilded and decked with fine precious stones, the streets are paved with pure gold as with glass; there is no dirt in them, no dung-heaps,' and so forth.[3]

Luther had laid down many excellent rules for useful pulpit discourses, and in his own sermons he had spoken in a style adapted to the people, vigorously and to the point. A preacher, he insisted, should not

---

[1] Schuler, i. 262. Schenk, p. 28.

[2] *Bergpostilla*, pp. 1–205[b]. ** See vol. xiii. pp. 505–507.

[3] Herrenschmidt, *Spiritus adveniens or The Christian Whitsun Sermons*, Wittenberg, 1610, Bl. B 4–C. G 2–G 3.

affect 'out-of-the-way scholarship, he should not use
Hebrew, Greek, or other foreign languages ; in church,
as at home in the house, the simple mother tongue
which everyone knows and understands should be
spoken.' [1] Soon, however, the same degenerate taste
which the Jesuit George Scherer had combated among
the Catholics set in among the preachers.[2] They
wanted to give their sermons a learned colouring,
and fell thereby, as was the case with the university professors in their lectures, too frequently into
mere pedantry, in which, according to the complaint
of a theologian, 'nothing of true godliness was to
be seen.' [3] All sorts of sayings from the Latin and
Greek classics were woven into the sermons. 'Very
ill,' said the Saxon Electoral court preacher Paul Jenisch
in 1610, at the grave of his colleague Polycarp Leiser,
'very ill could the dear man brook that a preacher
should adopt the new, strange, unwonted manner of
preaching, in which Plato, Xenophon, Pausanias,
Plutarch, Plautus, Terence, and other Ethnicorum
Sententiae, apothegmata, and such like ornaments
and fillings were introduced.' [4] In funeral sermons the
preachers were wont to allude to statements by Plato
and Juvenal in order to warn their hearers to be mindful
of death.[5] In a 'Christliche Trost- und Leichpredigt,'
which the pastor John Wecker delivered in 1611 on
Frau Martha von Gemmingen, it was shown from
Herodotus, Aristotle, Aelian, Herodian and other
authors, that the old pagans also lamented their dead.

[1] Schuler, i. 40 ff., 81 ff.   [2] See above, p. 463
[3] Schuler, i. 151, note.
[4] *Eine christliche Predigt*, &c.   Dresden, 1610, Bl. A 2 (nach E).
[5] Curtze, pp. 309–310.

This sermon must have lasted for hours, for it filled
sixty-four pages of print, besides fourteen pages which
were taken up with a ' blessing and last farewell,' and
eighteen pages of preface.[1]

Of equal, or even greater compass, were often the
numerous discourses held over defunct princes and
princesses. Caspar Ulrich, pastor at Zerbst, in 1610,
lamented Prince Frederick Maurice of Anhalt in a
sermon which filled eighty-six pages of print ; [2] at the
burial of the Saxon duchess Dorothea Susanna in
1592, the Weimar superintendent-general Antonius
Probus made a speech of more than seventy-five quarto
pages of print ; in honour of the dead woman, papists,
Calvinists and Sacramentarians were fiercely abused
in this discourse.[3]

Every death of a prince, great or small, was represented by the funeral orators as a special punishment
of God. 'We have lost,' said, for instance, Jacob
Runge in 1592, over the corpse of Duke Ernest Louis
of Pommernstettin, ' we have lost our Christian Church
Father, the pious father of our land, the house-father
of us all, our protector, our guardian, our chief, the
crown of our heads. And it is because of our sins and
ingratitude that God has taken him from us. God
Himself says in His Word that the subjects are the
cause of their sovereign's untimely death. We have
received our bread daily from the hand of his princely
grace, we have been fed and clothed by him.' [4] Eberhard

---

[1] Tübingen, 1611. Concerning all sorts of sermons which lasted from
two to four hours, see Diefenbach, p. 195.

[2] *Betrachtung bei Bestattung des Fürsten*, &c., Zerbst, 1610.

[3] *Symbolum Dorotheae Susannae*, &c., Jhena, 1592.

[4] Biederstedt, *Geist des pommerisch-rügenschen Predigtwesens*, Stralsund, 1821, pp. 4–5, 7.

Bidembach, Lutheran abbot at Bebenhausen, in his funeral discourse on Duke Christopher of Württemberg expressed the fear that ' God would take away all happiness and prosperity with this prince, and send all sorts of misfortune.' [1] The death of the Count Palatine John Casimir, in 1592, was interpreted in a similar manner by the Calvinist preacher John Strack. Mountains and valleys, foliage and grass, he said, would not be watered with dew again until, with him, they had bewailed the death of this ' Anointed of the Lord.' [2]

How greatly taste went astray in funeral sermons (' which all the world insisted on having preached for their dead ') in other respects also, is seen, for instance, from a sermon over a child of three years old, which the Rostock superintendent Luke Bacmeister preached in 1613, and had printed.[3] The pastor Jeremias Herfard. in 1618 preached a sermon on a stillborn son of Hans Wolf auf Pulsnitz, and described the course of the child's life.[4]

Soon also, even among the best preachers, a sickly jocose style came into vogue. The pious Valerius Herberger, preacher at Fraustadt, to whom it was a matter of most serious earnest to edify and improve his hearers, published in 1611, in six parts, a book entitled ' Geistliche Trauerbinden gewirket von lauter

---

[1] *Eine christlich tröstliche Predigt über weiland Christoph*, &c., Tübingen, 1569.

[2] *Eine christliche Leichpredigt über den Tod Joh. Kasimirs*, &c., Heidelberg, 1592.

[3] Franck, *Buch* 12, p. 173.

[4] Fraustadt, i^b . 550. A. Weyermann (*Nachrichten von Gelehrten*, &c., Ulm, 1798) gives the following account (p. 563) from a manuscript document : ' The preacher Christian Ziegler, in 1661, fell into disgrace with the widowed Frau Maria Polyxena von Geitzkofler, because he would not preach a funeral sermon on her deceased lapdog, and lost his post in consequence.'

erlesenen, schönen, körnigen, saftigen, schmackhaftigen, tröstlichen Leichpredigten.' For one funeral sermon on a young girl he took as text the old Catholic Christmas hymn which had passed into the Protestant collection, ' Ein Kindelein so löblich,' and explained how ' our children also in their last hours may trust in the new-born child Jesus, as is shown in this beautiful little song.' ' We consider this hymn,' he said, ' quite equal to the Holy Scriptures, for all the words in it are taken from the Bible. Our dear forefathers, like the bees in the meadows, flew about among all the Christmas roses with beautiful thoughts, and have gathered their Christ-honey in the little hive of this carol. This little song is a tasty, sweet and strong cordial, composed of all the little Christmas flowers in Holy Scripture.' In other funeral sermons he expatiated on such themes as ' A spiritual, strong conserve of roses for consumptive people, prepared from some of the consolation roses of the 39th Psalm ' ; ' A spiritual little hayrick, made up of faded human grass and stock gilliflowers ' ; ' Marzipan and heavenly bread for weeping parents, when they mourn for their dead children.' [1]

A funeral sermon of the Wittenberg preacher Röber bears the title ' Rosen- und Blumengeheimnis.' To his ' Christpredigt,' of the year 1615, Röber gave the title ' Des holdseligen lieben Jesuleins und Immanuels himmlisch Geburtszeichen oder prophetische Himmelsfigur ' ; he drew a parallel between the leading ideas of the text and horoscopic destinies.[2]

---

[1] Schuler, i. 292–296. Rhymes of all sorts strung together were also used as a means of riveting the attention of congregations ; examples of this are given by Diefenbach, p. 194.

[2] Tholuck, *Geist der Theologen Wittenbergs*, pp. 87–89 ; *Kirchliches Leben*, p. 137.

Christian morality was seldom dealt with from the pulpit. John Brenz was well-nigh the only important preacher who gave any attention to morals in his addresses, the only one, indeed, in the course of the whole century who devoted whole sermons to the general duties of men and of Christians, as well as to the special duties of particular vocations, and who took pains to connect dogmatic matter with practical life.[1]

Respecting offences against morality, which occurred in sermons, the Hessian preacher Hartmann Braun says : ' It is a bad thing when preachers have an unrestrained mouth, and do not spare modest ears, not only at drinking bouts, but even in the pulpit. Unchaste living, and unchaste, indecent words disfigure the sacred ministry and cause it to have a bad name.' [2] In 1591 there appeared a second edition of the ' Katechismus-oder Kinderpredigt,' for the Brandenburg-Ansbach land, ' collected and compiled for the great need of the young and simple children.' Each of the sermons deals with one of the Ten Commandments. In the sixth, the vices of whoredom and adultery are put forcibly before the eyes of the ' children.' Then it is said plainly ' Those who carry on whoredom are not proof against adultery. . . . this you will come to understand in good time ; for the present it is too difficult and high for you.' [3]

In spite of all the improprieties of the new pulpit oratory, all the confusion and bewilderment caused by the never-ending polemics and the zeal against the old-Church doctrine of good works, amid all the corruption of

---

[1] Schuler, i. 84–85. Schmidt, *Gesch. der Predigt*, p. 45.
[2] Hartmann Braun, *Zehn christliche Predigten*, pp. 85–86.
[3] Müller's *Zeitschr. für Kulturgesch.* Jahrg. 1874, p. 388.

taste passing from public life into preaching, and through preaching reacting again on life, it cannot be denied that a considerable portion of the sermon-literature which has come down to us is governed by a deeply earnest, religious spirit. Men like the distinguished Marburg theologians Andrew Hyperius and Nicholas Hemming, a pulpit of Melanchthon, gave the preachers much wise advice in their homiletics on Christian instruction, and the edification of congregations.[1]   Not a few of the preachers recalled to mind the superiority of the earlier Catholic times.

'Our ancestors under the papacy,' so preached, for instance, James Stöcker at Jena, 'always fasted on the evening before a high festival'; those intending to go to the Sacrament kept themselves strictly temperate and sober, so that they might better contemplate the high work of the redemption of the human race, and be able more heartily to thank the Son of God for it, as, indeed, is the duty of all Christ-believing children of God, and incumbent on their vocation. In what sort of way, however, we behave in this respect to-day is daily present to the sight, for each one says "We praise indeed the old world, but we live as it pleases ourselves." The nearer the holy season, and the more there is to be accomplished on behalf of our vocation, the more the world gets into our heads; they think there is no more need for them to be sober and temperate, and many of them drink and swill till past midnight; the rest rampage and play the fool about the streets, so that they are fit for nothing the next day.'[2]   'Under the papacy, most people before the time for work went early to hear Mass, neither master nor journeyman omitted this;

---

[1] Cf. Schuler, i. 95–112.   [2] *Spiegel christl. Hausszucht*, p. 335.

but nowadays artisans and labourers can scarcely stop working even to go to church once a week—early on Sunday for instance; if they were to stay to hear a sermon it would be too much time wasted from work, but if they often lie two or three days drunk in a beer or wine tavern, this does not injure their work!'[1] The preacher Sebastian Artomedes, at Königsberg, spoke in a similar strain: ' Under the papacy it was thought that if people did not hear a Mass every day from beginning to end they would have no good fortune, and no blessing the whole day. Then they went through their long, impure, false service with great devotion and patience ; now we find it tedious and wearisome to stay only half as long in church. Oh, how one day we shall feel the frost after the sun!'[2]

The more melancholy the condition of things became, the more frequently we meet with preachers who set themselves with fervent zeal to stem the downfall of morals, to pray, to warn, to exhort, to threaten, to condemn sin with deepest abhorrence, to point with vehement earnestness to the judgments of God. In spite of all their eccentricities and tastelessnesses, Strigenicius, Andrew Schoppius, James Stöcker, John George Sigwart, Erasmus Winter, and many others, exhibited zeal and earnestness of this description. Boldly, too, they hurled their words of blame against those of their own profession and against noble lords and princes when they saw religion and morality endangered by them. They interested themselves with warm fellow

---

[1] *Spiegel christl. Hausszucht*, p. 394. See Braun, *Zehn christl. Predigten*, p. 93.

[2] *Vier christliche und nützliche Predigten vom heiligen Segen und Friedewunsch*, Leipzig, 1903, p. 88 ; cf. p. 52.

feeling in the poor and the needy, they ranged themselves throughout on the side of the common people, and
did not shrink from open and resolute denunciation of
all oppression and tyranny over the lower classes.

It is astounding with what indefatigableness so
many preachers devoted themselves to the work of their
office in spite of their frequent and heavy complaints
of the small results that followed. Ambrose Blarer,
at the age of sixty-six, still preached every day in the
week, and two or three times every Sunday.[1] The
Quedlinburg preacher John Arndt wrote, in 1599, that on
all high and other festivals he had preached several times
a day, ' and though I had a number of listeners, not one of
them ever offered me a mouthful of bread '; ' they often
made me weary of preaching by their coarse behaviour
in church ; I often prayed that for God's sake they would
be still. I am sick of preaching; if it were God's will
I would cease preaching, not only here but anywhere.' [2]

Like Arndt, Paul Jenisch, a Saxon theologian,[3] also
polemised very seldom, and only when compelled to do
so, and then without bitterness, striving always to win
his opponents through love. Valerius Herberger, pastor
at Fraustadt from 1599, did not follow this good example.
Of his numerous and widely circulated writings the
' Evangelische Herzpostille ' was the first to be printed,
in 1613 ; this work contains much abuse of the Catholic
Church. The first volume of Herberger's celebrated
book, ' Magnalia Dei von den grossen Taten Gottes,
von Jesu, der ganzen Schrift Stern und Kern,' appeared
in 1601.[4] Of like popular style with Herberger's

[1] Keim, *Ambr. Blarer*, p. 140.
[2] Tholuck, *Lebenszeugen*, pp. 263–265.   [3] See Schenk, p. 24.
[4] Schmidt, *Gesch. der Predigt*, p. 90.   Tholuck, *Lebenszeugen*, p. 28 ff.

'Herzpostille' is the 'Postille' of John Gerhard, of Quedlinburg, first published in 1613. Another work by Gerhard, 'Meditationes sacrae oder heilige Betrachtungen, dadurch die rechte Gottseligkeit geweckt und der innerliche Mensch zum Wachstume gebracht werden kann,' published in 1603, was compiled chiefly from the Holy Scriptures, the works of St. Augustine, St. Bernard, St. Anselm, and from Tauler.[1]

Another preacher altogether averse to polemics was John Valentine Andreä, a pious man, whose faith was active in love, from 1614 to 1620 dean at Vaihingen, then superintendent-general at Calw († 1624 at Stuttgart). His autobiography is an important monument of the period.[2] Concerning the unceasing polemising he wrote :

> Auch hilft kein Zanken und Streitschrift,
> So unser Leben bleibt vergift ;
> Kein Buch Christum vertreten kann,
> Er will fromb Leut und Jünger han.

> Naught availeth quarrelling and strife,
> If poisoned still remains our life ;
> Christ by no book can represented be,
> He wants good folk and followers to see.

---

[1] 'The evangelical Church, though rich in sermons and postilles, was still poor in special books of edification—the first book of Arndt's *Wahrer Christentum* had only just appeared. This want, therefore, was still supplied from the ascetic writings of an Augustine, a Bernard, an Anselm, a Tauler, or Thomas à Kempis. Gerhard, too, owes to these luminaries of the Church his spirit and tone, in part also the subject-matter of his meditations. The language is flowing, tender, and sincere, as in the works of his precursors ; we hear the love strains of a *Jesu dulcis memoria*, and similar medieval devotional tunes, ringing through his pages.' Tholuck, *Lebenszeugen*, p. 187. Cf. Schmidt, p. 84.

[2] *Selbstbiographie J. B. Andreäs*, translated from the manuscript and accompanied with notes and contributions by Professor Seybold, Winterthur, 1799. ** Joh. Val. Andreae vita ab ipso conscripta. Ex autographo primum edidit F. A. Rheinwald, Berolini, 1849.

Under the heading ' Faith and Life,' he says :

'Tis faith does this ; faith gives the crown
That makes the entire world go down
Before us : yet love it is
That makes *us* our neighbours' servants,
As in Christ we plainly see.[1]

The pleasantest figure among all the great crowd of
' evangelical preachers ' is undoubtedly the above-mentioned John Arndt, called not seldom by the Catholics
also ' a Christian hero.'

Born in 1555, at Ballenstädt in the Anhalt-Bernburg
district, he attended the universities of Helmstädt,
Wittenberg, Strassburg and Basle, and in 1581 obtained
a post at the school of his native town. In 1583 he went
as pastor to the village of Badeborn. There, however,
because he opposed the abolition of the ceremony of
exorcism at baptism he was deposed from office in 1590,
and banished from the land. After this he officiated,
under much tribulation, in Quedlinburg, Brunswick,
Eisleben, and finally, from 1611, at Celle, as superintendent of the principality of Lüneburg († May 11, 1621).[2]
As an enemy of scholastic-polemical pulpit addresses
he insisted in his own sermons most especially on
' the cleansing of the heart, and on unfeigned love to God
and to one's neighbour ' ; he preached also that faith
must always be active in works of love.

His principal work, which, in Protestant circles, is

---

[1] Schmidt, p. 104. ** Besides the biography of Hossbach (*J. B.
Andreä und sein Zeit*, Berlin, 1819) see now the article by Henke in the
Allgemeine deutsche Biographie, i. 441 f., and Hefele in Wetzer und Welte's
Kirchenlexikon, i[2]. 821.

[2] ** *Friedr. Arndt, Joh. Arndt, ein biographischer Versuch*, Berlin, 1838 ;
Herzog's *Realenzyklopädie*, i[2]. 686 f. ; *Allgemeine deutsche Biographie*,
. 548 f. ; H. L. Pertz, *De Joanne Arndtio ejusque libris, qui inscribuntur
' De vero Christianismo*,' Hannov. 1852.

still in the present day a source of religious edification, is the ' Vier Bücher vom wahren Christentum,' of which the first book, the outcome of weekly sermons, appeared in 1605 ; the first complete edition of the work appeared in 1610.

It went deeply to the heart of this profoundly religious man that so many people, 'who were always bragging loudly of Christ and His Word,' 'led such un-Christian lives, just as if they were not dwelling in Christendom but in heathendom' ; that the fundamental doctrines of Christianity, original sin, redemption in Christ, a supernatural life of faith, and above all a faith showing itself in penitence and love, bore so little fruit ; that people did not concern themselves to fight against the evil within themselves, and to make ' heart, mind and spirit' conformable to Christ. To this ' Godless living and doing ' he attributed all the visitations which befell Germany at that period. ' From this cause there must needs come times of misery, war, hunger, and pestilence.' Instead of sounding a summons to war against the Catholics, he exhorted his fellow Protestants to earnest contrition and change of life. The aim and object of his whole work was ' that we should recognise the inherent, inborn abomination of original sin, that we should learn to know our own wretchedness and nothingness, that we should renounce ourselves and all our pretensions to merit, take all from ourselves and give all to Christ, so that He alone may be all and all within us, that He may work everything in us, create everything in us, because He is the beginning, middle and end of our conversion and salvation.' [1]

This innermost life-communion with Christ, wherein

[1] Edition of Pilger, Berlin, 1842, Introduction, pp. 3, 5, 9.

the Catholic teachers of the spiritual life had placed the essence of all asceticism and Christian perfection, was not apprehended by Arndt at all in the Catholic sense. He intended by his writings ' entirely to refute the doctrines of papists, Synergists and Majorites.' The article on justification by faith is also made as pointed and as extreme as possible. ' I protest also herewith that I wish this little book, just like all my other articles and prints, and also the article on free will, and the justification of the poor sinner before God, to be understood in no other way than according to the meaning of the symbolic books of the Churches of the Augsburg Confession, such as the first Augsburg Confession, the apology, the Smalcald articles, both the Catechisms of Luther, and the Formula of Concord.' [1] In conformity with this solemn protest, Arndt not only makes Luther's doctrine of justification the basis of his whole system of mysticism,[2] but narrows down ' the true Christian service of God,' in an un-Catholic sense, to a merely inward matter—*i.e.* to ' a pure recognition of God, a penitential recognition of the sins that have been committed, and a similar recognition of divine grace and forgiveness of sins.' [3]

This basic conception recurs frequently in the contemplations, and equally so in the prayers and the rhymed strophes which follow every section.[4] He classes Luther, as the restorer and purifier of Christian doctrine, with Christ Himself, with the Apostles, and the Church Fathers.[5] The belief in the utter corruption of human

---

[1] Edition of Pilger, pp. 9, 10.
[2] Pp. 43, 334 ff., 339 ff.   [3] P. 161.
[4] The contrast between ' law ' and ' gospel ' is very sharply emphasised in the lengthier songs at pp. 64 and 65.   [5] P. 281.

reason, which is so strongly insisted on by Luther, appears in a greatly modified form in Arndt. He concedes to the heathen ' a small spark of divine light,' or a trace and mark of natural witness to God, and insists so forcibly on active exercise of faith through works of love [1] that his teaching is hard to reconcile with the doctrine of justification by faith alone.

As Arndt nowhere puts forward the strict Lutheran controversial doctrines in an aggressive, polemical manner, so in most of his views he leans more to Tauler, Thomas à Kempis, and other medieval mystics than to Luther and the Protestant confessional writings. The very fact of the division of the work into four books, the occasional dialogue form, the contemplative style, the plain, often proverbial language, the contents and the phraseology of numerous passages, make it indubitable that Arndt took the ' little book on the imitation of Christ ' as his model is so far as he could do so consistently with his strongly Protestant fundamental conception, and that he also appropriated the teaching of the ' Imitation.'   Almost like a Catholic ascetic he describes [2] in connexion with the First Epistle to the Corinthians (xiii. 4 ff.) the ' fruits of Christian love,' the ' command to love one's enemies,' [3] the imitation of Christ [4] through humility, poverty, endurance, self-denial, and patient suffering, endurance of injuries and calumnies, hatred of sin, love of God, and active love of mankind.[5]   Like Thomas à Kempis, he returns perpetually to the practice of prayer as the most indispensable means of grace and of a truly spiritual life.   What he says on this subject is almost all Catholic.   With a

[1] Edition of Pilger, p. 217 ff.   [2] P. 217 ff.
[3] P. 198 ff.   [4] P. 401 ff.   [5] P. 407 ff.

certain sort of self-contradiction he stands up here [1] for
the externals of divine service. ' God,' he says, ' does
not need outward usages to awaken Him, but man, who
is by nature indolent, must be reminded by these outward
signs to think of the all-encompassing Fatherly love
of God.' Surpassingly beautiful and edifying, almost
taken from the old mysticism, is the fourth book : ' Von
den sechs Tagewerken Gottes und von dem Menschen
insonderheit.' Nevertheless it could as little replace
the fourth book of the ' Imitation of Christ ' as the pious
remembrance of Christ can replace the actual Presence
in the Sacrament of the Altar, the Holy Sacrifice of
the Mass and the Holy Eucharist—*i.e.* the Sacramental
life-communion with Christ.

The earnest, practical piety which brought Arndt in
some matters nearer to the Catholic point of view was,
nevertheless, sufficient to make many orthodox Lutherans suspicious. They made it a matter of accusation
against him that by his strict insistence on good works,
on active renewal of the inward man, on imitation of
Jesus, he curtailed the merits of Christ and destroyed the
power of all-justifying faith. From the pulpits he was
preached against as an enthusiast and a Synergist, in
confessionals the penitents were warned against him.
' The world is growing all too wicked,' Arndt wrote to
John Gerhard in 1607. ' I could never have believed
that there were such venomous, bad people among the
theologians.' ' I ask you to consider in a friendly way,' he
said in a letter to a burgomaster of Brunswick in 1608,
' what it is to accuse a man of heresy, of debauchery,
publicly before a whole parish, to call all his doing and
preaching jugglery and trash, to denounce him not

---

[1] Edition of Pilger, p. 541.

only as a most ignorant ass who has never studied
theology, and understands nothing, but also to lay him
under suspicion on account of his teaching.'[1] ' The
devil,' said the theologian John .Corvinus, ' would
reward Arndt for his heretical teaching.'[2] With like
irreconcilable animus he was attacked by the Tübingen
theologian Lucas Osiander the younger, who made him
out a papist, a Calvinist, a Schwenkfeldian, and a
Flacian, and described the spiritualised Christianity of
Arndt as so dangerous that Münzerian uproars and
infidelity might be brought into the country by it.[3]

The most peaceable and pious of men was not
secure against press censorship and persecution ; for
' the secret papism and fanaticism which was apparent
in many passages of Arndt's book of pretended true
Christianity must,' said a fugitive piece of the year
1619, ' be punished by the Christian authorities with
censure and condemnation.'[4]

---

[1] Tholuck, *Lebenszeugen*, pp. 266–268.   [2] *Ibid.* p. 273.
[3] Schmidt, *Gesch. der Predigt*, p. 84.   Spittler, *Gesch. von Württemberg*,
p. 234.   ** See also the Göttingen prize article of H. L. Pertz, quoted
above, p. 492 *n.* 2.
[4] *Was christlicher Oberkeit zu thun obliegt. Flugblatt* (without locality),
1619.

CHAPTER XI

BOOK CENSORSHIP—PRINTING AND BOOKSELLING—NEWSPAPERS

ONLY a few decades after the invention and spread of the art of printing, in 1479, the Cologne university obtained permission from Pope Sixtus IV to proceed with Church censorship against the printers, publishers and readers of heretical books.[1] The earliest censure ordinances issued in Germany were those of the Mayence archbishop Bertold von Henneberg, of March 22, 1485 ;[2] and of January 4, 1486; a special committee, appointed for the purpose, was instructed to examine all works before they were printed and sold.[3] Special papal orders connected with the censorship of books were issued in the years 1486, 1496, 1501, and 1515, to the effect that, under penalty of the ban and of definite money fines, nothing ' contrary to the Catholic faith, nothing Godless and productive of scandal,' was to be printed ; any books of the sort that had already been printed were to be burnt. By the edict issued at the Diet of Worms in May 1521, it was decreed on the part of the Empire that the whole of Luther's writings, as well as the numerous abusive pamphlets circulated

---

[1] Reusch, *Index*, i. 56.

[2] Contributed by H. Pallmann in the *Archiv für Gesch. des Buchhandels*, ix. 238–241.

[3] Reusch, i. 56–57.   ** J. Weiss, *Bertold von Henneberg, Erzbischof von Mainz*, Freiburg, 1889, 46 ff.

against the high clergy and the universities, and also all pasquils and caricatures, were to be destroyed ; and in future all books and writings in which there was the slightest mention of the Catholic faith were, before their first appearance in print, to be submitted to the approval of the acting diocesan bishop, and the theological faculty of the nearest university.[1]

Among the Catholic Imperial Estates, on the ground of the Worms imperial edict and the papal decrees respecting books, the most stringent ordinances were issued against all heretical writings in Bavaria and Austria. The university of Ingolstadt at the time of John Eck († 1543) not seldom had booksellers imprisoned for circulating Lutheran and other sectarian books ; two such offenders were not only expelled from the town but actually, with permission of Duke William IV, altogether banished from Bavaria.[2] A Bavarian religious mandate of 1548 ordained that books and writings which were pronounced by his Papal Holiness and the Chair of Rome misleading, and opposed to our Christian faith and wholesome doctrines, and to the decrees of the holy councils, were not to be sold or tolerated in houses ; whosoever acted against this decree was to be regarded as a contemner of the Christian Church, the Imperial Majesty and territorial prince, and punished in body and in goods. After the ' Tridentine Index of forbidden books ' had been published at Rome in 1564, Duke Albert V had it reprinted and distributed, and a regular catalogue made of books that it was allowable to read, and of those which were to be in future regarded as prohibited. Albert's successor, William V,

---

[1] Kapp, *Gesch. des deutschen Buchhandels*, pp. 528–538.
[2] Reusch, i. 85.

issued the order in 1580, that 'everybody in whose possession an heretical book should be found should be subjected to 'such punishment as would serve as a deterring example for many thousands'; in cases of death the bequeathed property was to be examined and the punishments attaching to the possessors of forbidden books were to pass over to the heirs.[1] At the instigation of the papal nuncio Felicianus Ninguarda there appeared at Munich, in 1582, an enlarged edition of the Trent Index of prohibited books.[2]

In Austria, in 1523, Ferdinand I forbade the reading and the sale of all 'new misleading books'; five years later he decreed that 'printers and sellers of sectarian, forbidden writings, who should set foot in the Austrian hereditary lands, were to be instantly punished with death by drowning, and their goods were to be burnt.'[3] The Emperor Rudolf II, in 1579, ordered nearly 12,000 German and 2000 Italian books of non-Catholic contents to be burnt by the executioner at Graz. At Vienna Protestant printers and publishers were forbidden residence; a special 'Inquisitorial book committee' was appointed to control the book market. When, in 1580, the Viennese bishop Caspar Neubeck was instructed by the government to prepare a book catalogue according

---

[1] K. Th. Heigel, ' Die Zensur in Altbayern ' in the *Archiv für die Gesch. des deutschen Buchhandels*, ii. 33–67. See *Archiv*, i. 176–180 ; Faulmann, pp. 239-240, 241 ; Kapp, pp. 558–562.

[2] Reusch, i. 472–480.

[3] *Ibid*. i. 84.   ** Busson (*Der Bücherfund von Palaus*, Wien, 1884, p. 8 f.) shows that in the last years of the Emperor Ferdinand the prevalent practice in Tyrol with regard to book censorship was of a lenient nature, deviating essentially from the severity of the letter. This state of things was altered when Ferdinand II, residing in Tyrol, carried on the government in person. Concerning the inspection of heretical books enforced in his time, see, besides Busson, 14 f., Egger, *Gesch. Tirols*, ii. 239, and, especially, Hirn, i. 182 ff.

to which the printers and publishers were to carry on business, he answered : ' There are so many bad books that it is impossible to count them ; at all the fairs and markets such quantities of strange and evil things are sold, pictures, songs, squibs, tracts and books in manifold dialects and languages, that it is impossible to draw up an accurate catalogue ; numbers of books and tracts are sold without the name of the author; numbers have titles and inscriptions which make them seem Catholic, while the contents are rabid against the orthodox religion ; numbers of mischievous Calvinistic and Flacianist books appear under the cloak of the Augsburg Confession.' It was not till 1582 that the fraudulent practice, already in general vogue, of printing Protestant writings with fictitious press-marks and with the names of Catholic writers was discovered at Vienna.[1]

---

[1] Fuller details occur in Th. Wiedemann, *Die kirchliche Bücherzensur in der Erzdiöcese Wien*, Vienna, 1873 ; cf. Calinich, pp. 222–243. ** The suppression of a writing of the Augustinian prior, Hoffmeister, by the Catholic council of Colmar, in 1540, is quite a special case. The pamphlet dealt in vehement language with the council and the Smalcaldian articles, in which Luther had expressed himself with such passionateness that ' even the most odious anonymous lampoons against the council had not by a long way equalled his language.' Hoffmeister remonstrated strongly against the confiscation of his work. He pointed out that till then ' all manner of printed matter had been allowed in the town of Colmar, and that no one had been forbidden to invent, write, buy or sell whatever he liked ' ; he described it as ' a piece of injustice to suppress his most orthodox book, in which he had attacked neither the town nor the neighbourhood.' He also offered to submit his work to the criticism of the university of Freiburg or the government at Ensisheim. But all was in vain. The council stuck to its decree, and caused his pamphlet to be destroyed, and this was done so effectually that at the present day there is only one single copy of it left. This copy is preserved in the town library of Colmar. ' That on this occasion,' says Paulus (*Hoffmeister*, p. 91), ' the town council was governed by the desire to support the new-religionist party cannot be supposed, for they had only shortly before, with a view to maintaining the old faith, appointed a first-rate Catholic preacher, the Dominican monk John Fabri. When, however, they assert that they only inhibited Hoffmeister's

As in Catholic districts all Protestant books, so in Protestant districts all Catholic books, were strictly prohibited, and the printers forbidden under penalty to publish them. [1]

At Strassburg Catholic writings were suppressed as early as in 1524.[2] At the bidding of a Nuremberg councillor, in 1543, a philosophical work by a Catholic scholar was mutilated—all such passages especially which seemed to touch Lutheran doctrine.[3] The council at Frankfort-on-the-Main exercised so strict a censorship that on December 4, 1562, it was necessary for Ferdinand I to make a special appeal to the bench in order to obtain permission for his daughter's Father Confessor ' to have a little tract of about five pages printed '; without leave from the council no printer in the place would undertake to do it.[4] At Rostock, in 1532, the printer of the ' Brethren of the Common Life ' was sent to prison, because he had used his printing press to the disadvantage of Protestantism, and had had transactions with the Catholic-minded Duke Albert

pamphlet on account of its violent language, we are well justified in doubting the statement. If the council had only been concerned to prohibit all fierce religious polemics, they would undoubtedly have also hindered the spread of the Lutheran writings. Such writings, however, and indeed the fiercest of them, as Hoffmeister points out in his letter to the council, could be freely printed and sold at Colmar at that time. Why, then, all at once this enforcement of the most stringent severity against a defender of the old faith ? ' Paulus answers to this that ' without doubt personal motives were at play. Only a short time before Hoffmeister had resolutely resisted the magistrate's intention of interfering in conventual matters. Hence it might well occur to the mortified councillors to make the disagreeable Augustinian suffer for his independent action.'

[1] ** Cf. Gretser, *Opp. omnia*, xiii., and the article of Paulus (?) in the *Innsbr. Zeitschr. für Kathol. Theologie*, 1900, p. 564 f.

[2] Döllinger, i. 548.

[3] Stieve, *Polizeiregiment in Bayern*, p. 18.

[4] The original in the *Frankfurter Archiv, Wahltagakten*, ix. 88.

of Mecklenburg, concerning the printing of the New Testament of Hieronymus Emser.

Three years before, Luther had already set his pen in motion concerning this Catholic translation of the Bible. ' The freedom of the Word,' which he claimed for himself, was not to be accorded to his opponent Emser. When his translation of the New Testament was prohibited by Catholic princes and rulers, ' partly on account of the marginal notes put in to emphasise the new doctrines, partly on account of certain libellous figures ridiculing and mocking the papal holiness,' Luther stirred up the people in his pamphlet ' Von weltlicher Obrigkeit ' (1523) not to obey such ' tyrants.' ' In Meissen, Bavaria, the Mark, and other places,' he wrote, ' the tyrants had issued an order that the New Testaments were to be delivered up to the magistrates ; now this was what the subjects were to do : not a page, not a letter was to be handed over by them at the risk of loss of salvation ; for all who did so were delivering up Christ into the hands of Herod, were acting as the murderers of Christ, or as Herods.' When, however, he learnt that Emser's translation with notes and glosses was to be printed by the ' Brethren of the Common Life ' at Rostock, he not only appealed himself to his follower, Duke Henry of Mecklenburg, with the request that ' for the glory of the evangel of Christ and the salvation of all souls ' he would put a stop to this printing, but he also worked on the councillors of the Elector of Saxony to support his action.[1] He denied the right and the power of the Catholic authorities to inhibit his books ; on the other hand he invoked the arm of the secular

---

[1] *Histor.-polit. Blätter*, xix. 390. Döllinger, i. 547 ; see our remarks vol. iii. p. 241 ff. ** See also above, p. 428.

authorities against all writings that were displeasing to him. Similarly Melanchthon demanded in the most severe and comprehensive manner the censure and suppression of all books that were hindering to Lutheran teaching.[1] The writings of Zwingli and the Zwinglians were placed formally on the Index at Wittenberg.[2] Instigated by Luther and Melanchthon, the Elector John of Saxony issued in 1528 the command : ' Books and writings of Sacramentarians, Anabaptists, and other sects deviating from Luther, are neither to be bought, sold or read in the land. All who are a party to this being done by strangers or acquaintances, in opposition to our order herewith issued, shall be taken into custody and punished according to the extent and nature of the connivance or transaction ; in every case by forfeiture of life and goods, if they are aware of such offences, and do not make them known.'[3]

In the strongly Protestant duchy of Saxony[4] the council of Leipzig, in 1539, by order of Duke Henry instructed all the printers neither to print nor publish anything new without his leave. Once a week two members of the council were to go round to the printers and see that ' nothing except what was in conformity to the evangel ' was being printed. For the better supervision of the press, the Elector Augustus of Saxony gave orders in 1571 that printing presses were only to be established in four places in the whole land, viz. at Dresden, Wittenberg, Leipzig, and at Annaberg, where the resident palace was. At Wittenberg printers and

---

[1] *Corp. Reform.* iv. 549 ; see Döllinger, i. 547, note.
[2] See proofs of this statement in Riggenbach, *Chronikon Pellicans*, p. xxxix.
[3] Döllinger, i. 549.   [4] See our remarks, vol. vi. p. 53 ff.

booksellers were placed under the censorship of the university ; in 1588 it was actually decreed that even books which had been passed by the Wittenberg university must receive in addition sanction at Dresden.[1]

Similar orders were issued against ' the books of the Zwinglians and other sects ' in Pfalz-zweibrücken, Baden, Württemberg and elsewhere.[2] An injunction of Duke Christopher of Württemberg, of 1557, prescribed heavy penalty on printers who should print anything new, especially in theology, without his knowledge. The publishers, on opening the cases of books which they received from Frankfort and from other fairs, were to submit all the books to the inspectors and not to sell anything without their approval—this on penalty of serious bodily punishment ; at stated times the book-shops were to be searched for forbidden goods. As ' sectarian books,' the sale of which was to be zealously repressed, Duke Frederick mentioned in 1601 the ' Calvinistic, papistical, Anabaptist, Schwenkfeldian books, and so forth.' [3]

In the recess of the Protestant assembly at Naumburg, in 1561, the following decree occurs : ' The Princes and Estates will not henceforth allow or tolerate the printing of any book which has not been diligently examined to see whether, not in the substance only, but also in the style and form of the language it coincides with the Augsburg Confession.' [4]

---

[1] Kapp, pp. 595–598.   [2] Proofs in Döllinger, i. 549 ff.
[3] Kapp, pp. 586–587.
[4] K. A. Menzel, *Neuere Geschichte der Deutschen*, ii. 383. According to this the domain of theology would actually have been closed for ever, and every further utterance on subjects connected with it would have had to be referred to this Confession, as though already settled by it beforehand. Greater bondage could scarcely be conceived than such subjection of the

As a rule the office of censorship was entrusted by the Protestant princes now to a court preacher, now to a consistorial councillor, now to the theological faculty of the university of the land ; sometimes the princes, in their own persons, exercised strong control. Duke Louis of Württemberg, for instance, boasted in 1585, ' he did not often let any writing be issued by his theologians which he had not supervised ' ; ' his councillors and ministers knew well that the controversial writings of his theologians could not be published until they had been read and approved by him.' [1]

If the religious views of the princes changed, the censorship changed also. Thus, for instance, the ' Corpus doctrinae ' of Melanchthon had passed muster for a long time in Saxony, but on the occasion of the crypto-Calvinistic controversies the Elector Augustus forbad the work being printed any longer in the land ; the press control, which Melanchthon had advocated against others, now hit him himself. The Leipzig bookseller Ernst Vögelin had to expiate in prison the offence of having printed a pamphlet composed in the spirit of the Melanchthonian party, and to pay a fine of 1000 florins ; he might think himself fortunate to escape half beggared to Saxony.[2]

In the Protestant towns numbers of preachers bestirred themselves zealously with the help of the municipal authorities to suppress the writings of all opposing parties.[3] ' When first Luther began to write

---

human spirit to this confessional creed. Further decrees of the censorship are mentioned by Menzel, ii. 253, 315, 445, 493, and iii. 23.

[1] ** Sattler, *Württemb. Gesch.* v. 125. Döllinger, i. 551.

[2] See our remarks, vol. viii. p. 187, and Döllinger, i. 551-552.

[3] Proofs in Döllinger, i. 554-556. The Saxon theologians, in 1607,

books, it was said,' so Frederick Staphylus recalled to
mind (1560), ' that it would be contrary to Christian
freedom if the Christian folk and the common people
were not allowed to read all sorts of books. Now, however, because the Lutherans themselves are falling
away from their faith, they are repeating the usage of
the old Church and forbidding the purchase and reading of the books of their opponents, and of apostate
members and sects.' [1]

How far the press control extended itself in Protestant towns is seen, for instance, from the ordinances
of the council of Basle. On August 3, 1542, this body
issued a decree which resulted not only in the prohibition
of the sale of an Alcoran, printed by Oporinus, and to
which regulations of Mohammed had been added, but in
the wholesale confiscation of the entire edition. Under
penalty of a fine of 100 florins no book was to be printed
without the consent of the council or of the censors.
In 1550 the booksellers received orders only to publish
works written in the German, Latin, Greek, and Hebrew
languages, and not those written in Italian, French,

actually prevented the printing of an article of Kepler on the comets.
Schuster, p. 180.

[1] *Vom rechten Verstande des göttlichen Wortes*, Neuss, 1560, Bl. E a ; see
Döllinger, i. 556. Of Protestant book censorship Kapp says (p. 552) :
' Luther tried to procure a prohibition of the Carlstadt writings in Saxony :
the same Luther, who considered that the papacy had not been by a long
way sufficiently reviled, written against, sung against, poetised against,
and painted against, in 1525 began already to call the censorship to the
help of his present position. The Lutherans hated the Zwinglians worse
than the Catholics, but both Lutherans and Zwinglians raged against
the Anabaptists and the so-called fanatical spirits. The Protestant
princes on their side loved and encouraged the censorship because, with its
help, they could suppress the well-merited complaint against their robbery
of Church property, or other self-interested deeds, or even criminal acts.
Finally, the patricians of the towns had in the censorship a mighty
weapon for the establishment of their own dominion.'

English or any other tongue. When the Antistes
(head-preacher) Sulzer and Professor Amerbach applied
to the council in 1553 for leave to print a French translation of the Bible from the original text, they were
told that ' When the manuscript was ready for print it
would be revised and examined to see if there were any
dirty, scandalous or abusive words in it.' [1] A year
before, Oporinus had been put in prison for printing a
pamphlet by Nausea.[2]

' The press police had an intolerably difficult and
withal, as was complained in almost all lands, almost
profitless work and trouble with the innumerable slan-
derous lampoons and libellous pamphlets and poems,
caricatures and squibs, that flooded the towns and
villages. The recesses of the diets at Nuremberg (1524),
at Spires (1529), at Augsburg (1530), at Ratisbon (1541)
issued stringent, but fruitless, enactments against
all press-produce of this sort.[3] The literature of libel

---

[1] Lutz, pp. 117–119. ' It cannot therefore be a matter of surprise
that Oporinus should have written indignantly to his friend Ampelander
at Bern : ' The devil has bombarded us with the new papacy, quod liber-
tatem evangelii renovati doctrina vix partam prorsus evertit : ut veteri
papatu iam plus libertatis sit, quam rebus publicis evangelicae doctrinae
restitutis etc.' p. 119. ** Earlier even than this, Sebastian Franck
complained in the preface to his *Weltbuch*, 1534 : ' We must all be of opinion
that there has been enough lying and flattering. But if this freedom
in writing is abolished, and people are not allowed to write against each
other, books will be full of lies and affectation. Formerly under the
papacy there was much more liberty to punish the vices of princes and
lords also : now all must be hushed up, or we are accused of seditiousness,
so tender has the latter-day world become. God have pity on it.' Sachse,
pp. 32–33, note.

[2] ** See Glast's *Tagebuch*, Basle, 1856, p. 94.

[3] ' Reichspressverordnungen,' in Kapp, p. 775 ff. It is a known fact
that at no time in the German Empire did caricatures and libellous writings
abound and compete with each other more than in the first half of the

and abuse became so extensive, that the imperial
police ordinance of 1548 issued the decree that 'the
printers, sellers, buyers, and even the owners of such
writings and pictures as had been published without
sanction of the censorship, should be taken into
custody, and in case of necessity, even put on the rack
and punished according to the extent of their offence.' [1]
Those printers who disobeyed the prescriptions of the
censors were threatened with deprival of their business
and a fine of 500 gold guldens.   But even this Draco-
nian ordinance remained a dead letter.   Then, as before,
a general *Kreisabschied* (decree of the provisional diet)
issued at Erfurt on September 27, 1567, complained
that ' The pamphleteers, lampoonists and libellers
succeed in stirring up such mistrust and irritation
between all classes, high and low, that an unforeseen
rising and much disaster may occur.'

In order to meet the question of unlicensed printing
presses from which, for the most part, these objectionable
publications issued, it was settled at the Spires Diet of
1570 that, in future, throughout the Roman Empire
of the German nation printing presses should only be set
up in the residential districts of princes, in university
towns, or in important imperial towns.   The grant of

---

sixteenth century, and this indeed in public more than in private life.'
Kapp, p. 541.   ' The spirit of libel and abuse was never more rampant
than at that period ; it knew no bounds and spared neither majesty, nor
things sacred, nor private life.'   Calinich, *Aus dem* 16. *Jahrhundert*, pp. 195,
196.   In vols. ii.–vi. (German) of our work there is overwhelming evidence
in proof of this statement.   ** Concerning *Schandbriefe* (accompanied as
a rule with a libellous picture) of the years 1536, 1537, and 1570, in the
county of Lippe, see A. Falkmann, *Graf Simon VI zur Lippe und seine
Zeit.   Erste Periode*, Detmold, 1869, p. 148.   Concerning the ordinances of
the diets see also Sachse, p. 39 ff.

[1] See Sachse, pp. 43–45.

a licence to a printer was to be dependent on previous proof and test of his respectability and trustworthiness ; each one was to bind himself by oath to observe the regulations laid down in the imperial recess.[1]   How it fared with the enforcement of these regulations is exemplified, for Austria at any rate, by a memorandum addressed by Caspar Neubeck, appointed bishop of Vienna, in 1577, to the Archduke Ernest. ' Formerly,' he said, ' only learned people, who could be trusted, were set up and recognised as printers ; now, however, people of all sorts—compositors, founders, moulders, letter painters, and others who have learnt nothing, who are masters neither of languages nor of materials— undertake the business of printing ; what sort of work is produced by this crowd of voracious printers is seen in the mass of forbidden tracts, irregular printing, false, incorrect forms.'   Not every ' trumpery printer ' should be allowed to print according to his own will and pleasure, but only respectable and suitable persons. ' All runaway, vagabond, feckless, riff-raff people, who do not know what else to turn to,' must be excluded from dealing with books.   At fairs, no book-dealers must be allowed to have secret stalls ; for this trade must be watched more closely than any other. ' Summa Summarum : a strong and perpetual system of inspec- tion must be instituted over such mischievous rabble, agitators, sedition-mongers, as are the book-printers, publishers, dealers, binders, &c., in order that in future the country may be secured against all their venomous transactions, and all people may remain more quiet and peaceful.' [2]

[1] Kapp, pp. 545–547, 779–783.
[2] See above, p. 500.

All ordinances were only 'turned into ridicule.' The police ordinance of November 9, 1577, recognised, with regard to the whole empire, the fact that of the earlier 'statutes' none had been kept, and that 'these scandalous books, writings, pictures, and suchlike were produced, printed, sold and distributed in greater and greater numbers.' [1] For Frankfort-on-the-Main, at the fairs of which town the liveliest book trade was carried on, the Emperor Rudolf, on March 23, 1579, issued an order to the effect that, ' Whereas all shops and stalls are filled with useless, misleading books, libellous pamphlets, poems and paintings, by which the people are led astray and embittered,' timely inspection is more than ever necessary. 'For this reason he had appointed the fiscal procurator of the Imperial Chamber at Spires, his commissioner of books, and with the help of the Frankfort council he was to examine printing-houses and book-shops, and to inflict suitable punishment on all transgressors of the enactments of the Empire. In the following year, with a view to facilitating the suppression of all defamatory writings and libellous poems, the cathedral dean of the Frankfort St. Bartholomew's Church was appointed second imperial commissioner of books.[2]

[1] Kapp, pp. 783–785.
[2] *Ibid.* pp. 615–616. Creditors often compelled their debtors to agree that in case of their not fulfilling their obligations they should submit to being attacked and persecuted by libellous pamphlets and caricatures. This evil custom had become so widespread that the imperial police ordinance of 1577 laid down the following regulation : ' It has been brought to our knowledge that debtors enter into agreements with their creditors or securities to the effect that in case of non-payment they allow themselves to be publicly lampooned in word, print, and picture. This scandal cannot be tolerated in a country ruled by justice and equity. We prohibit such clauses to be inserted in contracts, and command that all guilty of such lampooning be seriously punished.' *Ibid.* p. 541.

Individual princes, estates, and towns followed the lead of the Empire and the Emperor, and enacted the most stringent press ordinances and penal edicts against libellous literature, but all with equally slight result. 'All sorts of squibs, defamatory lampoons, libellous writings and songs,' says one of these edicts, issued in 1602 by Duke Frederick of Württemberg,' ' are being so widely distributed that at almost all public carousals and other gatherings they are declaimed and sung, as well as in street processions, and they are even taken out of the country.' [1]

The penal edicts were of so little use that Duke John Frederick increased their severity, and in July 1616 announced that he ' intended to proceed with unrelenting punishment of body and goods, or even, according to the nature of the offence, with death, against all transgressors of the decrees, and equally also against all such who knew of others transgressing and did not disclose their knowledge.' [2]   In the imperial towns also it was perpetually necessary to renew the prohibitions against ' defamatory writings, verses and lampoons '; at Strassburg, for instance, in the years 1590, 1592, 1602. [3]

The circulation of all sorts of abusive writings, chiefly directed against the Catholic Church, its representatives and followers, was for the most part effected by means of the hawker's trade, which had developed

---

[1] Reyscher, iv. 460.   [2] *Ibid.* v. 365–366.

[3] *Archiv für die Gesch. des Buchhandels*, v. 45.   Concerning several enactments against writings and caricatures of this sort, issued not only from political and ecclesiastical considerations, but also on the grounds of private justice, see A. Kirchhoff in the same *Archiv*, v. 157–161. At Leipzig, on one occasion, in 1589, a butcher's journeyman threatened his mistress with printing a pasquil.

more and more extensively ever since the beginning of the religious revolution. On market-places, in front of churches and council houses, in taverns, in the open streets, in university towns at the gates of colleges and bursas, the hawking booksellers, men of the lowest grades and riff-raff, touted for customers.[1]

It goes without saying that, by a hawking system of this description, all legitimate conditions and relations of the book trade must have been grievously injured, often indeed thrown into anarchy.

In many towns where printing and book-dealing had flourished highly in former times, these trades deteriorated more and more during the religious and political disturbances of the sixteenth century.

At Augsburg the ' newly discovered divine art ' had received a powerful impulse. Many of the works which appeared there in the last decades of the fifteenth and the first decades of the sixteenth centuries, especially those published by Günther Zainer, Antony Sorg, Hans

---

[1] Kapp, pp. 433–434, where the whole business is described. ' In this hawking trade young men were engaged who had failed in their callings and had nothing to lose : men who did not care to work hard, but yet wanted to enjoy their lives ; adventurers who let themselves be carried about on the agitated waves of the stream of the times, indifferent as to where they were landed or if they were landed at all ; and, finally, plotters of the pattern of Catilina. These book-dealers, full of hatred against all existing conditions, were particularly dangerous on account of their cleverness in selecting for distribution writings specially adapted to their ends. Their influence on the minds of the people was consequently immeasurable. Wherever during the Reformation period " anything was up," there the book-dealers hovered about like storm-birds. Battle and rebellion were the elements in which they throve best. It is only exceptionally that we hear of Catholic tracts and leaflets being hawked about by book-dealers ; as a rule it is only Lutheran and Lutherising writings that are circulated. Wherever one of these people is named, it is always a member of the revolutionary party.'

Schönsperger, Erhard Ratdolt, belong, as regards type, binding and illustrations, to the most brilliant specimens of this art. But after the third decade of the sixteenth century 'all this excellence came to an end.' Henry Steiner, the last representative of the typographical greatness of Augsburg, collapsed altogether in business in 1545, and died, as it seems, three years later in utter poverty. Ratdolt was the only one who at his death, in 1528, was in flourishing circumstances; all the other printers had to battle more or less with misery and need.[1] 'The Augsburg printers,' wrote the learned town warden, Mark Welser, in 1604, 'owing to want of means are not in the position to undertake any great work at their own expense.'[2] Welser founded an important printing company, from which, after 1595, numbers of works, many of them of lasting value, were issued.[3]

At Nuremberg Anthony Koberger had worked with twenty-four presses since 1470, had employed over one hundred journeymen, and had also given orders to foreign printers, especially at Basle, Strassburg and Lyons. He was the greatest bookseller of his time. After his death, in 1513, his extensive business was still carried on actively by some of his relations till 1525; after this date, however, the world-famous house declined to its end under the storms of the religious movement; the eldest son was a good-for-nothing fellow, who ended miserably; the youngest 'went to

[1] Butsch, *Bücherornamentik*, i. 23–25. Kapp, p. 126 ff.
[2] Kirchhoff, *Beiträge*, ii. 18.
[3] See present work, vol. xiii. p. 384 ; Kapp, pp. 134–135 ; Bursian, pp. 237–238. ' These specimens of printing distinguished by the beauty of the paper and the type, bear, after the town arms of Augsburg—the fir-cone—the inscription ' Ad insigne pinus ' (p. 238).

ruin' abroad ; a third made a living as goldsmith and dealer in gems ; 1526 saw the last work published under the name once so famous ; with the year 1541 this name disappears completely from the book trade. Nuremberg, formerly one of the most important centres of book-printing and bookselling, after 1541 could no longer boast of a single noteworthy printing establishment, but on the other hand was swarming with secret presses, which devoted themselves to the production of leaflets and pamphlets.[1]

The printing houses at Spires, Würzburg, Eichstätt, Esslingen and Ulm, which had produced many admirable specimens in the fifteenth century, sank during the sixteenth century into complete insignificance.[2]

Cologne, on the other hand, not only maintained its early position as a centre of printing and publishing, but won greater and greater renown in this respect up to the Thirty Years' War, and rivalled the best records of other towns both in the number of its printing firms and the importance of its productions.[3] It became the citadel of Catholic literary activity. The printing house founded by Henry Quentel († 1503) continued into the seventeenth century to exercise an important influence on learned life, especially that of the Lower Rhine district. The publishing book-dealer Gottfried Hittorp († 1565) set a considerable number of printing presses at work ; the largest bookseller was Franz Birckmann, whose business flourished for nearly 200 years, and who appeared regularly at the Frankfort

---

[1] Fuller details in O. Hase, *Die Koberger*, Leipzig, 1885. 'Nuremberg never again returned to the proud position which it had held up to the period of the Reformation.' Kapp, p. 143.

[2] Butsch, *Bücherornamentik*, i. 31.   [3] *Ibid*. ii. 36.

fairs with several assistants—in 1565 with eight. Among
the most renowned printing firms of Cologne were those
of Maternus Colinus (1555–1587) and of two of his
successors, who carried on business till after the middle
of the Thirty Years' War. The longest-established
printing and bookselling house at Cologne was the one
founded in 1516 by John Gymnich in the 'Einhorn
House,' which under frequently changing forms has
lasted on to the present day.[1] The business was carried on under the name of Gymnich till 1596 ; Antony
Hierat, who was connected with the family by marriage,
published in a comparatively short time 250 works,
among them many in folio, especially from the department of Catholic theology.[2]

At Mayence Franz Beham carried on comprehen-
sive work in the service of Catholic literature ;[3] in the
same cause the services of the firms of Adam Berg at
Munich, Weissenhorn at Ingolstadt, and Sebald Maier at
Dillingen reached an astonishing compass.[4]

Among the Protestant University towns of South
Germany, Tübingen and Heidelberg hold only a subordinate rank as regards printing and the book trade. A
publisher at Tübingen produced only slavish reprints ;[5]

[1] As Rommerskirchen's Buchhandlung und Buchdruckerei (J. Melling-
haus).

[2] Kapp, pp. 98–107. A tolerably comprehensive picture of Cologne
topography is given by J. J. Merlo in his work *Die Buchhandlungen und
Buchdruckereien ' Zum Einhorn,'* &c., Cologne, 1876. See also Von Bianco,
i. 207 f. Concerning Vienna see A. Mayer, *Wiens Buchdruckergeschichte*,
i. Vienna, 1883.

[3] See the valuable pamphlet of S. Widmann, *Eine Mainzer Presse der
Reformationszeit*, Paderborn, 1889.   ** See also above, pp. 285, 286.

[4] K. von Reinhardstöttner in the *Jahrb. für Münchener Gesch.* iv. 60.
• A history of these three printing and publishing firms would be at the
same time a piece of literary history of the land of Bavaria.'

[5] Kapp, pp. 168–170.

Heidelberg has only one single printer of note to boast
of, the Dutchman Hieronymus Commelin, who published there, in the years 1587–1598, Roman and Greek
Classics admirably got up.[1]

At Basle at the beginning of the sixteenth century
there were about twenty important printing houses
fully employed. John Amerbach († 1514) was one of
the most learned printers and publishers of his time;
his pupil, John Froben, with his father-in-law and
business manager Wolfgang Lachner (since 1520 an
opponent of the Lutheran movement) ranks among the
most important booksellers of all times. He worked
first with four, then with six, and finally with seven
presses, and for the most part published the Fathers
of the Church and theological works in folio; he was,
says Erasmus, ' a man admirable in all respects, formed
for the advancement of study.' After his death in 1527
the business could never keep up to its previous height.
Among the later Basle printers and publishers, John
Oporinus is almost the only one of note; in the years
1540–1568 he brought out 750 works, and extended his
book trade almost as far as to Italy; he died, however,
in ruined pecuniary conditions.[2]

The chief publisher of the writings of Zwingli and
the Zwinglians was Christopher Froschauer at Zurich
(† 1595), who was especially renowned for his numerous,
carefully got-up editions of the Bible, of which no less
than sixty-three in different languages are attributed to
him.[3]

---

[1] Faulmann, p. 258. Kapp, p. 176.
[2] Kapp, pp. 109–124, 287–288.
[3] *Ibid.* pp. 124–126. ** Vögelin, *Chr. Froschauer*, Zurich, 1840;
Rudolphi, *Die Buchdruckerfamilie Froschauer*, Zurich, 1859.

An extremely subordinate position was held by the
printing and publishing industries in most of the North
German Hanseatic towns. Bremen has not a single
printer worth naming. At Hamburg, in the first five
years after the Protestantising of the town there was
not a single printing house. In 1536 Franz Rhode, of
Marburg, migrated there, did a little publishing in this
and the following year, and then, not finding enough to
do at Hamburg, removed to Danzig. After this (showing how greatly the intellectual life of the place had
declined) it was twelve years before another printer
found his way there ; [1] only Joachim Löw, father and
son (1549–1589), deserve special mention as printers.[2]
Lübeck also, from the time of the religious innovation
to the end of the century, counted only two settled
printers.[3]

Of the North German university towns Greifswald,
Frankfort-on-the-Oder, and Königsberg scarcely come
under consideration. At Rostock, where formerly the
' Brethren of the Common Life ' had developed a lucrative printing trade, and in the years 1514–1524 three
printing houses had been simultaneously active,[4] in the
year 1558 the only printer left there, Ludwig Diez,
complained of want of work and wanted to go to
Copenhagen.[5]

At Leipzig, at the beginning of the sixteenth century,
the publishing firms had established far-reaching con-
nexions with the booksellers. In the second decade
there grew up in this town, under the firm of ' Pantzsch-
mann's Book Trade,' an extensive publishing society,

---

[1] Gallois, ii. 736, 780, 798.   [2] Kapp, p. 178.
[3] Ibid. p. 174.   [4] Lisch, Jahrbücher, iv. ix.-x 1 ff.
[5] Ibid. v. 154.

which had considerable pecuniary means at its command, and brought out quantities of humanistic writings and theological works, mostly in cumbersome folio volumes. After the spread of the religious disturbances, however, the Leipzig book trade went visibly backward ; the number of printing houses dwindled down to half what it had been before. The business which had been started under Duke George by Nicholas Wolrab in conjunction with several capitalists, after the introduction of Protestantism, in 1539, had a meretricious development, which continued for some years, till in 1552 it came to a disastrous end. Wolrab disappeared, and his wife had to be supported by municipal charity. Four other Leipzig printers also fell into the most wretched pecuniary conditions ; their businesses completely collapsed. The only two who maintained a reputable position were Valentine Bapst and his son-in-law Ernst Vögelin, who chiefly published theological and philological works, and, like Oporinus, at Basle, paid great attention to careful text and good binding.[1] In consequence of the crypto-Calvinistic controversies which broke out in Saxony he found himself obliged, in 1576, to fly from Leipzig.[2] Henning Grosse [2] also, the last noteworthy Leipzig publisher of the century, became involved in these controversies and was obliged to leave the town for a time.[3]

The first rank as a centre of printing and publishing, after the advent of Luther and the enormous spread of his multitudinous writings, was held by the university town of Wittenberg. As printers and publishers of these writings, especially of the translation of the Bible,

---

[1] Kapp, pp. 150–158.　** For Wolrab see above, p. 285.
[2] See above, p. 506.　　　　[3] Kapp, pp. 158–159.

Melchior Lotther and Hans Lufft († 1584) displayed the greatest activity.[1] Other workers besides these two were George Rhaw and many more, among whom Lucas Cranach, who carried on simultaneously a painter's workshop, an apothecary's shop, a printing business, and a paper and book trade, deserves special notice. The publishing trade of Wittenberg down to the end of the century was incomparably more important than that of Leipzig.[2]

The generally recognised centre of the German, indeed of the European, book trade in the sixteenth century was the fair at Frankfort-on-the-Main. There the booksellers gathered together for personal traffic, transacted their business arrangements, made their purchases from printers and publishers, and exchanged the products of their workshops. The paper trade was also carried on briskly at the fairs.[3]

An item of great importance in the sale of books was the fair catalogues,[4] which, since the autumn of 1564, had been published by the Augsburg retailer George Willer. These catalogues afforded on the whole a very good statistical basis for ascertaining the extent of literary

---

[1] See above, pp. 404 and 407.

[2] Kapp, pp. 171–172, 417 ff. In 1525 a Zwickau preacher said : ' All the world wants to trade in Dr. Martin Luther's books and grow rich by their means.' Burckhardt, ' Druck und Vertrieb der Werke Luther's,' in Riedner's *Zeitschrift für histor. Theologie*, xxxii. 456. The number of printed works issued under Luther's name in different years was as follows : in 1518, 20 ; 1519, 50 ; 1520, 123 ; 1521, 40 (comparatively few on account of the Worms Diet and Luther's detention in the Wartburg) ; 1522, 130 ; 1523, 180 ; altogether, 553 (p. 456).

[3] Kapp, p. 450 ff. ** See E. Kelchner, ' Die Frankfurter Buchhändlermesse ' in the *Mitteilungen des Vereins für Gesch. Frankfurts*, vi. (1881) 85 ff.

[4] ** Kirchhoff, *Beiträge*, ii. pp. 24–34.

activity, as well as for determining the position and importance, of the different branches of knowledge and of the literature of the day at different periods. But they by no means presented an infallible statement of the actually printed produce of each year. Whole groups of writings, pamphlets, satires, tales of ghosts and marvels, sermons printed singly and other publications of slighter compass, were only in rare cases thought worthy of enumeration. On the other hand, even at an early date much was put down in the catalogues which had never been printed at all, or only later, and in quite a different form.[1] Party considerations also entered into the construction of the catalogues. ' It is more from prejudicial motives than from carelessness,' wrote Peter Schmidt, of Frankfort, in 1590, ' that many distinguished books have often been left out.' He wished to obviate this evil by the publication of catalogues which should contain the titles of all books that were issued ' whether great or small, distinguished or otherwise.' However he did not get beyond the first series of 1590.[2]

After the year 1598 the Frankfort council published an official catalogue.[3] On the Catholic side there was repeated complaint—for instance, from the Emperor Rudolf II in 1608—that ' many Catholic books had been quite left out.' In consequence of this Catholic catalogues were also published, first of all in Mayence after 1606, and in Frankfort after 1614.[4]

In the years 1564–1600 the catalogues chiefly contain

---

[1] See Zarncke in Kapp, p. 787.

. Kapp, p. 483. ** See now especially the researches of Spirgatis, concerning which Freys in the *Histor. Jahrbuch*, xxiii. 480 f. speaks well.

[3] Schwetschke, viii. ff.

[4] *Ibid.* xviii. *Archiv für Gesch. des Buchhandels*, iv. 79.

books published in Germany and brought to the Frankfort fairs ; their number is no less than 21,941, and of these 14,478 are in the Latin language, which always preponderated, 6618 in German, 457 in French, 351 in Italian, and 37 in Spanish. Theology is the subject most strongly represented, and Protestant far more than Catholic theology. Next to theology comes history, then jurisprudence, and finally the medical science. From the last third of the century to the Thirty Years' War the number of books went on steadily increasing. The average number from 1576–1580 is close upon 487 ; from 1581–1585, 560 ; from 1586–1590, 724 ; from 1591–1595, 761 ; from 1596–1600, 803 ; from 1601–1605, 1334 ; from 1606–1610, 1413 ; from 1611–1615, 1544 ; in the two years 1616 and 1617, 3222 books were catalogued.[1]

But with the quantity the quality of the books by no means increased. ' What monstrosities in German writing,' wrote the famous Joseph Scaliger from Leyden in 1603 to Caselius, ' does not the Frankfort fair bring yearly to light ! Who has ever seen in all the rest of Europe so much or such shameless scribbling of incapable heads, as those books partly in German, partly in Latin, but all alike composed by German furies ? '[2] Significant

[1] According to Zarncke's tables in Kapp, pp. 791–792. Even Luther's friend John Mathesius complained of the overcrowding of the book-market. ' Of much writing of books there is no end, and there are numbers of idiotic doctors and teachers, and of these there are an innumerable multitude who make a trade and a business out of God's Word, and who stupefy and weary and bewilder themselves and others with all the many books they write.' ' The greater number of them do scarcely anything else than rail and gibe in their writings at princes and pious teachers, stab and hack and distress and mislead the Church.' *Postilla prophetica*, pp. 326, 327.

[2] Henke, *Calixtus*, i. 217, note 1. See present work, vol. xiii. p. 381.

also are the words of Geverhard (Gerhard) Elmenhorst, written from Hamburg to John Meursius on September 15, 1617 : ' It grieves me that we should have fallen on such times when the stupidest filth finds more buyers than does a serious book.' ' Verily, so soon as it is a question of a Greek author, there is scarcely a publisher to be found.' [1]

For the learned the writing of books was anything but a ' golden business.' While controversial literature, abusive pamphlets, tales of magic and marvels flourished so abundantly and not seldom realised large gains, the men of learning could not reckon on decent remuneration for their literary works. Very many of them, even the most eminent, had to renounce beforehand all thought of payment for their trouble. It was looked upon as an honourable exception when the great jurist Ulrich Zasius received fifty gulden from a Basle publisher in 1526 as an honorarium for one of his works. For a German ' Gospel Harmony ' which John Schwentzer had published, by Cyriacus Jacob, at Frankfort-on-the-Main in 1540 in 1200 copies, the bonus which the publisher paid for each copy was one kreuzer. Nicodemus Frischlin was constantly at a loss to find a publisher for his learned works ; he was obliged to have his Latin grammar and other writings printed at his own expense, and became involved thereby in debts. Peter Kopf, of Frankfort, one of the most important publishers of the time, thought it exorbitant of the learned Doctor Gregorius, in 1594,

---

[1] ' Doleo nos in haec tempora incidisse, in quibus ineptissima citius quam seria emptorem reperiunt.' ' Certe quoniam graecus est auctor, vix est qui eius editionem suscipere velit.' Kirchhoff, *Beiträge*, ii. 17.

to ask a payment of 100 thalers and five free copies for a work of over 100 folio sheets ; Gregorius was obliged to be content with fifty thalers and ten free copies. Marquard Freher, the publisher of German historical documents and other writings, received half a thaler (ninepence) for the folio sheet ; in 1607 he was willing to publish the miscellaneous writings of Willibald Pirkheimer in return for 100 free copies as only payment.

Quirinus Reuter, professor at Heidelberg, who sold his works at the rate of half a gulden for every sheet, remarked pathetically in a letter to Melchior Goldast on December 22, 1609 : ' Men of our condition do service to the booksellers ; they get the profits, but what do we get ? ' More bitterly still did the Heidelberg philologist and professor of history Janus Gruter complain in 1601 of the booksellers, who got everything for nothing, and would give nothing. Even the celebrated John Frederick Gronov of Hamburg received no real honorarium from the great publishing firm of the Elzeviers at Leyden for his comprehensive philological work.[1]

In order at least to get some payment for their work, or at any rate to get the expenses paid, the learned men and writers dedicated their works, with the most sub-

---

[1] Kirchhoff, *Beiträge*, ii. 109–111.   Strauss, *Frischlin*, p. 289 ; Kapp, pp. 312–317, 474 ; see the complaints quoted by Widmann (*Eine Mainzer Presse*, p. 18, note 2) of authors about their publishers.   For the illustrations of the works also the payment of the artists was often anything but lucrative.   When the highly esteemed Zurich printer and book-dealer Christopher Froschauer, in 1545, wanted to publish John Stumpf's *Swiss Chronicle*, he wrote to Badian at St. Gall : ' I have the best painter there is with me now in the house ; I pay him two groschen a week, and give him food and drink, and he does nothing else but draw figures in my Chronicle.' Kapp, p. 125.   ** Concerning the publishing difficulties of Catholic authors see above, pp. 285 and 293.

servient expressions of homage and the most fulsome
flattery, to some prince or great lord, to the magistrate
of a town or to other wealthy persons. This system of
dedication, which degenerated into a disgraceful form
of begging, especially after the last third of the century,
was encouraged by the publishers in order that they
might be relieved from the burden of paying bonuses.
Not seldom, however, the hopes built on patrons were
disappointed ; still more frequently the dedications only
brought a meagre sum, and on payment of a few florins
or thalers it was signified to the applicants never again
to presume ' to make themselves offensive by such
solicitations.' When Sigmund Feyerabend dedicated a
book on gymnastics to the council at Frankfort-on-the-
Main, he was left several weeks without an answer ; on
his asking ' if they intended to do anything favourable
for him ? ' the council decided ' That it had better
remain as it was.' Nicodemus Frischlin, in return for
the dedication of one of his Latin comedies, received
from the council at Strassburg, after long and expensive
waiting, the sum of twelve florins ; from other imperial
towns to which he dedicated comedies he is said to have
got only four thalers.[1]

As far as the outward get-up of the books is concerned, up to the time of the spread of the religious
disturbances, the great printers of Nuremberg, Augsburg, Strassburg, and especially Basle, had set great
store on faultless printing, beautiful type, and good
paper, and had employed the best critics of text and

[1] Kapp, p. 317 ff. Strauss, *Frischlin*, pp. 288–289. Concerning the
abuse of dedications see also Kirchhoff, *Beiträge*, ii. 113–115 ; ** and
present work, vol. xiii. pp. 342–343. This abuse had made such inroads
' that the preacher Gottfried Händel actually dedicated a Prayer-book
to our Redeemer Jesus Christ.' Kirchhoff, p. 115.

castigators. 'Froben,' writes Erasmus, 'spent enormous sums of money on text criticism and frequently also on the manuscripts by which finally the text was determined. The zealous honesty with which John Amerbach pursued this aim and the important sacrifices which he made for its attainment are especially evident in the correspondence which he kept up with Antony Koberger during the printing of the Bible and the postilles of Cardinal Hugo. These men collected around them hundreds of other workers, who, like themselves, recognised the high importance of the task they were engaged in, and exerted themselves for the development of their art.'[1]

Speaking generally, it may be said that with the progress of the religious quarrels the care formerly bestowed on the accuracy of text of books disappeared. Luther himself, even in 1521, had to complain of one of his Wittenberg publishers : 'I wish,' he said, 'I had sent him nothing German, so atrociously, so carelessly, so irregularly is it all printed, not to speak of the abominable types and paper'; he will not again, he adds, send anything to the press until he finds that these 'disgusting money-grabbers have learnt to think less of their own gains and more of the advantage of the readers !'[2] Willibald Pirkheimer complained in 1525 to John Grüninger at Strassburg, the printer of his translation of Ptolemy's geography, that the text was not printed in the proper order, that the notes and the text did not always correspond, that the misprints were

---

[1] See our remarks, vol. i. p. 21, and Kapp, pp. 309-311.   ** See also A. Mayer, *Wiener Buchdruckergeschichte*, pp. 1482-1882.   First half volume, Vienna, 1882.

[2] De Wette, ii. 41-42.

numerous, and that a scholar appointed to correct the proofs had not once been consulted. 'If I had foreseen all this I would rather have burnt my manuscript.' [1] In Italy also the printers would no longer go to the expense of scholarly correction; but in 'the disgrace of faulty printing, with which as a rule the worst possible get-up went hand in hand, Germany soon outstripped Italy and all other countries.' [2]

In the second half of the sixteenth century there were few firms left which distinguished themselves by accuracy of text and excellence of bookbinding and general get-up. Among these few were the great printers in Cologne, Oporinus at Basle, Vögelin at Leipzig, and Sigmund Feyerabend at Frankfort-on-the-Main. The latter for a long time commanded the whole Frankfort book trade, and employed for many of his publications the engravers Virgil Solis, Jost Amman and Tobias Stimmer.[3] He himself was by no means a learned publisher; the prefaces signed by his name are not from his pen; he wrote the most miserable German, and did not understand Latin.[4]

What George Klee wrote in 1589 was on the whole true: 'Book-printing was at the beginning an art so excellent that there was none to be compared with it,

---

[1] Kapp, pp. 90-91.   [2] *Ibid*. p. 312.

[3] See our statements, vol. xi. pp. 173, 174, note 2.   Butsch, ii. 21-22. ** See also H. Pallmann, *Sigmund Feyerabend*, Frankfort, 1881 ; E. von Ubisch, *Virgil Solis und seine biblischen Illustrationen für den Holzschnitt*, Leipzig, 1889, as also the article of F. H. Meyer in the *Archiv für Gesch. des Buchhandels*, xiv. (1891) 114 ff.

[4] Pallmann, p. 58 ff. The oldest counting-house book that has come down to us from the flourishing period of the Frankfort book trade is the 'Mess-register' (Fair catalogue) of Feyerabend for the year 1565, contributed by Pallmann in the *Archiv für Gesch. des Buchhandels*, ix. 9-40. He sold 560 copies of Ovid, text or translations ; 469 copies of the Bible (in various editions) ; 175 of Luther's *Hauspostille*, &c.

but now it has been turned into a common handicraft and trade.'[1] Taste and solidity in the binding and the general get-up of books deteriorated more and more ; this was especially the case after the second half of the century, and with the seventeenth century, as regards the average standard of work, regular anarchy set in.[2]

A new development in the department of book-dealing and of the Frankfort fair traffic, after the close of the sixteenth century, was the regular publication of newspapers (*Zeitungen*).

The name *Zeitung* began in the printed reports with the year 1505, and meant the same as ' report, news.' After the twenties and the thirties the number of these newspapers increased enormously, and up to 1599, 877 can be counted.[3] In the year 1567 the ' Neue Zeitungen ' had already acquired such importance among the people that the General Circle Diet at Erfurt,

[1] *Zeitschr. des Harzvereins*, xix. 370, note.

[2] Kapp, pp. 261–262.

[3] E. Weller, *Die ersten deutschen Zeitungen, herausgegeben mit einer Bibliographie von* 1505–1599, vol. cxi. of the publications of the Literary Society at Stuttgart.   See W. L. Schreiber, ' Die Entwickelung des Zeitungswesens ' in the *Beiblatt* of the *Deutsche Volksstimme*, Berlin, 1886, Nos. 27–30.   ** See also the interesting dissertation of R. Grashoff, *Die briefliche Zeitung des* 16. *Jahrhunderts*, Leipzig, 1877; Th. Sickel, ' Zeitungen des 16. Jahrhunderts,' in the *Weimarisches Jahrbuch für deutsche Sprache, Literatur und Kunst*, published by Hoffmann von Fallersleben and O. Schade, pp. 1, 2, Hannover, 1854, p. 344 ff. ; *Histor.-Jahrb.* xv. 304 f. ; Bücher, *Die Entstehung der Volkswirtschaft*, p. 167 f., and L. Salomon, *Geschichte des deutschen Zeitungswesen von den ersten Anfängen bis zur Wiederaufrichtung des deutschen Reiches*, vol. i. the 16th, 17th, and 18th centuries, Oldenburg, 1899.   There is no mention here of the report *Copia der Newen Zeytung auss Presily Landt*, which is in the Munich Court Library, although this report, printed at Augsburg in 1505 (4 folio sheets), is the first print (*Flugschrift*) known in Germany bearing the title *Zeitung*.   See also Quetsch, *Die Entwickelung des Zeitungswesens seit der Mitte des* 15. *Jahrhunderts*, Mainz, 1901.

on September 27 of that year, extended the decision of
the Augsburg Police Ordinances of 1548 [1] to include
these papers, because ' mistrust, sedition and other evils
in the holy Empire ' were to be feared on account of
them.[2] Up till then, and for a few ensuing decades,
these newspapers consisted only of single loose sheets,
which gave information concerning all events of special
importance and general interest. Little by little,
however, there were added under the name of ' Relationes ' consecutive accounts of the events of the world.
These appeared at first yearly, and later on twice a
year. The first publisher of these so-called ' Relations '
is Michael von Aitzing, or Eytzinger, who published
at Cologne from February 1580 to September 1583 a
' Relatio Historica ' of the contests between the Protestants and Catholics at Aix-la-Chapelle and in the
archbishopric of Cologne. As he found a good sale
for them he continued bringing out these ' Relations '
yearly or half-yearly till his death in 1598. Further
numbers followed in Cologne till 1601. These and
similar publications, although they had no connexion
with Frankfort either as regards their contents or
the place where they were printed, received the name
of ' Frankfort Messrelationen,' because they were
chiefly sent out from the fairs of that town.[3] In Frankfort itself Conrad Lautenbach, formerly preacher at
Heidelberg, founded, in 1590, the historico-political half-

---

[1] See above, p. 508 f.   [2] Kapp, pp. 780–781.

[3] Fr. Stieve, *Über die ältesten halbjährigen Zeitungen oder Messrelationen und insbesondere über deren Begründer Freiherrn Michael von
Aitzing*, Munich, 1881. There is no mention there of the *Messrelation*
of the Leipzig printer Abraham Lamberg. See *Archiv für Gesch. des
Buchhandels*, x. 250–256, where there are contributions from the *Historical Narrative of all Noteworthy Events since the Leipzig Michaelmas
Fair of 1605* (Anno 1606).'

yearly reports,[1] which seem to have been compiled from chiefly manuscript and printed newspapers.   The Frankfort post office secretary Andrew Striegel organised, in 1602, a ' joint enterprise,' ' in order,' he said, ' that the common people should not be so unfairly robbed of their money by the circulation of uncertain reports.'   In the earlier enterprises ' the despatches and letters were collected and swept together from the streets with a broom ' ;   on the other hand, his dear godfather, the postmaster, received ' the newspapers from all quarters and directions before others ' ;   he collected his contributions from the imperial post office.[2]

A further stage of progress in newspapers is marked by the monthly and weekly reports.   The Emperor Rudolf II is said to have organised, as early as 1597, the publication of a ' connected serial newspaper for whole months.'   This came out in monthly numbers at Augsburg, Vienna and Rorschach ;   at the latter place Samuel Dilbaum, of Augsburg, after 1597, published such periodicals in two to three quarto sheets.   The first printer who determined to supply the reading public weekly with the latest news was John Carolus at Strassburg.   The oldest-known ' year ' of the newspaper founded by him is demonstrably 1609, yet it is by no means the first, for the publisher states that he thinks ' by the Grace of God of continuing the editing of the " Ordinari Avisa," which has now been going on for several years.'[3]   The newspaper appeared

---

[1] *Relationes semestrales.*

[2] Faulmann, p. 389.   Opel, *Anfänge*, pp. 30-31.   The Frankfort ' Fair relations ' went on till the year 1806.

[3] ** Thus the beginning of the newspaper system in Germany may be fixed somewhere about the year 1600.   For England the date of the first newspaper can be proved to be 1622, for France, 1631.   It was much

in small quarto form ; its very lengthy title, surrounded by margins in woodcut, was as follows :—*Relation aller Fürnemmen und gedenkwürdigen Historien, so sich hin und wider in Hoch und Nieder Teutschland, auch in Frankreich, Italien, Schott- und Engelland, Hisspanien, Hungern, Polen, Siebenbürgen, Wallachey, Moldaw, Tirckey, &c., in diesem* 1609 *Jahr verlauffen und zutragen möchten. Alles auf das trewlichst, wie ich solche bekommen und zu wegen bringen mag, in Truck verfertigen will* ' (' Relation of all the important and memorable events which have happened here and there in High and Low Germany, also in France, Italy, Scotland and England, Spain, Hungary, Poland, Transylvania, Wallachia, Moldau, Turkey, &c., in this 1609th year. All related in the truest manner that I could learn and prepare in print '). The annual series contains what, in view of the still undeveloped condition of postal intercourse of that period, is a very remarkable number of contributions from seventeen European towns, among others Cracow, Amsterdam, Brussels, Pressburg and Venice ; Vienna and Prague are the most strongly represented ; next in rank come Cologne and Rome ; it is striking that London and Paris are quite left out. The publisher begs the reader to excuse certain oversights and faults because the ' compilation and publication had to be done hurriedly in the night.' [1] The Strassburg newspaper lived on under different publishers till 1682 certainly, possibly even longer.

later that newspaper advertisements were started. See the article of H. Schacht in the *Beilage zur Allgem. Zeitung,* 1899, No. 12.

[1] Opel found this annual series preserved almost complete in the university library at Heidelberg, and in his *Anfänge,* a work of great merit as regards the history of newspapers, he gives extracts from them.

With this enterprise of the Strassburg bookseller other schemes soon became connected; numbers of large towns received weekly papers, Frankfort, indeed, several; the dates, however, of the respective foundation years are difficult to determine, as only isolated numbers have been preserved from that period. The Basle printer, John Schröter, in 1611, published a periodical paper under the censorship of the town clerk.[1] Vienna possibly owned a newspaper as early as 1610; Frankfort, demonstrably, in 1615; Berlin in 1617.[2] Without doubt it is Protestant Germany that has by far the largest number of newspapers to show.

As early as at the beginning of the seventeenth century newspaper literature was used for drawing up surveys of contemporary events. We learn even from a Turkish proverb, says Gregorius Wintermonat, in 1609, in the preface to his 'Calendarium Historicum Decennale,' published at Leipzig, that 'the newspapers are the rudders of lords and potentates.' But to private persons also this newspaper information was an undeniable gain; it made good politicians, sharpened the powers of judgment and supplied experience.[3] The great multitude, however, jumped at the papers for quite other reasons. Even Fischart made fun of the 'newspaper-believing' credulous people and its craving for news.[4] The school-rector Sigmund Evenius complained later on that in families the fathers did not occupy themselves with the discipline and education of their children; they considered such employment ' a

[1] Ochs, vi. 823.
[2] Opel, *Anfänge*, pp. 65–152, 190–203. *Nürnbergische Zeitungen*, pp. 156–165; Münchener, pp. 204–240.
[3] Opel, p. 40.   [4] *Ibid*. p. 5.

robbery of the cheerful conversation and the excellent newspapers which were supplied in the markets, in the book and other shops or in the drinking-rooms, and which could not be fully read or understood in several hours, or indeed in whole days : this they think is the *summe necessarium*, the most needful thing.' [1]

Besides the printed newspapers there were also manuscript ones, which proved of special importance to the German trading class, for German trade was on such a far-reaching scale, extending even overseas in its enterprises, that it was essential for the merchants to get the latest news in the most expeditious manner possible. Consequently, in all the more important trading towns, such as Augsburg and Nuremberg, correspondence bureaus were established and put in communication with the business managers in other towns, from whence they received reports, and immediately after the post had come in they sent the intelligence to the business houses connected with themselves. Of the manuscript communications which the Nuremberg merchants Reiner Volckhardt and Florian von der Bruckh despatched by weekly messengers to Leipzig the yearly sets of 1587–1591 have been preserved. The richest of these extant collections consists of forty-eight volumes of all sorts of reports which came in the years 1568–1604 as ' Ordinari Zeitungen ' to those merchant princes the Fuggers of Augsburg.[2]

[1] Evenius, p. 33.
[2] Opel, p. 10 ff. The last-named collection is in the Vienna Court library. ** See Chmel, *Die Handschriften der Hofbibliotek*, i. Vienna, 1840, 347 f., and the article of Th. Sickel, p. 348 f., quoted above at p. 528 n. 3.

INDEX OF PLACES

INDEX OF PERSONS

END OF THE FOURTEENTH VOLUME